Japanese/Korean Linguistics

Volume 15

Japanese/Korean Linguistics

Volume 15

Edited by
Naomi Hanaoka McGloin
and Junko Mori

CSLI
PUBLICATIONS

Center for the Study of
Language and Information
Stanford, California

STANFORD LINGUISTICS ASSOCIATION

Copyright © 2007
CSLI Publications
Center for the Study of Language and Information
Leland Stanford Junior University
Printed in the United States
11 10 09 08 07   1 2 3 4 5

Library of Congress Cataloging-in-Publication Data

Conference on Japanese/Korean Linguistics (1st : 1989 : University of Southern California)
        Japanese/Korean Linguistics / edited by Hajime Hoji.
        Volume 15 / edited by Naomi Hanaoka McGloin and Junko Mori.
        p.   cm.
        Includes bibliographical references and index.
        ISBN-13: 978-1-57586-521-8
        ISBN-10:   1-57586-521-1
        ISBN-13: 978-1-57586-522-5 (pbk.)
        ISBN-10:   1-57586-522-X (pbk.)
    1. Japanese language—Congresses. 2. Korean language—Congresses.
3. Japanese language—Grammar, Comparative—Korean—Congresses.
4. Korean language—Grammar, Comparative—Japanese—Congresses.
5. Linguistics—Congresses. I. Hoji, Hajime. II. Stanford Linguistics Association.
III. Center for the Study of Language and Information (U.S.) IV. Title.
PL503.C6 1989
495.6–dc20   90-2550
                                               CIP

∞ The acid-free paper used in this book meets the minimum requirements of the American National Standard for Information Sciences—Permanence of Paper for Printed Library Materials, ANSI Z39.48-1984.

For a list of volumes in this series, along with a cumulative table of contents, please visit
http://cslipublications.stanford.edu/site/JAKO.html

CSLI was founded in 1983 by researchers from Stanford University, SRI International, and Xerox PARC to further the research and development of integrated theories of language, information, and computation. CSLI headquarters and CSLI Publications are located on the campus of Stanford University.

CSLI Publications reports new developments in the study of language, information, and computation. Please visit our web site at
http://cslipublications.stanford.edu/
for comments on this and other titles, as well as for changes and corrections by the authors, editors, and publisher.

Contents

Part III
Phonology and Morphology   197

Part IV
Processing and Acquisition   247

Part V
Syntax and Semantics   299

Acknowledgments

This volume contains most of the papers presented at the fifteenth Japanese/Korean Linguistics Conference, held at the University of Wisconsin-Madison, October 7-9, 2005. Thirty-three papers were selected by blind refereeing from 134 abstracts submitted. The number of abstracts submitted were well balanced between formal and functional, Japanese and Korean, and they represented a well balanced mix of sub-areas and languages.

We were most fortunate to have four excellent guest speakers: Masayoshi Shibatani (Rice University), Patricia Clancy (University of California at Santa Barbara), Chung-hye Han (Simon Fraser University) and Yoshiko Matsumoto (Stanford University). We are grateful for their insightful presentations, which enriched the intellectual excitement of the conference.

We are greatly indebted to the many scholars who support the conference by serving as referees. This year, fifty linguists from North America, Japan, Korea and Great Britain contributed their time and effort to make the reviewing process rigorous and fair. Presenters also came from all over North America, Japan and Korea. With almost 100 participants, we were able to enjoy lively discussions in a warm and congenial atmosphere.

This JK conference marked the retirement of Professor Noriko Akatsuka from UCLA. Professor Akatsuka is one of the founding members of JK, and the success of JK over the years owes a great deal to her vision and creative energy.

Organizing a conference is always a group effort. In particular, I would like to thank co-organizer Junko Mori for her help with many aspects of the conference organization, and graduate students Maki Shimotani and Kanae Nakamura for their help with the program booklet and the reception. I am also indebted to our departmental administrator Terry Nealon, who handled various matters above and beyond her regular duties. Without their help, the conference would not have run as smoothly as it did.

We would also like to express our appreciation to Dikran Karagueuzian, the Editor of CSLI publications, for his advice and support throughout the editing process. Graduate students, Maki Shimotani and Yan Wang, also lent support in formatting and indexing the volume.

The 15th Japanese/Korean Linguistics Conference was supported by grants received from the Anonymous Fund (University of Wisconsin-Madison), the Northeast Asia Council of the Association for Asian Studies (Japan Studies grant and Korean Studies grant), and the Korea Research Foundation. We are truly grateful for their generous support.

Naomi Hanaoka McGloin
University of Wisconsin-Madison

Discourse-Functional Correlates of Argument Structure in Korean Acquisition

PATRICIA M. CLANCY
University of California, Santa Barbara

1. Introduction[1]

The foundational assumption of a discourse-functional approach to grammar is that grammatical form is functionally motivated. Grammars are viewed as existing and evolving to meet the needs of their users; grammatical forms are analyzed in terms of the communicative functions they serve in discourse (Cumming and Ono 1997). Form-function patterns that are used with high frequency in discourse are seen as driving the process of grammaticalization over time (e.g. Givón 1979). In a discourse-functional framework, a modular view of grammar as encapsulated and inherently distinct from discourse cannot be maintained precisely because grammar is seen as arising from, and shaped by, discourse.

Another fundamental assumption of discourse-functional theory is that the relationship between grammar and discourse is highly systematic. Traditionally, sentence-level grammar has been regarded as exhibiting rule-governed systematicity, while discourse is characterized by variation and

[1] I am grateful to Pamela Downing and Soonja Choi for their many helpful comments on drafts of this paper. These data were collected with the support of a grant from the Social Science Research Council, Korea Program.

optionality (Du Bois 2003). In contrast, discourse-functional theory views the functional correlates of grammar as being sufficiently systematic to motivate the emergence and evolution of grammatical categories and structures. Discourse-based research has indeed documented remarkable systematicity in speakers' deployment of grammar in everyday talk. For example, one claim of Du Bois' (1987) work on Preferred Argument Structure is that speakers avoid using more than one lexical argument per clause; in fact, cross-linguistic research has shown that even though transitive sentences with two lexical arguments are perfectly grammatical, speakers rarely use more than one lexical argument with transitive verbs (Du Bois et al. 2003). This systematicity in the way that grammar is deployed in discourse is largely unavailable to conscious introspection and discoverable only in the aggregate, by analyzing sufficient amounts of discourse.

Taking a discourse-functional approach to grammar has important implications for acquisition theory, as well as for our understanding of the nature and scope of grammar. When grammar is used in discourse, forms and function are experienced together, by adults as well as by language-learning children. In a framework that views grammar as arising from discourse, it is assumed that our mental representations of grammar arise from our everyday experience with grammar in discourse. If we accept this discourse-functional assumption, it follows that the discourse functions of grammatical forms will also be mentally represented. In fact, this assumption is necessary to account for our ability to use grammatical forms appropriately in discourse in the first place. Thus grammar is seen as encompassing both form and function.

Functional approaches to the acquisition of grammar treat mastery of form-function relationships as central to the child's task of constructing a grammar (e.g. Bates and MacWhinney 1989, Slobin 2001). A discourse-functional perspective, in addition, emphasizes the frequency and distribution of forms and functions in discourse; to acquire native-speaker grammatical competence means to use grammatical forms for the same functions with approximately the same frequency and distribution in the same discourse contexts as other speakers. A discourse-functional framework thus expands the scope of 'grammar' to include consistent patterns of use that do not involve grammaticality vs. ungrammaticality. This, in turn, broadens our view of what the acquisition of grammar entails.

In sum, a discourse-functional approach emphasizes the functional correlates of grammar, as well as the systematic distribution of grammatical forms and their functional correlates in discourse. A particularly active area of research has been the semantic and discourse-pragmatic correlates of argument structure. In this paper, I will focus on three formal features of the grammar of argument structure: 1) argument realization, i.e. the surface forms used to encode arguments; 2) argument role, defined following Du

Bois (1987) in terms of the three core arguments S (subject of intransitive verbs), A (subject of transitive verbs), and O (direct object of transitive verbs); and 3) argument marking, including topic and case markers.

For each of these three formal features of argument structure, the following questions will be addressed: 1) What semantic and/or discourse-pragmatic functions are served by this formal feature in caregiver speech? 2) Is the distribution of form and function in caregiver speech systematic? 3) Do children's forms serve the same functions in discourse as are found in caregiver speech? and 4) Do the children's form/function relations show the same frequency and distribution found in caregiver speech?

Answers to these questions can provide the foundation for a discourse-functional analysis of argument structure and its acquisition. If the relationship between form and function is highly systematic in caregivers' speech, then children's acquisition of form may be functionally motivated. If the formal features of argument structure in children's speech serve the same functions found in caregiver speech, we will have evidence that form and function are being acquired together, i.e. that children's mental representations of argument structure incorporate discourse-functional information. In addition, if children are acquiring structural patterns that do not affect grammaticality, such as Preferred Argument Structure, we will have evidence that children are acquiring a broader set of regularities than is usually regarded as falling within the scope of the acquisition of grammar.

2. Methodology

2.1. Participants

The participants in this study are two Korean girls—Hyenswu (H) and Wenceng (W)—and their mothers, who were recorded at home engaged in everyday activities every other week for 13 months. At the start of the study, Hyenswu was 1 year and 10 months old (1;10), and Wenceng was 1;8 years old. Hyenswu's mother (HM) and Wenceng's mother (WM) were married to Korean graduate students living in Providence, Rhode Island. A female Research Assistant, a native speaker of Korean and graduate student in linguistics, recorded the 90-minute sessions and transcribed them as soon as possible following the recording; the transcripts were subsequently checked for accuracy a number of times by other native speakers. For purposes of this paper, data from 13 transcripts for each child at approximately one-month intervals have been analyzed.

2.2. Data Coding

The analyses of argument realization and argument role are based on S, A and O arguments of overt verbs in unembedded clauses. All of the children's unembedded clauses are included in the analysis. For each of the mothers, a sample of 1,050 unembedded clauses is analyzed, consisting of

350 clauses from the first four months, 350 from the next five months and 350 from the final four months of the study. The data for the analyses of argument realization and argument role are summarized in Table 1.

Speaker	Age	Clauses	Arguments
H	1;10-2;10	2,169	3,164
HM	adult	862	1,242
W	1;8-2;8	2,395	3,417
WM	adult	842	1,219

Table 1. Participants and Data

For the analysis of argument realization, four forms were coded, as presented in Table 2.

FORM	Examples
Ellipsis	*acci pwasse* '(Lit.) saw uncle', e.g. 'I saw Uncle.'
Noun	lexical categories (*chayk* 'book')
	proper names (*Wencengi, Hyenswu*)
	kin terms (*emma* 'mommy,' *appa* 'daddy')
Pronoun	demonstrative (*i-ke* 'this-thing', *ku-ke* 'that-thing')
	personal (*na* 'I', *ne/ni* 'you')
	interrogative/indefinite (*mwe* 'what/something')
Complement	*na ike halcwul ala* 'I know how to do this'

Table 2. Argument Realization: Coded Forms with Examples

Of the semantic and discourse-pragmatic properties of arguments that were coded, Table 3 presents the four that will be discussed in this paper.

VARIABLE	VALUES CODED
Animacy	human, pseudo-human (e.g. dolls, animal characters in stories), animate, inanimate, abstract, action
Contrast	contrasted/not contrasted with other referents. A referent is coded as contrastive if there is another referent in the verbal or nonverbal context bearing the same relation to the same verb or a parallel relation to a semantically similar verb (see Examples 1, 2, 10, 12-13 below).
Person	first, second, or third person
Prior Mention	new: first mention of the referent in the recording session given: the referent was mentioned in the prior main clause accessible: the referent was mentioned before the prior main clause

Table 3. Four Semantic and Discourse-pragmatic Properties of Arguments

For the analysis of argument role, each argument is coded as S, A, or O. The assessment of transitivity is context-specific, based on how a verb is used in a particular context; native speaker judgments were relied on for doubtful cases, including all clauses with *hata* 'do' that lacked an overt object or complement.

For the analysis of argument marking, the database has been expanded to include core arguments of verbs that are not overt. Noun phrases are coded as arguments of an implicit verb only when that verb could be assumed to be the same as the verb in the preceding main clause, as in NP answers to wh-questions. This expansion of the database was important for a full analysis of argument marking because both adults and children often answered wh-questions with case-marked nominals and no overt verb. All arguments in the database are coded for morphological markers; the analysis in this paper will be limited to nominative (*-ka/i*), topic (*-nun/(u)n*), and accusative (*-lul/(u)l* markers.

3. Results and Discussion

3.1. Argument Realization

Overall, the degree of systematicity in argument realization across speakers is remarkable, as we can see in Figure 1.

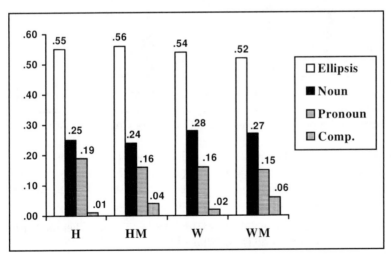

Figure 1. Proportional Frequencies of Forms for Argument Realization

Although the children in this study are very young, the proportional frequency of the surface forms that they use to encode arguments is already quite similar to that of their mothers. Only complements show a clear difference, with the mothers using a higher frequency of complements, most of which are object complements, compared with the children.

How can we account for the consistent distribution of forms in Figure 1? The basic claim of a discourse-functional approach is that argument realization is governed by semantic and discourse-pragmatic factors (Clancy 1993, 1997). In this section two of the strongest functional correlates of argument realization will be considered: contrast and prior mention.

Although ellipsis is the most frequent option for argument realization, making an effective contrast between the current argument and another referent requires an overt form rather than ellipsis. Figure 2 presents the proportional frequency of forms used for contrastive arguments.

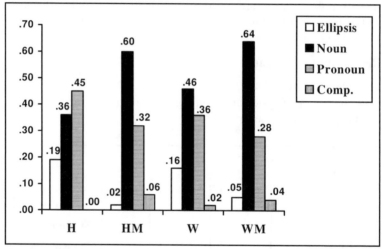

Figure 2. Proportional Frequencies of Forms for Contrastive Arguments

As Figure 2 shows, the mothers use similar proportions of forms to encode contrastive arguments. Contrastive complements are rare, as is the use of ellipsis in contexts in which a potential contrast exists. Nouns are the most frequent form, as in Example (1), followed by pronouns.

(1) Wenceng (2;2) is pretending to feed coffee to her doll; her mother has asked whether baby dolls can have coffee.
    Wenceng: ung.
        'Yeah.'

W's mother: cengmal? <u>wencengi</u> coffee mek-ulswuiss-e?[2]
                    really   Wenceng coffee eat-can-IE
                    'Really? Can Wenceng (=you) have coffee?'

The children, as Figure 2 shows, are different both from their mothers and from one another. For example, they are much more likely to ignore potential contrast, as their comparatively high rates of ellipsis reveal. They also use a higher proportion of pronouns to realize contrastive arguments than their mothers do, and Hyenswu uses a higher percentage of pronouns than Wenceng. The mother-child differences reflect the children's frequent use of contrastive self-reference with the first person pronoun *na*, whereas the mothers generally use the noun *emma* 'mommy' for self-reference. Hyenswu, who had a five-year-old sister, is more likely to use *na* for contrastive self-reference than Wenceng (38% vs. 28% of all contrastive referents, respectively). Example (2) is typical:

(2) Hyenswu (2;6) has been arguing with her friend Forum, who is visiting and wants to play with her Lego.
    Res. Asst: forum-to   com   kacko nol-key   hay.
                  Forum-also a.little with   play-RESUL do.IE
                  'Let Forum play with (your Lego) a bit too.'
    Hyenswu: . no. <u>na</u> ku-ke   ppay-llay.
                  no 1sg that-thing take.apart-VOL
                  'No. I'll take that apart.'

Despite these differences, both children are well on their way to adult usage. As Figure 2 shows, Hyenswu and Wenceng encode 81% and 82%, respectively, of their contrastive arguments with overt nouns and pronouns; the corresponding figure for both mothers is 92%.

In their realization of arguments, the mothers and children are also sensitive to the dimension of prior mention. The encoding of new information, i.e. referents not previously mentioned during the recording session, provides the clearest case in which nominal reference is expected. Figure 3 presents the distribution of forms used to realize new arguments. Almost all of the pronouns are deictic; complements are not included in this analysis.

---

[2] Abbreviations are taken primarily from Lee (1991).

ACC	accusative	INCHOA	inchoative
ANT	anterior	INT	intentional
CIRCUM	circumstantial	INTERR	interrogative
COMP	complementizer	NOM	nominative
CONN	connective	RESUL	resultative
DECL	declarative	TOP	topic
EXCL	exclamation	UNASSIM	unassimilated
IE	informal ending	VOL	volitional

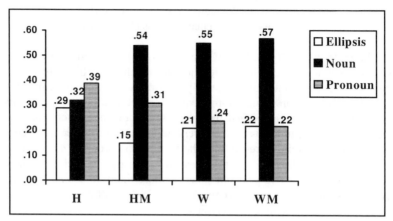

Figure 3. Proportional Frequencies of Forms for New Arguments

As Figure 3 shows, Wenceng and her mother have a very similar distribution of forms for new arguments. Predictably, nouns are by far the most frequent form used to introduce new information, as illustrated in (3):

(3) Wenceng's mother has been serving the Research Assistants coffee and cookies when Wenceng (1;11) says:
Wenceng:　emma,　<u>congi</u>　kaci-ko　　　o-kkey.
　　　　　　mommy　paper　bring-CONN　come-INT
　　　　　　'Mommy, I'll get some paper.'

When ellipsis and deictic pronouns are used for new arguments, the intended referent must be clarified by the nonverbal context. Compared to Wenceng and her mother, Hyenswu's mother is somewhat more likely to use deictic pronouns rather than ellipsis for new arguments. Hyenswu's distribution of forms for new arguments differs dramatically from the other speakers' usage, with a much lower rate of nominal reference and higher rates of elliptical and pronominal reference. In Example (4), she uses the deictic pronoun *yoke* 'this' for the first mention of a referent.

(4) Hyenswu (2;0) is trying to open a toy refrigerator door, and wants the Research Assistant to help her.
Hyenswu:　<u>yo-ke</u>　　ppay　　　　　cw-e.
　　　　　　this-thing　take.apart.CONN　give-IE
　　　　　　'Open this (for me).'

In sum, we have seen that the proportional distribution of forms for argument realization is highly systematic in adult speech, and is clearly related to the discourse functions of contrasting and introducing referents. The two children use overt nouns and pronouns for both of these functions, in proportions approximating their mothers'. Though still below three years of age, Wenceng is well on her way to acquiring the adult distribution of forms, as well as the functional motivations underlying that distribution. Hyenswu, though not distinguishing forms for first mentions as clearly as Wenceng and the adults, does use overt forms for contrastive referents.

Research on argument realization in other languages has yielded similar findings. For example, Kim (2000) reports that in a number of different languages, children's rates of subject ellipsis are best predicted by adult frequency rather than by typological characteristics such as whether the language in question is a 'pro-drop' language. Allen (2000), using functional variables including contrast and newness adapted from Clancy (1993), has found that argument realization in the speech of children acquiring Inuktitut, an Eskimo-Aleut language with argument ellipsis, also has a discourse-pragmatic basis. Thus there is cross-linguistic support for the two key findings of this section: that argument realization is motivated by semantic and discourse-pragmatic factors, and that children's patterns of argument realization closely match adult usage.

3.2. Argument Role

The argument roles S, A, and O are organized into grammatical categories in different ways cross-linguistically. In Korean, S and A arguments are usually treated alike; for example, both S and A receive nominative marking, while accusative marking is reserved for O arguments. In ergative languages, S and O both take absolutive marking, while A arguments are singled out for ergative marking. Discourse-functional researchers have sought to identify the functional correlates of these alignments. In his work on Preferred Argument Structure (1987), Du Bois proposes that the motivation for aligning S and O arguments is that both roles tend to accommodate new information, while the A role almost always conveys given information.

In this section I will address the functional correlates of argument roles S, A, O in these data. Do the mothers assign referents having certain semantic and discourse-pragmatic properties to particular argument roles? Are these assignments systematic? And do the children assign referents in discourse to S, A, and O argument roles in ways that reflect their caregivers' usage? I will focus here on three of the strongest correlates of argument role in the data: animacy, person, and prior mention.

With respect to animacy, there is a clear difference between the distributions of human (Figure 4) and inanimate (Figure 5) referents across S, A, and O argument roles. In Figure 4, we see that the majority of human referents are found in the A role and most of the others in the S role. The range of variation across speakers is remarkably narrow, and the children are very similar to their mothers.

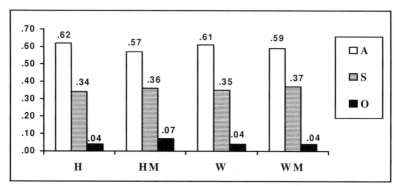

Figure 4. Distribution of Human Referents by Argument Role

Figure 5 gives the distribution of inanimate referents. Again, all four speakers have similar distributions. Inanimate referents are found most frequently in the O role, somewhat less often in the S role, and almost never in the A role. A typical example is (5), in which a human agent in the A role acts on an inanimate patient in the O role.

(5) Hyenswu (2;0) wants to remove the hairpin that her sister has on.
    Hyenswu: <u>hyenswu   ppin</u> ppay.
               Hyenswu pin   take.off.IE
               'Hyenswu (=I) will take off the pin.'

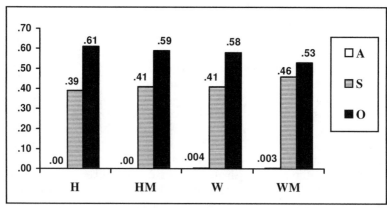

Figure 5. Distribution of Inanimate Referents by Argument Role

Clearly, animacy is a highly systematic correlate of argument role. Another, related correlate is person. The crucial distinction in the data is between first/second person referents (i.e. Speech Act Participants) and third person referents. Figures 6 and 7 illustrate this split.

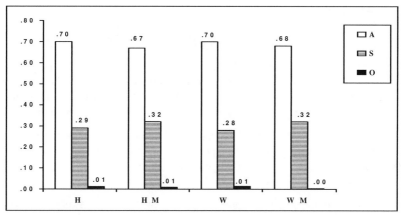

Figure 6. Distribution of First/Second Person Referents by Argument Role

As we see in Figure 6, the majority of first and second person referents are found in the A role and almost all the rest in the S role. The virtual absence of Speech Act Participants among referents in the O role is striking.

The distribution of third person referents is also strongly skewed across argument roles, as shown in Figure 7.

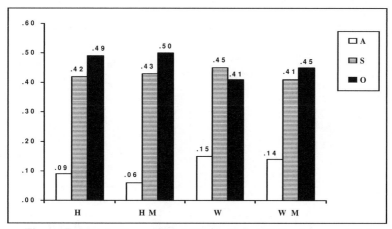

Figure 7. Distribution of Third Person Referents by Argument Role

As we can see in Figure 7, third person referents are usually assigned to the O role, as in Example (6), or to the S role.

(6) Wenceng (2;1) has been talking to her mother about food, and gets up to get some juice.
    Wenceng: emma   wencengi   <u>cwusu</u>   mek-ulkeya.
               mommy   Wenceng   juice   eat-will.IE
               'Mommy, Wenceng (=I) will drink juice.'

Compared with Hyenswu and her mother, Wenceng and her mother have a higher percentage of their third person arguments in the A role. This reflects their more frequent practice of reading from storybooks, which places third person story characters in the A role, as in the first clause of Example (7).

(7) Wenceng (2;1) is telling the story of Goldilocks from a storybook.
    <u>goldilock</u>-un   mwun-ul   yel-ko,   tule-ka-ss-e.
    Goldilocks-TOP   door-ACC   open-CONN   enter-go-ANT-IE
    'Goldilocks opened the door and went in.'

Thus the exceptions to the general exclusion of third person referents from the A role are themselves functionally motivated, in that they tend to be characteristic of a particular discourse genre.

The final correlate of argument role that I will consider here is prior mention, in particular, the distribution of new information. As prior research has shown (Clancy 1993, 2003), these data clearly exhibit Preferred Argument Structure, one feature of which is a skewed distribution of new information across argument roles. Figure 8 exhibits the constraint against new information in the A role (Du Bois 1987):

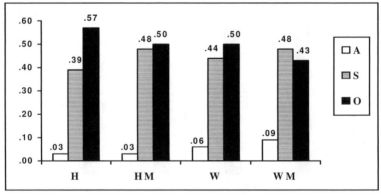

Figure 8. Distribution of New Referents by Argument Role

Although it is perfectly grammatical to place new information in the A role, Wenceng and her mother do so less than 10% of the time, and Hyenswu and her mother less than 5% of the time. As Figure 8 shows, all four speakers usually assign new referents to S and O roles. Typical examples are given in (8), in which new information appears in the S role, and (9), which has new information in the O role.

(8) Hyenswu (2;0) is looking at a book and sees a new picture.
    Hyenswu: <u>yenphil</u> yeki iss-ta.
                pencil   here exist-DECL
                'There's a pencil here.'

(9) Wenceng (2;5) stops singing a song and says:
    Wenceng: na cepttah <u>kicha</u> tha-pw-ass-e.
                1sg before train   ride-see-ANT-IE
                'I've had a ride on a train.'

In sum, it is clear that argument roles have strong semantic and discourse-pragmatic correlates, suggesting that the assignment of referents in discourse to argument roles is functionally motivated. The mothers and their children consistently assign human referents to S and A roles and inanimate referents to the O role; they also place first and second person referents in the A role, and third person referents and new information in S and O roles. The high degree of systematicity in adult usage means that children are presented with a consistent model of the relations between argument roles and the properties of referents. The early age at which the functional correlates of argument role appear indicates that the form-function relations involved are readily accessible to young children. Apparently, as they learn transitive and intransitive verbs, children learn what types of referents usually appear in which argument roles. Choi (1999) has documented similar patterns of animacy, person, contrast, and newness across S, A, and O arguments in Korean children and their caregivers. Transitive and intransitive argument structures thus appear to be acquired simultaneously with the semantic and discourse-pragmatic correlates of the argument roles S, A, and O.

At a general theoretical level, the systematicity of the correlates of argument roles S, A, and O supports the discourse-functional position that grammars are functionally motivated. As Du Bois (1987) has found, S and O are similar in these data in that both accommodate new information, a finding that is consistent with acquisition research on Preferred Argument Structure in other languages (e.g. Allen and Schröder 2003, Narasimhan et al. 2005). As we have seen, in these data S and O roles are also similar in that they tend to accommodate inanimate and third person referents, while the A role is usually limited to human referents, primarily Speech Act Participants. The almost exclusive assignment of human referents to A and S roles suggests a functional basis for the alignment of S and A as 'subject', as in Korean grammar. A key finding about argument role is that the children in this study acquire the semantic and discourse-pragmatic similarities shared by S and O arguments, which are not grammaticized in Korean, as readily as those shared by S and A arguments, which share subject word order and nominative casemarking in Korean. When such functionally motivated patterns of argument role alignment in discourse are grammaticized in word order or casemarking, they can serve as a functional basis for the acquisition of grammar.

3.3. Argument Marking

As we have seen thus far, both argument realization and argument role have clear semantic and discourse-pragmatic correlates. In this section, I will focus on two of the most common types of argument marking, nominative (*-i/ka*) and topic (*-nun/(u)n*), and will consider two functional correlates of these markers, contrast and focus.

In Korean, there is an inherent relationship between argument realization and argument marking: Only overt arguments can be marked. As noted in Section 2.2, for the analysis of argument marking the database has been expanded to include overt arguments that lack an overt verb, but only when the implicit verb can be assumed to be the same as that of the preceding main clause, as in answers to questions. Object complements, which take complementizers rather than accusative marking, e.g. *mek-ko siph-e?* 'eat-COMP want-IE'/'Do you want to eat?', are not included in this analysis.

Figure 9 presents the proportional frequencies of unmarked ('bare') arguments, arguments with nominative, topic, and accusative marking, and arguments with other markers, e.g. *to* 'also, even.'

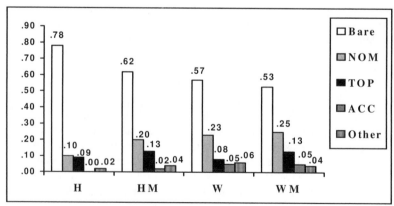

Figure 9. Proportional Frequencies of Argument Marking

As Figure 9 shows, the proportional distribution of argument markers for Wenceng and her mother is generally quite similar. Unmarked arguments are most common, nominative marking is more frequent than topic marking, and accusative marking is quite rare. Compared with Wenceng's mother, Hyenswu's mother has a slightly higher proportion of unmarked arguments and closer proportions of nominative and topic markers. Hyenswu, who is still at an early stage in acquiring argument marking, has a higher percentage of unmarked arguments than the other speakers and does not acquire the accusative marker during the year. Hyenswu uses almost the same proportions of nominative and topic marking; this may reflect, in part, her late acquisition of the -i allomorph of the nominative.

As we have seen, contrast is one of the major reasons for realizing arguments overtly in Korean; it is also generally recognized as one function of topic marking. Lee (1999), for example, proposes that contrastive topic marking encodes an explicit contrast between the marked argument and a specific set of contrasting items that the speaker currently has in mind. As noted in Section 2.2, an argument is coded as contrastive in these data if there is another referent in the verbal or nonverbal context bearing the same relation to the same verb or a parallel relation to a semantically similar verb. This coding captures cases involving an obviously contrastive referent that has been recently mentioned and/or is present in the discourse context.

Figure 10 presents the proportions of arguments coded as contrastive that are unmarked or marked with topic, nominative, accusative or other markers.

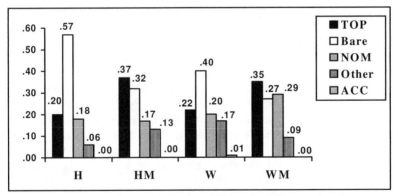

Figure 10. Frequencies of Marked and Unmarked Contrastive Arguments

As the figure shows, a notable proportion of overt arguments coded as contrastive remain unmarked; this is especially true for Hyenswu, who acquired argument marking more slowly than Wenceng. In comparison with the higher proportions of bare nominals in Figure 9, however, it is clear from Figure 10 that contrastive arguments are more likely to be marked, usually with topic or nominative markers. Contrast is apparently not one of the functions of the accusative marker, which is almost never used on contrastive arguments. The 'other' markers that appear on contrastive arguments include *to* 'even, also', *man* 'only', and *hako* 'with'.

The children's percentages of contrastive topic marking are lower than their mothers' percentages, perhaps because it is the mothers who usually take the initiative in labeling sequences, a frequent discourse context for the use of contrastive topics. Example (10) illustrates this context, as well as Wenceng's early acquisition of the questioner's role:

(10)　Wenceng (1;11) and her mother are looking at a storybook.

W's mother:	i-ke-**n**	mwe-ya?
	this-thing-TOP	what-be.IE
Wenceng:	/incomprehensible/	
W's mother:	ung.	
	'Yeah.'	
Res. Asst:	emma　　mwulkoki,	appa　　mwulkoki.
	mommy　fish	daddy　fish
	'Mommy fish, daddy fish.'	
Wenceng:	i-ke-**n**	mwe-ntey?
	this-thing-TOP	what-CIRCUM
	'What's this?'	
Res. Asst:	wencengi mwulkoki.	
	Wenceng　fish	
	'Wenceng (=baby) fish.'	

Rather than contrast, the function that is usually attributed to the nominative is marking focal information. While this is typically defined as new information, Lambrecht (1994) proposes that focus can be defined more precisely as information that the speaker asserts as unpredictable or non-recoverable. Such information can be seen as providing the answer to un-spoken questions, e.g. who performed a particular action. The marking of new information has been identified as one function of nominative marking in these data (Clancy 1995); the nominative is also used to mark unpredict-able information in question-answer sequences. In these data focal nomina-tives are found quite early in question-answer sequences, such as (11).

(11)　Wenceng (2;1) is looking at a torn page in a book.

RA:	aywu,　ccice-cy-ess-kwuna,	**nwu-ka**　　ccic-ess-ni?
	EXCL tear-INCHOA-ANT-UNASSIM	who-NOM tear-ANT-INTERR
	'Oh my, it's torn, who tore it?'	

W: wencengi-**ka**.
       Wenceng-NOM
       'Wenceng (= I) (did).'

The children, especially Wenceng, use nominative morphemes to mark wh-questions and their answers in rates comparable to their mothers' usage: H: 15.1%, HM: 10.8%, W: 17.8% and WM: 17.2%.

Nominative marking is also used contrastively in these data. As Figure 10 has shown, both mothers and children sometimes use nominative markers on contrastive arguments; in fact, the children use nominative marking about as frequently as topic marking on arguments coded as contrastive. Hyenswu often uses nominative marking when contrasting herself with others as an agent of actions, as in Example (12).

(12)   The Research Assistant has been cleaning her glasses with a tissue; now Hyenswu (2;7) wants to do it.
       Hyenswu: acwumma   yo-ke   **nay-ka**   hay cwu-kkey.
                  aunt   this-thing 1sg-NOM do.IE give-INT
                  'Auntie, I will do this (for you).'

Lee (1999) characterizes this usage, coded as contrastive in this study, as involving 'narrow' or 'exclusive' focus, noting that it corresponds to what Kuno (1973) treats as the 'exhaustive listing' interpretation of the Japanese nominative marker: 'It is X who ...'. Rather than a clear sense of contrast, Lee proposes, this usage highlights one of a set of evoked alternatives, leaving other alternatives 'shadowed' and implicit at the time of utterance.

In these data, only cases in which there is a specific alternative referent in the discourse context who is engaged in the same or a parallel action, e.g. the Research Assistant in (11), were coded as contrastive. As a result, the arguments with nominative marking in Figure 10 necessarily contrast with alternatives that are readily apparent in context. When the speaker mentions a specific alternative referent overtly, the contrast becomes fully explicit, as in Example (13).

(13)   Hyenswu (2;9) is assigning roles in pretend play with the Research Assistant.
       H: **ne-ka**   enni hay-ya-ci,   **nay-ka**   emma   ha-ci.
          2sg-NOM sister do-must-COMM 1sg-NOM mommy do-COMM
          'You be the sister, I'll be the mommy.'

The coding in this study presumably captures the more specific, and hence more obviously contrastive, end of the range covered by what Lee has analyzed as 'narrow focus' nominative marking.

Thus in addition to marking new information (Clancy 1995), nominative marking is used in these data for at least the following functions: 1) to mark information that is treated as unpredictable in the discourse context of wh-questions and their answers, and 2) to contrast the referent of the marked argument with a potential alternative in the discourse context.

In sum, the analyses in this section show that the children are already learning to use argument markers for the functions of contrast and focus found in adult usage. These results are consistent with prior research on the acquisition of Korean argument markers, which has found early 'narrow focus' use of the nominative marker and contrastive use of the topic marker (Lee 2001, Zoh 1982). As these findings imply, casemarking is not fully grammaticized in spoken Korean; neither adults nor children generalize nominative marking to all S and A arguments or accusative marking to all O arguments in everyday conversation. The distinction between marked vs. unmarked arguments is therefore available to serve a variety of semantic and discourse-pragmatic functions. Since the markers are necessarily associated with overt arguments, the functions they take on can be seen as arising, at least in part, from the properties of overt referents in discourse, such as marking contrastive information (Clancy 1995).

4. Conclusions

As we have seen, the three formal features of Korean argument structure addressed in this paper—argument realization, argument role, and argument marking—have clear discourse-functional correlates. Speakers realize arguments in ways that depend on the semantic and discourse-pragmatic properties of their referents. These properties also influence the assignment of referents to argument roles S, A, and O. Speakers add nominative and topic markers to overt arguments in ways that reflect and highlight the functions of their referents, such as conveying contrast and focus. The findings of this study thus provide support for the fundamental premise of discourse-functional theory: that grammatical form is functionally motivated.

Furthermore, the functional correlates of argument realization, argument role and argument marking that have been identified in this study are highly systematic. Argument realization, argument role, and argument marking have the same functional correlates across speakers from early on, and the frequency and distribution of forms and functions is quite similar. This systematicity provides support for another basic tenet of discourse-functional theory: that the functional correlates of grammatical form can serve as a basis for the processes of acquisition and grammatical change.

Interpreted in a discourse-functional perspective, systematicity in the frequency and distribution of the functional correlates of argument structure also implies that the children in this study are acquiring the forms and functions of argument structure together, on the basis of exposure to caregiver discourse. In order for both caregivers and children to produce the kind of systematic correlations between form and function found in this study, their mental representations of the grammar of argument structure must incorporate information about its semantic and discourse-pragmatic correlates.

Finally, the results of this study suggest that it is appropriate to expand the scope of 'grammar' to include discourse-level information about the frequency and distribution of the functional correlates of grammatical form. This discourse-functional definition of grammar—encompassing grammatical forms, their functional correlates, and the distribution of both in discourse—gives a fuller understanding of the task involved in the acquisition of grammar. As the analyses in this paper indicate, the acquisition of argument realization, argument role, and argument marking entails the mastery of a range of semantic and discourse-pragmatic properties of referents, as well as the conventional distributions of both. The fact that two-year-old children have made as much progress as has been found in this study implies that they, like discourse-functional linguists, treat grammar as a 'delivery system' for semantic and discourse-pragmatic information.

References

Allen, S. 2000. A Discourse Pragmatic Explanation for Argument Representation in Child Inuktitut. *Linguistics* 38:483-21.

Allen, S. and H. Schröder. 2003. Preferred Argument Structure in Early Inuktitut Spontaneous Speech Data. *Preferred Argument Structure: Grammar as Architecture for Function*, eds. J. Du Bois, L. Kumpf, and W. Ashby, 301-38. Amsterdam/Phildelphia: Benjamins.

Bates, E. and B. MacWhinney. 1989. Functionalism and the Competition Model. *The Crosslinguistic Study of Sentence Processing*, eds. B. MacWhinney and E. Bates, 3-73. New York: Cambridge University Press.

Choi, S. 1999. Early Development of Verb Structures and Caregiver Input in Korean: Two Case Studies. *International Journal of Bilingualism* 3:241-65.

Clancy, P. M. 1993. Preferred Argument Structure in Korean Acquisition. *The Proceedings of the Twenty-fifth Annual Child Language Research Forum*, ed. E. Clark, 307-14. Stanford University: CSLI.

Clancy, P. M. 1995. Subject and Object in Korean Acquisition: Surface Expression and Casemarking. *Harvard Studies in Korean Linguistics VI*, eds. S. Kuno, J. Whitman, Y-S Kang, I-H Lee, J. Maling, and Y. Kim, 3-17. Seoul: Hanshin.

Clancy, P. M. 1997. Discourse Motivations for Referential Choice in Korean Acquisition. *Japanese/Korean Linguistics 6*, eds. H. Sohn and J. Haig, 639-59. Stanford University: CSLI.

Clancy, P. M. 2003. The Lexicon in Interaction: Developmental Origins of Preferred Argument Structure. *Preferred Argument Structure: Grammar as Architecture for Function*, eds. J. Du Bois, L. Kumpf, and W. Ashby, 81-108. Amsterdam/Philadelphia: Benjamins.

Cumming, S. and T. Ono. 1997. Discourse and Grammar. *Discourse as Structure and Process*, ed. T. van Dijk, 112-37. London: Sage.

Du Bois, J. 1987. The Discourse Basis of Ergativity. *Language* 63:805-55.

Du Bois, J. 2003. Discourse and Grammar. *The New Psychology of Language: Cognitive and Functional Approaches to Language Structure*, ed. M. Tomasello, 47-87. Mahwah, NJ: Erlbaum.

Du Bois, J., L. Kumpf, and W. Ashby, eds. 2003. *Preferred Argument Structure: Grammar as Architecture for Function*. Amsterdam/Philadelphia: Benjamins.

Givón, T. 1979. *On Understanding Grammar*. New York: Academic Press.

Kim, Y. J. 2000. Subject/Object Drop in the Acquisition of Korean: A Cross-linguistic Comparison. *Journal of East Asian Linguistics* 9:325-51.

Kuno, S. 1973. *The Structure of the Japanese Language*. Cambridge, MA: MIT Press.

Lambrecht, K. 1994. *Information Structure and Sentence Form: Topic, Focus, and the Mental Representations of Discourse Referents*. New York: Cambridge University Press.

Lee, H. S. 1991. Tense, Aspect and Modality: A Discourse-Pragmatic Analysis of Verbal Affixes in Korean from a Typological Perspective. Doctoral dissertation, University of California, Los Angeles.

Lee, C. 1999. Contrastive Topic, A Locus of the Interface: Evidence from Korean and English. *The Semantics/Pragmatics Interface from Different Points of View*, ed. K. Turner, 317-42. New York: Elsevier.

Lee, C. 2001. Acquisition of Topic and Subject Markers in Korean. *Issues in East Asian Language Acquisition*, ed. M. Nakayama, 41-66. Tokyo: Kurosio.

Narasimhan, B., Budwig, N., & Murty, L. 2005. Argument Realization in Hindi Caregiver-Child Discourse. *Journal of Pragmatics* 37:461-95.

Slobin, D. I. 2001. Form-Function Relations: How Do Children Find Out What They Are? *Language Acquisition and Conceptual Development*, eds. M. Bowerman and S. Levinson, 406-49. New York: Cambridge University Press.

Zoh, M.-H. 1982. *Hankwuk Atong-uy Ene Hoyktuk Yenkwu: Chayklyak Mohyeng* [A Study of Korean Children's Language Acquisition: A Strategies Model]. Seoul: Seoul National University Press.

On the Grammaticalization of Motion Verbs: A Japanese-Korean Comparative Perspective

MASAYOSHI SHIBATANI[1] AND SUNG YEO CHUNG[2]
Rice University[1], *Osaka University*[2]

1. Introduction

Shibatani (forthcoming) shows that the converbal complex predicates involving verbs of coming and going in Japanese, as illustrated in (1) below, show interesting patterns of grammaticalization in both spatial and aspectual domains.[1] This synchronic study, however, leaves unexplored the question of the origins or the historical developments of these complex predicates. Furthermore, the parallel constructions in Korean shown in (2) pose a challenging question regarding the form-function correlation in these constructions, which is not obvious in the study of Modern Japanese. As shown in (2a) below, the *–te* converbal (or conjunctive) ending of Japanese corresponds to two conjunctive forms in Korean, *-Ø/-e/-a* and *–ko*. It is hoped that the following attempt at a Japanese-Korean comparative study sheds

---

[1] See Shibatani (forthcoming) for the demonstration that the *V-te iku/kuru* converbal complexes discussed in this paper form a unit of "word" in both phonological and syntactic senses. They are, however, not morphological words in the sense that they do not show lexical integrity characteristic of morphological words.

light on both diachronic and crosslinguistic issues involved in the evolution and the synchronic form-function patterns of complex predicates.

(1) Japanese[2]

    a. Boku-wa   Shinjuku-no   yuuryo toire-made Midori-o
       I-TOP   Shinjuku-GEN pay   toilet-to   Midori-ACC
       ture-te   **it**-te...
       accompany-CON go-CON
       'I took (take go) Midori to the pay toilet in Shinjuku and ....'

    b. Watasi oziisan,   obaasan,   otoosan-to   yo-nin
       I   grandfather grandmother   father-and   four-person
       kanbyoosi-te ki-ta-kara   yoku   sitteru-no   yo.
       care-CON   come-PAST-ABL well   know-NMNLZR FP
       'I know well, since I have cared for (care come) my grandfather,
       grandmother and father.'   (Haruki Murakami *Norwegian Wood*)

(2) Korean

    a. ne-lul   cesungsaca-ka
       you-ACC   messenger.of.the.other.world-NOM
       ep-e-ka-taka   **peli-ko**
       carry.on.the.back-CON-go-on.the.way throw.away-CON
       ka-n-ta-nun   il-to
       go-PRES-IND   that.thing-also
       '(there is no possibility of) throwing (you) away while the messenger
       from the other world carries you on his back'

    b. Na-nun ai-tul-uy   phyoceng-ul   hanahana
       I-TOP   child-PL-GEN   expression-ACC one.by.one
       ilk-e-ka-ss-ta.
       read-CON-go-PAST-IND
       'I went on reading the children's expressions one by one.'
           (Kim Joo Yong *Kokicapinun kaltaylul kkekkci anhnunta*)

These examples illustrate both spatial and aspectual use of the motion verbs. This paper is in the main concerned with the grammaticalization in the spatial domain. We will first make a critical appraisal of the widely-accepted scenario about the origins and the grammaticalization processes of these complex predicates. We will then tackle the question of

---

[2] Uncommon abbreviations: CCC = clause chaining constructions, CON = conver-bal/conjunctive ending, CPC = complex predicate constructions, CV = complex verb, EXP = experiential, FP = final particle, IND = indicative, NF = nonfinite marker, NMNLZR = nominal-izer.

form and attempt to show how the formal properties of the converbal complex predicates and the pattern of grammaticalization of them are correlated.

2. On the Origins of Converbal Complex Predicates

In his very influential paper, DeLancey (1991) recognizes the following three stages in the formation of serial verb constructions and their grammaticalization:

1. "Serialization" via dropping of the mark of subordination in the first verb in a clause chaining construction
2. "Auxilialization" – the loss by the grammaticalized verb of its phonological and morphological independence
3. "Morphologization" – the grammaticalized morpheme occurs as a finite verb inflection

This scenario for the grammaticalization of verbs from clause chaining constructions via verb serialization is based on the synchronic Lhasa Tibetan data of the following kind. First, the language has a clause chaining construction, whereby two clauses, one with a nonfinite verb form and the other with a finite verb form, are combined to form a compound sentence expressing sequentially ordered events.

(3) Kohs   las=ka   byas-**byas**   zas-pa   red
     he.ERG   work   did-NF   ate   PERF
     'He worked and ate; having worked, he ate.'

If the second verbs in such constructions happen to be 'come', 'go', and 'sit', the nonfinite marker in the first verb is optional, as in the following example:

(4) kho   'dir   gom=pa brgyab**(-byas)** yongs-pa   red
     he   here:LOC walked   (NF)   came   PERF
     'He walked (walk come) here.'

If, on the other hand, the second verbs are 'put' and 'finish', the nonfinite marker is obligatorily absent:

(5) Kho phyin   tshar-ba   red (obligatory absence of –*byas*)
     he   went   finish   PERF
     'He has gone.'

In addition, there are verbal suffixes functioning as inflectional endings, whose verbal origins appear to be still transparent; e.g., -*song* (go) = direct-evidential perfective; -*bzang* (put) = indirect-evidential perfective; -*byung* (get) = speaker as Goal perfective.

DeLancey's scenario above has been widely accepted among those engaged in grammaticalization research such as Lord (1993) and Hopper and Traugott (1993), as well as by those working on Japanese and Korean converbal complex predicates; e.g., Falsgraf and Park (1994), and Kim (1996). Falsgraf and Park (1994:224-225), for example, posit a direct historical link between the clause chaining constructions in (a) and the converbal complex predicates in (b) below:

(6) Japanese
    a. hayaku benkyoosi-te, ki-ta (CCC)
       quickly study:do-NF   come-PAST
       '(I) studied quickly, (then) came.'

    b. hayaku   benkyoosi-te ki-ta (CPC/grammaticalized)
       quickly   study:do-NF come-PAST
       '(I) have studied quickly to this point.'

(7) Korean
    a. say-ka   nal-a   na eykey=lo o-ass-ta (CCC)
       bird-SUBJ   fly-NF I   toward   come-PAST-DEC
       'The bird flew (and came) toward me.'
    b. say-ka   nal-a   o-ass-ta (CPC)
       bird- SUBJ   fly-NF   come-PAST-DEC
       'The bird came flying.'

Similarly, Kim (1966) envisions the following pattern of development for the auxiliarized verb forms in Korean:

(8) clause chains > serialization > auxiliarization
     鎖構文   連続動詞化   補助動詞化

Regarding "true" serial verbs, Foley and Olsen (1985) suggest the possibility of reanalysis from what is known as core-layer serialization (equivalent to VP or clausal-level serialization) to nuclear-layer serialization (equivalent to root or verb serialization) in order to account for the fact that the latter type of serialization typically occurs in OV languages.[3] The idea is that in OV languages the contiguity of the two relevant verbs facilitates the proposed reanalysis, but in VO languages an object nominal intervenes between the two verbs preventing them from serializing. That is, an OV lan-

---

[3] See Shibatani and Huang (forthcoming) for the discussion on the alleged distinctions between converbal complex predicates and serial verbs. It is shown in this paper that the widely-held definitions of serial verbs, e.g., Foley and Olsen (1985) and Aikhenvald (2006), intended to distinguish them from converbal complex predicates are neither consistent with empirical data nor coherent in the definition internal logic.

guage yields a verb sequence such as [**AXE** TAKE] = [GO], which can be reanalyzed as [AXE] [TAKE = GO] ('take an axe (and) go'→ 'bring an axe'), while a VO language would have an object NP intervening between the two verbs, as in [TAKE **AXE**] = [GO], which prevents TAKE and GO from serializing.[4]

Thus, for both DeLancey (1991) and Foley and Olsen (1985) verb contiguity is an important prerequisite for serialization and grammaticalization. However, that verb contiguity is not in fact a prerequisite for grammaticalization is easy to see. In (a) and (b) below, the second verbs have been grammaticalized across a converbal ending, and the Thai example in (c) indicates that grammaticalization can also take place across an object NP—in all these examples the finite verbs have lost their original lexical meanings and have gained a grammatical (i.e., aspectual) meaning.

(9) a. Kawa-no mizu-ga   hue-**te**   ki-ta. (Japanese)
        river-of   water-NOM   increase-CON   come-PAST
        'The river water has increased.'

    b. Turkish: *V-ip dur-* (V-CON STAY/STOP)
        yi-**yip** dur-'continue eating'
        bekle-**yip** dur- 'continue waiting'
        bak-**ip** dur- 'continue watching'

    c. khăw khìi **càkkayaan** pay rɯ̂ayrɯ̂ay
        he   ride   bicycle   GO   continuously
        'He keeps riding the bicycle.'

Phonological attrition and loss of morphological independence, or "auxilialization" in DeLancey's analysis, can also take place across a nonfinite or converbal ending as in the following examples, where the verb *iku* 'go' has lost its initial vowel and has been cliticized to the *-te* connective.

(10) a. Mattiboo-o   soko-ni narabe-**tette**   kure-ru? (narabe-te it-te)
         matches-ACC   there-at   line.up-CON.go-CON   give-PRES
         'Will you go on lining up the matches there?' (Haruki Murakami)

     b. Gohan tabe-**te**-ku? (tabe-te iku)
         meal   eat-CON-go
         '(Shall we) eat a meal (and go)?'

     c. De-**te**-ke! (de-te ike)
         exit-CON-go.IMP
         'Get out!'

---

[4] The correlation between OV order and nuclear-layer serialization has subsequently been disproved. In Oceanic languages, for example, one finds nuclear-layer serialization in VO languages—see Crowley (2002).

These observations and the fact that DeLancey's own Tibetan example in (4) above receives the same grammaticalized interpretation with or without the non-finite ending (according to DeLancey's observation) indicate that the Tibetan facts he presents are better understood if we reverse the processes 1 and 2 in his scenario. That is, the grammaticalization of verbs of 'go', 'come', 'put', etc. takes place across the nonfinite ending, and then the grammaticalized converbal complexes drop the nonfinite ending, some (with verbs 'put' and 'finish') obligatorily and others (with 'go', 'come', and 'sit') optionally.

A more serious problem for DeLancey's diachronic scenario and the Foley-Olsen reanalysis account, both of which are predicated on the structural property of verb contiguity, has to do with the valency property of the motion verbs, especially of the verb of going. That is, both verbs of 'go' and 'come' normally require a goal expression. In the case of 'come', the goal expression is typically omitted because it encodes lexically the information that the goal of the motion is the deictic center, typically the place of speech. But the verb 'go' normally requires an overt expression of a goal nominal. Indeed, DeLancey's Tibetan examples involving the main verb 'go' do specify a goal, as in the following examples:

(11) a. kho bod-la   'gro myong-ba red
        he Tibet-LOC   go EXP   PERF
        'He has been to Tibet.'

    b. nga khrom-la   phyin-tshar
       I   market-LOC   went-PERF
       'I've gone to the store.'   (DeLancey 1991:10-11)

In other words, if the converbal complex predicates (or verb serialization) involving the verb 'go' arise from clause chaining constructions or core-layer (or VP) serialization, in which the verb 'go' functions as a main verb, the desired verb contiguity does not normally obtain because the goal nominal intervenes between the first verb and the 'go' verb as in [book TAKE] = [school-to GO]. This structure is good for *hon-o mot-te gakkoo-ni iku* 'take a book and go to school', which is a core-layer juncture. The question is how to obtain the nuclear-layer juncture *gakkoo-ni hon-o mot-te iku* 'bring (take go) a book to school' from the structure in which a goal argument intervenes between TAKE and GO.

A usual response to this kind of argument is that those intervening elements are often deleted in actual discourse because of their old information status. But in reality an oblique nominal like a goal argument is rarely deleted, a least in written form, because of its low degree of predictability. In Japanese the *-te* converbal complex predicates became prevalent in the early 19th century, when they supplanted the former infinitival complex predicates completely at least in colloquial speech (e.g., tobi-yuku > ton-**de** iku 'go flying'; see below). The examination of a written text prior to this period indicates that the verb *iku* 'go' indeed typically occurs with a goal argument in its main verb function. Ihara Saikaku's *Kôshoku Ichidai Onna* (1686) contains twenty-one instances of the main verb *yuku* (or *iku*) 'go'. Of these, eighteen forms have an overt goal expression, and only two instances have an understood and elided goal expression. One is used in the expression type of *miti-o yuku* 'go on the road'. The same pattern obtains in Modern Japanese written form. Ito Sei's novel *Hanran* (1958) contains forty-five instances of the main verb *iku*. Of these, forty-one instances occur with a goal nominal, four with an understood and elided goal, and one with no goal expression. Thus, in both earlier Japanese and Modern Japanese, the main verb *iku* 'go' normally occurs with a goal argument. Thus the assumed omission of a goal argument rarely occurs at least in writing.

The other possible reply to our critique would say that the goal argument of a motion verb could be scrambled out of its normal position thereby allowing the two relevant verbs to come together. That is, an expression like (b) below is an input to grammaticalization according to this position.

(12) a. Taroo-ga   hasit-te,   gakkoo-ni   it-ta.
       Taro-NOM   run-CON   school-to   go-PAST
       'Taro went to school running.'
    b. Taroo-ga   gakkoo-ni hasit-te,   it-ta.
       Taro- NOM   school-to   run-CON go- PAST

While (12b) is a possible expression with a pause after *gakko-ni*, it is exceedingly rare, if ever, that we find in actual written discourse such a form, where two verbs belonging to two different clauses are brought together thanks to a displaced nominal argument. Similarly, even with the verb *kuru* 'come', whose goal argument is admittedly at best optional, we do not find many instances of the expression such as (6a) above, which Falsgraf and Park (1994) posit as a precursor of the converbal complex predicate involving *kuru*. This is true in both modern writings and those prior to the period when *–te* converbal complex predicates became prevalent.

Expressions similar to (6a) and (12b) could have occurred sporadically in casual speech, but the burden of proof rests on those who claim that such forms provide a basis for reanalysis or serialization. In order to maintain this position, it is not sufficient that forms like (6a) and (12b) occur sporadically in speech. The hypothesis must be embedded in a theory of reanalysis that tells us, among others, how prevalent the relevant expressions must be in order for them to motivate the hypothesized reanalysis. Neither Foley and Olsen (1985) nor DeLancey (1991) is backed by such a theory.

The only condition they assume for the reanalysis is verb contiguity, which, as we have seen above, is not essential for the formation of complex predicates or their grammaticalization.

Thus, while it is attractive to be able to connect the use of converbal endings in complex predicates and in clause chaining constructions of the following narrative-type, the proposals by DeLancey (1991) and Foley and Olsen (1985) have a flaw in their reasoning and also lack empirical support.

(13) Japanese converbal clause chaining construction

Sorekara	watasitati	itumono-yooni	syokudoo-de		gohan-o
and then	we	as usual	dining room-LOC		meal-ACC
tabe-**te,**	ohuro	hait-**te,**	sorekara	totteokino	zyootoono	wain
eat-CON	bath	enter-CON	and then	choicest	superior	wine
ake-**te**	hutari-de	non-**de,**	watasi-ga	gitaa	hii-ta	no
open-CON	two-by	drink-CON	I-NOM	guitar	play-PAST	FP

'And then we, as usual, ate our meal in the dining room, took a bath, and then opened the choicest super-quality wine (and we) two drank, (and) I played the guitar.' (Haruki Murakami *Norwegian Wood*)

(14) Korean clause chaining construction

Swutokkokci-lul	nwull-**e**	tayya-ey	mwul-lul	pat-**ko,**
faucet-ACC	push-CON	basin-LOC	water-ACC	catch-CON
pinwu	kephwum-ul	nay-**e**	elkwul-ey	palu-**ko,** ....
soap	lather-ACC	bring.out.CON	face-LOC	smear-CON
ssis-un		hwu...		
wash-PAST.ATTR		after		

'having pushed down the faucet (lever), and having caught the water in the wash basin, and having brought out the soap lather, and having smeared (it) on my face, I washed..., and then ...'

(Miri Yuu *Kacok sineyma*)

In view of the fact that the coordinate conjunction *and* in English forms coordinate structures at both clausal and NP levels, there does not seem any reason not to assume that converb endings in Japanese, Korean, and other languages form both clause chains and verb as well as VP junctures. With this possibility in mind, let us take a brief look at the history of the converbal complex predicates, again limiting our attention to those involving the two motion verbs of coming and going.

3. Brief History of the Japanese/Korean Converbal Complex Predicates

The *–te* converbal complex predicates are found in Old Japanese texts. But they appear limited in type and distribution. In the randomly chosen songs numbered 784 to 1810 of *Manyôshû*(万葉集)(A.D. 755-759), seventy converbal complex predicates involving *yuku* 'go' and *kuru* 'come' were found. Of these, fifty-two are connected by the infinitival or *–i/-Ø* connectives, and the remaining eighteen involve the *–te* conjunctive particle. Of the eighteen forms that occur in the *–te* form, three expressions alternate with the infinitival form. They are *ide-te kuru* 'exit-CON come', *sugi-te yuku* 'pass-CON go' and *naki-te yuku* '(bird) sing-CON go', whose infinitival variants are respectively *ide kuru*, *sugi yuku* and *nak-i yuku*. Though inconclusive with the limited amount of data examined for this study, forms such as *tob-i yuku* 'fly-go' and *yadori-te yuku* 'rest-CON go' appear to be respectively a non-alternating infinitival and a non-alternating *–te* form. Thus, while both infinitival converb forms and *–te* converb forms occur in Old Japanese, the former are a large majority. One notable fact is that the aspectual use of *kuru* and *yuku* is already seen in *Manyôshû*; e.g., *ake kure-ba* 'dawn come-COND (when it is dawning)', *yo-mo huke yuku-wo* 'night-too wear go-ACC (that the night wears on)'.

The infinitival forms gradually lose their ground as the predominant type of complex predicate throughout the history, and by the beginning of the 19th century, they are completely supplanted by *–te* forms at least in colloquial speech. The pattern of displacement is shown below:
(15)

Old Japanese: *Manyôshû* 『万葉集』 (755〜759)
Song 784〜Song 1819
    Infinitival forms 52
    -te forms   18
Classical Japanese: *Genjimonogatari* 『源氏物語』 (beg. of 11th C)
First three chapters
    Infinitival forms 34
    -te forms   4
Late 17th Century: *Kôshoku Ichidai Otoko* 『好色一代男』 (1682)
    Infinitival forms 19
    -te forms   23
Early 19th Century: *Ukiyoburo* 『浮世風呂』 (1809-1813)
In colloquial speech
    Infinitival forms 0
    -te forms   39
In stage directions: infinitival and *–te* forms alternate
Modern Japanese:
    -te forms are exclusively used in both written form and colloquial speech, infinitival forms occurring only in set phrases

---

While the presence of some early *-te* converbal complex predicates indicates their independent existence throughout the history of Japanese, the overall historical trend is characterizable in terms of replacement of the infinitival forms by the corresponding *-te* forms; e.g., *tob-i yuku > ton-de iku* 'fly go', *koe yuku > koe-te iku* 'pass go', *kaer-i kuru > kaet-te kuru* 'return come'.

Interestingly, a similar trend is observable in Korean, though at a much slower pace. Studies such as Kee-Kap Lee (1981), Seon-Yeong Lee (1992), and Seymotol Son (1996) indicate that in the Middle Korean period (15th century) stem compounding (i.e., those without any connectives) were more prevalent than *-Ø/-e/-a* connective forms, which we assume to correspond to Japanese infinitival forms. According to Seon-Yeong Lee's (1992) survey, there were 1,864 instances of the former type and 86 instances of the latter type. The *-ko* connective type, which we assume to correspond to Japanese *-te* constructions, arose much later in the history. While these studies examine a wider variety of complex verb types than ours here, the pattern of replacement is strikingly similar to that of Japanese converbal complex predicates with motion verbs. For example, the development pattern of *-ko iss-ta* '-CON be' corresponding to Japanese *-te i-ru* is as follows, according to Kee-Kap Lee (1981): *-e ista (-e issta)* was more productive than *-ko ista* in Middle Korean; the productivity of *-ko ista (-ko issta)* was low until 17th and 18th century; *-ko ista (-ko issta)* appears frequently in the literature beginning the 19th century. In Modern Korean the *-ko* connective is the only option with *iss-ta* 'be/exist', replacing older forms such as *sin-e-ista > sin-ko issta* 'have shoes on'. The following summarizes the general replacement pattern discernible from the works of the Korean scholars mentioned here:

(16)

Middle K (15th C)	Early Modern K (17th-19th C)	Modern K (19th C -)
tik-mekta		ccik-e-mekta
dip-eat		dip-CON-eat
cwuc-ancta	cwuc-e-ancta	cwuc-e-ancta
squat-sit	squat-CON-sit	squat-CON-sit
ci-ye-ota (end of 15th C)		ci-ko ota
carry-CON-come		carry-CON come
	tha-kata (beg. 16th C)	tha-ko kata
	ride-go	ride-CON go

Looking over the historical developments of the converbal complex predicates in Japanese and Korean, we recognize a trend of turning the relevant forms from less to more analytical. The same trend is seen in the converbal forms in the narrative-type clause chaining constructions (see (13) and (14)) such that the infinitival connectives (-Ø/-i) and the –Ø/-e/-a connectives are not used in colloquial speech of Modern Japanese and Modern Korean. The –te connective is used exclusively in Modern Japanese speech, and the –e-se or the –kon connectives are used in Modern Korean speech. Assuming that the infinitival connectives and their Korean counter- parts were used in older speech, there is a definite drift toward more ana- lytic forms in the converbal expressions at both verbal and clausal levels in both Japanese and Korean. Accordingly, notwithstanding our earlier con- clusion on the relationship between converbal complex predicates and clause-chaining constructions, the parallel historical developments between these two layers of connective expressions must be recognized.

4. On the Grammaticalization Pattern

One of the findings of Shibatani (forthcoming) is that the grammaticaliza- tion of the verbs of going and coming in Japanese converbal complex shows definite patterns in both spatial and aspectual domains.[5] The following table summarizes the pattern of decategorialization of the relevant verbs in the spatial domain.

	mieru	*rassyaru*	Valency	Fragments	Neg scope
main V *kuru* 'come'	○	×	○	○	N/A
arui-te kuru 'walk come'	○	△	○	△	both
de-te kuru 'exit come'	○	○	×	×	wide
tabe-te kuru 'eat come'	×	◎	×	×	narrow

(◎ = super, ○ = O.K., △ = grudgingly, × = no)

Table 1. Summary of the Decategorialization Pattern of *iku/kuru* 'go/come'

The verb *kuru* and *V–te kuru* in the table above stand for both *kuru* 'come' and *iku* 'go'. *Aruite-iku/kuru* 'walk go/come' represents the combi- nation of a motion verb and a manner of motion verb (*aruku* 'walk', *hasiru* 'run', *tobu* 'fly', *hau* 'crawl', etc.), *de-te iku/kuru* combinations of a motion verb and a change-of-location verb (*hairu* 'enter,' *agaru* 'ascend', *otiru*

---

5 See Shibatani (forthcoming) and Shibatani and Huang (forthcoming) for the discussion of the grammaticalization of motion verbs in the temporal (tense/aspect) domain.

'fall', *modoru* 'return', etc.), and *tabe-te iku/kuru* combinations of a motion verb and an action verb (*yasumu* 'rest', *taberu* 'eat', *utau* 'sing', etc.) These three represent points in the continuum of various other types of verbal combinations such as *densya-ni no-te iku* 'go riding the train', *akai syatu-o ki-te kuru* 'come wearing a red shirt', *hon-o kat-te kuru* 'come having bought a book', *ture-te kuru* 'come taking (someone) along', etc.

Consideration of space does not allow us to review all the phenomena examined in Shibatani (forthcoming), but, briefly, the honorific *mieru* '(lit.) visible' suppletes the main verb *kuru* 'come', *kuru* of *arui-te kuru* (walk-CON come) and that of *de-te kuru* (exit-CON come), but not that of *tabe-te kuru* (eat-CON come). *Rassyaru*, the abbreviated form of honorific *irassyaru* 'go, come, be', does not supplete the main verb *kuru*. It suppletes *kuru* of *arui-te kuru* rather grudgingly, its favorite target being *kuru* of the *tabe-te kuru* type expressions.

Let us now take a more detailed look at a couple of phenomena that are directly relevant in the examination of the Korean data. We are interpreting the pattern shown in Table 1 as evidence that *iku/kuru* in combination with action verbs like *taberu* 'eat' and *nomu* 'drink' are most advanced in the degree of grammaticalization, losing their lexical property of expressing a motion (movement in space) and becoming more like a deictic marker, based on the original deictic lexical meaning. The loss of the lexical motion meaning in these combinations is seen from the fact that expressions such as *tabe-te kuru* (eat-CON come) and *non-de iku* (drink-CON go) cannot describe a scene of someone's moving toward or away from the deictic center after eating, drinking, etc. Consider the following:

(17) a. #Taroo-ga   gohan-o   tabe-te   ku-ru.
       Taro-NOM   meal-ACC   eat-CON   come-PRES
       Intended for 'Taro is coming (here) after eating a meal.'

    b. Taroo-ga   gohan-o   tabe-te,   kotti-ni ku-ru.
       Taroo-NOM   meal-ACC   eat-CON   here-to   come- PRES
       'Taro is coming here having eaten a meal.'

(17a) cannot be used in describing a scene of Taro's coming toward the speaker (perhaps with a toothpick in his mouth) after eating a meal in a restaurant. Compare it with appropriate (17b), in which *kuru* is the main verb of a separate clause. (17a) can be contrasted with the following, where both expressions are perfectly capable of describing physical movements witnessed.

(18) a. Taroo-ga   arui-te   kuru.
       Taroo-NOM   walk-CON   come
       'Taro is coming on foot (walk come) (toward us).'

b. Taroo-ga   heya-kara   de-te   kuru.
Taroo-NOM   room-from   exit-CON   come
'Taro is coming out of the room.'

The above phenomenon shows that the motion verbs in the *arui-te iku/kuru* (walk-CON go/come) and the *de-te iku/kuru* (exit-CON go/come) type pattern alike and are more verb-like than those in the *tabe-te iku/kuru* (eat-CON go/come) type. Corollary to the loss of the lexical meaning of movement in space in the latter is the loss of the valency property of licensing a goal argument. Interestingly, the *de-te iku/kuru* (exit-CON go/come) type behaves similarly despite the retention of the motion meaning in the relevant verbs involved, indicating that this type of construction is ahead of the *arui-te iku/kuru* type in the relevant grammaticalization process.[6]

(19) a. Taroo-wa   gakkoo-ni   arui-te   it-ta.
      Taro-TOP   school-to   walk-CON   go-PAST
      'Taro walked (walk went) to school.'
   Cf. *Taroo-wa   gakkoo-ni   arui-ta.
       Taro-TOP   school-to   walk-PAST
       'Taro walked to school.'

b. *Taroo-wa   Hanako-no   heya-ni   zibun-no heya-o   de-te
    Taro-TOP   Hanako-of   room-to self-of   room-ACC   exit-CON
    it-ta.
    go-PAST
    (lit.) 'Taro exited (exit went) his own room to Hanako's room.'
   Cf. Taroo-wa   zibun-no heya-o   de-te,   Hanako-no   heya-ni
      Taroo-TOP   self-of   room-ACC exit-CON Hanako-of   room-to
      it-ta.
      go-PAST
      'Taro exited his own room and went to Hanako's room.'

c. *Taroo-wa   gakkoo-ni ringo-o   tabe-te   it-ta.
    Taro-TOP   school-to   apple-ACC   eat-CON   go-PAST
    (lit.) 'Taro ate (eat went) an apple to school.'
   Cf. Taroo-wa   ringo-o   tabe-te,   gakkoo-ni   it-ta.
      Taro-TOP   apple-ACC   eat-CON   school-to   go-PAST
      'Taro ate an apple and went to school.'

---

[6] There are many expressions of the *de-te iku/kuru* type in which a goal expression appears; e.g., *omote-ni de-te ik-u* (front-to exit-CON go-PRES) 'go out (exit go) to the front (of a house)', *nikai-ni agat-te ik-u* (second floor-to ascend-CON go-PRES) 'go (ascend go) to the second floor'. In these expressions, it is the converbs, not the motion verbs, which license the goal argument; c.f., *omote-ni deru* 'exit to the front', *nikai-ni agaru* 'ascend to the second floor'.

The valency phenomenon examined here together with the one examined above concerning the attrition of the movement meaning corroborates the grammaticalization/decategorialization pattern shown in Table 1.

Before turning to the Korean data, let us ask if even the *arui-te iku* (walk-CON go) type, which involves the most verb-like motion verbs according to Table 1, shows any sign of undergoing grammaticalization. We can answer this by examining the valency pattern. As mentioned earlier, the main verb *iku* 'go' typically requires a goal argument. However, this property of the main verb *iku* is not necessarily maintained in its use in the converbal complex, indicating that the relevant type of converbal complex is also undergoing grammaticalization. The following table lists the pattern of occurrence of a goal argument with the main verb *iku* and the one in the converbal complex found in a Japanese novel.

	Yes	No	Understood
Goal of the main verb *iku*	40	1	4
Goal of *–te iku*	8	5	2

Table 2. Occurrence of a Goal Argument (based on Ito Sei *Hanran*)

Although the total occurrence of those converbal complex predicates with and without a goal argument is small in the novel examined since the figures in Table 2 exclude all those *–te iku* forms that are aspectual in meaning, which do not take a goal argument, those that cannot take a goal argument, e.g., the *tabe-te iku* (eat-CON go) type, and those in which the converb licenses a goal argument, e.g., *hait-te iku* (enter-CON go) (see footnote 6). From this small sample, it is seen that a goal of the *–te iku* form occurs less often than that of the main verb *iku* indicating that even those combinations at the top of Table 1 are changing the valency property of the motion verbs involved—that is, from obligatory to optional.

Turning now to the Korean situation, we find it more difficult to show the parallel grammaticalization pattern, for the pertinent evidence here is not as robust as in Japanese. Yet, one can detect subtle differences in the degree of naturalness of the relevant expressions. First, consider the motion meaning of *ota/kata* 'come/go' in the following expressions. Just like the Japanese counterparts, (20a) and (20b) can describe a scene of Yenkyu's physical movement toward the speaker.

(20) a. Yenkyu-ka   kel-e-onta.
      Yenkyu-NOM   walk-CON-come-PRES
      'Yenkyu is coming on foot (walk come) (toward us).'

b. Yenkyu-ka   pang-eyse   na-onta.
Yenyku-NOM room-from exit-CON-come-PRES
'Yenkyu is coming out (exit come) from the room.'

c. Yenkyu-ka   pap-ul   mek-ko onta.
Yenkyu-NOM meal-ACC   eat-CON come.PRES
'Yenkyu is coming (here) (after) eating a meal.'

d. Yenkyu-ka   pap-ul   mek-ko, yeki-ey onta.
Yenkyu-NOM meal-ACC eat-CON   here-to come.PRES
'Yenkyu is coming here (after) eating a meal.'

Unlike the Japanese counterpart, (20c) appears acceptable as a sentence describing the scene of Yenkyu's coming toward the speaker after his eating a meal. However, this sentence seems slightly odd compared to (20a, b). The oddity of (20c) can also be detected by comparing it with (20d), which is perfectly acceptable without any special presupposition, which seems needed for (20c).

A similar observation can be made regarding the valency property of the motion verbs in the *mek-ko ota/kata* expressions. (21a) and (21b) below are perfect with a goal argument, as expected from the parallel Japanese forms.

(21) a. Kunye-nun hakkyo-ey tallye-wa-ssta/-ka-ssta.
     she-TOP   school-to run-come-PAST/go-PAST
     'She ran (ran come/go) to school.'

b. Kunye-nun hakkyo-ey pesu-lul   tha-ko   wa-ssta/ka-ssta.
    she-TOP   school-to bus-ACC   ride-CON come-PAST/go-PAST
    'She rode (ride come/go) a bus to school.'

c. Kunye-nun hakkyo-ey sakwa-lul   mek-ko wa-ssta/ka-ssta.
    she-TOP   school-to apple-ACC eat-CON come-PAST/go-PAST
    'She came/went to school (after) eating an apple.'

Again, unlike the Japanese counterpart, (21c) is acceptable. Yet, it is more marked than (21a, b) possibly requiring a pause after *hakkyo-ey* 'to school'. One can also see this subtle difference in acceptability by comparing (21b) with (22a) and (21c) with (22b) below:

(22) a. Kunye-nun pesu-lul   tha-ko   hakkyo-ey wa-ssta/ka-ssta.
     she-TOP   bus-ACC   ride-CON school-to come-PAST/go-PAST
     'She rode a bus and came to school.'

b. Kunye-nun sakwa-lul   mek-ko   hakkyo-ey wa-ss-ta/ka-ssta.
    she-TOP   apple-ACC eat-CON school-to come-PAST/go-PAST
    'She ate an apple and went to school.'

That is, (21b) is just as natural as (22a), but (21c), compared to (22b), appears more restricted in its use; for example, it requires a contrastive context (e.g., whether she ate an apple or not was at issue). (22b), on the other hand, is a neutral description of the two sequentially connected events and is usable in a broader context. From these observations, we predict that a goal argument would be less likely to occur in sentences with a *mek-ko kata* (eat-CON go) type predicate than in those with a *kel-e-kata* (walk-CON-go) type predicate.

Our interpretation of these findings is that Korean *ota/kata* 'come/go' in converbal complex are also undergoing grammaticalization similar to the Japanese counterparts, but at a much slower pace. An important point to recognize is that Korean also follows the Japanese pattern of showing a more advanced level of grammaticalization in the *mek-ko ota/kata* (eat-CON come/go) type than the other types of verb combinations. In Modern Korean, as in Old Japanese (see Section 3 above), there is a formal correlate between those undergoing grammaticalization, e.g., *mek-ko ota/kata* (eat-CON come/go) and those that are not, e.g., *kel-e-ota/kata* (walk-CON come/go), *na-ota/kata* (exit-Ø-come/go), whereby the former type is marked by a more explicit converbal ending (*-ko*) than the latter. The final section of the paper is an attempt to tie these two phenomena together under general functional principles.

4. On the Form and Grammaticalization Pattern of Converbal-Complex Predicates

The question of what factors drive grammaticalization has been raised by a number of people working in this area. Traugott and Heine (1991:9), for example, mention that "the form must be used frequently" for it to undergo grammaticalization. Heine, Claudi and Hünnemeyer (1991:29) recognize metaphorical extension as an important motivation for grammaticalization. In their own words: "grammaticalization can be interpreted as the result of a process that has problem solving as its main goal, whereby one object is expressed in terms of another." Of these two factors, metaphorical extension is not relevant here, for our cases dealt with in this paper are concerned with the grammaticalization of motion verbs in the spatial domain.

As for the frequency factor, situations are not as straightforward as Traugott and Heine (1991) put it. That is, determining the token frequency of constructions is not simple, since the frequency of use of a construction varies greatly depending on the specific lexical items involved. For example, in one recent Google count *hat-te iku* (crawl-CON go 這って行く) occurred 963 times, whereas the same Manner of motion + Motion combination of *arui-te iku* (walk-CON go 歩いて行く) yielded 623,000 instances. In ascertaining the token frequency, then, it is necessary to compare the frequency of different types of verb combination. The following table shows the token frequencies of the three combination types in a modern fiction in Japanese and Korean:

	Manner	Location change	Action
V-te iku/kuru V-CON go/come	23	109	6
V-e/ko ota/kata V-CON come/go	68	358	11

Table 3. Token Frequency of Three Combination Types
(Japanese; Ito Sei *Hanran*: Korean; Kim Joo Yong
Kokicapinun kaltaylul kkekkci anhnunta)

It is clear from the above table that frequency has little to do with the patterns of grammaticalization we have observed in Japanese and Korean. That is, the combination type of Action + Motion, e.g., *tabe-te kuru* (eat-CON come), that shows the most advanced degree of grammaticalization occurs least frequently in both Japanese and Korean.[7] Thus, neither frequency nor metaphorical extension appears to be a factor driving the grammaticalization phenomenon examined here. Below we will attempt a semantic account based on the notion of semantic congruity holding between the two events combined in the form of converbal complex.

Two events having the following kinds of property are semantically congruous:

(23)   (a) share participants,
(b) show spatio-temporal overlap,
(c) causally connected as in the combinations of Motion + Purpose, Cause + Effect, Action + Result,
(d) conventionally connected as in those events whose sequential occurrence is recognized as a cultural norm.

---

[7] It is likely that the high frequency of the Location change + Motion combination, especially in Korean, is related to the lexicalization of some of the relevant expressions instantiating this combinatorial pattern. For example, Korean *nata* 'exit' and *tulta* 'enter' must be used in combination with either *ota* 'come' or *kata* 'go' for expressions such as 'enter the room' and 'exit the room'. Furthermore, combinations of *tul-e-kata* (enter-CON go), *na-ota* (exit-Ø-come), etc. do not allow insertion of the topic particle *nun*, while other converbal complexes do. Notice that lexicalization is different from grammaticalization—the latter refers to a shift in meaning/function from lexical to grammatical.

Under this characterization, event combinations instantiating the Manner of motion + Motion pattern are semantically congruous if they share the actor, for there is complete spatio-temporal overlap in the executions of a manner of motion and a motion. When one walks, runs or swims, s/he is necessarily moving to some direction. Conversely, when one goes to someplace, s/he'd be typically doing so in some manner, e.g., walking, running, swimming. Compared to this, the combination of Action + Motion instantiates a combination of much less congruous events since there is typically no spatio-temporal overlap between eating and subsequently going to some place, for example. We would like to consider the combination of Location change + Motion to be intermediate in the degree of semantic congruity between these cases. Expressions like *hait-te iku* (enter-CON go) in Japanese and *na-ota* (exit-Ø-come) in Korean combine two events that show a spatio-temporal overlap, but not to the extent of Manner + Motion combinations. In the latter case, the two relevant events are coextensive, but in the former the overlap actually obtains only at the point of the threshold.

Based on this understanding of the notion of semantic congruity, we offer the following as a principle governing the grammaticalization pattern summarized in Table 1.

(24) Grammaticalization is facilitated in a semantically less congruous context.[8]

Various speculations can be entertained for the reason why grammaticalization is facilitated in a semantically less congruous context. It may be the case that lexical meaning is maintained more steadfastly in a semantically congruous context precisely because of the harmony in meaning with its environment. Semantic orphans, on the other hand, may be more prone to a (wilder?) shift in function. From the pragmatic point of view, semantically incongruous combinations more readily invite non-literal interpretations following the Grician maxims of conversation.

Before our final attempt to connect the grammaticalization pattern and the formal features of converbal complex predicates, we would like to posit the following principle governing the formation of a juncture.

(25) Semantically congruous events tend to form a juncture.

(25) is actually derivable from the more general iconicity principle of contiguity underlying the general tendency for similar entities or those that frequently occur next to each other to be expressed in contiguous form. (25) would predict that those events having some of the characteristics listed in

---

[8] See Shibatani and Huang (forthcoming) for the demonstration that this principle is also operative in the grammaticalization of motion verbs in the temporal (tense/aspect) domain.

(23) are more likely to be expressed in the form of a juncture such as converbal connectives, serial verbs, or other types of conjunctive expression than semantically less congruous events.

Finally, we would like to offer the following principle, which is a version of a more general principle first proposed in Shibatani (unpublished) as the "Principle of Functional Transparency": [9]

(26) Semantically less congruous junctures require a more explicit connective marking.

In both Modern Korean and Old Japanese, it is a semantically less congruous event sequence such as eating and then going/coming to some place that require more explicit marking of *–ko* (Modern Korean) and *–te* (Old Japanese). In Korean there are some expressions that allow either *–ko* or less explicit *–Ø/-e/-a* marking, e.g., *kac-ko-kata/ kaci-e-kata* (hold-CON go), *mwul-ko-kata/mwul-e-kata* (hold.in.the.mouth-CON go), *ep-ko-kata/ep-e-kata* (give.a.piggyback-CON go), *teyli-ko-kata/teyli-e-kata* (accompany-CON go). Possibly except for the last example, all these expressions depict situations in between semantically congruous event combinations and incongruous ones. There is a certain degree of overlap of the two events in these expressions such that the effect of the first event, e.g., holding something, overlaps with the motion, but not a total overlap as in the case of the combination of a manner of motion and a motion.[10] Our account is also consistent with the characterizations of the two types of Korean ending by Korean linguists such as: "*-e* is consolidating connective particle, and *–ko* is isolating connective particle" (Lee 2000:225 fn).

To conclude, the pattern of grammaticalization of motion verbs in converbal complex predicate constructions seen in Japanese (and the parallel pattern observed more subtly in Korean) and the formal properties of Modern Korean converbal complex predicates are related phenomena that are mediated by the concept of semantic congruity holding between the two events expressed in the converbal juncture form.

---

[9] The original formulation of the Principle of Functional Transparency reads as follows: "Less familiar or unusual situations require functionally more transparent coding".

[10] In serializing languages like Chinese and Thai, congruous events such as riding a bicycle and going to school allow verb serialization, but not incongruous events such as eating a meal and going to school. As predicted by (26), the latter combination requires an explicit conjunction. Cf. Chinese: *wǒ qí jǐaotàchē qù xúeixiào* '(lit.) I rode a bicycle went to school' and *wǒ chī fàn ránhou qù xúeixiào* 'I ate a meal **and then** went to school'.

References

Aikhenvald, A. 2006. Serial Verb Constructions in Typological Perspective. *Serial Verb Constructions: A Cross-linguistic Typology,* eds. A. Y. Aikhenvald and R.M.W. Dixon, 1-68. Oxford: Oxford University Press.

Crowley, T. 2002. *Serial Verbs in Oceanic: A Descriptive Typology.* Oxford: Oxford University Press.

DeLancey, S. 1991. The Origins of Verb Serialization in Modern Tibetan. *Studies in Languages* 15-1:1-23.

Falsgraf, C. and I. Park. 1994. Synchronic and Diachronic Aspects of Complex Predicates in Korean and Japanese. *Japanese/Korean Linguistics* 4, ed. N. Akatsuka, 221-237. Stanford: CSLI.

Foley, W.A. and M. Olsen. 1985. Clausehood and Verb Serialization. *Grammar Inside and Outside the Clause,* eds. J. Nichols and A. C. Woodbury, 17-60. Cambridge: Cambridge University Press.

Heine, B., U. Claudi and F. Hünnemeyer. 1991. *Grammaticalization: A Conceptual Framework.* Chicago: University of Chicago Press.

Hopper P.J. and E. C. Traugott. 1993. *Grammaticalization.* Cambridge: Cambridge University Press.

Kim, M-H. 1996. Mwunpephwa uy thul eyse ponun pocotongsa kwumun. *Tamhwa wa Inci* 2:126-146.

Lee, J-H. 2000. A Cognitive Approach to Connective Particles *–e* and *–ko*: Conceptual Unity and Conceptual Separation in Korean Motion Verbs. *Japanese/Korean Linguistics* 9, ed. M. Nakayama, 225-238. Stanford: CSLI.

Lee, K-K. 1981. The Historical Replacement of '-a' with '-ko' in the Ending System of Korean. *Language Research* 17-2:227-236. Language Research Institute, Seoul National University.

Lee, S-Y. 1992. *Kwuke yenkwu 110: 15seyki kwuke pokhaptongsa yenkwu* KwukeYenkwuhoy. Seoul National University.

Lord, C. 1993. *Historical Change in Serial Verb Constructions.* Amsterdam: John Benjamins.

Shibatani, M. Unpublished. Form and Function in Functional Linguistics. Colloquium Talk. Department of Linguistics, Rice University. (Fall, 2003)

Shibatani, M. Forthcoming. Grammaticalization of Motion Verbs. Paper Presented at the 2nd Oxford-Kobe Seminar in Linguistics, Kobe, Japan. September 28, 2004.

Shibatani, M. and L. Huang. Forthcoming. Serial Verb Constructions in Formosan Languages. Paper Presented at the 3rd Oxford-Kobe Seminar in Linguistics. Kobe, Japan. April 5, 2006.

Son, S.1996. *Kwuke pocoyongen yenkwu.* Seoul: Hankwuk Mwunhwasa.

Traugott, E. C. and B. Heine 1991. Introduction. *Approaches to Grammaticalization,* vol. 1. eds. E.C. Traugott and B. Heine, 1-14. Amsterdam: John Benjamins.

Part I

Discourse and Sociolinguistics

Prosodic Analysis of the Interactional Particle *Ne* in Japanese Gendered Speech

VICTORIA ANDERSON, MIE HIRAMOTO, AND ANDREW WONG
University of Hawai'i at Mānoa

1. Introduction

Gendered speech in contemporary standard Japanese has been well-researched (e.g., Ide 1982, McGloin 1990, Okamoto 1995a, Reynolds 1985, Shibamoto 1985). Studies of Japanese gendered speech reveal that women and men differ in their use of interactional particles, pronouns, lexical items, and discourse styles. However, the literature is sparser on the subject of the prosodic characteristics that differentiate masculine and feminine speech in Japanese, and the prosodic studies that exist mainly concern themselves with fundamental frequency (F0) rather than duration. Ohara (1992, 2001), Loveday (1986) and others have investigated women's use of high F0 and its social meanings. High F0 is generally associated with the expression of politeness, cuteness, and other positive feminine images (Loveday 1982, 1986, Ohara 1993, in press). Ide and Yoshida (1999), McGloin (1990), and Reynolds (1985) have also associated rising intonation and wide pitch range with feminine speech. On the other hand, little research has focused on possible differences in duration patterns in masculine and feminine speech. To begin to address this gap in research, the current paper investigates both F0 and duration characteristics of the interactional particle *ne* in gendered speech. In Section 2 we briefly summarize previous research on the gendered use of *ne*. Section 3 describes the methods we used to collect and analyze speech data for this study. Results are discussed in Section 4, and Section 5 presents our conclusions.

2. Gender-Neutrality and the Interactional Particle *Ne*

Researchers have established that the interactional particle *ne* is one of the most frequently used in Japanese (e.g., Cook 1988, 1992, Maynard 1997, Sreetharan 2004). *Ne* has been described as 'gender-neutral' (e.g., Ide and Yoshida 1999, McGloin 1990, Okamoto 1995b), meaning that unlike gender-exclusive particles such as *kashira* (feminine) and *zo* (masculine), *ne* is available to speakers of both genders. According to Ide and Yoshida, *ne* is neither gender "exclusive" nor gender "preferred" (1999:465). The assumption implicit in such a description is that *ne* functions in the same way for both genders. However, some recent studies have shown that men and women use *ne* in different discourse contexts (e.g., Okamoto 1995a, Sreetharan 2004). Sreetharan (2004:86) finds that NP+*ne* is moderately feminine, while VP/ADJ+*ne* is neutral. Cook (in press) and Shibamoto (1985) also find correlations between the use of certain lexical categories and gendered style. Utterances involving a nominal consistently sound more feminine than those involving a verbal. Thus, an utterance like *Hon ne* 'It is a book *ne*' is more feminine than an utterance like *Iku ne* 'I will go *ne*.'

In the same way that gendered speech styles use different lexical categories in combination with *ne*, gendered speech styles may assign distinct prosodic characteristics to *ne*. This possibility has yet to be explored, and as such forms the focus of the present study.

To gain a better understanding of possible gendered effects on the prosody of *ne*, we elicited stereotypically gendered speech from native speakers. Our particular focus here is language *ideology* rather than language *practice* per se. Cameron and Kulick (2003) discuss the importance of both in the study of language and gender, defining ideology as "representations of social types and their ways of speaking ...which circulate in a given society" (p. 135), and practice as "what we observe when we investigate the behavior of real people in real situations" (p. 135). To understand how people construct and perform identity through language practice, it is important to first be familiar with the ideological resources available to them, in terms of culturally agreed-upon stereotypes. In this study, we use *ne* as a tool with which to elucidate stereotypes about how Japanese men and women use prosody.

3. Speakers, Speech Materials, Methodology and Data Analysis

3.1. Speakers

Ten female and ten male native speakers of Japanese from the Kantoo area (Tokyo, Saitama, Western Chiba, and Eastern Kanagawa prefectures) participated in this study. All are considered by other native speakers to be monodialectal speakers of standard Japanese.[1] Participants' ages ranged between 23 and 35 for the female group, and 23 and 40 for the male group.

3.2. Speech Materials

Speech materials were developed so as to be 'gender-neutral'; that is, so that they could be uttered in either a masculine or a feminine speech style. *Ne* was placed in both channeling and backchanneling contexts. For the former, *ne* was situated in utterance-initial, -medial and -final positions. In the backchanneling context, *ne* occurs only in final position. Voiced segments were used as far as possible, to facilitate pitch tracking. Sentences one through four were presented to participants in written form.

(1) Sentence–Initial Channeling
    Participant: *Ne, Burugari-wa nan-no   burando?*
               ne   Bulgari-NOM what-GEN   brand
               'Say, what brand is Bulgari?'

(2) Sentence–Medial Channeling
    Participant: *Yuube ara moana-no mae-de ne, Yamada-san ni atta yo.*
           last night Ala Moana-GEN front-LOC *ne*, Yamada-san DAT meet-PST *yo*
           'Last night, I met Yamada-san in front of Ala Moana.'

(3) Sentence–Final Channeling
    Participant: *Gondoo-san rabo-de yoku miru ne.*
               Gondoo-san lab-LOC often see *ne*
               'Gondoo-san is often seen in the lab.'

(4) Sentence–Final Backchanneling
    Experimenter: *Mite, kono e   sugoku riaru janai?*
               look this picture very   real COP NEG
               'Look, doesn't this picture look real?'

    Participant: *Un, honmono mitai da ne.*
               yes real thing as if COP *ne*
               'Yeah, that looks real.'

---

[1] In the rest of this paper, the term "Japanese" will refer to standard Japanese, or Kantoo dialect.

3.3. Methodology

Each participant was recorded in a separate session. Participants were instructed to read utterances in two conditions: (i) in an explicitly masculine style, as though auditioning for a masculine role in a theater production; (ii) in an explicitly feminine style, as though auditioning for a feminine role in a theater production. Subjects practiced alone, and when comfortable, were recorded by the second author, in a sound-treated booth or quiet classroom. The order of sentences did not vary among subjects, nor did the order of speech styles. To control for possible effects of differences in intonational phrasing, speakers were rerecorded if they did not place an intonational phrase boundary (including pause) after *ne*, in each sentence.

3.4. Data Analysis

PitchWorks was used to digitize data at 11.025 kHz. For each sentence, a time-aligned waveform, pitch track and spectrogram were displayed. Duration, F0 maximum, and F0 minimum were measured for *ne* and for the sentence as a whole.

Figure 1 depicts speaker M1's utterance of Sentence (4), performed in a feminine style. Vertical arrows show the beginning and end of *ne*, as determined from the displays and the sound file. Figure 2 shows speaker M1's utterance of the same sentence, performed in a masculine style. Horizontal arrows show F0 minimum and maximum in *ne*.

3.5. Statistical Analysis

We submitted the data to two-factor, repeated-measures analysis of variance (ANOVA). Because inherent differences in F0 are expected between women and men, women were analyzed in one group, and men in another.

Two independent variables were investigated: *Gender Style* (role-played masculine style versus role-played feminine style), and *Sentential Position* (initial channeled, medial channeled, final channeled, and final backchanneled). Though interesting, sentential position is not the main focus here, and will be discussed in a future study.

Five dependent variables were analyzed: (i) duration of *ne* in milliseconds; (ii) duration of *ne* as a proportion of overall sentence duration; (iii) F0 range of *ne*, (iv) F0 maximum of *ne*, and (v) F0 minimum of *ne*.

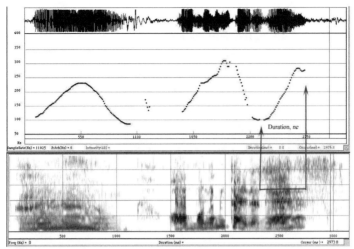

Figure 1. M1's Feminine Performance of Sentence (4)
Un, honmono mitai da ne. (Arrows refer to duration endpoints of *ne*.)

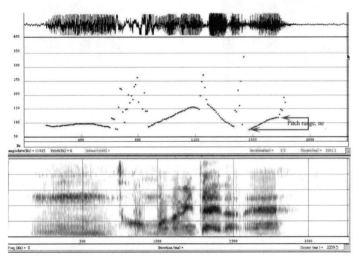

Figure 2. M1's Masculine Performance of Sentence (4)
Un, honmono mitai da ne. (Arrows refer to F0 minimum and maximum in *ne*.)

Though twenty speakers were recorded, data summarized here represent nine females and seven males. Two males declined to perform the feminine style; thus, the full data set was not available for them. Moreover, for one other male and one female, recording levels were often too low in amplitude at critical regions to permit reliable measurement of duration and/or F0.

4. Results and Discussion

4.1. Absolute and Relative Duration of *Ne*

Figure 3 shows results for mean <u>duration of *ne*</u>, in milliseconds. In this and the following summary figures, men's results are shown in the left-hand graph, while women's results are shown in the right-hand graph. In each graph, sentential position is arranged on the x-axis; the left-most pair of bars refers to sentence-initial position, the second pair to medial position, the third pair to final channeling position, and the fourth pair to final backchanneling position. Finally, for each sentential position, the bar on the left refers to the feminine style, while the bar on the right refers to the masculine style. Error bars reflect one standard deviation.

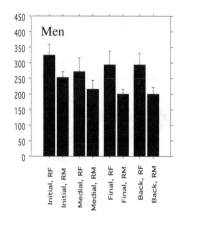 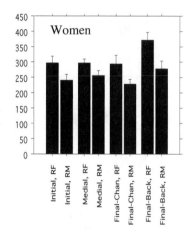

Figure 3. Absolute Duration of *Ne* in Milliseconds

ANOVA showed a statistically significant main effect of *Gender Style* on the <u>duration of *ne*</u>, for both the male group ($F(1,6)=7.366$; p=.0439) and the female group ($F(1,8)=20.452$; p=.0019). In each paired comparison, *ne* in the feminine style was of greater duration than *ne* in the masculine style.

For the women's group, there was also a significant main effect of *Sentential Position* on the <u>duration of *ne*</u> ($F(3,24)=3.505$; p=.0307). In the final backchanneling position, women made *ne* particularly long when performing the feminine style.

There was no significant interaction effect of *Sentential Position* by *Gender Style*, for either group.

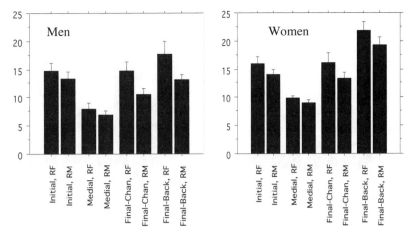

Figure 4. Duration of *Ne* as a Proportion of Sentence Duration in Percent

Figure 4 gives results for the relative <u>proportion of *ne*</u> as a percentage of the duration of the sentence. This measure was used in order to remove possible effects of differences in speech rate between or within speakers. ANOVA found a statistically significant main effect of *Gender Style* on proportion of *ne*, for both groups. (Men: $F(1,6)=8.340$; p=.0278. Women: $F(1,8)=8.391$; p=.0200.) For each RF vs. RM (role-played feminine vs. role-played masculine) pair, *ne* in the feminine style accounted for a greater proportion of the sentence than did *ne* in the masculine style.

There was also a statistically significant main effect of *Sentential Position* on <u>proportion of *ne*</u>, for both groups. (Men: $F(3,18)=22.725$; p<.0001. Women: $F(3,24)=33.128$; p<.0001.) In the male group, medial *ne* was shorter in duration than *ne* in other sentential positions. In the female group, medial *ne* was likewise shorter than elsewhere, and additionally, in final backchanneling position, *ne* was longer than elsewhere.

No significant interaction effect was found between *Sentential Position* and *Gender Style* on this measure, for either group.

4.2. F0 in *Ne*

Mean F0 ranges for *ne* as performed in feminine versus masculine styles are shown in Figure 5. We found a significant main effect of *Gender Style* on <u>F0 range of *ne*</u>, for both groups. (Men: $F(1, 6)= 6.798$; p=.0403. Women: $F(1,8)=7.155$; p=.0282.) For each RF vs. RM pair, the F0 range of *ne* was larger in the feminine style than in the masculine style. No significant main effect of *Sentential Position*, or interaction effect of *Sentential Position* by *Gender Style,* were found for this measure.

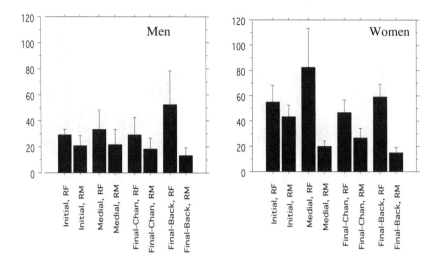

Figure 5. Mean F0 Ranges of *Ne*

Figure 6 provides means and error bars for the dependent variable F0 maximum in *ne*. ANOVA found a statistically significant main effect of *Gender Style* on F0 maximum, for both men and women. (Men: $F(1, 5)$= 24.633; p=.0042. Women: $F(1,8)$=12.264; p=.0081.) For each RF vs. RM pair, *ne* in the feminine style had a higher F0 maximum than did *ne* in the masculine style.

There was no main effect of *Sentential Position* on F0 maximum, for either group. However, there was a significant interaction effect, for the male group only, between *Sentential Position* and *Gender Style* ($F(3,15)$=3.539; p=.0406). For men, *ne* in the feminine style has a particularly high F0 maximum in the final backchanneling position.

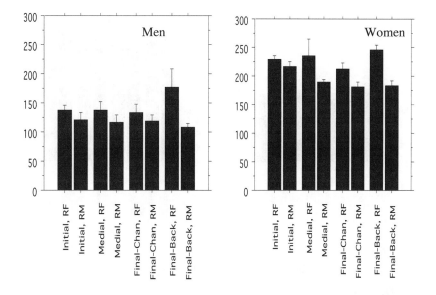

Figure 6. Mean F0 Maxima of *Ne*

Figure 7 summarizes means and standard error for the dependent measure <u>F0 minima in *ne*</u>. ANOVA showed a statistically significant main effect of *Gender Style* on F0 minimum, but unlike any of the foregoing results, this was true of the male group only ($F(1, 5)= 18.356$; $p=.0078$). For male speakers, *ne* in the masculine style was implemented with a lower F0 minimum than in the feminine style. There was also a significant interaction effect of *Sentential Position* by *Gender Style* for men ($F(3,15)=8.302$; $p=.0017$): in the final backchanneling position, men showed a greater difference between RF and RM styles than in other positions.

Women did not use a systematic difference in minimum F0 to differentiate gender styles ($F(1,8)=.212$; $p=.6575$).

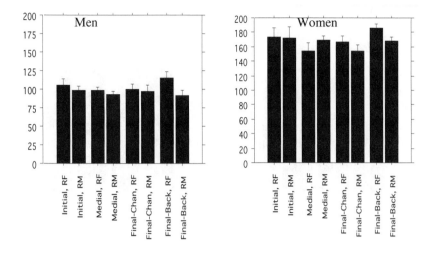

Figure 7. Mean F0 Minima of *Ne*

4.3. Discussion

Loveday (1986), and Ohara (1992, 2000) investigated differences in Japanese men's and women's language *practice*, focusing on F0 range over sentence spans. They found that F0 plays an important role in gender differentiation. Our results extend these findings to language *ideology*—native speakers' beliefs about stereotypical masculine and feminine speech. In this study we observe consistent differences between gender styles in the F0 characteristics of *ne*. We find that in the role-played feminine style, *ne* always has a higher F0 register and larger F0 range than in the masculine style. Women implement the F0 range difference by setting higher F0 ceilings in the feminine style, and lower ceilings in the masculine style, but do not use differences in the F0 floor to differentiate between the styles. Men use differences in both F0 ceiling and floor to indicate gender style differences; their implementation of the feminine style consistently has both higher F0 ceilings and higher F0 floors than the masculine style.

In addition, our findings show that gender stereotypes are also expressed via durational patterns. In these results, *ne* in the role-played feminine style always occupies a larger proportion of the utterance's duration than *ne* in the role-played masculine style. The pragmatic role of *ne* as an emphatic marker may underlie this difference in gender styles. Increased duration and F0 range often correlate with increased emphasis. In turn, increased emphasis is commonly thought to index femininity in Japanese.

5. Conclusion

In this study, prosodic features of stereotypical Japanese feminine and masculine speech styles were examined, by focusing on the F0 and duration characteristics of the interactional particle *ne*. *Ne* is used in both feminine and masculine speech, and has been called 'gender-neutral' for this reason. However, *ne* is not gender-neutral in terms of its prosody; it exhibits significantly different F0 and duration attributes as a function of gender style. Native speakers of Japanese raise their F0 register, and expand both the F0 range and the duration of *ne* in the feminine style. Speakers correspondingly contract the F0 range and duration of *ne* in the masculine style. These findings corroborate claims made in the existing literature regarding the F0 characteristics of Japanese women's language. In addition, these results empirically demonstrate that the relative duration of this interactional particle is also recruited as a linguistic resource in the performance of gender in Japanese.

References

Cameron, D. and D. Kulick. 2003. *Language and Sexuality*. Cambridge: Cambridge University Press.

Cook, H. 1988. Sentential Particles in Japanese Conversation: A Study of Indexicality. Doctoral dissertation, University of Southern California.

Cook, H. 1992. Meaning of Non-Referential Indexes: A Case Study of the Japanese Sentence-Final Particle *ne*. *Text* 12:507-539.

Cook, H. In Press. The Pragmatics of Japanese Sentence-Final Forms. *Japanese/Korean Linguistics 13*, ed. M. Hudson. Stanford: CSLI Publications.

Ide, S. 1982. Japanese Sociolinguistics: Politeness and Women's Language. *Lingua* 57:357-385.

Ide, S. and M. Yoshida. 1999. Sociolinguistics: Honorifics and Gender Differences. *The Handbook of Japanese Sociolinguistics,* ed. N. Tsujimura, 444-480. Oxford: Blackwell.

Loveday, L. 1982. Pitch, Politeness, and Sexual Role: An Exploratory Investigation into the Pitch Correlates of English and Japanese Politeness Formulae. *Language and Speech* 24:71-87.

Loveday, L. 1986. *Explorations in Japanese Sociolinguistics*. Philadelphia: John Benjamins.

Maynard, S. 1997. *Japanese Communication: Language and Thought in Context*. Honolulu: University of Hawai'i Press.

McGloin, N. 1990. Sex Difference and Sentence-Final Particles. *Aspects of Japanese Women's Language*, eds. S. Ide and N. McGloin, 23-41. Tokyo: Kuroshio.

Ohara, Y. 1992. Gender-Dependent Pitch Levels: A Comparative Study in Japanese and English. *Locating Power: Proceedings of the Second Berkeley Women and*

Language Conference, eds. K. Hall, M. Bucholtz, and B. Moonwomon, 469-477. Berkeley: Berkeley Women & Language Group.

Ohara, Y. 1993. Koe no Takasa Kara Ukeru Inshoo ni Tsuite. *Kotoba* 14:14-19.

Ohara, Y. 2000. *A Critical Discourse Analysis: Ideology of Language and Gender in Japanese*. Doctoral dissertation, University of Hawai'i.

Ohara, Y. 2001. Finding One's Voice in Japanese: A Study of the Pitch Levels of L2 users. *Multilingualism, Second Language Learning, and Gender*, eds. A. Pavlenko, A. Blackledge, I. Piller and M. Teutsch-Dwyer, 231-254. Philadelphia: Walter de Gruyter.

Ohara, Y. In Press. Exploring the Social Construction of Voice in Japanese: Pitch and Gender Displays in Conversations at Work. *Exploring the Myth of Japanese Women's Language*, eds. N. Adachi and J. Stanlaw. Honolulu: University of Hawai'i Press.

Okamoto, S. 1995a. "Tasteless" Japanese: Less "Feminine" Speech among Young Japanese Women. *Gender Articulated: Language and the Socially Constructed Self*, eds. K. Hall and M. Bucholtz, 297-325. New York: Routledge.

Okamoto, S. 1995b. Pragmaticization of Meaning in Some Sentence-Final Particles in Japanese. *Essays in Semantics and Pragmatics*, eds. M. Shibatani and S. Thompson, 219-246. Amsterdam: John Benjamins.

Reynolds, K. 1985. Female Speakers of Japanese. *Feminist Issues* 5:13-46.

Shibamoto, J. 1985. *Japanese Women's Language*. Orlando: Academic Press.

Sreetharan, C. 2004. Japanese Men's Linguistic Stereotypes and Realities: Conversations from the Kansai and Kanto Regions. *Japanese Language, Gender, and Ideology: Cultural Models and Real People*, eds. S. Okamoto and J. Smith, 275-289. Oxford: Oxford University Press.

Grammatical Features of Yokohama Pidgin Japanese: Common Characteristics of Restricted Pidgins

AYA INOUE

University of Hawai'i at Mānoa / East-West Center

1. Introduction[1]

A pidginized variety of Japanese called *Yokohamese* or *Japanese Ports Lingo* evolved during the reign of Emperor Meiji from 1868 to 1912, and largely disappeared by the end of the nineteenth century (Holm 1989:593). Hereafter this variety is referred to as Yokohama Pidgin Japanese, or YPJ. In this paper, I will describe the sociohistorical background and linguistic features of YPJ. Then I will examine if we could label YPJ as 'restricted pidgin' based on the common characteristics of restricted pidgins discussed in Siegel (in press) and Sebba (1997). Restricted pidgins are those that are used only for basic communication among people who do not share a common language. They are not the everyday language of any speech community. Siegel (in press) showed eight grammatical features that are shared by most restricted pidgins: a) virtually no productive bound morphology—inflectional or derivational, b) reduced number of adpositions and pronouns,

---

[1] I would like to thank Jeff Siegel for his valuable comments and encouragements. All remaining errors are of course my own.

c) reduced lexicon, d) no TMA markers—temporal adverbs used, e) preverbal negative markers, f) no complementizers, g) more reduplicated forms
(but reduplication not productive), and h) some bimorphemic question
words. Grammatical features of YPJ that are relevant to these eight features
will be introduced and examined. The influence from Chinese Pidgin English (CPE) will also be discussed.

2. Sociohistorical Background

The pidginized Japanese in Yokohama was produced by the contacts between Japanese and foreign nationals from abroad particularly in the Yokohama area at the time of the Meiji opening of Japan to the West (Miller
1967:266). According to a study on the formation of Yokohama Settlement
(Ishizuka 1996), Yokohama developed as an international trade city and a
port town of the capital, Tokyo, that served an important role in monopolis-
tic exporting of raw silk. The Tokugawa Shogunate (later on the Meiji government) allowed foreign nationals to borrow land, build buildings, and do
trading businesses only within the Gaikokujin-Kyoryuuchi (Foreign nationals' Settlement) for forty years from the opening of Yokohama port in 1859
until 1899. The Settlement was about 108 hectares in area. In 1860, six
months after the opening of the Yokohama port, only forty-four foreign
nationals (mainly English and Americans) were living in the settlement. In
eighteen years, the number of Europeans increased to 1,370. This meant
that combined with 1,850 Chinese, more than 3,000 foreign nationals were
living in the settlement then. In terms of nationality, the British were the
most representative followed by Americans and Germans. Many of the
foreign nationals were businessmen, doctors, teachers, and missionaries.
One-fourth were women who came to Japan as wives or tutors. Table 1
below shows the demographic data of the foreign nationals in the Yokohama Settlement from 1870 to 1897.

Year	1870	1878	1893	1897
British	513	515	808	869
American	146	300	253	372
German	76	175	151	208
French	83	120	133	274
Dutch	34	59	60	40
Total Europeans	***942**	**1,370**	**1,605**	**2,096**
Chinese		1,850	3,325	2,015
Total		**3,220**	**4,930**	**4,111**

Table 1. The Number of Foreign Nationals in Yokohama Settlement 1870 – 1897
(from Ishizuka 1996) [The number with * does not include the number of women.]

As Table 1 demonstrates, the number of Chinese represents a significant proportion in the demographic data. It is assumed that Chinese people played a significant role in the formation of YPJ although their role has not been discussed in the previous studies. Since the Tokugawa Shogunate and the Qing dynasty did not conclude their treaty, Chinese people could not officially enter Japan before 1871. Meanwhile, Chinese people entered Japan as employees of the foreign nationals who were from the countries with treaties. After the *Nissin tsuusyou jouki* 'Sino-Japanese Amity Treaty' was concluded on 1871, more Chinese migrated to Yokohama (Sugahara 1993). Most of the Chinese people who came to Yokohama were from Canton where CPE evolved in the early eighteenth century (Holm 1989:512). Concerning Chinese traders in the Settlement, Ishizuka (1996) stated that many of them did their business throughout the Pacific including places such as Shanghai, Hong Kong, and Singapore. In an autobiographical essay written by Theodate Geoffrey (Geoffrey 1926:7), who arrived in the Settlement in 1917, there is an anecdote about a Chinese baby nurse who spoke 'pidgin English.' The Chinese baby nurse greeted the author, 'How do, missy. You b'long ship side long time; you velly tired?' when she first met her. Two features of Chinese Pidgin English (CPE) are observed in this short discourse. They are the use of *belong* as copula and the zero copula. According to Baker (1987:183), the *belong* copula is an exclusively CPE feature and one which reflects Cantonese influence. As for the zero copula, it is one of the frequently found features in many other pidgins and creoles (Baker 1987:177). Taking these into consideration, it is very probable that Chinese people in the Settlement had used some CPE. Geoffrey (1926) also tells us that social interaction between foreign nationals and Japanese was limited to certain settings such as business negotiations and interaction with servants.

Niki (2001) revealed the social psychological attitudes of the English speakers toward YPJ by referring the articles in two major newspapers of those days for the English speakers in Yokohama settlement. Niki's discussion tells us about people with two opposing attitudes toward YPJ—those who designated YPJ as corrupted and vulgar, and those who believed in its usefulness. The review article in *The Japan Gazette* for the other orthodox textbook of Standard Japanese 'Kwaiwa Hen, Twenty-Five Exercises in the Yedo Colloquial' edited by Ernest M. Satow, mentioned YPJ as 'that odious jargon—the pidgin Japanese of Yokohama,' and also as 'the contemptible, vulgar, and to all but open port men, incomprehensible jargon that has flourished hitherto (*The Japan Gazette*: 1873, Oct. 21st).'

On the other hand, the review article of Atkinson (1879) in *The Japan Weekly Mail* argued that YPJ is very helpful for learners of Japanese as a foreign language and emphasized that the textbook is not for the small number of elites but for the public 'as regards this dialect [YPJ], no person can deny its marvellous compactness when finding the amount of multum it is capable of reproducing by so slight a pervo…', and applauded the anonymous author as one 'whom fame will soon lead forth to crown with public honours (*The Japan Weekly Mail*: 1873, Nov. 22nd).'

3. Linguistic Description of Pidginized Japanese in Yokohama

3.1. Data

The data is a word list and a set of example sentences from the small peda-gogical guide for the learners of YPJ: *Revised and Enlarged Edition of Ex-ercises in the Yokohama Dialect* (Atkinson 1879, hereafter referred to as '*Exercises*'). This small 40-page pamphlet was published anonymously, and the author later turned out to be a merchant who engaged in Commerce both in China and Japan. Although the amount of data contained in Atkinson (1879) is not comprehensive, as the author stated in the preface, it is enough to provide some idea of its lexicon and grammatical structure. Since YPJ is represented with English words (and pseudowords), two separate words were sometimes used to transcribe a word in YPJ. A good example is *cheese eye*, an adjective meaning 'little.' Apparently *cheese eye* derived from a Japanese adjective *chiisai* (little, small). In this paper, I will use a hyphen to combine such words as *cheese-eye* for the reader's convenience.

3.2. Phonology

As Holm (1989) pointed out, YPJ generally retained the CV syllabic struc-ture of Japanese. Since YPJ is mostly transcribed with a series of small English words that sound similar to the target Japanese words, it is difficult to see phonological features in the light of how and to what extent YPJ had phonological features in common with Japanese. Yet it is assumed that they were pronounced with English phonology on the basis of the English words. There is one interesting phonological aspect to point out about YPJ: how it reflects the characteristic feature of the Tokyo dialect spoken in those days. Unlike dialects of Japanese spoken in other areas, the Tokyo dialect used to have a salient phonological feature: they pronounced as /s/ which was pro-nounced in other dialects as /h/. *Sto/shto* (*hito* in other dialects) meaning 'human being', and *stoats* (*hitotsu* in other dialects) meaning 'one' are good examples. These features are being lost and only older speakers have this feature currently.

3.3. Lexicon

The lexicon of YPJ seems to be highly reduced. There are many cases where limited vocabulary was made use of to express various things and situations. For example, *daijoubu* in Japanese is usually used to describe a situation where no problems or dangers are involved. *Die-job* in YPJ, however, was used to depict 'being good' as in *die-job boto* 'a good sea boat', or 'being sound' as in *die-job mar* 'a sound horse.' Another example is the polysemy of the word *aboorah*. While *abura* in Japanese only designates 'oil', *aboorah* in YPJ refers to 'butter', 'oil', 'kerosene', 'pomatum' and 'grease.' *Aboorah* in YPJ is a good example of semantic extension as is frequently observed in pidgins. As Sebba (1997) explained, since pidgins need to place as small as possible a burden on their learners, the list of words should be as small as the function of the language will allow, and therefore, there will be a need to make the best use of the word-resources.

As Holm (1989:594) pointed out, YPJ contained words from a variety of languages such as *boto* 'boat' (> English *boat*), *piggy* 'go' (> Bazaar Malay *pergi*), though lexicon of YPJ mainly derived from Japanese, the superstrate language. Atkinson (1879:21) referred to the origin of the two words *chobber chobber* 'food, sustenance', and *bobbery* 'disturbance, noise' to 'pigeon English—a low and ungrammatical dialect, void of syntax—spoken between foreigners and Chinese.' Some words reflected loanwords from other European languages which had already been introduced by the time YPJ was evolved, such as *shabone* 'soap' (> French *savon*). Holm also states that some English derived words such as *nun-wun* 'the best' (> English *number one*) came from English via Chinese Pidgin English.

Some words in YPJ have a pragmatic origin. For example, a word for 'a dog' is *come-here*. It is not difficult to assume that Japanese people misunderstood the expression 'Come here!' that is often said to dogs, as the generic term of the creature. Another example is *high-high-mar* for 'racing pony.' *Hai-hai* is a typical interjection used when a rider hastens a horse in Japanese. These YPJ words are not similar to the Japanese words.

(1)   YPJ: come-here   high-high-mar
                 'dog'   'racing pony'

        J: inu   kyousouba

Subject pronouns in YPJ distinguish three persons (1st, 2nd, and 3rd) but there is no distinction in number. No example of object pronouns is observed in *Exercises*. There are no examples of adpositions and complementizers in the data.

1st person	watarkshee
2nd person	oh-my
3rd person	acheera sto

Table 2. Pronouns in YPJ

3.4. Morphology

There are several reduplicated forms in the data that do not originate from Japanese in the data: for example, *so-so* for the verb 'sew', *maro-maro* for 'to pass, to walk, to be not at home', and *sick-sick* for 'sick.' *So-so* and *sick-sick* are apparently from English 'sew' and 'sick' respectively for Japanese words for these words *nuu* and *byoukida* are not phonologically similar to them. Reduplication in YPJ does not seem to add any grammatical functions. YPJ data do not show evidence of bound morphology. There is one frequently observed compounding strategy with *sto/shto* 'person'. *Sto/shto* is added to any part of speech to describe and make the terms for professions.

(2) YPJ: ah-kye kimono **sto**, [2]   eeto high-kin **sto**
            red clothes (N.) person   thread look (V.) person
            'soldier'   'silk inspector'

     J: heitai   kinukensakan

Long words that consist of several components are sometimes observed in YPJ, and it is not very easy to determine the meaning of the words from the component morphemes. For example, the word for 'light house', *fooney high-kin serampan nigh rosokoo* is not easily understood at first glance, though it makes sense after a while.

(3) YPJ: fooney   high-kin serampan   nigh   rosoko
           ship   look   break   NEG   candle.
           'lighthouse'

     J: toudai
           'lighthouse'

3.5. Grammar

3.5.1 Article

There were no articles which exist in YPJ just as there are none in Japanese (Atkinson 1879:15).

3.5.2 Case Marking

All of the case markers found in Japanese were dropped.

(4) YPJ: Kooromar   aboorah   sinjoe.
           car   oil   give
           'Oil the carriage wheels'

---

[2] 'The British established a navy base in Yokohama from 1863 to 1875 to defend their settlements, and … the red uniforms of their soldiers were a common sight in the harbor area…' (Holm 1989:593).

J:	Kuruma-ni	abura-o	ire-ro.
	car-DAT	oil-ACC	put-IMP

'Put some oil into the car.'

3.5.3 Possessive Expression

No lexical item is used for possession in YPJ. Possessive relationships between two noun phrases is expressed simply by juxtaposition of the possessor (including pronouns) and the possessed.

(5)	YPJ:	acheera	sto	caberra- mono
		over-there	person	hat

'his hat'

	J:	achira-no	hito-no	kaburi-mono
		over there-GEN	person-GEN	hat

'that person's hat'

(6)	YPJ:	watarkshee	mar
		I	horse

'my horse'

	J:	watakushi-no	uma
		I-GEN	horse

'my horse'

Possession in Japanese is marked with the genitive case particle *–no* in the order of [possessor *-no* possessee]. Therefore, word order in YPJ is the same as Japanese except for the lack of the case marker *–no*.

3.5.4 Word Order

YPJ retained basic word order of Japanese, SOV. Direct and indirect objects always precede verbs both in YPJ and Japanese.

(7)	YPJ:	Mar	chobber-chobber	sinjoe
		horse	food	give

'Give the horse some feed.'

	J:	Uma-ni	esa-o	yare.
		horse-DAT	feed-ACC	give-IMP

'Give the horse some feed.'

3.5.5 Tense

There are not any tense/aspectual markers in YPJ. Tense is expressed by the context or by temporal adverbs such as *meonitchi* 'tomorrow,' *bynebai* 'later.' For example, future time is expressed by temporal adverb *bynebai* in (8).

(8) YPJ: Sigh-oh-narrow dozo **bynebai** moh-skosh cow
           good-bye   please by and by more little buy
           'Good-by and please buy some more (in the future).'
           [translation mine]

     J: Sayounara, douzo mata   kat-te   kudasai.
           good-bye   please again buy-CON   please
           'Good-by, and please buy something again.'

Bynebai is one of the features commonly attested in both Chinese Pidgin English and Melanesian Pidgin English (Siegel 2000). Considering the fact that there were a lot of Chinese people in the settlement, it may have been brought into YPJ via Chinese Pidgin English. Baker and Mühlhäusler (1996) made a list of first attestations of 106 selected features of Melanesian Pidgin English. The use of *by and by* as a preverbal marker as in (8) is also included in the table indicating that it was first attested in Chinese Pidgin English in 1878.

3.5.6 Negative

YPJ has a general negative marker *nigh* which follows the verb. There was also a negative predicate *arimasen* 'not to have, to be out'.

(9) YPJ: Oh-my nangeye tokey high-kin **nigh**.
           you   long   time   see   NEG
           'I haven't seen you for a long time.'

     J: Nagai aida   anata-to   at-te   (i)-nai.
           long   time   you-COM   see-CON   be-NEG

(10) YPJ: Bates **arimasen**?
           other be-NEG
           'Have you no others?'

     J: Betsu-no   (mono)-wa   ari-mas-en-ka?
           other-POS thing-TOP   be-PLT-NEG-Q
           'Do you have others?'

Although *Exercises* explains that the formation of the negative by the addition of *–en* or *–in* to verbs ending, *-en/ing* are added only to the two verbs, *arimas* and *walkarimas*. In both ways, the negation strategy of Japanese reflects the syntactic position of negative markers in YPJ.

3.5.7 Interrogative Sentences

As for the 'WH-questions', all the question words comes from Japanese (*doko* 'where', *nanny* 'what', *ikoorah* 'how much', *dalley* 'who'). In Japanese, there is no movement of a constituent associated with the formation of WH-questions, either. WH-question words replace noun phrases at the same position, and the question particle *ka* is added at the end of the sentence (Tsujimura 1996:185). YPJ employs the similar strategy as Japanese except that the question particle *ka* is dropped.

(11)   YPJ: Num wun sindoe **doko?**
                best   sailor   where
                'Where is the Captain?'

           J: Senchou-wa   doko (-desu-ka)?
                captain-TOP   where-PLT-Q

As is not observed in Japanese, a bimorphemic question word, *nanny sto* 'who', was also used as in (12) in addition to sets of monomorphemic WH-question words listed above.

(12)   YPJ: **Nanny sto** arimas, Watarkshee arimasen?
                what   person be   I   be-NEG
                'Who called when I was out?'

           J: watakushi-ga   i-nai   aida-ni   dareka-kara
                I-NOM   be-NEG a while-DAT   someone-OBL

                 denwa-ga   ari-mashi-ta-ka?
                 OBL telephone-NOM   be-PLT-PST-Q

4. Is YPJ a Restricted Pidgin?

Does YPJ share the common functional and structural features with other restricted pidgins? The sociohistorical background of YPJ tells us that the function of YPJ was restricted to the communication in the limited settings such as commerce and conversation with servants. Both Japanese and foreign nationals spoke other languages when they were with their peers. In the preface of *Exercises*, the author referred to YPJ as 'a means of communication between the native and foreign resident or visitor.' Thus YPJ was used only for basic communication among people who did not share a common language in a polyglot contact situation. The social environment of YPJ seems typical of the use of pidgin language.

    Siegel (in press) discussed eight grammatical features that most restricted pidgins share. These characteristics are found in Chinese Pidgin English, Greenlandic Pidgin, the Hiri Trading Languages, Nauru Pidgin English, Ndyuka-Trio Pidgin, Pidgin Delaware, Pidgin Hawaiian, Pidgin French of Vietnam and Russenorsk (Siegel in press:8). Out of the eight grammatical features, YPJ shares seven features (a) – (h) as demonstrated in Table 3 (see Section 3 for discussion). As for (e) preverbal negative marker, it is not observed in YPJ for the negative markers in YPJ are postverbal as in the superstrate language, Japanese.

Eight features commonly shared by restricted pidgins	Yes	No
a) virtually no productive bound morphology —inflectional or derivational	√	
b) reduced number of adpositions, pronouns	√	
c) reduced lexicon	√	
d) no TMA markers—temporal adverbs used	√	
e) preverbal negative marker		√
f) no complementizers	√	
g) more reduplicated forms than superstrate language	√	
h) some bimorphemic question words	√	

Table 3. Linguistic Features of Restricted Pidgins Observed in YPJ

Although negative markers occur before the verb in the majority of known pidgins, Sebba (1997:42) pointed out there are some exceptions to this, referring to Hiri Motu[3] in which the negator comes after the verb. Sebba provides an explanation of the exceptional case in Hiri Motu, saying that the presence of preverbal negator might be because of a universal preference among languages with SVO word order for preverbal modification, and it is not the case with languages with SOV word order. Since YPJ is also a language with SOV word order, YPJ serves as another evidence that the preverbal negator correlates with pidgins with SVO word order and portverbal negator with pidgins with SVO word order.

We have seen how the sociohistorical background and linguistic features of YPJ show the typical character of restricted pidgins so far. The next question is whether YPJ was stable enough to be called a pidgin. The fact that there existed a booklet for learners such as *Exercises* is good evidence that YPJ was a very stable variety and was recognized as a communication medium by many people. Also, people's attitudes towards YPJ—as illustrated in the review article on the *Exercises* (Atkinson 1879) published by the well established newspaper, *The Japan Weekly Mail*—is another piece of evidence that YPJ was recognized as a stable variety. In conclusion, YPJ is a variety that we can label "Restricted Pidgin" in terms of sociohistorical background, linguistic features, and stability.

5. Conclusion

The sociohistorical environment of the Yokohama Settlement in the late 19th century provided a typical situation where a restricted pidgin evolved: 1) limited social interaction between foreigners and the speakers of the superstrate language, Japanese, 2) a polyglot contact situation. Although the

---

[3] Hiri Motu is a pidgin based on Motu, an Austronesian language. It is spoken around Port Moresby in Papua New Guinea.

data in Atkinson (1879) is limited, it provides us enough data to observe the linguistic features shared by other restricted pidgins. The linguistic data and sociohistorical environment of YPJ tell us that there were a considerable number of speakers of Chinese Pidgin English in Yokohama in the late 19th century and CPE influenced the lexicon of YPJ.

Abbreviation

N.	noun	A.	adjective	V.	verb
NOM	nominative	ACC	accusative	DAT	dative
GEN	genitive	COM	comitative	OBL	oblique
NEG	negative	PLT	polite	VOL	volitional
PST	past	CON	connector	IMP	imperative
COMP	complimentizer	COND	conditional		
Q	question particle				

References

Atkinson, H. 1879. *Revised and Enlarged Edition of Exercises in the Yokohama Dialect.* Yokohama.

Baker, P. 1987. Historical Developments in Chinese Pidgin English and the Nature of the Relationships between the Various Pidgin Englishes of the Pacific Region. *Journal of Pidgin and Creole Languages* 2(2):163–207.

Baker, P. and P. Mühlhäusler. 1996. The Origins and Diffusion of Pidgin English in the Pacific. *Atlas of Languages of Intercultural Communication in the Pacific, Asia, and the Americas. Vol. II.1,* eds. S. Wurm, P. Mühlhäusler and D. Tryon, 551-594. New York: Mouton de Gruyter.

Geoffrey, T. 1926. *An Immigrant in Japan.* Cambridge: Houghton Mifflin Co.

Holm, J. 1989. *Pidgins and Creoles. Volume II: Reference Survey.* New York: Cambridge University Press.

Ishizuka, H. 1996. Yokohama Kyoryuuchizou no Keisei [The Formation of Yoko hama Settlement]. *Yokohama Kyoryuuchi to Ibunkakouryuu [Yokohama Settle ment and Intercultural Communication],* ed. Yokohamakaikousiryoukan, 3-30. Tokyo: Yamakawa Publishing.

Miller, R. A. 1967. *The Japanese Language.* Chicago, London: University of Chicago Press.

Niki, H. 2001. Nihon Hatsutoujyou no Hamuretto [When 'Hamlet' by Shakespeare was first introduced to Japan]. *Net Pinus.* 49, 16 April 2003. <http://www.yushodo.co.jp/pinus/49/h4.html/>.

Sebba, M. 1997. *Contact Languages: Pidgins and Creoles.* Basingstoke, Hampshire: Macmilan.

Siegel, J. 2000. Substrate Influence in Hawai'i Creole English. *Language in Society* 29:197–236.

Siegel, J. In press. Fiji Pidgins and Pidgins/Creole Origins. *Starting from Scratch*, eds. J. den Besten, M. Parkvall and P. Baker. London: Battlebridge.

Sugahara, K. 1993. Yokohama Chuukagai [The Yokohama Chinatown]. *Yokohama: Yokokhama shiritsutosyokanhou* [Yokohama: Monthly report of Yokohama City Library] 19:2–5.

Tsujimura, N. 1996. *An Introduction to Japanese Linguistics*. Cambridge: Blackwell.

Construction of Units and Interactive Turn Spaces in Japanese Conversation

SHIMAKO IWASAKI

University of California, Los Angeles

1. Introduction[1]

The key unit of language organization for talk-in-interaction is the turn-constructional unit (TCU) (Sacks et al. 1974, Schegloff 1996). However, the current understanding of TCUs does not account for coparticipant's intervention becoming relevant before a turn-constructional unit (TCU) reaches its possible completion. Therefore, this paper introduces an alternative framework to explain how the internal structure of a TCU in a turn at talk, in combination with the utilization of linguistic and nonlinguistic resources, facilitates collaborative participation in Japanese conversation. While affirming that turn construction is a result of multi-party, multi-contoured, and multi-modal production, I will show how the components and actions provided by recipients contribute to unit production in Japanese. Focusing on the mechanisms of interaction, I demonstrate that utterances are built incrementally and unit segmentation helps produce an interactive

---

[1] I thank my advisors Charles Goodwin and Emanuel Schegloff as well as Candy Goodwin, Makoto Hayashi, John Heritage, Shoichi Iwasaki, Shuya Kushida, and Aug Nishizaka for their insightful comments on earlier stages of this project. I appreciate Kuniyoshi Kataoka, the 15th JK conference participants, and all the other people who contributed to the development of this research. I am grateful to my partner ARI for his continued support and encouragement.

turn space, a particular space for participant's intervention, in which participants use multiple resources to shape collaborative turn constructions.
Though part of an ongoing research project, for this paper I will introduce
the phenomenon I am examining, elaborate and contextualize the analytical
framework I am developing, and then demonstrate the potentials of the
framework through a series of examples, which focus on interactions within
noun phrase construction, and the coordination of linguistic resources with
gaze shift, head nods, and hand gesture.

2. Phenomenon

Interaction within the turn organization framework is generally understood
to occur as speaker changes on possible completion of TCUs where transition is relevant.[2] However, as seen in Excerpt (1), participants intervene
prior to a transition-relevance place (TRP), and collaborate in the production of turns. Taken from a videotaped conversation between college students, Excerpt (1)[3] shows a single TCU produced by the speaker Gen,
marked by a speaker change, when Ami provides '*sooyuu mon nan da::.*'
The excerpt demonstrates that the participant intervenes in the midst of the
speaker's TCU, forming a sequence inside the TCU.

---

[2] Sacks et al. (1974) propose a mechanism for the organization of turn-taking which relied on
two components: TCUs and turn allocation, which deals with distributing turns at the end of
TCUs. At the possible completion of the TCU, marked by transition-relevance places (TRPs),
transition to the next speaker becomes relevant. TCUs are the smallest unit of turn organization
and either single- or multi-unit turns constitute possibly complete turns. In principle, no other
participant should take a next turn before the current speaker has reached the first possible
completion point in their TCU. For further discussion on units and TRPs, see Ford (2004).

[3] Transcripts are based on the following conventions. Japanese gloss symbols abbreviations:
CNJ = conjunctive; CON = conditional; COP = copula; GEN = genitive; INJ = interjection; IP
= interactional particles such as *ne. sa*, and *yo*; NOM = nominative; N = nominalizer; NPT =
nonpast tense; PT = past tense; QT = quotation particle; TL = title marker.
Transcription notation, adapted from Goodwin (1981) and Jefferson (2004), includes:

[ ]	overlapping talk	(( ))	transcriber's descriptions
(0.5)	length of silence in tenths of a second	-----	gazing toward the other party
(.)	micro-pause	.....	movement that brings gaze to
.	falling intonation		another
?	rising intonation	,,,,,	movement withdrawing gaze
,	continuing intonation, slightly rising		(absence of line) not gazing toward
_	level intonation		the other
h	exhalation	X	a point which gaze reaches the other
*h	inhalation; inbreath	y	brief glance toward the other
° °	portions quieter than the surrounding talk	nod	vertical head movement
=	contiguous utterances (no break or gap)	n	short and fast nod
-	cut-off	no::d	slow nod
:	prolongation of immediately prior sound	↗	direction of head movement
__	(underline) emphasis	{	onset of nod and gesture

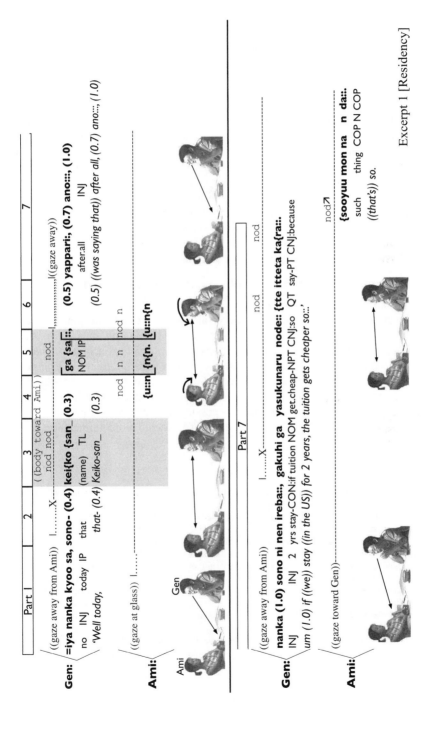

Part 1

	2	3	4	5	6	7

((gaze away from Ami)) |......X------|
               ((body toward Ami))
                  nod nod   nod |,,,,,,,,,,,,,,,|((gaze away))

Gen: =iya nanka kyoo sa, sono- (0.4) kei{ko {san_ (0.3)   ga {sa :;   (0.5) yappari;, (0.7) ano::;, (1.0)
    no INJ today IP that (name) TL   NOM IP   after.all   INJ
    'Well today, *that- (0.4) Keiko-san_* *(0.3)*   *(0.5) ((was saying that)) after all, (0.7) ano::: (1.0)*

                                  nod n n   nod n
((gaze at glass)) |.......   {u::n {n{n. {u::n{n

Ami:
          Gen

Part 7

((gaze away from Ami)) |......X------| nod   nod

Gen: nanka (1.0) sono ni nen ireba::, gakuhi ga yasukunaru node:: {tte itteta ka{ra::.
    INJ   INJ 2 yrs stay-CON:if tuition NOM get.cheap-NPT CNJ:so QT say-PT CNJ:because
    um (1.0) if ((we)) stay ((in the US)) for 2 years, the tuition gets cheaper so::'

                                  nod↗
((gaze toward Gen))------   {sooyuu mon na   n da::.
                                        such   thing COP N COP
Ami: *((that's)) so.*

Excerpt 1 [Residency]

Even though the speaker has not reached possible turn completion, participants sometimes actively join in and come to talk simultaneously. However, it does not mean that they become a legitimate next speaker of the next turn. Typically when recipients enter into the speaker's turn before its completion, it can be considered as interruption and treated as a turn-taking problem in need of repair. However, some linguistic features of Japanese facilitate segmentation in conversation that creates various caesuras within TCUs. The phenomenon demonstrated by Excerpt (1) suggests that the turn itself is permeable and open to the other participants who have conditional access to the turn. This phenomenon also suggests that Japanese TCUs are in fact composed of smaller components that can provide opportunities for collaborative achievement of talk between the speaker and coparticipants. Juxtaposing talk and other modalities, conversationalists are building units together. Consequently, TCUs need to be considered as multi-party, multi-contoured, and multi-modal constructions. After outlining the analytical frameworks I am using to explain this phenomenon, I will return to Excerpt (1) and examine it in detail, explicating how each component within the TCU contributes to its collaborative production.

3. Frames of Analysis for Collaboratively Constructed Units

In the phenomenon I am analyzing, participants enter into the turn, but do not become a legitimate next speaker at possible completion points where turn transition is relevant. Turns can be permeable and thus have parts where particular kinds of interventions and operations become relevant.[1] Based on studies of anticipatory completion in English, Lerner (1996) noted a similar phenomenon and introduced the concept of "semi-permeable" turns to describe recipient opportunities to conditionally enter into talk before the turn comes to recognizably possible completion.[2] However, I will demonstrate that in Japanese turns can be considered more permeable.

---

[1] Examining interaction in English, Schegloff (1979, forthcoming) and Goodwin (1979, 1980, 1981, 2002) identified interaction within a sentence. Both of their studies are an important foundation for my study. The possibility that discourse (multiple turns at talk) can occur within the boundaries of a single coherent sentence was first noted by Schegloff (1979), who revealed that a sequence of turns is inserted within the boundaries of a sentence exemplifying the local interactional determination of turn structure. What is traditionally considered as a sentence is opened up to include internal exchanges between the speaker and the recipient. Hayashi (2004) recently applied the notion of "discourse within a sentence" to Japanese conversation. Furthermore, among fine-grained analyses of turn construction, Goodwin (1979) demonstrates that a single sentence emerges in response to local contingencies and a sentence can be shaped and re-formed in the process of its utterance. Goodwin shows that a sentence produced within a particular turn at talk is determined by a process of interaction between participants and in response to recipient's behaviors, which is simultaneous with the production of the turn.

[2] See Hayashi (2003) for related studies of coparticipant completion in Japanese.

In fact, the grammatical structure of Japanese supports the notion of permeability. Previous studies of discourse-functional[3] and interactional linguistics[4] have noted 'fragmentation' in Japanese, based on the frequent use of words and phrases that are shorter than syntactically complete clauses.[5] Furthermore, even though within analyses of Japanese grammar, a constituent [noun phrase + nominal particle] is treated as a whole, several researchers have illustrated how noun phrases are produced separately from their particles.[6] Such studies corroborate my claim that grammar and segmentation facilitate the permeability of the turn.

Permeability allows unit segmentations with a finer granularity than conventional studies of Japanese turn-taking allow, and requires examining components smaller than TCUs. Even though the concepts of intonation units (IUs) (e.g. Chafe 1994, Iwasaki 1993a, 1993b, Iwasaki and Tao 1993, Matsumoto 2000, 2003), which mark breaks based on changes in intonation contour,[7] and pause-bounded phrasal units (PPUs) (Maynard 1989), which are identified by identifiable pauses,[8] offer additional ways of understanding smaller divisions, they do not adequately explain multi-party and multimodal TCU production. We need frameworks that can incorporate the interactional relevance of not only intonation and pauses, but also other nonlinguistic resources, and can provide a better way of understanding how turns are collaboratively produced from constituent components provided by both speakers and recipients. Building on conversation analytical frameworks and expanding grammatical analysis in relation to interaction, this paper introduces a vocabulary for describing interactions occurring within a TCU-in-progress.

Within a complete TCU, there can be smaller scale constituent components, which are produced by both speakers and participants. The negotiation of components is based on mutual orientation to multi-contoured at-

---

[3] E.g. Clancy et al. (1996), Iwasaki (1993a, b); Iwasaki and Tao (1993), and Maynard (1989).

[4] E.g. Fox et al. (1996), Tanaka (1999, 2000), and Thompson and Couper-Kuhlen (2005).

[5] Many of studies, identified in Footnotes 6 and 7, claim that Japanese is best characterized by 'phrases' rather than 'clauses' since it is often observed in conversational Japanese that speakers divide a clause up into constituent 'phrases.' For example, Fox et al. (1996) find that the scope of repetition during self-repair in Japanese is more local and phrase oriented than in English, which they argue parallels Maynard's (1989) findings on PPUs, and Iwasaki and Tao's (1993) findings on IUs. For further characterization of Japanese sentences, see Iwasaki and Ono (2002, to appear) and Ono and Iwasaki (2002).

[6] E.g. Hayashi (2003, 2004, 2005) and Ono et al. (1998).

[7] Intonation unit (IU) is a prosodic unit characterized by a stretch of speech uttered under a single intonation contour, which also corresponds with the flow of information (Chafe 1994).

[8] Pause-bounded phrasal unit (PPU) is characterized as a unit different from "idea unit." The definition of the PPU is lexical items plus function words such as particles set apart by identifiable pauses. PPUs are mostly accompanied by pause-predicting tone and/or pause-warning decreased speed, along with occasional stressed, rising intonation (Maynard 1989).

tenuation of talk and multi-modal resources mobilized in the course of unit construction. Component boundaries are marked by what I am provisionally calling *intervention relevance places*, where relevance is determined by the deployment of multiple resources in conjunction with the grammatical segmentation that is built into Japanese. Intervention relevance places are not TRPs, but function similarly at the component level of a turn. Activated intervention relevance places create *interactive turn spaces,* where participants operate on the emerging talk within a TCU that has not yet reached possible completion.[9] Within the interactive turn space recipients produce constituent linguistic components that provide a block for the speaker to continue in their TCU production. Through these constituent components, participants help co-construct the unfolding talk. In the next section, through several analytical examples, I will show how the components of utterance production make relevant a particular space of multi-party activity even though these components do not have a quality of recognizably possible completion.

4. Speaker Initiated Interactive Turn Spaces within a TCU

Segmentation and permeability facilitate participation that can be initiated by either speaker or recipients. For this paper, I will focus on the speaker-initiated interactive turn spaces, using two examples to demonstrate how an utterance is collaboratively produced by the speaker and recipients while monitoring each other to coordinate social action in interaction. Specifically, I analyze the interactional imports of constituent components that are noun phrases and responses toward them. I am developing a horizontal transcript system as an analytical device that allows us to see incrementally how both speaker and coparticipants monitor each other, orient themselves, and deploy multiple resources within an emerging talk in real time.[10] Using this device, I will provide an incremental account of how components are used to build a collaboratively produced TCU.

---

[9] Tanaka (1999, 2000) argues that interactional particles such as *ne* and *sa* in turn-internal positions invite the recipient to perform "back-channeling activity" at an "acknowledgement-relevance place." Similarly, Morita (2005) claims these same interactional particles mark "interactionally-relevant units" in conversation. Furthermore, Nishizaka (2005) discusses "*hannookikaiba*" (response opportunity places, ROPs), which occur after intonationally-stressed particles, such as case, adverbial, conjunctive, and interactional particles. In contrast, intervention relevance places can be initiated before particles and are triggered by multiple resources.

[10] Since this kind of horizontal transcript may be unfamiliar, I will briefly explain how it is organized in order to orient the readers. Each participant is assigned a series of tracks: nod/gesture, gaze, and speech (including Japanese gloss and English translations), each differentiated by font type. One TCU from the primary speaker is presented horizontally (from left to right), and the simultaneous actions of the participants can be compared in the vertical axis. The labels along the top identify the sequence of components that compose the TCU.

Returning to Excerpt (1), prior to this TCU Gen and Ami are discussing the impacts of having in-state resident status in California. Gen asked Ami if it is true that foreign students can be treated as state residents after living in the US for more than two years. Ami replied that it probably depends on the case. As soon as he hears Ami's response, Gen withdraws his gaze from Ami and starts his turn, with his gaze toward the table in front of them.

In the target segment, shown in Excerpt (1), Gen explains that the reason why he is inquiring is to verify information he received from a person named *Keiko-san*. I will analyze Excerpt (1) step by step to show how Gen's single TCU is constructed as both the speaker and the recipient hear and see it in real time. In **[Part 1]** Gen starts the sequence with a time formulation while gazing away from the recipient Ami. By starting this way, Gen projects that he is about to deliver a story, regarding his inquiry. The recipient Ami brings her gaze to Gen at this moment, which displays that she is an aligned recipient. In **[Part 2]** Gen starts moving his gaze to Ami, indicated by a dotted line, while producing the appositional *sono*, which projects that there is more to come. Cutting-off *sono,* he pauses a moment (0.4) while achieving mutual gaze, indicated by the X. Having a mutual gaze is important here because the speaker needs to see the recipient's stance toward the next element that he is about to produce. In **[Part 3]**, Gen leans towards Ami and produces the noun phrase while sustaining mutual gaze and nodding twice. The onsets of nods are indicated by curly brackets in the transcript. The component *keiko-san* becomes an operative component and multiple resources create an intervention relevance place for participation. Speaker's gaze shift, a (0.4) pause, posture shift (i.e. lean forward to the recipient), head movements, and level intonation (which is followed by a pause) activate an intervention-relevance place and initiate an interactive turn space. Notice that Gen's body shift accompanied with nods is produced on the production of the reference *Keiko-san* and before Ami's response, inviting an assertive recognition to confirm her alignment. In **[Part 4]**, there is a (0.3) pause. This indicates that the speaker waits for the recipient's recognition. Recognizing the relevance for intervention, Ami provides an invited response token *un* to fill the interactive turn space and provide Gen with a component for continuing the production of the TCU. The recipient also shapes the interactive turn space with multiple resources. In this case, Ami's recipient component is accompanied by nodding while sustaining her gaze toward the speaker.

The components provided by participants shape the unfolding talk. In **[Part 5]**, because Ami's component displays her recognition of the referent, Gen continues with his next component beginning with the nominal particle *ga*, which grammatically makes a link with the referent. Gen nods again while maintaining mutual gaze on the interactional particle *sa*, produced with vowel elongation (*sa::*), immediately following the nominative case marker *ga,* which invites the recipient to operate on the speaker's unit-so-far.[11] This action indicates that he is again creating an interactive turn space for Ami to participate in the action of not only establishing mutual recognition toward the referent, but also displaying her understanding of what the nominal particle *ga* projects (i.e. what the main character of Gen's story did). In **[Part 6]** when Gen hears and sees the participant's validation (i.e. response and nods), he withdraws his gaze, indicated by commas, marking the end of another component. Thus, in **[Part 7]** Gen continues constructing his unit until reaching possible TCU completion at *itteta kara::*. Throughout this final component, the recipient sustains her gaze toward the speaker and waits for him to complete his turn even though there are extended pauses in the production of Part 7. This reveals that pauses are neither the only indication of intervention relevance places nor the only key to activating interactive turn spaces. The recipient monitors the unfolding talk and orients to components made interactionally relevant by the speaker. As demonstrated, Gen's TCU production is collaboratively constructed by both the speaker and the recipient through careful coordination.

Furthermore, though this practice has been referred to as "try-marking" (Sacks and Schegloff 1979: For Japanese, Hayashi 2005, Ono et al. 1998), which is an interrogative check of alignment prior to proceeding, in this case Gen is doing something slightly different. How he refers to someone (*Keiko*) is very sensitive to the issue of what he has just been talking about, who he is talking to now, and what he is going to talk about. This is a component of his turn, which is more recipient designed than other parts of the turn. There is no rising intonational contour suggesting a question, but Gen pauses. Pausing for a moment and looking at the recipient to see whether there would be a token of "I'm with you" is achieved with different resources than generally associated with try marking. A momentary pause is employed in order to establish that both the speaker and the recipient are on the same track together in that moment of interaction.

To reinforce, the grey areas identified in Excerpt (1), corresponding to Parts 3 and 5, highlight how the noun phrasal component becomes operative and how relevant places for intervention and negotiation are created through the deployment of multiple resources. In the resulting interactive space, Ami's component provides an invited response with validations, like a question-answer adjacency pair (Schegloff, forthcoming), so that the speaker can move forward. Notice also that the recipient's constituent component is framed by gaze movements in Parts 2 and 6, and reinforced by nodding. Multiple actions are coordinated with Gen's emerging noun phrasal component to achieve collaborative participation.

---

[11] See Hayashi (2003, 2004, 2005) and Tanaka (1999) for how case and adverbial particles can be utilized in conversation. For discussion of interactional particles, see Maynard (1989), Morita (2005), and Tanaka (1999, 2000).

As Excerpt (1) illustrates, intervention-relevance places occur within the production of the noun phrase, but come before the next element, such as a nominal particle or a predicate. An intervention-relevance place is identified by linguistic and nonlinguistic resources, thus creating an interactive turn space wherein the recipient is expected to perform a relevant next action in the midst of the speaker's unit. Speaker initiation with prosodic and nonlinguistic means such as gaze shifts and head movements causes the noun phrase to be marked as an interactionally relevant component that the recipient is expected to operate on providing a component in the interactive turn space. After the recipient's relevant action, the speaker employs a next component, in the case of Excerpt (1) a nominal particle *ga*, to link with the marked noun phrase and continues the unfolding talk.

Closer consideration of the recipient's action demonstrates that the recipient component is a necessary part of the speaker's TCU construction. The vocalization *un* is often called *aizuchi* and characterized as one kind of continuer. Ami's use of *un* appears to be consistent with Schegloff's (1982) argument about continuers. In Excerpt (1) Ami's *u::n n n* allows Gen to move to the next constituent component. In other words, Gen is treating Ami's *u::n n n* as a warrant to now move forward after he held himself slightly in place (0.3) in Part 4. However, what makes this use of *un* different from continuers is that *un* occurs in the midst of unit construction, and it is elicited by the speaker's request for intervention. The recipient provides her response as the second pair part of the adjacency pair in a minimal manner. That is, there is a question-answer adjacency pair sequence in the midst of a single TCU. Furthermore, Ami nods while she is producing the token and sustains her gaze toward the speaker, reinforcing that the recipient is waiting for the further development of Gen's turn.

Excerpt (1) illustrated a recipient component that is similar to *aizuchi* responses. In the next example I will show another type of recipient component that can be supplied in a speaker initiated interactive turn space. Excerpt (2) is taken from a sequence where three participants are discussing the kinds of breakfast served at Denny's restaurants. It provides an example of a noun phrase with a modifier that is segmented into two entities and demonstrates a recipient component that results in choral co-production (Lerner 2002).

This example shows that the operative point is activated in the middle of the noun phrase construction. After his self-addressed question in **[Part 1]**, Gen starts shifting his gaze to Ami as he starts to produce the item that the demonstrative *are* projects. The end of the production of the attribute part *teiban no amerikan* becomes an intervention-relevant place when the speaker starts shifting his gaze toward Ami while moving his hand in **[Part**

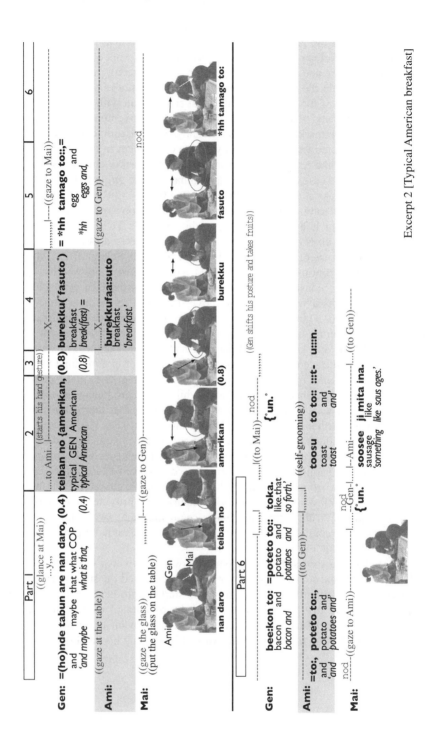

Part 1

1	2	3	4	5	6

Gen: =(ho)nde tabun are nan daro, (0.4) teiban no {amerikan, (0.4) burekku(°fasuto°) = (0.8) = *hh tamago to:;=
and maybe that what COP typical GEN American breakfast   egg and
'and maybe what is that, typical American break(fast)'   *hh eggs and,

Ami: ((glance at Mai)) ...y,... ((starts his hand gesture)) ...to Ami..! |------(gaze to Mai))------X.......,,,| |------(gaze to Mai))------
((gaze at the table))
=*hh
*hh burekkufaa:suto
breakfast
'breakfast'
--X----((gaze to Gen))--

Mai: ((gaze the glass)) ,,,,,,|------((gaze to Gen))------ nod
((put the glass on the table))

nan daro   teiban no   amerikan   (0.8)   burekku   fasuto   *hh tamago to:

((Gen shifts his posture and takes fruits))

Part 6

Gen: bee:kon to:; =poteto to:: toka.
bacon and potato and like.that
bacon and potatoes and so forth.'

Ami: =to:; poteto to:;, toosu to to:: ::t- u::n.
and potato and toast and and
'and potatoes and' toast and

nod ((to Gen))-----|,,,,,,| nod ,,,,,,,,|((to Mai))-------- ((self-grooming))

{°un.°   {°un.°

soosee ji mita ina.
sausage like
'something like sausages.'

--Gen--|--Ami---|---((to Gen))----
nod
--((gaze to Ami))-----|

Mai:

Excerpt 2 [Typical American breakfast]

2] and when he momentarily stops his utterance production in **[Part 3]**. Notice that the primary recipient Ami is not yet looking at Gen in [Parts 2 & 3]. The speaker uses gaze shift and a descriptive hand gesture, indicating a tray to put food on, to attenuate his claim to continue building components and invite the recipient to enter into the interactive turn space. After the (0.8) pause in [Part 3], Ami starts moving her gaze toward Gen and shares the interactive turn space producing the same word in unison in **[Part 4]**. This example also shows that the speaker is requesting the recipient's display of understanding, but the head noun (breakfast) is synchronized or co-produced rather than Ami simply providing a response such as *un*.

This Excerpt (2) demonstrates how participation other than requested *un* responses is used to fill the interactive turn space. Within the example, though it appears to be a similar type of participation, Ami's contribution of '*to: poteto to::*' represents a kind of anticipatory, coparticipant completion (Hayashi 2003, Lerner 1996, 2004), but is not a component provided to fill an interactive turn space because there is not a marked intervention relevance place prepared by the speaker at '*tamago to*' as we have seen in the prior cases. This component has a different kind of participation structure. Gen's gaze remains consistently toward Mai, not to Ami, and there are no gestures or pauses that solicit Ami's component. Ami's intervention is a preemptive move in locally emergent and recognizable action. In Part 5, '*tamago to::*' with a elongated particle *to::* syntactically projects a list-in-progress that Ami and Mai subsequently participate in formulating. Overall, these two cases demonstrate how the speaker initiates intervention from the coparticipants using segmented noun phrases in conjunction with multiple resources to create an interactive turn space that allows both speaker and the recipient to participate in TCU construction.

5. Discussion

This study develops a new way to explain how segmentation and unit construction facilitate collaborative participation in Japanese conversation. Like dancers who attune themselves to their partner, conversationalists use multiple resources and forms, creating a performance together. As illustrated in the Excerpts and summarized in Diagram (1), the production of a Japanese TCU is multi-party, multi-contoured, and multi-modal.

Within the TCU, turn components have 'directionality' (Schegloff 1996), which forms an underlying organizational shape. Directionality results not only from the temporality of talk, but also from the orientations by the participants to interactionally relevant places and ultimately to a possible completion point and possible speaker change. In conjunction with grammatical structures, components help coordinate the permeability of the TCU. Though participants have a normative orientation toward possible completion, at the same time they orient to the interactional relevance of components within a TCU, which are shaped by the multiple contours of attenuation and multi-modal resources. Each component also has projectability. When activated, intervention relevance places initiate an interactive turn space creating a sequence within a TCU, wherein the participant is expected to provide a constituent component that the speaker builds on to produce a complete TCU.

Diagram (1): Production of a TCU

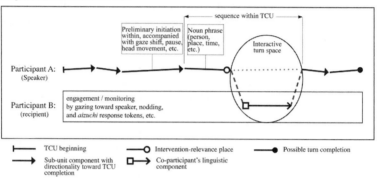

Constructing a TCU is a collaborative effort of building interactionally sensitive components. Both the speaker and recipient(s) orient to each next element of a TCU-in-progress. They monitor how each component contributes to what the prior component made relevant, how components modify what the prior talk made relevant, and what kind of next course of action components make relevant. For Japanese we cannot simply consider TCUs as a whole. Instead, we need to consider each component of the turn that contributes to the evolving meaning of a TCU, and eventually a turn.

The notions of constituent components, intervention relevance places, and interactive turn spaces expand our understanding of units at talk by allowing us to consider not only speakers, but the ways in which speakers and recipients collaborate to construct TCUs. In combination with a horizontal transcript system, these concepts help explicate a range of relevant resources and how they are employed to shape the production of units. While underscoring the perspective that a turn at talk reflects social interaction and is a contingent collaborative achievement of multiple participants, this study takes first steps toward understanding the ways in which the components provided by speaker and recipients inside a turn are organized verbally and bodily to facilitate the progressivity of turns at talk.

References

Chafe, W. 1994. *Discourse, Consciousness, and Time: The Flow and Displacement of Conscious Experience in Speaking and Writing.* Chicago: Chicago University Press.

Clancy, P. M., S. A. Thompson, R. Suzuki, and H. Tao. 1996. The Conversational Use of Reactive Tokens in English, Japanese, and Mandarin. *Journal of Pragmatics* 26:355-387.

Ford, C. E. 2004. Contingency and Units in Interaction. *Discourse Studies* 6:27-52.

Ford, C. E. and S. A. Thompson. 1996. Interactional Units in Conversation: Syntactic, Intonational, and Pragmatic Resources for the Management of Turns. *Interaction and Grammar*, eds. E. Ochs, E. A. Schegloff, and S. A. Thompson, 134-184. Cambridge: Cambridge University Press.

Fox, B. A., M. Hayashi, and R. Jasperson. 1996. Resources and Repair: A Cross-Linguistic Study of Syntax and Repair. *Interaction and Grammar*, eds. E. Ochs, E. A. Schegloff, and S. A. Thompson, 185-237. Cambridge: Cambridge University Press.

Goodwin, C. 1979. The Interactive Construction of a Sentence in Natural Conversation. *Everyday Language: Studies in Ethnomethodology*, ed. G. Psathas, 97-121. New York: Irvington Publishers, Inc.

Goodwin, C. 1980. Restarts, Pauses, and the Achievement of a State of Mutual Gaze at Turn-beginning. *Sociological Inquiry, 50*:272-302.

Goodwin, C. 1981. *Conversational Organization.* New York, NY: Academic Press.

Goodwin, C. 2002. Time in Action. *Current Anthropology* 43:S19-S35.

Hayashi, M. 2003. *Joint Utterance Construction in Japanese Conversation.* Amsterdam: John Benjamins.

Hayashi, M. 2004. Discourse within a Sentence: An Exploration of Postpositions in Japanese as an Interactional Resource. *Language in Society* 33:343-376.

Hayashi, M. 2005. Referential Problems and Turn Construction: An Exploration of an Intersection between Grammar and Interaction. *TEXT* 25:437-468.

Iwasaki, S. 1993a. *Subjectivity in Grammar and Discourse: Theoretical Considerations and a Case Study of Japanese Spoken Discourse.* Amsterdam: John Benjamins.

Iwasaki, S. 1993b. The Structure of the Intonation Unit in Japanese. *Japanese/Korean Linguistics*, ed. S. Choi, 39-53, vol. 3. Stanford, CA: CSLI Publications.

Iwasaki, S. and H. Tao 1993. A Comparative Analysis of the Intonation Unit in English, Japanese, and Mandarin Chinese. Paper presented at the 67th Annual Meetings of the Linguistic Society of America, Los Angeles, CA. Jan. 9, 1993.

Iwasaki, S. and T. Ono. 2002. 'Sentence' in Spontaneous Spoken Japanese Discourse. *Complex Sentences in Grammar and Discourse: Essays in Honor of Sandra A. Thompson*, eds. J. Bybee and M. Noonan, 175-202. Amsterdam: John Benjamins.

Iwasaki, S. and T. Ono. To appear. 'Sokujibun' · 'Hisokujibun': Gengogaku no Houhouron to Kiseigainen. *Bun to Hatsuwa*, eds. S. Kushida, T. Sadanobu, and H. Den. Tokyo: Hituzisyobo.

Jefferson, G. 2004. Glossary of Transcript Symbols with an Introduction. *Conversation Analysis: Studies form the First Generation*, ed. G. Lerner, 13-31. Amsterdam: John Benjamins.

Lerner, G. 1996. On the "Semi-permeable" Character of Grammatical Units in Conversation: Conditional Entry into the Turn Space of Another Speaker. *Interaction and Grammar*, eds. E. Ochs, E. A. Schegloff, and S. A. Thompson, 238-276. Cambridge: Cambridge University Press.

Lerner, G. 2002. Turn-sharing: The Choral Co-production of Talk-in-interaction. *The Language of Turn and Sequence*, eds. C. Ford, B. Fox, and S. Thompson. 225-256. Oxford: Oxford.

Lerner, G. 2004. Collaborative Turn Sequences *Conversation Analysis: Studies from the First Generation*, ed. G. Lerner, 225-256. Amsterdam: John Benjamins.

Matsumoto, K. 2000. Japanese Intonation Units and Syntactic Structure. *Studies in Language* 24:515-564.

Matsumoto, K. 2003. *Intonation Units in Japanese Conversation: Syntactic, Informational, and Functional Structures*. Amsterdam: John Benjamins.

Maynard, S. K. 1989. *Japanese Conversation: Self-contextualization through Structure and Interactional Management*. Norwood, NJ: Ablex.

Morita, E. 2005. *Negotiation of Contingent Talk: The Japanese Interactional Particles Ne and Sa*. Amsterdam: John Benjamins.

Nishizaka, A. 2005. Bunsansuru Bun: Sougokoui Toshiteno Bunpou. *Gengo* 4:40-47.

Ono, T. and S. Iwasaki. 2002. Toward an Understanding 'Sentence' in Spoken Japanese Discourse: Clause-combining and Online Mechanisms. *Culture, Interaction, and Language,* eds. K. Kataoka and S. Ide, 103-131. Tokyo: Hituzisyobo.

Ono, T., E. Yoshida, and M. Banno. 1998. It Takes Two to Dance: The Interactional Determinants of NP Intonation Units with a Marked Rising Intonation (*Hangimonkei*) in Japanese Conversation. *Japanese/Korean Linguistics* vol.7, eds. N. Akatsuka, H. Hoji, S. Iwasaki, S.-O. Sohn, and S. Strauss, 95-103, Stanford, CA: CSLI Publications.

Sacks, H., E. A. Schegloff. 1979. Two Preferences in the Organization of Reference to Persons in Conversation and Their Interaction. *Everyday Language: Studies in Ethnomethodology*, ed. G. Psathas, 15-21. New York: Irvington Publishers, Inc.

Sacks, H., E. A. Schegloff, and G. Jefferson. 1974. A Simplest Systematics for the Organization of Turn-taking in Conversation. *Language* 50:696-735.

Schegloff, E. A. 1979. The Relevance of Repair to Syntax-for-conversation. *Syntax and Semantics 12: Discourse and Syntax*, ed. by T. Givón, 261-286. New York: Academic Press.

Schegloff, E. A. 1982. Discourse as an Interactional Achievement: Some Uses of 'Uh huh' and Other Things that Come between Sentences. *Georgetown University Round Table on Languages and Linguistics 198, Analyzing Discourse: Text and Talk*, ed. D. Tannen, 71-93. Washington, DC: Georgetown University Press.

Schegloff, E. A. 1996. Turn Organization: One Intersection of Grammar and Interaction. *Interaction and Grammar*, eds. E. Ochs, E. A. Schegloff, and S. A. Thompson, 52-123. Cambridge: Cambridge University Press.

Schegloff, E. A. Forthcoming. *A Primer of Conversation Analysis: Sequence Organization.* Cambridge: Cambridge University Press.

Tanaka, H. 1999. *Turn-taking in Japanese Conversation: A Study in Grammar and Interaction*. Amsterdam: John Benjamins.

Tanaka, H. 2000. The Particles *Ne* as a Turn-management Device in Japanese Conversation. *Journal of Pragmatics* 32:1135-1176.

Thompson, S. A. and E. Couper-Kuhlen. 2005. The Clause as a Locus of Grammar and Interaction. *Discourse Studies* 7:481-505.

The Korean Topic Marker *nun* Revisited: *nun* as a Tying Device

KYU-HYUN KIM
Kyung Hee University

1. Introduction

In this paper, some of the discourse-organizational features of what is called the Korean topic marker *nun/un* (hereafter *nun*) are analyzed on the basis of a detailed examination of spontaneous conversational data. From a conversation-analytic perspective (Sacks et al. 1974), I examine sequential features that can be taken to 'motivate' the use of *nun* as part of a linguistic practice on the basis of which a range of social actions are sequentially organized. Drawing upon Sacks' notion of 'membership categorization device' (Sacks 1972), I propose that what is referred to by a *nun*-marked referent or what a *nun*-utterance is about is formulated as a categorizable or 'categorization-relevant' entity in the context of the category-linked knowledge evoked by the content of the post-*nun* predicate that attributes a particular trait to the *nun*-marked entity. Systematic attention is paid to how *nun*-utterances are triggered by or sequentially 'tied' to a feature of the prior or current context

(Sacks 1992).[1] The import of this tying practice evoking a category-implicated generic-specific link is found in a range of ways in which potentially face-impinging social actions are obliquely implemented on the basis of the interactional work made possible by it, such as indexing/soliciting responsiveness, negotiating the speaker's knowledgeability with regard to information he/she is entitled to, or incorporating the other's perspective in recipient-designed ways.

The data used for this study are audio-taped face-to-face conversations. *TA Meeting* is a conversation recorded during a meeting among teaching assistants teaching Korean at a university in the U.S. *G & S, S & H*, and *K & H* are conversations between friends,[2] and *Park S-H. Data* include conversations between graduate students at a university in Korea. Also included in the analysis are segments of overheard conversations that have been jotted down on the spot or immediately after the conversation took place.

2. *Nun*-Marked Referent As Categorization-Relevant

2.1. Attributing Membership Characteristic

One of the most salient semantic features of *nun*-utterances having a significant interactional import is that the speaker attributes a 'generic membership characteristic' to the given referent/event on the basis of his/her observation of an event or state that is proposed as attesting to such a trait. Consider fragment (1):[3]

(1) (Overheard Conversation)
((The mother (M) is looking for her son (Junho).))

    1 G: *cwunho hwacangsil ka-ss   -e.*
        Junho   bathroom go-ANT-IE
        "Junho is in the bathroom."

    2 M: *cwunho,*
        Junho
        "Junho."

→ 3 G: ***cay***   ***-nun*** *way hwacangsil-ul*   *ka-myen,*
        he (that:child)-TOP why restroom -ACC go-COND
        paci -ka   *pan-i*   *holttak*   *cec-e*   *-peli -nya,.*
        pants-NOM half-NOM completely wet-CONN-AUX-IE

---

[1] This is a two-part process of proposing an entity as categorization-relevant and subsequently attributing a quality or a trait that completes the categorization, which is reminiscent of the inference process associated with Kuroda's notion of 'categorical judgment' (Kuroda 1972).

[2] I thank Professor Hyo Sang Lee at Indiana University for providing me with this set of data.

3 The transcription notations used for this paper were adapted from Sacks et al. (1974):

//	Interruption	=	Contiguous utterances	--	Cut-offs
(0.0)	Intervals	(.)	Micro-pause	( )	Words/identities unclear
.	Falling intonation	,	Continuing intonation	?	Rising intonation
(( ))	Transcriber's remarks				

"How come **he,** whenever he goes to the bathroom, gets half of his pants all soaked with water?"

In the context preceding the cited conversation, the mother (M) was summoning her son, Junho, and the grandmother (G) tells her that he is in the bathroom. This sequence of talk triggers the grandmother's *nun*-utterance in which she brings up the child's habitual tendency to get his pants soaked with water whenever he washes his face. By referring to the child in a turn-initial component marked by *nun*, the grandmother brings up a trait that she has presumably observed repeatedly before and attributes it to the child as his 'problematic' generic behavioral feature. Note that, through this trait-attributing practice, the child has gained a new topical salience as a referent, and his conduct, formulated as 'complainable', has become a target of evaluation 'topic-initially'. This rather disjunctive turn of the event induced by the turn-initial *nun*-marked referent is made possible and warranted by way of being triggered by or 'tied' to the prior talk in which the child was mentioned with reference to his presence in the bathroom.

An important inference made possible through the *nun*-utterance is the common knowledge associated with the category of 'people managing their routine business of washing their face in the bathroom', which constitutes a background frame within which the *nun*-marked referent's conduct is to be compared and evaluated. The evocation of such category-linked knowledge (Sacks 1972) made possible by a *nun*-utterance seems to provide a basis on which a range of interactional work is implemented. In (1), the *nun*-marked referent ('the child'), formulated as a target to be evaluated in terms of the concomitantly evoked category-linked knowledge, is relevantly positioned as the party to be rebuked.

The specific-generic linkage evoked by a *nun*-utterance, often strongly imbued with the speaker's subjective evaluative stance that takes a proposed specific feature of the referent as an instance of its generic membership characteristic, furnishes the hearer with the opportunity to agree or disagree with the valence of the proposed generic feature in an affectively loaded way. In (1), for instance, the grandmother's *nun*-utterance was formulated as a complaint/rebuke to be acknowledged and shared by the addressee (the mother of the child) and possibly by the child himself, who was also in hearing range. With the addressee and the target referent being present, the grandmother's face-impinging *nun*-utterance projectively solicits responsiveness in such a way that it projects a trajectory of sequential development through which the participants are invited to collaboratively respond with an appreciative uptake as potential co-assessors in the direction of collectively rebuking the child. These interactional features of *nun* are also observed in fragment (2):

(2) (TA Meeting)

```
 1  J:  kuntey      ah  cham onul  lab worksheet-twu (.) hay-cwu
        by:the:way DM  RM   today lab  worksheet-ADD  do -give
 2      -eya        -tway-yo?  tap  -i   nawa    -ss  -eyo?
        -NECESS-OK  -POL  answer-NOM come:out-ANT-POL
        "By the way, Oh, are we also supposed to use the lab worksheet
        in class today? Is the answer key available?"
        ((Five lines omitted))
 9  K:  tuli -lkkey -yo.  cikum tap.
        give-MOD-POL  now  answer
        "I'll give (it) to you. Now the answer key."
10      (2.4)
→ 11  W: hangsang kim min-ki ssi -nun cwunpi -ka      tway  -iss.
        always   kim min-ki Mr.-TOP preparation-NOM become-exist
12      -e (0.5) ttak     meli sok  -ey  (i  -key)      ttak
        -IE      squarely head inside-LOC (this-thing:NOM) squarely
13      mwe      -ka  nao     -a hangsang.
        something-NOM come:out-IE always
        "Always Mr. Kim is ready. (0.5) He has his mind prepared and
        set to deal with any contingency at the right moment. Always."
14  S:  (naynnal--) kulen    -ke(h)kat(h)-ci       hh
        everyday    like:that-seem      -COMM
        "(Everyday--) You may think so (=but actually he is not like
        that)."
```

This conversation takes place during a loosely structured TA meeting. In the preceding context, J asked K, the TA coordinator, for a copy of the answer keys for practice materials. In line 9, K responds to J right away by delivering to him the requested answer keys. It is in response to this behavior of K that W, another TA, produces the *nun*-utterance as a compliment attributing a positive quality to K along the lines of applauding the efficiency with which he handles administrative affairs as the TA coordinator. The ascribed trait is formulated as a generic one that draws upon W's previous observation(s) of K's conduct that similarly indexes his professional readiness as head TA. This categorizing action takes place in the course of W's conveying the sense that K is being singled out and evaluated as a 'unique' incumbent of the concurrently evoked membership category 'TA' (e.g., as a TA who is always ready for contingencies).

As in (1), while being immediately responsive to the observed behavior, the *nun*-utterance projects a rich sequential context in which a range of responsive acts, such as co-assessment, appreciation, downgrading, disagreement, etc., becomes relevant as the co-participants can variably address in an affectively loaded way the link between the observed behavior and the generic trait proposed by W. Note, in this respect, that S, one of the co-present TAs, who also happens to be the wife of K, disputes the proposed generic trait being attributed to K (line 14: "You may think so (=but actually he is not like that)"). That is, S responds to W's characterization of K in such a way that she disputes it in a joking manner. On the basis of the preceding observations, we can say that, by disputing what W has proposed as a generic trait of K marked by *nun*, S is problematizing W's knowledge and experience on the basis of which K's observed conduct is tied to the proposed generic trait ascribed to him.

Fragments (1) and (2) illustrate that the *nun*-marked referent is singled out as a 'categorization-relevant' referent in the context of shared commonsensical knowledge; it is formulated as a target of evaluation whose 'unique' trait is to be described in the upcoming predicate component in comparison with (or in the context of) a concurrently evoked 'representative' membership characteristic commonly associated with the category of which the *nun*-marked referent is proposed as an incumbent. That is, in this process of categorization, *nun* evokes a category whose representative incumbent's membership characteristic serves as a background against which the *nun*-marked referent is evaluated as manifesting a particular 'generic' trait that deserves noticing and evaluation, e.g., as a unique, aberrant, typical, or non-fitting incumbent of the evoked membership category. Note that this categorizing or trait-attributing act is done as part of or for the purpose of a variety of affectively loaded interactional work such as complaining/rebuking (as in (1)) or complimenting (as in (2)), both in the context of asserting 'unique' membership characteristics of the *nun*-marked referents in terms of the commonsensically evoked category-bound activities inferred as the background frame.[4]

2.2. Dealing with Prior Talk

While in (1) and (2) the speaker makes a descriptive statement with *nun* in response to an observed behavior, which is formulated as an instance of the proposed trait being attributed to the *nun*-marked referent, there are contexts

---

[4] The membership category evoked by *nun* provides the speaker with the means of introducing and talking about the *nun*-marked referent in the context of claiming knowledge about the referent. As illustrated in (1) and (2), what the speaker offers with respect to the *nun*-marked referent is claimed as a 'generic' trait of the referent which presupposes the speaker's particular knowledge that is implicitly pitted against the commonsensical knowledge concurrently evoked by *nun*. The feature of *nun* indexing speaker entitlement is often highlighted 'for its own sake' in the context where the participants mainly orient themselves to claiming or disclaiming knowledge about a referent. A preliminary observation suggests, in this respect, that in a formal interview situation, *nun*-marked statements are massively used by the interviewee answering the interviewer's question. This would be in keeping with the preceding analysis in the sense that the interviewee is the more knowledgeable party vis-à-vis the interviewer about the given topic of the interview, and thus entitled to make a generic statement about it.

where a *nun*-utterance is not so much triggered by an event observed in the immediate context as produced to deal with the prior talk by way of being tied to some aspect of the prior talk as manifested by the speaker's responsive or counteractive stance displayed towards it (Kim 1993). Actually, it is often in such a context that the widely observed notion of 'contrastiveness' associated with *nun* could be analyzed in terms of the practice of evoking a category and category-linked knowledge. This practice provides a ground on which a range of social actions can be organized as a way of dealing with some aspect of the prior talk and initiating some counteractive action toward it by way of bringing up a referent inferentially tied to a referent implicitly or commonsensically envisaged or a previously mentioned referent via some shared or related membership characteristic associated with a category evoked by *nun*. Consider fragment (3):

(3) (Overheard Conversation)

   1 A: *ssoseyci sa -ss   -e?*
           sausage buy-ANT-IE
           "Did you buy sausage?"

→ 2 B: *ani. kkamppak   ic   -e   -mek-ess -e.*
           no for a moment forget-CONN-eat -ANT-IE

   3   *khulim chicu -nun sa -ss   -e.*
           cream cheese-TOP buy-ANT-IE.
           "No. I forgot. I bought **cream cheese** though."

B's *nun*-utterance occurs in a context where B responds to A in a dispreferred way; she responds negatively to A's question asking whether she has bought sausage ("No, I forgot"). B goes on to add that she did buy 'cream cheese', which, marked by *nun*, is proposed as an alternative to 'sausage' that she has forgotten to buy.

    The production of the *nun*-marked referent evokes a category of which 'sausage' and 'cream cheese' are asserted to be co-incumbents (i.e., edible grocery items that A wants). The introduction of the new referent 'cream cheese', which could be highly disjunctive, is thus warranted by the evocation of the category proposed as including as its member a previously mentioned referent 'sausage' as well. In other words, the informationally new *nun*-marked referent is tied to the previously mentioned referent via the evocation of the category that subsumes both. With the category being established linking the two referents, the speaker shifts the hearer's attention to the newly proposed incumbent ('cream cheese') which can be positively evaluated in the context of attempting to satisfy the interlocutor. This tying operation provides the speaker with the resource for performing a face-managing action obliquely, e.g., for mitigating the extent of her failure to do shopping as directed by the interlocutor (i.e., buy sausage) and for defending herself from the interlocutor's rebuke that might be subsequently forthcoming or for appeasing the interlocutor.

3. *Nun*-utterance as a Commentary

While the preceding discussion has mainly focused upon the cases in which the speaker's descriptive act primarily concerns the *nun*-marked referent per se, which is set up as a categorization-relevant entity by *nun*, there are contexts in which *nun*-utterances as a whole serve as a running commentary about a referent/event that has been established as the topic of the current interaction. In the following sections, two such contexts are examined with reference to some of the salient interactional features implicated by the category-evoking property of *nun*.

3.1. Incorporating Prior Utterance and Projecting Comparable Description in Recipient-designed Way

In fragment (4) below, the participants talk about Dodger Stadium, and in line 30, H produces a *nun*-utterance in response to S's question. Note that H's *nun*-utterance, while produced as a response to S's question, runs as a commentary about the current topic, i.e., Dodger Stadium, which was established as the topic of the conversation in the prior context:

(4) (S & H)
```
    29 S:  ... (0.7) kulekhey  khe   -yo?
                    that-much big:IE-POL
           "Is it that big?"
→   30 H:  ... (1.7) mwe kulehkey khu-ci    -n    anh -e. ...
                    well that:much big -NOML-TOP NEG-IE
           "Well, it isn't that big [Being so big, it is not]. ..."
```

In repeating the predicate of S's question ('is big') in his response, H 'reformulates' its content in the light of his own knowledge about and his experience associated with Dodger Stadium. This practice furnishes the sense that S's inquiry, which is apparently based on the inference made from the prior talk, is negatively responded to by H by way of being tied to what H knowledgeably presents as an empirically grounded generic feature of the stadium.

What is interesting in (4), in this respect, is that, in the subsequent context not shown in the fragment, H goes on to highlight the grandeur of Dodger Stadium by way of talking about the 'fantastic' aspects of the stadium (see H-S. Lee and K-G. Lee 2003). Note that if *nun* had not been used in H's utterance, the import of the utterance would have been limited to the denial of S's proposal of 'big size' as a property of the stadium. With *nun*, H goes on to evoke other positive generic features 'comparable' with the feature proposed by S ('big'), which can relevantly be brought up in relation to the category 'stadium' and its incumbent features concurrently evoked by the *nun*-utterance. With the descriptor 'big' used by S being incorporated in H's turn-in-progress in the course of being negated, it is still acknowledged as a 'positive' feature which provides a basis on which a comparable set of descriptors can be relevantly offered as ones sharing the same 'positive' membership features as the descriptor 'big'. This 'recipient-designed' practice (Sacks 1972) seems to have the effect of rejecting the interlocutor's version of description in an oblique fashion.

In the same vein, consider fragment (5), where the speaker of *nun* collaboratively rejects the interlocutor's self-commiserating comment halfway into her turn-in-progress:

(5) (Park S-H. Data)

> 26 H: *yey mwe (4.0) oykwuk   -eyse kongpwuha-ko*
>   yes what   foreign:country-LOC study   -CONN
>
> 27 *tolao -n   pwun -tul po-nikka   na-to*
>   return-ATTR person-PL see-REASON I -ADD
>
> 28 *naka -kosiph-eyo mak   palam-i*
>   go:out-want -POL without:reservation wind -NOM
>
> 29 *kwaynhi   tul   -e   //-kackwu*
>   without:reason come:in-CONN-CONN
>   "When I see those who return after finishing studies abroad, I
>   also feel like going abroad to study, totally filled with unrealistic
>   ideas."
>   [
> 30 S: *naka -lswu-man iss -umyen*
>   go:out-can -only exist-COND
>
> → 31 **palam kwaynhi   tu   -nun -ke   -n**
>   wind   without:reason come:in-ATTR-NOML-TOP
>
> 32 *ani -kwu   naka -myen   coh -ci.*
>   NEG-CONN go:out-COND great-COMM
>   "If you can go abroad, it's not **that you're filled with unrealistic
>   ideas**, but if you can go abroad it would certainly be great."

Here the *nun*-marked portion of S's utterance, which incorporates H's expression (lines 28-29: 'filled with unrealistic ideas'), is formulated as a parenthetical insert that is planted in the middle of her turn-in-progress ("…it's not that you're filled with unrealistic ideas, but…"). S, in responding to H's remark about her desire to go abroad to study, reformulates H's displayed self-commiseration in H's favor, i.e., by way of rejecting it in the context of proposing a perspective that puts her desire in a positive light. As in (4), the content of the *nun*-utterance incorporated from the interlocutor's (H's) turn provides material that the speaker initially rejects before proposing an alternative (and comparable) descriptor that shares the same descriptive category ('filled with unrealistic ideas' (line 31) vs. 'great' (line 32)).

That *nun* is often deployed in incorporating the other's point in the speaker's own turn-in-progress points to a recipient-designed way of disputing it obliquely, which is accomplished as a practice of tying the interlocutor's point to the speaker's own category-linked knowledge. The interlocutor's point, though being rejected, is formulated as instantiating a relevant member of the category being evoked whose 'category-relevance' is still acknowledged by the speaker's proposal of a 'comparable' feature as a trait that shares the same category as the one proposed by the interlocutor.

3.2. Bringing up Hither-to Not-fully-explicated Aspects of the Referent/event Being Talked About

In many contexts where *nun* is used, we find a sense in which the speaker re-opens the case that has already been closed, i.e., tapping into unmentioned aspects of what has already been wrapped up in the preceding contexts. The use of *nun* in this context provides us with the sense that the speaker is bringing up an aspect of the referent/event previously described that otherwise would have remained unexplained had it not been for the interactional need to address the interlocutor's move. This feature of *nun* that brings up a hither-to unexplicated aspect of the referent/event brings into relief the interactional motivation for doing so, e.g., soliciting agreement in rebuking, complimenting, or appeasing the interlocutor (as in (1), (2), and (3) respectively).

The speaker's practice of tapping into a particular aspect of the referent/event that could have been relevantly left untapped is also observed in story-telling contexts where the speaker highlights descriptive details or relatedness thereof as a way of strengthening the point of his/her story and justifying his/her stance displayed in the previous context. For instance, in fragment (6), the speaker is talking about the disappointment she felt about the apartment building she was moving in. In the immediately preceding context, G complained about the building not having an elevator:

(6) (G & S)
    45 G: *kulay   kac -kwu -se   -n,*
          be:so:CONN take-CONN-CONN-TOP
          "So then (=Having it being so),"
→ 46   *tto **kyeytan-un** yolehkey ccop -a*
          also stairs -TOP like:this narrow-CONN
    47   *kaci-kwu -nun iss -ci*
          take-CONN-TOP exist-COMM
          "**Stairs** also are narrow like this, you know, and so,"

48   ... *(1.0) ttak   pwass   -nuntey*
      squarely see:ANT-CIRCUM
      "... when we looked at it,"
      ((Three lines of G's turn omitted))
52 G: *kulikwu-nun tto,*
      and   -TOP also
      "and then, also,"
      ((G continues to tell the story.))

In line 46, G's *nun*-marked description ("Stairs are narrow ...") yields the sense that the speaker is tapping into an 'additional' negative aspect of the building she mentioned in the prior context in order to highlight the point of the story, i.e., the feeling of disappointment the speaker experienced about the building to which she was moving. With her complaining stance having been already displayed in the prior context with respect to the absence of an elevator, the use of *nun* in tapping into additional 'not-yet-mentioned' displeasing aspects of the building furnishes the speaker with a resource for further strengthening the ground on which her displayed complaining stance can be justified.

The frequent use of the adverb *tto* 'also' co-occurring with *nun*-utterances (lines 46 and 52) further suggests that the speaker is bringing up several of the not-yet-explicated aspects of the building. In this respect, the use of *nun* with a connective like 'so' or 'and then' could also be taken as signaling that the speaker is moving to the next stage of the story in such a way that any 'as yet unexplored' aspect of the event that has just been described in the preceding episode is going to be brought to bear upon the subsequent telling (see line 45 (*kulay kac-kwu-se-n* 'So then (=Having it being so)'), lines 46-47 (*ccop-a kaci-kwu-**nun*** 'narrow, and so') and line 52 (*kulikwu-**nun*** 'and then')).

The sense of going back to a previously described event and tapping into what might have been relevantly left unexamined is also associated with the context where *nun* is used for what H-S. Lee and K-G. Lee (2003) call a logical guidepost expression such as *sasil* 'in fact', as illustrated in fragment (7). In the preceding context, K has been talking about cheap PCs sold in Korea, saying that their quality is not good, as reflected by their low price. In recapping what he said about cheap PCs, K uses the logical guidepost expression *sasil* 'in fact' marked by *nun* in pointing out their low quality that does not deserve the label 'PC':

(7) (K & H)
    K: *sasil -**un**   phici-ka   ani -ci.*
       in fact-TOP PC   -NOM NEG-COMM
       "So in fact it is not a PC."

As shown by the English gloss that includes the discourse marker *so* (also see lines 45-47 in (6)), the use of *nun* with the guidepost expression provides us with the sense that the speaker is going back to what he said earlier in the manner of summarizing the whole point and bringing up an aspect thereof that has not been previously mentioned explicitly. Note in (7) that, without *nun*, the sense of tapping into what could have been left unmentioned (and presumably left as something to be inferred) would decrease dramatically.

The evocation of a category and category-linked knowledge associated with *nun* furnishes the speaker with the resource for organizing a wide range of actions variably tied to prior talk. This interactional feature seems to make it possible to extend the use of *nun* in the direction of highlighting the sense in which an aspect of an event that has been relevantly left unmentioned previously is newly tapped into for various interactional purposes, e.g., in order to further strengthen the point of the previous or forthcoming episode and justify the speaker's stance implicated in its telling or to address the interlocutor's move in a more efficient and justifiable manner.

4. Conclusion

Even though the interactional and sequential features of *nun* that I examined in this paper may seem to subsume different types of practice, they all share the same 'procedural' sense of the speaker's proposing a formulation of a categorization-relevant referent/event. This sense crucially draws upon a tying operation through which a category-relevant generic trait is proposed and ascribed to the referent/event by way of being tied to the prior talk.[5] With the speaker's claim of category-relevant knowledge is unchallengeably presupposed (H-S. Lee 1987), this process constitutes a practice on the basis of which a wide range of social action can be obliquely implemented in such a way that solicits the interlocutor's collusion and endorsement.

There is a need for a more detailed analysis of a range of practices in which *nun* is employed as a grammatical resource for various interactional work. The diverse positions where *nun* can be placed and an amazingly wide range of uses to which *nun* can be put seem to index particular directions in which some of these practice features of *nun* are being exploited and grammaticalized (H-S. Lee and K-G. Lee 2003). Further research on the role that *nun* plays in sequential organization will have implications for investigating how interaction bears upon the way *nun* gains unique functional

---

[5] Various semantic and functional notions traditionally associated with *nun*, such as givenness or aboutness (Chafe 1976), could be viewed as referring to some of the 'static' aspects of the dynamic interactional process enacted by *nun*.

properties and for illuminating the grammaticalization process *nun* is going through.

References

Chafe, W. L. 1976. Givenness, Contrastiveness, Definiteness, Subjects, Topics, and Point of View. *Subject and Topic*, ed. C. N. Li, 25-55. New York: Academic Press.

Kim, K-H. 1993. Topicality in Korean Conversation: Conversation-analytic Perspective. *Japanese/Korean Linguistics* 2, ed. P. Clancy, 33-54. CSLI, Stanford University,

Kim, K-H. 2000. The Korean Topic Marker *nun* in Conversation: Formulating Upshot in Orientation to the Immediate Context. Paper Presented as the WECOL 2000, California State University, Fresno.

Kuroda, S.-Y. 1972. The Categorical and the Thetic Judgment: Evidence from Japanese Syntax. *Foundations of Language* 9:153-85.

Lee, H-S. 1987. *Discourse Presupposition and the Discourse Function of the Topic Marker -nun in Korean*. Bloomington: Indiana University Linguistics Club.

Lee, H-S. and K-G. Lee. 2003. Highlighting through Marking Discontinuity and Independence: A Unified Account of the Uses of the Topic Particle *-nun* in Korean. Paper Presented at the 13th Japanese/Korean Linguistics Conference, Michigan State University.

Sacks, H. 1972. On the Analyzability of Stories by Children. *Directions in Sociolinguistics*, eds. J. J. Gumperz and D. Hymes, 325-45. New York: Holt, Rinehart & Winston.

Sacks, H. 1992. *Lectures on Conversation*. Vol. 1, ed. G. Jefferson. Oxford: Blackwell.

Sacks, H., E. A. Schegloff, and G. Jefferson. 1974. A Simplest Systematics for the Organization of Turn-taking for Conversation. *Language* 50:696-735.

Dealing With Changes: Discourse of Elderly Japanese Women

YOSHIKO MATSUMOTO
Stanford University

1. Introduction[1]

The speaker's age has been well-recognized as an important factor in analyzing the state and conditions of language use and development. However, in comparison to the extensive research achievements on the early years of life leading up to adulthood, the study of discourse and language used by (and to) the elderly is still underdeveloped. The decreased ability caused by age and illness has attracted more attention than the content and intention of elderly people's speech. It is conceivable that this inattention arises from a perception that old age is a less significant stage of one's life after the peak of adulthood, one that represents decline from full competence, linguistically and otherwise. However, such a perception would ignore the aspect of old age as the phase that displays the wealth of accumulated personal history and that has an identity of its own.

[1] This research was partly supported by a Japan Foundation Research Fellowship. I am grateful for generosity of the people who recorded their conversations, and for the research access provided by the Life Planning Center in Tokyo.

Some notable works in the last decade or so on language and the elderly have disputed the decrement view of aging, and they provide a valuable foundation for further research. These works were predominantly carried out in English-speaking contexts (e.g. Coupland, N., Coupland, J. and Giles 1991, Coupland and Nussbaum 1993, Hamilton 1994, Hamilton (ed.) 1999, Williams and Nussbaum 2000), or were quantitative studies of cross-cultural intergenerational communication (e.g. Giles et al. 2002, Ota et al. 2002). In-depth linguistic studies of the Japanese elderly discourse are few (Hamaguchi 2001, Matsumoto 2005), despite a large and growing population of elderly in Japan. The life expectancy of Japanese at birth is around eighty-five years for women and seventy-eight years for men (Ministry of Health, Labor and Welfare survey). As of September 2003, almost 20 % of the population of Japan were people over sixty-five years of age. These figures alone would make the Japanese elderly an important group to be understood better, rather than being dismissed on the basis of stereotypes.

Among the Japanese elderly population above age sixty-five, approximately 25% are in 'good' health and another 50% are in 'normal' health with no need for nursing. This means that three-quarters of the Japanese elderly population are in relatively good health; a fact that suggests that the numerous studies of the ill members of the elderly population (though undoubtedly important) do not reflect the general situation of the elderly.

Many studies on elderly speech have been conducted in the context of intergenerational discourse, largely that of first-time acquaintances, such as interviews by younger people (with some exceptions such as Hamilton's (1994) longitudinal interaction with an Alzheimer patient, and a peer gossip study by Saunders 1999). Such studies have found that the fact of old age and the associated hardships are foregrounded in the interactions. A frequent observation that characterizes speech of the elderly is 'painful self-disclosure' (Coupland, N., Coupland, J., and Giles 1991), in which unhappy personal information on one's ill health, immobility, disengagement, or bereavement is revealed, and the elderly often describe themselves in terms of negative stereotypes, which may be viewed as signs of being 'disengaged', 'egocentric' and 'grumbling.'

Although it is interesting to investigate the motives and effects of elderly speakers' disclosure of these personal events to first-time acquaintances (Bonnesen and Hummert 2002), it is possible that these negative and old-age focused characterizations of elderly discourse are heavily influenced by the settings of the conversations. Indeed, Coupland, N., Coupland, J., and Giles (1991) report more extensive use of 'painful self-disclosure (PSD)' by the elderly in intergenerational first-time acquaintance interviews than in a peer group setting. In a situation where participants do not share much in common – for example, if they did not gather for personal or professional purposes, but in response to the linguistic researcher's solicitation – it is possible that a clear age difference between the various speakers is an obvious and relatively uncontroversial property of the interlocutors that functions as a conversational topic. If the context remains at the level of introductions and small talk among non-intimates, we should not be surprised that the researcher finds the data to center around events stereotypically associated with age. Further studies on PSD (Coupland, N., Coupland, J., Giles, and Henwood 1991, Coupland, J., Coupland, N., and Grainger 1991) have shown that PSD among the elderly is often engendered by the younger conversation partners. From that finding, those studies have argued that elderly identities were interactionally manufactured in large part by the younger first-encounter interlocutors. If the situations are different, such as conversations with more familiar partners and interactional situations, a different analysis of the functions of PSD and different self-presentations of the speakers from the negative identities may well be observed.

This paper is a part of an endeavor to elucidate discourse practices of elderly people by examining the language of elderly Japanese women with particular attention to ways in which age, gender and individual personae are reflected and performed in their verbal interactions. In my discussion, I will focus on a discourse practice identified in previous studies as characteristic of elder speech, namely, 'painful self-disclosure' (Coupland, N., Coupland, J., and Giles 1991). In contrast to the first-time encounters of previous studies, this paper qualitatively examines informal conversations of three individual elderly Japanese women with acquaintances of peer and younger age groups. The data reveal that the interpretations that can be given to references to age and decline go beyond the stereotypical images of complaint and unhappiness, and present images of acceptance, awareness and ability to view their situation objectively, as well as the self-analysis needed to adjust one's established persona to the changing reality. The study cautions against associating a single pragmatic or social meaning to a linguistic sign or discourse practice and emphasizes the importance of considering a multitude of pragmatic and social meanings that are achieved in expressions of one's persona. It also encourages greater attention to the latter part of the life-span by illuminating the richness of the language and lives of people in an age group that is largely unstudied.

2. The Present Study

The examples I consider are from conversational data collected between summer 2001 and summer 2004 for a larger interdisciplinary exploration of the interactions of language use, old age and gender, with particular attention to verbal interactions of elderly women in Japan. The examination in this paper is based on two types of recorded informal conversations. One is peer conversations among elderly Japanese women (above sixty-five years of age)[2] who are in relatively good health and who share a common background to various degrees. The occasions were not set up solely for the purpose of this research, but there were other independent purposes, such as gatherings of friends, or volunteer work. Another type of recorded data is conversations between an elderly female speaker who participated in the peer conversations and the (middle-aged) researcher. The occasion was set up for the researcher to get in touch with the elderly individuals again about one and a half years after the previous peer conversation recordings. These follow-up conversations were led by the elderly speakers, and the researcher played the role of listener for the most part. The topics in both types of conversations varied, but included experiences of past trips and plans for future trips, food, shopping, sports, books, acquaintances' health and death, and family members' health condition.

One common feature that is noticeable in the ten 60 – 90 minute audiotape recordings of the peer interactions that I examined in Matsumoto (2005) is that the participants often laughed. This finding is similar to an observation by Ervin-Tripp and Lampert (1992) with respect to informal conversations among the younger people that they studied.[3] In my data of conversations of the elderly, the participants laughed often even during verbal interaction similar to 'painful self-disclosure'. Although the events and situations referred to in such conversations could be considered as painful and negative, the recorded conversations reveal that the stories were told comically and without apparent solicitation of sympathy.

The conversations with the researcher also contain many instances of laughter, but they are also illustrative of the elderly speakers' thought processes regarding past and present events, including those that resulted in what one may perceive as 'painful' changes in their lives, such as a husband's death and physical or mental inability. It should be noted that their 'painful self-disclosure' in these conversations, however, is accompanied with analytical annotations of their emotional responses to such changes, suggesting that their self-disclosure is not necessarily a simple sign of complaint or grumbling, but is part of the process of understanding and accepting changes in their lives.

In the following, I will present examples of such age-related disclosure, which is presented with laughter and humor, or with the speaker's self-

---

[2] As discussed by Eckert (1984), biological age is not necessarily an indication of the person's social age reflected in language, but I used sixty-five years of age for convenience in data collection.

[3] In Ervin-Tripp and Lampert, 8.3% of the turns occasioned laughter.

analysis, and discuss the meaning and effects of such interactions. The presented examples from the two types of conversational data suggest that has various meanings and effects. References to age and decline, rather than being simply stereotypical images of complaint and unhappiness, may be viewed as complex images of awareness, coping, and ability to view the unwelcome situation objectively. [4] It is hoped that the present study will indicate the depth and breadth of verbal interaction of older speakers, providing counterexamples to ageist stereotypes, and emphasizing the importance of examining naturally-occurring data from a variety of contexts in order to gain insights into language use and speakers' lives.

3. Examples

I will discuss in this paper: (1) a comical description of how speaker's (N's) husband died without making any sound, (2) an account of speaker's (K's) recent forgetfulness (3) a recounting of the incident that led the speaker of example 2 (K) to become forgetful, and (4) a description of the death of another speaker's (A's) husband. All can be categorized as PSD. The first two examples, (1) and (2), are from peer conversation data and the latter two, (3) and (4), are from conversations with the researcher. (1) and (4) are on the same topic of husband's death, and (2) and (3) are on the topic of K's forgetfulness.

The first example is from a ninety-minute conversation among senior volunteers who belong to a seniors' association affiliated with an organization called the Life Planning Center. When I visited the association, four senior volunteers, two female and two male, all aged above seventy-five, were gathered in a room to receive telephone calls from other elders who might seek a conversational companion over the phone. The volunteers were taking turns to perform this service. While they were waiting for phone calls, which were very few, they chatted among themselves.

In this segment of the conversation, two male participants were mostly quiet and listening. One of the female participants, N, had been talking about how lucky she was to receive the assistance of Dr. Hinohara, the founder of the Center, in advising with respect to her late husband's medical condition. N, the main speaker, is in her late seventies, while the other (female) participant, M, is in her early eighties. N's utterances are shown in bold face in your handout, and her utterances that are comical and/or that accompanied her chuckles are in small capitals. The designation '<laughter>' refers to some sustained laughing, while '<laugh>' marks a short and light laugh. The temporal positions of back channeling and laughs indicated

---

[4] Saunders (1999) also found that gossiping is used for the reasons of solidarity despite the common view of gossip as 'lazy small talk'.

in the translation in this and other excerpts are approximations due to the word order difference between Japanese and English.

(1) Husband's Death
N1: [tyanto sensei ga [moo teha   [tehai-site kudasatte
M1: [a   [a, mo, oisyasan mo [tyanto site,   [aa
T1:   [haa
N2: de sensei ga sugu tonndekite kudasutte [kangofu-san to [
M2:   [a   [aa
T2:   [aa
N3: sorede nee, nakunatte ne, nizikan hodo site odenwa ga [kakatte
M3:   [aaa
T3:   [aaa
N4: de dodesuka tte sensei mo nizikan mae ni nak
N5: sore mo hontoni ne, sobani itemo wakan nai gurai
N6: un tomo sun <laughter> tomo kyun tomo iwanaide [ne
M6:   [un
N7: ano <laugh> watasi mo sirooto desu kara [ne,
M7:   [un
N8: iki ga tomatteru nante.
N9: yome ga ne, [soba ni ite, otoosama ne, ikisiterassyaranai mitai
      desuyotte kara
M9:   [un
N10: eeee (animated) <laughter> nanteyutte ne
M10: <   laughter   > so.
N11: soide koosite, nn sinzooni naan tomo wakannai n desu ne.
N12: soide raifu puranningu sentaa ni sugu denwa simasita no.
N13: sositara ne < laugh >
N14: nanka anoo are tissyupeepaa o ne hana no sita ni nokkete
      [kuda.
M14: < laugh > [uun un
N15: nokketemo ne ugoiteru ka ugoitenai ka wakan nain desu.
N16: sositara, moo sensei to kangohu san ga sugu kite kudasatta[te,
M16:   [unn
N17: demo moo wakatta n desu ne moo
N18: kore wa moo damedatte < laugh >yuu koto ga ne
N19: daakara sensei no okage de nee, aan na.

TRANSLATION
N1: Dr. (Hinohara) had already made arrangements
M1: mm   mm already a doctor was already arranged to be sent, hmm

T1:   I see
N2: and the doctor rushed to my house with a nurse
M2:   ah   hmm
T2:   ah
N3: and y'know, about two hours after my husband passed away, I got
     a phone call
M3:   mmm mm
T3:   mmm mm
N4: and, Dr. Hinohara asked me 'how is he?', (and I said) two hours
     earlier
N5: and it was really, you wouldn't have noticed even if you were right
     next to him
N6: (my husband) didn't say a peep <laughter> or even a squeak
M6:   mm
N7: well <laughter> since I am a lay person, you know,
M7:   mm
N8: I couldn't imagine that he stopped breathing.
N9: my daughter-in-law was beside us and said 'Father (in-law)
     doesn't seem to be breathing,' so
M9:   uhuh
N10: 'Gee, really?' (animated voice) <laughter> I said
M10:<   laughter   >   I see.
N11: so, like this, um, (I touched) his heart, but I couldn't tell anything.
N12: so, I called the Life Planning Center right away.
N13: then <laugh>
N14: they told me that I should put a tissue paper under my husband's
     nose.
M14:   <laugh>   mm
N15: even when I put the tissue paper on him, I couldn't tell if it was
     moving.
N16: then, Dr. Hinohara's nurse came to our house right away
M16: <laughter>   I see
N17: but I understood then
N18: that my husband couldn't < laugh > be saved
N19: so, I'm thankful to Dr. Hinohara.

The theme of this stretch of narrative is bereavement, one of the core categories of self-disclosure associated with old age. The time of her husband's
death about ten years ago is recounted by N calmly with expressions of
gratitude to Dr. Hinohara, but her narrative becomes animated and even

comical when she describes the specifics of how she encountered her husband's death, and how she did not notice exactly when he died.[5] What is most striking in this example is her utterance numbered N6. The expression *un tomo sun to mo iwanai*, '[he] didn't say a peep', is a commonly used expression, literally meaning that someone does not say *un* or *sun*, and describes a state in which someone does not give even a slight verbal response. N may have expected to hear at least a slight sound at the last moment of her husband's life, but this was not what actually happened. She continues to express her surprise at this unexpected ending of her husband's life by adding *kyun tomo iwanai*, 'didn't even squeak'. The onomatopoeic *kyun* suggests a small creature, such as a mouse or a tiny dog, as the source of the sound. The association of a small creature's squeaks with one's husband's last moment, which would normally be expected to be described with dignity, is unexpected and humorous, illustrating N's surprise quite vividly, especially because N appears to be a proper and traditional upper-middle class homemaker. N discloses her memory of the very moment of her husband's death comically with laughter. She goes on to describe further her surprise and confusion with humor. N's reaction in N10 to the observation made by her daughter-in-law is given with an animated and vivid voice quality accompanied with laughter. The detail of testing breath by using a tissue paper in N14 adds another important but mundane aspect to the description of the situation, inviting a laugh. The humorous descriptions and laughs may be said to have contributed to the story telling of the important moment of N's husband's life by adding vividness of the situation, but a little laugh in N18, when she recounts her realization that her husband would not come back, seems different, giving the impression of resignation and acceptance.

The second example is an excerpt from a conversation among five women who had traveled overseas together. Four members were in their sixties at the time of recording, while K, the main speaker in this example, and N were in their mid seventies. One of the members invited all for a meal to talk over photographs from the last trip that all except K made. Just before the excerpt, the participants were talking about their past trips to Austria and K began to disclose her worry about her recent forgetfulness, which she presented as a possible sign of dementia, an impairment often associated with advanced age.

(2) Recent forgetfulness
[Talking about past trips in Europe]
K1: demo atasi nee, <cough>
K2: koo huuni, mukasi no bun wa kooyatte omoidasu kedo nee

---

[5] Five to ten years after a bereavement, according to Coupland, N., Coupland, J. and Giles (1991), seems to be the common time to start recounting the story.

X2:   un
K3: saikin no koto tasikani moo ne
K4: issyuno tihoo zya nai ka <laugh.voice>[to omoo.
N4:   iya atasi soona no yo
T4:   [iya iya minna onnasi ne
K5: katappasi kara [wasure tyau [no yo.   <laughter>
M5:   [onnasi onnasi
T5:   [ie, minna hontoni.   ne
K6: dakara nannen ni doko itta ka mo wasuretyatteru no <I'ter>
M6: onnasi onnasi
T6: moo syasin nannka

TRANSLATION
K1: but I, you know, <cough>
K2: like this, I can recall things from long past, like this, but
X2:   mm
K3: in terms of recent things, I really don't
K4: I almost think it's a kind of < laughing voice> dementia
N4:   I am like that, y'know
T4:   no, no, that's like everyone, right?
K5: I forget one after another.   <laughter>
M5:   same here, same here
T5:   everyone, really   right.
K6: So, I've forgotten where I went in which year <laughter>
M6: same here, same here
T6: y'know, photos and all

When K mentions the possibility of her developing dementia in K4, others jump into the conversation, repeatedly confirming that they all experience the same symptoms. These overlaps indicate the participants' involvement in the interaction. K's allusion to dementia and further reference to her forgetfulness can be understood as a serious self-disclosure of age-related health problems, but the possible gravity of the matter is lightened because of the accompanying light laughter, sounding as if she was just reporting somewhat disturbing facts that were also amusing.

The content of K's utterance can be viewed as a self-disparaging exaggeration, and, in that regard, it can be interpreted as comical, but K is the only person who is laughing. K's disclosure, however, elicited others' empathy. That outcome may be accounted for by the fact that K's conversants were her good friends who shared similar experiences and viewpoint. In fact, humorous self-disclosure has been observed as a method to display friendship and solidarity among English-speaking females in their late teens to 30's (Ervin-Tripp and Lampert 1992, Hay 2000, Rubin 1983). Here, as I note elsewhere (Matsumoto 2005), similar observations are made in conversations of elderly Japanese female friends. If K's conversants had not had such background, but were, for example, intergenerational first-time acquaintances, it would be less likely that K's utterance would have prompted as clear empathy as we see in this example.

In her conversation with the researcher, K gives an elaboration of the story behind her concern and utterance discussed in example (2). Talking about her recent high school reunion prompts her to recount the story. There is laughter here too as shown in the example, but it is also worthwhile to focus on the ways in which she analyzes her condition, the incident, and how she reconciles herself with the experience. Her story is extensive and cannot be fully discussed here, but lines K1, 6, and 11-14 in particular give a short summary of the incident, in which she relates that (K1) she experienced mental difficulties three years ago, (K6) it turned out to be acute depression, and (K11-14) she thinks that it was caused by her loss of confidence while working where she was treated as useless because of her old age. In a later interaction given after the dotted line, she concludes that she should become carefree and less uptight as she ages in order to avoid depression.

(3) More on K's forgetfulness

K1: tyoodo nee, hora san-nen mae ni tyotto, a atama okasiku-sityatta kara

K2: <LAUGHTER .... >
Y2: atama okasiku, nanka sonna hanasi detemasita nee. <laughter>

K3: damon da kara, moo kurasu-kai iku no ya de ne
Y3: aa aa

K4: anoo atama ga boo tto siteta kara, [de nan-nen de
Y4: [a, gobyooki ni natta n desu ka, sono toki,

K5: [ya atasi nee, dakara- nee,
Y5: sannen [mae

K6: ano sono utu, kyuusei ni utu ni natta tte kanji nanda kedo,
Y6: aa

K7: zibun de wakannai kedo, karui hossa, okosite

K8: atamano naka no itibubun dokka kowarete n zyanai kanaa to omou n desu kedo ne

K9: tonikaku hetoheto ni natte kaette kite,
Y9: ee

K10: asa, okirarenakatta desu yo ne

Y10:   a itinti, aruhi totuzen
K11: sigotosita toki ni, shokku ukete, sugoi jisinsoositu tte noka na
Y11:   ee
K12: nanka sooyuu me ni attyatte
Y12:   eeee   ee, ee
K13: aa, atasi moo toshiyoride yaku ni tatanai n danaa to omotte
K14: soide tukarete kaette kite
Y14:   aa

... ...

K15: tosi to tomo ni ruuzu ni natte ikanai to nee
K16:   honto honto
Y16: ikenai n daroo to omoimasu yo ne

TRANSLATION
K1: right about, y'know, three years ago, I sort of had my head mal-
      function,
K2: <laughter ....   >
Y2:   had your head malfunction, well I remember hearing a story like that.
      <laughter>
K3: because of that, I didn't want to go to a class reunion
Y3:   uh huh   uh huh
K4: since my head was fuzzy, [and in how many years
Y4:   [ah, did you become ill then?
K5:   [well I did, well y'know
Y5:   three years [ago
K6: um, well, depression -- it seems that I got a sudden depression
Y6:   oh
K7: I wasn't aware of it, but I got a light attack, and
K8: I have a feeling that a part of my brain is broken somewhere
K9: in any case, I came home totally exhausted,
Y9:   uh huh
K10: in the morning, I couldn't get up
Y10:   oh, a day, one day suddenly
K11: while I was working, I was shocked, I totally lost my confidence, I
      might say
Y11:   uh huh
K12: somehow I had such an experience
Y12:   right   yes, uh huh

K13: I thought that 'oh dear, I am already an old person and am not useful',
and
K14: then I came home tired,
Y14:   I see.

... ...

K15: one should become more carefree as one get older
K16:   absolutely
Y16: one should be, I think so

What K presents here can certainly be labeled as a series of 'painful self-disclosures' regarding the debilitating condition that she experienced three years ago. However, the overall impression is not of grumbling, or egocentricity as in the stereotyped views, of PSD and she is quite engaged in the objective analysis of what happened and what went wrong. She even gives herself advice on how to cope with the changes by changing her personal attitude.

In the forth example, among various topics that A talked about, including her favorite book, Pollyanna, she also recounts the death of her husband, which happened about 7 months earlier than the recording of the conversation.

(4) Death of A's husband
(Following conversations about A's favorite books including *Pollyanna*.)
A1: atasi mo zibun de ne, nootenki mitai na no, toko ga aru no ne
Y1:   <laughter   >

A2: sono mono ne. pareana no sei da.
Y2: <laughter   >

... ...

A3: odenwa kakatte kuru no yone otomodati kara
Y3:   ee ee

A4: anata doosite rassahru? tte kooyuu tyoosi nano yo
Y4:   ee ee

A5: soide mukoo ga sizunda koe nandesu yo
Y5:   ee ee

A6: atasi o nagusame yoo to omou kara
Y6:   ee ee ee

A7: sorega, mosimosi--? (in a high animated voice) <I'ter> hai hai?
Y7:   <laughter>

A8: e atasi? <laughter>
Y8: kyo kyonen no zyuuni-gatu desu ka?

A9: atasi? genki yo

Y9:   <laughter>
A10: nandaka atasi dotti ga (##) <l'ter> n daka wakan naku nattyatte
Y10:   <laughter>   dakedo ne

TRANSLATION
A1: I myself, seem like a total optimist, somewhat like that
Y1:   <laughter   >
A2: completely. It's Pollyanna's fault.
Y2: <laughter   >
… … …
A3: I get phone calls from my friends, y'know
Y3:   yes, uh huh
A4: 'how have you been doing? They say in this way
Y4:   uh huh
A5: and, they talk in a grave voice, as they try to console me
Y5:   yes   right
A6: but, (I say) 'hello? '(in a high animated voice) <l'ter> 'yes, yes?'
Y6:   <laughter>
A7: 'oh, me?' (I say) <laughter>
Y7: Was it in December las last year?
A8: 'me?' 'I'm fine.'
Y8:   <laughter>
A9: somehow I, which one is (##) <laughter> you don't know
Y9:   <laughter>   that's true, but

The excerpts in (4) gives a basic idea of how A deals with the painful change in her life. She tries to maintain her cheerful personality in coping with the period of bereavement, identifying herself with Pollyanna, whose character is synonymous with an almost excessive optimism in life. In contrast to K's approach of modifying her personality to deal with changes, A is focusing on emphasizing the helpful aspect of her own personal qualities to cope with the change. A's and K's strategies are different, but they both aim for positive outcomes and identities as they deal with changes in their lives.

4. Conclusion

Both types of conversational data, with peers and with a researcher/acquaintance, demonstrate that so-called painful self-disclosure should not automatically be taken as merely a sign of complaint or self-pity. The data also show a complex negotiation among the speaker's intention, social constraints, and expressions of personal and social identities in dealing with changes. This study illustrates at least two important points that are of broader significance in various sub-fields of linguistics; namely, (1) research data should come from various situations, not only from introspection, or a single type of setting such as short interaction between intergenerational first-time acquaintances, and (2) linguistic expressions and discourse practices tend to have multiple meanings and interpretations, and the speaker's intended meanings may not be one that a listener might suppose. More generally, it is my hope to encourage greater attention to the latter part of the life-span by illuminating the richness of the language and lives of people in an age group that is largely neglected and by offering evidence against the simple decrement-based 'ageist' view.

References

Bonnesen, J. L., and M. L. Hummert. 2002. Painful Self-disclosures of Older Adults in Relation to Aging Stereotypes and Perceived Motivations. *Journal of Language and Social Psychology* 21:275-301.

Coupland, J., N. Coupland, and K. Grainger. 1991. Intergenerational Discourse: Contextual Versions of Ageing and Elderliness. *Ageing and Society* 11:189-208.

Coupland, N., J. Coupland, and H. Giles. 1991. *Language, Society and the Elderly: Discourse, Identity and Ageing.* Oxford: Basil Blackwell, Inc.

Coupland, N. and J. F. Nussbaum (eds.). 1993. *Discourse and Lifespan Identity (Language and Language Behaviors Vol. 4).* Newbury Park, CA: Sage Publications.

Eckert, P. 1984. Age and Linguistic Change. *Age and Anthropological Theory*, eds. D. I. Kertzer and J. Keith, 219-233. Ithaca: Cornell University Press.

Ervin-Tripp, S. M. and M. D. Lampert. 1992. Gender Differences in the Construction of Humorous Talk. *Locating Power: Proceedings of the Second Berkeley Women and Language Conference* Vol 1, eds. K. Hall, M. Bucholtz, and B. Moonwomon, 108-117. Berkeley: Berkeley Women and Language Group.

Giles, H., H. Ota and K. A. Noels. 2002. Challenging Intergenerational Stereotypes across Eastern and Western cultures. *Linking Lifetimes: A global view of Intergenerational Exchange*, eds. M. S. Kaplan, N.Z. Henkin and A.T. Kusano, 13-28. Honolulu: University Press of America.

Hamaguchi, T. 2001. Co-construction of Meaning in Intergenerational Family Conversations: A Case of the Japanese Demonstrative Pronoun *Are*. Doctoral dissertation, Georgetown University.

Hamilton, H. Ehernberger. 1994. *Conversations With an Alzheimer's Patient: An Interactional Sociolinguistics Study.* Cambridge: Cambridge University Press.

Hamilton, H. E. (ed.). 1999. *Language and Communication in Old Age: Multidisciplinary Perspectives.* New York: Garland.

Hay, J. 2000. Functions of Humor in the Conversations of Men and Women. *Journal of Pragmatics* 32:709-742.

Matsumoto, Y. 2005. 'We'll be Dead by Then!' – Comical Self-disclosure by Elderly Japanese Women. *The Proceedings of the 30th Annual Meeting of the Berkeley Linguistics Society*, eds. M. Ettlinger, N. Fleisher and M. Park-Doob, 268-279.

Ota, H., H. Giles, and C. Gallois. 2002. Perceptions of Younger, Middle-aged, and Older Adults in Australia and Japan: Stereotypes and Age Group Vitality. *Journal of Intercultural Studies* 23:253-266.

Rubin, L. B. 1983. *Intimate Strangers: Men and Women Together*. New York: Harper and Row.

Saunders, P. A. 1999. Gossip in an Older Women's Support Group: A Linguistic Analysis. *Language and Communication in Old Age: Multidisciplinary Perspectives*, ed. H. E. Hamilton, 267-294. New York and London: Garland Publishing, Inc.

Williams, A. and J. F. Nussbaum. 2001. *Intergenerational Communication Across the Life Span*. Mahwah, NJ: Lawrence Erlbaum.

Where, How and Why Do Passives in Japanese and Korean Differ?
— A Parallel Corpus Account —

PRASHANT PARDESHI[1], QING-MEI LI[2], AND KAORU HORIE[3]

Kobe University[1], Tohoku University[2, 3]

1. Introduction[1]

There have been numerous contrastive studies on passive constructions in Japanese and Korean that reveal similarities and differences between the two (Chung 1993, Kim 1994, Oshima (to appear), Shibatani 1985, Washio 1993, inter alia). With regard to differences between passives in Japanese and Korean, the past studies have proposed that the Korean passive is more "restricted" than its Japanese counterpart. Shibatani (1985), for example, argues that the Japanese passive affords greater indirectness of the effect of the activity described by the verb stem on the referent of the subject than its Korean counterpart. Washio (1993) explains the differences between the possessive (or retained object) passives in Japanese and Korean in terms of an "inclusion/exclusion" relationship between the passive subject and the

---

[1] We would like to thank Matt Shibatani for his insightful comments and suggestions on the earlier version of this paper. Thanks are also due to Alan Hyun-Oak Kim, Satoshi Tomioka, and Andrew, Barke Shnji Ido, and Kanako Mori for their invaluable criticisms. The usual disclaimer applies. This study was supported in part by (i) a travel grant from the Tohoku University 21st Century Center of Excellence Program in Humanities (http://www.lbc21.jp/) and (ii) grants from Japan Society for the Promotion of Science (# 18520314, 18520290).

retained object. The passive subject in Korean can only have an "inclusion" relationship (typically inalienable possession) with the retained object, while in Japanese, the passive subject can have an "exclusion" relationship with the retained object including ownership, kinship, etc. in addition to possession. Further, Japanese also permits the so-called "indirect passive" wherein the subject of the passive is not an argument of the verb stem, which can even be intransitive, while Korean bars indirect passives altogether.

While the previous analyses make a substantial contribution to understanding similarities and differences between the passive constructions in Japanese and Korean, the issue as to how passives are actually used in connected text remains a mystery since most of the previous studies are based on passive sentences in isolation. The goal of this paper is to investigate how passives are used in Japanese and Korean in connected text and to shed light on their similarities and differences. We will focus on the differences especially, and attempt to answer the fundamental question: Where, how and why do the passive in Japanese and Korean differ?

2. Passives in Japanese and Korean: A Parallel Corpus Based Inquiry

In order to investigate the use of passive in Japanese and Korean in connected text we undertook a parallel corpus-based study using the Japanese novel entitled "MADOGIWA NO TOTTOCHAN" by Tetsuko Kuroyanagi and its translated version into Korean (as well as Chinese, English and Marathi). The story is a first person narration and was chosen on purpose to assess the effect of "subjectivity" in the use of passive expression. As a standard practice in typological study we used semantic criteria for identifying passive constructions since the formal properties of the construction vary from one language to another. We adopted the passive prototype proposed by Shibatani (1985) to identify passive constructions in the Japanese version and examine how their counterparts in Korean (and other languages at hand) are rendered. The passive prototype was also used to adjudge if the corresponding expression in the target language is passive or not. As for Korean, we have taken into consideration lexical, morphological and analytical passives as well (see Yeon 2003). The correspondence between passive expressions in Japanese and their counterparts in other languages is shown in Table 1 below.

Japanese	Korean	English	Chinese	Marathi
80	47/69	37/75	31/75	7/66

Table 1. Text Frequency of the Passive in TOTTOCHAN

The table reads as follows. The Japanese text has 80 tokens of passive. In Korean, corresponding to those 80 tokens of passives in Japanese, 69 were translated while the remaining 11 tokens were what we call "free translations" in which the translator has rendered the expression in a complete different way. Out of the 69 translated tokens in Korean, 47 were rendered as passive while the remaining 22 tokens were translated as active (read the figures in the table in a similar way for other languages).

From Table 1 it is clear that there is a conspicuous difference in token frequency of passives in Japanese and Korean despite the fact that the discourse content is the same. This difference cannot be ascribed to the presence of indirect passives or to the wider-scope of possessive or retained object passives in Japanese as compared to Korean since out of 80 tokens of passives in Japanese 79 are direct passive—a category that Korean shares with Japanese. Only one token of the possessive or retained object passive is attested while indirect passives are absent altogether. We carried out a thorough analysis of the data so as to uncover the mystery of where, how and why the passives in Japanese differ from their Korean counterparts.

For our analysis we adopted a tripartite functional/semantic classification of the passives proposed by Givón (1981), namely, "patient profiling" passive (PPP hereafter), "agent defocusing" passives (ADP hereafter) and "attributive" passives (ATP hereafter). PPP and ADP are related to a spatio-temporally bound event while ATP pertains to a time-stable state. To get a concrete idea of this classification, typical examples from Japanese cited in Masuoka (1991:106-107), which is the same in spirit as that of Givón (1981), are given below (English translations are ours).

(A) Patient profiling passive (PPP):

    (i)   Subject directly affected
        Watashi wa sono koto de oya ni shikarareta
        'I was scolded by my parents for that thing.'

    (ii)   Subject semi-directly affected
        Tarou wa densha no naka de tonari no hito ni ashi o fumareta
        'Taro had his foot stepped on by the person standing next to him in the train.'

    (iii)   Subject indirectly affected
        Hanako wa kodomo ni nakarete, yoku nerarenakatta.
        'Hanako was adversely affected by the child's crying and could not sleep.'

(B) Agent defocusing passive (ADP)
     Kaitouyoushi ga kaishuu sareta
     'Answer sheets were collected.'

(C) Attributive passive (ATP)

Hanako no ie wa kousou biru ni kakomarete iru

'Hanako's house is surrounded by skyscrapers.'

Adopting the afore-mentioned tripartite functional classification we analyzed the passive tokens in Japanese and Korean. The results of our survey are tabulated below in Table 2.

	PPP	ADP	ATP	Total
Japanese	55 (69%)	18 (22%)	7 (9%)	80 (100%)
Korean	32 (68%)	12 (26%)	3 (6%)	47 (100%)

Table 2. Functional Domain-wise Distribution

At first glance in Table 2, the passives in Japanese and Korean look alike. However, close scrutiny reveals subtle differences, especially in the domain of patient profiling passives on which we will primarily dwell in this paper.

2.1. Patient Profiling Passive (PPP)

Previous studies on Japanese/Korean passives envisage that "affectivity" is a crucial factor for foregrounding the patient and thereby recruiting patient profiling passives (cf. Chung 1993, Kim 1994, Shibatani 1985, Washio 1993). While our data does endorse this observation, it also reveals a striking fact that PPPs are equally prevalent in "non-affective" contexts as shown in Table 3 below.

		Affective		Non-affective	To-tal
		Adversative	Benefac-tive		
JPN.	Passive	28	2	25	55
KOR.	Passive	21	2	9	32
	Non-Passive	7	0	16	23
Breakup of expressions that are NOT rendered as passive in Korean					
Active		2	0	14	16
Free translation		5	0	2	7

Table 3. A Closer Look at PPPs in Japanese and Their Korean Counterparts

Table 3 reveals interesting similarities and differences in the use of the passive in Japanese and Korean. Let us first take a look at the affective category. The correspondence in the benefactive sub-category is perfect. As for the adversative sub-category, the correspondence is almost close to perfect. In Japanese, there are 28 tokens of adversative passives, of which 21 are rendered as passive in Korean while 7 are not rendered as passive. Out of these 7 non-passive tokens, 5 are free translations (which are non-comparable) while only 2 tokens are rendered as active, despite the fact that the patient is adversely affected.

Close scrutiny reveals that there are subtle differences in the construal of the adversative situation. High-transitivity predicates like *beat, kick, scold* are unequivocally construed as conveying adversity, both in Japanese and Korean, while low transitivity predicates like *oppose* and *see* are construed as adversative in Japanese, but not in Korean. The verb *see* shows interesting variation. Note the following examples.[2]

(1) J. jibun-dake-ga   but-are-tari   tsukitobas-are-ru-no-
     self-only-NOM   beat-PASS-etc.   shove-PASS-PRES-NOML-
     wa   iya   da
     TOP   dislike   COP

     K. caki honca-man   mac-ko   natongkulaci-ki-nun
     self-only   suffer-CONJ   tumble down-NOML-TOP
     silh-ess-umulo...
     dislike-PST-because

     E. 'She didn't like being the only one who got knocked about.'

(2) J. tsumetai-me-de   mir-are-te-iru-youna-mono-o
     cold-eyes-by   see-PASS-CONJ-be-like-NOML-ACC
     oborogeni-wa   kanji-te   ita
     faintly-PRT   feel-CONJ   be.PST

     K. honca-man   com   ssanulha-n   nunchong-ul
     herself-only   a little   cold sharp-ADN   look-ACC
     papko iss-nun   tushan,...
     receive-be-ADN like

     E. 'But deep down she felt she was considered different from other children.'

(3) J. soko-wa   dare-kara-mo   mir-are-nai-shi...
     there-TOP   anyone-from-NEG   see-PASS-NEG-CONJ

     K. keki-nun   nuku-hantey   tulkhi-l   yemlye-to   eps-ko...
     there-TOP   anyone-by   be found-ADN   worry-also   no-CONJ

     E. 'Nobody could see her there.'

(4) J. supai-ni naru-koto-o   hantai   sareta   kara-jya nakatta
     spy-become-NOML-ACC   oppose   do.PASS   hence-not:PST

---

[2] English translations are from "Totto-chan" translated by Dorothy Britton (Kodansha 1984).

K. Thai-ka   suphai-ka   toy-nun   kel
    Tai-NOM   spy-NOM   become-ADN NOML
    pantayhayse-ka-ani-ess-ta
    be against-NOM-NEG-PST-DECL

E. 'Not because he was against her being a spy.'

The foregoing difference can be arguably attributed to the degree of affectedness: verbs like *beat, kick, scold* imply a higher degree of affectedness resulting in visibly perceptible effect on the patient, while verbs like *oppose* and *see* lack such overt adversative effect on the patient implying a lower degree of affectedness. The verb *see* straddles the boundary between affectivity and non-affectivity in that in some contexts it is treated as adversative, while in other contexts it is not treated as such in Korean (cf. (2) and (3)). In sum, the notion of adversity is a scalar one. The verbs on the higher end of the adversity cline are unequivocally rendered as passive in both Japanese and Korean as in (1) while those on the lower end exhibit variation in the construal of adversity as in (4). These two extremes are being mediated by an ambivalent intermediate category endorsing the continuum nature of the cline (cf. (2) and (3)).

Most interestingly, our analysis reveals that striking differences between Japanese and Korean passives are attested in the domain of non-adversative passives that have largely gone unnoticed hitherto. Non-adversative passive assign topicality to the patient that outranks an agent on the "empathy" hierarchy a lá Kuno and Kaburaki (1977). We refer to such expressions as "perspectival" passives, which serve the function of maintaining topic continuity in discourse by depicting an event from the perspective of the narrator. Since these passives are sensitive to person effects we classified them into two groups: (i) those involving the narrator as a patient and (ii) those involving a non-narrator as a patient. The distribution of the perspectival or empathy-loaded passives is as shown in Table 4.

		Narrator as a patient	Non-narrator as a patient	Total
JPN.	Passive	13	12	25
KOR.	Passive	4	5	9
	Non-passive	9	7	16
Breakup of expressions that are NOT rendered as passive in Korean				
Active		7	7	14
Free translation		2	0	2

Table 4. Distribution of the Perspectival or Empathy-loaded Passive

From Table 4 it is clear that Japanese abounds with perspectival or empathy-loaded passives with as many as 25 tokens. Corresponding to these 25 tokens, only 9 are rendered as passive in Korean. The remaining 16 non-passive tokens include 14 active clauses and 2 free translations. This distribution exhibits sharp contrast with the affective domain (cf. Table 3) and this is an area where Korean conspicuously differs from Japanese. Representative examples of perspectival passives are in order. Example (5) involves the narrator (Tottochan) as a patient while (6) involves a non-narrator as a patient.

(5) J.   tottochan-wa   kouchousensei-ni   tsurer-are-te
         Tottochan-TOP   headmaster-by   take along-PASS-CONJ
         minna-ga   obentou-o   taberu   tokoro-o
         all-NOM   lunch box-ACC   eat   place-ACC
         mi-ni iku-koto   ni natta
         see-to go-NOML   became

   K.   kyocangsensayngnim-un   motwu-ka   cemsim-ul
        headmaster-TOP   everyone-NOM   lunch-ACC
        mek-nun   kos-ulo   thotho-lul   teyli-ko   ka-ss-ta
        eat-ADN   place-to   Totto-ACC   take-CONJ   go-PST-DECL

   E.   'The headmaster took Totto-chan to see where the children had
        lunch.'

(6) J.   shiranai otona-no-hito-tachi-kara   "dokono gakkouno seito?"
         unknown adult-of-people-PL-from   Which school-of pupil?
         toka   "dokokara kitano"-to   kik-are-ta-toki   chanto
         or   "where from?"-QUO   ask-PASS-PST-when   properly
         kotae-nakya naranakatta
         answer-had to

   K.   hok molunun   elun-tul-i   'enu hakkyo   haksayng-tul-ini?'
        unknown   adult-PL-NOM   which school   student-PL-Q
        latunci 'etise wa-ss-ni?'   lako   mwulu-myen
        or   where come-PST-Q   QUO   ask-if
        cenghwakhakey   taytapha-ci anhumyen antoy-ess-ta
        correctly   answer-must-PST-DECL

   E.   '…when strangers asked them what school they went to and where
        they were from, they had to answer politely.'

It is clear from the foregoing examples that Japanese consistently resorts to describing events from the perspective of the narrator or other characters in the story with whom the narrator empathizes, while Korean does so quite infrequently and inconsistently.

In the field of Japanese linguistics various scholars have discussed perspectival passives (see Kuno and Kaburaki 1977, Shibatani 2003, among others). Kuno and Kaburaki (1977:627) maintain that: "Passivization is used when the speaker wants to describe an event with the camera placed closer to the referent of the underlying object than to that of the underlying subject." Shibatani (2003:278) observes that when an action is directed to speaker's sphere, the passive is obligatory in Japanese (and possibly in some other languages).

In the face of distribution of perspectival passives as in Table 4, we argue that recruiting passives to depict an event from the "viewpoint" of the speaker or speaker's in-group member and maintaining topic continuity throughout the discourse is more salient in Japanese than in Korean. The empathy-loaded or perspectival passives are "subjective" in that they depict the event from the viewpoint of the speaker/narrator. We claim that the robust presence of non-adversative perspective-sensitive or empathy-loaded passives in Japanese is a reflection of a higher "degree of subjectivity" that Japanese entertains as compared to Korean.

We conducted another parallel-corpus based study with a Japanese novel called "KOKORO" by Souseki Natsume and its translated version in Korean (as well as English and Marathi). Similar results were attested as shown in Table 5.

Japanese	Korean	English	Marathi
339	164	102	42

Table 5. Distribution of Passive in KOKORO

Due to space constraints we will not go into details, but it should be added that more than a third of the total tokens of the passives attested in Japanese involve the narrator or his in-group member as a patient—an area where Japanese differs from Korean significantly as exemplified below.

(7) J.　iie　　　watashi-mo　kiraw-are-te-iru
　　　no　　　I-also　　　dislike-PASS-CONJ-be.PRES
　　　hitori-nan-desu
　　　one-NOML-COP

　　K.　anyo　na-to　　kui-ka　　silhehanun
　　　　no　　I-also　　he-NOM　dislike.ADN
　　　　salam-cwunguy　　hanayeyyo
　　　　person-among　　one.COP

　　E.　'Certainly not. I am like all the rest in his eyes.'

From the two parallel-corpus based studies described above it is clear that Japanese abounds with passive constructions in comparison to Korean (or the other languages under scrutiny). More specifically, Japanese differs from Korean conspicuously in the domain of perspectival or empathy-loaded passives, which are used to depict the event from the viewpoint of the speaker/narrator in a non-adversative context for maintaining topic continuity in discourse. Based on these facts, we claim that Japanese entertains a higher degree of subjectivity than Korean. In other words the robust presence of semantically neutral perspective-sensitive passives in Japanese is a reflection of a high degree of subjectivity that Japanese entertains as compared to Korean.

In sum, recruiting passive constructions to depict an event from the speaker's perspective is more conspicuous in the case of Japanese than Korean. Previous studies on passives in Japanese and Korean have fallen short of uncovering these crucial differences since they have confined their attention to passive sentences in isolation. The notion of subjectivity holds the key to understanding these crucial differences.

2.1.1 Repercussions of Subjectivity: Supporting Evidence

It should be added that the repercussions of the notion of subjectivity are not confined to the use of passives alone but are also observed in other domains of the grammar such as (i) use of the inverse *come* construction in the case of directed motion events involving the speaker as a goal and (ii) use of the lexical inverse *kureru* benefactive construction in the case of a transaction event involving the speaker as a beneficiary as exemplified below (see Kuno and Kaburaki 1977, Shibatani 2003). In both of these, Korean differs from Japanese as shown in example (8) and (9).

(8) J.   Ken-ga   boku-ni   tegami-o   {*kaita/kai-te   kita}
      Ken-NOM   I-DAT   letter-ACC   wrote/write-CONJ   came

   K.   Kheyn-ga   na-eykey   phyenci-lul   {ssessta/sse   wassta}
      Ken-NOM   I-DAT   letter-ACC   wrote/write.CONJ   came

     'Ken wrote me a letter.'

(9) J1. Taroo-ga   boku-ni tegami-o   kai-te   {*yatta/kureta}
      Taro-NOM   I-DAT   letter-ACC write-CONJ   gave
     'Taro wrote a letter for me.'

   J2. boku-ga Taroo-ni   tegami-o   kai-te   {yatta/*kureta}
      I-NOM   Taro-DAT   letter-ACC   write-CONJ   gave
     'I wrote a letter for Taro'.

   K1. Thalo-ka   na-eykey phyenci-lul   sse   cwuessta
      Taro-NOM   I-DAT   letter-ACC   write.CONJ   gave

'Taro wrote a letter for me.'

K2. nay-ka   Thalo-eykey phyenci-lul   sse   cwuessta
    I-NOM   Taro-DAT   letter-ACC   write.CONJ gave

'I wrote a letter for Taro.'

The foregoing differences are also arguably attributed to the higher degree of subjectivity that Japanese entertains as compared to Korean. Uehara (2006) reports that Japanese and Korean differ in the encoding of motion events, mental states, and deference expressions and argues that these differences stem from the difference in the degree of subjectivity (also see Pardeshi, Li, and Horie (to appear)).

Having accounted for the major area of conspicuous difference between passives in Japanese and Korean, let us take a look at the remaining two categories of passives, namely, agent defocusing passives (ADP) and attributive passives (ATP).

2.2. Agent Defocusing Passives (ADP)

Agent defocusing passives are used for suppressing the agent phrase and are a neutral depiction of an event from an objective perspective as pointed out by Masuoka (1991). In the Japanese text 18 tokens of this category were attested out of which 12 are rendered as passive, 4 are rendered as active and 2 are freely translated in Korean. Example (10) is a case where Japanese and Koran behave alike while (11) is a case where they differ.

(10)J. eigo-wa   subeteno   gakkou-no   jyugyou-kara
        English-TOP   all   school-of   curriculum-from
        hazus-are-ta
        remove-PASS-PST

   K.   yenge-nun   cekkwuk-uy   ene-la-nun
        English-TOP   enemy country-of   language-QUO-ADN
        iyu-lo   motun   hakkyo   swuep-eyse
        reason-by   all   school   lesson-from
        paycey-toy-ess-ta
        drop-PASS-PST-DECL

   E.   'Since English had become the enemy language, it was dropped
        from the curriculum of all the schools.'

(11)J. gakunen-betsuni   dashimono-ga   kentou-sare-ta
        grade-by   play-NOM   discuss-PASS-PST

   K.   aitul-un   haknyen   pyello   mwutay-ey
        children-TOP grade   according to   performance-DAT

olli-l   cakphwum-ul yelsimhi   kemthohay-ss-ko,....
put-ADN play-ACC enthusiastically discuss-PST-CONJ

E. 'They all discussed what sort of program they should put on for
their end-of-year performance.'

In (11), Korean uses an unmarked active construction rather than a marked
passive construction.

DeLancey (1981) introduces two psychological notions—attention flow
(AF) and viewpoint. AF determines the linear order of NP's in a sentence,
while viewpoint is a mechanism to alter the natural AF. The relative preference for objective, unmarked active construction in Korean can be interpreted as a sign of a lesser degree of subjectivity.

2.3. Attributive Passives (ATP)

Amongst the three functional domains under discussion, attributive passives
are the least frequent. In Japanese 7 tokens are attested of which 3 are rendered as passive in Korean, 1 as active and the remaining 3 as freely translated.

(12)J. gakkou-wa ima honou-ni tsutsum-are-te-i-ta
    school-TOP now flame-by surround-PASS-CONJ-be-PST

 K. hakkyo-nun cikum hwayem-e hwipssa-ye iss-ta
    school-TOP now   flame-by surround-PASS.be-DECL

 E. 'The school that had been the headmaster's dream was enveloped
  in flames.'

If we assume that the primary/core function of the passive is agent defocusing as envisaged by Shibatani (1985), the marginality of attributive passives
is quite natural since states are devoid of an agent. The statistical marginality of attributive passives can be interpreted as an indication of their peripheral nature.

3. Summary and Conclusion

In this paper we have demonstrated where, how and why do the passives in
Japanese and Korean differ. Focusing on the differences, we claimed that
the cross-linguistic variation at hand stems from the degree of "subjectivity"
that a language entertains—the higher the degree of "subjectivity" of a language, the wider and more profound are the ramifications of such speech act
participant (SAP) related phenomena and vice versa. Under our proposal,
Japanese is more subjective than Korean. Recall that in a highly subjective
language like Japanese it is obligatory to use passives when the speaker or
the participant with whom the speaker empathizes with is on the receiving

end of an action—affected or not affected by it—while the same restriction is not so strong in Korean. Recruiting passives to depict an event from the viewpoint of the speaker or an in-group member and maintaining topic continuity throughout the discourse seems to be more salient in Japanese than in Korean. In sum, the notion of "subjectivity" may hold the key to understanding these cross-linguistic differences, not only in regard to passives, but also in other domains of grammar.

Abbreviations

ACC: Accusative	ADN: Adnominal	CONJ: Conjunctive
COP: Copula	DAT: Dative	DECL: Declarative
NEG: Negative	NOM: Nominative	NOML: Nominalizer
PASS: Passive	PL: Plural	PRES: Present
PRT: Particle	PST: Past	Q: Question
QUO: Quotation	TOP: Topic	

References

Chung, T. 1993. The Affected Construction in Korean and Japanese. *Japanese/Korean Linguistics* 3:154-170.

DeLancey, S. 1981. An Interpretation of Split Ergativity and Related Patterns. *Language* 57:626-657.

Givón, T. 1981. Typology and Functional Domains. *Studies in Language* 5.2:163-193.

Kim, K. 1994. Adversity and Retained Object Passive Construction. *Japanese/Korean Linguistics* 4:331-346.

Kuno, S. and E. Kaburaki. 1977. Empathy and Syntax. *Linguistic Inquiry* 8(4):627-672.

Masuoka, T. 1991. Jyudouhyougen to Shukansei [Passive and Subjectivity]. *Nihongono Boisu to Tadousei* [Voice and Transitivity in Japanese], ed. Y. Nitta, 105-121. Tokyo: Kuroshio.

Oshima, D. To appear. Adversity and Korean/Japanese Passives: Constructional Analogy. *Journal of East Asian Linguistics*.

Pardeshi, P., Q-M, Li, and K. Horie. To appear. Being on the Receiving End: A Tour into Linguistic Variation. *Diversity in Language: Perspectives and Implications*, eds. Y. Matsumoto, D. Y. Oshima, O.W. Robinson, and P. Sells. Stanford: CSLI.

Shibatani, M. 1985. Passives and Related Construction: A Prototype Analysis. *Language* 61:821-848.

Shibatani, M. 2003. Directional Verbs in Japanese. *Motion, Direction and Location in Language: In Honor of Zygmunt Frajzyngier,* eds. E. Shay and U. Seibert, 259-286. Amsterdam: John Benjamins.

Uehara, S. 2006. Toward a Typology of Linguistic Subjectivity: A Cognitive and Cross-linguistic Approaches to Grammaticalized Deixis. *Subjectification: Various Paths to Subjectivity,* eds. A. Athanasiadou, C. Canakis and B. Cornillie, 75-117. Berlin: Mouton de Gruyter.

Washio, R. 1993. When Causatives Mean Passive: A Cross-linguistic Perspective. *Journal of East Asian Linguistics* 2:45-90.

Yeon, J. 2003. *Korean Grammatical Constructions: Their Form and Meaning.* London: Saffron Books.

A Claim-of-Reanalysis Token *e?/e-* within the Sequence Structure of Other Repair in Japanese Conversation

MAKI SHIMOTANI
University of Wisconsin-Madison

1. Introduction[1]

In naturally occurring conversation, the speakers engage in projecting a forthcoming action with reference to the sequential organization, the emerging structure of a turn and so on. Turn-initial items especially have been considered significant in how the following turn will unfold and what kind of actions will be accomplished (See Sacks et al. 1974). They have also been considered important because 'they are a prime location for the placement of sequential markers that convey some relation between what the current speaker is about to say and what the previous speaker has said' (Heritage 2002:196-197). This paper investigates the non-lexical token '*e*' in Japanese conversation, which frequently occurs at a turn-initial position.

'*E*' has generally been categorized as a 'filler' or 'interjection particle' and analyzed as a marker to indicate the speaker's affects such as surprise. These analyses are based on the speaker's cognitive treatment of informa-

---

[1] I am grateful to Naomi H. McGloin and Junko Mori for organizing the 15th JK at UW-Madison. Especially, I thank Junko Mori, who read the earlier version of this paper and guided me in completing this paper. My thanks also go to Cecilia Ford, Makoto Hayashi, Yan Wang, Beth Schewe, and the audience at JK 15th. All remaining errors are my responsibility.

tion that he/she receives, and they emphasize the speaker's psychological process (see Takubo 1994, etc.). Yet, few have considered the interactional roles of '*e*' in talk-in-interaction and the sequential environments where '*e*' is employed to accomplish the speaker's actions.

This paper provides the preliminary findings of the workings of the short-length utterance of '*e*', specifically the cases of *e-* with cutoff and *e?* with rising pitch. In particular, by employing Conversation Analysis (CA) as an analytical tool (Sacks et al. 1974), I investigate the sequential environments where '*e*' occurs. By describing such sequential environments of '*e*' and its turn structure in detail, I also analyze the interactional roles that '*e*' plays to accomplish the speaker's actions in talk-in-interaction.

2. Background

It has been pointed out that the meanings of a linguistic form used in conversational discourse must be analyzed in terms of both informational status and interactional roles (Schiffrin 1987, Maynard 1993). '*E*' is one such form that occurs in conversational discourse. Yet, the past studies have only focused on informational status (i.e. the speaker's psychological processing of information) ignoring the interactional roles of '*e*' (see Takubo and Kinsui 1997, Togashi 2004, etc.). More specifically, '*e*' has been analyzed as an indication of 'receipt of new information' that is contradictory or irrelevant to the information that the speaker already has. Thus, it tends to be understood as the speaker's expression of surprise, exclamation, unexpectedness, etc. These analyses are insightful; however, these expressions of the speakers' psychological status are provided essentially relying on the researchers' intuitive analyses rather than empirical analyses of the data. In other words, their analyses are based on discrete sentences, which are constructed in order to explain their cognitive models (Takubo and Kinsui 1997:259) but not to examine the context and actual conversational sequence in which '*e*' occurs. Thus, in the past studies, it is unclear what psychological feelings such as surprise can be expressed by '*e*' in what context.

This paper positions itself as methodologically and epistemologically different from the past studies. In particular, I examine naturally occurring conversational data and analyze the sequential environments in which '*e*' occurs and its turn structures. Then, I aim to investigate the function of '*e*' in talk-in-interaction, which can be assumed from the conversational sequences and the turn structures.

3. Data

The data consists of twenty-four casual conversations.[2] The participants are native speakers of Japanese who are close friends, colleagues, or previously unacquainted people. The length of these conversations is approximately five hours in total. First, take a look at the following two examples:[3]

(1) WU4

1. E: *°nanka- kureta,° nanka- mora (hh) chatta (hh) hh hm hm*
    'Um (she) gave (it to me), um I got (it from her).'

2. → D: *e?*

3. E: *moratt (hh) chat(hh)ta hhh*
    'I got (it from her).'

4. D: *a- so(hh) na no [hh?*
    'Oh, Is that so?'

(2) Danjo-byodo

1. A: *↑demo nanka (.) ke- kekkon shitai tte yuu jan=*

2. *=hitori gurashi no [otoko no hito tte yoku.*
    'But um I hear that (they) want to get married.'
    '(I mean) the men who are living by themselves''(I hear so) often'

3. B: *[°un un°* ((nodding three times)) =
    'uh huh'

4. → B: *=e-* (.) *sore wa kaji o yat[te morau tame*
    '*e-* that's because they receive a favor of (women's) housekeeping'

5. A: *[yatte hoshii kara de [shoo?*
    '(They) want (women) to do housekeeping, right?'

6. B: *[u::n.*
    'I see.'

As argued in the past studies, it may be possible to analyze '*e*' in these examples as the speaker's expression of surprise or as an indication of contradiction or irrelevance between the received information and the information that the speaker already has. However, whether or not the speaker used '*e*' to express his/her surprise and whether or not the other participant understood it as contradiction are unknown to the researchers.

Now consider the conversational sequence in which '*e*' occurs in these cases. The free-standing *e?* in line 2 in (1) and *e*-prefaced utterance in line 4 in (2) play the role of repair initiator to clarify what the other participant has said in the prior turn. In other words, they demonstrate that the speaker has some trouble in hearing or understanding what the other has said in the prior

---

[2] Twenty of them are digitally recorded and transcribed by myself or by a graduate student at UW-Madison. Four others are videotaped conversations, which were provided by Junko Mori.

[3] The gloss in each example is omitted due to the space limitation. The transcription convention is based on Sacks et al. (1974).

turn (i.e. Other Initiated (OI) Repair, Schegloff et al. 1977). Table 1 shows the overview of the occurrences of '*e*' in OI repair sequences (i.e. *e*- OI repair) and the 'boundary cases' (Schegloff 1997) of *e*- OI repair, which I will discuss in Section 5.

Other Initiated Repair	Boundary Cases of OI Repair	Total
52	87	139

Table 1. The Occurrences of '*e*' in OI Repair Sequences vs. Boundary Cases

OI repair is in general understood as next turn repair initiation (NTRI), which specifies a trouble source (TS) in the immediately prior turn uttered by the other participant (Schegloff et al. 1977). Yet, '*e*' by itself does not locate what or where the TS is. In that sense, '*e*' is characterized as an 'open' class repair initiator such as *pardon?* (Drew 1997). Unlike *pardon?* in English, however, '*e*' is rarely free-standing;[4] I found only 7 cases out of 52. In the rest of the cases, '*e*' is followed by additional turn constructional unit(s) (TCU(s), Sacks et al. 1974) as in (2). It is also interesting to note that all free-standing cases have rising intonation rather than cutoff, while the cases of '*e*' with additional TCU(s) have cutoff. Table 2 shows the occurrences of free-standing *e?* and *e*- with additional TCU(s).

Free-standing *e?*	*e*- + additional TCU(s)	Total
7	45	52

Table 2. The Occurrences of Free-standing e?/e- and e?/e with Additional TCU(s)

In what follows, I will analyze the sequential structure of the cases of '*e*' with additional TCU(s), i.e. *e*-prefaced OI repair. And I will discuss my findings about the interactional workings of '*e*'.

4. *E*-Prefaced Other Initiated Repair

4.1. The Sequential Structure of *e*-Prefaced OI Repair

Most *e*-prefaced OI repair utterances are preceded by acknowledgment tokens, alignment expressions or assessment expressions of the interlocutor's prior turn.[5] That is, unlike the typical cases of OI repair, which immediately follow a turn containing a TS (i.e. NTRI), *e*-prefaced OI repair and its TS are often separated by its producer's acknowledgment tokens toward the prior turn. Thus, *e*-prefaced OI repair is typically 'delayed within (or past) the next turn position relative to the TS' (cf. Schegloff 2000).

---

[4] Ohama (2001) also demonstrates that the occurrences of free-standing '*e*' in her data are surprisingly few; she shows that 9 out of 114 cases were free-standing.

[5] The free-standing *e?*, which rarely occurs, is often preceded by a gap rather than acknowledgment, alignment or assessment tokens.

In (2) above, B first provides minimum acknowledgment tokens, °*un un*° in line 3 towards what A said before. Then, B initiates a repair with '*e*' followed by an additional TCU, providing her candidate understanding of A's utterances. Thus, the *e*-prefaced OI repair in line 4 and its TS in lines 1 and 2 are not immediately adjacent to each other, indicating delayed OI repair.

Example (3) also illustrates this typical pattern of delayed OI repair.

(3) WU3
1. TS→ C: *nanka::(1.4) nanka-* ⌈*shoogakko go nensee*⌉ *no on'nanoko (.)*
   'Um, like ⌈fifth-grade elementary school⌉ girls'

2. *futari ga:: atashi no (.) koto mite cho: bakushoo sun no:*
   'Looking at me, the two girls burst into laughter'

3. *(0.5) e- de- nani- nani tte kiitara::,*
   'So, I asked (them) "what? what?" then'

4. *tsu:: ka sa:: sono mune hazukashiku nai no:: toka itte:::,*
   'They say "aren't you ashamed of your breasts" or something and...'

5. *patto irenakya warawarechau yo? toka iwarete hh*
   'I was told "if you don't use padding, you'd be made fun of" or something and..'

6. ASS→ K: *hh so:re wa hh iya da na:::=*
   'That's nasty.'

7. OI→ *=e- demo shoogaku(.)go nen- (0.5)go nense- ima go nensee::?*
   '*e*- but (are they) fifth grade pupils in elementary school?'

In line 6, K provides an assessment, *sore wa iya da na::*, to C's story. Immediately after that, K initiates an *e*-prefaced OI repair in line 7, which identifies the TS in line 1. K's assessment separates the *e*-prefaced OI repair from its TS turn; thus this sequence of repair resulted in a delay. Table 3 shows the cases of *e*-prefaced OI repair as an NTRI and as a delayed OI.[6]

	NTRI	Delayed OI	Total
e-prefaced OI repair	3	42	45

Table 3. The Occurrences of *e*-prefaced OI repair: NTRI vs. Delayed OI

Considering these cases, the typical sequential organization of *e*-prefaced OI repair can be schematically illustrated as follows:

---

[6] Schegloff (2000) and Wong (2000) treat OI repairs as 'delayed' if either a silence or other talk intervenes between an OI and its TS (cf. Schegloff et al. 1977). Here, following Schegloff (2000) and Wong (2000), I categorize silence-prefaced OI repairs as 'delayed'.

```
Turn(s) 1   Speaker A:   [Repairable utterance]   ((TS))      ←────┐
Turn 2      Speaker B:   [acknowledgment, alignment, assessment tokens]
Turn 3  →   Speaker B:   e- + extended TCU(s)    ((Repair))   ____│
Turn 4      Speaker A:   [Repair]
```

Figure 1.

Figure 1 indicates that B, within Turn 2, is providing minimum acknow-ledgement, alignment, or assessment tokens toward what A has said in Turn(s) 1. And, in Turn 3, B initiates *e*-prefaced OI repair. Therefore, by placing '*e*' after his/her acknowledgment, B claims his/her 'reanalysis' of A's problematic utterance in Turn(s) 1. By this means, '*e*' serves to project B's repair initiation.

In the next section, I focus on the *e*-prefaced OI repair sequence and analyze the sequential relationship between *e*-prefaced OI repair and its TS.

4.2. The Trouble Source in *e*-Prefaced OI Repair Sequences

In 4.1, we observed the cases of *e*-prefaced OI repair in which the additional TCU identifies what the TS is. However, the TS in an *e*-prefaced OI repair sequence is not always clearly identified by the additional TCU. This phe-nomenon is very similar to 'open' class repair initiators in English (Drew, 1997), as noted in Section 3. According to Drew (1997), 'open' class repair initiators do not specify a TS in the prior turn(s). He argued that they are employed to resolve 'certain kinds of troubles which a participant may have in understanding not so much what the other said, as why he/she said it.' (p. 72) Many cases of *e*-prefaced OI repair in Japanese conversation illustrate a strikingly similar conversational sequence. Observe (4).

(4) WU4

1. Turn1   A: °*ore*° *manga toka yomanai   nda yone:: an'ma ne::*
                   'I don't read comics etc.'   'not very much'

2. Turn2   B: *a::[:::::::::,*
                   'Oh, I see.'

3.   A: [*heh heh*   ← expected explanation

4.   (0.67)

5. Turn3 → B: *e-* (.) *nanka-*=
                   '*e-*   um-'

6. Turn4   A: =*autodoa kee da kara   ne. eh heh heh*
                   'Because I am an outdoor-type person, you know.'

7.   B: *a::: sokka sokka.*
                   'Oh:: I see I see'

Here, by placing '*e*' after her acknowledgment and a silence, it seems that B projects that there is some problem in the prior turns. However, neither *e*- nor its extended TCU, *nanka*, specifies what the TS is.

Now consider what a possible TS is in this conversational sequence. Before line 1, A asks B if she reads comics, and B answers that she does. On the other hand, A's utterance in line 1, says that he does not. Thus, A's and B's utterances are contrasting; so sequentially, A's explanation of why he does not read comics may be expected in the following turn (= line 3) (cf. Ford, 1994); however, A ends up laughing instead. This may cause B to find a sequentially problematic connection between what A said in Turn 1 and what has been talked about before, although she first aligns herself to A's turn by producing an acknowledgment token *a:::::::* in line 2 (= Turn 2). The 0.67-second silence in line 4 may have resulted from B's reanalysis of the sequentially problematic connections in the prior turns. B then produces *e*- in line 5 (= Turn 3) followed by an extended TCU that displays a hesitation, *nanka*-. The projectability of these tokens might have allowed A to anticipate what was problematic for B and to provide a possible reason in response to B's repair initiation in line 6 (= Turn 4).[7] As suggested in Ford (1994), the emergence of *because* in English conversation indicates a potential problem in the prior turns. This analysis may also apply to the emergence of causal connective particle *kara* (because) in A's utterance in line 6 (see Mori 1999). Thus, A's employment of *kara* may have been triggered by the *e*-prefaced OI repair in line 5, which has projected a possible TS.

The following fragment also illustrates a case of *e*-prefaced OI repair that indicates a sequentially problematic connection between what the other said in the prior turn and his talk previous to it. Before the segment in (5), N asks H about his future plans. In response to N, H, who is currently taking an advanced course in video production at a university, says that he wants to do a job related to video production. However, he states that it is hard to get such a job and continues to line 1.

(5) Hosaka1

1.	H:	*yappa* (0.3) *kitsui desu yone?* °=*yappa*°*sore dakede ikiteiku no*
2.		*tte. tabun hu*[*h heh heh*=
		'I guess it's tough. Isn't it?' '(I mean it is tough to) lead a normal life maybe (if we have) that kind of job only'
3.	N:	[*soo na-* 'That's so-'

---

[7] Although *e*- and *nanka* produced by B appear to project that B may extend her turn, what she might have been going to add in her extended turn in line 5 is of course unknown. It might have been something other than repair initiation. Yet, from A's perspective, '*e*' and B's hesitation are at least regarded as repair initiation (Junko Mori, personal communication).

4.   H: *=wakannaidesu kedo=*
'I don't know, though.'

5.   N: *=he:::*
'Oh yeah?'

6.   H: *imeeji tekini.*
'As an impression.'

7.   N: *hu::::n.*
'I see.'

8.   H: *dakara ma (0.2) arien   no wa (.) sono-   terebi gyookai toka.*
'So, what is possible (for me) is the TV station world, etc.'

9.   N: *un un*
'uh huh'

10.   H: *soo yuu hookoo ga attara (°nantonaku aru no°) kana tte.*
'If there is such an option, I wonder if there may be (a job
I can get) somehow.'

11.   N: *hu:::n=*
'I see.'

12. [Turn1] H: *=tada NHK   tatakarete n de h[u heh heh heh*
'But NHK is being criticized.'

13. [Turn2] N: *[hh soo da ne*
'That's right'

14. [Turn3]→ N: *e-(hh) NHK[ni hairitakatta   no ?*
'e- You've wanted to work for NHK?'

15. [Turn4] H: *[huh huh huh huh*

16.   *cho- ichiyo- (.) chotto kyoomi ga atta kana tte kanji de.*
'A little, or to some extent, I was sort of interested in (NHK).'

From line 1 through 10, H tells N that the world of TV stations may be a
possible place for him to work in the future. As H's talk proceeds, N aligns
herself as a recipient of his talk by producing various kinds of news-receipt
tokens such as *un un*, *hu::n* and *he:::* (see Mori 2006). More specifically, in
line 10, H's gradually weakened volume and clear final intonation seem to
indicate the closing of the informing sequence. And N's news-receipt token
hu:::n without any additional talk in line 11 appears to have facilitated the
closing of H's informing sequence. H then makes a topic shift by employing
connective word *tada* in line 12. NHK is an abbreviation of *Nippoin Hosoo
Kyoku* (Japan Broadcasting Station), which is one of the biggest TV stations
in Japan. Thus, from H's view of the sequence, this topic shift seems to
have been sequentially as well as topically coherent to his own previous talk.
Yet, it does not seem to be sequentially coherent from N's view. In other
words, hearing H's topic shift, N first seems to align herself as a recipient
by producing an agreement expression *soo da ne* in line 13 (= Turn2). But,
in the immediately following turn, N suddenly suspends her alignment as a

recipient and initiates *e*-prefaced OI repair in line 14. Thus, it may seem that N has experienced some problem finding the sequential connection between H's topic shift in line 12 and what he said in the prior turns. N's extended *e*-prefaced turn in line 14, *NHK ni hairitakattano?*, also indicates that she does not have any problem in hearing and understanding what H said in the prior turns. Rather it provides N's candidate understanding of the sequentially problematic connection.

As a summary of this section, '*e*' occurs in the sequential environments where there is a problem not only in hearing/understanding what the other participants said but also in sequential disconnection between the prior turn(s) and the turns previous to it. Thus, '*e*' is frequently employed as a token that initiates a repair. The speaker claims his/her reanalysis of the prior turn and/or of the prior sequential connection and projects a repair initiation of the sequentially problematic utterance and/or connection.

5. Boundary Cases of *e*-Prefaced OI Repair Sequences

This section discusses the 'boundary cases' of *e*-prefaced OI repair. Schegloff (1997: 502) refers to 'boundary cases' as follows:

> [Boundary cases] generally look like our emerging phenomenon, even if they do not turn out to be instances of it. In specifying what makes them "look like," we learn about our phenomenon; and in specifying why nonetheless they "are not," we learn as well.

The boundary cases of *e*-prefaced OI repair are in fact similar to *e*-prefaced OI repair in terms of their sequential structure. Yet, they differ from *e*-prefaced OI repair in that there does not seem to be a TS in the prior turns. More specifically, even if there seems to be a TS, it is in fact not one of those which we have observed above, i.e. a single word/phrase TS and/or a sequentially problematic connection between what the other participant said in the prior turn and what has been talked about previous to it. Through examining the similarities and differences between the cases of *e*-prefaced OI repair and those which are not, we will be able to further learn what the speaker is doing with the token '*e*'. In what follows, focusing on these boundary cases, I will elucidate what 'actions' other than 'repair' can be accomplished by employing the sequentially unique structure of *e*-prefaced OI repair.

5.1. Disagreement

The following example shows the sequential structure of *e*-prefaced OI repair that displays the speaker's disagreement with the other participant.

(6) Danjobyodo

1.	A:	*demo sa:: soo da yona::, sore o maa, demo sore ga*
2.		*sa::, zutto ie ni inai to::, shakai ni sa:[:,*
3.	B:	[*un un*
		'uh huh'

4. |Turns1| A: *kooken   dekiru kodomo ga sodatanai ka tte ittara*

5.   *mata soo de mo nai kara::*

A's lines 1 to 5: 'But, that's right, well but it's not always the case that, if women aren't at home, they cannot raise their children to be able to contribute to the society.'

6.		(2.2)
7.	A:	*janai?h*
		'right?'

8. |Turn2| B: *a:::,*

9. |Turn3| B: *e- demo sugoku:: yuushuu   de::,* (>> continues)

               'yeah... *e-* but very brilliant and:: (>> continues)'

From lines 1 through 5, A provides her opinion about working women. However, A cannot get any response from B, which results in a 2.2-second silence in line 6. Thus, A solicits B's agreement response using *janai?* in line 7. In response to A, B first provides a minimum acknowledgment towards A's opinion. But then B produces *e-* and continues her turn with the connective *demo*. By employing the sequential structure of *e*-prefaced OI repair with elongated prosody (*e- demo sugoku::*) *and te*-infinitive form (*yuushuu de::*), the speaker projects her upcoming turn to state her opinion, which is based on his/her reanalysis of what the other said in the prior turns. As Schegloff (1997) notes, since 'other repair' itself may be used as a vehicle for displaying disagreement, the sequential structure of *e*-prefaced OI repair can be a resource to display the speaker's disagreement with the other participant.

5.2. Topic Extension/Expansion/Shift

Example (7) demonstrates that by employing the sequential structure of *e*-prefaced OI repair, the speaker tries to accomplish his/her actions of extending the topic of the conversation. Before line 1, B asks A why he wanted to take the United Nations' Official English Test. A answers:

(7) Hasebe2

1.   A: *ano::eigo no benkyoo suki datta kara:: nde::*

                 'Well, because I liked studying English and so..'

2.   (2.3)

3.   A: *ano::ma- dooshitemo hoshii tte yuu wake ja nakatta [nda kedo::*

                 'I don't mean that I extremely wanted it (= a qualifying score on the English Test) but'

4. AKN   B: [*un un un*
                                                  'yeah'

5. FPP→   B: *e- demo kiwametai tte kanji desu ka=*
                      '*e-* but you mean you wanted to study (English) thoroughly?'

6. SPP→   A: *=tte yuu ka mokuhyoo attara* [*ii kana::to omotte*
                      'I mean, I thought it is good if I have an aim'

7. AKN   B: [*un:::*
                                        'yeah'

8. FPP→   B: *e- doregurai amerika ni wa iru ndesu ka?*
                      '*e-* How long have you being staying in the U.S.?'

9. SPP→   A: *a- boku- daka-* (0.5) *boku::ano::: kugatsu   kara kiteru ndesu yo.*
                      'I have been (here) since September'

In lines 1 through 3, A answers B's first question. Hearing A's answer, B provides her claim of understanding in line 4. Then, B uses '*e*' to initiate another question-answer sequence relevant to A's answer in the prior turns in line 5. Similarly, in line 8, B employs the same sequential structure of *e*-prefaced question and answer. These adjacency pairs in lines 5/6 and lines 8/9 are superficially similar to the *e*-prefaced OI repair sequence structure as shown below.

Turn(s) 1		Speaker A: ((Talk))
Turn 2		Speaker B: minimum acknowledgment tokens
Turn 3	FPP	Speaker B: *e-* + additional TCU(s) ((= Question))
Turn 4	SPP	Speaker A: ((Answer))

Figure 2.

The *e*-prefaced first pair parts (FPP) in lines 5 and 8 (= Turn 3) do not seem to be produced in order to resolve a TS. Rather it seems that, by prefacing the FPP with '*e*', B claims her reanalysis of A's answer and elaborates on her understanding of the specifics of A's prior turns. '*E*', which is the first component in the FPP, seems to indicate that the speaker's question is not produced out of the blue but is based on his/her reanalysis of what the other speaker said in the prior turn. This employment of *e*-prefaced FPP, forming a sequentially similar structure to the *e*-prefaced OI repair sequence, can often become a connective device between the talk in Turn(s) 1 and that in Turn 4 in Figure 2. This is because a question, which is the second component in the *e*-prefaced FPP, requires an answer as its second pair part (SPP). Therefore, this sequence structure serves to accomplish the speaker's action of smoothing the speaker transition and extending/expanding/shifting the current topical sequence.

Even when the speaker transition is unsuccessful, however, the speaker also employs a sequentially similar structure to the *e*-prefaced OI repair in order to project his/her action of 'changing' a topic. Observe (8).

(8) University

1.	E:	*awanai hito niwa hontoni awanai* =
		'We don't see those whom we don't see'
2.	M:	= *u::n,*
		'yeah'
3.		(0.7)
4.	M:	*so:: da ne::*
		'That's right'
5.		(2.1)
6.	T:	°*un so::dane::*°
		'yeah, that's right'
7.		(0.5)
8.	M:	°*hu::n.*°
9.		(1.4)
10.	T:	°*.hhhh*° °*e::::*[*:::*°
11.	E:	[°*un*°
		'yeah'
12.		(2.3)
13.	M:	°*nanka aru kana::*°
		'I wonder if there is something (else) to talk about)'
14.		(1.2)
15.	➔T:	*e-*(.) *ano::* (0.9) °*ii desu ka*°
		'*e-* um, is it okay?'
16.	M:	*un*
		'yeah'
17.	T:	*ano:: amerika:: ni ite::,*
		'Well, when I was in America, (continues)'

'loop sequence' (Iwasaki, 1997)

In (8), before line 1, M, E, and T talked about the people whom they see on campus. After M's acknowledgment in line 2, long silences occur several times. The participants also produce, in a whispery voice, some agreement tokens °*so::da ne::*° in lines 4 and 6, and hesitant expressions °*hu:::n*° in line 8, and °*nanka aru kana::*° in line 13. These tokens indicate a failure to continue the prior topic and transition to the next speaker. As a result, they consist of a 'loop sequence' to negotiate the next floor holder (Iwasaki 1997). Ohama (2001) argues that '*e*' in such a conversational sequence may signal the speaker's turn-taking strategy to mitigate initiating a topic aggressively or voluntarily. Thus, the speaker may be able to accomplish his/her action of changing a topic in a mitigated way in order to resolve the discontinuation of the prior topic. More precisely, by placing '*e*' at a turn initial position, the speaker can display his/her topic initiation as if he/she were reanalyzing the prior talk. By doing so, the speaker can then demonstrate that the additional TCU, which often forms a question (FPP), is not out of the blue although the question itself may not be related to the prior topical sequence.

These boundary cases of '*e*' can only be understood when we consider the speaker's actions in a range of conversational sequences. Thus, it is worth pointing out that '*e*' is not only the speaker's expression of surprise, exclamation, or unexpectedness, but it also plays a role in accomplishing the speaker's various actions in talk-in-interaction.

6. Conclusion

Through examining the sequential environments where '*e*' occurs, this study has demonstrated various interactional aspects of '*e*' produced in a sequence of conversation. Specifically, I have argued that '*e*' can be characterized as a 'claim-of-reanalysis' token which serves to project the speaker's action of repair initiation. I have also showed that *e*-prefaced OI repair is typically delayed within (or past) the next turn relative to a possible trouble source because '*e*' as a repair initiator and its TS are separated by acknowledgment tokens. Therefore, the sequential organization of *e*-prefaced OI repair is uniquely structured and remarkably different from the generally recognized OI repair sequence of NTRI.

By employing this sequentially unique structure of *e*-prefaced OI repair, the speaker accomplishes various actions other than 'repair' itself. In particular, I have demonstrated that an *e*-prefaced question can be a device to connect between prior turns and following turns and serve to expand/extend the current topical sequence. Also, when the speaker negotiates agreement with the other participant, the employment of '*e*' may serve as the speaker's display of disagreeing with the other participant. Moreover, an *e*-prefaced question can indicate the speaker's initiation of a new topic in a mitigated way in order to solve the failure of continuing the prior topic and unsuccessful speaker transition.

Finally, the characteristics of '*e*' may be easily integrated into an expression of the speaker's surprise, or exclamation towards received information. Yet, this analysis may not elucidate how it plays a role in a range of conversational sequences and what actions can be accomplished by using it. Although there may be more actions which can be accomplished by employing *e*-prefaced OI repair, I hope to have shown that the function of '*e*' is fundamentally backward looking in the conversational sequence; thus by making use of such characteristics of '*e*' and the sequential structure of *e*-

prefaced OI repair, speakers try to accomplish various kinds of actions in talk-in-interaction.

References

Drew, P. 1997. 'Open' Class Repair Initiators in Response to Sequential Sources of Troubles in Conversation. *Journal of Pragmatics* 28:69-101.

Ford, C. E. 1994. Dialogic Aspects of Talk and Writing: Because on the Interactive-edited Continuum. *Text* 14:531-554.

Heritage, J. 2002. Oh-prefaced Responses to Assessments: A Method of modifying Agreement/Disagreement. *The Language of Turn and Sequence*, eds. C. Ford, B. Fox and S. A. Thompson, 196-224. New York: Oxford University Press.

Iwasaki, S. 1997. The Northridge Earthquake Conversations: The Floor Structure and the 'Loop' Sequence in Japanese Conversation. *Journal of Pragmatics* 28:661-693.

Maynard, S. 1993. *Discourse Modality: Subjectivity, Emotion and Voice in the Japanese language*. Philadelphia: John Benjamins.

Mori, J. 1999. *Negotiating Agreement and Disagreement in Japanese Conversation. Connective Expressions and Turn Constructions*. Philadelphia: John Benjamins.

Mori, J. 2006. The Workings of the Japanese Token *Hee* in Informing Sequences: An Analysis of Sequential Context, Turn Shape, and Prosody. *Journal of Pragmatics* 38:1175-1205.

Ohama, R. 2001. 'E' no Danwa Kinoo. *Hiroshima Daigaku Daigakuin Kyouiku-gakubu Kenkyuka Kiyou* 50:161-170.

Sacks, H., E. A. Schegloff, and G. Jefferson. 1974. A Simplest Systematics for the Organization of Turn-taking for Conversation. *Language* 50:696-735.

Schegloff, E.A., G. Jefferson, and H. Sacks. 1977. The Preference for Self-correction in the Organization of Repair in Conversation. *Language* 53:361-382.

Schegloff, E. A. 1997. Practice and Actions: Boundary Cases of Other-Initiated Repair. *Discourse Processes* 23:499-545.

Schegloff, E. A. 2000. When 'Others' Initiate Repair. *Applied Linguistics* 21:205-243.

Schiffrin, D. 1987. *Discourse Markers*. Cambridge: Cambridge University Press.

Takubo, Y. 1994. Towards a Performance Model of Language. *Onseigengo Johoshori* 1-3:15-22.

Takubo, Y and S. Kinsui. 1997. The Discourse Management Function of Fillers in Japanese. *Speech and Grammar*, eds. Spoken Language Working Group, 257-279. Tokyo: Kuroshio Shuppan.

Togashi, J. 2004. *Nihongo Daiwa Hyoushiki no Kinou*. Doctoral dissertation, Tsukuba University.

Wong, J. 2000. Delayed Next Turn Repair Initiation in Native/Non-native Speaker English Conversation. *Applied Linguistics* 21:244-267.

Cognition through the Lens of Discourse and Interaction: The Case of -*kwun,* -*ney,* and -*tela*

Susan Strauss and Kyungja Ahn

The Pennsylvania State University and CALPER (Center for Advanced Language Proficiency Education and Research)

I. Introduction[1]

This paper confirms and builds on findings in Strauss (2005), which presents the sentence enders –*kwun, -ney,* and –*tela* as members of a natural class of evidential (specifically mirative) markers, referred to as "cognitive realization markers." Each form will be shown to signal that an instantaneous shift has taken place within the speaker's consciousness, and each form marks and makes visible a distinctive aspect of such cognitive realization. That is, both –*kwun* and –*ney* mark an instantaneous shift in the present or at the moment of speech; -*tela* marks an instantaneous consciousness shift that occurred in the past—usually emerging in the recounting of a past time narrative. The discussion presented here resonates in part with previous work by H. Sohn (1994, 1999), K. Lee (1993), and H. Lee (1993), but differs essentially in that we present a unified analysis for

---

[1] Research for this project was partially funded by The Penn State University Center for Advanced Language Proficiency Education and Research (CALPER) through a grant from U.S. Department of Education (CFDA 84.229A P229A020010). The authors are grateful to the participants at the 15th Japanese/Korean Linguistics Conference, and especially to Kaoru Horie, Kyu-hyun Kim, and Byong-jin Lim for their helpful comments and thought provoking questions.

135

each form, all of which is based on a macro-/micro-level examination of a large corpus of authentic spoken discourse.

2. Previous Accounts of *–kwun, -ney,* and *–tela*

H. Sohn (1994, 1999), K. Lee (1993), and H. Lee (1993) provide discussions of at least two of the three target forms. H. Sohn (1994, 1999) treats all three, indicating that *–kwun* and *–ney* are apperceptive mood markers, where *–kwun* signals discovery and confirmation and *–ney* signals counterexpectation; *–tela* is discussed as a marker of retrospective mood, indicating that the speaker has directly witnessed or experienced an event. The sentence enders are treated by K. Lee (1993) in the following way: *-Kwun* is said to signal that the speaker becomes aware of something that s/he had been previously unaware of, *-ney* indicates that the speaker has a commitment toward a proposition, and then finds that proposition to be wrong (p. 29) [essentially, 'counterexpectation'], and *–tela* is discussed simply as a "non-committal marker," with no explicit mention of retrospection or direct experience. H. Lee (1993) addresses *–kwun, -ney,* and the declarative sentence ender *–ta* all as markers of newly perceived information; he does not discuss *–tela* as a relevant target form. In H. Lee's analysis, the three forms differ in that *–kwun* marks "unassimilated" information that is non-factual and non-informative, *-ney,* information that is factual but non-informative, and *–ta* information that is both factual and informative.

Thus, we find an implicit, and at times, explicit tendency to consider the target forms as markers of epistemic modality, given that the core notions surrounding the analyses deal with "commitment," "factuality" and/or "confirmation." At the very least, we find a tendency in the literature to conflate epistemic modality, i.e., the "belief state of the speaker" with evidentiality, i.e. "the knowledge state of the speaker," (e.g., H. Lee 1985, 1991, 1993).

The analysis put forth in Strauss (2005), based on a different corpus of spoken data different from the present one,[2] is that the three markers rest squarely in the domain of evidentiality, and more specifically, mirativity, which linguistically marks new, unexpected, or unassimilated information. DeLancey (2001:369-370) operationalizes mirativity as follows: "[I]t marks both statements based on inference and statements based on direct experience for which the speaker had no psychological preparation."[3] Through the unified analysis proposed in Strauss (2005) and maintained

---

[2] Strauss (2005) is based on 8.88 hours of spoken data from different sources than those used in the present study.

[3] For early work on mirativitty, see McCawley (1973), Akatsuka (1985), Slobin and Aksu (1982), and Aksu-Koç and Slobin (1986).

here, we will demonstrate that the three mirative markers under investigation reflect systematic patterns of cognition which have come to serve specific interactional and pragmatic functions in discourse. We will also postulate gender-related skewings related to the three forms.

3. Data and Methodology

The data used for this study has been summarized below in Table 1.

Dataset	# minutes	-*kwun*	-*ney*	-*tela*
achimmatang 1 (TV)	60	6	24	10
achimmatang 2 (TV)	60	7	22	22
CJ homeshopping (TV)	120	4	18	21
achimmatang 3 (TV)	60	10	16	21
ppoppoppo (5 episodes) (TV)	105	17	18	6
Pastor Cen: Sermon ("family")	40	4	0	7
Pastor Cen: Sermon ("Prayer")	20	0	0	1
F-t-F conversation	55	4	15	25
Frog story 1	25	0	1	4
Frog story 2	25	0	1	0
mwuesitun mwule poseyyo 1 (TV)	45	10	27	6
acwu thukpyelhan achim 1 (TV)	55	3	16	7
mwuesitun mwule poseyyo 2 (TV)	45	4	12	15
acwu thukpyelhan achim 2 (TV)	55	6	15	13
Korean TA Meeting	60	23	10	22
achimmatang 4 (TV)	60	2	21	6
achimmatang 5 (TV)	60	5	54	23
LG homeshopping (TV)	120	6	42	8
seysanguy achim (TV)	120	5	46	19
TOTAL	1190 (20 hrs)	116	358	72/ 236

Table 1. Corpus Summary: 20 hours/ Approx. 200,000 Words

As noted, the corpus consists of approximately 20 hours or 200,000 words of naturally occurring spoken discourse. Our datasets include television programs such as *achimmatang* (5 broadcasts), *mwesitun mwule poseyyo* 'Ask us Anything' (2 broadcasts), home shopping programs, and five episodes of the children's show *ppoppoppo*. We have also included face-to-face conversations, elicited narratives, as well as two religious sermons.

These datasets represent a wide array of speakers from a variety of social backgrounds, engaged in interactive talk with varied sets of interlocutors. The majority of the data involves dialogic or multi-party interaction; the religious sermons and elicited narratives are predominantly monologic. All data were Romanized to allow for narrow transcription according to a substantially modified set of conventions for conversation analysis (For a list of typical CA transcription conventions, see Atkinson and Heritage 1984). Such a transcription methodology captures relevant prosodic features (e.g., sound stretches, intonational contours, volume shifts) as well as pauses, and immediately contiguous and overlapping speech at turn boundaries.[4]

Once all datasets were transcribed, we conducted a search for the target tokens, the results of which appear in Table 1. Note that the column for –*tela* includes the grand total of all –*tela* tokens from the coprus, i.e., 236. Of these, only 72 were categorized as "cognitive realization markers." The remaining tokens of –*tela* were found to fit within approximately five other pragmatic/functional categories; these other functions will be addressed in a later study through CALPER.

4. –*Kwun, -ney,* and –*tela:* Evidential (Mirative) Markers

Following Strauss (2005), we propose that –*kwun, -ney,* and –*tela* all signal that the speaker has undergone a cognitive shift—as a result of directly perceiving something (through any one of the five senses) or through an inferential trigger. –*Kwun* and –*ney* both mark a present time cognitive shift or one that occurs at the moment of speech, while –*tela* marks a shift which took place in the past. What distinguishes –*kwun* from –*ney* is that –*kwun* marks a punctual realization while –*ney* signals that the speaker has undergone an immediate logical inductive process that engenders an attendant cognitive shift. Examples (1) and (2) from our corpus will illustrate for –*kwun* and –*ney*, respectively.

(1) From *acwu thukpyelhan achim* 2—*KWUN:* **(present punctual realization)** ((The two hosts, Cayyong and Ywunyeng are discussing the benefits of speaking English))

Cayyong: …•*hh e:: ye:^nge ca:^l hamyen cohunikka:+ e^ccaysstu:n*
             ye:^nge kongpwunu:n a^itul com ha:^myen co:hciyo.
             ' ···Uh. I think speaking English well is a good thing. So, if kids study English, that would be great.'

Ywunyeng: *ney:*
             'm hm'

Cayyong: *kuntey •h pwu^monimto ka:^thi hasimye:n te*
             cay[missul kekwuyo
             'If parents studied English together with their kids, it would be more fun.'

Ywunyeng: [*yey::*
             'm hm'

---

[4] We use the Yale system of Romanization throughout. For a complete list of transcription conventions for Korean, see CALPER workbooks (i.e., Strauss et al. (in progress)).

COGNITION THROUGH THE LENS OF DISCOURSE AND INTERACTION / 139

Cayyong: *yey:: •hh ye:/\telpsi: sa:/\sipsampwuni**kwu:n**yo:/*
Yes. It's 8:43 -***KWUN***. ((Cayyong had just noticed the clock))

The punctual realization in (1) occurs as Cayyong, one of the program hosts, notices the clock and realizes the exact time, thus breaking his on-going conversation. The excerpt in (2), illustrating *–ney*, also involves a realization that centers on the time of day. However, the cognitive shift here is qualitatively different from that in (1). That is, in (2) Danny, a character from the children's show *ppoppoppo*, had been concentrating heavily on his work, but suddenly hears the cry of a wolf—a signal to him that it is no longer daytime. His concomitant realization that it is now nighttime is triggered by his inference from that single piece of evidence, i.e., the wolf's cry.

(2) From *ppoppoppo*—**NEY: (process of inductive logic)**
((a clock is ticking; its hands move quickly from 12:00 noon to 9 o'clock; Danny is sitting on a bench and taking notes. Suddenly, he hears a wolf howling))

Danny: *e::/ pe:/\lsse pa:/\m**iney**:/*
Oh. It's nighttime already! -**NEY**

Bobby: Wha:^t (.) ti:^me i:^s i:t.

((Dolly sings and dances with a big clock (picture), indicating 9 o'clock))

Dolly: Wha:^t (.) <u>time</u> is it. ((singing))

Chorus: Wha^t time is it <u>now</u>::^^

Dolly: I::^t's <u>ni::^ne</u> o'clo::ck.

Chorus: I::^t's <u>ni::^ne</u> o'clo::ck.

Examples (3) and (4) will further illustrate the distinction between *–kwun* and *–ney*. In (3), two hosts of *achimmatang*, Kumhuy (f) and Pemswu (m), are discussing the family members of one of the guests, Chanho. Chanho had indicated that he has no photos of his family as a group, but that he was able to locate a picture in which both of his parents appeared together. Pemswu then immediately recognizes it as Chanho's parents' wedding photo.

(3) From *achimmatang 3*-- <u>***KWUN*: (present punctual realization)**</u>

Chanho: *a^penimhako e^me:nimhako ku:^ttay ta^ngsiey sa:^cini e^psekaciko, •hhh ku^namalatwu ka:^ciko na:^wasssupnita:.*
'We don't have (any pictures of my older sister), so we just brought one of my father and mother together.'

Kumhuy: *>kunikka< nwu:^na sa^cinun e^pskwu, •hhh (.) i^ncey pwu^monimi ha^mkkey cci^kusyesste:n=*

'So, you don't have any of your older sister's pictures, but you have one of your parents taken together.'

Pemswu: =_a: kye^lho:n (.) [sa^cini__kwun__yo/_
            'Oh, it's a wedding photo--_KWUN._'

Kumhuy: [_a::/_
                             Oh::

Kumhuy: •_h pwu^moni:m kye^lho:n_
            'It's your parents' wedding photo.'

In contrast with the punctual realization marked by –_kwun_, -_ney_ serves as a linguistic signal which exhibits a cognitive process on the part of the speaker, in which s/he pieces together facts, observations, or inferences that ultimately lead to a context-relevant conclusion or understanding. This is evident in (4), from the television program _mwuesitun mwule poseyyo_ 'Ask us anything.' Here, the guest Yoseyp, has just provided information to the audience and the two hosts regarding statistics of "the world's happiest nations." Upon hearing that Korea ranked number 23 in the world, the host, Insek, expressed his surprise through a –_ney_-marked assessment, revealing the logical process that he has just gone through.

(4) _mwuesitun mwule poseyyo 2_ – **NEY: (process of inductive logic)**

Yoseyp: _itu:^ngi:, (0.2) aceylupai^ca:n_ [Azerbaijan] _iesskwu:^yo:/ (.)_
            sa:^mtungi naicili^a [Nigeria].
            'The second happiest nation was Azerbaijan and the third, Nigeria.'

Audience: _a_[_:::_

Yoseyp: [_ha:^nkwukun i:^sip sa:^mwi._
            'Korea (ranked) 23rd.'

Insek: [_e sa:^ngtanghi nophney:^yo. >wuli<to:/_
            'Oh, we ranked pretty high—**NEY'**

Audience: [_a:::_

Yoseyp: _ku^lehcyo:. (.)_ •_hh o:^sip sa^kaykwukiesssupni:ta:. (hh) (hh)_
            (hh) ((giggles)) •_hh ku^leni[kka cwu^ngkan cengto:^yesscyo:._
            'Right. Participants were nationals from 54 countries. So, Korea was in the middle.'

That –_ney_ indicates the cognitive process of induction is supported by the fact that it frequently co-occurs with logical connectors such as _kulem, kulemyen,_ and _kulayse_ (see Strauss 2005), all of which translate loosely as a conclusion marker meaning "then" or "so." Further, even when such connectors are not overt, many –_ney_-marked utterances can easily be prefaced by "so...,", "then...," or "that means that..."

Now, while *–kwun* and *–ney* signal an immediate realization in the present or at the moment of speech, the third marker *-tela* signals an immediate realization that occurred in the past. Like *–kwun, -tela* signals a punctual realization. Excerpts (5) and (6) will illustrate. In both examples, the *–tela*-marked utterances occur in the midst of a past time narrative in which the speaker is recounting an emotionally charged incident; in both cases, *–tela* emerges at the very upshot of the story as the speaker verbalizes the crucial realization.

In (5), Mrs. Kim, is telling of a car accident that occurred as a result of her husband having suffered a sudden heart attack while he was driving.

(5) From *acwu thukpyelhan achim 2—TELA* **(past punctual realization)**

S. Kim: *cha:^ka kapca:^ki:, (.) •h ha:^nccokulo
            ki:^wullecitelakwuyo::/ •hh >kunikka< mak cha:^ka ma:k
            ssay- (.) ta^lliko issnu:ntey::, •hh pwu^tichi:llye:ko::, (.)
            ku^lay[senu:n*

            'Suddenly our car (that my husband was driving) tilted to
            one side--TELA. And we were about to collide with other
            cars that were coming...

In (6), Hyeswuk is recounting the details of how her three-year old son disappeared from a pre-school outing. And, once again, the utterance marked with *–tela* contains the very piece of information that signals an unexpected and shocking discovery.

(6) From *achimmatang 3—TELA* **(past punctual realization)**

Hyeswuk: *•hhh ce:msi:^mu:l+ e: ye^lhansikye:^ngey to:cha^ku:l
            hay:^se: (.) •hh °e:° cemsi^mul ye:^ltwusikye:^ngey
            me:^kkwuyo:/ •hh ha:nsi:^ si:^popwu:nkka^ci
            se:^nsay:ngnimi: •hh °e° nay:^lyekal si:^kani ta: toy:^nke
            ka^thayse=se^nsayngnim=mye:^chsieyyo:. i^layse: (.) •hhh
            h:^ansi si:^popwu:nieyyo:. ha:^l ttay:, •hh a:^ilul mo:^la:se:,
            •hh ye^ki: (0.2) pey:^nchika: (.) sey:^kayka i:^ssketunyo:/ i:^
            pey:^nchiey: mo:^lase ka^thi a^nchyesseyo:. •hhh a:^nchiko:,
            ka:^nsi^kul ttu:^tecwu:ko:, •hh se:^nsay^ngni:m sey:^pwu:n
            cwu:^ngey ha:^npwu:nkkeyse:, •hh (.) ye:^ki:, (.)
            ya:^kswutheka i:^ccokey i:^ssketun[yo:/ •hh ye:^ki mwu:^l
            ttu^le o:^llakasi:^ko:, •hh twu:pwu:^nu:n, •hh ye:^kise:, (.)
            a^itul ka:^nsikul ttu^tecwuko kye:^sye:sseyo:. •hhh ku^liko: (.)
            mwu::^lul me:^killye:kwu: (0.2) to:^lasese po:^nikka:n, (.)
            •hhh e-(.) ye:ngkwa:^ngima:n e:^pstelanun ke^eyyo:.*

            '(Teachers and kids) arrived (there) at around 11 am and had
            lunch at about noon. When the teachers thought it was time to

go, (one child) asked what time it was. So one of the teachers said that it was 1:15. Then, the teachers made the children sit down on three benches around here. They unwrapped snacks for the children and one of three teachers went to the mineral spring here to get water. One teacher went up to get water and two teachers unwrapped the children's snacks. *When the teachers looked back to give water (to the children)*, they found only Yengkwang wasn't there -- **TELA**.'

The punctual nature of the discoveries in (5) and (6) is underscored by the adverbs which immediately precede each discovery, i.e., in (5), *capkaci* 'suddenly' [our car tilted to one side] and in (6) the adverbial clause *...tolasese ponikkan ...*'when they looked back [Yengkwang was gone].

5. Pragmatics of Evidentials

On the basis of only the foregoing excerpts, it is clear that the target markers actually have little to do with factuality, informativeness, confirmation, or commitment toward a proposition. Further, we have found no evidence suggesting counter-expectation as an epistemic feature underlying the use of *–ney*.

In fact, a counter-expectation reading for *–ney* might lead to problematic interpretations, since the majority of utterances in our data that are marked with this form tend to be expressions of empathy, compliments, encouragement, positive assessments and the like, as summarized in Table 2 below. Note that 68% of all *–ney* tokens in this corpus co-occur with positive interactional moves.

INTERACTIONAL MOVE with -*ney*	n=358
Empathy	103 (29%)
Compliment	65 (18%)
Assessment	
Positive	29 (8%)
Negative	12 (3%)
Positive affect	8 (2%)
Encouragement	8 (2%)
Other	
Positive	31 (9%)
Negative	38 (11%)
Neutral	64 (18%)
TOTAL positive moves with -*ney*	244 (68%)

Table 2. Summary of Interactional Moves Marked with *–ney*

Excerpts (7) through (11) exemplify some of these moves; due to space constraints, we present only the single lines marked with *–ney*.

(7) *achimmatang 4* ('Morning Yard') [COMPLIMENT]

Kumhuy: ⁰*e::::⁰(.) >apenim acwu< (.) ca:::l sayngkisyessney^yo=*
'Oh, your father was really handsome—**NEY**.'

(8) *acwu thukpyelhan achim 2* ('Very special morning') [COMPLIMENT]

Swukkyeng: *cal e^wullisineyyo.* [(hh) (hh) ((giggles))
'It looks good on you—**NEY**.'

(9) *mwuesitun mwule poseyyo* ('Ask us Anything') [POS. ASSESSMENT]

Mihwa: •hh *a:wu::: (.)ne^mwu kway:^nchanhney.*
'Wow. It is really good—**NEY**.'

(10) *CJ Home shopping* [POS. ASSESSMENT]

Cengswu: *e: cha^m i^ppuney:yo:.*
'Yes. They look great—**NEY**.'

(11) *achimmatang* ('Morning Yard') [EMPATHY]

Kumhuy: *ku^ccoktwu oy:^lo:pkey sa:sye:^ssneyyo:[: ⁰(ennitwu:)⁰*
'You, too, ((Kwica)) have lived lonely–**NEY**.'

By positing an underlying meaning of counter-expectation for *–ney,* the interactional moves in (7) through (11) would lose their pragmatic strength as compliments, expressions of positive affect, or empathy, especially given that the interlocutor would be oriented to the speaker's stance of 'contrary to a previous expectation' (e.g.,'it looks good on you, → pragmatic inference: 'but I didn't really think it would,' or 'your father was really handsome, → pragmatic inference: 'but I didn't really think he would be').

In this paper and elsewhere, we have instead posited that the core meaning/function of *-ney* is that of a mirative marker, signaling new, unexpected (not counter-to-expectation), or unassimilated information apprehended through a process of inference and inductive logic based on contextually-situated evidence. This was observed as a core conceptual pattern in examples (2) and (4). The core conceptual pattern of *–kwun*, on the other hand, simply involves an instantaneous and punctual realization. Example (7') below presents the identical utterance as in (7), only this time marked with *–kwun*.

(7') *achimmatang 4*

Kumhuy: ⁰*e:::⁰(.) >apenim acwu< (.) ca::l sayngkisyesskwunyo=*
'Oh, your father was really handsome—**KWUN**.'

The pragmatic force of (7) is dramatically different from that of (7'). The former, as originally delivered by the speaker, constitutes an expression that is clearly addressee-centered, serving as a positive politeness strategy (Brown and Levinson, 1987) on the part of the television host vis à vis her guest. The latter, altered by a switch in mirative forms, is more speaker-centered, constituting a spontaneous exclamation of surprise engendered by the immediate and punctual perception of a single piece of evidence, i.e., the physical appearance of the guest's father. That one mirative marker carries with it a concomitant logical process of inductive reasoning grounded in contextually situated evidence, in contrast with the other that marks only a punctual realization, accounts for the marked pragmatic distinctions engendered by these two seemingly similar sentence enders.

Having observed distinctions in the pragmatic force behind *–kwun* and *–ney*, and the corresponding functions that these take on in talk-in-interaction, and having observed the emotional intensity underlying *–tela* as represented in examples (5) and (6), it became relevant to ascertain whether gender might play a role in the distribution of the target forms across the various datasets in our corpus.[5] Table 3 below presents preliminary results from this dimension of our study.

Dataset	*-kwun*		*-ney*		*-tela*	
	M	**F**	**M**	**F**	**M**	**F**
achimmatang 1 (TV)	3	3	12	12	1	4
achimmatang 2 (TV)	5	2	2	20	3	6
CJ homeshopping (TV)	3	1	6	11	1	1
achimmatang 3 (TV)	7	3	3	13	4	6
ppoppoppo (TV)	7	6	6	7	0	0
F-t-F conversation	0	4	0	15	0	3
mwuesitun mwule poseyyo 1 (TV)	1	9	4	23	0	2
acwu thukpyelhan achim 1 (TV)	3	0	7	9	2	3
mwuesitun mwule poseyyo 2 (TV)	4	0	11	0	0	0
acwu thukpyelhan achim 2 (TV)	3	3	6	9	0	4
Korean TA Meeting	0	23	0	9	0	6
achimmatang 4 (TV)	1	1	8	13	0	1
achimmatang 5 (TV)	3	2	24	30	1	9
LG homeshopping (TV)	0	6	1	39	0	2
seysanguy achim (TV)	2	3	15	31	0	9
TOTAL	**42**	**66**	**105**	**241**	**12**	**56**
Ratio m : f use of target tokens	**1:**	**1.6**	**1:**	**2.3**	**1:**	**4.7**

Table 3. Gender Distribution of *–kwun, -ney,* and *–tela*

Note that the datasets included in Table 3 represent all but Pastor Cen's sermons; we have excluded these from this segment of our analysis because the target tokens produced in the sermons emerge within the context of reported speech, and, in many cases, the gender of the reported speaker is irrelevant and/or ambiguous.

---

[5] The authors thank Byong-jin Lim for raising this question.

While it is clear in the table that the number of mirative tokens produced by female speakers exceeds that produced by male speakers, the results are admittedly inconclusive at this level of our study; we have not examined with precision the ratio of male to female speakers in each individual dataset nor have we yet examined in depth each interactional context in which the target forms were uttered. What is certain, however, is that the relative frequency of each female-produced mirative increases according to mirative type. That is, the ratio of production of the target forms by female speakers increases from 1 in 1.6 for –*kwun* to 1 in 2.3 for –*ney,* and to 1 in 4.7 for –*tela.* It would appear preliminarily that –*tela* produced by male speakers is relatively rare, in comparison with –*kwun* and –*ney.* This could be due to what appears to be the highly emotional charge that –*tela,* as a cognitive realization marker, carries in past time narrative. The pragmatics of Korean evidentials and epistemic modality is still under investigation by Strauss (in preparation).

6. Conclusion

Previous work on the target markers has provided a solid foundation for the current study. Building on the insights of H. Sohn (1994, 1999), K. Lee (1993), and H. Lee (1985, 1991, 1993), we have examined the target forms from a macro-/micro-perspective as they emerge within a variety of discursive contexts involving a wide range of interlocutors culled from a different corpus than that used in Strauss (2005). We maintain the same unified analysis as that posited in the earlier paper, i.e., one that is based on core conceptual patterns for each marker, and have extended the findings to include a number of pragmatic implications.

In this paper, we hope to have demonstrated to what degree close examination of discourse in talk-in-interaction can make visible and render salient particular aspects of speaker cognition. We have also touched on the interrelationships between cognition and emotion and between evidentiality and politeness, illustrating how cognitive realization markers pattern discursively in expressions of surprise, unexpectedness, positive evaluation, empathy, compliments, and intense emotion associated with unexpected discovery.

References

Akatsuka, N. 1985. Conditionals and the Epistemic Scale. *Language* 61:625-639.
Aksu-Koç, A. A. and D. I. Slobin. 1986. A Psychological Account of the Development and Use of Evidentials in Turkish. *Evidentiality: The Linguistic Coding of Epistemology,* eds. W. Chafe and J. Nichols, 159-167. Norwood, NJ: Ablex.
Atkinson, J. M. and J. Heritage. 1984. *Structures of Social Action: Studies in Conversation Analysis.* Cambridge: Cambridge University Press.

Brown, P. and S. Levinson. 1987. *Politeness*. Cambridge: Cambridge University Press.

DeLancey, S. 2001. The Mirative and Evidentiality. *Journal of Pragmatics* 33:369-382.

Lee, H. 1985. Consciously Known but Unassimilated Information: A Pragmatic Analysis of the Epistemic Modal Suffix -kun in Korean. *Proceedings of the Annual Meeting of the First Pacific Linguistics Conference*, eds. S. DeLancey and R. Tomlin, 183-210. University of Oregon.

Lee, H. 1991. Tense, Aspect, and Modality: A Discourse-pragmatic Analysis of Verbal Suffixes in Korean from a Typological Perspective. Doctoral dissertation, UCLA.

Lee, H. 1993. Cognitive Constraints on Expressing Newly Perceived Information, with Reference to Epistemic Modal Suffixes in Korean. *Cognitive Linguistics* 4:135-167.

Lee, K. 1993. *A Korean Grammar on Semantic Pragmatic Principles*. Seoul: Hankwuk Mwunhwasa.

McCawley, N. A. 1973. Another Look at *No, Koto,* and *To*: Epistemology and Complementizer Choice in Japanese. *Problems in Japanese Syntax and Semantics*, eds. J. Hinds and I. Howard, 178-212. Tokyo: Kaitskusha.

Slobin, D. and A. Aksu. 1982. Tense, Aspect, Modality, and More in Turkish Evidentials. *Tense-aspect: Between Semantics and Pragmatics*, ed. P. Hopper, 185-200. Amsterdam: John Benjamins.

Sohn, H. 1994. *Korean*. London: Routledge.

Sohn, H. 1999. *The Korean Language*. Cambridge: Cambridge University Press.

Strauss, S. 2005. Cognitive Realization Markers in Korean: A Discourse-Pragmatic Study of the Sentence-ending Particles *–kwun, -ney,* and *–tela*. *Language Sciences* 27:437-480.

Strauss, S. et al. In Progress. *A Discourse-pragmatic Approach to Korean Language, Culture, and Society* (for CALPER).

Strauss, S. In Preparation. The Pragmatics of Evidentials and Epistemic Modality in Korean.

Part II

Grammaticalization

Different Faces of Equality: Grammaticalization of Equative Comparatives in Korean

SEONGHA RHEE
Hankuk University of Foreign Studies

1. Introduction[1]

The grammatical notion of comparison seems to be among the conceptual primitives but its linguistic manifestations are diverse across many languages. This paper addresses the grammaticalization processes of 'equative comparatives' (Heine 1997), largely equivalent to English *like* and *as*, and their uses in Present Day Korean (PDK). It also presents interesting aspects that surfaced in the course of their grammaticalization, some conforming to the commonly attested grammaticalization principles while some deviating from them. Even though their interesting grammaticalization processes merit in-depth research, especially because there are multiple forms for the same or similar function, they have received little attention to date either individually or collectively, and this paper intends to fill the gap.

[1] This research was supported by the Research Grant of Hankuk University of Foreign Studies. Special thanks go to Professor Linda Fitzgibbon for kindly reading and commenting on an earlier version of this paper. All errors, however, are mine.

In PDK, there are six markers of equative comparative, i.e. *kathi, chelem, man(khum), taylo, tapkey* and *tus*[2] as shown in (1).[3]

(1) a. ku   ai-nun   appa-mankhum   khu-ta
     the child-Top father-EqCom   be.tall-Dec
     'The child is as tall as its father.'

    b. kunye-nun ku-chelem   ttokttokha-ta
      she-Top   he-EqCom   be.smart-Dec
      'She is smart like him / as smart as he is.'

    c. kunye-nun aki-kathi   kwiyep-ta
      she-Top   baby-EqCom   be.cute-Dec
      'She is cute like a baby / as cute as a baby is.'

    d. ney   mal-taylo   cham coh-ta
      your   word-EqCom   very be.good-Dec
      'It is good as you said.'

    e. ku-nun   senpi-tapkey   sal-ass-ta
      he-Top   scholar-EqCom   live-Pst-Dec
      'He lived as a (true) scholar.'

    f. pi-ka   o-l-tus   ha-ta
      rain-Nom come-Pros.Adn-EqCom   do-Dec
      'It looks like rain.'

2. Grammaticalization

Equative comparatives date back to the earliest Korean data in Hankul orthography, i.e. the 15th century, the Middle Korean (MidK) period, and they are still productively used in Modern Korean (ModK). In this section we investigate their lexical and structural sources.

2.1. Lexical and Structural Sources

The equative comparatives under discussion have diverse lexical sources as shown in Table 1. It is noteworthy that the majority, i.e. four out of six,

---

[2] There are other markers of equative comparative in dialectal varieties, such as *meylo, maylo, maychilo, maynchilo, manki, tholem,* and numerous others (see Lee 2003), whose grammaticalization processes this paper does not address for interest of space.

[3] The transcription of the Korean data follows the Extended Yale Romanization System (Rhee 1996) to allow for old orthographic notations. The abbreviations used in gloss are: Acc: accusative; Adn: adnominal; Advz: adverbializer; Attm: attempt; Comp: complementizer; Conn: connective; Dec: declarative; Emph: emphatic; End: sentential ending; Eq.Com: equative comparative; Exclam: exclamative; Imp: imperative; Inst: instrumental; NF: non-finite; Nom: nominative; NP: noun phrase; Poss: possessive; Pres: present; Pros: prospective; Pst: past; Stat: status; and Top: topic.

have nominal sources, making reference to various aspects of a physical entity.

Form	Lexical Source	Characteristics
kathi	kath- 'be same'	adjective denoting identicalness
tapkey	tav- 'be qualified as'	defective adjective
chelem	thyey 'body'	Sino-Korean noun
man(khum)	man 'amount'	defective noun
taylo	tA 'place'	defective noun
tus	tus 'shape'	defective noun

Table 1. Lexical Sources of Equative Comparatives

A comparison of their source structures shows a common feature that they largely make use of adverbializers such as *-lo, -i,* and *–key* as shown in Table 2. This has to do with the fact that adverbializer is a common device for phrasal or clausal connection in Korean.

Form	Structural Source	Literal Meaning
kathi	kath + i 'ADVZ'	in the same manner
tapkey	tav +key 'ADVZ'	qualified as
chelem	thyey + lo 'INST/STAT'	with/as the body
man(khum)	man + (kom 'EMPH')	the exact amount
taylo	tA + lo 'INST/STAT'	with/as the place
tus	tAs	shape

Table 2. Structural Sources of Equative Comparatives

2.2. Formal Change

The complexity in the historical development of the forms of each equative comparative is such that a comprehensive description of the developmental path is well beyond the scope of this paper. We will briefly describe their historical development.

Among the earliest forms is *kAthi,* an adverbialized adjective *kath-* 'be identical', which later developed into 'be similar' (Rhee 2004). There were numerous variants, and especially in the 18th century data diverse forms such as *kAschi, kAchi, kAtthi, kAsthi,* etc. are all attested. However, in ModK only *kathi* is used.

Another equative comparative with a long history is *tapkey,* a combination of a derivational suffix *-tav-* 'be qualified as, be equal to, be tantamount to, be a good exemplar of, etc.' and the manner adverbializer *-key.* However, the further lexical origin of *-tav-* is unclear but it is hypothesized as 'be same' by some researchers (e.g. Huh 1975, Kim 1998, Kim 1996). The phoneme /v/ disappeared in ModK as a result of a general phonological change, and in all the words containing it, the phonemic value has changed into either /b/ or /w/. A variant form of the derivational suffix -tAv-, surviving in a very few fossilized lexical forms, is -lAv-. There was a change in the relative productivity of the two competing adverbializers -key and -i, the latter having been used more productively in early Korean (Rhee 1996). Thus the historically earlier form of tapkey is tAvi.

It is noteworthy that chelem was derived from a Sino-Korean noun thyey 'body', whose ModK counterpart is the palatalized chey. It first occurred in the mixed orthography of Chinese thyey and an instrumental -lo in the 16th century. It showed some variation between thyelo and chyelo in the 18th century, and only the palatalized variant survives in ModK.

The historical development of man and mankhum is complex. The ModK function of these two forms as equative comparative is to mark 'limit' and 'degree', and their historical origin goes back to man/ma/maskam, which meant 'amount' in the 15th century data. The attested variations are man/mankom in the 16th century, makom in the 17th century, manchi in the 18th century, and mankhum from the 19th century. A development worth noting is that from the 18th century, the productive particle man denoting 'only' began to be used as a result of split from mankhum. This man with the delimitation function and the man with the equative comparative function are in the relationship of homophony or polysemy (or even heterosemy, if we assign different grammatical categories to them), but we shall not go into the detail of this delimiter particle here.

Taylo is a combination of the defective noun tA/ta 'place' and the instrumental suffix -lo. It is attested in the 16th century in the form of taylo and its variant form tAylo is attested in the 18th century, which was more commonly used in the 19th century. However, from the 20th century only the first variant form, taylo, is used as a result of a general orthographic and phonological change in Korean that eliminated the phoneme /ɔ/ of the vowel 'A', splitting it into three different vowels /a/, /ə/ and /U/.

Finally, tus was originally a defective noun denoting 'shape' or 'state', occurring in the form of tAs in MidK, and often occurring with a light verb ha- 'do'. It has remained stable in form except for the general historical change that occurred to its vowel as noted above.

As is evident in the historical development of the equative comparatives in the preceding section, all these acquired the grammatical function, albeit through different paths and at different rates, from the MidK, i.e. the 15th through the 16th centuries.

2.3. Semantic Change

In general, semantic change is concomitant of grammaticalization and sometimes it is even considered a prerequisite of grammaticalization. Interesting semantic changes are observable in the development of equative comparatives.

As for *kathi,* the semantic change pattern can be characterized as in (2), an instance of semantic generalization gradually losing the degree of likeness (Rhee 2004). The examples are as in (3).

(2) identicalness > similarity > non-dissimilarity
    identicalness > emphatic

(3) a. sinsa-kathi   yeyuypalukey   hayngtongha-yla
    gentleman-EqCom   courteously   behave-Imp
    'Act courteously like a gentleman.'

   b. saypyek-kathi   talli-e-o-ass-ta
    dawn-EqCom   run-NF-come-Pst-Dec
    '(He) came very early in the morning.'

The semantic change of *tapkey* can be characterized as in (4) and its examples are as given in (5).

(4) identicalness > similarity > qualification/membership

(5) a. pulkun yen-s   koc-An   yenyenhi kos-tap-tota
    red   lotus-Poss flower-Top smoothly flower-EqCom-Exclam
    'The red lotus flower is smoothly beautiful/fragrant.'
                              (Twusienhay I: 7.2; 1481)

   b. ku-nun   tayhaksayng-tap-ta
    he-Top   college.student-Eq.Com-Dec
    'He is truly a college student (e.g. intelligent, etc.).'

The semantic change with *chelem* is an instance of generalization from identicalness to similarity, in the sense that 'body' designates the extreme level of identicalness as does English *self.* The change from similarity to assumed similarity is an instance of subjectification. The semantic change pattern of *chelem* is as in (6) and some of the examples are given in (7).

(6) body > shape > similarity > assumed similarity

(7) a. syonpatang-thyelo stey-lAl   mAnt-Ala
    palm-EqCom   patch-Acc make-Conn
    'Make a patch in the shape of a palm (of a hand), and then ...'
                              (Twuchangbang 29; 1663)

b. amwukes-to   molu-nun   kes-chelem   hayngtongha-n-ta
   nothing-even not.know-Adn   thing-EqCom   behave-Pres-Dec
   '(He) behaves as if he did not know anything / pretends ignorance.'

As for *man* and *mankhum,* its development can be characterized as an instance of metaphor along the ontological continuum of [SPACE > TIME > QUALITY]. There is the subjectification phenomenon as well in the sense that some parts of the semantic change involve attribution of dynamicity, value, scalarity/relativity, and even causation, which are tied to the speaker's subjective judgments. The semantic change patterns are as in (8), and their partial uses are as exemplified in (9) and (10).

(8) man: amount > duration > degree > worth
    mankhum: amount > duration > degree > limit > cause/reason

(9) a. wupak-i   golf-kong-man   ha-ta
       hail-Nom   golf-ball-EqCom   do-Dec
       'The hail is as big as golf balls.'

    b. ku yenghwa-nun po-l-man   ha-ta
       the movie-Top   see-Adn-EqCom   do-Dec
       'The movie is worth watching.'

(10) a. mek-ul-mankhum   mek-ess-ta
        eat-Adn-EqCom   eat-Pst-Dec
        '(I) ate as much as I would like to eat.'

     b. cil-i   coh-un-mankhum   pissa-ta
        quality-Nom   be.good-Adn-EqCom   be.expensive-Dec
        'It is expensive as much as /because it is good.'

The semantic development of *taylo* involves metaphorization from SPACE to QUALITY and CONCRETE to ABSTRACT as shown in (11). There is subjectification involved in the change as we can see attribution of dynamicity and scalarity/relativity. Some of the examples are given in (12).

(11) place > shape/quality/circumstance > fulfillment > conformity > exclusivity > emphatic

(12) a. yelay   kyesi-n   tAy-lAl   molA-zAvangita
        Buddha   exist-Adn   place-Acc   not.know-End
        '(I) do not know the place where Buddha is.'
                                        (Sekposangcel II, 11:10; 1495)

     b. iss-nun-taylo   noh-a-twu-ela
        exist-Adn-EqCom   leave-NF-keep-Imp
        'Leave it as it is.'

Finally, *tus* does not show any substantial semantic change. According to MidK data, especially in the Buddhist scripture commentaries, *tus* often corresponds to the Chinese *ye* 'similar' or *yuye* 'very similar', *sa* 'similar' or to the Korean *kAt-* 'be same/similar'. Since its syntactic environment warrants its analysis as a noun, albeit defective, we can assume the change as one from 'a shape having similarity' to 'in similarity to'. One aspect of the semantic development of *tus* is that it can be used for clausal connection equivalent to English *as if*, even though its meaning is ambiguous between factual and counterfactual descriptions.

3. Issues for Discussions

3.1. Layering and Specialization

If we look at the development of equative comparatives, their geneses are almost simultaneous despite the absence of evidence of mutual interaction in replacing their precedents in Old Korean. This is a state of affairs exhibiting an extreme case of 'layering' (Hopper 1991, Hopper and Traugott 2003). On the other hand, they show delicate semantic differences, and therefore, even though some of them are often interchangeable, the substitution often renders some level of semantic difference or of awkwardness. Therefore, there is a level of specialization according to their fine-grained subdivision of the functional domain, with a few members of the category being more dominant than others, a case of 'specialization' (Hopper 1991, Hopper and Traugott 2003). The specialization is organized along the variables of meaning and morpho-syntactic structure as shown in Table 3.[4]

Form	Semantic Focus	Host	Frequency	ParticleRanking
kathi	similarity in shape	NP	2,172	62/184
takpkey	qualification	NP	N/A	N/A
chelem	(faked) similarity in quality	NP	14,783	28/184
mankhum	reaching standard	NP, Adn	3,832	59/184
taylo	establishing standard	NP, Adn	3,540	48/184
tus	shape/appearance	V, Adn	13,780	N/A

Table 3. Specialization of Equative Comparatives

---

[4] The token frequency is based on the KAIST-KORTERM Corpus (13.6 million words), in which *tapkey* is not searchable as an independent linguistic unit. The particle ranking is based on National Academy of the Korean Language (2002), in which *tapkey* and *tus* are not classified as particles, and their rankings are thus not available.

As noted above, the functional specialization of these forms in subdivided domains is such that their substitution may show semantic differences as shown in (13) and (14).

(13) a. kusalam-mankhum mek-ess-ta
    b. kusalam-chelem mek-ess-ta
      he-EqCom   eat-Pst-Dec
      a: '(I) ate as much as he did.' [amount]
      b: '(I) ate as he did.'   [appearance]

(14) a. ton-i   ku-mankhum iss-umyen ne-n   pwuca-ta
    b. ton-i   ku-taylo   iss-umyen ne-n   pwuca-ta
      money-Nom that-EqCom   exist-if   you-Top rich.person-Dec
      a: 'If you have that much money, you are rich.' [fulfillment of standard]
      b: 'If the money is still there, you are rich.'   [established standard]

The difference in the examples in (13) is due to the fact that *mankhum* focuses on the referenced entity's reaching the quantitative standard, whereas *chelem* focuses on the similarity or identicalness in quantity or state. Likewise, the difference in (14) is due to the fact that *taylo,* unlike *mankhum,* focuses on the established standard. This type of subtlety is present in most of the equative comparatives.

3.2. Universal Paths and Grammaticalization Channels

The grams of equative comparatives came from diverse source lexemes of different conceptual and grammatical domains as discussed in 2.1. However, all these forms, through sense attraction by virtue of conceptual affinity, proceeded to the grammaticalization of a single grammatical function. This state of affairs lends support to the grammaticalization principle called 'the Universal Path' as proposed by Bybee et al. (1994) or 'Grammaticalization Channels' as proposed by Heine and Reh (1984).

    Indeed, in a brief survey through grammaticalization lexicons and elsewhere we see that there are diverse, yet similar, source lexemes as in (15).

(15) a. German *wie* 'how?' > *wie* 'like'
    b. Spanish *como* 'how?' > *como* 'like'
    c. Mandarin Chinese *you* 'exist' > *you* 'like, as ... as'
    d. Twi *sɛ* 'resemble' > *sɛ* 'as ... as' (Lord 1993)
    e. Tamil *poola* 'be similar with' > *poola* 'like, as' (Lehmann 1989)
    f. Idoma *ka* 'say' > *kɛ* 'like' (Lord 1993)
    g. English OE *all-swá* 'wholly so' > *as* (OED)
    h. English OE *líc* [OTeut 'body' > *like* (OED)
    i. Thai *yàaŋ* 'way, manner' > *yàaŋ-kàb* ['way/manner-with'] 'as if'
      (Bisang 1998)

j. Kenya Pidgin Swahili *namna* 'manner' > *namna* 'like, as' (Heine and Kuteva 2002)

In view of the development of Korean equative comparatives and those attested in other languages, we can construct a hypothetical path followed by the equative comparatives in the course of their grammaticalization as in Figure 1.

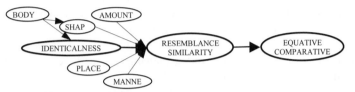

Figure 1. Grammaticalization Paths of Equative Comparatives

3.3. Borrowings in Source Lexemes

Borrowed lexemes are less likely to grammaticalize into grammatical markers since they are often associated with specific genres and styles and consequently a low use frequency (Rhee 1996). The low frequency of Sino-Korean words in contrast with native Korean words is well illustrated in the following state of affairs of Sino-Korean words in the Korean lexis.

(16) About 55-70% in the entire ModK vocabulary
      About 50% in the top 1,000 frequent content words
      About 5% in the top 100 frequent morphemes
      Only one in the 800 particles/endings, i.e. *chelem*

As shown in (16) the fact that *chelem,* despite its Sino-Korean origin, was grammaticalized is noteworthy. As a matter of fact, the lexical origin has become completely opaque in ModK due to its extensive grammaticalization processes. Another factor that contributed to the resultant opacity is a rare and seemingly unmotivated phonological addition, i.e. from /če/ to /čərəm/, contra the Parallel Reduction Hypothesis (Bybee et al. 1994), according to which grams lose semantic content and phonological volume in parallel in the course of grammaticalization.

3.4. Source Characteristics

The next issue for discussion is the source characteristics of the equative comparatives. From the morphosyntactic point of view, their co-occurrence patterns follow our expectation that they would retain the characteristics of their source constructions (the 'Persistence Principle'; Hopper 1991, Hopper and Traugott 2003). For instance, those equative comparatives of nominal sources may allow for NP-hosts as instances of compounding, or Adnominal-hosts as instances of relativization. This is well observed by *mankhum* and *taylo*. Similarly, *kathi* of an adjectival source does not allow for Adnominal-hosts, which is also expected from the Persistence Principle.

However, there are instances that are not in consonance with this expectation. For example, *chelem,* which has a nominal source, does not allow for an Adnominal-host. In ModK all adnominal phrases or clauses must accompany a semantically vacuous noun *kes* 'thing' to host the equative comparative *chelem.* Likewise, *tus,* also having a nominal source, cannot take an NP-host, and can take finite or non-finite verb as its host, both of which are against the expectation. We might suspect their original idiosyncratic behavior as being responsible, but a full explanation as to these anomalies should await a further investigation.

Another aspect of source characteristics is the phonological shapes. Among the most common principles relating to the phonology of grammaticalizing forms is Formal Erosion (Bybee et al. 1994, Heine et al. 1991, Lehmann 1995[1982]). The equative comparatives *taylo, kathi, tus,* and *tapkey* did not undergo much phonological change other than following other general phonological changes that occurred in the history of Korean. There are no reductive processes involved. Though this does not strictly conform to the Parallel Reduction Principle or Formal Erosion, the degree of violation by these forms may be said to be minimal. However, *mankhum* and *chelem* have undergone additive processes, a sheer violation of the Parallel Reduction Principle or Formal Erosion.

Still another aspect of the source characteristics relates to their semantics. The six markers of equative comparative, in a situation of conflict of interest because of their shared grammatical function, exhibit delicate division of labor by each specializing in more fine-grained grammatical subfunctions resorting to such notions as scalarity, identicalness, similarity, conformity, concomitance, etc. in contemporary Korean. Their current semantics may be characterized in the following terms. *Mankhum* still has the 'amount' meaning inherited from the source. *Chelem* does not have the 'body' meaning, and has undergone the most extensive semantic bleaching. Consequently it is used most frequently. *Kathi* still has the 'be same/similar' meaning and retains the source meaning most transparently. Possibly attributable to its formal and semantic transparency, it is used least frequently. *Taylo* still has the 'standard/background' meaning inherited from the source. *Tus* still has the 'shape' meaning (or more frequently the 'appearance' meaning), its function extending to include factual and counterfactual description of appearance, and it is used in high frequency. *Tapkey* still retains the original 'qualification' or 'qualified membership' meaning, thus undergoing minimal semantic change. Since it is predominantly used for an adjectival derivation by hosting a noun and as many words derived from such a process have been fossilized as independent lexical items, its use is highly restricted.

All these descriptions of current semantic characteristics point to the facts that most of them retain, though in varying degrees, the original semantics of the source lexemes, and that the speed of semantic change is by no means uniform.

4. Conclusion

In this paper we have looked at the six equative comparatives used in ModK. Drawing upon historical data from the MidK literature and a contemporary corpus, this paper attempted to trace and contrast the developmental paths of these equative comparatives, focusing on their genesis with respect to lexical and structural sources, on their conflict of interest in the same functional domain, which was resolved by specializing in subdivided functions, and on their observance and/or violation of grammaticalization principles widely subscribed to in grammaticalization scholarship, such as universal path, persistence, parallel reduction and formal erosion. The diversity presented by the grammaticalization history of these grammatical forms shows different faces hidden behind the cover label of equality.

References

Bisang, W. 1998. Adverbiality: The View from the Far East. *Adverbial Constructions in the Languages of Europe*, ed. J. van der Auwera, 643-812. Berlin: Mouton de Gruyter.

Bybee, J. L., R. D. Perkins, and W. Pagliuca. 1994. *The Evolution of Gramar: Tense, Aspect and Modality in the Languages of the World.* Chicago: Chicago University Press.

Heine, B. 1997. *Cognitive Foundations of Grammar.* Oxford: Oxford University Press.

Heine, B., U. Claudi and F. Hünnemeyer. 1991. *Grammaticalization: A Conceptual Framework.* Chicago: University of Chicago Press.

Heine, B. and T. Kuteva. 2002. *World Lexicon of Grammaticalization.* Cambridge: Cambridge University Press.

Heine, B. and M. Reh. 1984. *Grammaticalization and Reanalysis in African Languages.* Hamburg: Helmut Buske.

Hopper, P. J. 1991. On Some Principles of grammaticalization. *Approaches to Grammaticalization*, eds. E. C. Traugott and B. Heine, Vol. 1, 17-35. Amsterdam & Philadelphia: John Benjamins.

Hopper, P. J. and E. C. Traugott. 2003[1993]. *Grammaticalization.* Cambridge: Cambridge University Press.

Huh, W. 1975. *Wuli Yeysmalpon: 15-seyki Kwuke Hyengthaylon* [Old Korean Grammar: 15th Century Korean Morphology]. Seoul: Saem Publishing.

KAIST KORTERM Corpus, http://morph.kaist.ac.kr/kcp/ accessed September 2005.

Kim, J.-A. 1998. *Cwungseykwukeuy Pikyokwumwun Yenkwu* [A Study of Comparative Constructions in Middle Korean]. Seoul: Thaehaksa.

Kim, C. S. 1996. *Kwukeuy Tanehyengsengkwa Tanekwuco Yenkwu* [A study of Korean word formation and word structure]. Seoul: Thaehaksa.

Lee, K. 2003. *Kwuke Pangen Mwunpep* [Grammar of Korean Dialects]. Seoul: Thaehaksa.

Lehmann, C. 1995[1982]. *Thoughts on Grammaticalization.* Newcastle: LINCOM Europa.

Lehmann, T. 1989. *A Grammar of Modern Tamil.* Pondicherry: Pondicherry Institute of Linguistics and Culture.

Lord, C. 1993. *Historical Change in Serial Verb Constructions.* Amsterdam/Philadelphia: John Benjamins.

National Academy of the Korean Language. 2002. *Hyentay Kwuke Sayong Pinto Cosa: Hankwuke haksupyong ehwi sencengul wihan kicho cosa* [A Use Frequency Survey of Modern Korean: A pilot survey for selection of Korean educational vocabulary]. Seoul.

Rhee, S. 1996. Semantics of Verbs and Grammaticalization: The Development in Korean from a Cross-Linguistic Perspective. (Doctoral dissertation, The University of Texas at Austin.) Seoul: Hankuk Publisher.

Rhee, S. 2004. How Far Likeness Can Go: Grammaticalization of *kath-* in Korean. Paper Presented at Berkeley Linguistics Society 30. February 13-16, 2004.

From Classifier Construction to Scalar Construction: The Case of the Japanese *N hitotu V-nai* and *N 1-numeral classifier V-nai* Constructions

OSAMU SAWADA

University of Chicago

1. Introduction[1]

In Japanese, when we count things, a numeral classifier is attached to the numeral. The shape or nature of the thing to be counted determines the numeral classifier to be attached. In this sense, Japanese numeral classifiers are morphemes which are similar to *sheet* in the phrase *a sheet of paper* or *cup* in the phrase *a cup of coffee* in English. Observe (1) below:

(1) Taro wa   kuruma o   ni- dai   ka-tta.
    Taro Top   car   Acc two-NCL (vehicle) buy-Past
    'Taro bought two cars.'

In (1), the classifier *dai* (vehicle) is attached to the numeral *ni* 'two'. *Dai* is used because the classifier semantically agrees with *kuruma* 'car.' The Japanese numeral classifiers appear in various syntactic environments.[2]

[1] I am very grateful to Naomi McGloin, Mutsuko Endo Hudson, Yoshiko Matsumoto, Chris Kennedy, Anastasia Giannakidou, Keiko Yoshimura, Brent de Chene, Kojiro Nabeshima, Alan Yu, Harumi Sawada, Jun Sawada and the participants at the 15th J/K Linguistics Conference for their valuable comments and suggestions.

However, there are two types of construction that contain numeral classifiers that are not used for counting things and are only used with the negative *nai* 'not'. This paper focuses on these two types of Japanese scalar constructions, the N *hitotu* V-*nai* and N 1-numeral classifier V-*nai* constructions. The paper examines (i) what kinds of syntactic, semantic, and pragmatic characteristics each construction possesses and (ii) the process of grammaticalization from a numeral classifier to a scalar particle in the two constructions.

Typical examples of the N *hitotu* V-*nai* construction and the N 1-numeral classifier V-*nai* construction are illustrated in (2) and (3), respectively (Scalar Prt stands for a scalar particle and NCL stands for a numeral classifier).

(2) Taro   wa   biiru   *hitotu*   nom- e-   *nai.*
   Taro   Top   beer   Scalar Prt   drink can   not
   'Taro cannot even drink beer.'   (event scale)

(3) Taro   wa   biiru   i-   *ppai*   nom- e-   *nai.*
   Taro   Top   beer   one   NCL (cup)   drink can   not
   'Taro cannot even drink beer.'   (event scale)
   'Taro cannot drink beer at all.'   (emphasis of negation)

As I argue below, although the N *hitotu* V-*nai* construction (=2) and the N 1-numeral classifier V-*nai* construction (=3) share some characteristics, they must be regarded as different constructions (Fillmore et al. 1988, Goldberg 1995, Kay 1990) in terms of multifunctionality and degree of grammaticalization.

From the viewpoint of multifunctionality, the former construction has only one function—'event scale', as shown in (2). The latter construction, on the other hand, has (maximally) two functions—'event scale' and 'emphasis of negation',as shown in (3).[3]

From the standpoint of grammaticalization, I will argue that the N *hitotu* V-*nai* construction is more grammaticalized than the N 1-numeral classifier V-*nai* in terms of decategorization. More specifically, I will argue that *tu* of *hitotu* in the former construction (=2) has totally lost its function as a numeral classifier to become a new scalar particle, *hitotu* 'even' by combining

---

[2] The syntactic environments of numeral classifiers are usually classified into the following three construction types: pre-nominal, post-nominal, and appositive (Mizuguchi 2004:62-63).

[3] The 'event scale' function is, roughly, a function that forces the hearer to posit contextually relevant events other than the text proposition, as in the case of the Japanese scalar adverb *sae* or the English one *even*. The 'emphasis of negation' function, on the other hand, emphasizes the negativity of the text proposition, which can be paraphrased by a Japanese negative polarity expression, such as *zenzen...nai* or an English one such as *not...at all*.

with the minimal numeral *hito* 'one.' (The numeral classifier *tu* can count things that are inanimate and separable, but not animate or inseparable things.) The classifier *ppai* in *i-ppai* in the latter construction (=3), on the other hand, still retains the characteristics of a numeral classifier.

It is important to notice that the *tu* in *hitotu* can also function as a numeral classifier, as in the following sentence (INANI stands for inanimate).

(4) Kono doresu ni wa simi hito- tu   nai.
 This dress in Top stain one-NCL (INANI, separable) not-exist
'There is not even a stain in this dress.'   (event scale)
'There is not a stain in this dress at all.' (emphasis of negation)

In (4), the morpheme *hito-tu* is the same as *i-ppai* in the sense that it is one of the many numeral classifiers. In other words, (4) is parallel to (3). This means that while (2) belongs to the N *hitotu* V-*nai* construction, (4) belongs to the N 1-numeral classifier V-*nai* construction. The two constructions that I analyze here can be classified as follows:

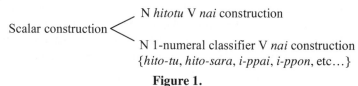

         N *hitotu* V *nai* construction
Scalar construction
         N 1-numeral classifier V *nai* construction
         {*hito-tu, hito-sara, i-ppai, i-ppon*, etc…}

Figure 1.

2. Previous Analyses of the N *hito-tu* V *nai* Construction

Nabeshima (2003) and Sakamoto (2002) base their analyses on the presupposition that the pair of sentences (2) and (3) belong to the same construction, viz., the N *hito-tu* V-*nai* construction. They seem to regard *hito-tu* as just a representative of various cases of **one+numeral classifier** constituent (Sakamoto 2002:30). It is important to notice that what they call the N *hito-tu* V *nai* construction corresponds to what I call the N 1-numeral classifier V nai construction.[4]

Nabeshima (2003:88-90) states within the framework of construction grammar (Fillmore et al. 1988, Kay 1990, Kay and Fillmore 1999) that N *hito-tu* V-*nai* construction should be considered as an independent construction (form-meaning pairing) because it possesses the following five unique characteristics:

(5) (a) No case marker appears in this construction.
 (b) This construction is always used in a negative environment.

---

[4] Nabeshima (2003) actually calls the construction as the '…*hito-tu*…*nai*' construction. The first variable corresponds to N and the second variable corresponds to V. It is the same construction as the 'N *hito-tu* V *nai*' construction which Sakamoto (2002) posits.

(c) Scalarity is involved in this construction.

(d) Even activities (e.g. *aisatu* 'greeting') can be counted by *hito-tu* in this construction.

(e) This construction has a (pragmatic) meaning of 'terrible!' or 'wonderful!'

The following examples illustrate these five characteristics (note that (d) is only for the example of *hito-tu*).

(6) Kare wa kakezan   hito-tu deki-nai.   (Nabeshima 2003:89)
    He Top multiplication one NCL can not
    'He cannot even multiply.'

(7) Sakana i- ppiki sabak -e -nai.   (Nabeshima 2003:83)
    Fish   one NCL   cook   -can-not
    'You cannot even cook fish.'

Sakamoto (2002) points out that there are two interpretations in the N *hito-tu* V-*nai* construction, viz., the 'modal' and the 'absolute negation' interpretations.[5] She further argues that the basic meaning of the construction lies in the modal interpretation, whereas the interpretation of absolute negation interpretation is peripheral, as in the following examples.

(8) Heya no   katazuke hito-tu   sunde inai.
    Room Gen clearance one NCL   finish not
    'I haven't even finished clearing up the room.'

(9) Otya i-ppai   dasi- tekure- naka-tta.
    tea one NCL (cup) serve give   not   PAST
    'He (she) didn't even serve me tea.'
    'He (she) didn't serve me a cup of tea at all.'   (Sakamoto 2002:30)

According to Sakamoto (2002), in (8) there is only one interpretation, i.e. the modal interpretation, while in (9) there are two interpretations: the modal interpretation and the absolute negation interpretation.[6] She concludes from this fact that the modal interpretation is more basic than that of the absolute negation.[7]

Although previous analyses posit only one construction, I will argue that each of the pairing of the sentences (2)-(3), (6)-(7), and (8)-(9) belongs to a different construction from each other in terms of multifunctionality

---

[5] 'Modal interpretation' corresponds to my notion of event scale function.

[6] It seems that there is no absolute negation interpretation in (9) because of the pragmatic condition, which I consider in section 6.

[7] It seems that this is not necessarily the case, because there are examples that have only what she calls "the absolute negation" interpretation, as I will argue in section 6.

and the degree of grammaticalization. The former examples (=(2), (6), and (8)) belong to the N *hitotu* V-*nai* construction and the latter (=(3), (7), and (9)) belong to the N 1-numeral classifier V-*nai* construction.

3. The Similarities between the Two Constructions

This section argues that the N *hitotu* V-*nai* (=2) and the N 1-classifier V-*nai* (=3) constructions share four constructional characteristics that are essentially different from ordinary numeral classifier constructions such as (1).

3.1. Occurrence of Minimal Number

The first characteristic is concerned with the fact that in the two constructions, the number is limited to <u>one</u>, *hito* or *iti*, as in the following examples:

(10) a. *Hanako wa syatu   {iti- /*ni-} mai   ka- e-   nai.
      Hanako Top shirt   one/ two   NCL (thin flat) buy can not
      'Hanako cannot even buy two shirts.'

      b. *Hanako wa   syatu {hito-/*futa-} tu   ka- e-   nai.
        Hanako Top shirt   one /   two   NCL (inanimate) buy can not
        'Hanako cannot even buy two shirts.'

3.2. Negativity

The second characteristic is concerned with the fact that the two constructions can only appear in a negative environment, as in (11). This means that *hitotu* and '1-classifier' are negative polarity items (NPIs).

(11) a. Anata wa otya {hitotu   / i-ppai}   dasa-nai.
      You   Top tea   Scalar Prt   / one-NCL (cup)   serve not
      'You do not even serve tea.'

      b. *Anata   wa   otya {hitotu   /i- ppai}   dasu.
        You   Top tea   Scalar Prt /one classifier (cup)   serve
        '(lit.)You even serve tea.'

It is important to notice that these two characteristics, the existence of a minimum number and the negativity, are correlated with each other from the standpoint of function (Israel 2001). As Israel (2001:302) argues, a lexical item that denotes a minimum value in scale tends to become an emphatic NPI.

3.3. Appearance of Noun without Determiner

The third characteristic is concerned with the fact that syntactically, the noun followed by a classifier in the two constructions is a noun without determiner:

(12) Jiro wa biiru {i- ppai   / hitotu}   dasa-nai.
Jiro top beer   one NCL (cup)/ Scalar Prt serve not
'Jiro does not even serve beer.'

(13) *Jiro wa sono biiru   {i- ppai   / hitotu}   dasa-nai.
Jiro Top the beer   one NCL(cup)/ Scalar Prt} serve not
'Jiro does not even serve the beer.'

Example (13), but not (12), is ill-formed because the noun *biiru* 'beer' is preceded by the determiner *sono* 'the'.

3.4. Non-existence of Case Markers

The fourth characteristics is concerned with the fact that neither the nominative case maker *ga* nor the accusative case marker *o* appears in the two constructions. If either is inserted, the sentence becomes ungrammatical, as shown in (14b) and (15b).

(14) a. Taro wa biiru {hitotu   / i-ppai}   nom -e -nai.
Taro Top beer   Scalar Prt/ one NCL (cup) drink can not
'Taro cannot even drink beer.'

b. *Taro wa biiru o   {hitotu   / i-ppai}   nom -e -nai.
Taro Top beer ACC Scalar Prt / one NCL (cup) drink can not
'Taro cannot even drink beer.'

c. Taro wa   biiru o   itt-pai   mo   nom -e -nai.
Taro Top beer ACC one-NCL (cup) even drink can not
'Taro cannot drink even one glass of beer.'

(15) a. Tiri   hito-tu   nai.
Dust   one NCL not-exist
'There is not even a dust.' / 'There is not a dust at all.'

b. *Tiri   ga   hito-tu   nai.
Dust   Nom one NCL not-exist
'There is not even a dust.' / 'There is not a dust at all.'

c. Tiri   ga   hito-tu   mo   nai.
Dust   Nom one NCL even not-exist
'There is not even one dust.'

Sentence (14b) and (15b), but not (14a) and (15a), are ungrammatical because the nominative case marker *o* or *ga* appears in it. (14c) and (15c) are acceptable because the sentences belong to an ordinary numeral classifier construction.

The above discussion suggests that the two syntactic characteristics analyzed in sections 3.3 and 3.4 are motivated by **meaning**: the noun without a determiner or a case marker in the two constructions does not denote **instance** but **type,** in the sense of Langacker (1991: 55ff.).

4. The Differences between the N *hitotu* V-*nai* and N 1-numeral classifier V-*nai* Constructions

This section discusses the difference between the N *hitotu* V-*nai* and N 1-classifier V-*nai* constructions mainly from a semantic viewpoint.

4.1. The Semantics of the N *hitotu* V-*nai* Construction

The following examples belong to the N *hitotu* V-*nai* construction:

(16) Saikin   isogasii node   sanpo   hitotu   deki-nai.
These days busy   because   walk   Scalar Prt can not
'Because I am busy these days, I cannot even take a walk.'

(17) Hanako wa   ryoori   hitotu   deki -nai.
Hanako Top   cooking Scalar Prt   do-can-not
'Hanako cannot even cook.'

(18) Ano fuufu wa   kodomo hitotu   manzoku-ni sodate   rare-nai.
That coupleTop child   Scalar Prt well   bring up can not
'That couple cannot even bring up a child well.'

(19) Saikin   no   wakamono   wa   aisatu   hitotu   deki-nai.
These days Gen young people Top   greeting Scalar Prt can not
'These days, young people cannot even offer a greeting.'

These examples show that the N *hitotu* V-*nai* construction has the following function:

(20) The N *hitotu* V-*nai* construction is a construction which shows that even the lowest-ranked event (=E1) is not realized among various contextually related events that are ordered on the same scale.

According to scalar entailment, if the lowest ranked event is not realized, all the other events which are higher than the E1 are not realized either, as shown in Figure 2:

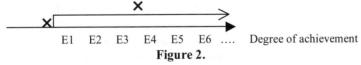

              E1   E2   E3   E4   E5   E6   ....   Degree of achievement
Figure 2.

I refer to this function as an **event scale** function, because the event in question (=E1) is construed relative to other related events (E2, E3, E4...).

As I discuss bellow, *tu* in this construction has lost its function of numeral classifier and become the independent scalar particle *hitotu* by combining with the minimum numeral *hito* 'one'. It is possible to take the view that *tu* in (16)–(19) is not a numeral classifier because when it does serve as such, it is never used for counting activity nouns, such as *sanpo* 'walking', *aisatu* 'greeting', *ryoori* 'cooking' and *uta* 'song.'

4.2. The Semantics of the N 1-numeral classifier V-*nai* Construction

The following examples belong to the N 1-classifier V-*nai* construction:

(21) Taro no   fudebako ni wa   enpitu itt- pon   nai.
    Taro Gen pencil box in Top pencil one NCL (elongated) not-exist.
    'There is not even a pencil in Taro's pencil case.'
    'There is not a pencil in Taro's pencil case at all.'

(22) Kanojo wa   ryoori itt- pin   tukur-e -nai.
    She   Top   dish   one NCL (food) make can not
    'She cannot even cook.'
    'She cannot cook at all.'

The above examples demonstrate the hypothesis that the N 1-classifier V-*nai* construction has the following multiple functions:

(23) The N 1-numeral classifier V-*nai* construction has the functions of **event scale** and **emphasis of negation.**

The following examples must be regarded as the N 1-numeral classifier V-*nai* construction, because in (24) we can find the function of emphasis of negation, in which the quantity of N is involved:

(24) Kanojo no   kao ni wa simi   hito-tu   nai.
    She   Gen face to Top blemish one NCL (INANI, separable) not-exist
    'There is not even a blemish on her face.'   (event scale)
    'There is not a blemish on her face at all.'   (emphasis of negation)

5. Two Kinds of Semantic Functions and their Scalarity

In the previous section, I argued that the N *hitotu* V-*nai* construction has only one function, viz., the function of event scale, while the N 1-classifier V-*nai* construction has (potentially) two functions, i.e. the function of event scale and that of emphasis of negation. How can we explain this asymmetry in terms of scalarity? I argue that while the N *hitotu* V-*nai* construction can only posit a qualitative scale, the N 1-classifier V-*nai* construction can posit both a qualitative scale and a quantitative scale simultaneously. The qualitative scale is based on pragmatic information, while the quantitative scale is based on semantic information, as shown in the following figures:

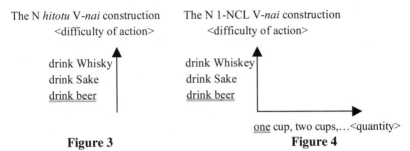

Figure 3   **Figure 4**

The relation between the two functions and their scalarity can be summarized as follows:

(25) The function of event scale has a qualitative (or pragmatic) scale, which is sensitive to context.

(26) The function of emphasis of negation has a quantitative (or semantic) scale, which is based on the number of N.

Which of these two functions a sentence serves can be determined by the following tests:

(27) Test 1: The sentence has the function of event scale if the constituent 1-NCL can be replaced by *mo* or *sae* 'even.'

(28) Test 2: The sentence has the function of emphasis of negation if the constituent 1-NCL can be followed by *mo* or *sae* 'even.'

For example, the above tests predict that sentence (2) has a function of event scale, but not the function of emphasis of negation:

(29) Taro wa biiru {mo   /?*hitotu   mo}   nom- e- nai.
    Taro Top beer   Scalar Prt (even)/ Scalar Prt Scalar Prt drink-can-not
    'Taro cannot even drink beer.'

6. The Functional Distribution of the N *hitotu* V-*nai* and the N 1-numeral classifier V-*nai* Constructions

Table (30) shows the possible distribution patterns of the two constructions:

(30)	Event scale	Emphasis of negation
(Type A) N *hitotu* V-*nai* construction	YES	NO
(Type A) N 1-NCL V-*nai* construction	YES	NO
(Type B) N 1-NCL V-*nai* construction	YES	YES
(Type C) N 1-NCL V-*nai* construction	NO	YES

It is possible to observe the following two points from the above table. First, the N *hitotu* V-*nai* construction has only one function, whereas the N 1-numeral classifier V-*nai* construction is multifunctional. Second, although the N *hitotu* V-*nai* construction can have two functions as a constructional meaning, it sometimes can have only one function, as shown in Type A and Type C. This is because there are the following well-formedness conditions for the two functions:

(31) Plural events condition: In order to have the function of event scale, there must be the presupposition that relevant plural events must be posited.

(32) "To some quantity" condition: In order to have the function of emphasis of negation, there must be a presupposition that the speaker can pragmatically posit many (or some) Ns.

Let us now look at each of the three types. In Type A the reading of event scale is acceptable, but the reading of emphasis of negation is not:

(33) Kare wa aisatu hitotu deki-nai. (Type A)
He Top greeting Scalar Prt cannot
'He cannot even offer a greeting.' (event scale)
'*He cannot offer a greeting at all' (emphasis of negation)

(34) Hanako no heya ni wa rajio iti- dai nai. (Type A)
Hanako Gen room to Top radio one NCL (flat object) not-exist
'There is not even a radio in Hanako's room.' (event scale)
'??There is not a radio at all in Hanako's room.'(emphasis of negation)

The reason why (34) has only the function of event scale is due to the violation of the well-formedness condition in (32).

In Type B, the reading of event scale and that of the emphasis of negation are both acceptable:

(35) Ziro wa syatu iti- mai ka- e- nai. (Type B)
Ziro Top shirt one NCL (sheet-like) buy can not
'Ziro cannot even buy a shirt.' (event scale)
'Ziro cannot buy a single shirt at all' (emphasis of negation)

In Type C, the reading of the emphasis of negation, but not that of event scale, is acceptable:

(36) Sora ni wa kumo hito-tu nai. (Type C)
Sky to Top cloud one NCL not-exist
'*There is not even a cloud.' (event scale)
'There is not a single cloud at all.' (emphasis of negation)

The reason why (36) has only one function is due to the violation of the well-formedness condition in (31).

7. From Classifier to Scalar Construction: The Process of Grammaticalization

In this section we will consider the difference between the N *hitotu* V-*nai* construction and the N 1-numeral classifier V-*nai* construction from the viewpoint of the following process of grammaticalization:

(37) Although the N 1-classifier V-*nai* construction is grammaticalized to some extent to be a scalar construction, the function of classifier partially remains. The N *hitotu* V-*nai* construction, on the other hand, is **de-classified** to become an independent scalar construction. There is no morphological boundary between *hito* and *tu* and the word *hitotu* becomes a single scalar adverb.

For example, *tu* in the N *hitotu* V-*nai* construction (=2) has totally lost the function of numeral classifier to become the independent scalar particle *hitotu* 'even' by combining with the minimum numeral *hito* 'one', while *ppai* in the N 1 numeral classifier V-*nai* construction (=3) still retains the characteristic of numeral classifier, because there still remains a semantic agreement between the noun *beeru* 'beer' and *ppai* 'cup.'

(37) is also supported by the fact that the N 1-numeral classifier V-*nai* construction can have not only an event scale reading but also an emphasis of negation reading. The N *hitotu* V-*nai* construction, on the other hand, has only an event scale reading.

8. Conclusion

In this paper I argued that while the N *hitotu* V *nai* construction has only the function of event scale, the N 1-numeral classifier V-*nai* construction can have two functions of event scale and emphasis of negation. I showed that in terms of scalarity, the event scale function posits a qualitative scale and the function of emphasis of negation posits a quantitative scale. I also argued that the difference of multifuctionalitity between the two constructions is due to the degree of grammaticalization.

Why can only *hitotu* be decategorized from a numeral classifier to a scalar particle? Probably, this is because *tu* is the most abstract numeral classifier in Japanese. The numeral classifier *tu* can count any kind of things or objects which are inanimate and separable. From the viewpoint of grammaticalization, it is possible to consider that *tu* is the most likely to loose the function of a numeral classifier. The following figure shows the grammaticalization from the classifier construction to the scalar constructions.

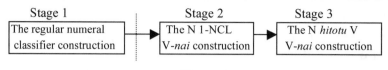

Figure 5.

References

Fillmore, C.J., P. Kay, and M.C. O'Connor. 1988. Regularity and Idiomaticity in Grammatical Constructions: The Case of '*Let Alone*'. *Language* 64:501-538.

Goldberg, A. 1995. *Constructions: A Construction Grammar Approach to Argument Structure*. Chicago: University of Chicago Press.

Hopper Paul. J. and E. C. Traugott. 2003. *Grammaticalization* (second edition). Cambridge: Cambridge University Press.

Israel, M. 2001. Minimizers, Maximizers and Rhetoric of Scalar Reasoning. *Journal of Semantics* 18: 297-331.

Kay, P. 1990. Even. *Linguistics and Philosophy* 13:59-111.

Kay, P. and C. J. Fillmore. 1999. Grammatical Constructions and Linguistic Generalizations: The What's X Doing Y Construction. *Language* 75:1-33.

Langacker, R. W. 1991. *Foundations of Cognitive Grammar. Vol.2. Descriptive Application*. Stanford: Stanford University Press.

Matsumoto, Y. 1993. Japanese Numeral Classifiers: A Study on Semantic Categories and Lexical Organization. *Linguistics* 31: 667-713.

Mizuguchi, S. 2004. Nihongo no Ruibetusi no Tokusei (The Characteristics of Japanese Numeral Classifiers). *Ruibetusi no Taisyo* (Contrastive Analyses of Classifiers) eds. Y. Nishimitu and S. Mizuguchi, 61-77. Tokyo: Kuroshio Publisher.

Nabeshima, K. 2003. "Hitotu V nai" Koobun ni tuite: Nihongo ni okeru Kobun Bunpoo no Itirei to site. (On the "....hitotu V nai" Construction: As One of the Example of the Construction Grammar Approach) *Nihongo Bunpo Gakkai Dai 4kaitaikai Happyo Ronbunsyuu* (*Proceedings of the Fourth Conference of the Society of Japanese Grammar*):83-92.

Sakamoto, T. 2002. Suryosi 'Hitotu' no Imi to Yoho; 'N hitotu V nai' Koobun o Tyusin ni. (Meaning and Use of Numeral Quantifier *hito-tu*: Focusing on the 'N hitotu V nai' Construction. *Conference Handbook of the 124th General Meeting of Linguistic Society of Japan*:30-35.

Sawada, O. 2005. The Possible Semantic Diversity of the Comparative Constructions in English and Japanese: A Construction-based Approach. Paper Presented at the 9th International Cognitive Linguistics Conference, Yonsei Univerisity.

Sawada, O. In Press. The Multi-functionality of English and Japanese Scalar Distance Constructions: A Semantic Map Approach. *Papers from the 40th Annual Meeting of the Chicago Linguistic Society*.

From Quotative Conditionals to Emotive Topic Markers: A Case of *tteba* and *ttara* in Japanese

RUMIKO SHINZATO[1] AND SATOKO SUZUKI[2]
Georgia Institute of Technology[1], Macalester College[2]

I. Introduction[1]

Compared to earlier days when a topic marker in Japanese was automatically equated with *wa* vis-à-vis the subject marker *ga* (Kuno 1973, *inter alia*), the scope of topic marker studies has expanded to include various other topic markers. Some representative studies include: *tte* (Maynard 2002, R. Suzuki 1999, S. Suzuki 1998), *nante* (S. Suzuki 1998), *nara* (Takanashi 1995), *tteba* (Saegusa 1999) and *ttara* (Hayes and Shinzato 2001). Interestingly, all these topic markers either implicate a speech act verb, *i(f)u*[2], or conditional particle *ba*[3]. Of these, this paper will focus on the lat-

---

[1] We would like to thank John Haiman, Kyoko Masuda, and Timothy Vance for reading and giving feedback on our earlier drafts. We would also like to thank the audience at the 15th J/K conference for their comments, especially Kaoru Horie and Sung-Ock S. Sohn. Any errors are our own.

[2] For the presentation of pre-modern examples, we used *ifu, ihe-ba, ihi* with an intervocalic consonant, but for modern examples, we used *iu, ie-ba, and ii*.

[3] This recalls the English expression of *speaking of X*, and Haiman's (1978) famous paper, *Conditionals are topics*.

ter two, the quotative conditionals, *tteba* and *ttara*, both of which include *i(f)u* and *ba*.

The purposes of this paper are twofold. First, from a diachronic perspective, it delineates the developmental path of *tteba* and *ttara*, and by doing so, touches upon issues relevant to grammaticalization such as (inter) subjectification and scope increase. Second, it brings into focus the semantic contrast seen in the (older) unreduced (i.e., *to i(h)e-ba*, and *to it-tara*) vs. (more innovative) reduced (i.e., *tteba* and *ttara*) forms (cf. 'layering' in the sense of Hopper 1991), and relates this contrast to Bolinger's (1968) concept of 'semantic bifurcation'.

2. A Diachronic Perspective

2.1. Developmental Paths

Diachronically, *tteba* and *ttara* are derived from quotative conditionals as shown in (1). Both consisted of the quotative particle, *to*, the verb of saying *i(f)u* (*ihe* and *ihi* are conjugational variants), and the conditional particle *ba*.

(1) a. ...*to*   *ihe -ba*   >   *tteba*
        QT   say-COND

   b. ...*to*   *ihi-* (*tara/tare*)- *ba*   >   *ttara*[4]
        QT   say-PERF-COND

At the 1st stage, these original strings only expressed conditional/temporal meanings, as in 'If/When saying X, then Y happen(s/ed).'

(2) X {*to ihe-ba* / *ihi-(tara/tare)-ba*} Y
    'If/When saying X, then Y'

Here, what comes before the quotative particle *to* is something said by someone, and thus has a referential value. For instance, in (3), *to ihe-ba* is added to what was uttered by someone, in this case, *Kaguyahime*, and it is followed by a consequent clause, thereby forming a temporal relationship. The same quotative characteristics apply to (4) as well.

(3)   [*'Oya to koso*   *to ihe-ba*,   [*Okina*, *'Ureshikumo*
       omohitatematsure']   *notamahu mono kana' to ihu.*]
       [I only think of you   QT say-COND   Okina said, 'I am so happy to
       as my (real) father]   hear what you said!]
       'When (Kaguyahime) said, "I only think of you as my real father,"
       then Okina said, "I am so happy to hear what you said!"' (*Taketori*
       Monogatari Ca. 9C-10C)

---

[4] The *-tara* based etymology comes from Sakakura (1993) and the *-tare*-based etymology is adopted from Yoshida (1971).

(4)   *Ko ha nani zo to* **ihi-tare-ba**   *shika no ifu nari to ifu.*
       this TP what KP QP say-PERF-COND   buck   SB   cry   CP   QT   say
       '(Referring to strange sounds) when I asked what it is, (he/she) said
       it is the buck crying'' (*Kagerō Nikki* 974)

In contrast to the 1ˢᵗ stage where the relationship between X and Y is
characterized as conditional or temporal, at the 2ⁿᵈ stage, the X-Y relationship expresses that of a topic-comment. Importantly, X is prompted by the
previous discourse. For instance, in example (5), the second person reiter-
ates what was introduced in the previous utterance, *sosō* 'mistake. Likewise,
in example (6), the second person repeats what was mentioned in the first
person's utterance, *keiko no iranē mono* 'things which need no practice'.
In a broad sense, *to ihe-ba* and *to ifu-tara* still function as quotes, but rather
than designating the conditional/temporal protasis, they take on the role of a
topic for the following clause.

(5)   Mankō   '*Honni*   *sosō*   *wo*   *mōshimashi-ta*'
              really   mistake   OB   say-PST
              'I made a mistake saying it.'

      Agemaki '*Sosō*   **to-ihe-ba**,   *watashi   mo   sosō   ga at-ta   wai
      na.*'
              mistake   speaking of   I   also   mistake SB have-PST SP SP
              'Speaking of a mistake, I made one, too' (*Sukeroku* 1839)

(6)   '*Keiko   no iranē   mono   nishite...*'
      rehearsing GN need-not thing   as
      'Something which needs no rehearsing...'

      '*keiko   no kakara-n mono* **to-ifu-tara**, *Chūshingura, Hiragana,*
      rehearsing GN take-not thing   speaking of <name>   <name>
      'Speaking of things which need no rehearsing, they are Chushingura,
      Hiragana,..' (*Ukiyoburo* 1809)

The 3ʳᵈ stage maintains the same topic-comment relationship, with yet
new developments: [1] X no longer has to be prompted by the previous context; [2] *to ihe-ba* and *to ifu-tara-ba* appear in their reduced forms as *tteba*
and *ttara*; [3] X typically denotes a human being (often with a pronoun)
with strong relevance to the speaker himself in the sense that the comment
is highly judgmental and subjective. In (7), the word *okusan* appended by
teba was not prompted by the previous utterance; it is a third person subject
to whom the speaker attributes his own personal evaluation. The speaker
regards her demeanor to be inappropriate and unwelcome. Similarly, in (8)
the speaker's evaluative comments are expressed for a third person subject.

(7) *Okusan **teba** (=tteba) watashi no ashimoto kara atama no teppen made*
    wife TP   I   GN toe   from head   top   to
    jirojiro mitete, totemo iyana   waraikata wo shita no.
    stare look very unpleasant smile   OB did NM
    '(To my surprise), your wife [marked with *tteba*] stared at me from the
    top of my head to my toe and sneered.' (*Ukigumo* 1949)

(8) *Sonna mono, itsu ni nattara kabureru yōni naru n da ka shireya shinai*
    no ni, [I don't know when I will be able to wear it, but]
    *otōsama-**ttara**   kinō   katte-oide- ninat-ta   no   yo ...*
    father-TP   yesterday buy-come-HOR-PST NM SP
    'my father, but (to my surprise), bought a hat for me yesterday.'
    Okashina otōsama deshō? [Isn't he funny?] (*Kaze Tachinu* 1938)

Stage 1	Stage 2	Stage 3
X *to ihe-ba* Y	X *to i(h)e-ba* Y	X *tteba* Y
X *to ihi-tara-(ba)* Y	X *to it-tara-(ba)* Y	X *ttara* Y
X= direct quote of others	X=prompted by others	X =a noun (mostly
X could be a clause	X could be a phrase	human)
temporal /conditional	topic/comment rela-	topic/comment
relation	tion	relation

Table 1. Developmental Path of Quotative Conditionals

Following from the developmental paths above, the next subsection will discuss their implications on theories of grammaticalization.

2.2. Theoretical Implications on Grammaticalization

From the perspective of grammaticalization, the developmental paths in Table 1 involve changes in three domains. First, they show phonological reduction where the initial unreduced strings coalesce as a reduced form, as shown in (1). This is consistent with a generally held view in grammaticalization literature (Lehman 1995 [1982], Traugott and Hopper 1993).

The second of the three domains is semantic. In the 1st stage an external world occurrence is matter-of-factly described, while in the 3rd stage, the topic marker adds emotive coloring to the comment. This shift is in line with what Traugott's unidirectional hypothesis referred to as 'subjectification in grammaticalization'. Traugott (1995:32) states:

> 'Subjectification in grammaticalization' is, broadly speaking, the development of a grammatically identifiable expression of the speaker belief or speaker attitude to what is said ... forms and constructions that at first express primarily concrete, lexical, and objective meanings come through

repeated use in local syntactic context to serve increasingly abstract, pragmatic, interpersonal, and speaker-based functions.

Whereas the first two domains follow the generally accepted parameters of grammaticalization, the third domain, structure, does not. Givón (1979) and Lehmann (1995 [1982], ch. 4.3) have observed that the scope decreases with grammaticalization. However, the paths here clearly show a syntactic scope increase. The positional shift to an outer and more peripheral positions, and non-embeddability of a later function into an earlier function, as in Minami (1974) (i.e., a topic cannot be embedded in a conditional clause), are indicative of scope increase (see Shinzato (forthcoming) for further discussion on syntactic scope increase). In this respect, the present study corroborates Tabor and Traugott (1998) and Onodera (2004) in reevaluating syntactic scope decrease as a definite criterion of grammaticalization.

3. A Synchronic Perspective

3.1 Differences between two topic markers

The Stage 2 unreduced forms and the Stage 3 reduced forms coexist in the current language and both function to mark topic/comment relation (cf. 'layering' in Hopper 1991). However, there are some notable divergences, as summarized below.

(9) X *to i(h)e-ba/it-tara* Y:
     (a) X has been recently introduced (or evoked) in the discourse.
     (b) The X-Y relationship is pre-established. Y is expected.

   X *tteba/ttara* Y:
     (c) X may or may not be recently mentioned.
     (d) Y is counter to expectation.

The first difference has already been mentioned in section 2. When the unreduced forms (X *to i(h)e-ba* Y and X *to it-tara* Y) are used, X tends to have been recently introduced in previous discourse as illustrated in examples (5) and (6) which we saw earlier. In the current usage, *to ie-ba* and *to it-tara* may be used without prior mention of the topic entity as in (10).

(10) *Shōgatsu*   **to it-tara**   *owarai desu.*
     New-Year speaking of   comedy CP
     'Speaking of the New Year, it is time for comedies.' (*Nobu* 417.net)

This sentence is used at the top of a web page, so there is no prior mention of *shōgatsu* 'new year.' However, even though it is not textually evoked, it is evoked nonetheless. (10) is taken from a web diary written on January 3rd. Since the New Year is a culturally significant holiday in Japan and people often take the first three days off from work, *shōgatsu* is expected to be in the reader's mind on January 3rd. By using *X to it-tara* 'if one says X; speaking of X,' the writer is treating X as if it has been textually evoked.

Based on the foregoing, we can conclude that X in *X to i(h)e-ba/it-tara* is part of the speaker's current consciousness. When X is textually evoked in the immediately preceding discourse, or when X is contextually evoked and can be assumed to be in the current consciousness, *X to i(h)e-ba/it-tara* can be used. On the other hand, the reduced forms (*X tteba/ttara Y*) do not have such contextual restrictions on X. X is 'given' by virtue of being a topic, but it does not have to be recently introduced.

The second difference between the unreduced forms (*X to i(h)e-ba/it-tara Y*) and the reduced forms (*X tteba/ttara Y*) pertains to the relation between X and Y. With the unreduced forms, the relationship is pre-established. The relation can be phrased as 'Given X, Y is expected' or 'Speaking of X, Y naturally comes to mind.' For example, the speaker of (10) assumes (or at least presents himself to assume) that people naturally think of comedies when the topic is the New Year holiday as many comedy programs are broadcast during the first three days of the New Year in Japan.

On the contrary, with the reduced forms (*X tteba/ttara Y*) Y is usually counter to expectation. For example, given the topic 'teacher' in (11), the expectation is that she be decently dressed. The comment (that she is wearing revealing clothes) betrays the expectation.

(11)   *Kono sensei*   ***tteba*** *shōgakkō*   *no kyōshi na noni*
        this   teacher TP   elemntary:shool   GN teacher CP although
        sugē   *bī*   *konshasu na fuku kite-ru*   *n*   *da yo ne.*
        awfully body conscious CP clothe is-wearing NM CP IP IP
        'This teacher ***tteba*** is wearing awfully revealing clothes even though she is an elementary school teacher.' (*Untitled* 2001:1)

(12)   *Yuka*   *ni wa sō-iu*   *ki*   *wa nai*   *kara*   *tte*
        <name> in TP that-kind intention   TP not-exist   so   QT
        kotowat-ta   *noni,*   *Harue-san*   ***tara(=ttara)***
        decline-PST   although Ms.-<name>   TP
        hijōshiki   *ni*   *shashin*   *made*   *oite-itte*
        thoughtless AV. photograph   even   leave-go
        'Although I declined (the proposal of an arranged marriage) saying that Yuka does not have that kind of intention, Harue ***ttara*** even left the photograph (of the potential groom) - so thoughtless! (*Kanai* 1995: 335)'

3.2. Counter to Expectation and Emotivity

From where does this meaning of counter-to-expectation come? Further, as seen in the above examples, sentences with *tteba* and *ttara* convey the speaker's feelings of surprise, disbelief, disapproval, and/or animosity. How did these emotions come to be embodied in these topic markers?

In exploring these questions, Quinn (forthcoming) gives us some insights. He theorizes that the Old Japanese sentence-final particle *mo* is related to the inter-clausal *mo*, which denotes inclusion 'also.' He argues that the meaning of inclusion, when what is included is something out of the ordinary, naturally leads to expressions of emotions such as surprise, ironic doubt, and despair, in the Old Japanese sentence-final particle *mo*.

We argue that this line of inferencing can be applied to the expressions in question. *X to i(h)e-ba/it-tara* literally means 'if I say (or one says) X.' Its meaning is best conveyed in English as 'speaking of X.' The expression highlights and calls attention to X. In the case of *X to i(h)e-ba/i-ttara*, this highlighting or attention-calling makes sense. Since X has just been introduced to the conversation/text, or X is a prominent entity in the extralinguistic context, drawing attention to such a new or prominent entity is a reasonable, and expected thing to do.

However, in the case of the reduced form, *X tteba/ttara*, X is neither new nor prominent necessarily. Calling attention to such an entity is an aberration from an appropriate way to introduce a topic. We believe this apparent irregularity is pragmatically motivated. Just like Quinn's account, we assert that the factor of 'counter expectation' plays a role here. We propose the following inferencing: The speaker highlights and calls attention to X even though X is neither new nor prominent > There must be a reason to call attention to X > X must be out of the ordinary and/or newsworthy > X must have attributes that are counter to one's expectation.

Because of this inferencing, Y in *X tteba/ttara Y* functions to express something about X that is counter to one's expectation. And when something is counter to one's expectation, one is likely to have an evaluative attitude or emotional reaction towards it. We argue that this is why *X tteba/ttara* is associated with emotivity.

3.3. Semantic Bifurcation

The semantic divergence between older, unreduced forms (*to i(h)e-ba* and *to it-tara*) and innovative, reduced forms (*tteba* and *ttara*) recalls the concept of 'bifurcation' proposed by Bolinger (1968:110-111). A phonetic change may result in coexisting older and new forms. When these two forms are reinterpreted to be semantically different, and the difference in meaning crystallizes in speech registers of a sizeable number of speakers, then semantic 'bifurcation' results. In concrete terms, he (ibid:110) describes the bifurcation process of the *burned* and *burnt* pair as follows:

> If I use *burned* as the past of the verb *to burn* and you happen to prefer *burnt*, and our conversation turns on the subject of something charred and

you refer to it as burnt, I may suspect that you are in possession of a formula that I lack, whereby a thing gets burned and ends up burnt...Perhaps my impression is supported by the length of the words – *burned* takes longer to say, it sounds like something going on, while *burnt* is short, like something finished.

Vance (2002) applies Bolinger's concept of bifurcation to his study of Japanese compound verbs which resulted in a phonetic split and subsequently in separate dictionary entries. Specifically he dealt with 13 pairs of compound verbs which consisted of a verbal stem, *(C)i*, followed by another verb. A phonetic change produced the *(C)i~/Q/* alternation. Vance found the member of a pair with the reduced form more colloquial and emphatic than the original regular stem member. What is particularly interesting for the present paper is the difference between *hikikomu* and *hikkomu*. Almost all of Vance's native speaker respondents said that the unreduced form *hikikomu* is transitive and that the reduced form *hikkomu* is intransitive. This suggests that the unreduced form refers to the process of pulling someone in, while the reduced form represents the end result of the inward movement, or a retreat (See Jacobsen (1992) for the correlations of transitivity/intransitivity and process/end result). This is reminiscent of Bolinger's account of *burned* and *burnt* as indicating on-going process vs. end result.

As implicated in Bolinger's analysis and also in Haiman (1985), isomorphism goes hand-in-hand with iconicity. We believe that the unreduced, long phonetic forms are more in line with the nature of quotation they still maintain ('persistence' as in Hopper 1991). The topic that *to i(h)eba* and *to it-tara* mark is a quote of what has just been introduced to the discourse. It is as if by using a quotative expression *to i(h)e-ba/it-tara*, the speaker extracts the topic from the preceding discourse or from the external context and brings it into the place of conversation. Since the topic has just been introduced to the speaker's consciousness, it takes some time before it is completely assimilated. Further, the proposition of the sentence is not presented as the speaker's original idea, but as a pre-established concept that belongs to the conventions of the world. So, the speaker communicates little emotional involvement with and is distanced from the proposition. We believe this temporal, spatial, and psychological distance is iconic with the phonetic length of the form. In contrast, the reduced form appends to what has long been assimilated in the speaker's mind (i.e., a personal familiar entity that has already been residing in the speaker's mind), and the comment for that entity is presented as the speaker's original idea, thus implicating the high endorsement by and the strong emotivity of the speaker. The instantaneity, proximity, and attachment are consistent with the short phonetic form. Additionally, the mora obstruent is noted for its forceful and emphatic tone (Nasu 1995)[5]; therefore, the reduced forms, *tteba* and *ttara* are doubly suitable for inducing emotivity. It is only natural that an emotionally charged statement with a sharp accusatory tone seen in (11) and (12) takes the reduced form, not the unreduced form (cf. Hui 2003).

When a similar semantic bifurcation between short and long forms exists, there may be tendencies for the short form to be more expressive than the long form. This contrast is also observed in the Kansai dialect of Japanese and in Korean. Horie and Kondo (2004) note that of the two negation forms, *n* and *hen* in the Kansai dialect, the short form *n* has become specialized to express the speaker's subjective attitude. The short form is preferred when the speaker wants to impose his/her will on the addressee more strongly.

Sohn and Park (2003) compare the two most frequently used forms of indirect quotations in Korean: the short form *–tay* and the long form *–ta(ko) ha-*. They observe that while the speaker focuses more on the source of relevant information in using the long form, s/he is likely to express his/her subjective involvement such as emotion and evaluation when using the short form. Their iconicity-alluded remark (ibid: 116) that "the conceptual distance between narrative and narrated speech is greater with the long form than with the reduced form" is in line with the view presented here.

4. Conclusion

This paper was a study of the two quotative conditionals, *to i(h)e-ba*, and *to it-tara*. Diachronically, we have delineated the developmental paths of these quotative conditionals to topic markers. We then analyzed the paths in the framework of the grammaticalization theories. The paths do conform to the general tendencies recognized in the theories such as phonetic reduction and subjectification, but they come at odds with the advocated position of the syntactic scope decrease, since they vouch for the syntactic scope increase.

Synchronically, we compared the coexisting older unreduced and newer reduced phonetic variants. We pointed out their semantic difference as 'expected' vs. 'counter-expected' topic-comment relationships. Incorporating the concept of isomorphism, we attempted to explain the difference to be iconically motivated.

We hope the present study contributes in expanding the scope of the study of topic markers in Japanese by offering a data-driven account of less

---

[5] In her research on the speech of male speakers in Japanese, Sreetharan (2004: 285) observes that there may be a correlation between rude or gruff speech and 'hyper-geminated' forms (that is, forms with a mora obstruent). This supports the association of mora obstruents with forceful and emphatic tone.

studied expressions. We also hope that the present study contributes to the study of grammaticalization with new data from Japanese.

References

Bolinger, D. 1968. *Aspects of Language*. New York: Harcourt, Brace, and World.

Givón, T. 1979. *On Understanding Grammar*. New York: Academic Press.

Haiman, J. 1978. Conditionals Are Topics. *Language* 54:564-589.

Haiman, J. 1985. *Natural Syntax*. Cambridge: Cambridge University Press.

Hayes, S. T. and R. Shinzato. 2001. Jōken no Setsuzoku Joshi kara Danwa/taijin Kinō no Joshi e -- *Tara, Ttara* no Bunpōka. *New Directions in Applied Linguistics* 2, eds. M. Minami and Y. S. Alam, 127-142. Tokyo: Kuroshio Shuppan.

Hopper, P. J. 1991. On Some Principles of Grammaticalization. *Approaches to Grammaticalization*, ed. E. C. Traugott and B. Heine, 17-36. Amsterdam and Philadelphia: John Benjamins.

Horie, K. and M. Kondō. 2004. Subjectification and Synchronic Variation: Two Negation forms in Kansai Dialect of Japanese. *Language, Culture, and Mind*, eds. M. Achard and S. Kemmer, 445-459. Stanford: CSLI.

Hui, H. 2003. Hanashi Kotoba ni Okeru 'To Ieba' 'To Ittara' no Imi Kinō Henka. *Dai-ikkai Nagoya Daigaku Nihongo Kenkyō Shōkai Yokōshū*: 30-33.

Jacobsen, W. 1992. *The Transitive Structure of Events in Japanese*. Tokyo: Kuroshio Shuppan.

Kuno, S. 1973. *The Structure of the Japanese language*. Cambridge, MA: MIT Press

Lehmann, C. 1995[1982]. *Thoughts on Grammaticalization*. München: LINCOM.

Maynard, S. K. 2002. *Linguistic Emotivity*. Amsterdam: John Benjamins Publishing Co.

Minami, F. 1974. *Gendai Nihongo no Kōzō*. Tokyo: Taishukan Shoten.

Nasu, A. 1995. Kyōchōka to Tokushu Mōra no Sentaku: Onomatope o Chūshin ni. Paper Presented at Kansai On'inron Kenkyūkai (PAIK), May 15th, Kobe University.

Onodera, N. 2004. *Japanese Discourse Markers*. Amsterdam/Philadelphia: John Benjamins.

Quinn, C. Jr. In press. *Mo* than Expected: From Textual to Expressive with an Old Japanese Clitic. *Emotive Communication in Japanese*, ed., S. Suzuki. Amsterdam/Philadelphia: John Benjamins.

Sakakura, A. 1993. *Nihongo Hyōgen no Nagare*. (Iwanami Seminaa Bukkusu 45). Tokyo: Iwanami Shoten.

Saegusa, R. 1999. Teidai no 'Tteba', 'Ttara'. *Hitotsubashi Daigaku Ryūgakusei Sentā Kiyō*, vol. 2:1-11.

Shinzato, R. Forthcoming. (Inter)subjectification, Japanese Syntax and Syntactic Scope Increase. (to appear in *Journal of Historical Pragmatics*).

Sreetharan, C. S. 2004. Japanese Men's Linguistic Stereotypes and Realities: Conversations from the Kansai and Kanto Regions. *Japanese Language, Gender, and Ideoplogy: Cultural Models and Real People*, eds. S. Okamoto and J. S. Shibamoto Smith, 275-289. New York: Oxford University Press.

Sohn, S.-O. and M.-J. Park. 2003. Indirect Quotations in Korean Conversations. *Japanese/Korean Linguistics,* volume 11, ed. P. M. Clancy, 105-118. Stanford: CSLI.

Suzuki, R. 1999. Multifunctionality: The Developmental Path of the Quotative *tte* in Japanese. *Cognition and Function in Language*, eds. B. A. Fox, D. Jurasky and L. A. Michaelis, 50-64. Standard: CSLI.

Suzuki, S. 1998. *Tte* and *Nante*: Markers of Psychological Distance in Japanese Conversation. *Journal of Pragmatics* 29:429-462.

Tabor, W. and E. C. Traugott. 1998. Structural Scope Expansion and Grammaticalization. *The Limits of Grammaticalization*, eds. A. G. Ramat and P. Hopper, 229-272. Amsterdam/Philadelphia: John Benjamins Publishing Company.

Takanashi, S. 1995. Hisetsutekina X *Nara* nitsuite. *Fukubun (jō)*, ed. Y. Nitta, 167-187. Tokyo: Kuroshio Shuppan.

Traugott, E. C. 1995. Subjectification in Grammaticalization. *Subjectivity and Subjectivisation*, eds. D. Stein and S. Wright, 31-54. Cambridge: Cambridge University Press.

Traugott, E. C. and P. Hopper. 1993. *Grammaticalization*. Cambridge: Cambridge University Press.

Yoshida, K. 1971. *Gendaigo Joshi Jodōshi no Shiteki Kenkyū*. Tokyo: Meiji Shoin.

Vance, T. 2002. Semantic Bifurcation in Japanese Compound Verbs. *Japanese/Korean Linguistics 10,* eds. N. M. Akatsuka and S. Strauss, 365-377. Stanford: CSLI.

Frequency Effects in Grammaticalization: From Relative Clause to Clause Connective in Korean

SUNG-OCK SOHN
University of California, Los Angeles

1. Introduction[1]

A corpus-based approach to grammaticalization reveals that frequency analysis based on large collections of language production can provide evidence for language change. Increased frequency of a construction over time offers statistical proof for grammaticalization (Hopper and Traugott 2003). This paper investigates the role of frequency in grammaticalization by examining the evolution of the clause connective -*nuntey* 'and, and so, then, but, however' in Korean, as illustrated in (1) and (2) below.

(1) Relative clause: 'the place where ...'
    kalbi cal   ha-**nun tey** a-sey-yo?
    kalbi well   do-nun tey   know-Subj Honorific-POL
    'Do you know a good place for *kalbi* (Korean barbecue)?'[2]

---

[1] I would like to express my gratitude to Professor Kyu-Dong Yurn for his insightful comments on historical texts. The Yale system is used in this paper for the transcription of Korean.
[2] Literally, sentence (1) means 'Do you know a place which makes *kalbi* very well?'.

(2) Clause connective 'and; but; however; while'
pi-ka   o-**nuntey**   wusan-i   eps-eyo.
rain-NM   fall-nuntey   umbrella-NM   not have-DEC-POL
It is raining *nuntey,* I don't have an umbrella.'

As shown in the above examples, *-nuntey* is used in a variety of syntactic and semantic contexts. For instance, *-nuntey* in (1) functions as a prenominal relative clause which consists of *-nu* (indicative mood)-*n* (relativizer) and the head noun *tey* 'place' (H. Sohn 1999:306). The head noun *tey* in (1) functions as the grammatical object of the sentence, as shown in English translation.[3] In (2) *-nuntey* is used as a clause connective which provides circumstantial background for the main clause event (K. Lee 1993, H. Lee 1999). Note further that in (2) what precedes the connective *-nuntey* and what follows it express a contrastive relationship, similar to 'but' in English as shown in the translation (i.e., 'It's raining, but I don't have an umbrella.'). Thus, many scholars have identified the connective *-nuntey* as a contrastive marker (cf. H. Choi 1965, H. Kim 1992, Y. Park 1999).[4] In addition, *-nuntey* is often used in utterance-final position without being followed by a main clause (cf. Y. Park 1999).

The polysemy of *-nuntey* is further observed in the ambiguous meaning of the following example (3).

(3) anc-ki   silh-**untey**   anc-ula-ko   hay-yo.[5]
sit-NOM   dislike-nuntey   sit-IMP-QT   say-POL
a. '(He) is telling me to sit down although I don't want to.'
b. '(He) is telling me to sit down in a place where I don't want to.'

In the above, the meaning of *-nuntey/-untey* is ambiguous between a concessive/contrastive meaning as in (3a) and the lexical meaning 'place' as in (3b). The locative particle *-ey* 'at; in' can be added after *-nuntey/-untey* for the interpretation of (3b).[6]

Previous studies of *-nuntey* focus on its synchronic variations and discourse functions in contemporary Korean (C. Ha 2003, H. Lee 1999, K. Lee 1993, Y. Park 1999). Although these studies describe cognitive and semantic/pragmatic functions of *-nuntey* in modern Korean, there has been little attempt at a corpus-based analysis of its diachronic development from the perspective of grammaticalization. Using a large-scale corpus drawn from

---

[3] The place noun *tey* is a defective noun which requires a modifying element.
[4] H. Lee (1999) claims that many contrastive *-nuntey* clauses serve to provide a background situation as well.
[5] The variants of *-nuntey* include *-untey/ntey* attached to adjectives.
[6] The Korean orthography requires a space before *tey* for a 'place' meaning.

Sejong historical texts,[7] this paper examines the emergence of the clause connective -*nuntey* and its grammaticalization path.

The historical data for this study consists of a total of 28 documents ranging from the earliest records written in Korean (i.e., fifteenth century) until the nineteenth century (total of 3,453,941 words). In addition, spoken corpus (157, 546 words) drawn from naturally occurring conversation is used to examine a frequency effect in grammaticalization and phonological reduction.[8]

2. Historical Development of -*nuntey*

The analysis of the *Sejong* historical corpus reveals that both the relative clause and the clause connective -*nuntey* coexisted in the earliest historical records written in Korean. -*Nuntey* is found in the fifteenth century texts with variants such as -*(u)ntAy*, -*nAntAy*, and -*nuntAy*.[9] The contexts where -*nuntey* occurs in are quite similar to those of modern Korean. It is observed in the following two contexts: i) in a relative clause construction (including adnominal clause) which modifies the head noun *tey* whose lexical meaning is 'place; location', and ii) at a clause connective position where -*nuntey* expresses a background circumstance for the following main clause event. Consider example (4) where -*nuntey* functions as relative clause 'the place where...'.

(4) wang-i   kenik-i   po-si-kon   thayca ka-si-**n   tAy**
     king-NM   *kenik*-NM   see-SH-and   prince go-SH-RL place
     ka-lye   hA-te-si-ni
     go-in   order to d o-RT-SH-and
     'The king saw *Kenik* (Buddha's servant) and wanted to go to <u>the place</u> <u>where</u> the prince went.' [*sekposangcel* 1447]

In the above, the defective noun *tAy* (> *tey*) 'place' is preceded by a noun modifying form -*n* (relativizer), and functions as the head noun of the relative clause. It is used as a locative argument of the verb *ka*- 'to go'.

While the use of -*nuntey* as relative clause (i.e., 'place' meaning) is quite prevalent in the fifteenth century texts, example (5) shows that -*nuntey* functions as clause connective.

(5) kwangcelmwuin-tAlh-An sayngsa-i   cangwenhA-**n tAy**
     kwangcelmwuin-PL-TOP   longevity-NM   long-<u>nuntey</u>

---

[7] The *Sejong* corpus has been compiled since 1998 under the auspice of the National Academy of the Korean Language.
[8] The spoken corpus is based on Sung-Ock Sohn's personal compilation.
[9] The symbol 'A' in the Korean transcription refers to the vowel '*alay* (low) a' in middle Korean, which is equivalent to the vowel 'a' in contemporary Korean.

cinsil-s   cikyen eps-e
truth-INTER   wisdom not exist-and
'They (*kwangcelmwuin*) have longevity, but they don't have wisdom
for the truth.' [*pephwakyeng* 1463]

The use of *-nuntey* in (5) does not express a place meaning, but behaves like
a contrastive connective.

Although both the relative clause construction and the clause connective
are attested in the earliest records written in Korean, there is evidence that
the clause connective *-nuntey* originates in the relative clause construction.
Specifically, frequency analysis of the *Sejong* historical corpus reveals a
consistent pattern over time in the distribution of *-nuntey*.

2.1. Statistical Results

Table 1 below illustrates the overall frequency of *-nuntey* and its distribution in relative clauses and clause connectives in the fifteenth through nineteenth century.[10]

Period	Text size	Raw Frequency	Normal- ized	Relative clause	Clause connective
15th C.	710346	81	114	79/81(97.5%)	2/81 (2.4%)
16th C.	265278	59	222	31/59 (52.5%)	28/59 (47.6%)
17th C.	399755	106	265	41/106(38.7%)	65/106 (61.1)
18th C.	1010364	952	942	18/95 (18.9%)	77/95 (81.1%)
19th C.	480126	592	1,233	8/59 (13.6%)	51/59 (86.4%)

Table 1. Frequency of *-nuntey* in 15th C. through 19th C.

For the distributional pattern of relative clause vs. connective *-nuntey*, raw
frequency was used for the fifteenth through seventeenth century. For the
eighteenth and nineteenth century since the raw frequency is large, the size
is reduced to one tenth size. Thus, a total sampling of 95 tokens are used for
the eighteenth century and 59 tokens for the nineteenth century. Every one
tenth is chosen according to a chronological order. In addition, each occurrence of *-nuntey* is analyzed according to its function, i.e., relative clause vs.
clause connective. For instance, in the fifteenth century texts, out of a total
of 81 raw tokens there were only two instances of *-nuntey* as clause connective whereas the rest were used as relative clauses (2.4% vs. 97.5%). In the

---

[10] For an accurate count of frequency in Table 1, original Chinese version as well as Korean
texts were examined. The normalized frequency is based on the occurrence per one million
words.

sixteenth century, the ratio of relative clauses and clause connectives is 52.5% vs. 47.5%, showing a drastic increase in the use of clause connective. The normalized frequencies (Biber 1995:75-76) in Table 1 reveal that there are noticeable changes in the semantic and syntactic distribution of -*nuntey* over five centuries. Specifically, three important facts are observed in Table 1. First, the use of -*nuntey* in relative clauses is predominantly more frequent than the use of the clause connective construction in early texts. Second, there is an overall increase in the frequency of -*nuntey*, in particular in its use in the clause connective position over time. Third, the use of -*nuntey* in relative clauses decreases whereas its use as clause connective continues to increase over time.

The statistical result is illustrated in Figure 1 and Figure 2 below.

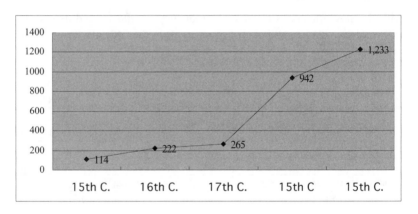

Figure 1. Overall Frequency of -*nuntey*

As illustrated in Figure 1, the historical development of -*nuntey* exhibits that overall the frequency of -*nuntey* increases over time. For instance, the normalized frequency of -*nuntey* in the fifteenth century is 114 tokens, in the sixteenth century 222 tokens, 265 tokens in the seventeenth century, 942 tokens in the eighteenth century, and 1,233 tokens in the nineteenth century.

In addition, Figure 2 exhibits the ratio of relative clause (-*nu-n tey*) and the clause connective (-*nuntey*). The relative clause construction is predominantly more frequent than the use of the clause connective construction in the fifteenth and early sixteenth centuries. Out of a total of 81 raw frequency of -*nuntey* in the fifteenth century, only two tokens are found in the connective function. In particular, in *welinsekpo* (1459) and *nungem* (1461), all the instances of *tey* except for the lexical use (e.g., *han-tey* 'outside' *kaon-tey* 'in the middle') occur in a relative clause construction. Out of a total of 31 tokens of *-nuntey* (12 tokens in *welinsekpo* and 19 tokens in *nungem*), there was no instance of the clause connective *-nuntey*. These texts reflect the earliest writing in Korean, and the dominating frequency of the relative clause *-nuntey* in the fifteenth century texts indicates that the clause connective *-nuntey* is a later development than that of the relative clause construction. The overall increase in the frequency of *-nuntey* over time as shown in Figure 1 is thus the result of the increase of the clause connective *-nuntey*; the relative clause becomes grammaticalized into clause connective.

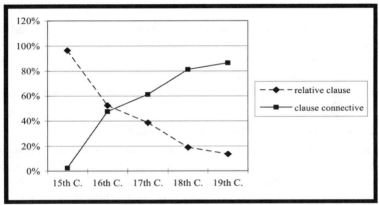

Figure 2. Distribution of *-nuntey*

The distribution of *-nuntey* in the fifteenth century shows a sharp contrast with that of *-nuntey* in modern Korean. Table 2 below based on Ha (2003) illustrates the distribution of *-nuntey* in modern written discourse.

	Relative clause	Clause Connective	Utterance-final	Lexical-ized	Total
Frequency	28	77	26	4	**135**
Percent	20%	57%	20%	3%	**100%**

Table 2. The distribution of *tey* in written discourse (Source: Ha 2003)

As indicated in Table 2, the clause connective *-nuntey* is more frequently used than relative clause constructions in modern Korean. While 77 out of a total of 135 tokens of *-nuntey* (57%) are found in clause connectives, only 28 instances of *-nuntey* (20%) are used in relative clause constructions.[11] Considering that utterance-final use of *-nuntey* is an extended form of the

---

[11] In Table 2, the lexicalized use of *tey* includes examples such as *kulen tey* 'such a place'.

clause connective, the percent of the connective *-nuntey* is much higher than 57%.[12]

Cross-linguistic evidence reveals that a place noun tends to develop into a locative meaning and locative markers are a common source for causal markers (Heine & Kuteva 2002:239). Supporting evidence for the locative significance of *-nuntey* is shown in the co-occurrence of *-nuntey* with the locative particle *-yey* (> *-ey*) 'at; in', as shown in (6).

(6) namo alay   isy-om-kwa   han   **tAy-yey**   isy-om-kwa
    tree under be-NOM-and   outside place-LOC   be-NOM-and
    'Being under a tree and being <u>outside place</u>, and ...' [*welinsekpo* 1459]

In the above, the *-nuntey (< -ntAy)* form occurs with the locative particle (*-yey* > *-ey* 'at; in') and functions as the locative argument of the existential verb *isi-* 'to exist'. The locative meaning of *-nuntey* is reinforced by the subsequent locative particle *yey*. The co-occurrence of the connective *-nuntey* with the locative particle is frequently observed in modern Korean as well.

2.2. Ambiguity Between Place and Background
Another crucial piece of evidence for the development of the clause connective *-nuntey* from the relative clause is the existence of the ambiguity of the *-nuntey* construction in middle Korean texts. Note that in the following example drawn from the fifteenth century text, the meaning of *-nuntey* is ambiguous between the interpretation of a relative clause ('the place where') and that of a clause connective.

(7) kamaoti se-s-nyek hAy picwi-yeys-nA-**n tAy** nAlkay mAloy-nola
     cormorant west-INS-side sun shine-PST-<u>nun tey</u> wing dry-in order to
     koki cap-nAn tolh-ay kAtAkhA-yas-tota
     fish catch-RL ditch-LOC full-PST-DEC   [*twuhaycho* 1481]

     (a) 'At <u>a place where</u> sun is shining from the west, there are lots of cormorants drying their wings in a ditch where people catch fish.'

     (b) '<u>While</u> sun is shining from the west, there are lots of cormorants drying their wings in a ditch where people catch fish.'

In the above, there are two possible readings: a relative clause (i.e., 'at a place where sun shines') as in (7a) and a clause connective which expresses backgrounding information as in (7b).[13] In other words, the propositional content of the *-nuntey* clause serves not only as a location for the situation

---

[12] See Y. Park (1999) for the discourse function of the utterance-final *-nuntey*.
[13] While most Korean scholars interpret the meaning of *tey* as 'place' in (7), U. Lee (1990:47) notes that it is ambiguous between relative clause and clause connective meanings.

in the following clause, but can be interpreted as circumstantial information for the subsequent situation. Given the inherent lexical meaning of *tey* 'place', it seems quite natural that the source meaning of -*nuntey* 'the place' gives rise to a locative meaning. Once -*nuntey* acquires a locative meaning, it permits further semantic interpretations such as backgrounding or circumstantial information for a main clause event.

The ambiguity of (7) above indicates that -*nuntey* was being grammaticalized in the fifteenth century from the relative clause to clause connective. The full semanticization and grammaticalization of -*nuntey* to clause connective is evidenced when -*nuntey* is no longer interpreted as place or locative. For instance, consider the following instance of -*nuntey* in the early sixteenth century.

(8) salAm mek-ul   kes-to   eps-**un tAy**
     people eat-RL   thing-even not exist-<u>nun tey</u>
     sto   etuy   ka mAl   mek-ul khongtip   kacyeo-lyo
     again where   go horse eat-RL bean-leaves bring-INT
     'While there is nothing for people to eat; where can I go and fetch bean leaves for horses?' [*nokeltay* 1517]

In the above, the meaning of place is no longer associated with *tey*. The -*nuntey* marked clause above serves as the ground for the following rhetorical question (i.e., "There is nothing for people to eat-*ntAy;* where can I find and bring bean leaves for horses?").

The connective -*nuntey*, introducing a main clause, invites the conversational inference that a negative or dispreferred situation would follow (cf. Y. Park 1999). Such an inference seems to have played a major role in the grammaticalization of -*nuntey* as clause connective. In such cases, the main function of -*nuntey* is to express circumstantial or backgrounding information for the main clause situation.[14] The conversational inference associated with -*nuntey* (e.g., circumstantial information or the grounds for the situation) becomes dominant over the meaning of 'the place where' from the seventeenth century.

The diachronic evidence presented here points to four stages of grammaticalization. These are illustrated in Table 3 below.

---

[14] See H. Lee (1999) for a figure-ground approach to the grammaticalization process.

Stage	Syntactic position	Function/meaning
I	Lexical noun	*Tey* is used as a lexical noun meaning 'place'.
II	Relative clause *-nu-n tey*	*Tey* functions as the head of a relative clause 'the place where'.
III	Adverbial clause *-nu-n tey-(ey)*	The locative meaning of *tey* gives rise to a new meaning (i.e., circumstance) in certain contexts.
IV	Clause connective *-nuntey*	The relative clause *-nu-n tey* is reanalyzed as clause connective *-nuntey*.

Table 3. Linguistic Evolution of *-nuntey*

In Stage I, *tey* is used as a lexical noun, but in Stage II it attaches to the preceding relativizer *-nu-n* and functions as the head noun of a relative clause. Stage III is a transitional phase from relative clause to clause connective. While the meaning of *tey* in Stages I and II expresses a concrete, physical location, in Stage III *tey* indicates a circumstance.

Note that a major morpho-syntactic change is involved in the development of the connective *-nuntey* out of a relative clause construction. The reanalysis from a relative clause into clause connective *-nuntey* is accompanied by a reduction in a morpho-syntactic boundary between the modifier *-nu* (indicative) *-n* (relativizer) and the head noun *tey* ('place'). As a result, the morpho-syntactic boundary between *-nun* and *tey* becomes obscured at Stage IV. The morpho-syntactic fusion is also reflected in the orthography of contemporary Korean. That is, when *tey* expresses a lexical meaning of place (e.g., Stages I, II and III), the Korean orthography requires a space between the preceding word and *tey*, whereas the connective *-nuntey* in Stage IV above is spelled without any spacing.

Furthermore, in early stages *tey* refers to a specific and physical content such as 'place' (Stage I and II). However, as it is grammaticalized further, its semantic entity moves toward a more abstract level, indicating circumstantial information for the following main clause event (Stage III and IV).

The development of the connective *-nuntey* out of a relative clause involves syntactic contiguity of the relativizer *nu-n* and the defective noun *tey* 'place'. As discussed in Hopper and Traugott (2003:87-93), the semantic changes arising out of contiguity in linguistic contexts are known as "associative" or "conceptual metonymic". The semantic change from a lexical noun describing a physical location to a grammatical marker of clause connective involves the association of a physical location with a more abstract concept of circumstantial information. As the frequency of this association increases within a speech community over time, the relative clause *-n-un tey* is reanalyzed as a clause connective (*-nuntey*).

The discussion thus far indicates that the clause connective *-nuntey* derives from a relative clause construction. Based on the sharp increase in the frequency of *-nuntey* in Table 1, the grammaticalization of relative clause into clause connective appears to take place actively around the sixteenth century, though the first instance of the clause connective *-nuntey* is observed in a fifteenth century text.

3. Phonological Reduction and Frequency Effects

With increased frequency, the boundary between the erstwhile relativizer *-nu-n* (> *-nun*) and the head noun disappears, leading to the reanalysis (*-nu-n + tey* > *-nuntey*) as reflected in modern orthography.

The "reduction effect" in frequently used items (Bybee and Hopper 2001) is further observed in a phonological contraction in relatively recent conversational data. The spoken corpus for this study shows that when -*nuntey* is attached to the demonstrative predicate *kuleh-* 'be such a way', the form (*kulen-tey* 'by the way; but') is often contracted into *kuntey,* as illustrated below.

(9) pwa cwu-l   salam-i   hwaksilha-myen nah-ul   swu-to   iss-ci
     take care-RL person-NM be sure-if give   birth-RL DN-also exist-COM
     kuntey kulehci-ka   anh-unikka
     but   be such a way-NM not-because
     'If I can be sure to find someone who can take care of my baby, then I could have a baby. But since that's not the case ....'

In the above, the discourse connective *kuntey* derived from the full form *kulentey* connects two discourse segments with a contrastive meaning. While the full and reduced forms seem to be interchangeable in (9) above, the reduced form is preferred over the other in spoken discourse.[15]

Table 4 illustrates the skewed frequency of the full form (9.4%) and the reduced form (90.6%) in naturally occurring conversation. These results are taken from Sohn spoken corpus which contains approximately 23 hours of naturally occurring conversation.

	Full form	**Reduced form**	**Total**
Frequency	93 (9.4%)	896 (90.6%)	989

Table 4. Frequency of *kulentey* and *kuntey*

---

[15] The discourse connective *kulentey/kuntey* is used to shift from one topic to another.

As illustrated in Table 4, the reduced form is predominantly more frequent than the full form in spoken discourse. The frequency of the reduced form is nearly ten times higher than that of the full form. It is also to be noted that the full form *kulentey* includes both the discourse connective and a referential usage. Specifically, out of a total of 93 instances of *kulentey* in Table 4, 59 instances are discourse connective whereas the rest (34 tokens) are used for referential meaning such as a place noun or pro-predicate 'be such a way'. On the other hand, all the instances of the reduced from *kuntey* are used as discourse connective as shown in (9). In other words, when *kulentey* retains its referential meaning (i.e., *kulen tey* 'such a place'), it does not get reduced. This suggests that the frequency effect is constrained by the original lexical meaning. Consider the following example where the full form *kulen tey* retains its original lexical meaning of 'place'.

(10) taumey   mwe   target-ina **kulen tey**   ka-se sa-ya-kess-ta.
    next time what   target-or <u>such place</u>   go-and buy-OBLG-will-DEC
    'Next time, I will have to buy one at a place like Target.'

In (10) above, it would be unacceptable to use the reduced form *kuntey* in the place of the full form (*kulen tey*). The resistance to phonological reduction is due to the original lexical meaning of *tey* 'place'. In other words, *kulentey* is subject to phonological reduction only in contexts where its referential meaning is lost.

The phonological reduction of the discourse connective *kulentey* supports the notion that frequency of use affects sound change (Bybee and Hopper 2001). Since -*nuntey* combined with the demonstrative predicate *kuleh*- 'be such a way' is more frequently used as a discourse connective than for referential meaning (i.e., 'such a place'), the discourse connective is more likely to undergo a formal reduction.

4. Conclusion

Using statistical evidence for the frequency of -*nuntey* drawn from a large corpus of historical data, this paper examined the empirical evidence for the grammaticalization of the clause connective -*nuntey* from the erstwhile relative clause construction. Statistical analysis of the historical corpus has illustrated that in early texts (15th C.-16th C.), -*nuntey* is predominantly more frequent in relative clauses than as a clause connective. Its frequency in relative clauses, however, has decreased sharply over the past five centuries whereas the use of -*nuntey* as a clause connective has become dominant over time. This skewed distribution provides empirical evidence for the diachronic cline from relative clause 'the place where' to clause connective.

The frequency effect in the grammaticalization of -*nuntey* is manifested in reanalysis and a formal reduction. With increased frequency, a morphosyntactic boundary between the erstwhile relativizer -*nu-n* and the head noun (*tey*) disappears, leading to the reanalysis of relative clause (-*nu-n* + *tey* 'the place where') into clause connective (-*nuntey*).

The polysemy associated with -*nuntey* in contemporary Korean reflects the meanings of -*nuntey* in various stages of the grammaticalization of -*nuntey*. The development of -*nuntey* from the earlier relative clause construction ('the place where') to the clause connective follows the general tendency of grammaticalization. It also follows the general regularity of semantic changes (from referential to subjective) found in the process of grammaticalization.

Finally, this study demonstrates the frequency effect in grammaticalization by examining the phonological reduction of the discourse connective *kulentey* (> *kuntey*) 'by the way'. The corpus-based analysis of the discourse connective has shown that the reduction takes place only when the lexical meaning of the source form is lost, suggesting that reduction effect is constrained by semantics. In short, this study illustrates that quantitative corpus study is a useful tool in providing empirical evidence for a suspected grammaticalization.

References

Biber, D. 1995. *Dimensions of Register Variation*. Cambridge University Press.

Bybee, J. and P. Hopper. (Eds.) 2001. *Frequency and the Emergence of Linguistic Structure*. Amsterdam: John Benjamins Publishing.

Ha, C. 2003. Tey Ccaimwel-uy Mwunpephwa Kwaceng Yenkwu (A Study on the Grammaticalization Process of the Tey Constituent Sentence). *Hangul* 261:97-121. Seoul: Korea.

Heine B. and T. Kuteva 2002. *World Lexicon of Grammaticalization*. Cambridge: Cambridge University Press.

Hopper, P. and E. G. Traugott. 2003. *Grammaticalization*. Cambridge: Cambridge University Press.

Lee, H. 1999. Grammaticalization of the Korean Connective -*nuntey*: A Case of Grammaticalization of Figure-ground Relation. Paper Presented on the First New Reflections on Grammaticalization Symposium. Potsdam, Germany.

Lee, K. 1993. *A Korean Grammar: On Semantic-Pragmatic Principles*. Seoul: Hankwuk Mwunhwasa.

Lee, U. 1990. *Wulimal Iumssikkuth-uy Thongsicek Yenkwu* (A Diachronic Study of Connective suffixes in Korean). Seoul: Emwunkak.

Park, Y. 1999. The Korean Connective -*nuntey* in Conversational Discourse. *Journal of Pragmatics* 31:191-218.

Sohn, H. 1999. *The Korean Language*. Cambridge: Cambridge University Press.

Part III

Phonology and Morphology

Prosodically Conditioned Ellipsis and Lexical Integrity in Sino-Japanese Morphology

HITOSHI HORIUCHI
The University of Texas at Austin

1. Introduction[1]

Lexical Integrity is a general property of grammatical words such that no syntactic process is allowed to refer to their subparts (Spencer 1991, Bresnan 2001). Bresnan and Mchombo (1995) (hereafter B&M) propose the following objective criteria.[2]

(1) Criteria for Lexical Integrity

    a. **inbound anaphoric islands**: subparts of words disallow an anaphoric use. E.g. *McCarthy-ism*, **him-ism*

    b. **phrasal recursivity**: subparts of words disallow arbitrarily deep embedding of syntactic phrasal modifiers. E.g. [A *happi*]-*ness*, **[AP quite happi]-ness*, **[AP more happy than sad]-ness*

    c. **conjoinability**: subparts of words cannot be coordinated. E.g. *joyful-ness and cheeri-ness*, **joyful- and cheeri-ness*

---

[1] I would like to thank Leo Hanami for proofreading an earlier draft of this paper.
[2] I ignore B&M's other criterion called extraction (i.e. subparts of words disallow extraction such as topicalization or relativization) since it is not relevant to our discussion.

    d.   **gapping**: subparts of words cannot be gapped. E.g. *John liked the play and Mary, the movie.* **John liked the play, and Mary dis- it.*

These criteria can be used to identify grammatical words in most cases, but there are apparent exceptions to conjoinability (1c) and gapping (1d), as B&M point out. Specifically, subparts of complex nouns in Italian and Dutch can be coordinated (Booij 1985, Nespor 1984: e.g. *infra- e ultra-suoni* 'infrasounds and ultrasounds', *Freund- oder Feind-schaft* 'friendship or hostility').

B&M's solution to the problem is to assume that the apparently sublexical conjoining and gapping involve a phonological process called **Prosodically Conditioned Ellipsis (PCE)** rather than a syntactic process. For example, *infra-e ultra-suoni* is analyzed as involving an ellipsis of a phonological word in the first conjunct (i.e. *infra-ₗᵥsuoni e ultra-ₗᵥsuoni*: N.B. ᵥₗ__ represents a phonological word).

The goal of this paper is to defend B&M's criteria of lexical integrity and their PCE analysis of the apparent exceptions to the criteria, based on Japanese data. In particular, I will defend a hypothesis about the lexical integrity of a type of Sino-Japanese (S-J) morpheme complex (Horiuchi 2004) and explain the apparently sublexical conjoining and gapping on the basis of a PCE analysis.

In Section 2, I will introduce the S-J morpheme complexes dealt in this paper, two incompatible hypotheses about their grammatical wordhood, and a problem of apparently sublexical conjoining and gapping. A PCE analysis of the conjoining/gapping is presented in Section 3. The PCE analysis predicts a prosodic ambiguity of a class of S-J morpheme complex. In Section 4, I argue for existence of the prosodic ambiguity and present how to resolve it, to support our PCE analysis.

2. Problem: Apparently Sublexical Conjoining and Gapping in Sino-Japanese Morpheme Complex

In this paper, I examine S-J morpheme complexes, which are made up of a **Temporal Morpheme (TM)** combined with a preceding S-J **Verbal Noun (VN)**. There are two types of TMs that are morphologically distinct.

(2)   Two types of TMs:
    a.   **TM1**: directly concatenated with the preceding VNs (cf. temporal affix: Hoshi 1997)
        E.g.   *kenkyuu*   +   {*tyuu/go/izen/*...}
             research   during/after/before/...
        'during/after/before research'

b. **TM2**: intervened by the morpheme *no* when combined with the preceding VNs (cf. temporal noun: Shibatani and Kageyama 1988)

E.g. *kenkyuu* (+ *no*) + {*sai/ori/...*}
　　 research　NO　　　　　case/occasion/...
'in case of/on the occasion of research'

　　Horiuchi (2004) proposes the following hypothesis about the grammatical wordhood of the S-J morpheme complex. I will refer it to as Hypothesis 1.

(3)　Hypothesis 1: A TM is not an independent word but a suffix (i.e. [VN-TM]) under a verbal projection, while it is a full-fledged word (i.e., [VN][TM]) under a nominal projection.

Hypothesis 1 reflects the fact, with respect to inbound anaphoric islands, that a VN alone can be replaced by a pronoun under a nominal projection (4a, 4a'), which requires a genitive case marking within it, while the VN disallows replacement by a pronoun under a verbal projection (4b, 4b'), which allows a verbal case such as a Nominative or an Accusative on the arguments.[3]

(4)　Mary-wa　　iroirona　　gengo-no　　　kenkyuu$_i$-o　　sita.
　　 Mary-TOP　　various　　language-GEN　research-ACC　did
　　 'Mary studied various languages.'

　　a.　kanojo-no　　Ainugo-no　　sore$_i$　　izen,
　　　　 her-GEN　　　Ainu-GEN　　it　　　　before
　　　　 (John-wa　　ronbun-o　　happyoo-sita.)
　　　　 John-TOP　　paper-ACC　　presentation-did
　　　　 'Before her research of Ainu, (John presented his paper.)

　　b.　*kanojo-ga　　Ainugo-o　　sore$_i$　　izen,
　　　　 her-NOM　　　Ainu-ACC　　it　　　　before

　　a'.　kanojo-no　　Ainugo-no　　sore$_i$　　no-sai,
　　　　 her-GEN　　　Ainu-GEN　　it　　　　NO-case
　　　　 (John-wa　　ronbun-o　　happyoo-sita.)
　　　　 John-TOP　　paper-ACC　　presentation-did
　　　　 'In case of her research of Ainu, (John presented his paper.)'

　　b'.　*kanojo-ga　　Ainugo-o　　sore$_i$　　no-sai,
　　　　 her-NOM　　　Ainu-ACC　　it　　　　NO-case

---

[3] Horiuchi (2004) discusses the correlation between case marking and category in Japanese.

Hypothesis 1 also reflects the fact, with respect to phrasal recursivity, that a VN alone allows modification by an adjectival phrase in a nominal projection (5a, 5a'), while it does not in a verbal projection (5b, 5b').

(5) a. John-no   sono ronbun-no   kibisii hihan go,
       John-GEN   the paper-GEN   severe criticism after
       (Mary-ga   syohyoo-o kaita.)
       Mary-NOM   review-ACC wrote
       '(Mary wrote a review) after John's severe criticism of the paper.'

    b. *John-ga   sono ronbun-o   kibisii hihan-go
       John-NOM   the paper-ACC   severe criticism-after,

    a'. John-no   sono ronbun-no   kibisii hihan no-sai,
       John-GEN   the paper-GEN   severe   criticism   NO-
                                          case,
       (Mary-ga   syohyoo-o kaita.)
       Mary-NOM   review-ACC wrote
       '(Mary wrote a review) in case of John's severe criticism of the paper.'

    b'. *John-ga   sono ronbun-o   kibisii hihan no-sai,
       John-NOM   the paper-ACC   severe criticism NO-case,

Under Hypothesis 1, both types of TMs in (2) behave equally as words or suffixes. Nevertheless, application of the criteria of conjoinability or gapping leads to the following alternative hypothesis.

(6) Hypothesis 2: TM1 is a suffix (i.e. [VN-TM1]), while TM2 is a word (i.e. [VN][TM2]).

Regarding conjoinability, VN (+TM1) or (VN+) TM1 cannot be coordinated in (7a, 8a), while VN (+TM2) or (VN+) TM2 can in (7b, 8b).

(7) a. *John-ga ainugo-o   kenkyuu-   to   tyoosa-tyuu
       John-NOM   Ainu-   research-   and   survey-mid
       ACC
       'during John's research and survey on Ainu'

    b. John-ga ainugo-o   kenkyuu-   to   tyoosa-no-sai
       John-NOM   Ainu-   research-   and   survey-NO-
       ACC   case
       'in case of John's research and survey on Ainu'

(8)   a.   *John-ga ainugo-o   kenkyuu-tyuu   to   –go
            John-NOM   Ainu-   research-mid   and   –after
            ACC
            'during and after John's research on Ainu'

       b.   John-ga   ainugo-o   kenkyuu-no-sai   to   -ori
            John-NOM   Ainu-   research-NO-case   and   -occasion
            ACC
            'in case of and on the occasion of John's research on Ainu'

Regarding gapping, TM1 cannot be gapped in (9a) while TM2 can in (9b).

(9)   a.   *(John-wa)   ainugo-o   kenkyuu-~~tyuu~~,
            John-TOP   Ainu-ACC   research-~~during~~,
            (Mary-wa)   maorigo-o   tyoosa-tyuu,
            Mary-TOP   Maori-ACC   survey-during,
            (ronbun-o   happyoo-sita.)
            paper-ACC   presentation-did
            '(John presented a paper) during his study of Ainu
            and (Mary) during her survey of Maori.'

       b.   (John-wa)   ainugo-o   kenkyuu-~~no-sai~~,
            John-TOP   Ainu-ACC   research-~~NO-case~~,
            (Mary-wa)   maorigo-o   tyoosa-no-sai,
            Mary-TOP   Maori-ACC   survey-NO-occasion,
            (ronbun-o   happyoo-sita)
            paper-ACC   presentation-did
            '(John presented a paper) in case of his study of Ainu
            and (Mary) on the occasion of her survey of Maori.'

Since every VN+TM complex in (7) through (9) appears under a verbal projection, Hypothesis 1 should predict that every TM is just a suffix and cannot explain the word-like behavior of TM2. To maintain Hypothesis 1, one must explain the apparently sublexical conjoining and gapping in (7b), (8b) and (9b).[4]

3. A Prosodic Analysis of Conjoined/Gapped Elements

Regarding the two incompatible hypotheses given above, my position is that Hypothesis 1 but not Hypothesis 2 should be maintained, since no explana-

---

[4] In nominal projections, the VN+TM complex also shows the same behavior as the one in (7) through (9) regarding conjoinability and gapping, though the illustration is omitted due to the space limit. In the nominal projections, Hypothesis 1 predicts that the TM is a word, in spite of the nonword behavior of TM1.

tion for data (1) and (2) can be found under Hypothesis 2, while an explanation for the apparently sublexical conjoining and gapping in (3) through (5) can be given by assuming the following phonological process, which is based on a rule-based definition proposed by Booij (1985).

(10) Prosodically Conditioned Ellipsis (optional)
Omit X iff (i) there is an identical string as X in another conjoined part, (ii) $X = w^m$ $m \geq 0$ (where w is a phonological word), and (iii) X is adjacent to a conjunction or a clause boundary.

The Prosodically Conditioned Ellipsis (PCE) in (10) is a phonological process, which allows a phonological word (or phrase) to be elided under the identity with another phonological word (or phrase). The phonological word may coincide with a grammatical word, but only the former is subject to the phonological process.[5]

Given the PCE, the data (7, 8) that serve to motivate Hypothesis 2 in (6) are reanalyzed as follows.

(11) a. *[$_w$kenkyuu-~~tyuu~~] to [$_w$tyoosa-tyuu] (cf. 7a)
research-~~during~~ and survey-during

b. *[$_w$kenkyuu-tyuu] to [$_w$~~kenkyuu~~-go] (cf. 8a)
research-during and ~~research~~-after

(12) a. [kenkyuu-$_w$~~no-sai~~] to [tyoosa-$_w$no-sai] (cf. 7b)
research-~~NO-case~~ and survey-NO-occasion

b. [$_w$kenkyuu-no-sai] to [$_w$~~kenkyuu-no~~-ori] (cf. 8b)
research-NO-case and ~~research-NO~~-occasion

Under PCE analysis, the elided elements (i.e. *no-sai, kenkyuu-no*) in (12) can be taken as phonological words, which happen to coincide with subparts of grammatical words. In contrast, elements that cannot be elided (i.e. *tyuu, kenkyuu*) in (11) are taken as nonprosodic constituents.

The data (9a, 9b), which also serve to motivate Hypothesis 2, are given an alternative account by PCE. It provides the same kind of operation as gapping (i.e. elision), but the former is a phonological process rather than a syntactic process. Thus, the elided element, *no-sai*, in (9b) is taken as a phonological word rather than a subpart of a grammatical word. In contrast, a nonelided element, *tyuu*, in (9a) is not counted as a phonological word.

As above, under PCE analysis, apparent conjoining or gapping is counted as a prosodic ellipsis, so that I can avoid the problem of sublexical

---

[5] (10iii) excludes a possibility of ellipsis of VN (e.g. *John-wa ainugo-o no-sai, ...*).

conjoining or gapping and do without abandoning Hypothesis 1. The result of PCE analysis suggests that a TM1, a TM2, or a VN alone does not form a phonological word.[6] Interestingly, under PCE analysis, phonological word-hood is given to a segment made up of a TM2 and the preceding morpheme *no* (e.g. *no sai*) or the one made up of a VN and the following morpheme *no* (e.g. *kenkyuu no*). That is, PCE analysis predicts the prosodic ambiguity of VN *no* TM2: $_w$VN-*no*, and $_w$*no*-TM2. The following will demonstrate that the prediction is borne out, from a phonological viewpoint, to support PCE analysis.

4. Prosodic Ambiguity of VN *no* TM2 and Its Resolution

I assume here that the prosodic ambiguity of the VN *no* TM2 discussed in this section arises from and is resolved by the following mechanism.

(13)　Prosodic Ambiguity Resolution: suppose that a phonological requirement, A, allows $_w$VN-*no*, while another phonological requirement, B, allows $_w$*no*-TM2. The following requirement rankings disambiguate the prosodic constituency of VN-*no*-TM2.
　　　a. Requirement A >>Requirement B: [$_w$VN-*no*-TM2]
　　　b. Requirement B >>Requirement A: [VN-$_w$*no*-TM2]

In short, I assume that prosodic ambiguity can be attributed to two competing phonological requirements and resolved by their ranking.

4.1. Requirement A: Nonfinality

Let us begin with Requirement A in (13). It licenses $_w$VN-*no* as a phonological word. I assume that it is Nonfinality, a requirement that no prosodic head should be final in phonological words (Kubozono 1995, Prince and Smolensky 1993, Tanaka 2001). It predicts that no phonological word can have a lexical accent on its final mora, assuming that a prosodic head contains the lexical accent (In Japanese, the lexical accent is a pitch fall (') from H(igh) to L(ow)). Following Nasu (2001), I argue that every noun must be followed by a particle to maintain Nonfinality and to obtain the status of phonological word. Consequently, $_w$VN-*no*, a subset of Noun + Particle, should form a phonological word.

　　Nasu's first argument is based on the accent associated with a class of mimetic words. A mimetic word such as *(pika)pikaQ, (poki)pokiQ*, or

---

[6] The fact that a VN or a TM2 alone cannot serve as a phonological word can be illustrated by comparing the following ill-formed examples with well-formed ones in (12a, 12b).
(i) *kenkyuu-no-~~sai~~ to tyoosa-no-sai
(ii) *kenkyuu-no-sai to ~~kenkyuu~~-no-ori

(koro)koroQ appears to violate Nonfinality in that the lexical accent falls onto the final mora, as follows.

(14) a. (pika)pika'Q   b. (poki)poki'Q   c. (koro)koro'Q
'glistening'   'snapping'   'rolling'

> N.B. Q stands for part of a long consonant or a geminate. It forms a mora with a preceding CV string. That is, *kaQ*, *kiQ*, and *roQ* are made up of one mora, respectively.

However, such a mimetic word, in fact, conforms to Nonfinality by assuming that Noun + Particle forms a phonological word. In fact, each mimetic word in (14) must be followed by the particle *to*, when it is used as an independent word, as in (15).

(15) (pika)pika't-*(to), (poki)poki't-*(to), (koro)koro't-*(to)

Another argument put forth by Nasu is based on the following fact. An unaccented noun, *hasi*, is ambiguous and associated with distinct meanings. The meaning of *hasi* is determined or disambiguated when the noun followed by a nominative case-particle like *ga* is associated with different accents, as in (16).

(16) a. ha'si-ga (H'LH)   b. hasi'-ga (LH'L)   c. hasi-ga (LHH)
chopstick-NOM   bridge-NOM   edge-NOM

In particular, the fact that not only the meaning of *hasi* (LH) but also its accentuation (i.e. *hasi'* or *hasi*) cannot be determined without being followed by a particle, as in (16b, 16c), suggests that attachment of the particle is a part of the phonological word-formation of nouns. Furthermore, unless Noun + Particle serves as a phonological word, one cannot explain the lexical accent on the final mora of the noun *hasi* in (16b), causing a violation of Nonfinality.

4.2. Requirement B: Pre-*no* Deaccenting Rule

Next, I assume that Requirement B in (13), which licenses $_w$*no*-TM2 as a phonological word, is a phonological rule called Pre-*no* Deaccenting (McCawley 1968, Poser 1984), as follows.

(17) Pre-*no* Deaccenting
$[_{N1} …\mu'] \, no \, [_{N2} …] \rightarrow [_{NP} …\mu \, no \, …]$

This rule predicts that a lexical accent on the final mora of a noun is deprived by the subsequent particle *no*. For example, a noun like *uma* (LH) 'horse', which can place its lexical accent on the final mora when it is followed by a particle like *ga* (i.e. *uma'-ga*: LH-L), is de-accented if it is followed by the genitive particle *no*, as in *uma-no* (LH-H) '(the) horse's'.

To explain why Pre-*no* Deaccenting licenses the phonological word-dhood of ${}_w$*no*-TM2, let us consider the prosodic function of the particle *no*. On the one hand, the particle *no* serves to deprive a lexical accent from the preceding noun. On the other hand, it serves to preserve a lexical accent of the subsequent noun. In general, the deprivation (or loss) of the lexical accent takes place when a unit smaller than a word is demoted from a word, while the preservation of lexical accent takes place when a unit larger than a word is built from words. Kubozono et al. (1997)'s classification of N-N compounds is based on the loss or the preservation of the lexical accent in their member nouns, as follows.

(18) A Classification of Prosodic Constituency in N-N Compounds

	N1	N2
a) word	lost	lost
b) phrase	preserved	preserved
c) subphrase?	lost	preserved

According to the classification, a typical N-N compound is formed when the member nouns lose their lexical accents as in (18a). In contrast, a phrase-like N-N compound is formed when the member nouns preserve their lexical accents as in (18b). In addition to these two types of N-N compounds, Kubozono et al. claim that there exists a type of N-N compound whose first member loses its lexical accent and whose second member preserves it, as in (18c), although there is no type of N-N compound whose first member preserves its lexical accent and whose second member loses it. The following examples correspond to (18a), (18b), (18c), respectively.

(19) a. *sa'ttyaa* (HLLL) + *seiken* (LHHH)
        Thatcher   +   administration
        = [${}_w$*sattyaa-se'iken*] (LHHH-HLLL)
        'the Thatcher administration'

    b. *sa'ttyaa* (HLLL) + *syusyoo* (LHH)
        Thacher   +   premier
        = [${}_w$*sat'tyaa-${}_w$syusyoo*] (HLLL-LHH)
        'Prime Minister Thatcher'

    c. *nyu'u* (HL) + *karedonia* (LHHHH)
        new   +   Caledonia
        = [*nyuu-${}_w$karedonia*] (LH-LHHHH) 'New Caledonia'

Let us go back to the function of the particle *no*. Proposing classification (18), Kubozono et al. point out that the function of the particle *no* patterns with the third type of N-N compound (18c) in that it deprives a lexical accent from the preceding noun and preserves a lexical accent of the subsequent noun. Or, in other words, the function of the particle *no* is to deprive phonological wordhood from the preceding noun and to preserve phonological wordhood for the subsequent noun. To satisfy both the deprivation and preservation of phonological wordhood, I assume that the particle *no* forms a phonological word with the subsequent noun and it does not form a prosodic constituent with the preceding noun, as shown in (20a). Similarly, the same prosodic constituency is given to the VN *no* TM2, as in (20b).

(20) a. *uma'* (LH)   +   *no*   +   *i'tiba* (HLL)
          Horse   +   GEN +   Market
          = [*uma-ₙno-i'tiba*] (LH-H-HLL) 'a horse market'

      b. *kenkyuu* (LHHH)   +   *no* + *sa'i* (HL)
          research   +   NO + case
          = [*kenkyuu-ₙno-sa'i*] (LHHH-H-HL)
          'in case of research'

The above discussion explains why Pre-*no* Deaccenting licenses the phonological wordhood of ₙ*no*-TM2. The particle *no* cannot attach to the preceding noun to form a phonological word, since it contributes to complex phonological constituency (18c), avoiding an impossible accent pattern.

References

Booij, G. E. 1985. Coordination Reduction in Complex Words: A Case for Prosodic Phonology. *Advances in Nonlinear Phonology,* eds. H. van der Hulst and N. Smith, 143-160. Dordrecht, Holland: Foris.

Bresnan, J. and S. A. Mchombo. 1995. The Lexical Integrity Principle: Evidence from Bantu. *NLLT* 13:181-252.

Horiuchi, H. 2004. Lexical Integrity, Head Sharing and Case Marking in Japanese Temporal Affix Constructions. In *Proceedings of the International LFG 04 Conference.* http://cslipublications.stanford.edu/LFG/9/lfg04.html

Kubozono, H. 1995. Constraint Interaction in Japanese Prosody: Evidence from Compound Accent. *Phonology at Santa Cruz 4*:21-38.

Kubozono, H., J. Ito, and A. Mester. 1997. On'in-koozoo kara Mita Go to Ku no Kyookai [The Phonological Boundary between Word and Phrase: An Analysis of Japanese Compound Noun Accentuation]. *Onsei to Bunpoo 1 [Speech and Grammar 1],* ed. Onsei Bunpoo Kenkyuukai [Spoken Language Working Group], 147-166. Tokyo: Kurosio Publishers.

McCawley, J. D. 1968. *The Phonological Component of a Grammar of Japanese.* Hague: Mouton.

Nasu, A. 2001. Onomatope no gokeisei to akusento [Word formation and Accent in Onomatopoeia]. *Nihongo Nihon-bunka Kenkyuu [Studies on Japanese language and Culture]* 11:9-24.

Nespor, M. 1984. The Phonological Word in Italian. *Advances in Nonlinear Phonology,* eds. H. van der Hulst and N. Smith, 193-204. Dordrecht: Foris.

Poser, William. 1984. *The Phonetics and Phonology of Tone and Intonation in Japanese.* Doctoral dissertation, MIT.

Prince, A. and P. Smolensky. 1993. Optimality Theory: Constraint Interaction in Generative Grammar. Manuscript, Rutgers University and University of Colorado, Boulder.

Spencer, A. 1991. *Morphological Theory.* Oxford: Blackwell.

Tanaka, S. 2001. The Emergence of the 'Unaccented': Possible Patterns and Variations in Japanese Compound Accentuation. *Issues in Japanese Phonology and Morphology,* eds. J. van de Weijer and T. Nishihara, 159-192. Berlin: Mouton de Gruyter.

The Feature Hierarchy of Korean Consonants in Speech Errors

Busan College of Information Technology

1. Introduction

Consonants take up a central part in phonological theories of speech sounds. Many have poured out genuine efforts in characterizing their substructures according to the phonetic features associated, and applied feature geometric findings to give meaningful accounts of various phonological processes.

On the other hand, the research on speech error has gained popularity among linguists over decades, as the slips data provide useful evidence regarding the structure of linguistic units and their interactions in the mind. However, in Korean, relatively few have attempted to incorporate such a psycholinguistic result into developing their theoretical framework. Little has been known about which consonant features play a dominant role in speech production. It is also unknown whether unmarked features in phonology do function as weak or covert elements by the influence of marked counterparts in adjacency.

So, the current paper aims to deepen our knowledge of consonantal features, highlighting their functional roles during a speech production based on slips of the tongue from a natural corpus.

210

2. The Study

2.1. Speech Error

Whether conscious or unaware, people participate in making speech errors in everyday conversation. Dell (1986: 286) defined speech errors as "unintended, nonhabitual deviations from a speech plan." Thus, simple repetitions, hesitations, stutterings, and inappropriate utterances are unable to be qualified as slips of the tongue. The speaker's insufficient, or habitually erroneous expressions are also far from speech errors. According to Poulisse (1999), there are two criteria in determining speech errors. First, there must be an error as a result of certain problems in performance like a lack of attention. Second, the error must be repairable by the speaker.

In collecting slips of the tongue, some researchers have used a pen-and-paper method, often tape-recording the errors. Others employ a tongue-twisting experiment to detect spontaneous errors. The former method has been criticized for being variant in the ability of detecting errors relative to listeners, whereas the latter for orienting errors to be artificial and restricted in pattern. Recently, criticisms on impressionistic transcription by the researcher have increased, as some cast doubts on the transcriber's capability of perceiving actual sound changes due to his or her own perceptual biases. In particular, Frisch and Wright (2002) and Pouplier and Goldstein (2004) suggest that there exist not only categorical but also gradient changes requiring careful instrumental measurements in speech error experiments.

2.2. Methods

The slips data for the current study were collected from talks on the radio and TV, and from natural dialogues engaged or overheard. I have utilized a pen-and-paper method, writing down the error-carrying sentences or phrases verbatim. For precise encoding, part of the errors were tape-recorded and transcribed carefully after multiple listening.

After having monitored slips for over three years, I was able to gather a total of 350 substitution errors of consonants caused by a shift into a neighboring, incorrect segment. Of 350 slips, 222 errors (63%) occurred in spontaneous speech, and the remaining 128 (37%) in a reading mode. In most cases, the speakers seemed to be well aware of their slips in production as there existed a brief moment of a pause or an on-time correction by the speaker. For instance, 291 errors (83%) were self-corrected by the speaker immediately after the release of a slip during the speech. This extremely high proportion of self-corrections on time seem to play a significant role in minimizing possible perceptual biases or prejudices that the transcriber might have, so that the data which didn't go through thorough phonetic analysis could be as reliable as possible.

2.3. Results

The overall pattern of interactions between the target and intruding segments in errors are illustrated in Table 1. Each row in Table 1 shows the extent of all the intruding segments with which the target consonant was replaced, while each column refers to the extent of all the target segments for which the intruding consonant was substituted.

For instance, a labial stop /p/ in target form was erroneously replaced with a homorganic nasal and aspirated stop /m, p^h/ for 5 times each, with other lax stops and affricate /t, k, c/ 3 times on average, and with a velar glide once. However, as the intrusion, /p/ was involved in errors by substituting for /m/ 8 times, /k/ 5 times, /p^h/ 4 times, /t/ twice, and /p', c, mj^1/ once each. All these substitution errors of /p/, whether it played as the target or intrusion, were restricted to the interactions between segments carrying the same place feature [+labial] or whose laryngeal configurations were lax.

The aspirated counterpart /p^h/ was also changed into either labials varying in a laryngeal or manner type (9 slips, 64%), or heterorganic aspirated segments (5 slips, 36%). Among the 8 intrusive errors of /p^h/, the majority of them were concerned with substituting for /p/.

In contrast, substitution errors of the tense /p'/ were numbered only 5 – 2 target errors into a homorganic stop and 3 intrusions for /p^h/. Similarly, the errors of /p^h, p'/ exhibit an interrelation between segments sharing the same place feature of [+labial] or with a marked glottal feature.

On the other hand, the nasal /m/ was usually paired with a labial stop, or other nasals at a different place of articulation. It also showed an infrequent substitution with a liquid or glide in errors, implying the importance of such manner features in common as [+nasal] and [+voice].

The results in Table 1, first, demonstrate that consonant substitution in slips of the tongue is a rather complicated phenomenon, requiring a detailed analysis using place, manner and laryngeal features.

Second, there existed an asymmetry in the substitution rates of obstruents depending on their laryngeal type. That is, lax consonants had the highest frequency of substitution errors both as the target and intrusion (T: 174, I: 155), whereas aspirated consonants had an intermediate number of errors (T: 47, I: 47), and tense counterparts had the least (T: 10, I: 7). The

---

[1] Glides /j, w/ are not assumed as a consonant in this paper, nor are they even when preceded by another consonant. Based on speech error data, Kang (2003) hypothesized that they be generated from the nucleus like a vowel, but they can be associated with the onset during the speech production planning due to the option provided at the periphery of the nucleus.

	p	t	k	c	s	h	pʰ	tʰ	kʰ	cʰ	p'	t'	k'	c'	s'	m	n	ŋ	l	j	Cj	w	Total
p	–	3	4	2			5									5						1	20
t	2	–	2	22	3			4								1	4		4				42
k	5	2	–	2	2				2							2	4	4	5				28
c	1	13	4	–	24					9									1	2	k-3		57
s		2	3	13	–	1				6									2				27
h		2		1	2	–																	5
pʰ	4						–	1	2	2	3					2							14
tʰ		1						–	1	4													6
kʰ									–				1										1
cʰ				12	8		1	3	1	–											pʰ-1		26
p'							1				–	1											2
t'												–											0
k'									1	1			–										2
c'										1		1		–									2
s'					2					1					–						s-1		4
m	8															–	1	4	1	1			15
n		3	2	1	2											4	–	10	11	1			34
ŋ			6	2	1											3	12	–	10				31
l		6	2	2	1											1	5	2	–	1			20
j						1														–			2
Cj	m-1	cʰ-1	h-1	k2,pʰ1	h-1				k-1												–		9
Cw										kʰ1,pʰ2												–	3
Total	22	33	25	59	46	2	8	8	7	24	3	2	1	0	1	19	26	20	34	4	5	1	350

Table 1. Confusion Matrix for Korean Consonants. (350 tokens: Target (vertical) vs. Intrusion (horizontal))

errors of the lax series were three times over the sum combined by the aspirated and tense. Moreover, almost a half of all the errors were caused by the lax obstruents.

This asymmetry among the obstruents seems to be partly attributable to the rate of frequency. Lexical items that carry the lax series in the base form are the most common, and thus most frequently spoken and heard during a speech, which maximizes the possibility of engaging in slips of the tongue. In contrast, lexical words including a fortis consonant in the underlying representation are relatively small in number, and thus, tense as well as aspirated segments will have a relatively low chance of being substituted in speech production. However, the apparent fewer violations by the tense than the aspirated sounds unresolved due to the lack of the full-scaled research on the frequency bias in relation to the segment type.

The sums of the target and intrusion rates for each consonant are as in the following:

C

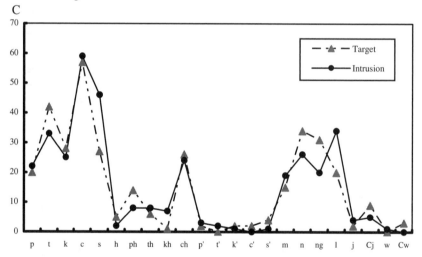

Figure 1. Target and Intrusion Rates for Korean Consonants

As seen in Figure 1, typical errors occurred in association with lax obstruents, nasals, and a liquid. In contrast, aspirated obstruents showed a relatively smaller distribution of slips, while tense consonants involved in errors were the least in number with only 17. In particular, the lax fricative /s/ and liquid /l/ were found to function as an intruding segment much more often than as the target with a difference of 19 and 14 respectively. On the other hand, the alveolar stop /t/, alveolar and velar nasals /n, ŋ/ turned out to be fairly weaker segments with a higher tendency of replacement by intruding segments.

3. Discussion

First of all, the frequency rates of occurrence were found to be greatly varied relative to consonant type, and this asymmetry seems largely attributed to the differences across place, manner and laryngeal features associated. To examine the hierarchy of feature distribution, I chose 12 features individually – labial, alveolar, palatal, velar, stop, sibilant, nasal, liquid, voice, spread glottis, stiff vocal cords, and constricted glottis –, and grouped them into 3 categories, namely, place, manner and laryngeal, as in (1):

(1) The 12 features chosen
    a. Place: labial, alveolar, palatal, velar
    b. Manner: stop, sibilant, nasal, liquid
    c. Laryngeal: voice, spread glottis, stiff vocal cords, constricted glottis

You can see the full picture of feature assignment across each phoneme from the table in (2). The Korean consonants consist of labials, alveolars, palatals, and velars in terms of the place of articulation, and their manner and glottal characterizations are just as indicated in the table below:

(2) Korean consonants[2]

	Labial				Alveolar							Palatal				Velar			
	p	p'	pʰ	m	t	t'	tʰ	s	s'	n	l	c	c'	cʰ	j	k	k'	kʰ	ŋ
Stop	+	+	+	-	+	+	+	-	-	-	-	+	+	+	-	+	+	+	-
Sibilant	-	-	-	-	-	-	-	+	+	-	-	+	+	+	-	-	-	-	-
Nasal	-	-	-	+	-	-	-	-	-	+	-	-	-	-	-	-	-	-	+
Liquid	-	-	-	-	-	-	-	-	-	-	+	-	-	-	-	-	-	-	-
Voice	-	-	-	+	-	-	-	-	-	+	+	-	-	-	+	-	-	-	+
Spread	-	-	+	-	-	-	+	+	-	-	-	-	-	+	-	-	-	+	-
Stiff	-	+	+	-	-	+	+	-	+	-	-	-	+	+	-	-	+	+	-
Constricted	-	+	-	-	-	+	-	-	+	-	-	-	+	-	-	-	+	-	-

---

[2] Although Korean has 21 consonants in its inventory, the glide /w/ and fricative /h/ were excluded in counting the number of tokens, because their occurrences were extremely low in frequency, and they were associated with either more than two places of articulation or none. Besides, substitutions with a cluster of consonants that often occurred in association with a palatal glide were also removed from the calculation. Therefore, the total number of tokens included for the analysis of feature variation was 325 errors.

To determine a featural value for controversial segments, I further used the slips data as crucial evidence for the appropriate feature specification. For example, Kim (1997, 1999, 2001) argues that Korean affricates are alveolars, rather than a palato-alveolar as traditionally assumed, with findings from her articulatory and acoustic study. However, the slips data indicate that out of 14 slips for the palatal glide /j/, the majority (11 slips, 79%) originated from an unlawful interchange between an affricate /c/ and /(C)j/ or between /cʰ/ and /Cʰj/, respectively, as exemplified in (3).³ Such a high propensity between the affricates and palatal glide cannot be taken into account unless we assume the two share the same place feature, namely [+palatal].

(3)

    a. /c/→/j/: sɛ.lo konjancʰənjakce ... koɲcaŋ-cʰənjakce-lɨl   silsiha-jə
        new   *error*   factory-contract-Obj perform-Conj
        'As they perform a new factory contract,'
    b. /lj/→/c/: a.cu so.caŋ ... so-ljaŋ-ɨ   pjən.hwa-ka   sɛn.ki.nɨn
        very *error* small-amount-of change-Subj   occur-Conj
        'A very small amount of change occurs, and '
    c. /cʰ/→/pʰj/: ~pʰjən.pu ... cʰəŋ.pu-sal.in-ɨl   cə.ci.lɨn
            error   contract-murder-Obj   commit-Comp
        '(To cover her love affair, she) hired a contract murderer'
    d. /kʰj/ → /cʰ/ : jək.sa-e   ta   pal.cʰə ... pal.kʰjə-cip.ni.ta
        history-in   all   *error*   be revealed-become
        'All will be revealed in the history'

Moreover, Iverson (1983) and Kang (2000) point out that /s/, despite being a lax, has a heavy aspiration, more equivalent to the aspirated series. In line with this claim, the slips data showed that /s/ interacted with an aspirated (15 slips, 21%) more often than a lax stop, and also exhibited a wider range of selection even with a heterorganic segment /cʰ/ (14 slips, 19%), with which a typical lax is prohibited to interact. The observed correlation between a lax /s/ and aspirated /cʰ/, as shown in (4), supports the view above that the /s/ is [-stiff vocal cords] as a lax, but [+spread glottis] like an aspirated.

(4)

    a. /s/→/cʰ/ : sin.cəp cʰal.lim ... sal.lim-ɨl   cʰa.rjəs'.sɨp.ni.ta
        new   *error* housekeeping-Obj prepared

---

³ The slips are transcribed phonemically in this paper, omitting an allophonic variation like a voiced stop or flap [ɾ] in an intersonorant environment.

'(We) prepared a new housekeeping (after marriage)'
b. /cʰ/→/s/: cʰwekɨn sǝŋnjǝn ... c̲ʰǝŋnjǝn s̲ilǝp-i cɨŋkaha-nɨn
recenty error young people unemployment-Sub increase
'Recently, unemployment for young people increases'
c. /tʰ/→/s/: apʰɨ-ɾiɾako-nɨn saŋsaŋ-to mot s̲ɛs'.... mot h̲ɛs'-ki t'ɛmune
sick-will-Comp imagine-even not error not do-because
'Since (I) didn't even think that (he) would be sick,'

Besides, in accordance with Clements (1999), I treat affricates as identical to stops, rather than a composite of a stop + fricative. In fact, affricates maintain not only the 3-way distinction of lax, tense, and aspirated, but they are subject to various phonological processes, just like a genuine stop. However, the slips data also indicate that fricatives were used predominantly as substitutes for affricates, and vice versa, as revealed in Table 1. As a result, to capture a high correlation in substitution errors between fricatives and affricates, I add the terminology of sibilants in place of [+strident], just as I label stops as [stop], instead of [-continuant], to ease the conceptualization.

When analyzed in accordance with the feature specifications in (2), Korean consonants were found to be violable in the order of Place (207) > Manner (177) > Laryngeal (119), as illustrated in Figure 2:

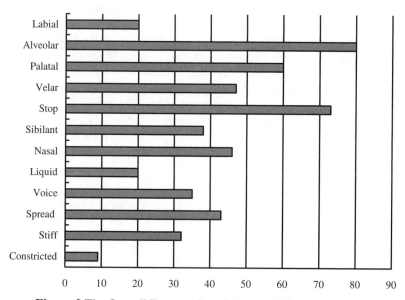

Figure 2 The Overall Frequencies of Feature Deletion in Errors

That place features are the most susceptible to errors seems to have a cross-linguistic validity, as previous pen-and-paper research usually came up with a similar outcome, irrespective of languages in corpora (Wan 1999, Jaeger 1992, Berg 1985, Dell 1980).

However, the current study is of importance in a sense that it shows a clear and complete within-category ranking that previous studies fail to clarify: namely for Place (alveolar > palatal > velar > labial), Manner (stop > nasal > sibilant > liquid) and Laryngeal (spread glottis > voice > stiff vocal cords > constricted glottis).

Among the 4 place features, [alveolar] was the most vulnerable to feature change, and thus equipped with the least capability of preserving itself. In a way, this supports the basic tenet of underspecification, where alveolar (or coronal) is regarded as the least marked or unmarked place of articulation (Mohanan 1993, Paradis and Prunet 1991). Since alveolars are represented as unmarked, unspecified in terms of place feature, they are more likely to be targeted by adjacent segments at a marked, specified place of articulation during speech production.

However, contrary to a widely assumed place assimilation ranking of velar > labial > alveolar in Korean (see Jun 1996, Iverson and Kim 1987), a velar in target form was less often replaced with a nonvelar than [labial] with a nonlabial. The current result suggests labial could be the most marked member in the place class of Korean, and a more careful research on phonological processes and their asymmetrical relationship concerning place would be worth trying.[4]

When it comes to manner, [stop] was the most influenced and thus weakest feature, whereas [liquid] was subject to deletion least of the time as the most marked. Given that categories with the largest inventory such as alveolars and stops became the primary target in error as the unmarked, the size of inventory or frequency (meaning that the bigger the category is, the more frequent it may appear) seems more or less inversely correlated with markedness. That is, high frequent sounds are typically replaced by less frequent or more marked counterparts in slips of the tongue (see Goldrick 2002).

---

[4] Many agree that a morpheme-final labial can assimilate to a following velar like /ip'wear'+ko'and'/ → [ipko], [ikko] in a fast speech, but a velar doesn't assimilate to a following labial, as in /kuk'soup'+pota'better than/see' / → [kukpota],*[kuppota]. That is why a velar is considered higher than a labial in markedness hierarchy. However, I've noticed that people do pronounce a coda velar as a labial in assimilation to a following labial, as in /cʰɛk'book'+pota/→[cʰɛkpota] , [cʰɛppota]. Why not people stop assimilating a velar into a labial, while they do so the other way around? Isn't that impression originated from a naïve judgment that a labial using lips sounds more marked than a coronal and velar, whose main articulator is the tongue?

However, the inventory itself cannot be served as the sole determiner of markedness ranking in substitution. The feature [sibilant] is associated with 5 phonemes, larger than [nasal], which contains three. However, the latter with a smaller inventory turned out to be replaced more often than the former. In addition, [palatal], [velar], and [labial] have the same inventory size, but their substitution outcomes varied significantly.

In the case of laryngeal features, [spread glottis] was found to be the most frequently deleted, while [constricted glottis] the least. When compared with the others, the feature [constricted glottis] was hardly involved in error with such a low frequency rate as 9 in total.[5] Besides, the feature [stiff vocal cords], which has the largest inventory with 9 members in it, violated less frequently than [spread glottis] or [voice], as many of the errors ended up pertaining the [stiff] feature by changing into a tense or an aspirated.

4. Conclusion

Consonants have been one of the key issues in the study of Korean language. However, few attempt to test the theories of Korean consonants in the use of psycholinguistic evidence. I have gathered 350 consonant-related errors from natural talks or readings, and analyzed them in terms of segment types, and features involved.

The results indicate, first, that alveolars are the unmarked or the least marked consonants in Korean, in the sense that they show the highest vulnerability in contact with other segments, signaling the lowest tendency to preserve itself (see De Lacy 2002 and Goldrick 2002 for further discussion). In contrast, velars and labials function as more marked consonants, and the labials were found to the highest in the strength of preservation. So far, velar stops have been claimed to be more marked than coronals and labials with respect to assimilation processes. The current psycholinguistic outcomes point out that more study is needed to verify the hierarchy of consonant place.

Secondly, there exists asymmetry in the markedness of consonantal features, and the rankings were found to be in the order of Laryngeal > Manner > Place. The more errors it tends to attract, the less marked status it may have.

In particular, the [constricted glottis] feature was the most resistant to feature change, while [alveolar] and [stop] were the most susceptible to

---

[5] Kang (2004) mentions that the feature [constricted glottis] is not only redundant but also misleading in characterizing Korean consonants. She insists rather [stiff vocal cords] is the feature distinguishing the tense from lax, as well as the lax from the tense and aspirated combined.

substitution as the least marked features, partly due to their larger inventories and more chances of pooling unlawful exchanges between the target and intrusion. Nevertheless, the inventory alone can't account for the observed ranking that goes to the opposite of the inventory size or for the categories with the same number of inventory.

References

Berg. T. 1985. Die abbildung des sprachproduktionprozesses in einem aktivationsflussmodell. Untersuchungen an deutschen und englischen. Versprechuern. Doctoral dissertation. University of Braun-Schweig.

Clements, G. N. 1999. Affricates as noncontoured stops. *Item order in language and speech*, eds. O. Fujimura, B. Joseph & B. Palek, 271–299. Prague: Charles University Press.

De Lacy, P. 2002. The formal expression of markedness. Doctoral dissertation. University of Massachusetts at Amherst.

Dell, G. 1980. Phonological and lexical encoding in speech production. Doctoral dissertation. University of Toronto.

Frisch, S. A. and R. Wright. 2002. The phonetics of phonological speech errors: An acoustic analysis of slips of the tongue. *Journal of Phonetics* 30:139–162.

Goldrick, M. A. 2002. Patterns of sound, patterns in mind: phonological regularities in speech production. Doctoral dissertation. Johns Hopkins University.

Iverson, G. K. 1983. Korean S. *Journal of Phonetics* 11:191–200.

Iverson, G. K. and K-H. Kim. 1987. Underspecification and hierarchical feature representation in Korean consonantal phonology. *CLS* 23(2): 182–198.

Jaeger, J. 1992. Phonetic features in young children's slips of the tongue. *Language and Speech* 35:189–205.

Jun, J. 1996. Place assimilation is not the result of gestural overlap: evidence from Korean and English. *Phonology* 13:377–407.

Kang, K-S 2000. On Korean fricatives. *Korean Journal of Speech Sciences* 7(3): 53–68.

Kang, K-S. 2003. The status of onglides in Korean: evidence from speech errors. *Studies in phonetics, Phonology and Morphology* 9(1):1–15.

Kang, K-S. 2005. Laryngeal features for Korean obstruents revisited. *Studies in Phonetics, Phonology and Morphology* 10(2):169–182.

Kim, H. 1997. The Phonological Representation of Affricates: Evidence from Korean and other languages. Doctoral dissertation. Cornell University.

Kim, H. 1999. The place of articulation of Korean affricates revisited. *Journal of East Asian Linguistics* 8:313–347.

Kim, H. 2001. The place of articulation of the Korean plain affricate in intervocalic position: an articulatory and acoustic study. *Journal of the International Phonetic Association* 31(2):229–257.

Mohanan, K. P. 1993. Fields of attraction in phonology. *The last phonological rule*, ed. J. Goldsmith, 61–117. Chicago: University of Chicago Press.

Paradis, C. and J-F Prunet. 1991. *Phonetics and phonology: the special status of coronals*. San Diego: Academic Press.

Pouplier, M. and L. Goldstein. 2004. Asymmetries in the perception of speech production errors. *Journal of Phonetics* 33(1):47–75

Wan, I-P. 1999. Mandarin Phonology: Evidence from speech errors. Doctoral dissertation. State University of New York at Buffalo.

Rock Rhymes in Japanese Hip-Hop Rhymes

NATSUKO TSUJIMURA, KYOKO OKAMURA, AND STUART DAVIS
Indiana University

1. Introduction[1]

It is well known that Japanese poetry, such as Haiku and Tanka, is largely conditioned by mora count. For example, Haiku consists of three lines with 5, 7, and 5 moras in each line; while Tanka is formed by five lines with 5, 7, 5, 7, and 7 moras. Traditional Haiku and Tanka poetry is sampled in (1-2), where mora breaks are indicated by hyphens.

(1)   a.   Hu-ru-i-ke-ya   b.   Sa-mi-da-re-o
                   Ka-wa-zu-to-bi-ko-mu   A-tsu-me-te-ha-ya-shi
                   Mi-zu-no-o-to   Mo-ga-mi-ga-wa

(2)   A-ra-za-ra-mu
        Ko-no-yo-no-ho-ka-no
        O-mo-i-de-ni
        I-ma-hi-to-ta-bi-no
        A-u-ko-to-mo-ga-na

---

[1] We are grateful to Shigeto Kawahara for sharing his work with us. All errors are our responsibility.

What is essential in the poetry in (1) and (2) is the number of moras per line. The individual moras in the different lines are not required to be composed of identical or similar sounds. Thus, there does not seem to be anything like the notion of rhyme in Haiku, Tanka, and other Japanese poetry tradition. (cf. Kawamoto 2000)

Given this tradition, it is interesting to note that Japanese hip-hop music, as investigated by Kawahara (2002, 2005a, 2005b) has developed a notion of rhyme. While the rhyming pattern demonstrated in Japanese hip-hop is somewhat different in nature from its English counterpart, as we will discuss in detail in this paper, the resemblance is readily observed in the parts of two sample songs from Dragon Ash in (3-4) where the rhyming parts are underlined.

(3)   machija nayameru juudaiga
         naihu nigiri aitewa juutaida
                 .....
         sonnauchini yumeou monodooshi
         tekundara zettee morochooshi ii

         temeeno ketsuwa temeede motsubekida
         soitsuga wakaru yatsuwa totsugekida   (from "21st Century Riot")

(4)   owari aru jinnseidemo yookosoo
         tukamitorerusa kyookoso
                 .....
         tinbaarando humishimeru daichio
         in da round moyasu akaichio

         konomachide tashikani saiteru
         yuri ashitani maiteru   (from "Yurino Hanasaku Bashode")

In this paper, we will examine what Zwicky (1976) calls "rock rhymes" in their applications to Japanese hip-hop rhyming. We will maintain that Japanese hip-hop rhymes involve a system of what can be termed "moraic assonance". We shall first review two observations concerning the nature of the hip-hop rhyming in Japanese from Kawahara's (2002) discussion of the topic. We will then place the nature of Japanese hip-hop rhymes in the context of Zwicky's (1976) discussion on imperfect rhymes, and show that Japanese hip-hop exemplifies a system of imperfect rhyme that is best termed as moraic assonance. We will further examine cases where moraic assonance does not seem to hold, and suggest that moraic assonance most frequently occur with moras whose cores are vowels. Finally, we shall discuss instances in which pronunciation of words is modified in performance so that they can better rhyme. Our investigation reported in this paper is based on the examination of a single artist, Dragon Ash.

2. Minimality and Extrametricality in Japanese Hip-Hop Rhymes

Kawahara (2002) discusses basic principles underlying the Japanese hip-hop rhymes. Two of his principles that are of relevance to this paper are a bimoraic requirement and extrametricality. English perfect rhymes are normally recognized when the part of a word from the stressed vowel to the end is identical in the two rhyming words, as in *sigh* and *pie*, *tight* and *sight*, and *awful* and *lawful*. Kawahara observes that in Japanese hip-hop songs, at least two moraic elements must rhyme. He states this principle as the Minimality Principle in (5), and gives examples in (6-7) where the underlined moraic elements are pronounced identically.

(5)   Minimality: Rhymes should consist of the agreement of at least two moraic elements. Moraic elements are vowels and coda consonants.

(6)   soshite te ni ireyooze satsut<u>aba</u>
        mitero ore no sokojik<u>ara</u>

(7)   kyoomo T-shatsu ni shibumeno g<u>ooru</u>d<u>o</u> ch<u>ee</u>N
        shanpan banban akete s<u>ooru</u> t<u>oree</u>N

The principle of extrametricality allows for a rhyming domain to contain an "extra" element at a line's end, as in (8); and it also enables a long vowel to rhyme with its short counterpart, as in (9). Both examples are taken from Kawahara, and angle brackets are added to indicate extrametricality.

(8)   a.   Ittuno doori no aarii m<u>ooni</u><n>
                yume kara samereba uso no y<u>ooni</u>

        b.   hadani karamu nurui k<u>aze</u>
                toroketeru karada wo hurui t<u>ate</u><ru>

(9)   nani ka ga haj<u>imari</u> s<u>o</u><o>
        so k<u>imari</u> m<u>o</u>
        nani mo nai shizen no sh<u>igusa</u>
        ga toori sugi kisetsu no f<u>iruta</u><a>

3. Japanese Hip-Hop Rhymes as Moraic Assonance

Assuming the principles of minimality and extrametricality we now turn to an examination of the nature of Japanese hip-hop rhymes as found in the lyrics of the group Dragon Ash. Japanese hip-hop rhymes are an instantiation of what are called imperfect rhymes in the poetry literature. In his discussion of imperfect rhymes from a linguistic perspective, Zwicky (1976) gives a traditional classification of imperfect rhymes in terms of how they deviate from perfect rhymes.

(10)   Zwicky's (1976) classification of imperfect rhymes in English

a. One or more of the matched vowels is unstressed:
   kiss – tenderness, scenery – tapestry

b. Vowels following the stressed one do not match
   face – places

c. Consonance – stressed vowels do not match but the consonants do
   off – enough, stop – up

d. Assonance – stressed vowels match but the following consonants do not
   wine – times, sleepin' – dreamin'

Technically speaking, none of these terms applies to the notion of rhyme that emerges from the Japanese hip-hop lyrics because Japanese is not a stress-accent language, nor does one find vowel reduction processes that can be at issue in English rhymes. In fact Kawahara (2005a) notes that a rhyme domain in Japanese hip-hop tends to have its own melody independent of the lexical accentuation of the words. This is indicated in the example from Kawahara (2005a) in (11) where the rhyming words are shown in parentheses.

(11)   Example of intonation on Japanese hip-hop rhyme

a. Geijyuts wa (bakuhatsu)   cf. bakuhatsi
         | |
         H L

b. Ikiruno ni (yakudatsu)   cf. yakudatsu
         | | | |
         H L   H L

In order to see the nature of Japanese imperfect rhyme in hip-hop, consider the rhyming pairs from the Dragon Ash lyrics.

(12)   Hip Hop rhymes in Dragon Ash

a.   mo tsu be ki da -- to tsu ge ki da

b.   ko o do o -- bo o do o

c.   sa i go ni -- ta i no ni

d.   ju u da i ga -- ju u ta i da

e.   se ma i to ko -- de ka i ko to

f.   shi n ji ta i -- ka n ji ta i

g.   ba su ja k ku -- ka su ja p pu

These Japanese imperfect rhymes seem to illustrate Assonance mentioned in (10d) but it should be applied in the context of mora. We shall call it a principle of "moraic assonance". In examining the data in (12), we see that the moraic elements are identical in each rhyming pair, where core moraic elements are understood to be a vowel, moraic nasal, or the first member of a geminate. The non-moraic consonant, namely the onset consonant of a mora, may or may not be identical. In (12b), for example, the first rhyming mora pair *ko* and *bo* agree in vowel but differ in the quality of the onset consonants. This is most telling in (12e) where all moraic elements in the rhyming pair, namely, the vowels in these cases, are completely identical, but all the onset consonants in the rhyming pair differ. The term "moraic assonance" thus seems most appropriate to capture the rhyming pattern of Japanese hip-hop. Notice that in the examples in (12) the moraic elements in the rhyming pairs are identical whether the moraic element is a vowel, as in (12a-e), or a moraic nasal as in (12f). An exception to this seems to be the different geminate consonants in (12g) where a moraic core element [k] is paired off with another moraic core element [p], where each of [k] and [p] is the first consonant of a geminate. However, one can view this as not being exceptional under a traditional abstract view of geminate consonants as being represented by the Q-element. (cf. Vance 1987) Thus, we find the generalization that the Japanese hip-hop songs are subject to moraic assonance which requires that moraic core elements in a rhyming pair be identical, where a moraic core element is either a vowel, moraic nasal, or the first member of a geminate.

A further observation that argues for the notion of moraic assonance in Japanese hip-hop rhyme, at least as performed by Dragon Ash, is that the rhyming pairs virtually always have the same number of moras (ignoring the possibility of a final extrametrical mora). This is shown in the examples in (12) above as well as the further examples in (13).

(13)   Identical number of moras for each rhyming pair

     a.   wa ga -- wa da   (from "Glory")

     b.   so ma ri -- to ba ri   (from "Glory")

     c.   ki ka n no ta i yo -- ki ga n to a i o
                             (from "Yurino Hana Saku Bashode")

     d.   ta shi ka ni sa i te ru -- a shi ta ni ma i te ru
                             (from "Yurino Hana Saku Bashode")

e.   mo tsu be ki da -- to tsu ge ki da
                  (from "21st Century Riot")

The requirement that rhyming pairs have the same number of moras distinguishes hip-hop rhyme (at least as manifested by Dragon Ash) from rhymes in English, where identical word length is not required for two words to rhyme. In English, words having different number of syllables can constitute rhymes as long as the stressed vowel and every sound after it is identical. Thus, pairs like *end – offend* and *tore – adore* are good rhymes even though the rhyming words do not have the same number of syllables. It is also clear from the data in Zwicky (1976) that even imperfect rhymes in English do not have to be of the same length. Examples include *kiss – tenderness* and *underfed – kid*. Thus, the notion of moraic assonance in Japanese hip-hop seems to impose a requirement on the forms in a rhyming relation that they have the same mora length.

As much as this state of affairs in Japanese hip-hop rhymes may seem unique, our findings together with Kawahara's (2002) preliminary observations are reminiscent of (though not identical to) what Zwicky (1976) calls "rock rhymes" in his investigations of rhyming in English rock music. Zwicky notices that there is a great deal of deviance from traditional classifications of rhyming patterns in rock lyrics, and describes such deviant behavior in terms of the principles that he calls "subsequence rhyme" and "feature rhyme". Crucially, characterizations of Japanese hip-hop rhymes that we have discussed thus far can also be captured on the basis of these two principles. First, subsequence rhymes are defined in (14).

(14)   **Subsequence rhyme**: X counts as rhyming with XC, where C is a consonant (X may end with a consonant itself, as in *pass-fast*, or with a vowel, as in *go-load*). In a relatively infrequent variant on this principle, internal subsequence rhyme, X counts as rhyming with CX (as in *proud-ground* and *plays-waves*).
                                         (Zwicky 1976:677)

Given this definition, extrametricality in (8-9) is characterized as an instance of subsequence rhymes: that is, subsequence rhymes generally add extra phonemes after the rhyming part of one of the words, and this is precisely what extrametricality is intended to capture. The nature of added elements, however, perhaps should be interpreted somewhat differently in the case of Japanese so that any addition is based on mora, rather than phonemes. Some examples of extrametrical elements from Dragon Ash lyrics are given in (15),

(15)   Extrametricality in Dragon Ash lyrics

    a. dooshita -- dooshita<chi>   (from "Glory")

    b. kanjitai -- panchirai<n> (from "Yurino Hana Saku Bashode")

Second, Japanese hip-hop rhymes do not normally pay attention to the nonmoriac consonant at the onset of each mora. As shown by examples like that in (12), the nonmoriac consonants in the rhyme do not have to be identical, though they can be. Nonetheless, as noted by Kawahara (2005a,b) there seems to be a certain similarity between two nonmoraic consonants in a rhyme that are not identical. The role of similarity is well captured by Zwicky's second principle, feature rhymes, which is defined in (16).

(16)   **Feature rhyme**: segments differing minimally in phonological features count as rhyming. The segments may be vowels (as in *end-wind*) or consonants (as in *stop-rock*); the feature in question can even be syllabicity (as in *mine-tryin'*).   (Zwicky 1976:677)

To illustrate this type of rhyme in actual songs, Zwicky (1976:692) gives the examples in (17-20).

(17)   My experience was limited and <u>underfed</u>,
    You were talking while I <u>hid</u>,
    To the one who was the father of your <u>kid</u>.
                (Dylan, 'Love is Just a Four Letter Word')

(18)   Well, the technical manual's <u>busy</u>
    She's not going to fix it up too <u>easy</u>
                   (Joni Mitchell, 'Electricity')

(19)   Blackbird singing in the dead of <u>night</u>
    Take these broken wings and learn to <u>fly</u>
    All your <u>life</u>
    You were only waiting for this moment to <u>arise</u>
          (Dylan, 'It's Alright Ma (I'm only Bleeding)')

(20)   Me and my gal, my gal, <u>son</u>,
    We got met with a tear gas <u>bomb</u>
                    (Dylan, 'Oxford Town')

In (17) and (18) the vowels that are involved in the rhyming pairs are not identical but can sometimes be perceived to be at least similar in that they only differ by one feature. The examples in (19) and (20) involve similarity of consonants rather than identity. Such "perceptual similarity" may lead to "identity" in actual performance as the musician may modify the pronunciation of the nonmatching sounds so that they are perceived as identical.

The recent work of Kawahara (2005a, 2005b) on Japanese hip-hop has largely focused on the similarity relation between the nonmoraic consonants of two units in a rhyming relation. In examining cases in hip-hop lyrics where the matching nonmoraic consonants in the rhyme are not identical, Kawahara notes certain tendencies such as a coronal obstruent to be matched with another coronal obstruent or a voiced consonant to be matched with another voiced consonant. From this observation, he makes a larger theoretical claim arguing that this finding confirms the role of similarity in a phonological grammar as mediated by Steriade's (2001a, 2001b) P-Map mechanism. While the data from Dragon Ash lyrics show similar tendencies in the matching of nonmoraic consonants in rhyming pairs, we note, as Zwicky (1976) does, that results of similarity studies varies with task, experimental conditions, and subject population. On the other hand, one fairly common phenomena found in Japanese hip-hop lyrics, mentioned by Kawahara (2005b), though not incorporated in his study, is the observation that a nonmoraic (or onset) consonant corresponds with the absence of a consonant in many of rhyming pairs. Examples from Dragon Ash are given in (21).

(21) Examples of rhyming pairs where nonmoraic consonants have a null correspondence (the relevant rhyming part is underlined)

  a. i ta mi ga -- hi ka ri ga
            (from "Yurino Hana Saku Bashode")

  b. ji ka n to ta i o n -- ki ka n no ta i yo o
            (from "Yurino Hana Saku Bashode")

  c. da ke ma shi te -- ka ke a shi de
            (from "Yurino Hana Saku Bashode")

  d. yo o sha na ku -- yo ko ja na ku
            (from "My friends's Anthem")

  e. de ka i o to -- se ka i go to   (from "Bring It")

This type of relation is not reported to be found in English imperfect rhymes, but is quite common in Japanese hip-hop. While such forms may be problematic for a similarity account, they do provide additional evidence for the principle of moraic assonance in Japanese hip-hop rhymes where the notion of mora plays a crucial role.

4. Issues

While we have discussed that the minimality and extrametricality principles as well as moraic assonance constitute a major characteristics of Japanese hip-hop rhymes, we find possible counterexamples to these in our data. In our discussion earlier, it has been observed that hip-hop rhymes may contain an extra mora that is not matched with anything at the end of a word. Two examples from Dragon Ash have been given in (15) to illustrate it. According to Kawahara (2002), since extrametricality is restricted to the "periphery of the form", instances should not be found where a penultimate mora is considered extrametrical, as Kawahara schematizes in (22).

(22)   *CV <CV> CV
              ⟍ |
           CV   CV

Precisely the type illustrated in (22) has been observed in our sample. This is shown in (23-24).[2]

(23)   rensashite hiraku mi ra i   ga
                               | |
        sonosakiga   mi ta i <n> da
                               (from "Yurino Hana Saku Bashode")

(24)   menomaeni   ka su ka   na
                               | |
        demo tashikana kachi ka <n> ga
                               (from "Yurino Hana Saku Bashode")

In each of (23-24), the extrametricality surfaces in the penultimate mora. In fact violations of extrametricality seem to always involve a moraic nasal. One of the songs, "Glory", has the recurring rhyming of CaCa such as *naka*, *taka*, *utaga* and *waga*, and one of the target words is *nanka*, which is a shortened form of *nanika*. As the schema in (25) describes, the non-edge extrametricality that appears in the penultimate mora is a moraic nasal.

(25)   CaCa: naka, utaga, waga, wada, mada
            | ⟍
           na <n> ka

While the data in (23-24) are exceptional to extrametricality in that there is a nonperipheral mora that is outside the rhyming domain, it seems to be a

---

[2] Examples of the following type that resemble a violation of extrametricality in (13-14) are also found. However, if only the final two moras are considered the rhyming domain, as is required by the Minimality Requirement, this example should not be viewed as violating extrametricality.

(i)   umareiku sennennkino sa i syo   ni
                                   | |
        nomikomarenai   yo <o> ni

regular pattern that such nonperipheral extrametricality tends to involve a moraic nasal.

A second related problem concerns the principle of moraic assonance. Under moraic assonance, the expectation is that the moraic elements of two rhyming units be identical. This is illustrated by the Dragon Ash data in (12), (13), and (21). Occasionally, however, there are examples where moraic assonance does not hold, as is shown by the examples in (26-27) from the lyrics of "Yurino Hana Saku Bashode", where the moras at issue are capitalized.

(26)   hidoku yaseta koOyao
         hosiga aseta koNyamo

(27)   ikinukunowa koNnande
         daremoga mina soOnande

In each example, the capitalized moras, one being a vowel and the other a moraic nasal, are intended to rhyme, but they don't; and hence, assonance is not observed. Such examples, however, seem to be more common involving pairing of a vowel and a moraic nasal. In fact, we find several examples of the same sort in our sample, as is illustrated in (28).

(28)   a.   ju n ba n ni -- ju u ma n shi   (from "Glory")

        b.   to o a ke ro -- do n da ke no   (from "Glory")

        c.   ku u ka n ni -- ju n ba n ni   (from "Glory")

        d.   ji ka n to ta i o n -- ki ka n no ta i yo o
                                          (from "Yurino Hana Saku Bashode")

        e.   ko n na n de -- so o na n de
                                          (from "Yurino Hana Saku Bashode")

This may suggest that while the principle of moraic assonance is stronger for moras whose core element is a vowel, its deviant pattern may also form a certain regularity.

These apparent counterexamples bring up the issue of modification of pronunciation in the actual performance of the lyrics. In our investigations of some of Dragon Ash songs we note that they modify their pronunciation of lyrics during performance in such a way that rhyming is achieved. A rather drastic example of this is given in (29).

(29)   saa kakenukeyooze dooshita
         yuri no moto tudotta dooshitachi
         yo ima dakara koso tooshi dashi
         don't stop tomo ni mezasu eekooe e ikoo   (from "Glory")

In (29) the vowel sequences of the underlined rhyming domain in the first three lines are identical, with the second and third lines contain extrametricality, but the English phrase in the last line, "don't stop", is modified in pronunciation so that it rhymes with the first three lines: in fact, "don't stop" sounds exactly like "dooshita" in performance. Other examples of English words that involve altering pronunciation are given in (30-31).

(30)   hai ni intoro bai ni <u>sindoo o</u>
        makiokosu Lilyda <u>sindoroo</u><mu>

(31)   mune hukuramasite <u>kanjitai</u>
        kono omoio <u>panchi rai</u><n>

The last words of the second line in (30) and (31) are English words "syndrome" and "punch line", respectively. While the final mora of these words seem to be extrametrical in the rhyming scheme, upon listening to the actual songs, they are virtually inaudible.

To be clear, modification in pronunciation is not restricted to loan words, as the examples in (32-33) illustrate.

(32)   suusennen himitsuno <u>beeru</u>
        tsutsumareta michinaru <u>sukeeru</u>
        toodaikara naniga <u>mieru</u> doodai
        kyoodaieno <u>eeru</u>   (from "Yurino Hana Saku Bashode")

(33)   sonna nakani yume ou <u>monodooshi</u>
        tekundara zettee <u>morochooshi ii</u>   (from "21th Century Riot")

The four underlined words in (32) are intended to be targets of rhyming. Notice that the third word *mieru* is a Japanese verb to mean "see", and does not appear to rhyme with the rest of the words perfectly. In order to keep the rhyming pattern, however, the musician pronounces it as *mieeru*, lengthening the second mora of the verb. In (33) the last two moras, ii, in the second line, which is a Japanese word, is obviously an extra element while what precedes it perfectly rhymes with *monodooshi*. In this case, since these extra vowels are identical with the final vowel of the rhyming element in the second line, *morochooshi*, it is not detectible in performance, nor is it perhaps even relevant, whether the vowel gets strictly lengthened.

5. Conclusion

In this paper we have proposed that Japanese hip-hop musicians use the principle of moraic assonance in their rhyming scheme. This principle can be seen as combining the traditional notion of mora count in Japanese poetry with the western notion of assonance (vowel identity) in poetry. Thus, rhyming units in Japanese hip-hop lyrics ideally should have an identical number of moras and the corresponding moraic elements should agree in quality. We have noted slight deviations from this scheme, but they are often compensated for by modified pronunciation in performance. Japanese hip-hop rhymes then can be seen as a Japanese interpretation of the foreign notion of rhyme.

References

Kawahara, S. 2002. Aspects of Japanese Hip-hop Rhymes: What They Reveal about the Structure of Japanese. In *Proceedings of Language Study Workshop*. http://people.umass.edu/kawahara/hiphop_prose.pdf#search=%22Aspects%20of%20Japanese%20Hip-hop%20Rhymes%22

Kawahara, S. 2005a. Linguist's Delight: Similarity, Half-rhyme, and Hip hop. Presentation, University of Massachusetts, June 17.

Kawahara, S. 2005b. Linguist's Delight: Similarity, Half Rhymes, and Hip Hop, Manuscript, University of Massachusetts.

Kawamoto, K. 2000. *The Poetics of Japanese Verse: Imagery, Structure, Meter*. Tokyo: University of Tokyo Press.

Steriade, D. 2001a. The Phonology of Perceptibility Effects: The P-map and Its Consequences for Constraint Organization. Manuscript, UCLA.

Steriade, D. 2001b. Directional Asymmetries in Place Assimilation. *The Role of Speech Perception in Phonology,* eds. E. Hume and K. Johnson, 219-250. San Diego: Academic Press.

Vance, T. 1987. *An Introduction to Japanese Phonology*. New York: SUNY Press.

Zwicky, A. 1976. Well, This Rock and Roll Has Go to Stop. Junior's Head Is Hard As a Rock. *CLS* 12:676-697.

On Neutral Vowels in Korean Vowel Harmony

GWANHI YUN

University of Arizona

1. Introduction[1]

The status of neutral or transparent vowels with respect to vowel harmony has long attracted much attention and research in the field of the interface between phonology and phonetics. Thus, it might be helpful and interesting to look into the neutral vowels in other languages such as Hungarian and Finnish in order to better understand Korean vowel harmony.

1.1. Neutral Vowels in Hungarian and Finnish Vowel Harmony

One of the most well-known cases of neutral vowels (henceforth, NV) comes from Hungarian vowel harmony (Benus 2005, Gafos and Benus 2003, Ringen 1988, Ringen and Vago 1998). In Hungarian, the backness of the suffix vowel ([a] vs. [e]) is determined by the backness of the preceding stem vowel, as is illustrated in (1).

---

[1] I would like to thank Diana Archangeli and Jeff Mielke for their comments and suggestions, and the subjects for their time. I am also grateful to Michael Kenstowicz, Donca Steriade, Adam Albright, Edward Flemming, Stuart Davis, Young-Gie Kim-Renaud, and Yoonjung Kang for their feedback. All remaining errors are my own.

(1)		-nak/nek	-na:l/ne:l
		dative 'to'	adessive 'at'
ha:z	'house'	ha:z-nak	ha:z-na:l
város	'city'	város-nak	város-na:l
föld	'earth'	föld-nek	föld-ne:l
öröm	'joy'	öröm-nek	öröm-ne:l

Front vowels such as [i,e] seem not to be involved in back harmony as is seen in (2). That is why such vowels have been called 'transparent' or 'neutral' in the sense that they do not block vowel harmony. In traditional phonological theories, their special status has been handled by their being unspecified with respect to harmonic feature [±back] (Ringen and Vago 1998).

(2)	papír	'paper'	papír-nak
	kávé	'coffee'	kávé-nak

However, recent phonetic experiments show different results which reveal that they are not really neutral. Gafos and Benus (2003) and Benus (2005) argue that Hungarian transparent vowels such as [í,i,é,e] are actively involved palatal vowel harmony. They further claim that "the [±back] harmonizing feature is manifested on the NVs by systematic phonetic difference in the horizontal position of the tongue body". For example, the phonemically identical NVs in back contexts are articulated further backward than those in front harmony contexts as a result of significant difference in coarticulation as is illustrated in (3).

(3)	viz-nek	'water'	vs.	hid-nak	'bridge'
	hotel-nak	'hotel'	vs.	hotel-nek	

On the basis of articulatory and acoustic data from NV, Benus (2005) suggests that the fine degree of articulatory backness in the stem-final vowel is phonologized, and that it participates in determining (or *triggers*) the [±back] form of the suffix.

Finnish shows vowel harmony patterns similar to Hungarian's (Kim 2005, Ringen 1988), The backness of suffix vowels agrees with the backness of preceding stem vowels, as is shown in (4).

(4)	[-back]	pöydä-llä	'table', adessive
	[+back]	pouda-lla	'clear weather', adessive

However, Kim's (2005) acoustic study of NV in Finnish revealed patterns different from what Benus and Gafos reported for Hungarian. Kim found that neutral vowels [i, e] undergo coarticulation only, and do not participate in vowel harmony, suggesting that Finnish NVs do not need to be phonologically specified for [±back]. Kim suggests further that the phonetic realization of Finnish NVs should be attributed to a language particular phonetic implementation component, independent of the phonological grammar. For example, the NVs such as [i, e] in (5) showed no significant difference in F1 values, indicating no significant influence from surrounding harmony contexts.

(5)   [-back]   säde-ttä   'ray', partitive
                    tädi-llä   'aunt', adessive
       [+back]   sade-tta   'rain', partitive
                    Kati-lla   (woman's name), adessive

In summary, there are two positions about the status of neutral vowels in vowel harmony; so-called Hungarian NVs are not transparent in vowel harmony but trigger vowel harmony, while Finnish NVs are not phonologized but undergoes coarticulation only.

1.2. Korean Vowel Harmony

Korean exhibits an interesting type of vowel harmony, as shown in (6) (Sohn 1999). According to Sohn, it is a (nonautomatic) assimilatory process whereby one vowel becomes harmonious with another one in the neighboring syllable. That is, Yang or "bright" vowels (/a,o/) pattern with other Yang vowels, while Yin or "dark" vowels (/ə, u..../) pattern with other Yin vowels. Sohn points out that this type of vowel harmony exists "only in the ə/a alternation in verbal suffixes (6a), in onomatopoeic and mimetic expressions, including color terms, which are often called sound symbolism (6b), and in some prefixal alternations (6c)."

(6)   a. cwuk-essta   'died'   nol-assta   'played'
          t'wi-ela   'Jump!'   cap-ala   'Catch (it)!'
          cwu-eto   'though gives'   po-ato   'though sees'

       b. phongtang   'with a plop'   phungteng
          cholangkelita 'slop'   chulengkelita

       c. say-kkamahta 'deep black'   si-kkemehta
          hay-malkahta 'glossy white'   huy-melkehta

Of interest is that Yin (or neutral) vowel /i/ and neutral vowel /ɨ/ occur either with Yang vowels or with Yin vowels like NVs in other languages, as is illustrated in (7).

(7) Neutral vowels in vowel harmony

a. Yang vowels	b. Yin vowels		c.Pattern
[podɨɾapta]	[pudɨɾəpta]	'be soft'	o..ɨ..a/u..ɨ..ə
[talgɨɾak]	[təlgɨɾək]	'with a rattling noise'	a..ɨ..a/ə..ɨ..ə
[pandɨlgəɾida]	[pəndɨlgəɾida]	'shine'	a..ɨ..ə/ə..ɨ..ə
[polgɨcokcok]	[pulgɨcukcuk]	'reddishly'	o..ɨ..o/u..ɨ..u
[k'omciɾakkərida]	[k'umciɾəkkərida]	'move a little'	o..i..a/u..i..ə
[komsildɛda]	[kumsildɛda]	'wriggle a little'	o..i..ɛ/u..i..ɛ

Here an interesting question is whether or not the intervening (transparent-looking) vowels [ɨ, i] are coarticulated with the surrounding Yang or Yin vowels, showing significant differences like Hungarian or unlike Finnish NVs. Do Korean NVs show the evidence that they actually participate in vowel harmony with significantly different coarticulation or reveal non-significant difference of coarticulation?

2. Goals and Hypotheses

First, this paper aims to probe into phonetic-fine details of NVs to see if Korean NVs are different in different harmony contexts like Hungarian NVs or to see if they show only coarticulation with surrounding harmonic vowels like Finnish NVs. Secondly, we aim to provide an answer to the question: could Korean NVs be phonologically relevant in vowel harmony? That is, do variants of Korean NVs need different phonological specification or should this just be left to an independent phonetic implementation component? To pursue these goals, the following hypotheses will be tested.

H1   Korean NVs participate in vowel harmony at subphonemic phonetic details as a result of coarticulation effects from surrounding vowels.

H2   Korean NVs in stems without suffixes show the difference in fine degrees of height articulation, triggering vowel harmony.

3. Ultrasound Experiments

3.1. Methods

Two Korean speakers (male and female) aged in their 30s, participated in the production experiments. They read the word list in (7) five times, and ultrasound images were taken. The tongue body shapes were quantified in Excel. First, in order to quantify the tongue shape, a concentric radial grid was placed over the ultrasound images which are marked with pixels. Then, the values of the (xy) coordinates were measured at about ten points along the tongue shape line. The origin was moved from the top left to the bottom left. Then the average of 5 tokens was calculated in 10 points of tongue shape. These adjusted averages created the smooth tongue body line with Excel as is illustrated in (8) below.

3.2. Results

3.2.1 Hypothesis 1 : Coarticulation of NVs in Harmony Contexts

The graphs in (8) show the average tongue body lines of NVs in both vowel harmony contexts from speaker 1. The similar patterns obtained from Speaker 2. The square-shaped lines represent the tongue shapes of [ɨ] (8a-d) and [i] (8e-f) in Yang vowel contexts, while the triangle-shaped lines represent the tongue body shapes of [ɨ] (8a-d) and [i] (8e-f) in Yin vowel contexts. The thin lines represent the tongue shapes of both NVs in mono-syllabic words, i.e. non-harmonic words.

(8) Average tongue body lines from 5 tokens

(a) [podɨɾapta] vs. [pudɨɾəpta]   (b) [talgɨɾak] vs. [təlgɨɾək]

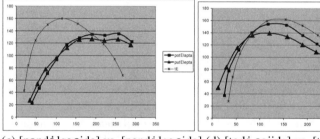

(c) [pandɨlgəɾida] vs. [pəndɨlgəɾida] (d) [todɨɾajida] vs. [tudɨɾəjida]

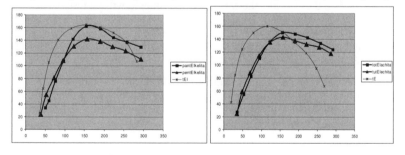

(e)[k'omciɾakkərida]vs.[k'umciɾəkkərida]   (f)[komsildɛda] vs. [kum-sildɛda]

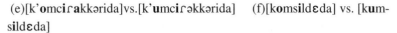

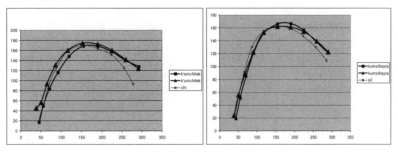

Overall, /ɨ/ in both the harmonic contexts shows considerably anticipatory coarticulation from the following alveolars (8a-d), whereas /i/ seems to undergo little coarticulation (8e-f). That is, the neutral vowel /ɨ/ is articulated fronter than the same vowel in monosyllabic words in both harmonic contexts, but the other neutral vowel /i/ is articulated almost in the same position as that in monosyllabic control words in both harmonic contexts. These results might be more evidence for the claim that /i/ is the most resistant to coarticulation because /i/ is considered to be articulated with active tongue dorsum raising toward the palatal zone where it causes large amounts of contact (Recasens 1990, Recasens and Romero 1997).

However, contrary to expectations, there was no significant difference in tongue body positions for neutral vowels between Yang vowel contexts and Yin vowel contexts (p.>0.05 for two speakers at two points of vectors). These results do not support hypothesis (1), and thus indicate that the height of tongue body of neutral vowels is phonetically *neutralized* in harmony contexts even though NVs like /ɨ/ are articulated further front than in monosyllabic words. However, more speakers are needed to increase the likelihood of significance.

3.2.2 Hypothesis (2): Neutral Vowels in Stems

The graphs in (9) show the relative tongue body height of NVs in Yang and Yin vowel contexts for speaker 1. Similar patterns were obtained from Speaker 2. Squares represent the tongue shapes of [ɨ] (9a-d) and [i] (9e-f) in stems without suffixes, while triangles represent the tongue body shapes of [ɨ] (9a-d) and [i] (9e-f) in stems without suffixes. We can expect that if NVs are phonologized and trigger vowel harmony according to hypothesis (2), tongue body height of NVs in stems with Yin vowels might be higher than that of identical NVs in stems with Yang vowels.

(9) Tongue body height of NVs in stems without suffixes
(a) [podɨ] vs. [pudɨ]   (b) [talgɨ] vs. [təlgɨ]

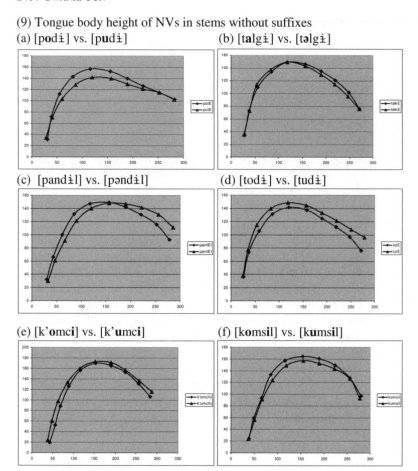

(c) [pandɨl] vs. [pəndɨl]   (d) [todɨ] vs. [tudɨ]

(e) [k'omci] vs. [k'umci]   (f) [komsil] vs. [kumsil]

Contrary to expectations, the results are very similar to those with re-gard to Hypothesis (1). There was no significant difference in tongue body height of NVs in both the stems (p.>0.05 for one speaker at two points of vectors). There was little significant difference in coarticulation from the preceding vowel or consonants. These results confirm that Korean NVs, if ever, show anticipatory rather than carryover coarticulation. In sum, these results do not support Hypothesis (2) and show that Korean NVs are more similar to Finnish NVs than to Hungarian NVs.

4. Acoustic Experiments on F1 Coarticulation

4.1. Neutral Vowels in Harmony Contexts

To confirm the articulatory properties of NVs with phonologically and phonetically neutral status, we conducted acoustic experiments to test the identical hypothesis (1). Hypothesis (1) is to see if Korean NVs undergo significantly different degree of coarticulation from surrounding harmonic contexts. Specifically, it is expected that /ɨ, i/ in Yang vowel contexts will be articulated with a lower tongue position than those in the Yin vowel environments as a result of height coarticulation, showing higher F1 values. For acoustic experiments, two native Korean subjects (male and female) participated in production of the same stimuli in (7) five times and their sounds were recorded in the phonetics lab. F1 values of /i/ and /ɨ/ were compared between in Yang and Yin vowel contexts in order to see how low F1 is. In total, 290 tokens were analyzed and F1 values were measured at three time points of the vowels (i.e. onset, medial, offset) with PRAAT.

The graphs in (11) show the F1 coarticulation patterns of NVs in Korean from speaker 1. Similar patterns were obtained from Speaker 2. The diamond-shaped lines represent the gradual change of F1 values of [ɨ] (11a-d) and [i] (11e-f) in stems with Yang vowels, while the square-shaped lines represent the gradual change of F1 values of [ɨ] (11a-d) and [i] (11e-f) in stems with Yin vowels.

(11) F1 coarticulation of neutral vowels in harmony contexts
(a) [podɨɾapta] vs. [pudɨɾəpta]   (b)[talgɨɾak] vs.[təlgɨɾək]

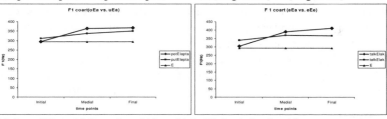

(c) [pandɨlgəɾida] vs. [pəndɨlgəɾida] (d) [polgɨcokcok] vs. [pulgɨcukcuk]

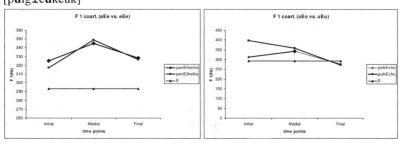

(e)[k'omciɾakkərida] vs. [k'umciɾəkkərida]   (f)[komsildɛda] vs. [kum-
sildɛda]

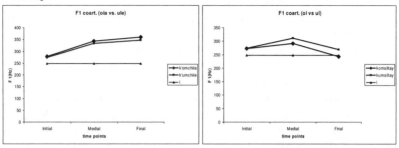

The results show that the two neutral vowels are not significantly different between in Yang vowel contexts and in Yin vowel contexts (p. > 0.05)
as illustrated in (11a)-(11f). They do not support Hypothesis (1). That is,
although the vowels exhibit consistent anticipatory coarticulation (11a, b, e),
the differences are small and not contrastive enough to allow phonologically
different specifications. Unlike Finnish vowel harmony (Kim 2005) or Hungarian vowel harmony (Gafos & Benus 2003), Yang and Yin vowels do not
seem to consist of phonetically natural classes in vowel harmony. Thus, it is
not easy to determine whether neutral vowels belong to Yang or Yin vowel
classes, or to specify the two vowels in a phonologically different manner.

4.2. Neutral Vowels in Stems

We also attempted to confirm articulatory results about NVs in stems without suffixes. So Hypothesis (2) was tested through acoustic experiments.

Results showed that stem-final neutral vowels reveal little significant
difference in F1 values. This does not support H (2) (p.>0.05 for 2 speakers), indicating that Korean NVs do not trigger vowel harmony and so need
not be phonologically differently specified like Hungarian NVs.

5. Discussions

5.1. The Phonetic Neutralization of Phonologically Neutral Vowels

In a language with fully productive vowel harmony it is not possible to separate the effect of V-to-V coarticulation from vowel harmony. Vowel harmony and coarticulation are intertwined in the phonetics of neutral vowels
(Gafos & Benus 2003). However, Korean VH has a lot of exceptions and is
not productive. So Korean NVs may show only coarticulation effects. The
results about H (1) show that phonologically neutral vowels are also phonetically transparent. The failure to support H (2) also suggests that they do
not trigger vowel harmony like Hungarian NVs but are similar to Finnish

NVs, indicating that Korean NVs need not be specified as phonological features like Hungarian NVs.

A naturally arising question is why Korean NVs are truly transparent, and do not undergo significantly different degrees of coarticulation in different vowel harmony contexts? There might be two possible explanations. One is related to the fact that Korean vowel harmony is not productive. Thus, the vowel harmony is truly morphologically (or lexically) specified at word level, not involving the stem or affix level. Or it might be necessary to divide the lexical classes according to relative productivity or frequency of the application of vowel harmony as sublexical domains. The other reasonable explanation may involve phonetic or articulatory factors with respect to neutral vowels. That is, Korean NVs are phonetically (articulatorily) strikingly robust and so the most resistant to coarticulation from the surrounding harmonic vowels. Thus, they do not belong to either class phonologically and need not have different phonological specification by way of [±Yang] feature or whatever harmonic feature. Some might wonder about the possibility of use of ATR/RTR feature in vowel harmony. So they might argue that neutral vowels such as [i, ɨ] are all [ATR] and lexically specified, while the vowels actively participating in vowel harmony are all [RTR]. The reason why neutral vowels are transparent both phonologically and phonetically may be that Korean vowel harmony occurs only on the [RTR] tier. I will leave this issue open for further research because it might be prerequisite to define the status of [ATR/RTR] of Korean vowels in terms of articulatory or acoustic properties.

5.2. The Phonetic Neutralization of Phonologically Neutral Vowels

As is seen in (11a, b, e), the consistent coarticulation patterns reveal anticipatory rather than carryover effects (11c), consistent with Öhman (1966). Anticipatory effects involve articulatory preprogramming, while carry-over effects are considered mechanical and attributable to the mass and inertia of articulators (Henke 1966, MacNeeilage and DeClerk 1969, Recasens 1984, Whalen 1990). As in Keating (1996), if we adopt two-level model theories and coarticulation is left only at language-specific phonetics, it is difficult to expect the directionality of anticipation effects here in Korean neutral vowels. English shows carryover effects over anticipatory effects in physiological and acoustic aspects (Huffman 1986).

So I follow Whalen's (1990) position that anticipatory effects are programmed, and Barry (1992) that cross-linguistically different low-level phonetic processes such as gestural weakening or overlap are to some extent under the cognitive control of the speaker and low-level phonetic variation may not be accounted for entirely by phonetic theory, but by phonological theory as well. Although the neutral vowels are not allowed to be specified in phonological representations, the directionality of coarticulation patterns implies that formal constraints on V-to-V coarticulation can be intertwined with phonological constraints as suggested by Gafos (2002) along with a relevant ranking such as V2-to-V1, Vowel Harmony >> IDENT (target) >> V1-to-V2.

(13) Constraints on gestural coordination

a.   IDENT (target) : The gestural target of an input segment must be preserved in its output correspondent.

b.   V1-to-V2 : The release of the V1 gesture must be synchronous with the onset of the V2 gesture.

c.   V2-to-V1 : The onset of V2 gesture must be synchronous with the target of the V1 gesture.

6. Conclusions

The first contribution of this study is that it reveals the phonetic nature of two neutral vowels, in that they do not belong to any harmonic vowel classes and that they are not phonologically specified in featural composition (Kirchner 1997, Smolensky 1993). Thus, the locality condition in Korean vowel harmony need not be invoked or violated because Korean NVs are both phonologically and phonetically neutral, supporting relativized locality (Kiparsky 1981) rather than strict locality (Gafos 2002, Ni Chiosan and Padgett 2001). Second, despite the neutral status of the NVs, this study shows that the directionality of V-to-V coarticulation can still be formulated in gestural phonology grammar.

This research awaits further investigation into the coarticulation patterns of NVs. First, we need to look into different types of vowel harmony in verb classes or in the words beginning with NVs to see if there is any difference according to lexical classes. Second, it might be interesting to see the effects of speech rate on the degree of coarticulation of NVs.

References

Barry, M. 1992. Palatalization, Assimilation and Gestural Weakening in Connected Speech. *Speech Communication* 11:393–400.

Benus, S. 2005. Dynamics and Transparency in Vowel Harmony. Ultrafest III, the University of Arizona, Tucson, April 14–16, 2005.

Gafos, A. 2002. A Grammar of Gestural Coordination. *Natural Language and Linguistic Theory* 20:269–337.

Gafos, A. and S. Benus. 2003. On Neutral Vowels in Hungarian. 15th ICPhS, Barcelona.

Henke, W. L. 1966. Dynamic Articulatory Model of Speech Production Using Computer Simulation. Doctoral dissertation, MIT.

Huffman, M. K. 1986. Patterns of Coarticulation in English. *UCLA Working Papers in Phonetics* 63:26–47.

Keating, P. A. 1996. The Phonology-phonetics Interface. *Interfaces in Phonology*, ed. U. Kleinhenz, 262–278. Berlin: Akademic Verlag.

Kim, Y. 2005. Finnish Neutral Vowels: Subcontrastive Harmony or V-to-V Coarticulation? Talk presented at LSA 79, Oakland, CA, January 6-9, 2005.

Kiparsky, P. 1981. Vowel Harmony. Manuscript, MIT.

Kirchner, R. 1997. Contrastiveness and Faithfulness. *Phonology* 14: 83–111.

MacNeliage, P. F. and J. L. DeClerk. 1969. On the Motor Control of Coarticulation in CVC Monosyllables. *Journal of the Acoustical Society of America* 45:1217–1233.

Ni Chiosain, M. and J. Padgett. 2001. Markedness, Segments Realization, and Locality in Spreading. *Segmental Phonology in Optimaility Theory*, ed. L. Lombardi, 118–156. Cambridge: Cambridge University Press.

Öhman, S. 1966. Coarticulation in VCV Utterances: Spectrographic Measurements. *Journal of the Acoustical Society of America* 39:151–168.

Recasens, D. 1984. Vowel-to-vowel Coarticulation in Catalan VCV Sequences, *Journal of the Acoustical Society of America* 76:1624–1635.

Recasens, D. and Romero, J. (1997). An EMMA Study of Segmental Complexity and Articulatory-acoustic Correlations for Consonants. *European Journal of Disorders Communication* 30:203-212.

Ringen, C. O. 1988. *Vowel Harmony: Theoretical Implications*. New York: Garland.

Ringen, C. O. and R. M. Vago. 1998. Hungarian Vowel Harmony in Optimality Theory. *Phonology* 15:393–416.

Smolensky, P. 1993. Harmony, Markedness, and Phonological Activity. Manuscript, University of Colorado, Boulder [ROA-87].

Sohn, H. 1999. *The Korean Language*. Cambridge: Cambridge University Press.

Whalen, D. H. 1990. Coarticulation is Largely Planned. *Journal of Phonetics* 18:3–35.

Part IV

Processing and Acquisition

Object Control in Korean: Structure and Processing

NAYOUNG KWON AND MARIA POLINSKY
University of California San Diego

1. Introduction[1]

Control is a dependency between two argument positions where the referential properties of the overt controller determine the referential properties of the silent controllee (represented as a gap below), as in (1).

(1) Craig Venter$_i$ tried   [___$_i$ to capture the code of life]
      controller   controllee

The controller can appear in the subject position as in (1) (subject control) or in the object position of the matrix clause, as in (2) (object control):

(2) Craig Venter persuaded investors$_i$ [___$_i$ to fund the genome project]
                        controller   controllee

[1] This project was supported in part by NSF grant BCS-0131946 to the second author and by the Center for Research in Language at UCSD. We are grateful to Shin Fukuda, Norbert Hornstein, Robert Kluender, Phil Monahan, Hajime Ono, Eric Potsdam, Peter Sells, Mieko Ueno, and audiences at the JK-15, University of Maryland, and Zentrum für allgemeine Sprachwissenschaft in Berlin for helpful discussions of this paper. All errors are our responsibility.

Traditional analyses of control assume that such constructions are base generated with an invisible subject in the complement clause (or no subject at all, depending on a particular theory). More recently, an analysis of control has been proposed which subsumes control under A-movement and thus assimilates control to raising. The two structures are less unlike than they appear under the traditional view, differing only in whether or not the matrix position is thematic (as in control) or not, as in raising (Hornstein 2003).[2]

The derivational analysis of control has received strong support from the phenomenon of backward control. Under backward control, the referential identity of the silent matrix controllee crucially depends on the identity of the overt controller in the embedded clause. This phenomenon, where the silent controllee is structurally higher than the overt controller, is represented in the hypothetical English example below:

(3) Craig Venter persuaded ___$_i$ [investors$_i$ to fund the genome project]
controllee controller

Such a structure is incompatible with base generation (the silent element in the matrix clause is in violation of binding conditions and the distribution of PRO), and does indeed call for a movement analysis. A movement derivation of backward object control would look like (4b) (noncrucial details omitted). The difference between forward and backward control is simply in the choice of the link in the movement chain: the tail under forward control, the head under backward:

(4) a. [$_{VP}$ persuade investors [$_{CP}$ to [$_{TP}$ ~~investors~~ [$_{vP}$ ~~investors~~ fund the project]]]]

b. [$_{VP}$ persuade ~~investors~~ [$_{CP}$ to [$_{TP}$ ~~investors~~ [$_{vP}$ investors fund the project]]]]

While backward control has been found in a number of languages,[3] it is still possible that the attested cases can be accounted for by a different analysis than movement. What kind of analysis may be available? Many languages with purported backward control have null pronominal subjects and some also allow null pronominal objects. The presence of *pro*-drop suggests an alternative to the movement analysis: the silent element in the matrix clause may be a null pronominal co-indexed with the subject of the embedded clause. As long as the two positions are not in a c-command rela-

---

[2] For earlier proposals that control and raising are not as distinct as they are made to be, see Bolinger (1961), Langacker (1995).

[3] Backward subject control has been attested in Tsez, Malagasy, and Circassian (Polinsky and Potsdam 2002, 2003, 2006). Backward object control has been attested in Brazilian Portuguese (Farrell 1995), Malagasy (Potsdam 2006), Japanese (Harada 1973, Kuroda 1978), and Korean (Monahan 2004).

tion, such co-indexation should be possible and, given the right semantic or pragmatic conditions, would yield the control interpretation (Dowty 1985, Jackendoff and Culicover 2003, among many others). The crucial difference between the two possible analyses then comes down to the difference between Obligatory Control with movement and Non-Obligatory Control with coerced coreference between two argument expressions.

This paper will compare the two analyses against a family of object control constructions in Korean. Korean is particularly relevant to the debate between the two approaches because it has subject and object *pro*-drop (Kim 2000) and shows an intriguing variation under object control.

In what follows, Section 2 introduces the relevant object control structures. Section 3 presents the syntactic- and semantics-based analyses of Korean object control. Then the two analyses are compared using syntactic considerations (Section 4) and processing evidence (Section 5). Conclusions and general discussion follow in Section 6.

2. Object Control in Korean

Object control in Korean involves the matrix verbs *seltukhata* 'persuade', *kwonyuhata* 'suggest' (and some others), and the complement clause headed by the complementizer -*tolok* (see Kim 1978, 1984 for evidence that it is a complementizer). The construction is illustrated in (5), with the missing argument represented again as a gap:

(5) Chelswu-ka Yenghuy-lul /eykey [__ tomangka-tolok] seltukhayssta
    Chelswu-NOM Yenghuy-ACC/DAT   run_away-COMP persuaded
    'Chelswu persuaded Yenghuy to run away.'

The apparent controller, preceding the embedded clause, can be either in the accusative or dative case (we will not consider the dative in this paper). The construction shows all the relevant properties of obligatory control such as selectional restrictions, uniqueness of the controller, and sloppy interpretation under ellipsis (Monahan 2004).

This construction, which we will refer to as ACC1, alternates with two other constructions, illustrated in (6) and (7) below.

(6) Chelswu-ka [__ tomangka-tolok] Yenghuy-lul seltukhayssta
    Chelswu-NOM   run_away-COMP Yenghuy-ACC persuaded
    'Chelswu persuaded Yenghuy to run away.'   *ACC2*

(7) Chelswu-ka ___ [Yenghuy-ka tomangka-tolok] seltukhayssta
    Chelswu-NOM   Yenghuy-NOM run_away-COMP persuaded
    'Chelswu persuaded Yenghuy to run away.'   *NOM*

The second accusative construction (ACC2) differs from ACC1 in the order of the complement clause and the accusative DP. The construction in (7), referred to as NOM, has a silent object in the matrix clause, determined by the argument structure of the matrix verb. The reference of that object is determined by the overt nominative DP which, as shown by constituency tests, binding, and quantifier float, is a constituent of the embedded clause (Monahan 2004).

All three of these constructions are relatively rare: in the Sejong corpus of 10 million sentences, they occur only 233 times, of which ACC1 occurs 97 (41%), ACC2, 38 (16%), and NOM, 98 times (43%).

3. Two Analyses of Korean Object Control

The relationship between ACC1, ACC2 and NOM has been analyzed as either syntactic control or as semantic control. Under both analyses that have been proposed in the literature, the three constructions are viewed as derivationally related. For now, we will keep this as a working assumption and we will return to it in sections 4 and 6.

3.1. Syntactic Analysis

Under the syntactic analysis, which treats control as raising into a theta-position, the matrix and embedded DP form an A-chain. In both accusative constructions (ACC1, ACC2), the tail of the chain is deleted, instantiating forward control. In NOM, the head of the chain is deleted, thus instantiating backward control (Monahan 2004).

(8) ACC1

John [$_{VP}$ Mary$_k$-ACC [$_{CP}$ [$_{TP}$ ___$_k$ [$_{VP}$ leave]]-$_{COMP}$] persuaded]
                                                    A-chain

(9) ACC2 (possibly scrambled?)

John [$_{XP}$ [$_{CP}$ [$_{TP}$ ___$_k$ [$_{VP}$ leave]]-$_{COMP}$]$_j$ [$_{VP}$ Mary$_k$-ACC t_j persuaded]
                                                       A-chain

(10) NOM (the position of the gap uncertain)

John [$_{VP}$ ___$_k$ [$_{CP}$ [$_{TP}$ Mary$_k$-NOM [$_{VP}$ leave]]-$_{COMP}$] persuaded]
                                   A-chain

The difference between the two forward patterns may be due to scrambling. However, at this point it is not entirely clear which of the accusative constructions is basic and which, if any, is derived by scrambling. Frequency data above may suggest that ACC1 is basic (hence more common than the presumably scrambled version), but there may be many reasons for this distribution. Next, if frequency were taken seriously, it is somewhat puzzling that the presumably scrambled structure (ACC2) is so frequent.

While scrambled OSV sentences occur in only about 1.5% of the Sejong corpus data, the ratio of ACC1 to ACC2 is about 2.5:1, which makes ACC2 inexplicably widespread for a case of scrambling.

In summary, at this point it is hard to rule out either direction of derivation (ACC1→ ACC2 and ACC2→ACC1), and it is possible that both constructions are base generated.

3.2. Semantic Analysis

The semantic analysis of control relies on the fact that Korean has subject and object *pro*-drop. This analysis assumes that the silent element in all three control constructions is a null pronominal. Then the overt DP is analyzed as being co-indexed with a null pronominal, via a meaning postulate (Agent-to-Agent). In those instances where the coindexation is impossible, the null pronominal is interpreted nonreferentially (Choe 2006, Cormack and Smith 2004).

According to this analysis, ACC1 is the basic structure, with the accusative DP in the specifier of VP, and the control complement adjoined to V' as shown in (11). The accusative DP c-commands the nominative DP in the embedded clause. The control interpretation is achieved by the meaning postulate which links the agent of the embedded proposition and the persuadee of the matrix (Cormack and Smith 2004):

(11)   John $[_{VP} [Mary_1$-ACC$]$ $[_{V'} [_{CP} [_{TP} pro_2$ leave$]$-COMP$]$ persuaded$]$

Although Korean has object *pro*-drop, the structure in (11) is incompatible with the null pronominal in the specifier position coindexed with the embedded subject (12).

(12)   *John $[_{VP} [pro_1]$ $[_{V'} [_{CP} [_{TP}$ Mary-NOM$_2$ leave$]$-COMP$]$ persuaded$]$

The apparent violation of Condition C in (12) seems to be remedied by local scrambling (within the VP). Under such scrambling, the control complement appears in the specifier of VP, and the matrix DP adjoins to V':

(13)   John $[_{VP} [_{CP} [_{TP} DP_1$ leave$]$-COMP$]$ $[_{V'} [DP_2$-ACC$]$ persuaded$]$

In this structure, either of the coindexed DPs can be expressed by a null pronominal. If the null pronominal appears in the embedded clause, the result is ACC2, if in the matrix, NOM:

(14) a.   John $[_{VP} [_{CP} [_{TP} pro_1$ leave$]$-COMP$]$ $[_{V'} [DP_2$-ACC$]$ persuaded$]$

   b.   John $[_{VP} [_{CP} [_{TP} DP_1$ leave$]$-COMP$]$ $[_{V'} [pro_2$-ACC$]$ persuaded$]$

The control interpretation is crucially achieved by the meaning postulate; when a referential antecedent of the null pronoun is not available, *pro* is interpreted arbitrarily (Choe 2006).

4. Syntax or Semantics? Structural considerations

4.1. Scrambling

Cormack and Smith (2004) stipulate that local scrambling obviates the binding violation shown in (12). The data in Choe (2006) suggest that the accusative DP which follows the *tolok*-complement (as in ACC2) may have different binding properties than the preposed accusative DP in ACC1. There seem to be two issues involved here: first, the general import of local scrambling in Korean, second, the difference between ACC1 and ACC2. Thus scrambling is a crucial analytical component of the semantic analysis.

There are at least two reservations about scrambling, one general, and the other specific to Korean. On a general level, many arguments in favor of scrambling can be shown to be empirically flawed or inconclusive (Fanselow 2001). Theoretically, the concept of A-scrambling conflicts with a number of accepted minimalist assumptions, and base generation of alternative orders may be a better solution (Fanselow 2001).

Even if we ignore this general reservation, something is rotten in the state of Korean scrambling. Researchers often assume that Korean scrambling is a copycat of Japanese scrambling, and the latter is reported to change binding conditions, including condition C (Nemoto 1991). In Korean, however, scrambling has an effect on A binding (Choi 2001) but not on condition C binding (Johnston and Park 2001). In relatively uncomplicated examples, which are expected to reproduce the effects found in Japanese, there is no change in condition C despite the difference in word order—in both (15a) and (15b), 'he' and 'Chelswu' must be disjoint:

(15) a. Yenghi-nun ku-lul   Chelswu-uy   pang-eyse   mannassta
        Yenghi-TOP him-ACC   Chelswu-GEN room-at   met
        'Yenghi met him$_{i/*j}$ in Chelswu's$_j$ room.'

   b. Yenghi-nun Chelswu-uy   pang-eyse   ku-lul   mannassta
        Yenghi-TOP Chelswu-GEN room-at   him-ACC   met
        'Yenghi met him$_{i/*j}$ in Chelswu's$_j$ room.'

Thus the reliance on scrambling may be problematic, which makes things more difficult for the semantic analysis. To minimize this problem, one could pursue the possibility that ACC1 and ACC2 are both base generated. That still leaves unanswered the question of why the more exotic construction, NOM, must be based on ACC2, not ACC1. The syntactic analysis does not rely on scrambling: the A-movement relation between the overt controller and silent controllee holds regardless of the constituent order.

4.2. Embedded Subject Restriction

The syntactic and semantic analyses achieve the control interpretation by very different means. According to the syntactic analysis, if a matrix empty category c-commands a constituent of the embedded CP, only the embedded subject could be coindexed with it. On the other hand, according to the semantic analysis, since no c-command holds, the meaning postulate should allow for the embedded agent, regardless of its grammatical function, to be coindexed with the matrix object DP (cf. Monahan 2005).

Turning now to a sentence where the embedded subject is not an agent but a patient, we find that the syntactic analysis correctly predicts that this subject will form a dependency with the matrix object. On the other hand, the semantic analysis incorrectly predicts that the agentive argument (the by-phrase in (16)) will be coindexed with the matrix argument.

(16) Tom-un $\_\_\_{j/*k}$ [Mary$_j$-ka Bob$_k$-ey uyhay chwuycay-toy-tolok]
Tom-TOP Mary-NOM Bob-by interview-PASS-COMP
seltukhayssta
persuaded
'Tom persuaded Mary to be interviewed by Bob.'
NOT: 'Tom persuaded Bob to interview Mary.'

4.3. Distributive Quantification

Distributive quantifiers provide another tool of distinguishing between the two analyses. In the syntactic analysis, distributive quantifiers should be possible in the embedded clauses. In the semantic analysis, true distributive quantifiers should be impossible because they would bind a pronominal (Monahan 2005). The syntactic analysis makes the right prediction:[4]

(17) Tom-un [ai-tul-i motwu-ka swukcay-lul ha-tolok]
Tom-TOP child-pl-NOM every-NOM homework-ACC do-COMP
seltukhaessta
persuaded
'Tom persuaded every child to do the homework.'

4.4. Disruption of c-Command

In summary, primary linguistic evidence based on c-command relations supports the syntactic analysis of Korean object control. If this analysis is

---

[4] Cormack and Smith (2004) account for these empirical facts by proposing that Korean lacks true quantifiers and uses indeterminate pronouns instead. At this point it is too early to tell if this is a viable approach.

on the right track, the three object control constructions can be accounted for in the following manner:

(18) a. DP-ACC [~~DP-NOM~~ V-tolok] persuaded   ACC1
   b. [~~DP-NOM~~ V-tolok]$_{(i)}$ DP-ACC (t$_i$) persuaded   ACC2
   c. ~~DP-ACC~~ [DP-NOM V-tolok] persuaded   NOM
   c.´ [DP-NOM V-tolok] ~~DP-ACC~~ persuaded   NOM

As the discussion above shows, there are reasons to doubt the application of scrambling in (18b), which is why it is shown as hypothetical. The base position of the deleted head of the chain in the nominative construction is unclear, and we present both possibilities in (18c, 18c').

5. Syntax or Semantics? Processing considerations

5.1. Processing Predictions

The two analyses compared here make different predictions concerning the processing of the three constructions. In order to flesh out these predictions, let us revisit those components of the syntactic or semantic analysis that may have processing consequences.

First, research on scrambling/word order variation shows that scrambling imposes an additional processing load—this has been amply demonstrated for OSV sentences in Japanese (Mazuka et al. 2002, Miyamoto and Takahashi 2002, Ueno and Kluender 2003;). Thus, scrambling has to be taken into consideration. Second, processing favors the order in which the filler precedes the gap (anaphora); the opposite, cataphoric, order, in which the gap precedes the filler, incurs a greater processing cost (Gordon and Hendrick 1997, Kazanina and Phillips 2004, Sturt 2003).[5] The two analyses apply these criteria in the following way:

	Syntactic analysis	Semantic analysis
ACC1	anaphora	base structure, anaphora
ACC2	cataphora	scrambling, cataphora
NOM	possibly cataphora (18c)	scrambling, anaphora

Table 1. Scrambling and Anaphora in Object Control

The analyses then make different processing predictions for the three constructions. According to the semantic analysis, ACC2 should incur the heaviest processing cost because it shows both scrambling and cataphora. Only scrambling applies in NOM, which should therefore be faster than

---

[5] Of course there are other considerations, for example, frequency. Assuming that the more frequent a construction, the faster it should be processed, ACC1 and NOM should not differ in terms of processing, and ACC2, which is less common, should impose a heavier processing load. This prediction is not borne out.

ACC2 but slower than ACC1. According to the syntactic analysis, ACC1 should be faster than NOM and ACC2. Given the uncertainties with the basic order of the overt DP and embedded clause, it is hard to make a direct comparison between ACC1 and ACC2 or between ACC2 and NOM. The predictions are summarized below (> means 'slower than'):

Syntactic analysis	Semantic analysis
ACC2 > ACC1 (cataphora)	ACC2 > NOM > ACC1
NOM > ACC1 (cataphora?)	(cataphora and scrambling)

Table 2. Predictions Made by The Two Analyses

5.2. Reading Time Experiment

To test which analysis makes correct predictions, we conducted a reading time experiment with ACC1, ACC2, and NOM as target structures. An example sentence is given below.

Example: "The marketing department persuaded the leading actress to appear on a popular talk show to advertise the movie."

ku	yenghwasa -uy	hongpothim -i	yenghwa	hongpo -lul	wuyhay
that	production -GEN	marketing- dept-NOM	movie	advertising -ACC	for
W1	W2	W3	W4	W5	W6
"The marketing department ....to advertise the movie."					

Table 3. Opening Frame

ACC1	heroine -ACC	popular	talk_show-to	appear -comp	persuaded
NOM	heroine -NOM	popular	talk_show-to	appear -comp	persuaded
ACC2	popular	talk_show -to	appear-comp	heroine -ACC	persuaded
	W7	W8	W9	W10	W11
"...persuaded the leading actress to appear on a popular talk show"					

Table 4. Target Regions

5.2.1 Participants

Twenty-three native speakers of Korean participated in the experiment. At the time of study, subjects were undergraduate students, graduate students, or post docs at either Korea University or UCSD (17 males, 7 females; mean age 25). The subjects were compensated for their participation.

5.2.2 Materials

There were forty sets of sentences of three conditions: ACC1, ACC2, and NOM patterns. Sentences were pseudo-randomized and were split into four lists using a Latin-square design so that each subject would read only one condition per set. Seventy filler sentences were added to the list.

5.2.3 Procedure

The experiment was run on PsyScope. Stimulus presentation was word by word, self-paced, and non-cumulative. After the final word of each sentence, a yes/no comprehension question followed all the sentences including the fillers. There was a practice session with eight sentences before the experiment. The JMP IN statistical package was used for analyzing the data.

5.2.4 Results

The overall correct answer rate was 89%. Statistical analysis was conducted with control pattern as an independent variable and response to comprehension question as a dependent variable. There was no effect of pattern type ($F(2, 22)=0.92$, $p < 0.41$).

The overall reading time (RT) results are given in Figure 1. When analyzing the RTs, word by word statistical analysis was conducted only between ACC1 and NOM patterns. For a comparison with ACC2, whose word order did not match that of ACC1 and NOM, RTs between W7 and W10 were collapsed.

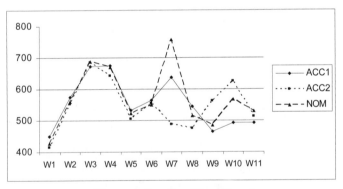

Figure 1. Reading Time Results

Both analyses correctly predicted NOM to be more difficult than ACC1; NOM was significantly delayed at W7 (757 vs. 639 ms), [$F(1, 22) = 7.25$, $p < 0.013$], at W10 (567 vs. 493 ms), [$F(1, 22) = 5.6$, $p < 0.027$] and at W11 (529 vs. 492 ms), [$F(1, 22) = 4.6$, $p < 0.042$].

The statistical analysis of collapsed RTs from W7 to W10 showed a significant effect of control type [$F(2, 22) = 3.86$, $p < 0.026$]. The effect, however, came solely from the difference of the NOM pattern (2195 ms) when compared to the ACC1 (2001 ms) and ACC2 patterns (2014 ms). Pairwise comparison showed that ACC1 and ACC2 did not differ from each other [$F_{(1, 22)}$ =0.37, $p < 0.55$] but that NOM and ACC2 were significantly different [$F_{(1, 22)}$ =5.54, $p < 0.026$]. At W11, there was just a marginal effect of control pattern [$F_{(2, 22)}$ =2.67, $p < 0.08$].

5.2.5 Discussion

Both the syntactic and semantic analysis correctly predicted the NOM pattern to be more difficult to process than the ACC1 pattern. The semantic analysis did not fare well on the overall prediction: ACC2 was as fast as ACC1 and NOM was the only outstanding pattern that caused a significant delay. Recall that if scrambling caused processing difficulty for NOM, then ACC2 also should have been more difficult to process than ACC1. However, ACC1 and ACC2 did not differ from each other in the reading time experiment. This suggests that either scrambling does not cause processing difficulties (unlike other cases where it has been shown to do so) or the constructions in question are not related by scrambling. Only the NOM pattern differed from both ACC1 and ACC2: NOM > ACC1/ACC2. This general finding provides another argument against the semantic analysis, which predicted the order ACC2 > NOM > ACC1.

Beyond this result, however, neither analysis did particularly well. Recall that in formulating the predictions of each analysis, we anticipated deleterious effects of cataphora. The results do not support this prediction; in particular, ACC2, which is the clearest case of cataphora, did not show any reading time delay. At this point, we cannot offer a definitive explanation of this result, but we would like to point out a possible reason for it. In principle, cataphora seems more difficult because it requires the parser to hold in working memory an expression with no/minimal referential content and associate it later on with a more contentful expression. However, negative effects of cataphora (known primarily from English) can be offset by some other effect. What could that be? In a head-final language, there is a preference for putting longer constituents to the left of the shorter ones (Yamashita and Chang 2001); in the Korean control constructions, this would entail putting the embedded *tolok*-clause before the accusative DP (ACC2).

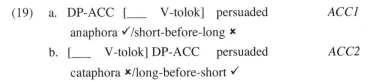

(19)   a. DP-ACC [___   V-tolok]   persuaded   *ACC1*
             anaphora ✓/short-before-long ✘

        b. [___   V-tolok] DP-ACC   persuaded   *ACC2*
             cataphora ✘/long-before-short ✓

If the long-before-short preference and anaphora preference cancel each other out, this would correctly predict that ACC1 and ACC2 should not differ in RTs—precisely the result obtained in this experiment. What exactly then causes the significant slowdown in NOM? If the position of the gap is to the left of the *tolok*-clause, then the deleterious effects of cataphora may be felt and cannot be offset by the presence of an overt segment as in (20). This may account for the results of this experiment.

(20) ___ [DP-NOM V-tolok] persuaded *NOM*

Although this explanation is attractive and may help us solve the question concerning the position of the gap in the nominative construction, it is extremely tentative. Basing an entire structural account on this reading time result alone would be premature. More fine-grained experimental measures may provide us with a more definitive solution to the question of where the gap in NOM is located—before or after the embedded clause.

6. Conclusions

In this paper, we examined three Korean object control constructions with the complementizer *–tolok*: with the overt accusative controller in the matrix clause either preceding or following the embedded clause (ACC1, ACC2), or with the overt nominative controller in the embedded clause (NOM).

We considered two analyses that have been proposed to account for these constructions. In the semantic analysis, base generated *pro* is argued to be coindexed with the overt controller via a meaning postulate. In the syntactic analysis, an A-chain linking two thematic positions is proposed; in ACC1 and ACC2, the tail of the chain is deleted, while in NOM, the head undergoes deletion.

Structural considerations and processing evidence favor the syntactic analysis. This in turn means that Korean object control supports the growing body of empirical evidence for backward control and the theoretical approach to control as raising into a thematic position. If this approach is pursued, it is important to answer the following question: In an A-chain, what motivates the deletion of the head in some cases and the tail in others, resulting in the ACC-NOM contrast? Most other languages with backward control do not show the alternation as Korean does; rather, particular verbs occur only in the forward or only in the backward pattern. For other types of movement, it has been proposed that the choice is driven by phonological considerations (Bošković 2002, Nuñes 2004), but it remains to be seen if these considerations are sufficient to account for the ACC-NOM contrast in Korean object control.

Our processing findings cast doubt on the scrambling relation between the two constructions with the overt controller in the matrix clause (ACC1 and ACC2). On a more general level, the processing findings offer additional support to theoretical proposals rejecting scrambling as theoretically and empirically untenable (Fanselow 2001). With respect to Korean, assuming that ACC1 and ACC2 are both base generated, it is possible that only one of those constructions is actually Obligatory Control (ACC1), while the other instantiates Non-Obligatory Control. This would account for slight differences between ACC1 and ACC2 noted by some researchers (for example, Non-Obligatory Control examples in Choe 2006 all involve ACC2). If this possibility is on the right track, the syntactic and semantic approaches may both be needed — as long as their division of labor is done correctly.

References

Bolinger, D. 1961. Syntactic Blends and Other Matters. *Language* 37:366-381.

Bošković, Ž. 2002. On Multiple Wh-fronting. *Linguistic Inquiry* 33:351-383.

Choi, H.-W. 2001. Binding and Discourse Prominence: Reconstruction in "Focus" Scrambling. *Optimality-Theoretic Syntax*, eds. G. Legendre, J. Grimshaw and S. Vikner, 143-169. Cambridge: MIT Press.

Choe, H.-S. 2006. On (Backward) Object Control in Korean. *Harvard Studies on Korean Linguistics* XI: 373-386. Kyunggi: Hanshin Pub.

Cormack, A., and N. Smith. 2004. Backward Control in Korean and Japanese. *University College of London Working Papers in Linguistics* 16:57-83, London: UCLWPL.

Dowty, D. 1985. On Recent Analyses of the Semantics of Control. *Linguistics and Philosophy* 8:291–231.

Fanselow, G. 2001. Features, θ-roles, and Free Constituent Order. *Linguistic Inquiry* 32:405-437.

Farrell, P. 1995. Backward Control in Brazilian Portuguese. *Proceedings of the Eleventh Eastern States Conference on Linguistics*, eds. J. Fuller, H. Han and D. Parkinson, 116-127. Ithaca, NY: Cornell University.

Gordon, P., and R. Hendrick. 1997. Intuitive Knowledge of Linguistic Coreference. *Cognition* 62(3):325-370.

Harada, S.-I. 1973. Counter Equi-NP Deletion. *University of Tokyo Research Institute of Logopedics and Phoniatrics Annual Bulletin* 7:113-147.

Hornstein, N. 2003 On Control. *Minimalist Syntax*, ed. R Hendrick, 6-81. Oxford: Blackwell.

Jackendoff, R., and P. Culicover. 2003. The Semantic Basis of Control in English. *Language* 79:517-556.

Johnston, J., and I. Park. 2001. Some Problems with a Lowering Account of Scrambling. *Linguistic Inquiry* 32:727-732.

Kim, Y.-J. 2000. Subject/Object Drop in the Acquisition of Korean: A Cross-linguistic Comparison. *Journal of East Asian Linguistics* 9:325-351.

Kim, N.-K. 1978. Tolok Sentential Complements in Korean. *Papers in Korean Linguistics: Proceedings of the Symposium on Korean Linguistics*, 137-147. Columbia: Hornbeam Press.

Kim, N.-K. 1984. *The Grammar of Korean Complementation.* Honolulu: Center for Korean Studies, University of Hawaii.

Kazanina, N., and C. Phillips. 2004. On-line Processing of Universal vs. Language-Specific Constraints. Paper presented at 10th AMLaP, Aix-en-Provence, France.

Kuroda, S.-Y. 1978. Case Marking, Canonical Sentence Patterns and Counter Equi in Japanese. *Problems in Japanese Syntax and Semantics*, eds. J. Hinds and I. Howard, 30-51. Tokyo: Kaitakusha.

Langacker, R. W. 1995. Raising and Transparency. *Language* 71:1-62.

Mazuka, R., K. Itoh, and T. Kondo. 2002. Cost of Scrambling in Japanese Sentence Processing. *Sentence Processing in East Asian Languages*, ed. M. Nakayama, 131-166. Stanford: CSLI.

Miyamoto, E. T., and S. Takahashi. 2002. Sources of Difficulty in Processing Scrambling in Japanese. *Sentence Processing in East Asian Languages*, ed. M. Nakayama, 167-188. Stanford: CSLI.

Monahan, P. 2004. Backward Object Control in Korean. *WCCFL* 22:356-369.

Monahan, P. 2005. Backward Object Control in Korean. Manuscript. University of Maryland.

Nemoto, N. 1991. Scrambling and Conditions on A-Movement. *WCCFL* 10:349-358.

Nuñes, J. 2004. *Linearization of Chains and Sideward Movement.* Cambridge: MIT Press.

Polinsky, M., and E. Potsdam. 2002. *Backward Control. Linguistic Inquiry* 33:245-282.

Polinsky, M., and E. Potsdam. 2003. Backward Control: Evidence from Malagasy. *Proceedings of the Eighth Meeting of the Austronesian Formal Linguistics Association*, eds. A. Rakowski and N. Richards, 257-272. Cambridge, MA: MITWPL.

Polinsky, M., and E. Potsdam. 2006. Expanding the Scope of Control and Raising. *Syntax* 9.

Potsdam, E. 2006. Backward Object Control in Malagasy. *WCCFL* 25.

Sturt, P. 2003. The Time-course of the Application of Binding Constraints in Reference Resolution. *Journal of Memory and Language* 48:542-562.

Ueno, M., and R. Kluender. 2003. Event-related Brain Indices of Japanese Scrambling. *Brain & Language* 86:243-271.

Yamashita, H., and F. Chang. 2001. "Long before short" Preference in the Production of a Head-final Language. *Cognition* 81(2):B45-B55.

The Acquisition of Relative Clauses in Japanese: A Comparison with Korean

HIROMI OZEKI[1] AND YASUHIRO SHIRAI[2]
University of Tokyo[1], *University of Pittsburgh*[2]

1. Introduction[1]

Although many studies have investigated the acquisition of relative clauses in postnominal relative clause languages, not many studies have investigated prenominal relative clauses. Kim (1987) and Ozeki and Shirai (2005, 2007) showed that Korean and Japanese relative clauses, which are prenominal, develop very differently from English relative clauses. Still, what is lacking in this area is an "intra-typological approach" (Slobin 1997). Slobin states that there are two kinds of crosslinguistic methodology. The first takes advantage of typology as a means of holding many factors constant, exploring the effects of "fine-grained differences"; he calls this the "intra-typological approach". The second approach, which he calls the "cross-typological approach," compares languages of different types, seeking universals on the one hand, and typological specific factors on the other. Relative clause constructions in Japanese and Korean are very similar, but

---

[1] We are grateful to Kevin Gregg, K. Seon Jeon and Hae-Young Kim for their helpful comments on a draft of this paper. We would also like to thank the participants at the 15th Japanese/Korean Linguistics Conference for their comments and suggestions.

have one important difference: Korean overtly marks relative clauses in verb morphology, whereas Japanese does not. In this paper, we make an intra-typological comparison between Japanese and Korean to investigate the effect of fine-grained differences and how they affect the acquisition of relative clauses. We compare the results from our study with those of Kim (1987), which reported a detailed analysis of the study of spontaneous speech data from three Korean children.

Ozeki and Shirai (2005) showed that relative clauses in Japanese develop very differently than in English in that the semantics and functions of early relative clauses are very different. Diessel and Tomasello (2000), who analyzed spontaneous speech data from English-speaking children, showed that the prototype of English relative clauses is presentational relative clauses that modify the copula complement of a copula clause, and assert new information concerning the referent established in the presentational clause (Diessel and Tomasello 2000:137), as in example (1):

(1) Here's a tiger [that's gonna scare him]. (Nina 3;1)

In contrast, Ozeki and Shirai reported that Japanese children used relative clauses as typical restrictive relative clauses right from the beginning. They found that the prototypical relative clauses that Japanese children use early modify abstract nouns and pronouns such as *mono* 'thing', *tokoro* 'place', *no* 'one' with stative/generic predicates, and have a function of naming a referent, as in (2):

(2) [Kore ireru] mon doko ni   aru? (Sumi 2;03)
    This put.in thing where Loc² exist
    'Where is the thing [which you put this in]?'

Ozeki and Shirai explained these differences as follows: In Japanese, all noun modifiers are placed prenominally, and sometimes it is not easy to distinguish between noun modification by words, phrases, and clauses (Kato 2003, Teramura 1980). As a result, Japanese children's relative clauses are extended from adjectival modification, which they have already acquired, and therefore there is no discontinuity observed of the sort that is seen in relative clause acquisition in English.

Kim (1987) reported similar characteristics in the acquisition of Korean relative clauses, but there are some interesting differences, which may be attributed to subtle differences between the two relative clause constructions in Japanese and Korean. In what follows, we examine these similarities and

---

² List of abbreviations: Acc = accusative, Dat = dative, Dec = declarative, Dim = diminutive, Ind = indicative, Int = interrogative, Loc = locative, Nom = nominative, Part = particle, Pres = present tense, Rel = relative, Ret = retrospective, Top = topic.

differences and attempt to explain them by the competing notions of overt marking and formal complexity.

2. Characteristics of the Noun-Modifying Constructions in Japanese and Korean

Relative clauses in Korean and Japanese have in common that they are prenominal and have no relative pronoun; that is, they are both very meager in grammatical marking of relativization. However, one major difference between Japanese and Korean lies in verb morphology. In Japanese, both relative clauses and matrix clauses have the same verb form as in (3), whereas in Korean, relative clauses require tense-aspect forms that are different from matrix clauses as in (4). In other words, Japanese does not morphologically mark a relative clause, whereas Korean does.

(3) a. Kinoo   ano hito   ni   atta.
       Yesterday   that person-Dat   meet-Past
       'Yesterday (I) met that person.'

     b. [kinoo   atta]   hito
       yesterday   meet-Past   person
       'the person [(I) met yesterday]'

(4) a. Ecey   ku salam-ul   manna-ass-ta.
       yesterday   that person-Acc   meet-Past-Ind
       'Yesterday (I) met that person.'

     b. [ecey   manna-ass-te-n]   salam
       yesterday   meet-Past-Ret-Rel   person
       'the person [(I) met yesterday]'   (Kaplan and Whitman 1995:30)

Another important fact about Korean relative clauses is that the suffix -(u)n, one of the three suffixes that are used on verbs in relative clauses (as in 5b), is used also as the prenominal adjectival ending (as in 5a), though it is not used when an adjective is used as a predicate in matrix clauses. In Japanese, there is no such formal similarity between adjectives and verbs in relative clauses, because adjectives take the same ending regardless of whether they are used as a predicate or a prenominal modifier, which is distinct from a verbal ending.[3]

---

[3] In Japanese, there is another adjective-like element called *keiyoo doosi*, variously translated into English as 'verbal adjective', 'adjectival noun', or '*na*-adjective', which changes form depending on whether it is used as a noun-modifier or as a predicate. Interestingly, children's acquisition of this class of words is slow. Miyata (2001) shows that the acquisition of *keiyoo doosi* is delayed compared with adjectives.

(5) a. [pala-n]   sakwa
    green   apple
    'green apple'

   b. [Yumi-ka   tta-n]   sakwa
     Yumi-Nom pick-Rel.Past apple
     '(the) apple that Yumi picked'   (Kim 1997:339)

In sum, prenominal adjectives and relative clauses share structural characteristics in Korean; that is, the function of noun modification is explicitly marked, which is not the case in Japanese.

3. Previous Crosslinguistic Research

Clancy et al. (1986) conducted a comprehension experiment with Korean children, and compared the results with published studies on relative clause comprehension in English (e.g. Sheldon 1974, Tavakolian 1981) and Japanese (e.g. Hakuta 1981, Harada et al. 1976). They reported that 'in Japanese, there was a markedly higher frequency of errors on center-embedded sentences than there was in Korean', which they attributed to the lack of overt marking (Clancy et al. 1986:247).

From the result of Clancy et al., one might suggest that the acquisition of Korean relative clauses, which have overt marking, is easier than Japanese relative clauses. However, the other side of the coin is that Korean overtly marks relative clauses, which makes them morphologically more complex than Japanese. Slobin (1973) suggests that a structure is acquired early if its form-meaning relationship is overtly marked. However, often times overt marking of form-meaning relationships results in formal complexity i.e., they are in a trade-off, as Slobin (1979:189) wrote: 'there are universal constraints on the degree to which a language system can be compact and still be meaningful and processible.' In this paper, we investigate how these variables of simplicity vs. overt marking influence the acquisition processes of relative clauses in Korean and Japanese.

4. Method

4.1. Data

Longitudinal data of spontaneous speech from three boys are analyzed. Data from Tai (Miyata 2000) and Taa (Kokuritsu Kokugo Kenkyujo 1982a, 1982b) are typical longitudinal data transcribed from the recordings of caretaker-child interaction. Sumi's data come from a large-scale published corpus of diary data (Noji 1973-1977), which represent almost all the utterances produced by a child from birth to age six. In this paper we analyzed the data up to age 3;11. Tai's and Sumi's data are available on the

CHILDES Database (MacWhinney 2000, Oshima-Takane and MacWhinney 1998).

Children	Age range	Number of relative clauses
Tai	1;5-3;1	68
Taa	0;11-3;11	148
Sumi	0;0-3;11	309

Table 1. Data Analyzed for Japanese Children

4.2. Data Analysis

All sentences containing relative clauses were extracted and coded. We included all the instances of a finite clause modifying a head noun except for the clauses of 'outer relationship' (Teramura 1969, 1975) for which a gap within the relative clause does not exist, as in the case of appositive clauses in English. (Japanese permits this type of noun-modifying clauses; see Matsumoto 1997). The repetitions of the caretaker's and the child's own utterances that appeared within three utterances of the original were excluded from the analysis of the children's speech.

We compared our results from Japanese children with Kim's (1987) results from data of spontaneous speech from three Korean children. Kim also excluded from analysis what we called outer relationship, which she called appositive clauses.

Children	Age range	Number of relative clauses
Wenceng	1;8-2;9	112
Polam	1;6-2;6	100
Ciman	1;10-3;5	294

Table 2. Korean Children Analyzed by Kim (1987)

5. Results and Discussion

5.1. Emergence of Relative Clauses

First, there was a major difference in the emergence of relative clauses in Korean and Japanese. Kim reported that for each Korean child, after adjectives as predicates emerge, adjectival noun-modification and relative clauses emerge almost simultaneously between 1;9 and 2;1. In Japanese, adjectives also appear as predicates first, and then adjectival noun-modification emerges between 1;6 and 1;8, and relative clauses emerge four or five months later, between 1;10 and 2;2.

Korean-speaking children			Japanese-speaking children		
Child	Prenominal adjectives	Relative clauses	Child	Prenominal adjectives	Relative clauses
Wenceng	1;9	1;9	Tai	1;6	1;10
Polam	1;11	2;0	Taa	1;8	2;1
Ciman	2;1	2;1	Sumi	1;8	2;2

Table 3. Emergence of Prenominal Adjectives and
Relative Clauses in Korean and Japanese

Although we need more data to generalize from these results, it appears that:

• The emergence of relative clauses in Korean, which coincides with prenominal adjectival modification, is earlier than that of Japanese.

• Prenominal adjectives emerge later in Korean than in Japanese.

Kim explained that simultaneous emergence of prenominal adjectives and relative clauses is due to the fact that Korean relative clauses share the same morphological marking with prenominal adjectives. This explanation is supported by our Japanese data because Japanese, which does not overtly mark these structures uniformly, does not exhibit the same pattern, and because there is a few-month delay for relative clauses. On the other hand, late emergence of prenominal adjectives in Korean can be attributed to overt marking on predicate adjectives, which makes them as complex as relative clauses, and that may be why Korean acquisition of prenominal modification itself is delayed.

5.2. Head Nouns of Early Relative Clauses

Kim reported that in Korean, the head nouns of early relative clauses are always -*kes* 'one/thing', and lexically determinate head nouns appear a few months later.

(6) [Yeki kki-nun] ke eti iss-e?   (Ciman, 2;8)
    here insert-Pres thing where exit Int?
    'Where is the thing [that (I) insert here]?'   (Kim 1987:125)

Kim reported that for the first two or three months after the emergence of relative clauses, head nouns used in relative clauses are exclusively –*kes,* and that other indeterminate head nouns such as -*tey* 'place' emerge after the emergence of lexically determinate head nouns in relative clauses.

In Japanese, we also observed that the head nouns of early relative clauses include more indeterminate head nouns such as *mono* 'thing' or -*no* 'one' than lexically determinate head nouns. However, Japanese children use both types of head nouns from the early stages of relative clause use. (For example, thirty-five percent of the head nouns during the first three months of relative clause use were lexically determinate head nouns). Therefore, in Japanese, there seems to be no time lag between the emergence of indeterminate and determinate head nouns. Furthermore, Japanese children start to use relative clauses with various indeterminate head nouns—not only -*no* (which roughly corresponds to -*kes* in Korean) but also *mono* 'thing', *yatu* 'thing', *tokoro* 'place'. Japanese children do not show a *no*-only stage, corresponding to Korean children's *kes*-only stage.

(7) [Mamagoto asobu] no doko   ni   aru ne ?   (Sumi 2;3)
    House   play   one where Loc exist-Part
    'Where is the thing with which (we) play house?'

(8) Kore ne   [moratta] yatu.   (Tai 2;1)
    This Part was:given thing
    'This is the thing I was given.'

(9) [Taa-tyan ga   kanda] tokoro doko nano?   (Taa 2;7)
    Taa-dim-Nom bit   place where-Part
    'Where is the place that Taa bit?'

One possible explanation for this difference between Japanese and Korean may lie in the form-function transparency of indeterminate head nouns. Japanese -*no* is used not only as "one" or "thing", but also as a complementizer, genitive case marker, appositive case maker and final particle very frequently, whereas its Korean equivalent -*kes* does not have the latter three functions.[4] Furthermore, Japanese children produced several other head nouns equivalent to "one" or "thing", such as *mono, yatu*, which is not the case for Korean. Therefore, the form-function transparency of -*no* in Japanese is lower than that of -*kes* in Korean, both in terms of their function and of availability of synonymous forms. This may contribute to the lack of a *no*-only stage in Japanese, unlike Korean.

Another possible explanation for this asymmetry is that Japanese children use prenominal modification for several months before producing relative clauses, with various adjectives and head nouns, so that at the time of the emergence of relative clauses they are already familiar with the noun-

---

[4] See Horie (1998) for further discussion of -*no* and -*kes*.

modifying construction. As a result, they can use verb-modifiers with various head nouns. In Korean, children start to use both adjectival-modifiers and verbal-modifiers at the starting point of the noun-modifying construction, and both modifiers are formally complex. Due to this formal complexity, Korean children may have to start with simple structures with a simple head noun.

5.3. Relativization for 'Here and Now'

Kim highlights early emergence and frequent use of relativization on copula complements of matrix sentences in Korean, as in the following example (Kim 1987:148).

(10)   I   ke-n   [sicang-eyse   sa-n]   ke-ya.   (Wenceng 2;6)
       this one-Top   marketplace at   buy-Past one be-Dec
       'As for this one, (it is) the one that (we) bought at the marketplace.'

Kim (1987:166) states:

> One thing that immediately attracts our attention ... is the early emergence and high frequency of relativization on copular complements... For all three Korean-speaking children, the category Copular Complement occupies the highest percentage of the total relative-clause-containing complex NPs.

What is interesting in this regard is the fact that "an overwhelming majority of utterances containing relative clauses attached to copula complements begin with demonstratives" (Kim 1987:167) such as "this one" or "that one".

Kim points out that both Korean and English children start to use relative clauses modifying copula complements in the structure "This/That/Here is X", and argues that one possible explanation is young children's universal tendency to talk about the 'here-and-now'. Our data also show that Japanese children's relative clauses modifying copula complements are almost exclusively in "This/That is X" structures. Therefore, it may be argued that this structure (i.e. relative clauses modifying copula complements in 'This/that is X [Relative Clause]') is universally early.

At the same time, however, there was a subtle difference. In Japanese, the frequency of relative clauses modifying copula complements is not so high. Among all the relative clauses used, the ratio of copula complements, which are mostly in 'This/that is X' structure in both languages, was 34.6 percent in Korean, and was 14.1 percent in Japanese. How can we account for this difference?

To characterize the earliest relative clause production in our data from Japanese children, we analyzed the first ten relative clauses produced by each child. An average of 72 percent of their earliest relative clauses modify a head noun that is not present in the context of interaction, or something that the child or the caretaker cannot find, as in the following examples:

(11) [kore ireru] mon doko ni   aru?   (Sumi 2;03)
      this put:in thing where-Loc exist
      'Where is the thing [which you put this in]?'

(12) [Hikidasi ni   aru] no tyoodai   (Sumi 2;4)
      drawer   Loc exist one give:me
      'Give me the one in the drawer'

(13) [katta] *no   zidoosya wa ?   (Taa 2;2)
      bought one car   Top
      '(Where is) the car (we) bought?'

Thus, in Japanese, children's earliest relative clauses were often used to identify the referent in the context where the child asks about something that he cannot find in his presence, asks for it, tells caretakers that he cannot find it, or explains about it, rather than talking about the 'here-and-now'.

This result can also be attributed to our earlier observation that Japanese children use prenominal modification for several months before producing relative clauses, and are already familiar with the noun-modifying construction so that once relative clauses emerge, they can use verb-modifiers with more cognitively complicated function. All three Japanese children, at the stage when they start to use prenominal adjectives, use them to state the attribute of the things that are in their immediate surroundings. It may be that Japanese children have already passed the 'here-and-now' stage which Korean-speaking children seem to be at when they start to use relative clauses.

6. Summary and Conclusion

To summarize, we found that there are three noteworthy differences between Japanese and Korean relative clause acquisition:

(a) In Korean, prenominal adjectives and relative clauses emerge almost simultaneously. In Japanese, prenominal adjectives emerge earlier than in Korean, but the emergence of relative clauses is later than in Korean.

(b) In Korean, children first exclusively use relative clauses with the head noun -kes, and after several months, they start to use relative clauses with lexically determinate head nouns. In Japanese, although children use indeterminate-head relative clauses frequently, they use relative clauses with lexically determinate head nouns as well right from the emergence of relative clauses.

(c) In Korean, relative clauses modifying copula complements (with "This is X + Relative Clause" structure) emerge early and are used in the highest frequency. In Japanese, copula complement-head relative clauses are not used in such high frequency; instead children use relative clauses to identify a referent that is not visible in the context of interaction.

Kim suggests that the formal similarity between adjectival modification and relative clauses and the overt marking of relative clauses are the reasons relative clauses emerge quite early, together with adjectival modification in Korean. Our results from Japanese support this explanation because in Japanese, where verbs and adjectives are formally quite distinct, relative clauses emerge much later than adjectival modification, as summarized in finding (a). The findings in (b) and (c) show that in Japanese, once relative clauses emerge, children can use them freely, which we suggest is due to formal simplicity in Japanese relative clauses in that verb morphology is identical to that in matrix clauses, and to the later acquisition of relative clauses than prenominal adjectives. Japanese children have already become used to noun-modifying construction at the time of the emergence of relative clauses, so formally they can use them with various head nouns from the early stages and functionally they can use relative clauses in contexts other than the 'here and now'.

From these findings, we may say that in relative clause acquisition in Korean and Japanese, overt marking and simplicity may interact: On the one hand, overt marking may help children to find the function of the form so that it can accelerate the emergence of the relevant structure (as in the case of Korean relative clauses). On the other hand, accelerated emergence and its formal complexity due to overt marking seems to constrain children's production at early stages; that is, a lack of functional differentiation through overt marking may delay the emergence of the structure in question (as in the case of Japanese relative clauses), but once the form emerges, formal simplicity can facilitate children's use of the form in more adult-like manners.

References

Clancy, P., H. Lee, and M. Zoh. 1986. Processing Strategies in the Acquisition of Relative Clauses: Universal Principles and Language-Specific Relativizations. *Cognition* 14:225-62.

Diessel, H. and M. Tomasello. 2000. The Development of Relative Clauses in Spontaneous Child Speech. *Cognitive Linguistics* 11:131-151.

Hakuta, K. 1981. Grammatical Description versus Configurational Arrangement in Language Acquisition: The Case of Relative Clauses in Japanese. *Cognition* 9:197-236.

Harada, S. I., T. Uyeno, H. Hayashibe, and H. Yamada. 1976. On the Development of Perceptual Strategies in Children: A Case Study on the Japanese Child's Comprehension of the Relative Clause Constructions. *Annual Bulletin, Research Institute of Logopedics and Phoniatrics, University of Tokyo* 10:199-224.

Horie, K. 1998. On the Polyfunctionality of the Japanese Particle 'no': From the Perspectives of Ontology and Grammaticalization. *Studies in Japanese Gram-maticalization: Cognitive and Discourse Perspectives*, ed. T. Ohori, 169-192. Tokyo: Kurosio.

Kaplan, T. I. and J. B. Whitman. 1995. The Category of Relative Clauses in Japanese, with Reference to Korean. *Journal of East Asian Linguistics* 4:29-58.

Kato, S. 2003. *Nihongo Syuusyoku Koozoo no Goyooronteki Kenyuu* [A Pragmatic Analysis of Japanese Noun Modifying Constructions]. Tokyo: Hitsuji Shoboo.

Kim, Y. J. 1987. The Acquisition of Relative Clauses in English and Korean: Development in Spontaneous Production. Doctoral dissertation, Harvard University.

Kim, Y. J. 1997. The Acquisition of Korean. *The Crosslinguistic Study of Language Acquisition, Vol.4*, ed. D. I. Slobin, 335-443. Mahwah, NJ: Lawrence Erlbaum Associates.

Kokuritsu Kokugo Kenkyujo [National Institute of Language Research]. 1982a. *Yoozi no Kotoba Siryoo (3): Issaizi no Kotoba no Kiroku* [Child Language Data (3): A Record of Language by a One-Year-Old]. Tokyo: Shuuei Shuppan.

Kokuritsu Kokugo Kenkyujo [National Institute of Language Research]. 1982b. *Yoozi no Kotoba Siryoo (4): Issaizi no Kotoba no Kiroku* [Child Language Data (4): A Record of Language by a One-Year-Old]. Tokyo: Shuuei Shuppan.

MacWhinney, B. 2000. *The CHILDES Project: Tools for Analyzing Talk. Third Edition*. Mahwah, NJ: Lawrence Erlbaum Associates.

Matsumoto, Y. 1997. *Noun-modifying Constructions in Japanese: A Frame-Semantic Approach*. Amsterdam: John Benjamins.

Miyata, S. 2000. The TAI Corpus: Longitudinal Speech Data of a Japanese Boy Aged 1;5.20 – 3;1.1. *Bulletin of Aichi Shukutoku Junior College* 39:77-85.

Miyata, S. 2001. The Development of NP-Structure. *A Crosslinguistic Study for the Universal Developmental Index: Report of the Grant-in-Aid for Scientific Research (A)(2) (1999-2000) Supported by Japan Society for the Promotion of Science and the Ministry of Education, Science, Sports and Culture*, 124-137.

Noji, J. 1973-1977. *Yooziki no Gengo Seekatu no Zittai, I-IV*. [The Language Development of a Child, I-IV]. Hiroshima: Bunka Hyooron.

Oshima-Takane, Y. and B. MacWhinney. (eds.) 1998. *CHILDES Manual for Japanese, 2nd ed.* McGill University and Chukyo University.

Ozeki, H. and Y. Shirai. 2005. Semantic Bias in the Acquisition of Relative Clauses in Japanese. *Proceedings of the 29th Annual Boston University Conference on Language Development*, eds. A. Brugos, R. Clark-Cotton and S. Ha, 459-470. Somerville, MA: Cascadilla Press.

Ozeki, H. and Y. Shirai. 2007. The Consequences of Variation in the Acquisition of Relative Clauses: An Analysis of Longitudinal Production Data from Five Japanese Children. *Diversity in Language: Perspectives and Implications*, eds. Y. Matsumoto, D. Y. Oshima, O. W. Robinson and P. Sells, 243-271. Stanford, CA: CSLI Publications.

Sheldon, A. 1974. On the Role of Parallel Function in the Acquisition of Relative Clauses in English. *Journal of Verbal Learning and Verbal Behavior* 13: 272-281.

Slobin, D. I. 1973. Cognitive Prerequisites for the Development of Grammar. *Studies of Child Language Development*, eds. C. A. Ferguson and D. I. Slobin, 175-208. New York: Holt, Rinehart and Winston.

Slobin, D. I. 1979. *Psycholinguistics*. 2nd ed. Glenview, IL: Scott, Foresman and Company.

Slobin, D. I. 1997. The Universal, the Typological, and the Particular in Acquisition. *The Crosslinguistic Study of Language Acquisition. Vol. 5: Expanding the Contexts*, ed. D. I. Slobin, 1-39. Hillsdale, NJ: Lawrence Erlbaum Associates.

Tavakolian, S. 1981. The Conjoined-Clause Analysis of Relative Clauses. *Language Acquisition and Linguistic Theory*, ed. S. Tavakolian, 167-187. Cambridge, MA: MIT Press.

Teramura, H. 1969. The Syntax of Noun Modification in Japanese. *The Journal-Newsletter of the Association of Teachers of Japanese* 6:64-74.

Teramura, H. 1975. Rentai Syuusyoku no Sintakusu to Imi: Sono 1 [Syntax and Semantics of Noun Modification, No.1]. *Nihongo Nihonbunka* [The Japanese Language and Culture]: Osaka Gaikokugo Daigaku 4:71-119.

Teramura, H. 1980. Meisi Syuusyoku-bu no Hikaku [Comparison of Noun Modifiers]. *Nitieigo Hikaku Kooza (2): Bunpoo* [Lectures on Contrastive Studies of Japanese and English (2): Grammar], ed. T. Kunihiro, 221-260. Tokyo: Taishukan.

Inalienable Possession Relation in Processing Korean Double Accusative Constructions

KYUNG SOOK SHIN
University of Hawai'i at Mānoa

1. Introduction[1]

While processing languages the parser utilizes various sources of information such as syntactic, semantic, phonological, and pragmatic factors. There are, however, cross-linguistic differences in how the factors exert their effect and interact with each other. For example, in Indo-European languages such as English and German, word order, verb meaning, and inflectional morphology are crucial sources of information to generate syntactic and semantic structures of sentences (MacWhinney et al. 1984). East Asian languages such as Korean and Japanese have different syntactic properties from Indo-European languages in some respects – crucial sources of syntactic information such as verbs and complementizers appear late in the sentence, word order is relatively free, and arguments can be omitted in a sentence. In head-final languages, case marking is an important source of information concerning sentence structures (Carlson

---

[1] I would like to thank William O'Grady, Amy Schafer and Ho-Min Sohn for their valuable comments and suggestions. All remaining errors are my own.

and Tenenhaus 1988, Kim 1999, Miyamoto 2002). For example, a nominative-marked noun phrase is the subject of its clause and an accusative-marked noun phrase is the object of its clause. Moreover, in a sequence of two noun phrases with identical case markers, the second one is typically taken to be the signal of the beginning of a new clause (Uehara 1997, Miyamoto 2002), as shown in (1) and (2).

(1) Yenghi-ka [s Chelswu-ka naka-ss-ta-ko] malhayssta[2]
    Yenghi-NOM Chelswu-NOM go out-PAST-MOOD-COMP said
    'Yenghi said Chelswu went out.'

(2) Yenghi-ka Chelswu-lul [s sonyen-ul ttayli-n] namca-eykey ponaysta
    Yenghi-NOM Chelswu-ACC boy-ACC hit-REL man-DAT sent
    'Yenghi sent Chelswu to the man who hit the boy.'

In sentence (1), the first nominative noun phrase, *Yenghi*, is the subject of the main clause and the second nominative noun phrase, *Chelswu*, is the subject of the embedded clause. And in sentence (2), the first accusative noun phrase, *Chelswu*, is the object of the main clause and the second accusative noun phrase, *sonyen* (boy), is the object of the embedded clause.

But it is not the case that the second accusative noun phrase is always an object of an embedded sentence. Sometimes, it is an object of a main clause since Korean has a monoclausal double accusative construction that includes two accusative noun phrases, as seen in (3).

(3) *Double Accusative Construction*
    Yenghi-ka Chelswu-lul meli-lul ttayli-ess-ta
    Yenghi-NOM Chelswu-ACC head-ACC hit-PAST-DEC
    'Yenghi hit Chelswu's head.'

In sentence (3), the two accusative noun phrases, *Chelswu* and *meli* (head), are parts of a double accusative construction.

It is well known that there are semantic constraints on double accusative constructions. In double accusative constructions, the two accusative noun phrases should enter into an inalienable possession relation.

---

[2] The following abbreviations were used to gloss Korean sentences: ACC=accusative, COMP=complementizer, DAT=dative, DEC=declarative, INST=instructive, MOOD=mood marker, NOM=nominative, PAST=past tense, REL=relative clause maker.

(4) *Inalienable Possession Relation*[3]
Yenghi-ka   Chelswu-lul   meli-lul   ttayli-ess-ta
Yenghi-NOM Chelswu-ACC head-ACC hit-PAST-DEC
'Yenghi hit Chelswu's head.'

(5) *Alienable Possession Relation*
*Yenghi-ka   Chelswu-lul   namtongsayng-ul ttayli-ess-ta
Yenghi-NOM Chelswu-ACC brother-ACC   hit-PAST-DEC
'Yenghi hit Chelswu's brother.'

(6) *No Semantic Relation*
*Yenghi-ka   Chelswu-lul   haksayng-ul ttayli-ess-ta
Yenghi-NOM Chelswu-ACC student-ACC hit-PAST-DEC
'Yenghi hit Chelswu's student.'

The sentence in (4) is grammatical since the two accusative noun phrases, *Chelswu* and *meli* (head) enter into an inalienable possession relation. In contrast, the sentences in (5) and (6) are ungrammatical since *Chelswu* and *namtongsayng* (brother) enter into an alienable possession relation in (5) and *Chelswu* and *haksayng* (student) do not enter into any semantic relations in (6).

Double accusative constructions have an important effect on on-line sentence processing in Korean. This is one of the main factors which cause local ambiguities in processing a sequence of two accusative noun phrases. For example,

(7) *Inalienable Possession Relation*

a. Yenghi-ka   Chelswu-lul   meli-lul...
   Yenghi-NOM Chelswu-ACC head-ACC

b. Yenghi-ka   Chelswu-lul   meli-lul   ttayliessta
   Yenghi-NOM Chelswu-ACC head-ACC hit

c. Yenghi-ka   Chelswu-lul [s meli-lul ttayli-n] namca-eykey ponaysta
   Yenghi-NOM Chelswu-ACC head-ACC hit-REL man-DAT   sent

---

[3] The possession relations can be sub-classified in detail. Inalienable possession relations manifest a body-part relation (e.g., *Yenghi's hand*), a part-whole relation (e.g., *table's leg*), an attribute-holder relation (e.g., *Yenghi's character*), a time-event relation (e.g., *yesterday's weather*) and a locative relation (e.g., *the patch's strawberry*), while alienable possession relations indicate an interpersonal relationship (e.g., *Yenghi's father*) and a possessor-possessee relationship (e.g., *Yenghi's book*) (Chappell and McGregor 1996, Nichols 1988).

(8) *Alienable Possession Relation*

a. Yenghi-ka   Chelswu-lul   namtongsayng-ul...
Yenghi-NOM Chelswu-ACC brother-ACC

b. Yenghi-ka   Chelswu-lul [s namtongsayng-ul...
Yenghi-NOM Chelswu-ACC brother-ACC

(9) *No semantic Relation*

a. Yenghi-ka   Chelswu-lul   Swuni-lul...
Yenghi-NOM Chelswu-ACC Swuni-ACC

b. Yenghi-ka   Chelswu-lul [s Swuni-lul...
Yenghi-NOM Chelswu-ACC Swuni-ACC

In sentence (7a), the first two noun phrases, *Chelswu* and *meli* (head) enter into a possible inalienable possession relation. In this case, they can be constituents of a double accusative construction as we can see in (7b), or they can be arguments of a biclausal construction where the second accusative noun phrase, *meli* (head) is the object of an embedded clause as in (7c). In contrast, the two accusative noun phrases which enter into either an alienable possession relation (*Chelswu* and *namtongsayng* (brother)) as in (8a) or no semantic relation (*Chelswu* and *Swuni*) as in (9a) are not ambiguous – the second accusative noun phrase is the object of an embedded clause.

In sum, even though case marking is an important source of information in Korean sentence processing, the sequence of two accusative noun phrases generates local ambiguities, especially when the two noun phrases enter into a potential inalienable possession relation. For example, two accusative-marked noun phrases which permit an inalienable possession relation can have two interpretations: a monoclausal interpretation where the second accusative noun phrase is an argument of a double accusative construction or a biclausal interpretation where the second accusative noun phrase is an argument of an embedded clause.

The purpose of this study is to investigate (1) whether native speakers of Korean initially solve the local ambiguity with only the help of grammatical information associated with case markers (Autonomous Models: Frazier 1989, Frazier and Rayner 1982), or whether they also initially use semantic information, especially involving the nature of the possession relation in double accusative constructions (Interactive Models: Trueswell et al. 1994), and (2) if semantic information has an effect on initial syntactic ambiguity resolution, how the syntactic and semantic information interact with each other in processing the ambiguous sentences which have a sequence of two accusative noun phrases.

2. Experiment

2.1. Subjects

Fifty-four native Korean speakers participated in the experiment. Forty subjects were undergraduates at a university in Korea and the others were undergraduates or graduates at the University of Hawai'i. They were quite naïve with respect to the purpose of the experiment and considered the comprehension questions as the main part of this experiment. They received a small payment for their participation.

2.2. Materials

Twenty-four sets of center-embedded relative clauses were constructed by using a Korean corpus program from the 21st Century Sejong Project, each containing a sequence of two accusative-marked noun phrases.

(10) a. Inalienable Condition
    Mina-ka   Jinhi-lul   meli-lul   iywuepsi   ttayli-n
    Mina-NOM Jinhi-ACC head-ACC without reason hit-REL
    kkangphay-eykey ponay-(e)ss-ta
    gangster-DAT   send-PASt-DEC
    'Mina sent Jinhi to the gangster who hit (her) head without reason.'

   b. *Alienable Condition*
    Mina-ka   Jinhi-lul   enni-lul   iywuepsi   ttayli-n
    Mina-NOM Jinhi-ACC sister-ACC without reason hit-REL
    kkangphay-eykey ponay-(e)ss-ta
    gangster-DAT   send-PASt-DEC
    'Mina sent Jinhi to the gangster who hit (her) sister without reason.'

   c. *Unrelated Condition*
    Mina-ka   Jinhi-lul   hayngin-ul iywuepsi   ttayli-n
    Mina-NOM Jinhi-ACC passerby-ACC without reason hit-REL
    kkangphay-eykey ponay-(e)ss-ta
    gangster-DAT   send-PASt-DEC
    'Mina sent Jinhi to the gangster who hit a passerby without reason.'

The relative clause constructions were designed to test three different types of semantic relations – in the Inalienable Condition the two accusative noun phrases potentially enter into an inalienable possession relation, in the Alienable Condition they potentially enter into an alienable possession relation, and in the Unrelated Condition the two noun phrases enter into no plausible relation.

    The target sentences were split into three lists balancing all factors in a Latin-Square design. Each list contained 24 target sentences and 48 fillers, which were pseudo-randomized so that at least one filler item intervened between two targets. The target sentences in each list consisted of 8 tokens of each of the 3 conditions. The fillers included sentences with a variety of structures and different length. Subjects were evenly assigned to three lists.

2.3. Hypotheses

The test sentences are center-embedded relative clause constructions in which the first accusative noun phrase is the object of a main clause, and the second accusative noun phrase is the argument of an embedded clause. While comprehending the test sentences on-line, however, the sentences in the Inalienable Condition are potentially ambiguous at the second accusative noun phrase: they can be interpreted as monoclausal double accusative constructions or as biclausal center-embedded relative clause constructions. This local ambiguity can be resolved when the head noun is encountered, as it provides the information that the sentence is a biclausal relative clause construction. In the Alienable or Unrelated Conditions, the sentences are not ambiguous: the second accusative noun phrase is initially interpreted as the object of an embedded clause.

Two patterns of reading times can be predicted. First, if the parser uses only case information, it will take the second accusative-marked noun phrase to be an object of an embedded clause and thus insert a clause boundary before the second accusative-marked noun phrase. Under this assumption, there is no difference in reading times across the three conditions. Secondly, if the parser is sensitive to the nature of the possession relation, it would initially consider the Inalienable Condition to be a monoclausal double accusative construction. In this case, the reading time patterns of the Inalienable Condition would be different from those of other conditions since a clause boundary is not inserted before the second accusative noun phrase and the monoclausal interpretation would have to be changed into a biclausal interpretation at the head noun of the relative clause. The predictions can be summarized as follows:

(11) *Hypotheses*

Hypothesis 1: If the parser uses only case information, there will be no difference in reading times across the three conditions.

Hypothesis 2: If the parser uses possession relations, the Inalienable Condition will show different reading times from other conditions.

2.4. Procedure

A self-paced reading task was used in the study. Table 1 illustrates how each word in each type of sentence was presented on a computer monitor.

Frame 1	Frame 2	Frame 3	Frame 4	Frame 5	Frame 6	Frame 7
NP-Nom	NP1-Acc	NP2-Acc	Adverb	Rel Cl	Head Noun	Verb
Mina-ka	Jinhi-lul	meli-lul enni-lul hayngin-ul	iywuepsi	ttayli-n	kkangphay-eykey	ponayssta
Mina-Nom	Jinhi-Acc	head-Acc sister-Acc passerby-Acc	without reason	hit-Rel Cl	gangster-Dat	sent

'Mina sent Jinhi to the gangster who hit (a) (her) head without reason.'
(b) (her) sister
(c) a passerby

Table 1. Regions for the Self-paced Reading Presentation

Test sentences were presented word-by-word on the screen and the subjects can see the next word to the right of the previous word position by pressing a button.[4] As each new word appeared, the preceding word disappeared. The amount of reading time (RT) the participant spent on each word was recorded as the time between button-presses. After the final word of each sentence, a comprehension question appeared which asked about information contained in the preceding sentence. Participants pressed one of two buttons to respond "Yes" or "No." No feedback was given for the responses. It took about 30 minutes to finish the whole experiment.

2.5. Data Analysis

Each subject's responses on comprehension questions were analyzed to examine whether they understood the test sentences. Reading times falling beyond cutoffs established for each subject at mean plus three standard deviations were replaced with those cutoff values. The number of trimmed reading times was less than 2.5% of the total 9072 test data. Repeated measures ANOVAs and paired t-tests were performed separately at each word position.

---

[4] A button box was used to record the participants' reading times more precisely.

2.6. Results and Discussion

The overall rate of correct answers to a total of 72 comprehension questions was more than 95 percent, which indicates the participants read the test sentences carefully.   Figure 1 shows the reading times per region.   A repeated measures ANOVA for the first two words revealed that there was no significant difference across the three conditions [$F(2,53) = .881, p = .7659$], [$F(2,53) = 1.153, p = .1765$].

At the third word position where the second accusative noun phrase appears, the Inalienable Condition seems to show shorter reading times than other conditions but the difference is marginally significant [$F(2, 53) = 0.957, p = .560$].

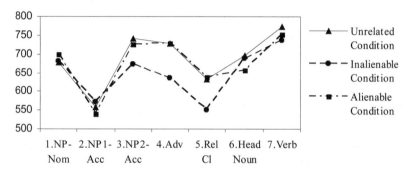

Figure 1. Reading Times for Each Region in
Embedded Clauses with Two Accusative NPs

At the fourth and fifth noun phrases, however, the Inalienable Condition was shorter than other conditions [$F(2,53) = 1.303, p = .0428$], [$F(2,53) = 1.581, p = .015$].   This means that the subjects were sensitive to the inalienable possession relation, and needed less time to process the noun phrase in the Inalienable Condition than in the other conditions.

At the head noun, there was no significant difference in reading times among the three conditions [$F(2,53) = .829, p = .8611$].   But, the comparison of reading time increase between the fifth word and the sixth word showed a statistically significant difference among the three conditions.   The Inalienable Condition showed a greater increase in reading time than the other conditions [$F(2,53) = 3.346, p = .0361$].   Presumably the subjects needed more time to revise their initial analysis of the Inalienable Condition from a monoclausal analysis to a biclausal analysis.   This suggests that the Inalienable Condition is initially considered to be a double accusative construction, and at the head noun, it is reinterpreted as a biclausal construction. This reanalysis causes reading time to increase.

At the seventh word position, no significant difference was found among the three conditions [$F(2,53) =.817, p = .8783$].

3. General Discussion

This study investigated how native speakers of Korean process the potentially ambiguous sentences which contain a sequence of two accusative noun phrases. The results of the experiment indicated that they are sensitive not only to the grammatical information associated with case markers but also to the nature of the possession relation in processing the sentences. Relative clauses with an inalienable possession relation showed the shortest reading time at the words in the embedded relative clause and the greatest increase in reading time at a head noun of a relative clause compared to other constructions. The reading time patterns may suggest that an inalienable possession relation induced the parser to take a sequence of two accusative noun phrases as constituents of a double accusative construction and later reanalyze it as a part of an embedded clause.

As discussed above, the sequence of two accusative noun phrases is potentially ambiguous – they can be either part of a monoclausal double accusative construction or arguments of a biclausal construction. Then, why were they initially taken to be constituents of a double accusative construction? The frequency of the sequence of two accusative noun phrases in a Korean corpus consisting of 1,504,077 words showed an interesting fact. Among a total 101 sequences of two accusative noun phrases, 22 entered into inalienable possession relations and the rest did not enter into any plausible semantic relation.[5] When two accusative noun phrases entered into an inalienable possession relation, they appeared in double accusative constructions (19 times) more frequently than in biclausal constructions (3 times). In contrast, when two accusative noun phrases did not enter into any semantic relation, they occurred in biclausal constructions (64 times) more frequently than in double accusative constructions (15 times).[6] This supports that the frequency of the semantic relation may be one of main factors which influence the comprehension of the sentences (MacDonald et al. 1994, Trueswell et al. 1994) with two accusative noun phrases.

Another interesting finding is that the Inalienable Condition was faster than other conditions at the two word positions following the second accusative noun phrase. One possibility is that the reading time patterns

---

[5] The sequence of two accusative noun phrases entering into an alienable possession relation was not found in the data.

[6] The 15 sentences were different types of double accusative constructions where one of the accusative-marked noun phrases denoted location, time, or goal.

reflect the spillover effect of inalienable possession relation: the effect of the semantic relation appears at the next word positions. Another possibility is that the differences in the reading times among the three conditions may be related to the differences in the syntactic memory cost for the conditions. Unlike the Inalienable Condition, the other conditions are initially taken to involve a biclausal construction so that a clausal boundary is inserted before the second accusative noun phrase. At this point, the first two noun phrases (the nominative noun phrase and the first accusative noun phrase) which are parts of a main clause remain partially processed until the incomplete head-dependency relationships are resolved at the head noun. Holding the incompletely processed noun phrases in working memory increases working memory cost (Gibson 1998), leading to increase the reading times of the following words until the head noun appears.

The experimental results suggest evidence supporting the Interactive Model (Trueswell et al. 1994) in that the native speakers of Korean incrementally process sentences by using various sources of information – the grammatical information associated with case marking, the nature of semantic relations between two accusative noun phrases, and the frequency of each type of semantic relation.

Even though possession relations are common in human languages, how the semantic relations are relevant to linguistic phenomena can differ cross-linguistically. Moreover, double accusative constructions exist in a typologically varied set of language. For example, some languages such as Japanese do not have double accusative constructions, even though possession relations involve in some syntactic constructions. A comparative study to examine how semantic relations such as possession are used in processing the languages could shed light on how the parser employs language specific strategies in comprehending their languages.

References

Carlson, G. N. and M. K. Tenenhaus. 1988. Thematic Roles and Language Comprehension. *Syntax and Semantics 21,* ed. W. Wilkens, 263-300. New York, NY: Academic Press.

Chappell, H., and W. McGregor. 1996. *The Grammar of Inalienability: A Typological Perspective on Body Part Terms and the Part-whole Relation.* New York: Mouton de Gruyter.

Frazier, L. 1989. Against Lexical Generation of Syntax. *Lexical Representation and Rrocess,* ed. W. D. Marslen-Wilson, 505-528. Cambridge, MA: MIT Press.

Frazier, L., and K. Rayner. 1982. Marking and Correcting Errors during Sentence Comprehension: Eye Movements in the Analysis of Structurally Ambiguous Sentences. *Cognitive Psychology* 14:178-210.

Gibson, E. 1998. Linguistic complexity: Locality of syntactic dependencies. *Cognition* 68:1-76.

Kim, Y. 1999. The Effects of Case Marking Information on Korean Sentence Processing. *Language and Cognitive Processes* 14:67-714.

MacDonald, M.C., N. J. Pearlmutter, and M. S. Seidenberg. 1994. The Lexical Nature of Syntactic Ambiguity Resolution. *Psychological Review* 101:676-703.

MacWhinney, B., E. Bates, and R. Kliegl. 1984. Cue Validity and Sentence Interpretation in English, German and Italian. *Journal of Verbal Learning and Verbal Behavior* 23:127-150.

Miyamoto, E. T. 2002. Case marker as clause boundary inducers in Japanese. *Journal of Psycholinguistic Research* 31:307-47.

Nichols, J. 1988. On Alienable and Inalienable Possession. *Honor of Mary Haas: From the Haas Festival Conference on Native American Linguistics,* ed. W. Shiley, 557-609. Berlin: Mouton de Gruyter.

O'Grady, W. 2005. *Syntactic Carpentry: An Emergentist Approach to Syntax.* Mahwah, NJ: Erlbaum.

Trueswell, J. C., K. T. Michael, and M. G. Susan. 1994. Semantic Influence on Parsing: Use of Thematic Role Information in Syntactic Ambiguity Resolution. *Journal of Memory and Language* 33:285-318.

Uehara, H. 1997. Judgments of Processing Loads in Japanese: The Effects of NP-ga Sequences. *Journal of Psycholinguistic Research* 26:255-263.

Gap-filling vs. Filling Gaps: Event-Related Brain Indices of Subject and Object Relative Clauses in Japanese

MIEKO UENO[1,2] AND SUSAN M. GARNSEY[2]

University of California, San Diego[1]
University of Illinois, Urbana-Champaign[2]

1. Introduction[1]

The fundamental question we aim to address in this paper is how syntactically distinct languages are processed in the brain. By investigating such a question we hope to find language-universal and -specific aspects of sentence comprehension and thereby to narrow the gap between linguistic and cognitive neuroscientific approaches to language. Event-related brain potentials (ERPs) are useful in this endeavor, as they reveal millisecond-by-millisecond changes in neural activity during language comprehension.

This study investigates the processing of Japanese subject vs. object relative clauses using both self-paced reading times and ERPs. We compare the processing of gap-filler dependencies in Japanese relative clauses to the processing of filler-gap dependencies in English. We discuss theoretical and experimental background on English and Japanese relative clauses in Section 2 and report our reading-time and ERP experiments in

---

[1] This work was supported by the University of Illinois Research Board and by an NIMH postdoctoral fellowship (T32 MH19554) to the first author.

Sections 3 and 4. Section 5 discusses the implications of the experimental results followed by a conclusion in Section 6.

2. Background

2.1. English vs. Japanese Relative Clauses

Consider subject and object relative clauses in English in (1).

(1) a. Subject relative (SR)
the reporter [who$_i$ ___$_i$ attacked the senator]
FILLER GAP

    b. Object relative (OR)
the reporter [who$_i$ the senator attacked ___$_i$]
FILLER   GAP

A number of studies show that ORs are harder to process than SRs in English (e.g. reading times: King and Just 1991; ERPs: King and Kutas 1995; fMRI: Caplan et al. 2001). The explanation for this is often tied to the notion of filler-gap dependencies. In the psycholinguistic literature, the displaced wh-element is called a "filler" while its canonical position is called a "gap". The filler and its gap are said to be dependent on each other, as the interpretation of a gap involves associating it with its filler (cf. Fodor 1989). While the filler and its gap are immediately adjacent to each other in SRs, there are words between them in ORs, and this linear filler-gap distance is said to be the source of difficulty (e.g. Gibson 1998). Alternatively, however, it is also possible to look at the filler-gap distance in terms of hierarchical syntactic structure shown in Figure 1. There are more syntactic nodes between the filler and its gap in ORs than in SRs, and this structural distance can be another source of comprehension difficulty (O'Grady 1997).

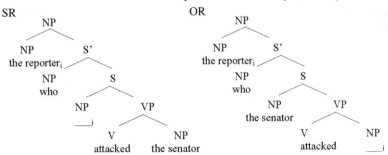

Figure 1. Syntactic Structures for SRs and ORs in English

Japanese relative clauses are different from English relative clauses in several ways. First, they are prenominal, as shown in (2). Second, there is no relative pronoun in Japanese, and the head noun functions as the filler in word-by-word sentence processing. Thus, the gap precedes the filler in Japanese.

(2) a. Subject Relative (SR)

   [___ 議員を   非難した]   記者

   [___senator-ACC   attacked]   reporter

     GAP   FILLER

   'the reporter who [___ attacked the senator]'

   b. Object Relative (OR)

   [議員が   ___   非難した]   記者

   [senator-NOM   ___   attacked]   reporter

                         GAP   FILLER

   'the reporter who [the senator attacked ___]'

In addition to the prenominal structure and absence of overt markers indicating the beginning or end of the relative clause, Japanese allows *pro-drop*. Thus there is a temporary ambiguity up until the head noun position regarding whether a particular sentence fragment will be a relative clause or a mono-clausal sentence. In other words, a relative clause like (2a) can be interpreted initially as a mono-clausal sentence as in (3), but then when the head noun appears, it becomes clear that there is a relative clause instead.

(3) *pro*議員を   非難した

    pro senator-ACC   attacked

    '(Someone) attacked the senator'

In terms of linear distance, SRs involve a longer linear gap-filler distance than ORs in Japanese, as shown in (2). This is exactly the reverse of English relative clauses. However, Japanese relative clauses are argued to have hierarchical structures similar to English as shown in Figure 2, with a covert operator (instead of a relative pronoun) coindexed with both the head noun and the gap (e.g. Kaplan and Whitman 1995).

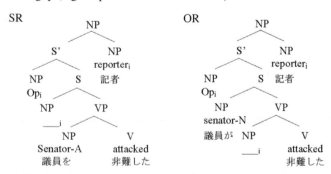

Figure 2. Syntactic Structures for SRs and ORs in Japanese

Thus despite surface differences between the two languages, in both languages ORs involve a longer structural distance than SRs. Therefore, unlike English, linear and structural distance accounts yield different predictions for Japanese, in that a linear distance account predicts a higher processing cost for SRs while a structural distance account predicts a higher processing cost for ORs.

2.2. Previous ERP Research on English Filler-gap Dependencies

As discussed in Section 2.1, ORs are typically harder to process than SRs in English, possibly due to a longer linear or structural filler-gap distance. This section reviews relevant ERP studies in English. ERPs consist of positive and negative voltage peaks termed 'components', and ERP effects are examined in terms of differences in polarity (e.g. N for negative or P for positive), poststimulus latency, amplitude, and distribution over the scalp between experimental and control conditions. Some of the components occur in both slow (differences lasting several seconds) and phasic (differences a few 100 msec in duration) forms.

Earlier studies on the processing of filler-gap dependencies in relative clauses and wh-questions (e.g. King and Kutas 1995, Kluender and Kutas 1993) argued that associating a displaced wh-filler with its gap increases working memory load, and that this processing cost is reflected in an ERP component known as left anterior negativity (LAN: negative deflection of voltage that is larger at the frontal regions of the scalp, often left-lateralized) between the filler and the gap.

Instead of or in addition to LAN effects, recent studies have reported P600 effects (positive peak at around 600 msec poststimulus onset). For instance, Kaan et al. (2000) compared embedded yes-no and wh-questions and found P600 effects at the pre-gap position. They argued that although the P600 had previously been attributed specifically to syntactic reanalysis, their results showed that it can also indicate syntactic integration difficulty in general, in their case the process of integrating a wh-filler into a sentence. A more recent study (Phillips et al. 2005) has reported the combination of both LAN and P600 effects in English wh-questions.

2.3. Previous Reading Time Research on Japanese Relative Clauses

In English, there is wh-movement (and resulting filler-gap dependencies) in both wh-questions and relative clauses, but in Japanese wh-words typically stay *in situ* and thus wh-questions are syntactically distinct from relative clauses. Previous ERP studies of Japanese have investigated wh-questions (e.g. Ueno and Kluender 2003), but not relative clauses, to the best of our knowledge. However, reading time studies of Japanese relative clauses (Ishizuka et al. 2003, Miyamoto and Nakamura 2003) have shown that ORs take longer to read than SRs at or starting at the head noun position. Given the shorter linear gap-filler distance in Japanese, this may suggest that the structural distance account is more promising.

2.4. Predictions

Given the above, we wanted to test whether LAN (and/or P600) effects reflecting filler-gap associations in English would replicate with gap-filler associations in Japanese, and whether these effects in Japanese would correlate with linear or structural distance. If gap-filler association is like filler-gap association, we should see LAN effects between gap and filler possibly followed by P600 effects at the filler. Additionally, if linear distance is more important, we should see more processing costs indexed by these ERP effects for SRs than ORs. On the other hand, if structural distance is more important, we would see ERP effects indexing difficulty in ORs, as suggested by the reading time studies discussed in Section 2.3.

3. Experiment 1: Self-paced Reading Times

Experiment 1 used the self-paced reading task to examine reading times for the experimental stimuli as a first step, in order to determine whether our stimuli would show the same pattern of results as previous studies.

Stimuli consisted of pairs of sentences with singly-embedded (a) subject relatives (SRs) and (b) object relatives (ORs), as shown in (4).

(4)   a. Subject Relatives (SRs)

[新任の 議員を 非難した] 記者には 　　長年の 　相棒が 　　いた。

new   senator-ACC attacked   reporter-DAT-TOP long-term colleague-NOM existed

'The reporter [who attacked the new senator] had a long-term colleague.'

b. Object Relatives (ORs)

[新任の 議員が 　　非難した] 記者には 　　長年の 　相棒が 　　いた。

new   senator-NOM attacked reporter-DAT-TOP long-term colleague-NOM existed

'The reporter [who the new senator attacked] had a long-term colleague.'

In order to confirm that nouns used at the head noun position were equally plausible as the subject or the object of the relative-clause verb, 20 native speakers of Japanese (who did not participate in Experiment 1 or 2) rated sentences created by replacing the gap with the corresponding head noun, as in 'The reporter attacked the senator' vs. 'The senator attacked the reporter', on a scale from '1' (strange) to '5' (natural). There were no significant differences in the ratings [$F_1(1,18) = 1.02$, p > .1; $F_2(1,78) = 2.58$, p > .1] regardless of whether the head noun was used as the subject (mean rating = 4.4) or the object (4.3). Another norming study was conducted to test whether the verbs used in the sentences were transitive-biased. The 69 different verbs used in the relative clause of the stimulus sentences and 31 filler verbs were combined and pseudo-randomized. Ten native speakers of Japanese, a subset of those who had already participated earlier in either Experiment 1 or 2, were presented with the verbs and asked to type the first sensible sentence that came to mind. Collapsed across participants, 96% of the sentences with the relative-clause verbs contained overt direct objects, showing that these verbs were highly transitive-biased. (Interestingly, 35% of the sentences had subject-drop in the total absence of discourse context.)

Eighty sets of experimental sentences were placed in a Latin square design to create two parallel lists. 80 filler sentences were added to each list, and then sentences in these two lists were pseudorandomized and divided into 5 blocks of 32 sentences each.

Forty native speakers of Japanese were timed in a word-by-word self-paced non-cumulative reading task. Stimuli were presented in the center of the computer screen in Japanese characters one word at a time. Yes/no comprehension questions were presented after each sentence to ensure that participants were paying attention.

Reading times were trimmed so that data points beyond 2 standard deviations from the relevant subject x condition x position cell mean were replaced with the corresponding cutoff value, affecting 5% of the data. For each sentence position as well as for the post-relative clause region, a repeated measures ANOVA was conducted with 'relative clause type' as a within-group factor, and either 'subject' (with 'list' as a nested factor) (F1) or 'item' (with 'item group' as a nested factor) (F2) as a random factor.

Figure 3 shows the trimmed reading times by sentence position.

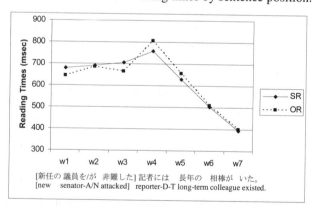

Figure 3. Trimmed Reading Times for Each Sentence Position

In the relative clause region (words 1-3), SRs took longer to read than ORs at the first word position [F1(1,38) = 4.74, p < .05; F2(1,78) = 8.10, p < .01], although items were completely identical across conditions at this position. There was no significant difference at word 2 [Fs < 1]. At word 3 (the relative clause verb, 'attacked'), however, SRs took longer than ORs, but this was reliable only in the item analysis [F1(1,38) = 2.27, p > .1; F2(1,78) = 8.25, p < .01]. In the post-relative clause region (words 4-7), ORs took longer than SRs at the head noun (word 4) [F1(1,38) = 5.60, p < .05; F2(1,78) = 4.79, p < .05], and also at the following word 5, though only marginally so [F1(1,38) = 2.89, p < .1; F2(1,78) = 3.30, p < .1]. There were no significant differences at word 6 [Fs <1] or word 7 [F1(1,38) = 1.19, p > .1; F2(1,78) = 1.01, p > .1]. When reading times for the entire post-relative clause region (w4-w7) were collapsed together, ORs were read significantly more slowly than SRs [F1(1,38) = 8.24, p < .01; F2(1,78) = 6.99, p < .01].

Slow reading times in word 1 must have been due to noise, given that the word in that position was identical in both conditions. The slowdown did not continue on the following word and so will be ignored in the remainder of discussion. At word 2, different case-markers (nominative in ORs and accusative in SRs) on the noun did not lead to reading time differences, even though it is more typical to start a sentence with a nominative- than accusative-marked noun. However, in the self-paced reading paradigm effects are often delayed a word, so we could speculate that the accusative-marked noun in SRs caused a slowdown one word later at word 3, although the difference was reliable only by items. Upon reaching the head noun position, ORs took longer than SRs at the head noun (word 4) and the following word (word 5) and when the reading times across the entire post-relative clause region were combined (words 4-7). Thus there seems to be a reliable processing cost to ORs, starting from the position which clearly indicates the relative clause structure. This replicates the previous studies in support of the structural distance account.

4. Experiment 2: ERPs

Experiment 2 investigated ERPs in response to SRs and ORs. Thirty-three native speakers of Japanese participated in the study. The stimuli were identical to Experiment 1, but instead of self-paced presentation, they were presented at a rate of 650 msec per word. The electroencephalogram (EEG) was recorded from 25 electrodes.

ERP waveforms were examined using two-word averages to reveal phasic effects, and four-word averages for longer-lasting effects. The statistical analyses were done separately on midline (Fz, Cz, Pz), parasagittal (AF3/4, F3/4, FC3/4, C3/4, CP3/4, P3/4, PO7/8), and temporal (F7/8, FT7/8, T3/4, T5/6) electrodes as well as on individual electrodes, using 'relative clause type', 'anteriority', 'hemisphere', and 'subject' (with 'list' as a nested factor) as factors.

Sentences were compared at the relative clause region (relative clause+head noun), to see how gap-filler dependencies in Japanese relative clauses were processed, and at the post-relative clause region (head noun+remainder of the sentence), to see whether there were any effects after the gap was filled by the head noun.

Visual inspection of the relative clause region showed bi-lateral anterior negativity at the relative-clause verb and head noun position of ORs (Figure 4). ANOVAs performed in the latency window of 300 to 1250 ms after the onset of the relative clause verb 'attacked', encompassing the 300-600 msec (standard latency for LAN) windows of both 'attacked' and 'reporter-DAT-TOP', revealed a significant or marginal main effect of relative type in the midline [$F(1, 31) = 7.36$, $p < .05$] and parasagittal [$F(1, 31) = 3.04$, $p < .1$] arrays. Additionally, there was a marginal interaction between condition and anteriority in the midline array [$F(2, 30) = 3.04$, $p < .1$]. ANOVAs run on individual electrodes in the same latency window revealed a significant main effect of relative clause type at Fz, AF3, F4, FC4, and C4, as well as a marginal main effect at Cz, F3, and C3. These effects indicated that ORs were more negative than SRs, especially at frontal regions.

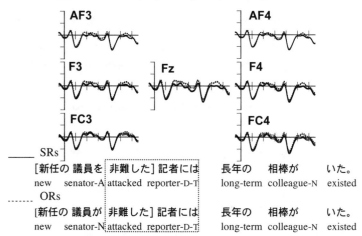

Figure 4. ERPs from Frontal Electrodes to the Relative
Verb and Head Noun Positions of SRs vs. ORs

Figure 5 shows the comparison at the post-relative clause region. Visual inspection of these four-word averages showed a long-lasting continuous positivity to ORs, starting at about 500 ms poststimulus onset of the head noun and continuing throughout the epoch to the sentence end. ANOVAs performed in the latency window of 500 ms to 2950 ms poststimulus onset (starting at the head noun and continuing to the end of the sentence) revealed a significant or marginal main effect of relative clause type in all three arrays [midline: $F(1, 31) = 7.77$, $p < .01$; parasagittal: $F(1, 31) = 4.82$, $p < .05$; temporal: $F(1, 31) = 3.36$, $p < .1$], as well as a significant relative clause type x anteriority interaction in the temporal array [$F(3, 29) = 3.38$, $p < .05$]. ANOVAs run on individual electrodes in the same time window revealed a significant main effect of relative clause type at Fz, AF4, T4, C4, T5, T6, CP3, P3, and P4, as well as a marginal main effect at Cz, C3, PO7, and PO8. These effects indicated that ORs were more positive than SRs, especially at centro-posterior sites.

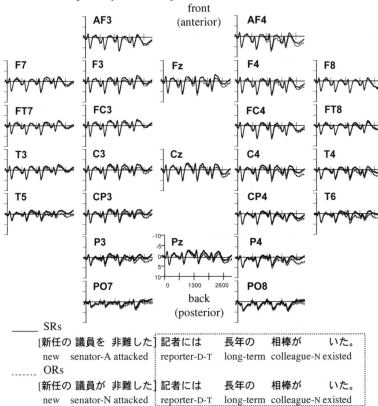

Figure 5. ERPs from All Electrodes to the
Post-relative Clause Region of SRs vs. ORs

To summarize, ORs elicited bilateral anterior negativity at the relative verb and head noun positions and continuous centro-posterior positivity from the head noun to the sentence-end, compared to SRs. The anterior effect has the typical latency and scalp distribution for anterior negativity, a variant of LAN. The centro-posterior effect has a reasonable scalp distribution for a P600 effect, but shows a steady long-lasting positive shift instead of a local peak. However, LAN effects have been reported in both local and long-lasting versions (e.g. King and Kutas 1995, Kluender and Kutas 1993), and the same might be true for P600 effects. In fact, Van Petten and Kutas (1991) reported a slow positive shift in response to syntactically incoherent sentences, such as *Be place prefer the was city it and sure be perfume*, and more recently, Casado et al. (2005) reported a long-lasting positive shift for a phrase structure reallocation process in Spanish. These effects are argued to index syntactic processes typically related to the P600, and the positivity effect in our experiment may be a similar variant.

The anterior negativity observed during the relative clause may be due to the demands placed on working memory by both the storage of a gap and its subsequent retrieval for gap-filling (cf. Kluender and Kutas 1993). On this interpretation, the parser recognizes the gap in ORs upon seeing a transitively biased verb immediately following a nominative-marked noun, since there is no object in the usual position. This leads to processes that tax working memory until the object-gap in the relative clause is filled by the head noun. The parser would also recognize a gap in SRs at either the accusative-marked noun or the relative clause verb (as a scrambling interpretation is possible at the noun position itself) of SRs, but this seems to be easier, as indicated by the ERP results.

Another possible explanation has to do with differences in the likelihood of subject- and object-drop in Japanese. It is much more common to drop subjects than objects with transitively biased verbs like those used in this experiment (as shown in our norming test). If the sentence is parsed as a simple mono-clausal sentence up until the head noun, at the relative clause verb the ORs appear to be missing an object, while SRs appear to be missing a subject. Since missing objects are less common, the appearance of a missing object in the ORs may contribute to greater processing cost.

The continuous positivity starting at the head noun is more clearly due specifically to relative-clause processing, since there is no longer any ambiguity. Consistent with previous results obtained by Kaan et al. (2000), this positivity seems to index the greater syntactic integration costs of filling object-gaps. This fits well with the structural distance account, in that the object gap position is more deeply embedded and thus more structurally distant from the head noun, leading to more retrieval and integration costs.

5. General Discussion

The two experiments reported here have shown that Japanese ORs are harder to process than SRs. In both reading times and ERPs, the extra processing cost was clearly shown starting at the head noun and continuing to the end of the sentence.

Our reading time study replicated the results of previous studies finding that ORs took longer to read than SRs starting at the head noun position. Our ERP study showed further that similar ERP components were elicited by English and Japanese ORs: anterior negativity effects between filler and gap or gap and filler and positivity effects when and after the gap was filled. If we interpret the anterior negativity effect in the relative clause region as associated with gap-filler dependencies, we could further say that the pattern of results suggests similar parsing operations for both filler-gap and gap-filler dependencies. However, as discussed in Section 4, there is an alternative possible interpretation of the anterior negativity that is not specifically about relative clause processing. Therefore, what we can say with more certainty is that gap-filler association in Japanese relative clauses seems to involve a long-lasting integration process after the filler, as indexed by the continuous positivity in ORs. If we take this approach and assume that the continuous positivity indicates greater syntactic integration cost for ORs, both ERP and reading time data are more consistent with a structural rather than linear distance account of relative clause processing difficulty in Japanese.

We have been focusing on the linear vs. structural distance accounts, but we are aware that this is not the only possible interpretation. It could be that the discourse prominence of subjects over objects causes the extra processing cost to ORs. Some linguists have proposed that Japanese relative clauses do not involve syntactic movement and that gaps are actually *pro*s instead of traces (e.g. Murasugi 2000). On this interpretation, a cataphoric relationship links the gap and the filler at the head noun. Then rather than gap-filler distance (either linear or structural), what actually matters is that the subject *pro* is easier to link cataphorically with the head noun than the object *pro*, possibly due to its discourse prominence. Related to this, several ERP studies (e.g. Cowles et al. 2003, van Berkum et al. 2003) have reported anterior negativity and/or P600 effects in the establishment of anaphoric links. Cowles et al. (2003), in particular, reported a sustained anterior negativity when the parser is carrying referential ambiguity, as well as a P600 effect when that referential gap was filled. Thus the present results could be linked with this type of interpretation, and we hope to move the discussion forward by exploring more types of filler-gap/gap-filler dependencies in our future research.

6. Conclusion

To conclude, our experiments have shown that Japanese ORs are harder to process than SRs. Our data also suggest that gap-filler association in Japanese relative clauses involve a long-lasting integration process after the filler, as indexed by the continuous positivity to ORs. Finally, both ERP and reading time data seem more consistent with a structural distance account than a linear distance account, at least for Japanese relative clauses.

References

Caplan, D., S. Vijayan, G. Kuperberg, C. West, G. Waters, D. Greve, and A. M. Dale. 2001. Vascular Responses to Syntactic Processing: Event-related fMRI Study of Relative Clauses. *Human Brain Mapping* 15:26-38.

Casado, P., M. Martín-Loeches, F. Muñoz, and C. Fernández-Frías. 2005. Are Semantic and Syntactic Cues Inducing the Same Processes in the Identification of Word Order? *Cognitive Brain Research* 24:526-543.

Cowles, H. W., M. Kutas, and R. Kluender. 2003. Different ERP Results from Identical Sentences: The Importance of Prior Context in Sentence Processing. Poster presented at the 16th Annual CUNY Conference.

Fodor, J. D. 1989. Empty Categories in Sentence Processing. *Language and Cognitive Processes* 4:155-209.

Gibson, E. 1998. Linguistic Complexity: Locality of Syntactic Dependencies. *Cognition* 68:1-76.

Ishizuka, T., K. Nakatani, and E. Gibson. 2003. Relative Clause Extraction Complexity in Japanese. Poster presented at the 16th Annual CUNY Conference.

Kaan, E., A. Harris, E. Gibson, and P. Holcomb. 2000. The P600 as an Index of Syntactic Integration Difficulty. *Language and Cognitive Processes* 15:159-201.

Kaplan, T. I., and J. B. Whitman. 1995. The Category of Relative Clauses in Japanese, with Reference to Korean. *Journal of East Asian Linguistics* 4:29-48.

King, J. W. and M. A. Just. 1991. Individual Differences in Syntactic Processing: The Role of Working Memory. *Journal of Memory and Language* 30:580-602.

King, J. W. and M. Kutas. 1995. Who Did What to When?: Using Word- and Clause-level ERPs to Monitor Working Memory Usage in Reading. *Journal of Cognitive Neuroscience* 7:376-395.

Kluender, R. and M. Kutas. 1993. Bridging the Gap: Evidence from ERPs on the Processing of Unbounded Dependencies. *Journal of Cognitive Neuroscience* 5:196-214.

Miyamoto, E. and M. Nakamura. 2003. Subject/object Asymmetries in the Processing of Relative Clauses in Japanese. *Proceedings of the 22nd West Coast Conference on Formal Linguistics*, eds. G. Garding and M. Tsujimura, 342-355. Somerville, MA: Cascadilla Press.

Murasugi, K. 2000. An Antisymmetry Analysis of Japanese Relative Clauses. *The Syntax of Relative Clauses*, eds. A. Alexiadou, P. Law, A. Meinunger, and C. Wilder, 231-263. *Amsterdam*: John Benjamins.

O'Grady, W. 1997. *Syntactic Development*. Chicago: Chicago University Press.

Phillips, C., N. Kazanina, and S. Abada. 2005. ERP Effects of the Processing of Syntactic Long-distance Dependencies. *Cognitive Brain Research* 22:407-428.

Ueno, M. and R. Kluender. 2003. On the Processing of Japanese Wh-questions: Relating Grammar and Brain. *Proceedings of the 22nd West Coast Conference on Formal Linguistics*, eds. G. Garding and M. Tsujimura, 491-504. Somerville, MA: Cascadilla Press.

van Berkum, J., C. M. Brown, P. Hagoort, and P. Zwitserlood. 2003. Event-related Brain Potentials Reflect Discourse-referential Ambiguity in Spoken Language Comprehension. *Psychophysiology* 40:235-248.

Van Petten, C. and M. Kutas. 1991. Influences of Semantic and Syntactic Context on Open and Closed Class Words. *Memory and Cognition* 19:95-112.

Part V

Syntax and Semantics

On What Makes Korean HOW Island-Insensitive

DAEHO CHUNG
Hanyang University

1. Introduction[1]

This paper is concerned with the difference between HOW and WHY in Korean with respect to island-sensitivity. As shown in (1) and (2), the apparent adjunct wh-phrase *ettehkey* 'how' does not show island effects, while adjunct *way* 'why' does:

(1) a. [<u>ettehkey</u> yoliha-n]   yangkoki-ka masiss-ni?
       how   cook-ADN   mutton-NOM delicious-QE
       'Q mutton that is cooked how is delicious?'

    b. [yangkoki-lul <u>ettehkey</u> yoliha-myen] ku   citokhan naymsay-ka
       mutton-ACC how   cook-if   that nasty   smell-NOM
       epseci-ni?
       disappear-QE
       'Q if you cook mutton how, that nasty smell disappears?'

[1] This paper is an abridged and revised version of Chung (2005). Some modification is made, in particular in relation to the discussions in Section 3. I would like to thank all the audience at the 15th J/K Linguistics Conference. I would also like to thank professors Chung-hye Han and Pil Young Lee for valuable discussions and comments on this work. I alone am responsible for any errors.

(2) a. *[Tom-ul <u>way</u> ttayli-n] yeca-ka kamok-ey ka-ess-ni?
  T.-ACC why beat-ADN woman-NOM jail-to   go-PAST-QE
  'Q a woman who beat Tom why was imprisoned?'
 b. *[salam-ul   <u>way</u>   ttayli-myen]   kamok-ey   ka-ni?
  man-ACC   why   beat-if   jail-to   go-QE
  'Q if you beat a person why, you're imprisoned?'

Ettehkey resides in a relative clause in (1a) and in a conditional clause in (1b). Both sentences are fine. The sentences in (2) show that *way* is not allowed in such island environments. The fact that *ettehkey* and *way* display different syntactic behaviors is somewhat unexpected because adjunct wh-phrases are generally believed to be island-sensitive. The difference needs to be somehow explained.

There have been several analyses entertained to explain the island-insensitivity of *ettehkey*: T. Chung's (1991) ECP (Empty Category Principle) account based on a VP adjunct analysis, D. Chung's (1996) binding account based on a nominal analysis, Yang's (1997) ECP account based on a d-linking analysis, and D. Chung's (1999) ECP account based on a predicate analysis. In this paper, I point out some non-trivial problems with such analyses, and propose an alternative (nominal) analysis, in which *ettehkey* is decomposed into *e-tte-ha-key* 'Det-N-do-adverbializer', as in (3), based on the morphological paradigm that Korean wh-phrases display.

(3) *ettehkey* → *e-tte-ha-key* 'Det-N-do-adverbializer'

The presence of the nominal element N enables *ettehkey* to be wh-scope-licensed via binding, accounting for the island-insensitivity of Korean HOW.

2. Previous Approaches and their Problems

In this section, I will review some previous approaches to the island-insensitivity of Korean HOW. Let us first discuss T. Chung's (1991) ECP account based on a VP adjunct analysis of *ettehkey*.

2.1. T. Chung's (1991) ECP Account Based on a VP Adjunct Analysis of *Ettehkey*

T. Chung (1991) claims that Rizzi's (1990) conjunctive ECP is responsible for the HOW vs. WHY difference in Korean. According to T. Chung, adverbs take different positions depending on their types, as schematically shown in (4), where manner or instrumental adverbs are generated VP-internally, spatio-temporal adverbs are generated higher than manner or instrumental adverbs but still within VP, and causal adverbs are generated VP-externally.

(4) (= slightly modified from T. Chung 1991:244, (11))

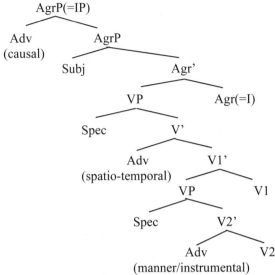

Manner or instrumental adverbs are taken as sisters of V2, spatio-temporal adverbs as those of V1', and causal adverbs as adjuncts of AgrP.

Now let us see how the conjunctive ECP explains the contrast between HOW and WHY. All adverbs, including causal adverbs, are head-governed. The causal adverb is head-governed by Agr, while all other adverbs are head-governed by V1 or V2 in the structure. In addition, all adverbs, except for causal adverbs, are *specially a-governed* by the subject due to the c-command relation. T. Chung (1991) motivates this special a-government relation from the so-called plural agreement between subject and adverbs, as discussed in Choe 1988, Kuh 1987, Song 1975, 1988, etc. That is, adverbs may bear the dummy plural marker *-tul* when the subject is plural. Thus, all adverbs, except for causal adverbs, are island-insensitive because they satisfy the ECP, without having to resort to the regular antecedent government relation. As a manner adverb, *ettehkey* is island-insensitive. In contrast, *way* is island-sensitive as a causal adverb.

T. Chung's (1991) structure in (4) seems very natural. However, as pointed out in D. Chung (1999), the analysis faces several non-trivial problems. First, causal adverbs can also host a dummy plural marker:

(5) (= T. Chung's (16))
   {encey-tul/etiey-tul/ettehkey-tul/way-tul}   o-ess-ni?
   when-PL/where-PL/ how-PL/why-PL   come-PAST-QE
   'When/where/how did (you-Pl) come?'

If the c-command relation matters in the licensing of the dummy plural marker, -tul, then the subject should be higher than the causal adverb at least at some point of the derivation,

Second, T. Chung (1991) generates causal adverbs in a position higher than the subject position so that it cannot be specially antecedent-governed by the subject. Notice, however, that a subject can appear higher than causal adverbs, as in the example (6):

(6) Kim kyoswu-uy   nonmwun-i   way   palphyotoyci anh-ess-ni?
     Kim professor-GEN   paper-NOM   why be;presented NEG;do-PAST-QE
     'Why was Professor Kim's paper not presented?'

We might say that the subject in (6) is generated lower than way and scrambled to the overt position at a later stage.[2] However, it is generally observed that clause-internal scrambling remedies binding violations. Thus, if, as T. Chung claims, a subject may antecedent-govern adverbs in its c-command domain, then causal adverbs should be allowed in islands whenever the subject is scrambled over them. But this is not true, as shown in (7) and (8):

(7) *ne-nun   [e$_i$ [Kim   kyoswu-ka   way palphyoha-n] nonmwun-ul
     you-TOP   Kim   professor-NOM   why present-ADN   paper-ACC
     ilk-ess-ni?
     read-PAST-QE
     'Q you read the paper that Professor Kim presented why?'

(8) *[Kim kyoswu-ka   nonmwun-ul way   palphyoha-myen]
     Kim   professor-NOM   paper-ACC   why   present-if
     salamtul-i   silmangha-keyss-ni?
     people-NOM   disappointed-will-QE
     'Q People will get disappointed if Professor Kim presents his papers why?'

There are some other problematic aspects to T. Chung's (1991) analysis, but I would like to refer the audience to D. Chung's (1999) comments on T. Chung (1991).

2.2. D. Chung's (1996) Binding Account Based on a Nominal Analysis of *Ettehkey*

Now let us briefly look at D. Chung's (1996) analysis. Working from Lee's (1993) analysis of causative ending -key as nominalizer -ki plus

---

[2] Even if subjects are assumed not to undergo scrambling as claimed in Saito (1985), the grammaticality of a sentence like (7) is still problematic since there will be no difference between causal adverbs and other adverbs with respect to the c-command relation with subjects.

postposition -*ey* meaning 'at', Chung (1996) decomposes *ettehkey* into predicate *etteh* plus nominalizer -*ki* plus postposition -*ey*, as shown in (9).

(9) ettehkey → etteh-ki-ey
              -NMZ-at

As it contains a nominal element, *ettehkey* can have its [+wh] scope in terms of binding along the lines of Baker (1970), Reinhart (1995), Tsai (1991, 1994), etc.

One crucial problem with this analysis is that predicate *etteha* 'to be how' itself is island-insensitive as well as *ettehkey*, as shown in (10):

(10) [e$_i$ [sanghwang-i   *etteh(a)*-ta-ko]   pokoha-n]   kyengchal-i
      situation-NOM to;be;how-DE-C report-ADN police-ACC
      haykotoy-ess-ni?
      be;fired-PAST-QE
      'Q the police officer who reported that the situation is how was fired?'

Notice that *etteha* does not contain -*key*, but it is still island-insensitive. Thus, D. Chung's (1996) claim that *ettehkey* is island-insensitive because of the nominal property of the adverbial ending -*key* does not seem to be accurate.[3]

2.3. Yang's (1997) ECP Account Based on a D-linking Analysis of *Ettehkey*

Let us now discuss Yang's (1997) d-linking analysis. According to Yang, wh-elements with *ette* or *etteha* are d-linked and thus *ettehkey* is d-linked. Being d-linked, *ettehkey* does not have to move, vacuously satisfying the ECP (Pesetsky 1987).

This line of approach, however, faces the following problems. First, Korean wh-elements with no *ette(ha)* are freely d-linkable as well, as shown in (11):

(11) ku   cwungey {nwukwu/mwues/eti/encey, etc.}
     that among   who/what/where/when
     'among them, who/what/where/ when, etc.'

Second, wh-elements with *ette(ha)* are not necessarily d-linked. For example, the sentences in (12) can be uttered with no prior linguistic context:

---

[3] T. Chung's (1991) analysis cannot explain the grammaticality of (10), either, since *etteh* here is not a VP adjunct.

(12) a. (To a friend you just saw)
yocum   <u>ettehkey</u> cinay-ni?
recently   how   spend-QE
'How are you these days?'

   b. (Looking at your damaged car bumper)
<u>etten</u>   nom-i   ilen   cis-ul   ha-ess-e?
which   guy   such   thing-ACC   do-PAST-QE
'What rascal did this?'

Third, wh-elements in islands are not necessarily d-linked. (13), for example, can be uttered without any previous context.

(13) a. yocum   [nwu-ka   e$_i$ ssu-n]   chayk$_i$-i   cal   phal-li-ni?
Recently   who-NOM   write-ADN   book-NOM   well sell-PASS-DE
'Q. the book that who wrote sells well these days?'

   b. Tom-i   [mues-ul   mek-ese]   pay-ka   aphu-ni?
T.-NOM   what-ACC   eat-because   stomach-NOM   sick-QE
'Q. Tom is sick because he ate what?'

Thus, d-linking does not seem to be directly connected with the syntactic behavior of *ettehkey*.

2.4. D. Chung's (1999) ECP Account Based on a Predicate Analysis of *Ettehkey*

Now turn to D. Chung (1999), where *etteha* and *ettehkey* are analyzed as predicates (the latter being a small clause predicate). Predicates side with arguments rather than with adjuncts in the sense that they both participate in theta-identification, while adjuncts do not. Thus, it is claimed that argument or predicate wh-elements are theta-identified in situ and need not move, while adjunct wh-elements are not theta-identified in situ and need to move for scope licensing.

It may be correct to analyze *etteha* and *ettehkey* as predicates, based on various morpho-syntactic behaviors. However, it does not seem to be correct to claim that predicate wh-elements are licensed by theta-identification and need not be a-governed or need not be locally linked. Notice that predicate movement does display island effects, as shown in the sentences in (14), which are cited from Baltin (1989):

(14) a. *How intelligent did she wonder whether he was?

   b. *How eager did her campaign staff wonder whether she was?

   c. *How afraid of dogs did they ask if he was?

Observe also that predicate phrases in Korean cannot be extracted across a clause boundary, not to mention out of an island, as illustrated in (15):

(15) a. *[o-ess-ta-ko]ᵢ   Mary-ka   [Sue-ka eᵢ]   malha-ess-ta.
     come-PAST-DE-C M.-NOM   S.-NOM   say-PAST-DE
     (Intended) 'Mary said that Sue came.'

  b. *[o-ess-ta-ko]ᵢ   na-nun   [Mary-ka [Sue-ka eᵢ]
     come-PAST-DE-C I-TOP   M.-NOM S.-NOM
     malha-ess-nunci]   alkosiph-ta.
     say-PAST-QE   want;to;know-DE
     (Intended) 'I want to know if Mary said that Sue came.'

To sum up, all the analyses thus far proposed bear some non-trivial problems, calling for an alternative analysis.

3. A Revised Nominal Analysis

In this section, I propose a nominal analysis of *ettehkey*, but the nominality does not come from the ending *-key* but from some other sub-component of the wh-element.

3.1. On Wh-Morphology in Korean

First, note that at least some Korean wh-elements are morphologically complex. As discussed in D. Chung 1996, a lot of Korean wh-elements start with *e(n)-*, as illustrated in (16a):

(16) Wh-elements (=adapted from D. Chung 1996:140, his (16))
    a. Wh-elements with *e(n)*
       eti/encey/elma(<enma)/enu (N)/*etten* (N)/*etteha/ettehkey*
       where/when/how much/which/to be how/how

    b. Wh-elements with no *e(n)*
       nwu(kwu)/mwues/mwusun (N)/*myech* (CL)/*way*
       who/what/what (N)/how many/why

What is the grammatical status of the string *e(n)-* in (16a)? Is it just a coincidence that more than half of the Korean wh-elements start with this? My answer is no. Rather, I would like to analyze the string *e-* or *en-* as a determiner or a determiner-like element that modifies or takes as its complement a nominal element that follows.

    The determiner analysis of *e(n)-* receives supporting evidence from the following phenomena. First, the string *e(n)-* has a paradigmatic relation with other determiner-like elements, as pointed out in D. Chung (1996:143, (19)):

(17) a. *etteh(a)-key*   'how'
    ileh(a)-key   'this way'
    celeh(a)-key   'that way'
    kuleh(a)-key   'that way'

   b. *encey*   'when'
    icey   'this time or now'
    cecey   'that time'
    kucey   'that time or the day before yesterday' cf. *ecey* 'yesterday'

   c. *ette(ha)n*   'which'
    ile(ha)n   'this kind of'
    cele(ha)n   'that kind of'
    kule(ha)n   'that kind of'

Korean seems to have an *i/ku/ce/e* N pattern at least for some wh-elements, just as Japanese has a *ko/so/a/do* N pattern.[4,5] With a paradigmatic relation being confirmed, at least some Korean wh-elements should be viewed as complex. For example, *encey* and *eti* should be analyzed as in (18):

(18) a. *encey* 'when' > *enu-cey* 'ENU-time'

   b. *eti* 'where' > *enu-tey* 'ENU-place', etc.

---

[4] Wh-element *mues* also seems to have a similar pattern, if *-es* in *mues* is etymologically identical to *-kes* (see Kim 1997:387, where *mues* is analyzed as *musus-kes*).

(i)   *mues*   'what'
    ikes   'this (thing)'
    cekes   'that thing over there'
    kukes   'that thing'

[5] Similarly, Japanese displays a *ko/so/a/do* N pattern at least for some wh-elements. Hoji (1995) maintains that *da* or *do* in the question words like *dare, doko,* and *dono* has a paradigmatic relation with other demonstrative-like elements in Japanese, i.e., *ko* 'this,' *so* 'that,' and *a* 'that over there,' as exemplified below:

(i)   a. *dare*   'who'
      kore   'this thing'
      sore   'that thing'
      are   'that thing over there'
    b. *doko*   'which place' 'where'
      koko   'this place'
      soko   'that place'
      ako   'that place over there'
    c. *dono* N   'which N'
      kono N   'this N'
      sono N   'that N'
      ano N   'that N over there'

Hoji (1995) further notes that *n* in *nani* and *naze* is historically related to *d*.

Another piece of evidence for the determiner analysis of *e(n)-* comes from the fact that *enu* 'which' can modify some wh-elements but not those that start with *e(n)-*. As exemplified in (19), *enu* can go with wh-elements *nwukwu* 'who' or *mwues* 'what' but not with *encey* 'when', *eti* 'where', *elma* 'how much', or *ettehkey* 'how'.

(19) a. *enu {nwukwu/mwues}*
    which who/what

  b. **enu {encey/eti/elma/ettehkey,* etc.}
    which when/where/how much/how, etc.

The contrast can be easily explained under the determiner analysis of *e(n)-*. Since it is itself a determiner, *e(n)-* in the wh-elements in (19b) resists an additional determiner of the same type.

3.2. Application to *Ettehkey* 'how' and *Etteh* 'to be how'

Once *e(n)-* in wh-elements is analyzed as a determiner, then wh-element *ettehkey* 'how' should be morpholgocially decomposed into at least two subcomponents: *e* plus *ttehkey*. Notice further that the wh-element ends with the so-called adverbializer *-key*, and this ending must be hosted by a verb. *H* in *ettehkey* can be analyzed as a reduced form of the verb *ha* 'do'. As shown in (17a), *ettehkey* in fact can be pronounced as *ettehakey*, though this latter form sounds archaic. Refer to D. Chung (1999) for additional verbal properties that *ettehkey* displays. Thus, *ettehkey* should be decomposed into four sub-parts, as in (20). Similarly, predicate wh-element *etteha* 'to be how' should be analyzed as *e-tte-ha*, as in (21):

(20) *e-tte-ha-key*
    DET-N-do-adverbializer

(21) *e-tte-ha*
    DET-N -do

The second element, i.e. *tte*, is diagnosed as a nominal element because the first element, i.e. *e-*, as a determiner, requires a nominal element to be modified and the third element, i.e. *ha*, as a transitive verb, requires a nominal complement.[6]

Given this (revised) nominal analysis, *ettehkey* and *etteha* can take advantage of a binding option in their wh-scope licensing. (Reinhart 1995, Tsai 1991, 1994, etc.). It can be assumed that binding is germane to nomi-

---

[6] The verb *ha* may take some apparently adverb-like elements, so-called onomatopoeic adverbs, e.g. *penccekha* 'flash'. Notice, however, an accusative case marker can attach to such elements: *penccek-ul ha*. Thus, it is clear that the verb *ha* takes some sort of nominal complement. I thank Pil Young Lee for informing me of these facts.

nal elements since the referential index is confined to nominals. The lack of island effects for *ettehkey* and *etteha* now follows, as schematically illustrated in (22):[7]

(22)

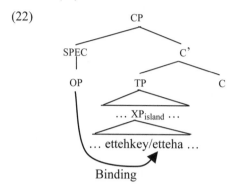

A syntactic island does not block the binding relation between the question operator and these nominal wh-elements within the island since binding is basically constrained by c-command.

In contrast, *way* 'why' is not a nominal element and the binding option is unavailable for the scope interpretation. It has to resort to the movement option. Thus, when it resides in an island, while its scope position outside the island, it necessarily crosses an island, leading to an island violation. Wh-elements in (16b), except for *way*, are themselves nominal elements or modify a nominal element, and the lack of island effects for these wh-elements also naturally follows.

References

Baker, C.L. 1970. Notes on the Description of English Questions: The Role of an Abstract Question Morpheme. *Foundations of Language* 6:197-219.

Baltin, M. 1989. Comments on Cinque's Paper "The Respective Scope of Long and Successive Cyclic Movement." Paper presented at the Second Princeton Workshop on Comparative Grammar. Princeton University.

Choe, H.-S. 1988. Restructuring Parameters and Complex Predicates: Transformational Approach. Doctoral dissertation, MIT.

Chung, D. 1996. On the Representation and Licensing of Q and Q-Dependents. Doctoral dissertation, University of Southern California.

Chung, D. 1999. On the Licensing of HOW. *Studies in Generative Grammar* 9.2:337-360.

Chung, D. 2000. On the Categorial Status of Interrogatives and Some Theoretical Implications, *Ene* 25.4:723-743.

---

[7] In Chung (1996, 2000), I claimed there is a DP layer over CP for interrogative clauses based on the various nominal properties of question clauses. I ignore the DP layer in this paper.

Chung, D. 2005. Why is HOW in Korean Insensitive to Islands?: A Revised Nominal Analysis. *Studies in Modern Grammar* 39:115-131.

Chung, T. 1991. On Wh-Adjunct Extraction in Korean. *Harvard Studies in Korean Linguistics IV*, eds. S. Kuno, J. Whitman, I.-H. Lee, S.-Y. Bak, and Y.-S. Kang, 241-248. Cambridge, MA: Dept. of Linguistics, Harvard University.

Hoji, H. 1995. Demonstrative Binding and Principle B. *Proceedings of the Northeast Linguistic Society* 25:255-271.

Kim, M.-S. 1997. *Wulimal Ewonsacen* (The Korean Etymology Dictionary). Seoul: Thahaksa.

Kuh, H. 1987. Plural Copying in Korean. *Harvard Studies in Korean Linguistics II*, eds. S. Kuno, I.-H. Lee, J. Whitman, S.-Y. Bak, and Y.-S. Kang, 239-250. Cambridge, MA: Dept. of Linguistics, Harvard University.

Lee, K. 1993. *A Korean Grammar on Semantic-Pragmatic Principles.* Seoul: Hankwukmwunhwasa.

Pesetsky, D. 1987. Wh-in-situ: Movement and Unselective Binding. *The Representation of (In)definiteness*, eds. E. Reuland and A. ter Meulen, 98-129. MIT Press.

Reinhart, T. 1995. Interface Strategies. *OTS Working Papers of Theoretical Linguistics 95–002.* Utrecht, Netherlands: Utrecht University.

Rizzi, L. 1990. *Relativized Minimality. Linguistic Inquiry Monograph 16.* Cambridge, MA: MIT Press.

Saito, M. 1985. Some Asymmetries in Japanese and their Theoretical Consequences, Doctoral dissertation, MIT.

Song, S.-C. 1975. Rare Plural Marking and Ubiquitous Plural marker in Korean. *CLS* 11:536-546.

Song, S.-C. 1988. *Explorations in Korean Syntax and Semantics. Korean Research Monograph 14.* Berkeley: Institute of East Asian Studies, University of California.

Tsai, W.-T. 1991. On Nominal Island and LF Extraction in Chinese. *MIT Working Papers in Linguistics 15*, eds. L. Cheng and H. Demirdash, 239-274. Cambridge, MA: MIT.

Tsai, W.-T. 1994. On Economizing the Theory of A-bar Dependencies. Doctoral dissertation, MIT.

Yang, H.-K. 1997. Uymwun Pwukaewa Semceyyak (Interrogative Adjuncts and Island Constraints). *Studies in Generative Grammar* 7(1):67-81.

NPI Licensing in Korean Modal Constructions

ILJOO HA
University of Wisconsin-Madison

1. Introduction[1]

The Korean possibility modal form *–(u)l swu iss-* is ambiguous between a root reading and an epistemic reading.

(1) Mary-ka   maykcwu-ul   masi-l swu iss-ta.[2]
    M-nom   beer-acc   drink-mod-decl.
    a. Mary is capable of drinking beer.
    b. It is possible that Mary will drink beer (given what is known).

As shown in (2) and (3), the modal sentence is still ambiguous with two types of Korean negation.

---

[1] This is a revised version of a talk given at the 15th J/K conference held at the University of Wisconsin-Madison, October 7-9, 2005. I thank the audience at the conference for their helpful comments. I would also like to thank Mürvet Enç, Yafei Li and Vivian Lin for their comments and suggestions. All remaining errors are my own.
[2] The modal form '*-(u)l swu iss-*' is composed of three elements. An adnominal suffix '*–(u)l*', a noun '*swu*' and a copula '*iss-*'. I will discuss each morpheme in detail later. For now, the modal form is glossed as Modal.

(2) Mary-ka   maykcwu-lul   **an**   masi-l swu iss-ta.
     M-nom   beer-acc   Sneg drink-mod-decl.
     a. 'Mary is capable of not drinking beer.'   (root > neg)
     b. 'It is possible that Mary will not drink beer.'   (epistemic > neg)

(3) Mary-ka   maykcwu-lul   masi-**ci an**-ul swu iss-ta.
     M-nom   beer-acc   drink-Lneg-mod-decl.
     a. 'Mary is capable of not drinking beer.'   (root > neg)
     b. 'It is possible that Mary will not drink beer.'   (epistemic > neg)

The negation marker *an* can come either before a verb as in (2) or after a verb accompanied by a particle *ci* as in (3). These two types of negation are called Short-form negation (S-negation) and Long-form negation (L-negation) respectively in the literature. The sentences above show that the ambiguity is still preserved with both types of negation. Interestingly, when the subject *Mary* is replaced with an NPI *amwuto* 'anyone' as in (4), the root modal reading is no longer available.

(4) Amwuto   maykcwu-lul   **an**   masi-l swu iss-ta. / masi-**ci an**-ul swu iss-ta.
     Anyone   beer-acc   Sneg drink-mod-decl.   drink-Lneg-mod-decl.
     a. 'It is possible that no one will drink beer.'   (epistemic reading)
     b. Intended: 'No one is capable of drinking beer.'   (*root reading)

The aim of this paper is to provide an analysis for the lack of the root reading in the modal construction (MC) in (4). Specifically, I propose that the semantic ambiguity in Korean possibility MCs is due to structural ambiguity between a root MC and an epistemic MC, and that the lack of the root reading in (4) is due to the failure of NPI licensing in the root MC.

I propose a syntactic analysis of Korean possibility MC in Section 2, where I argue that the MC is a subtype of Korean existential constructions (EC). In Section 3, I show how the proposal accounts for the lack of the root reading in (4). In Section 4, I provide evidence in favor of my analysis. Section 5 extends my analysis to another construction in Korean.

2. The structure of the Possibility Modal Construction

I argue that the (un-)availability of certain readings in (4) is closely related to the structural properties of the possibility MC. Specifically, I propose that the structure of possibility MCs is identical to the structure of Korean ECs.

2.1. The Structures of Korean Existential Constructions

Harasawa (1994) classifies Japanese ECs into three semantic types. The following sentences are Korean counterparts of Harasawa's classification.

(5) Kuisin-i   iss-ta.   (Absolute EC)
     Ghost-nom be-decl.
     'Ghosts exist./ There are ghosts.'

(6) Pang-ey   aitul-i   iss-ta.   (Locative EC)
Room-dat   children-nom   be-decl.
'Children are in the room./There are children in the room.'

(7) Mary-ka   cha-ka   iss-ta.   (Possessive EC)
M-nom   car-nom   be-decl.
'Mary has a car.'

(5) expresses the existence of *kuisin* 'ghost' in an absolute sense. (6) expresses the location relationship between *aitul* 'children' and *pang* 'room', i.e. where the children are located. In (7), *cha* 'car' and *Mary* are in the relationship of possessor-possessee.

There has been research regarding the source of these different meanings. The literature is divided mainly into two groups. One is the different-*be* approach (e.g. Kishimoto 2000, Kuno 1973) and the other is the same-*be* approach (e.g. Muromatsu 1997, Tsujioka 2002). According to the former approach, there are two types of copulas, one meaning 'be/exist' and the other meaning 'have'. Thus, the meaning difference between (6) and (7) is attributed to two lexically different verbs. Under the latter view, on the other hand, there is only one type of copula, the 'be/exist' type copula. According to Tsujioka (2002), for example, the meaning difference between (6) and (7) lies in the structure of the precopular NP. Structures in (8) represent Korean counterparts of her analysis of Japanese.

(8)   a. Absolute EC   b. Locative EC   c. Possessive EC

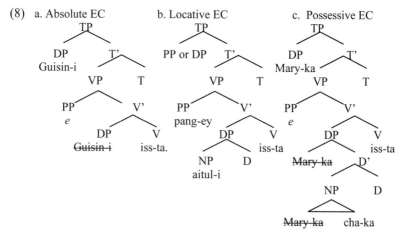

Under Tsujioka's analysis the three types of EC share a basic structure in which both the locational PP and the theme DP are projected within the maximal projection of the unaccusative copular verb. In (8b), which is a locative EC, either the locational PP or the theme DP can move to spec/TP to be the subject of the sentence. In the absolute EC in (8a), since the locational PP is absent, the theme DP raises to spec/DP. The possessive EC in (8c) is different from the previous sentences in that it has a more complex DP structure. In (8c), both the possessor *Mary* and the possessee *cha* are projected inside the DP.

Based on Szabolcsi's (1994) analysis of Hungarian possessive DPs and possessive constructions, Tsujioka argues that the complex DP in (8c) is similar to Hungarian possessive DPs and proposes the following structure for the possessive DP in Japanese.[3]

(9)[$_{DP}$ [$_{PossP}$ (Alienable) possessor [$_{NP}$[$_{N'}$ (Inalienable) possessor Possessee]]]]

In (9), the base position of the possessor depends on its (in)alienable relationship with the possessee. While an alienable possessor is base-generated in spec/PossP, an inalienable possessor is generated as a complement of a possessee noun. The inalienable possessor is theta-marked directly by the possessee noun. On the other hand, an alienable possessor receives a possessor role from the null head of PossP.

2.2. The Structure of the Possibility MC in Korean

This section provides structures for Korean possibility MCs on the basis of Tsujioka's analysis of ECs.

The traditional analyses often decompose the possibility modal form -*(u)l swu iss-* into three independent morphemes: the adnominal suffix '-*(u)l*', the noun *swu* 'ability/possibility' and the existential copula *iss-* 'be/exist' (Nam and Ko 1993, Sohn 1999). In these works, the noun *swu* is called a bound noun (BN) since its syntactic distribution is highly limited.

(10) a. [Mary-ka   maykcwu-lul   masi-l]   **swu**   **iss**-ta.
M-nom   beer-acc   drink-Adn   BN   exist-decl.
i. 'Mary is capable of drinking beer.'
ii. 'It is possible that Mary will drink beer.'
b. *[Mary-ka   maykcwu-lul   masi-l]   swu   ha-ta.
M-nom   beer-acc   drink-Adn   BN   do-decl.
c. *Swu   iss-ta.
BN   exist-decl.

The bound noun *swu* in (10a) is only meaningful when it is preceded by an adnominal clause and is followed by the existential copula. The sentence does not make any sense if the bound noun lacks either the copula as in (10b) or the preceding adnominal clause as in (10c). For this reason, Sohn

---

3 The possessive DP structure in (9) is a simplified version of Tsujioka's original structure in which a functional projection is located between PossP and NP. It is omitted here since it is not crucial to the current purpose of the paper.

(1999) suggests that this type of bound noun construction is a non-analyzable atom, that is, a lexicalized item.

However, the decomposition of the possibility MCs reveals its close structural relation with Korean ECs. If we ignore the locational PP, both MCs and ECs minimally consist of a noun and an existential copula. Based on this, I argue that possibility MCs and ECs in Korean share the same structure in which an unaccusative copular verb takes a DP as its complement. I propose that the ambiguity of the possibility MCs between a root reading and an epistemic reading is structural. Specifically, I suggest that epistemic MCs have the structure of absolute ECs while root MCs have the structure of possessive ECs.

(11) a. Epistemic MC (= Absolute EC)   b. Root MC (= Possessive EC)

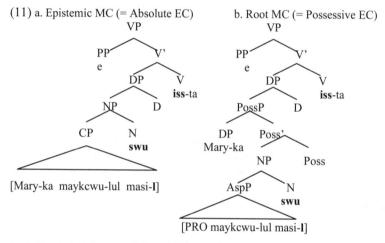

(11) illustrates the possibility MCs in (1). In both (11a) and (11b) the existential copula takes a DP as its complement. However, the internal structure of the DP in each construction is quite different.

The DP in (11a) consists of an adnominal clause which projects CP and the bound noun *swu* 'possibility'. I propose that the adnominal suffix '-(u)l' is the head of CP and the adnominal CP is in the complement position of the bound noun. My proposal is based on its structural closeness to Korean noun complement constructions.

(12) [DP [NP [CP Mary-ka sihap-eyse iki-l] hwaklywul]]
       M-nom match-loc win-**And** percentage
'Chances that Mary will win the match.'

(12) is a gapless noun complement construction in which the adnominal clause corresponds to the *that*-complement clause in English. Based on this, the adnominal suffix '-(u)l' has been traditionally analyzed as a comple-

mentizer. Under this view, the precopular DP in (11a) is nothing but a gapless noun complement construction whose head noun is a bound noun.

On the other hand, the precopular DP in (11b) is a possessive DP in which *Mary* is a possessor and *swu* 'ability' is a possessee. As in the possessive EC in (8), the possessor DP *Mary* is base-generated in spec/PossP. Note that the adnominal clause in (11b) is not CP but AspP. I propose that the adnominal suffix '-*(u)l*' in (11b) is the head of AspP. In other words, I argue that Korean has two homophonous suffixes '-*(u)l*'. One is a complementizer and the other is an aspectual marker.

Evidence for this difference in categories comes from the fact that the adnominal clause in (11b) is not able to accommodate tense.

(13) a. [$_{CP}$ Mary-ka maykcwu-lul masi-**ess**-ul]   swu   iss-ta.
        M-nom   beer-acc   drink-**past**-Adn(comp) BN   exist-decl.
        'It is possible that Mary drank beer.'   (^{OK}epistemic / *root)
     b. Mary-ka [$_{AspP}$ maykcwu-lul masi-l]   swu   iss-**ess**-ta.
        M-nom   beer-acc   drink-Adn(asp) BN   exist-**past**-decl.
        'Mary was capable of drinking beer.'   (*epistemic/ ^{OK}root)

(13a) has a past tense marker within the adnominal clause and it yields only an epistemic reading. Meanwhile a root reading is available only if the tense marker is located outside of the adnominal clause as shown in (13b). The lack of the root reading in (13a) remains unexplained if we assume that the adnominal clause of root MCs is a full-fledged CP which can accommodate TP. The lack of the root reading in (13a) and the epistemic reading in (13b) can be accounted for under the hypothesis that epistemic MCs have an adnominal clause headed by a complementizer and root MCs have an adnominal clause headed by an aspectual head which is lower than TP.

Also note that the AspP in (11b) has a PRO subject. An overt subject would not be licensed because the AspP lacks tense which checks off the Case/EPP feature of the subject. One might argue that the subject *Mary* can be base-generated within the AspP and cyclically move to spec/PossP and spec/TP. But this option is not available since the movement would violate Chomsky's (1981) *Theta-Criterion*. The subject would be theta-marked twice by the verb *masi-* 'drink' in the base-generated position which is spec/VP and by the head of PossP in the intermediate position.

In sum, in this section I have proposed that Korean possibility MCs are nothing but a subtype of Korean ECs. Specifically, I have argued that epistemic MCs have the structure of absolute ECs and root MCs have the structure of possessive ECs. In this analysis, Korean epistemic MCs are biclausal while root MCs are mono-clausal, in that the former has two CPs and the latter has only one.

3. Analysis

Recall that the possibility MC in (1) is ambiguous between a root reading and an epistemic reading. Interestingly, placing an NPI *amwuto* 'anyone' in the subject position disambiguates the sentence. This was shown in (4), which is reintroduced in (14).

(14) **Amwuto** maykcwu-lul **an** masi-l swu iss-ta. / masi-**ci an**-ul swu iss-ta.
   Anyone   beer-acc   Sneg drink-mod-decl. / drink-Lneg-mod-decl.
   a. 'It is possible that no one will drink beer.'   (epistemic modal)
   b. Intended: 'No one is capable of drinking beer.'   (*root modal)

I argue that the (un)availability of the readings in (14) depends on whether the negation in each construction is able to license the subject NPI or not. In other words, I propose that the root reading in (14) is missing because neither S-negation nor L-negation in root MCs can license the subject NPI.

To illustrate my proposal, I adopt Sohn's (1995) analysis of Korean NPI licensing in which NPIs are licensed in overt syntax via a feature-checking mechanism. He proposes that an NPI has a strong [+neg] feature and must have its feature checked off through spec-head agreement. He assumes that while the L-negation projects NegP, the S-negation *an* is an affix adjoined to V. (15) illustrates the positions of these two types of negation in Korean.

(15)

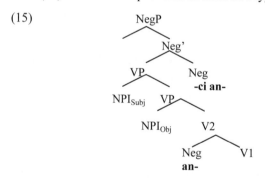

In the case of L-negation, a subject or an object NPI has its feature checked through spec-head agreement by moving to spec/NegP. In the case of S-negation, since the affixal negation does not project NegP, Sohn argues that the relevant NPIs must be licensed in situ. This is because the NPIs can be in a spec-head relation with S-negation only in their in situ positions. As shown in (15), the subject as well as the object is in a spec-head relation with V2 which contains the S-negation.

(16) and (17) illustrate how NPIs are licensed in the two types of MC under Sohn's analysis, given the structures just posited for the epistemic and root MCs.

(16) Epistemic MC

a. [$_{DP}$ [$_{CP}$ **amwuto**$_i$ [$_{VP}$ t$_i$ maykcwu-lul **an**   masi]-l]   swu] iss-ta
    anyone   beer-acc   Sneg drink-Adn BN exist

b. [$_{DP}$ [$_{CP}$ **amwuto**$_i$ [$_{NegP}$ t$_i$ [$_{VP}$ t$_i$ maykcwu-lul masi-] **ci an**-]-ul] swu] iss-ta.
    anyone   beer-acc   drink- Lneg-Adn BN exist

'It is possible that no one will drink beer.'

(17) Root MC

a.*[$_{DP}$ [$_{PossP}$ **amwuto** [$_{NP}$ [$_{AspP}$ [$_{VP}$ PRO makcwu-lul **an** masi]-l]   swu]]] iss-ta.
      anyone   beer-acc   Sneg drink-Adn BN exist

b.*[$_{DP}$ [$_{PossP}$ **amwuto** [$_{NP}$ [$_{AspP}$ [$_{NegP}$ [$_{VP}$ PRO makcwu-lul masi-] **ci an**] -ul]
      anyone   beer-acc   drink- Lneg-Adn

swu]]] iss-ta.
BN   exist.

Intended: 'No one is capable of drinking beer.'

(16) and (17) illustrate the internal structure of the precopular DPs in MCs. In (16), the subject NPI *amwuto* is base-generated in spec/VP inside the adnominal clause. The NPI is licensed either in its in situ position as in (16a) or in spec/NegP as in (16b). Thus, (16) yields an epistemic reading. In (17), on the other hand, the NPI is base-generated in spec/PossP. Recall that the adnominal clause in the root MC projects AspP, and that spec/VP is filled with PRO. Thus, the NPI in (17a) fails to be licensed by S-negation since they are never in a spec-head relation throughout the derivation.

The case is the same in (17b) where L-negation is used. Being generated in a position higher than NegP, the NPI in spec/PossP would have to undergo lowering to spec/NegP to check off its [+Neg] feature. However, current syntactic theory bans lowering other than reconstruction. As a result, a subject NPI base-generated in spec/PossP as in the root MC cannot be license by S-negation or L-negation, because it is structurally higher than both. This is why the root reading is not available in (14).

4. Supporting Evidence

This section provides two types of evidence in favor of my analysis.

4.1. Object NPIs

Unlike subjects, objects in an epistemic MC and a root MC are base-generated in the same position, that is, spec/VP inside the adnominal clause (See (11) and (15)). Thus, it is expected that a possibility MC with an object NPI should yield both a root reading and an epistemic reading, since the object NPI can be licensed in both types of MC. (18) and (19) confirm this.

(18) Epistemic MC

a. [$_{DP}$ [$_{CP}$ Mary-ka$_i$ [$_{VP}$ t$_i$ **amwukesto an**   masi]-l]   swu] iss-ta
    M-nom   anything Sneg drink-Adn BN exist

b. [DP [CP Mary-ka$_i$ [NegP **amwukesto$_j$** [VP t$_i$ t$_j$ masi-] **ci an-**]-ul] swu] iss-ta.
   M-nom   anything   drink-Lneg-Adn BN   exist
   'It is possible that Mary will drink nothing.'

(19) Root MC

a. [DP [PossP Mary-ka [NP [AspP [VP PRO **amwukesto an** masi]-l] swu]]] iss-ta.
   M-nom   anything Sneg drink-Adn BN exist

b. [DP [PossP Mary-ka [NP [AspP [NegP **amwukesto$_j$** [VP PRO t$_j$ masi-] **ci an**] -ul]
   M-nom   anything   drink- Lneg-Adn
   swu]]] iss-ta.
   BN   exist.
   'Mary is capable of not drinking anything.'

(18) and (19) are minimally different from (16) and (17) in that (18) and
(19) have the object NPI *amwukesto* instead of the subject NPI. In contrast
to the root MC with a subject NPI in (17), (19) is grammatical. In (19a), the
object NPI can have its feature checked off against S-negation in its in situ
position (See (15)). The NPI in (19b) is able to have its feature checked off
by moving to spec/NegP. My analysis successfully accounts for the subject-
object asymmetry in terms of NPI licensing found in Korean root MCs.

4.2. Negative Existential Copula *Eps-* and the Clause-mate Condition

My analysis predicts that Korean possibility MCs, being either mono-
clausal or bi-clausal, should interact with the clause-mate condition, which
states that both negation and an NPI must be in the same clause. This subsection illustrates how this prediction is borne out.

So far, we have seen possibility MCs in which modals scope over negation. This is due to the configuration in which both types of negation are
located inside the adnominal clause which is syntactically lower than the
bound noun *swu* 'possibility/ability' (See (11)). For reverse scope readings
where negation scopes over modals, the existential copula *iss-* 'exist' has to
be negated.

(20) a. Mary-ka   maykcwu-lul   masi-l   **swu**   **eps-**ta.
       M-nom   beer-acc   drink-Adn BN   not.exist-decl.
       'Mary is not capable of drinking beer.'   (Neg > root)
     b. Mary-ka   maykcwu-lul   masi-l   **li**   **eps-**ta.
       M-nom   beer-acc   drink-Adn BN   not.exist-decl.
       'There is no possibility that Mary will drink beer.' (Neg > epistemic)

Two comments are in order. First, the verb *eps-* 'not exist' is a special form
of the negative counterpart of the existential copula *iss-*. Second, as shown
in (20b), the epistemic MC, when yielding a reading where negation scopes
over the modal, uses a different bound noun, *li,* which also means 'possibility' just like *swu.* I attribute this to one of the idiosyncratic subcategoriza-

tion properties of the negative copular verb *eps-*. I assume that (20b) has the same structure as epistemic MCs with the bound noun *swu*.

Now, consider (21) and (22), where each sentence has a subject NPI or an object NPI.

(21) a. **Amwuto** maykcwu-lul masi-l   swu   **eps**-ta.
       Anyone   beer-acc   drink-Adn   BN   not.exist-decl.
       'No one is capable of drinking beer.'
    b. Mary-ka   **amwukesto** masi-l   swu   **eps**-ta.
       M-nom   anything   drink-Adn   BN   not.exist-decl.
       'Mary is not capable of drinking anything.'

(22) a. *****Amwuto** maykcwu-lul masi-l   li   **eps**-ta.
       Anyone   beer-acc   drink-Adn   BN   not.exist-decl.
       Intended: 'There is no possibility that anyone will drink beer.'
    b. *Mary-ka   **amwukesto** masi-l   li   **eps**-ta.
       M-nom   anything   drink-Adn   BN   not.exist-decl.
       Intended: 'There is no possibility that Mary will drink anything.

The sentences in (21) are root MCs having a subject NPI or an object NPI. They are fully grammatical, yielding readings where negation scopes over the root modal. On the other hand, the epistemic MCs in (22) are ungrammatical, whether the NPI is in subject or object position.

The contrast between (21) and (22) follows straightforwardly from my analysis. Under my proposal, a root MC is mono-clausal while an epistemic MC is bi-clausal, in that the adnominal clause in the former is AspP lacking TP, while the one in the latter is a full-fledged CP. Therefore the NPIs and the negative copula in (22) are not in the same clause. This violates the clause-mate condition, which requires negation and an NPI to be in the same clause. Thus, the sentences in (22) are ruled out. On the other hand, the negative copula in (21) has no problem licensing both the subject NPI and the object NPI since the negative verb and the NPIs are under the same CP.

5. Another Bound Noun Construction

One final example that validates my analysis comes from a different bound noun construction found in Korean. Just like *swu*, the bound noun *cek* 'event, experience' also requires an adnominal clause and an existential copula.

(23) Mary-ka   pati-lul   ha-**n**   **cek**   **iss**-ta.
      M-nom   party-dat   do-Adn   BN   exist-decl.
    a. 'There is an event such that Mary had a party.'
    b. 'Mary has had an experience of having a party.'

In (23), the bound noun *cek* is preceded by an adnominal clause headed by a suffix '-*(u)n*' and is followed by the existential copula *iss-*.[4] Interestingly, the meaning of the sentence is ambiguous between (23a) and (23b). I will call (23a) the event-*cek* reading and (23b) the experience-*cek* reading.

My analysis, if it is on the right track, makes the following prediction. Being structurally similar to Korean possibility MCs, (23) should have two different structures, one like an absolute EC and the other like a possessive EC. Thus, each reading in (23) is derived from two different ECs. Let us suppose that the event-*cek* reading has a structure similar to absolute ECs and the experience-*cek* reading has a structure similar to possessive ECs. If my analysis is correct, the pattern of NPI licensing in (23) should be exactly the same as the one in the possibility MCs.

The examples below confirm this prediction. First, I predict that a sentence such as (23) with a subject NPI and S-negation should lack the experience-*cek* reading.

(24) **Amwuto** pati-lul **an** ha-n cek iss-ta.
    Anyone party-acc Sneg do-Adn BN exist-decl.
    a. 'There is an event such that no one had a party.'
    b. Intended: *'No one has an experience of having a party.'

As shown in (24), the experience-*cek* reading is indeed missing.[5] This is because the subject NPI in the possessive EC cannot be licensed by the S-negation since they cannot establish a spec-head relation.

Second, I predict that for a sentence such as (23) with an object NPI, both readings will be available. This is because objects in both constructions are projected inside VP, and can therefore be licensed either in situ for S-negation or by moving to spec/NegP for L-negation. (25) illustrates this.

(25) Mary-ka **amwukesto** **an** mek-un cek iss-ta.
    M-nom anything Sneg do-Adn BN exist-decl.
    a. 'There is an event such that Mary ate nothing.'
    b. 'Mary has had an experience of not eating anything.'

Finally, it is predicted that if a *cek* sentence has the negative existential copula, it should yield only the experience-*cek* reading.

(26) a. **Amwuto** pati-lul ha-n cek **eps**-ta.
      Anyone party-acc do-Adn BN not.exist-decl.

---

[4] Different bound nouns are subcategorized for different adnominal suffixes in Korean. While *swu* requires an adnominal clause headed by the suffix '–*(u)l*', *cek* requires a clause headed by the morpheme '-*(u)n*'.

[5] L-negation also patterns with S-negation here. Due to space considerations, the relevant example is omitted.

    i. Intended: *'There is no event such that anyone had a party.'
    ii. 'No one has had an experience of having a party.'

b. Mary-ka   **amwukesto** mek-un   cek   **eps**-ta.
M-nom   anything   eat-Adn BN not.exist-decl.
    i. Intended: *'There is no event such that Mary ate anything.'
    ii. 'Mary has had no experience of eating anything.'

In (26), the event-*cek* readings are missing. This is predicted since the subject/object NPIs and the negative existential copula in an absolute EC, which is responsible for the event-*cek* reading, are located in different clauses. This violates the clause-mate condition and the absolute EC is ruled out.

6. Summary

I suggested that the semantic ambiguity between the epistemic reading and the root reading in Korean possibility MCs is due to structural ambiguity between an epistemic MC and a root MC. I also argued that both types of MC are subtypes of the EC--absolute EC and possessive EC, respectively. I have shown that the MCs lack certain readings depending on the positions of NPIs and negation and that the (un)availability of certain readings follows from my analysis of Korean MCs.

References

Chomsky, N. 1981. *Lectures on Government and Binding*. Dordrecht: Foris.

Harasawa, I. 1994. A Pragmatic View of *V-te-iru* and *V-te-ar-u*. *Journal of Pragmatics* 22:169-197.

Kishimoto, H. 2000. Locational Verbs, Agreement, and Object Shift in Japanese. *The Linguistic Review* 17:53-109.

Kuno, S. 1973. *The Structure of Japanese Language*. Cambridge: MIT Press.

Muromatsu, K. 1997. Two Types of Existentials: Evidence from Japanese. *Lingua* 101:245-269.

Nam, K-S. & Ko, Y-G. 1993. *Pyocwun Kwuke Mwunpeplon*. Seoul: Tap Publish Company.

Szabolcsi, A. 1994. The Noun Phrase. *The Syntactic Structure of Hungarian*, eds. F. Kiefer and K. E. Kiss, 179-274. San Diego: Academic Press.

Sohn, H-M. 1999. *The Korean Language*. Cambridge: Cambridge University Press.

Sohn, K-W. 1995. Negative Polarity Items, Scope, and Economy. Doctoral Dissertation, University of Connecticut.

Tsujioka, T. 2002. The Syntax of Possession in Japanese. Doctoral Dissertation, Georgetown University.

In Search of Evidence for the Placement of the Verb in Korean and Japanese

CHUNG-HYE HAN
Simon Fraser University

1. Introduction[1]

One of the most frequently used arguments for or against verb-raising to inflection (INFL) is the placement of the verb with respect to certain type of adverbs or negation (Emonds 1978, Pollock 1989). For example, 'verb-adverb' order is taken to be evidence for verb-raising in French (1), and 'adverb-verb' order is taken to be evidence for INFL-lowering in English (2).

(1) Jean embrasse souvent Marie. / *Jean souvent embrasse Marie.
     Jean kisses   often   Marie / Jean often   kisses   Marie

(2) John often kisses Mary. / *John kisses often Mary.

But in a head-final language like Korean and Japanese, the string order between the verb and such diagnostic elements is uninformative, as the verb will occur to their right whether it raises or not, as in (3).

(3) a. Tori-ka   cacwu maykcwu-lul masi-n-ta.
         Tori-NOM often beer-ACC   drink-PRES-DECL
         'Tori often drinks beer.' (Korean)

---

[1] The work reported here is part of a larger project with Jeffrey Lidz and Julien Musolino. I thank the audience at JK 15 for helpful comments and questions. This work was supported by SSHRC Standard Research Grant #410-2003-0544.

b.   Tori-ga   sibasiba biiru-o   nom-u
Tori-NOM often   beer-ACC drink-PRES
'Tori often drinks beer.' (Japanese)

Since string order cannot be used as evidence for or against verb-raising, syntacticians have had to resort to other ways to make the case for the placement of the verb. Using data pertaining to wide range of phenomena including coordination, scrambling, null objects, and NPI licensing, arguments in both directions have been made, with some arguing that there is verb-raising and others arguing that verb-raising does not occur.

In this paper, I reevaluate the arguments presented in the literature to demonstrate the placement of the verb in Korean and Japanese, and show that none of them are conclusive as all of the data intended to support a verb-raising analysis are compatible with a non-verb-raising analysis and vice-versa (Section 2). I then motivate scope of short negation and quantified object NP as potentially being a good test for verb placement, if the language has a clitic-like negation that associates with the verb in syntax. It will be shown, however, that the extant literature on this topic reports conflicting judgments on crucial data, making it impossible for us to draw any conclusions (Section 3). I will conclude with a speculation on what this conflicting situation in the literature implies for the acquisition of verb placement and the grammar of head-final languages. In the remaining of the paper, to streamline and simplify the presentation, all the examples and discussions will be based on Korean. When the original arguments in the literature are based on facts in Japanese, I have duplicated them here using Korean examples.

2.   Reevaluation of Arguments in the Literature on the Placement of the Verb

2.1.   Null Object Constructions (NOCs)

Otani and Whitman (1991) argue that the fact that NOCs in Japanese (and Korean) appear to allow a sloppy reading, as illustrated in (4), is evidence for verb-raising. They propose that through verb-raising, NOCs result in an empty VP, and that this results in a structure analogous to VP ellipsis in English, which can have a sloppy reading, as in (5).

(4)   A: John-un **caki-uy pyenci-lul** pely-ess-ta.
John-TOP self-GEN letter-ACC discard-PST-DECL
'John threw away self's letter.'

B: Mary-to **[e]** pely-ess-ta.
Mary-also   discard-PST-DECL
'Mary$_j$ also threw out self$_j$'s letters.' (sloppy reading)
'Mary also threw out John's letters.' (strict reading)

(5) John threw away his letter; Mary did [$_{VP}$ e] too.

Hoji (1998) however shows that the sloppy-like reading in NOCs is not the genuine sloppy reading attested in a VP ellipsis structure. While English VP-ellipsis examples generally have sloppy readings available, the corresponding Korean NOCs do not always do so, as illustrated in (6) and (7). Hoji concludes that sloppy-like readings in NOCs arise because of the way the content of the null argument is recovered from discourse, and therefore the NOC examples with sloppy-like readings have no bearing on the issue of verb-raising.[2]

(6) A: Every Korean couple consoled each other.

    B: Every American couple did too. ($\sqrt{}$sloppy)

(7) A: Motun hankwukin khepul-i   **selo-lul**
    every Korean   couple-NOM each other-ACC
    wilohayecwu-ess-ta.
    console-PST-DECL
    'Every Korean couple consoled each other.'

    B: Motun mikwukin khepul-to   **[e]** wilohayecwu-ess-ta.
    every American couple-also   console-PST-DECL
    'Every American couple consoled them, too.' ($\sqrt{}$strict, *sloppy)

2.2. Scrambling and Coordination

Koizumi (2000) argues that the verb raises all the way up to COMP in Japanese (and Korean), using examples from coordination and scrambling. According to Koizumi, 'Subject [Object and Object] Verb' coordinate structure is derived through VP-coordination, with across-the-board (ATB) verb-raising at least to INFL, as illustrated in (8), and '[Subject Object] and [Subject Object] Verb' coordinate structure is derived through IP coordination, with ATB verb-raising to COMP, as illustrated in (9). Importantly, the coordinate structures (VP and IP below) can be scrambled, supporting the fact that they form constituents.

(8) Mary-ka   [$_{VP}$ [motun sakwa-lul t] kuliko [motun panana-lul   t]]
    Mary-NOM   every apple-ACC   and   every banana-ACC
    mek-ess-ta.
    eat-PST-DECL
    'Mary ate every apple and every banana.'

---

[2] Arguments against NOCs as evidence for overt verb-raising are also provided in S.-W. Kim (1999), with examples of NOCs with a non-empty VP that nevertheless have a sloppy reading.

(9) [$_{IP}$ [Mary-ka   motun sakwa-lul t] kuliko [Nancy-ka   motun
        Mary-NOM every apple-ACC   and   Nancy-NOM every
     panana-lul   t]] mek-ess-ta.
     banana-ACC   eat-PST-DECL
     'Mary ate every apple and Nancy ate every banana.'

But similar examples can be constructed where the material shared by the two conjuncts contains more than just the verb, as in (10). This means that the ATB extraposition can target more than just the verb, making the kind of data Koizumi provides a sub-case of a more general phenomenon, not relevant to the issue of verb-raising.[3]

(10) a. Mary-ka   [[motun sakwa-lul] kuliko [motun panana-lul]]
          Mary-NOM every   apple-ACC and   every   banana-ACC
          culkepkey mek-ess-ta.
          joyfully   eat-PST-DECL
          'Mary ate every apple and every banana joyfully.'

      b. [[Mary-ka   motun sakwa-lul] kuliko [Nancy-ka   motun
          Mary-NOM every apple-ACC and   Nancy-NOM every
          panana-lul]] culkepkey mek-ess-ta.
          banana-ACC joyfully   eat-PST-DECL
          'Mary ate every apple and Nancy ate every banana joyfully.'

In fact, the derivation of all these examples with apparent ATB extraposition may not involve a rightward syntactic movement of the material in the ATB extraposed position. D. Chung (2004) has shown that plurality-dependent expressions such as plural-marked adverbs are licensed in an ATB extraposed position as in (11a) when the same expressions cannot be licensed in each conjunct as in (11b). The contrast in (11a) and (11b) shows that the two examples cannot be derivationally related and poses a serious problem for the rightward ATB raising analysis in general for the examples discussed in this section.[4]

(11) a. John-un   nonmwun-ul kuliko Mary-nun chayk-ul   yelsimhi-tul
          John-TOP article-ACC   and   Mary-TOP book-ACC hard-PL
          ilk-ess-ta.
          read-PST-DECL
          'John read the article hard and Mary read the book hard.'

---

[3] See Fukui and Sakai (2002) for a critique of Koizumi's arguments on string-vacuous verb-raising in Japanese.

[4] I thank Daeho Chung for pointing this out to me.

  b. John-un nonmwun-ul yelsimhi(*-tul) ilk-ess-ko   Mary-nun
     John-TOP article-ACC hard-PL   read-PST-CONJ Mary-TOP
     chayk-ul yelsimhi(*-tul) ilk-ess-ta.
     book-ACC hard-PL   read-PST-DECL
     'John read the article hard and Mary read the book hard.'

2.3. NPI Licensing

In a negative sentence, an NPI can appear in both subject and object positions, as in (12) and (13). Descriptively, NPIs are possible as long as there is a licensor (negation) in the same clause (Clause-mate Condition, H.-S. Choe (1988)). Y.-S. Choi (1999) takes this as evidence for verb-raising. Assuming that negation is a clitic on the verb, he argues that NPIs in both subject and object positions are licensed because they are in the scope of negation once the verb moves up along with the cliticized negation.

(12) a. John-un **amwukesto an** mek-ess-ta.
        John-TOP anything   NEG eat-PST-DECL
        'John didn't eat anything.'

     b. John-un **amwukesto** mek-ci **ani** ha-yess-ta.
        John-TOP anything   eat-CI Neg do-PST-DECL
        'John didn't eat anything.'

(13) a. **Amwuto** kwaca-lul **an** mek-ess-ta.
        anyone   cookie-ACC NEG eat-PST-DECL
        'Nobody ate the cookies.'

     b. **Amwuto** kwaca-lul mek-ci **ani** ha-yess-ta.
        anyone   cookie-ACC eat-CI NEG do-PST-DECL
        'Nobody ate the cookies.'

    It can be shown however that scope of negation and NPI licensing domain do not always go together, and so NPI licensing has no bearing on the issue of verb-raising. First, as we will see in section 3, Korean speakers do not agree on judgments concerning the scope of negation and argument quantified phrases (QPs), but there is no disagreement as to the status of sentences with NPIs like (12) and (13). Second, in sentences with inherently negative predicates, NPIs are licensed even though the negative predicate does not take scope over it, as shown in Chung and Park (1997) with examples as in (14).

(14) a. **Motun mwulken-i** chayksang-wiey **eps-ta**.
        every thing-Nom desk-on   not_exist-Decl
        'Nothing is on the desk.' ($\sqrt{}$every>neg, *neg>every)

     b. **Amwukesto** chayksang-wiey **eps-ta**.
        any thing   desk-on   not_exist-Decl
        'Nothing is on the desk.'

Third, Chung and Park show that some NPIs, such as *celtaylo* 'absolutely', cannot be in the scope of negation, even though it requires a clause-mate negation to be licensed, as illustrated in (15).

(15) a. Ku-nun **celtaylo** kukos-ey ga-ci **ani** ha-yess-ta.
     he-Top absolutely there-to go-Ci Neg do-Past-Decl
     'It is absolutely true that he did not go there.'
     '*It is not the case that he absolutely went there.'

   b. Ku-nun **celtaylo** kukos-ey **an** ga-ss-ta.
     he-Top absolutely there-to Neg go-Past-Decl
     'It is absolutely true that he did not go there.'
     '*It is not the case that he absolutely went there.'

2.4. Coordination of an Untensed and a Tensed Conjunct

J. Yoon (1994) makes an argument against verb-raising, using coordinate structures conjoining an untensed clause and a tensed clause. Yoon proposes that while the coordinate structure instantiates clausal conjunction at IP-level when tense is specified in all the conjuncts, as in (16), it instantiates VP-level conjunction as in (17) when tense is specified only on the verb in the last conjunct, and that the inflections on I and C combine with the verb in the final conjunct by lowering onto the appropriate places in morphology.

(16) $[_{IP}$ [John-i pap-ul mek-ess-ko] [Mary-ka kulus-ul
     John-NOM meal-ACC eat-PST-CONJ Mary-NOM dishes-ACC
     chiwu-ess]]-ta.
     clean-PST-DECL
     'John ate the meal and Mary cleaned the dishes.'

(17) John-i $[_{VP}$ [pap-ul mek-ko] [kulus-ul chiwu]]-ess-ta.
     John-NOM meal-ACC eat-CONJ dishes-ACC clean-PST-DECL
     'John ate the meal and cleaned the dishes.'

   Yoon provides three supporting arguments for his proposed coordinate structures. First, NPI *amwuto* ('anyone') is licensed in (18a) with VP-level coordination because it is in the same clause as negation *ani*. But in (18b), with IP-level coordination, *amwuto* is not licensed as it is not in the same clause as *ani*.

(18) a. **Amwuto** $[_{VP}$ [pap-ul mek-ko] [kulus-ul chiwu-ci]] **ani**
     anyone meal-ACC eat-CONJ dishes-ACC clean-CI NEG
     ha-yess-ta.
     do-PST-DECL
     'No one ate the meal and cleaned the dishes.'

b. * [$_{IP}$ [**Amwuto** pap-ul   mek-ess-ko] [kulus-ul   chiwu-ci
anyone   meal-ACC eat-PST-CONJ dishes-ACC clean-CI
ani ha-yess]]-ta.
NEG do-PST-DECL
'No one ate the meal and cleaned the dishes.'

Second, in (19a), scrambling of *pap-ul* ('meal-ACC') is fine because it adjoins to VP, and from there it properly binds its trace, in the sense of Saito's (1985) Proper Binding Condition. But in (19b), scrambling of *pap-ul* is ruled out because it has moved into the fist clausal conjunct, and from there it cannot properly bind its trace in the second clausal conjunct.

(19) a.   John-i   **pap-ul**   [$_{VP}$ [chayk-ul ilk-ko]   [t
John-NOM meal-ACC   book-ACC read-CONJ
mek]]-ess-ta.
eat-PST-DECL
'John read the book and ate the meal.'

b. * [$_{IP}$ [John-i   **pap-ul**   chayk-ul ilk-ess-ko]   [t
John-NOM meal-ACC book-ACC read-PST-CONJ
mek-ess]]-ta.
eat-PST-DECL
'John read the book and ate the meal.'

Third, while negation in (20a) can scope over both conjuncts or the second conjunct, it can only scope over the second conjunct in (20b). For Yoon, this contrast follows from the distinction between VP- and IP-level coordination.

(20) a.   John-i   [$_{VP}$ [pap-ul   mek-ko] [kulus-ul   chiwu-ci]] **ani**
John-NOM   meal-ACC eat-CONJ dishes-ACC clean-CI   NEG
ha-yess-ta.
do-PST-DECL
'John didn't eat the meal and clean the dishes.'
'John ate the meal but didn't clean the dishes.'

b.   [$_{IP}$ [John-i   pap-ul   mek-ess-ko]   [kulus-ul   chiwu-ci
John-NOM meal-ACC eat-PST-CONJ dishes-ACC clean-CI
ani ha-yess]]-ta.
NEG do-PST-DECL
'John ate the meal but he didn't clean the dishes.'

J.-B. Kim (1995) however demonstrates that while coordination of two tensed clauses is a real case of coordination, coordination of an untensed conjunct with a tensed one is a case of clausal adjunction. Under this analysis, Yoon's NPI example with VP coordination (18a) can be reanalyzed as a structure with an IP adjunct containing a *pro* subject, as in (21). In this structure, the NPI is licensed as it is in the same clause as the negation.

(21)

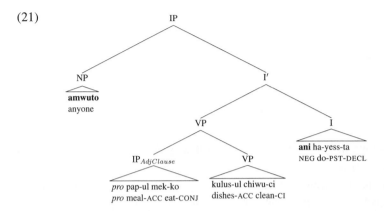

Further, under the adjunction approach to untensed conjuncts, scrambling facts are accounted for without appealing to Saito's Proper Binding Condition. Scrambling out of the tensed clause conjoined with an untensed clause is predicted to be possible because this is a case of local scrambling across an adjunct clause, as in (22).

(22) John-i   **pap-ul**   [$_{IP}$ **pro** chayk-ul   ilk-ko]   **t** mek-ess-ta.
John-NOM meal-ACC   book-ACC read-CONJ   eat-PST-DECL
'John read the book and ate the meal.'

The ambiguity concerning the scope of negation in (20a) can also be accounted for under the adjunction analysis, where the untensed conjunct is an IP adjunct containing a *pro* subject, as in (23). The ambiguity can be seen as part of a general phenomenon having to do with the interpretation of matrix negation in complex sentences, in which either the matrix clause or the embedded clause is negated.

(23) John-i   [$_{IP}$ **pro** pap-ul   mek-ko] kulus-ul   chiwu-ci **ani**
John-NOM   meal-ACC eat-CONJ dishes-ACC clean-CI NEG
ha-yess-ta.
do-PST-DECL
'John didn't eat the meal and clean the dishes.'
'John ate the meal but didn't clean the dishes.'

With the untensed conjunct as an adjunct clause, the verb in the final tensed clause can combine with inflections through verb-raising as well as INFL-lowering, as illustrated in (24). Therefore, coordination of an untensed conjunct with a tensed one does not have any bearing on the issue of verb-raising.[5]

(24)

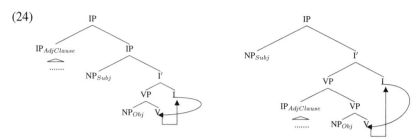

3. Scope of Short Negation and Object QP as Evidence for Verb Placement

Korean has two types of negation: long negation in a postverbal position, and short negation in a preverbal position. These two types of negation occupy distinct syntactic positions, as they can both occur in a sentence, as in (25).

(25) Toli-ka   maykcwu-lul **an** masi-ci **ani** ha-yess-ta
     Toli-NOM beer-ACC   NEG drink-CI NEG do-PST-DECL
     'Toli didn't not drink beer.' (Toli drank beer)

Because of three independent facts about Korean, scope interaction between short negation and object QP can be used as a diagnostic for verb placement. First, Korean, as in Japanese, exhibits frozen scope. That is, in a sentence with canonical SOV order as in (26) with subject and object QPs, only the reading in which the subject scopes over the object is available (S.-H. Ahn 1990, Hagstrom 2000, Y. Joo 1989, K.-W. Sohn 1995).

(26) **Nwukwunka-ka manhun salam-ul**   piphanhay-ss-ta.
     someone-NOM   many   person-ACC criticize-PST-DECL
     'Someone criticized many people.' (some > many, * many > some)

Second, object NP raises out of VP, as it must precede VP-adjoined adverbs such as *cal* ('well'), as in (27) (Hagstrom 2000, 2002).

(27) a.   Toli-ka   **maykcwu-lul cal** masi-n-ta.
          Toli-NOM beer-ACC   well drink-PRES-DECL
          'Toli drinks beer well.'

     b.   * Toli-ka   **cal maykcwu-lul** masi-n-ta.
          Toli-NOM well beer-ACC   drink-PRES-DECL
          'Toli drinks beer well.'

---

[5] Storoshenko (2004) goes through arguments presented in the literature regarding verb-raising in Japanese and shows that none of them are conclusive.

Third, short negation has the morphosyntactic status of a clitic (Y.-S. Choi 1999, H. Han and M.-K. Park 1994), as in many Romance languages (Cinque 1999), and is treated as a unit with the verb in overt syntax. It must occur immediately before the verb, as in (28).

(28) a. Toli-ka   maykcwu-lul cal   **an**   **mas-in-ta**.
         Toli-NOM beer-ACC   well NEG drink-PRES-DECL
         'Toli doesn't drink beer well.'

     b. * Toli-ka   maykcwu-lul **an**   cal   **mas-in-ta**.
         Toli-NOM beer-ACC   NEG well drink-PRES-DECL
         'Toli doesn't drink beer well.'

Taken together, these facts suggest that scope facts in sentences containing both short negation and object QP as in (29) could provide a clear test for the height of the verb.

(29) Tori-ka   **motun** chayk-ul   **an**   ilk-ess-ta.
      Tori-NOM every   book-ACC NEG read-PST-DECL
      'Tori didn't read every book.'

Given scope freezing, the scope of argument QPs will be determined in their surface positions without recourse to QR or reconstruction, and so the scope of negation and the object QP will reflect the position of negation, relative to the object QP in the clause structure. And, given object raising and Neg-cliticization, the availability of Neg>objectQP reading will be evidence for verb-raising.

Although the predictions are clear, we cannot draw any conclusions regarding verb-raising based on what is reported in the extant literature, because the scope judgments reported in the literature for sentences containing negation and quantified argument NPs often conflict with each other. For instance, Hagstrom (2000) and J.-H. Suh (1989) report that sentences like (29) only have 'every > neg' reading, whereas Y.-K. Baek (1998) and J.-B. Kim (2000) report that they are ambiguous between 'every > neg' and 'neg > every' readings.[6]

4. Conclusion: Implications for the Grammar

I have shown that none of the arguments in the literature for verb-raising or INFL-lowering in Korean is definitive, and the data used in the argumentation has explanations consistent with either analysis. I have further shown that though scope of short negation and an object QP can be a good test for demonstrating the height of the verb, conflicting judgments reported in the literature makes it impossible for us to draw any conclusions.

---

[6] Storoshenko (2004) also found that conflicting scope judgments are reported in the literature on Japanese sentences with negation and argument QPs.

I speculate that this conflicting situation in the literature is not an accident, but a reflection of the fact that evidence regarding the verb placement in a head-final language like Korean and Japanese is truly hard to come by, not only for linguists developing an analysis of verb placement but also for children acquiring the language. This lack of evidence then raises a question as to how Korean and Japanese children acquire verb placement. This question is taken up in Han et. al. (2005). Building upon the idea that insufficient input can lead to distinct grammars in a single speech community, a widely postulated idea in diachronic syntax literature (Kroch 1989, Pintzuk 1991, Santorini 1992, Taylor 1994) and in language acquisition literature (Roeper 1999, Yang 2003), they hypothesize that there are two populations of Korean speakers: one with verb-raising and one without. Under this hypothesis, the paucity of relevant evidence may result in a situation where one group has scope judgments consistent with verb-raising grammar and another group consistent with INFL-lowering grammar.

References

Baek, J. Y.-K. 1998. Negation and Object Shift in Early Child Korean. *The Interpretive Tract*, volume 25 of *MIT Working Papers in Linguistics*, 73–86. Cambridge: MITWPL.

Choe, H.-S. 1988. Restructuring Parameters and Complex Predicates: A Transformational Approach. Doctoral Dissertation, MIT.

Choi, Y.-S. 1999. Negation, its Scope and NPI Licensing in Korean. *Proceedings of ESCOL*, eds. R. Daly and A. Riehl, 25–36. Ithaca, NY: Cornell University.

Chung, D. 2004. A Multiple Dominance Analysis of Right Node Sharing Constructions. *Language Research* 40:791–811.

Chung, D. and H.-K. Park. 1997. NPIs Outside of Negation Scope. *Japanese/Korean linguistics*, volume 6, eds. H.-M. Sohn and J. Haig, 415–435. Stanford: CSLI.

Fukui, N., and H. Sakai. 2003. The Visibility Guideline for Functional Categories: Verb Raising in Japanese and Related Issues. *Lingua* 113:321–375.

Hagstrom, P. 2000. Phrasal Movement in Korean Negation. *Proceedings of SCIL*, volume 9, 127–142. Cambridge: MITWPL.

Hagstrom, P. 2002. Implications of Child Error for the Syntax of Negation in Korean. *Journal of East Asian Linguistics* 11:211–242.

Hahn, K.-J. P. 1981. The Development of Negation in One Korean Child. Doctoral Dissertation, University of Hawaii.

Han, C.-H., J. Lidz, and J. Musolino. 2005. Verb-raising and Grammar Competition in Korean: Evidence from Negation and Quantifier Scope. Manuscript, Simon Fraser University, University of Maryland, Indiana University. Based on a talk presented at *Workshop on UG Principles and Input Data: How do we get Plato's Heaven into Skinner's Box?*, Michigan State University in East Lansing, Aug. 1-2, 2003.

Han, H., and M.-K. Park. 1994. The Syntax of Negation in Korean and its Development in Child Language. *Proceedings of ESCOL*, 152–162.

Joo, Y. S. 1989. A Cross-linguistic Approach to Quantification in Syntax. Doctoral

Dissertation, University of Wisconsin, Madison.

Kim, J.-B. 1995. On the Existence of NegP in Korean. *Harvard Studies in Korean Linguistics*, volume 6, 267–282.

Kim, J.-B. 2000. *The Grammar of Negation: A Constraint-based Approach.* Stanford: CSLI.

Kim, S. 1999. Sloppy/strict Identity, Empty Objects, and NP Ellipsis. *Journal of East Asian Linguistics* 8:255–284.

Koizumi, M. 2000. String Vacuous Overt Verb Raising. *Journal of East Asian Linguistics* 9:227–285.

Kroch, A. 1989. Function and Grammar in the History of English Periphrastic *do*. *Language variation and change*, eds. R. Fasold and D. Schiffrin, Current Issues in Linguistic Theory 52, 133–172. Amsterdam, Philadelphia: Benjamins.

Otani, K., and J. Whitman. 1991. V-raising and VP-ellipsis. *Linguistic Inquiry* 22:345–358.

Park, M.-K. 1998. Negation and Placement of Verb in Korean. *Language Research* 34:709–736.

Pintzuk, S. 1991. Phrase Structures in Competition: Variation and Change in Old English Word Order. Doctoral Dissertation, University of Pennsylvania.

Roeper, T. 1999. Universal Bilingualism. *Bilingualism: Language and Cognition* 2:169-186.

Santorini, B. 1992. Variation and Change in Yiddish Subordinate Clause Word Order. *Natural Language and Linguistic Theory* 10:596–640.

Sohn, K.-W. 1995. Negative Polarity Items, Scope and Economy. Doctoral Dissertation, University of Connecticut.

Storoshenko, D. R. 2004. Negation Scope and Phrase Structure in Japanese. Master's thesis, Simon Fraser University.

Suh, J. 1989. Scope Interaction in Negation. *Harvard Studies in Korean Linguistics*, volume III, 527–536. Department of Linguistics, Haravard University.

Taylor, A. 1994. The Change from SOV to SVO in Ancient Greek. *Language Variation and Change* 6:1–37.

Yang, C. 2002. *Knowledge and Learning in Natural Language*. Oxford.

Yoon, J. H.-S. 1994. Korean Verbal Inflection and Checking Theory. *The Morphology-Syntax Connection*, volume 22 of *MIT Working Papers in Linguistics*, 251–270. Cambridge: MITWPL.

Temporal Order in Japanese *Toki-ni* Sentences: An Event-Structural Account

MAKIKO IRIE

The University of Texas at Austin

1. Introduction

This paper explores temporal readings associated with sentences containing *toki-ni* "when." After reviewing the variety of temporal interpretations available for *when* sentences in English, I examine Japanese *toki-ni* sentences and point out that their readings range over four types, Subevent, Sequence, Overlap and Reversed Sequence. Similarities and differences between *when* and *toki-ni* noted here will lead us to a working hypothesis that makes use of Moens-style Event Nuclei as the default temporal frame that *toki-ni* invokes.

2. English *When*

In this section, I review on what has been said about the temporal semantics of *when* in English, for the purpose of laying background knowledge of the phenomena I will be discussing.

2.1. Three Readings of *When*

When sentences give rise to a variety of temporal interpretations, as shown in (1) through (4).[1] For the sake of simplicity, I focus on *when* sentences with the past tensed main clause.

(1)   a. When the Smiths threw a party, they invited all their friends.

      b. When John broke his leg, he made a pair of crutches.

(2)   When John destroyed all the documents, everybody was away.

(3)   We were crossing the street when John noticed us.

(4)   When we were in New Orleans, it was raining all day.

I shall call the three readings as Subevent, Sequence and Overlap respectively. The mnemonic names reflect how the main clause eventuality is interpreted with respect to the when clause eventuality.

(1a) represents Subevent, where the main clause describes a (proper) subevent of the when clause eventuality. Characteristically, this reading requires that the clauses refer to one event, where the when clause depicts the whole and the main clause elaborates some part of it. (1b). is an example of Sequence, where the when and main clause eventualities are ordered in sequence so as the latter follows the former. (2) through (4) involve Overlap relations in two different ways. In (2), the main clause eventuality temporally includes the *when* clause eventuality. In (3), contrastively, the *when* clause eventuality temporally includes the main clause eventuality.

2.2. State Clauses and the Availability of Overlap

It has been pointed out that Overlap and non-overlap readings (Sequence and Subevent) are distributed depending on an aspectual property of the clauses, namely Event-State distinction.[2] In particular, an Overlap reading obtains for sentences with at least one State clause in it. If there is only one State clause in the sentence, the State clause eventuality temporally extends including the non-State clause eventuality, and not vice versa. Finally, if both clauses contain State eventualities, then the *when* clause eventuality temporally includes the main clause eventuality.

These points are shown in (2) through (4) above. (2) contains a State eventuality in the main clause, which temporally includes the non-State eventuality in the *when* clause. In (3), the reverse holds. In (4), it is the *when* clause eventuality that includes the main clause eventuality.

2.3. Subevent, Sequence and Non-durative Predicates

It has been implicitly assumed that the non-Overlap readings, namely Subevent and Sequence, remain ambiguous until pragmatic or extra-

---

[1] These examples are taken from Heinämäki (1978:36) and Hinrichs (1986:74-75) and slightly modified.

[2] Heinämäki (1978), Hinrichs (1986), Moens (1987), Partee (1984), and Sandström (1993).

linguistic information is provided. That is, grammatical devices are not able to distinguish them. Hence, (1a) and (1b) could receive the intended interpretation (Subevent for a. and Sequence for b.) only as the reader knows how the events described in the sentence are usually ordered.

In the meantime, this is only so when the *when* clause contains a durative predicate, as Sandström (1993) notes. With a non-durative predicate such as *turn the key*, Sequence is the sole available interpretation, as is shown in (5).

(5)   When I turned the key, the car started.

2.4. Beyond Temporal Order: Consequentiality

Besides the above-described temporal properties, it has sometimes been addressed that the main and *when* clause eventualities are subject to a stronger pragmatic requirement than the mere ordering relation. This idea has lead to an informal modeling of the semantics of *when* as proposed in Moens (1987), to be introduced immediately. Specifically, he argues that Sequence is licensed only when the main and *when* clause eventualities stand in a Consequentiality relation, roughly defined as "completion of the main clause eventuality is included in the set of result states that ensue from the *when* clause eventuality."[3]

The following pair shows this point.

(6)   a. !When my car broke down, the sun set.

   b. When my car broke down, I called AAA for help.

Moens (ibid) reports (6a) as odd, due to unrelatedness between the two events described in the sentence. The main clause eventuality in (6b) occurs as a result of the when clause eventuality, and the sentence is more improved compared to (6a). The above observation of Moens's suggests that the main clause eventuality in a Sequence *when* sentence must hold a strong consequential link to the *when* clause eventuality.

The device Moens (1987) introduces for such linking is a complex internal structure for eventualities, which he calls Event Nucleus (EN). EN provides a template using which an eventuality is conceptualized. A complete EN exhaustively includes preparatory process, culmination point and consequent state. Moens defines *when* to be a function that takes any non-State eventuality and yields a complete EN, complete with preparatory process, culmination point and consequent state. (Moens (ibid:77)) He then posits that the main clause eventuality in a *when* sentence must be integrated to some part of the EN. Hence, a main clause Event in a *when* sentence can either be a consequent state (1b) or a preparatory process (1a) of

---

[3] This is an informal characterization that suffices the present discussion. Galitou and Ligozat (2000) formally explore Consequentiality.

the *when* clause eventuality.

The relevant examples are repeated below.

(7) a. When the Smiths threw a party, they invited all their friends.

b. When John broke his leg, he made a pair of crutches.

(=(1))

Not permitted are cases in which the main clause describe an eventuality that is completely independent of the *when* clause eventuality, such as (6a).

Meanwhile, it is left implicit in Moens' analysis how *when* sentences involving a State clause is to receive a proper interpretation. A possible way to deal with it is to assume, as is standard, that a State includes the current reference time, against which the main clause eventuality is interpreted. Insofar as this semantics of State predicates overrides the semantics of *when*, one successfully obtains the Overlap reading independent of how one would like to interpret *when*.

3. Properties of *Toki-ni*

Based on what has been introduced in the previous section concerning *when*, this section explores its Japanese equivalent *toki-ni*. *Toki-ni* "when" consists of a noun *toki* "time" and an optional postposition *-ni* "at". The adverbial head sits clause finally, and the adverbial clause must always precede the main clause, as shown in (8) through (10).

(8) [[...toki(-ni)] ...]

(9) Mary-ga kaer-ta   *toki-ni* John-ga tuk-ta
     M-NOM return-TA time-at J-NOM arrive-TA
     "When Mary left, John arrived"

(10) *John-ga tuk-ta   Mary-ga kaer-ta   *toki-ni*
     J-NOM arrive-TA M-NOM return-TA time-at
     "John arrived when Mary left"

As I did for English, I focus on *toki-ni* sentences with the past tensed main clause.[4]

3.1. Similarities to *When* (1): State Clauses and the Availability of Overlap

Much like English, State-Event distinction plays a crucial role in distinguishing between Overlap and non-Overlap readings. Thus, *toki-ni* sentences containing at least one State clause are interpreted as Overlap.

---

[4] There are debates as to whether *–ru* and *–ta* are "tense" markers or denote something else, for example perfectivity. See Hasegawa (1998) for discussion. The present analysis does not hinge on what these morphemes strictly mean. So throughout the paper I call them "tense markers" and gloss them as nonpast and past respectively.

(11) Mary-ga kaer-ta   *toki-ni* John-ga ne-tei-ta
    M-NOM return-TA time-at J-NOM arrive-PROG-TA
    "When Mary left, John was sleeping"

(12) Mary-ga ne-tei-ta   *toki-ni* John-ga tuk-ta
    M-NOM sleep-PROG-TA time-at J-NOM arrive-TA
    "When Mary was sleeping, John arrived"

(13) Mary-ga ne-tei-ta   *toki-ni* ame-ga   fur-tei-ta
    M-NOM return-TA time-at rain-NOM fall-PROG-TA
    "When Mary was sleeping, it was raining"

Yoshimoto and Mori (2002) make the above point in their attempt to give a uniform analysis of various kinds of Japanese complex sentences. Their contention as to *toki-ni* sentences is that event order in a *toki-ni* sentence is determined on the bases of Event-State distinction as well as tense marking of the predicates involved.[5] They state that State *toki-ni* clauses may invoke the Overlap reading of the sentence, while Event *toki-ni* clauses must trigger a sequential interpretation (ibid:314).

They do not provide examples in their work, but straightforward cases are (11) through (13) above.

3.2. Similarity (2): Subevent, Sequence and Non-durative Predicates

Turning now to *when* sentences involving two Event clauses, the Subevent-Sequence indeterminacy discussed above is also available for Japanese, again depending on extra-grammatical factors.

(14) a. Enkai-o   hirak-ta   *toki-ni* kyaku-o   yob-ta
        Party-ACC get_off-past time-at guest-ACC call-past
        "When we threw a party, we invited guests"

    b. Kossetu-si-ta   *toki-ni* matsubazue-o tukur-ta.
        Break_bone-do-past time-at crutch-ACC   make-past.
        "When I broke a bone, I made a pair of crutches"

Along with English, a non-durative *toki-ni* clause does not show indeterminacy in this respect. As can be seen in (15), a *toki-ni* sentence with a non-durative *toki-ni* clause only has the Sequence reading.

(15) Akuseru-o   hum-ta   *toki-ni* kuruma-ga ugok-ta
    Accel_pedal-ACC step_on-past time-at car-NOM   move-past
    "When I stepped on the gas, the car started"

As shown above, *toki-ni* and *when* sentences exhibit a number of commonalities with respect to their temporal interpretations.

---

[5] The effect of embedded tense marking will be discussed in the next subsection.

3.3. Difference from *When* (1): Temporal Proximity in Place of Consequentiality

Similar though they are, *when* and *toki-ni* do not always parallel. I would like to point to two such differences. First, the Consequentiality requirement appears to be much weaker in Japanese.

(16) Kuruma-ga koware-ta *toki-ni* hi-ga   oti-ta
     Car-NOM break-past time-at sun-NOM fall-past
     "When my car broke down, the sun set"

Rather than being odd, the acceptability of the sentence is conditioned by the proximity of two eventualities. That is, the sunset must occur as soon as my car breaks down for this sentence to be felicitous, but it is not necessary that the former is an eventuality ensuing from the latter, as is required for English.

3.4. Difference from *When* (2): Reverse-Sequence

Another major difference between *toki-ni* and *when* is the fact that embedded tense marking in *toki-ni* sentences gives rise to an additional temporal reading. Tohsaku (1999:443) makes the following observation.[6]

(17) a. Tokyo-e ik-ta   *toki-ni* tikatetu-ni   nor-ta.
       Tokyo-to go-nonpast time-at subway-DAT ride-past
       "When I went to Tokyo, I rode the subway"

    b. Tokyo-e ik-u   *toki-ni* sinkansen-ni   nor-ta.
       Tokyo-to go-nonpast time-at bullet_train-DAT ride-past
       "When going to Tokyo, I rode the bullet train"

Tohsaku puts forth that when the *toki-ni* clause bears a past tense, temporal interpretation of the sentence exhibits the Sequence reading, where the *toki-ni* clause eventuality precedes the main clause eventuality. Note, in passing, that this reading is also available for the equivalent construction in English. as (17b) exemplifies, a nonpast tense in the *toki-ni* clause indicates that the *toki-ni* clause eventuality is not finished by the time at which the main clause eventuality takes place. Forward sequence of events is not available where the embedded tense does not harmonize with the main clause past tense. The interpretation that (17b) does have is one in which the *toki-ni* clause eventuality includes the main clause eventuality as its proper subevent. One may subsume this example to the Subevent reading discussed earlier, saying that Japanese embedded tenses can induce such an interpretation.

(18), however, is not compatible with the approach I just suggested.

---

[6] The examples are slightly modified by deleting punctuations and honorification-marking items that are immaterial to the present discussion.

(18) a. Basu-o   ori-ta   *toki-ni* ryookin-o   haraw-ta
        Bus-ACC   get_off-past time-at   money-ACC pay-past
        "When I got off the bus, I paid the fare"

     b. Basu-o   ori-ru   *toki-ni* ryookin-o   haraw-ta
        Bus-ACC   get_off-nonpast time-at money-ACC pay-past
        "When I was getting off the bus, I paid the fare"

The paying takes place after the getting off of the bus occurs in (18a), whereas in (18b) these two events realize in the reverse order. Temporal interpretation associated with (18b) is not exactly the same as Subevent, as the *toki-ni* clause event is non-durative and cannot have internal subevents. I regard that (18) represents a reading unavailable in English and call it as Reverse-Sequence. Reverse-Sequence involves the embedded (*toki-ni*) clause eventuality temporally following the main clause one. It consists of two separate events, unlike, as with Subevent, one big eventuality including another small one. This seems to be a proper description of (18b), as the payment occurs before getting off and paying fares can hardly be considered as a sub-component of getting off the bus.[7] Also to mention is that the verb in (18) is non-durative. As we have seen, Subevent requires that the *toki-ni/when* clause eventuality is durative. Thus, Reverse-Sequence seems to be an independent reading unique to *toki-ni* sentences.

4. Discussion: The Role of Event Nuclei in *Toki-ni* Sentences

We have seen that *toki-ni* shares basic properties with *when*, but is different from it in two respects. First, *toki-ni* is not so Consequentiality-oriented as *when* is. Secondly, the fourth reading Reverse Sequence is available in a limited environment.

     The three-fold readings of *when*, as well as the Consequentiality requirement associated with Sequence, allow a semi-formal explanation using Moens' EN. It is not straightforward, however, how these characteristics pertaining to *toki-ni* would be accounted for using existing mechanisms. For the lack of the Consequentiality requirement, the notion of consequent states is inherent to EN, and it would be difficult to use EN without using Consequentiality. For Reversed-Sequence, it would not fit into EN regardless of how we use it. This is because EN requires that the main clause eventuality be integrated into either the preparatory process or consequent state of the main clause eventuality. The main clause eventuality cannot be linked to the consequent state of the *when* clause eventuality, as the former temporally precedes the latter. Moreover, the preparatory process option is not possible because the main clause eventuality describes a separate event

---

[7] It would naturally be a subcomponent of having a bus trip. In that case a different verb would have to be used and one would be asking a different question.

from the *when* clause does.

For a conclusive analysis, I remain agnostic in this paper. What I am able to suggest is a flexible use of Moens' EN, so that an EN is called upon as it is possible. When EN is not available, for reasons ranging from semantic to pragmatic, a secondary rule takes effect that places the main clause eventuality as temporally close as possible to the *when* clause eventuality.

Let us see how it may work with the discussed cases of *toki-ni*, with a relevant example repeated. A *toki-ni* sentence containing at least one State clause would not invoke an EN for the reason speculated above; the meaning of State predicates overrides the meaning of *toki-ni*, so one gets Overlap no matter what.

(19) Mary-ga kaer-ta   *toki-ni* John-ga ne-tei-ta
     M-NOM return-TA time-at J-NOM arrive-PROG-TA
     "When Mary left, John was sleeping"
     (=(11))

With a *toki-ni* sentence with a durative past-tensed *toki-ni* clause, an complete EN can be called upon to offer both preparatory process and consequent state, resulting in Subevent or Sequence, whichever is pragmatically preferred.

(20) a. Enkai-o   hirak-ta   *toki-ni* kyaku-o   yob-ta
        Party-ACC get_off-past time-at guest-ACC call-past
        "When we threw a party, we invited guests"

     b. Kossetu-si-ta   *toki-ni* matsubazue-o tukur-ta.
        Break_bone-do-past time-at crutch-ACC   make-past.
        "When I broke a bone, I made a pair of crutches"
        (=(14))

If a *toki-ni* clause is non-durative and past-tensed, the only option for it is to offer an EN with only the consequent state, as the eventuality itself does not extend over time to include the preparatory process.

(21) Akuseru-o   hum-ta   *toki-ni* kuruma-ga ugok-ta
     Accel_pedal-ACC step_on-past time-at car-NOM   move-past
     "When I stepped on the gas, the car started"
     (=(15))

A *toki-ni* sentence involving a durative nonpast-tensed *toki-ni* clause is able to receive the Subevent reading but not Sequence, the durative part functioning as an EN that only has the preparatory process.

(22) Tokyo-e   ik-u   *toki-ni* sinkansen-ni   nor-ta.
     Tokyo-to go-nonpast time-at bullet_train-DAT ride-past
     "When going to Tokyo, I rode the bullet train"

(=(17b))

If the *toki-ni* clause is non-durative in the same situation, no EN is available, lacking both the preparatory process and consequent state. If this happens, the secondary rule to place the main clause eventuality as temporally close as possible to the *when* clause eventuality. This is how we obtain Reverse-Sequence.

(23) Basu-o   ori-ru   *toki-ni* ryookin-o   haraw-ta
     Bus-ACC get_off-nonpast time-at money-ACC pay-past
     "When I was getting off the bus, I paid the fare"
     (=(18b))

Finally, if making use of a complete EN is not preferred because of pragmatic reasons, that option is not chosen. The secondary rule is then executed, positing only that the main clause eventuality to be in the closest vicinity of the *when* clause eventuality.

(24) Kuruma-ga koware-ta *toki-ni* hi-ga   oti-ta
     Car-NOM   break-past time-at sun-NOM fall-past
     "When my car broke down, the sun set"
     (=(16))

This should contrast with its English equivalent (6a), which is pragmatically ill formed.

5. Concluding Remarks

We have seen that English *when* and Japanese *toki-ni* give rise to at least three representative readings, Subevent, Sequence and Overlap. Overlap solely obtains when a *when/toki-ni* sentence contains at least one State clause. In English, if the *when* clause is non-durative, Sequence is the only available interpretation. Japanese *toki-ni* sentences have more varieties; the readings in such an environment range over Subevent, Sequence and an additional one, Reversed Sequence. When there is no State clause in the sentence, a *when/toki-ni* sentence may either be interpreted as Subevent or Sequence (Forward or Reversed), depending on the embedded tense and extra-linguistic information in the context. Towards the end of our observation, we saw that the Consequentiality requirement is rather weak for *toki-ni* than it is for *when*. Recognizing the above little-addressed findings as potentially important in furthering our knowledge about the semantics of *toki-ni*, I proposed a working hypothesis that makes use of Moens' Event Nuclei as the default temporal frame invoked by *toki-ni*, together with a secondary rule that places the main clause eventuality as temporally close to the *when* clause eventuality.

References

Bach, E. 1986. The Algebra of Events. *Linguistics and Philosophy* 9:5-16.

Galiatou, E. and G. Ligozat. 2000. A Formal Model for the Representation of Processes having an Internal Structure. Manuscript, University of Athens and Paris-Sud University.

Hasegawa, Y. 1998. Tense-Aspect Controversy Revisited: The -TA and -RU forms in Japanese. Manuscript, University of California at Barkley.

Heinämäki, O. 1978. Semantics of English Temporal Connectives. Doctoral Dissertation, The University of Texas at Austin.

Hinrichs, E. 1986. Temporal Anaphora in Discourses of English. *Linguistics and Philosophy* 9:63-82.

Moens, M. 1987. Tense, Aspect and Temporal Reference. Doctoral Dissertation, University of Edinburgh.

Partee, B. H. 1984. Nominal and Temporal Anaphora. *Linguistics and Philosophy* 7:243-286.

Sandström, G. 1993. *When*-Clauses and The Temporal Interpretation of Narrative Discourse. Doctoral dissertation, University of Umeå.

Tohsaku, Y-H. 1999. *Yookoso!: An Invitation to Contemporary Japanese*. Boston, McGraw Hill.

Yoshimoto, K and Y. Mori. 2002. A Compositional Semantics for Complex Tenses in Japanese. *Proceedings of the Eighth International HPSG Conference*, eds. F. van Eynde and D. Beermann, 300-319. Stanford: CSLI Publications.

Scrambling, Resumption and Scope of Neg

KIYOKO KATAOKA
Nihon University, College of Economics

1. Introduction[1]

The thesis in (1) has been widely assumed regarding the so-called 'scrambling' construction in Japanese, i.e. sentences with the word order of *Object-Subject-Verb* (Miyagawa 2001, Saito 1992, 2003, and others).

(1) Every 'scrambled' object is base-generated in its theta-position inside the VP (or *v*P in the recent frame work).

[1] I am very grateful to Hajime Hoji, Yukinori Takubo, and Ayumi Ueyama for their careful comments and insightful suggestions for the materials of the paper. I also deeply appreciate the intensive discussions with Christopher Tancredi at the final stage of the paper. I have greatly benefited from the patient help and support by Daisuke Bekki, Junichi Hayashishita, Ai Kawazoe, Tomohide Kinuhata, Maki Irie, Yasuhiko Miura, Kanae Mori, Satoru Muraoka, Toshio Matsuura, Iwao Takai, Daiki Tanaka, Sanae Tamura, Yukiko Tsuboi, Emi Yamada, and especially Emi Mukai for her help at the last minute. They always responded to my surveys willingly and gave me valuable comments. Lastly, I would like to thank to the organizing committee members and the participants at the 15th Japanese/Korean Linguistics Conference.

I argue, on the basis of observations involving negation, and making crucial use of 'resumption', that the sentence-initial object in the scrambling construction (henceforth *ScramObj*) should be 'base-generated' in its surface position when it shows A-properties, in line with Ueyama (1998) and contrary to (1).

The organization of the paper is as follows: In this section, I provide an observational generalization that a 'scrambled' object with A-properties (henceforth *A-ScramObj*) cannot be in the scope of Neg, though the scope relation between Neg and a QP is generally observed to be ambiguous. In section 2, I first examine the two *Movement* analyses that maintain the thesis in (1). I discuss the *A-movement* analysis for the *A-ScramObj* by Miyagawa (2001) and others, and the *derivational* analysis of Saito (2003) for A/A'-properties of the scrambling construction, and then point out problems they face in giving an account for that generalization. In section 3, I show that the *base-generation* analysis of Ueyama (1998) can give an account for the generalization without any problem. In section 5, I provide a further argument for our conclusion, making use of the QP-scope interpretations. Section 6 concludes the paper.

1.1. Scope (Un)ambiguity in a Scrambling Case

The scope relation between Neg and a QP is ambiguous in Japanese (Kuno 1980 and others). As observed in (2), the subject NP as well as non-subject NPs can be in the scope of Neg, and the ambiguity continues to obtain in their 'scrambled' counterparts as in (3).[2]

(2) a. [$_{QP1}$ itutuizyoo-no ginkoo]-ga Toyota-ni   yuusisi-**nak**-atta (koto)
       five:or more-GEN bank-NOM   Toyota-DAT finance-Neg-Past (Comp)
       'Five or more banks did not finance Toyota.'
       QP_1>Neg, Neg>QP_1

   b. UFJ-ginkoo-ga [$_{QP1}$ itutuizyoo-no kigyoo]-ni yuusisi-**nak**-atta (koto)
       UFJ bank-NOM five:or more-GEN company-DAT finance-Neg-Past (Comp)
       'UFJ Bank did not finance five or more companies.'
       QP_1>Neg, Neg>QP_1

(3) a. Toyota-ni [$_{QP1}$ itutuizyoo-no ginkoo]-ga yuusisi-**nak**-atta (koto)
       Toyota-DAT 5:or:more-GEN bank-NOM finance-Neg-Past (Comp)
       QP_1>Neg, Neg>QP_1

---

[2] The two interpretations for (2a), for instance, can be informally described as (i), which concerns the number of the banks which did not finance Toyota, and (ii), which concerns the number of the banks which financed Toyota.

   (i)   *QP > Neg* : 5 or more *x* (*x*= bank) NOT (*x* finance Toyota)
   (ii)   *Neg > QP* : NOT 5 or more *x* (*x*= bank) (*x* finance Toyota)

b. [$_{QP1}$ itutuizyoo-no kigyoo]-ni UFJ-ginkoo-ga yuusisi-**nak**-atta (koto)
   5:or:more-GEN company-DAT UFJ Bank-NOM finance-Neg-Past (Comp)
   $QP_1 > Neg, Neg > QP_1$

However, as observed in Kataoka (2004 and 2006a), in regard to the scrambling construction, the *Neg>QP* reading cannot obtain if the bound variable anaphora interpretation (henceforth, *BVA*) is forced to obtain between the object QP$_1$ and the dependent term *soko* 'it' in the subject NP, as in (4a). The ambiguity disappears as well if what seems to be 'resumption' is involved, as in (4b).[3] (4) should be compared with (3b) above.

(4) a. [Itutuizyoo-no kigyoo]$_{QP1}$-ni   [soko-no torihiki-ginkoo]-ga
         five:or:more-GEN-company-DAT   it-GEN-dealing:bank-NOM
         yuusisi-**nak**-atta.
         finance-Neg-Past
         'To five or more companies, its own bank did not finance.'[4]
         with *BVA*, *Neg > *QP$_1$*

     b. [Itutuizyoo-no kigyoo]$_{QP1}$-ni   UFJ-ginkoo-ga   *soko*-ni
         five:or:more-GEN-company-DAT   UFJ Bank-NOM   it-DAT
         yuusisi-**nak**-atta.
         finance-Neg-Past
         (Lit.)'To five or more companies, UFJ Bank did not finance it.'
         *Neg > *QP$_1$*

1.2. The A-scrambled Object Cannot be in the Scope of Neg

The scrambling construction displays A'-properties such as reconstruction effects as in (5a), and A-properties such as the absence of weak crossover effects as in (5b) (Saito 1992, Ueyama 1998, among others).

(5) a. Soko$_i$-no torihikisaki-ni [itutuizyoo-no kigyoo]$_{QPi}$-ga tousisi-ta.
         it-GEN client-DAT five:or:more-GEN company-NOM invest-Past
         'To its$_i$ client, [each of five or more companies]$_i$ invested.'
         ^{ok}*BVA*

---

[3] As we discuss it later, what is referred to as 'resumption' in Japanese displays a totally different distribution from the one in the standard sense (Ross 1967, Sells 1984). In this paper, I use the term 'resumption' as a purely descriptive term. See section 1.2 for some relevant discussion.

[4] There are some speakers who find acceptable the *Neg>QP* reading for the example involving BVA like (4a), and some of them accept it fairly easily. The fact that most of such speakers, who readily accept the scrambling examples with resumption (see footnote 6), do not find the reading available for examples with resumption, like (4b), suggests that the speakers in question are taking the relevant scrambling construction as an instance of A'-scrambling case and that the BVA in (4a) is based on what Ueyama (1998) calls 'co-I-indexation', which is in a way sensitive to the precedence relation at PF between QP and dependent term, and not contingent upon an LF-c-command relation. Further elaboration on and substantiation of the suggested account will have to wait for a separate occasion.

b.　[Itutuizyoo-no kigyoo]$_{QP_i}$-ni soko$_i$-no torihikisaki-ga tousisi-ta.

　　five:or:more-GEN company-DAT it-GEN client-NOM invest-Past

　　'To [each of five or more companies]$_i$, its$_i$ client invested.'

　　^{ok} *BVA*

Given the general assumption that a QP α must c-command a dependent term β at pre-QR position in order for a BVA to obtain between α and β (Hoji 2003, Reinhart 1983, Ueyama 1998), the subject must c-command the object at pre-QR position in (5a), and the object must c-command the subject at pre-QR position in (5b), respectively, in order for the BVA to obtain.

It is generally agreed that the Scope Rigidity Principle is operative in Japanese, disallowing the c-command relation between the maximal projections XP$_1$ and XP$_2$ to be altered by any LF-movement (Hoji 1985, Huang 1982).[5] Given the Principle and the observation above, the two distinct c-command relations at LF between the subject and the object should be available for the sentences in the scrambling construction: the one where the subject c-commands the object, and the other where the object c-commands the subject, at LF. The former is A'-scrambling, with its *ScramObj* showing A'-properties ((5a)), and the latter A-scrambling, with its *ScramObj* showing A-properties ((5b)).

In addition to the (un)availability of BVA (Yoshimura 1992), the (im)possibility of resumption can be a clue to diagnose A/A'-scrambling. It is first pointed out in Hayashishita 1997, and further discussed in Hoji and Ueyama 1998, 2003 and Hoji 2003 that resumption in Japanese is compatible with A-properties but not with A'-properties. If we embed a resumption (*soko*) in (5b), as in (6), the BVA is possible, which means that the object in (6) is then a *ScramObj* with A-properties (henceforth, *A-ScramObj*). However, if we embed a resumption in (5a), the BVA is not possible as in (7). For the BVA to obtain in (7), the object in (7) is forced to be 'reconstructed' showing A'-properties. (Hereafter, a *ScramObj* with A'-properties will be referred to as *A'-ScramObj*.)[6]

---

5 The Scope Rigidity Principle is indispensable in order to give an account for the unavailability for the object NP to take wide-scope over the subject NP in the 'non-scrambling' construction. Given the general thesis that the scope relation between α and β is determined on the basis of their c-command relation at LF, the LF-representation in (ii-a) should be made unavailable.

(i)　　QP1-NOM QP2-ACC V　 * QP$_2$ > QP$_1$, ^{ok} QP$_1$ > QP$_2$

(ii)　a.　LF1: [QP$_1$-NOM [QP$_2$-ACC [$_{VP}$ t_1 [... t_2 ... V]]]]

　　　b.　LF2: [QP$_2$-ACC [QP$_1$-NOM [$_{VP}$ t_1 [... t_2 ... V]]]]

6 Although there have been conflicting views on the acceptability of resumption in the scrambling construction (Saito 1985 vs. Ueyama 1998), I would like to report that it is accepted by

(6)   [Itutuizyoo-no kigyoo]$_{QPi}$-ni   soko$_i$-no   torihikisaki-ga
        five:or:more-GEN company-DAT   it-GEN   client-NOM
        soko-ni tousisi-ta.
        it-DAT   invest-Past
        'To five or more companies$_i$, its$_i$ client invested *to it.*'
        (with *BVA*)

(7)   *Soko$_i$-no torihikisaki-ni [itutuizyoo-no kigyoo]$_i$-ga
        it-GEN   client-DAT   five:or:more-GEN company-NOM
        soko-ni tousisi-ta.
        it-DAT   invest-Past

Hoji and Ueyama (1998, 2003) show that the resumption in Japanese is allowed only when an operator movement occurs at LF just as in the case of the English *tough* construction, where a null operator is said to function to induce Predication. Hoji and Ueyama (2003) propose that resumption in Japanese is an overt category that appears in the launching site of a covert IP-adjunction (i.e. operator movement). (Hoji and Ueyama 2003:Section 4)

Given the above, the object in (4a) must be an *A-ScramObj* when the BVA is forced, and the object in (4b), with resumption, must also be an *A-ScramObj*. Thus these observations can be subsumed under the generalization in (8).[7]

(8) Generalization: An *A-ScramObj* cannot be in the scope of Neg.

1.3. The Goal of the Paper

The goal of this paper is to argue against the *Movement* analyses for *A-ScramObj* put forth under the thesis in (1), and support the *base-generation* analysis of the *A-ScramObj* proposed in Ueyama 1998, by considering how (8) could be accounted for under these approaches. I will assume, without further discussion, that the scope of α is its c-command domain at LF (Reinhart 1983), and that Neg is in the VP (or *v*P)-adjoined position at LF (Klima 1964, Pollock 1989).

---

the majority of speakers (16 out of 19) with whom I have consulted in my surveys. The source of judgmental variation on resumption in Japanese is discussed in Hoji (2003: Section 3).
[7] The negative counterpart of (6), in (i), disallows the *Neg* > *QP* reading, and this is as expected since the *ScramObj* must be an *A-ScramObj*, due to the BVA *and* the resumption.
(i)   [Itutuizyoo-no kigyoo]$_{QPi}$-ni soko$_i$-no torihikisaki-ga *soko*-ni tousisi-**nak**-atta.
        five:or:more-GEN company-DAT it-GEN client-NOM it-DAT invest-Neg-Past
        with *BVA(QP$_i$, soko)*, * *Neg* > *QP$_i$*, ^{ok}*QP$_i$* > *Neg*

2. *Movement* Analyses for A-scrambling

2.1. *A-movement* Analysis (Miyagawa 2001 and others)

I will first examine the *A-movement* analysis of *A-ScramObj* (Miyagawa 2001 among others), where the *A-ScramObj* is assumed to move to its surface position from its theta-position by *A-movement*.

2.1.1 Blocking of LF-lowering by Neg for A-moved NP

An A-moved NP is said to undergo 'quantifier-lowering' (May 1977); (9a) allows the reading in (9b). It is claimed that the narrow scope for *someone* in (9a) obtains by *someone* adjoining to the lower IP at LF, being inside the c-command domain of *likely* at LF.

(9) a. Someone is likely to address the rally.
     b. It is likely that someone will address the rally.

It is pointed out, however, that the lowering of an A-moved NP is blocked by a negative predicate (Lasnik and Saito 1991); (10a) does not allow the reading in (10b).

(10) a. Someone is unlikely to address the rally.
      b. It is unlikely that someone will address the rally.

If we accept this analysis and assume that the lowering of an A-moved NP is blocked by Neg, the absence of *Neg>QP* for an *A-ScramObj*, which is generalized as in (8), could be accounted for under the assumption that the *A-ScramObj* is moved from its theta-position by *A-movement*. Thus it seems that we can give an account for the generalization in (8) under the *A-movement* analysis for the *A-ScramObj*.

2.1.2 Problem for *A-movement* Analysis: 'Resumption'

As mentioned in section 1.2.1, however, resumption in Japanese is compatible with A-properties but not with A'-properties (Hayashishita 1997, Hoji 2003, Hoji and Ueyama 1998, 2003). The *A-movement* analysis of an *A-ScramObj* would therefore have a consequence that resumption should be an overt category which appears in the position occupied by the *A-movement*-trace, and how that could be expressed in theoretical terms is not clear.

Furthermore, according to Hoji and Ueyama (1998, 2003), the resumption in Japanese under discussion is allowed only when an operator movement at LF is involved. Thus, if we assume the *A-movement* analysis of an *A-ScramObj*, it would imply that the overt category in the position of the *A-movement*-trace must involve *A'-movement* (operator movement) at LF, and it is not clear what kind of element that would or could be analyzed as.

2.2. *Derivational* Analysis for A/A'-properties (Saito 2003)

The *derivational analysis* of A/A'-properties of Saito (2003) adopts the following assumptions: (i) Every *ScramObj* is derived by an optional movement operation (Saito 2003: Section 1 and 3.2). (ii) Adopting a copy and deletion analysis of movement by Chomsky (1993), chains, which are formed by movement of features, are interpreted as they are formed, and the deletion for interpretation applies as soon as a chain is formed in the derivation (Saito 2003: Section 1 and 3.1). (iii) As a consequence of (ii), the D-feature of *ScramObj* is retained only in its theta-position at LF, and every *ScramObj* is therefore substantially 'reconstructed' at LF. (Saito 2003: Section 3.2 and 4).[8]

Those assumptions adopted by Saito (2003), however, do not make a prediction correctly, regarding the scope relation between Neg and an NP, specifically, the absence of the *Neg>NP* reading for the *A-ScramObj*, as exemplified by (4).

He assumes, making recourse to (ii) above, that, in order for formal relations underlying the A/A'-properties (such as BVA) to be established, the relevant features are checked derivationally at some stage of the derivation. Suppose that a scope relation between α and β is assumed to obtain based on the c-command relation among the relevant features at some stage of the derivation. Since he assumes that every *ScramObj* is base-generated in its theta-position, the relevant feature of the *ScramObj* could be in the c-command domain of Neg while it occupies its theta-position. Under a derivational theory of Neg-QP interactions, one would be led to expect, contrary to fact, that every *ScramObj* could be in the scope of Neg.

If a scope relation were determined on the basis of the LF-representation, we would face the same problem. He assumes that the D-feature of every *ScramObj* is retained only in its theta-position and thus every *ScramObj* must be 'reconstructed' to its theta-position at LF, leaving aside VP-internal scrambling cases. Even an A-*ScramObj* would therefore be in the c-command domain of Neg at LF. We would thus fail to predict the absence of *Neg>NP* for the *A-ScramObj*.

---

[8] Saito (2003) assumes as follows: In the scrambling construction, what actually moves are the bundle of features, such as P(honetic)-feature and D-feature, which makes it possible for the NP to have a 'reference'. In the case of scrambling across the subject, only the P-features of the 'scrambled' object are retained in the sentence-initial position at LF, and its D-feature is retained only in its theta-position, but not at the landing site, at LF (Saito 2003:Section 3.2). For the cases of VP-internal scrambling, however, he maintains that the D-feature of the 'scrambled' object can remain at the landing site, since its landing site is within the projection of its theta-role assigner and therefore selected for the D-feature. (Saito 2003:Section 5.2)

3. *Base-generation* Analysis for A-scrambling (Ueyama 1998)

Let us now turn to the *base-generation* analysis of *A-ScramObj* by Ueyama (1998). We show that it gives an account for all the observations above without any problem. The most crucial aspects of Ueyama's proposal that are relevant here can be summarized as in (11).

(11)   a.   The *A-ScramObj* is base-generated in its surface-position c-commanding the subject.

        b.   The *A-ScramObj* involves a null-operator movement, like the one in the English *tough* construction, establishing a syntactic relation between the theta-position and the *A-ScramObj*, as an instance of Predication (Ueyama 1998:Sec. 2.4.3, 2.5.2, & 5).

3.1. Absence of *Neg>QP* for A-scrambled Object

The generalization in (8), as observed in (4a, b), is as predicted. First, in (4a), with the BVA, the object QP must c-command the subject NP at pre-QR position. Under the *base-generation* analysis, the *ScramObj* QP then is assumed to be base-generated in its surface position c-commanding the subject NP. Now if we assume that the base-generated position of the *A-ScramObj* is outside the c-command domain of Neg, as extensively argued in Kataoka 2004 and 2006a), the schematic LF of (4a) will be (12) after QR.

(12)   LF: [QP_1-DAT [t_1 [$_{IP}$ Op_j [$_{IP}$ [$_{NegP}$ [$_{Neg'}$ [$_{VP}$ [... *soko* ...]-NOM t_j V] [$_{Neg}$ -nai]]]]]]

The *ScramObj* in (4a) is therefore always outside the c-command domain of Neg throughout the derivation, given that movement is never downward, thus making the *Neg>A-ScramObj* impossible, as desired.

3.2. Resumption Under *Base-generation* Analysis

The unavailability of *Neg>ScramObj* in (4b), where the *ScramObj* is *A-ScramObj* with resumption, can also be given an account. As stated in (11b) above, Ueyama (1998) assumes the null operator movement at LF for the *A-ScramObj*, and, according to Hoji and Ueyama (2003), resumption is an overt counterpart of the null operator which appears in the launching site of a covert IP-adjunction, as mentioned in 1.2 above. Thus the fact that resumption is possible only with the *A-ScramObj* is precisely what is expected. The LF of (4b) should therefore be as schematized below, and the *ScramObj* cannot be in the c-command domain of Neg throughout its derivation as well as the one in (4a). See the parallelism between (12) and (13).

(13)   LF: [QP_1-DAT [t_1 [$_{IP}$ ***soko***-DAT$_i$ [$_{IP}$ [$_{NegP}$ [$_{Neg'}$ [$_{VP}$ NP-NOM t_i V] [$_{Neg}$ -nai]]]]]]]

4. A Supporting Argument for the *Base-generation* Analysis: QP-scope Interpretation

In support of the conclusion reached above, another argument can be provided based on QP-scope interpretations which involve a wide-scope distributive reading (DR).

4.1. A-scrambled Object and Resumption

It is generally observed that the scope relation between the subject and the object is unambiguous in the non-scrambling construction in Japanese. As observed in (14), the DR for the object QP_2 over the subject QP_1 (henceforth, $DR(QP_2>QP_1)$) cannot obtain, while the DR for the subject QP_1 over the object QP_2 can.

(14)   [Itutuizyoo-no ginkoo]$_{QP1}$-ga   [mittuizyoo-no kigyoo]$_{QP2}$-ni
       five:or:more-GEN bank-NOM   three:or:more-GEN company-DAT
       kitaidoori   yuusisi-ta.
       as:expected   finance-Past
       'Five or more banks financed three or more companies as expected.'
       *$DR(QP_2>QP_1)$, $DR(QP_1>QP_2)$

This follows if we assume: (i) the subject asymmetrically c-commands the object at LF in the non-scrambling construction (Hoji 1985, 2003), (ii) in order for $DR(QP_1>QP_2)$ to obtain, QP_1 must c-command QP_2 at LF (Reinhart 1983, Hayashishita 2004), and (iii) the Scope Rigidity Principle holds in Japanese (see 1.2 and footnote 5).

On the other hand, the scope relation is ambiguous in the scrambling construction.

(15)   [Mittuizyoo-no kigyoo]$_{QP2}$-ni   [itutuizyoo-no ginkoo]$_{QP1}$-ga
       three:or:more-GEN company-DAT   five:or:more-GEN bank-NOM
       kitaidoori   yuusisi-ta.
       as:expected   finance-Past
       'Three or more companies, five or more banks financed as expected.'
       $^{ok}DR(QP_2>QP_1)$, $^{ok}DR(QP_1>QP_2)$

Given the assumption (ii) above, the object QP_2 in (15) must c-command the subject QP_1 at LF when $DR(QP_2>QP_1)$ obtains, while the subject QP_1 in (15) must c-command the object QP_2 when $DR(QP_1>QP_2)$ obtains. Thus the availability of the *DR (the ScramObj QP_2 > the subject QP_1)* is taken as an instance of A-property, and the availability of the *DR (the subject QP_1 > the ScramObj QP_2)* is considered to be an A'-property.

Now if resumption is embedded in (15), the *DR (the ScramObj QP_2 > the subject QP_1)*, which corresponds to an A-property, is possible to obtain. However, the *DR (the subject QP_1 > the object QP_2)*, which corresponds to an A'-property, is not possible with resumption, as pointed out in Hayashishita 1997.

(16) [Mittuizyoo-no   kigyoo]$_{QP2}$-ni [itutuizyoo-no ginkoo]$_{QP1}$-ga
      three:or:more-GEN   company-DAT   five:or:more-GEN bank-NOM
      kitaidoori   *soko*-ni yuusisi-ta.
      as:expected it-DAT   finance-Past
      'Three or more companies, five or more banks financed it as expected.'
      a. ^{ok} { *resumption soko*-ni & $DR(QP_2>QP_1)$}
      b.   * { *resumption soko*-ni & $DR(QP_1>QP_2)$}

4.2. Absence of *Neg>QP* for A-scrambled Object

Consider the negative counterpart of example (15), given in (17).

(17) [Mittuizyoo-no kigyoo]$_{QP2}$-ni   [itutuizyoo-no ginkoo]$_{QP1}$-ga
      three:or:more-GEN company-DAT   five:or:more-GEN bank-NOM
      yuusisi-**nak**-atta.
      finance-Neg-Past
      'Three or more companies, five or more banks did not finance.'
      *{$DR(QP_2>QP_1)$ & $Neg>QP_2$}, ^{ok}{$DR(QP_1>QP_2)$& $Neg>QP_2$}

If we make the QP$_2$ an *A-ScramObj* by forcing $DR(QP_2>QP_1)$, the QP$_2$ cannot be in the scope of Neg. Notice that $Neg>QP_2$ is possible with $DR(QP_1>QP_2)$.

If resumption is added to (17), as in (18), it forces the QP$_2$ to be an *A-ScramObj*, just as the DR for QP$_2$ does in (17). The QP$_2$ then cannot be in the scope of Neg.

(18) [Mittuizyoo-no kigyoo]$_{QP2}$-ni   [itutuizyoo-no ginkoo]$_{QP1}$-ga
      three:or:more-GEN company-DAT   five:or:more-GEN bank-NOM
      soko-ni   yuusisi-**nak**-atta.
      it-DAT finance-Neg-Past
      (Lit) 'Three or more companies, five or more banks did not finance it.'
      ^{ok}{'resumption' *soko*-ni & $DR(QP2>QP_1)$}, but then *$Neg>QP_2$

Notice again that, since the *ScramObj* QP$_2$ must be an *A-ScramObj* in (18), the DR for the subject QP$_1$, i.e., reconstruction effects, is no longer available in contrast to (17).

The observations above, which show parallelism with the BVA cases, also confirm the generalization in (8), and corroborate the conclusion reached above. If we assume that the *A-ScramObj* QP is base-generated in its surface position c-commanding the subject, the necessary condition for the DR is satisfied: the *ScramObj* QP necessarily c-commands the subject QP at LF, making the DR possible only for the *ScramObj* QP over the subject QP. The resumption-related paradigms are also as expected as discussed in section 3.2, and the absence of the *Neg>NP* reading for the *A-ScramObj* QP is as predicted since the *A-ScramObj* is outside the c-command domain of Neg throughout the derivation.

5. Conclusion

We have examined three analyses of the scrambling construction proposed in the field in relation to the absence of *Neg>A-ScramObj* as generalized in (8), and shown that the *base-generation* analysis of Ueyama (1998) can give an account for the generalization without any problem, but not the *A-movement* analysis of Miyagawa (2001) among others nor the *derivational* analysis for A/A'-properties of Saito (2003).

The considerations given above (see also Kataoka 2006b) for further arguments) suggest that we should abandon the widely accepted thesis that every *ScramObj* should be 'base-generated' in its theta-position, and adopt the thesis that the *ScramObj* is 'base-generated' in its surface position when it shows A-properties, in line with Ueyama (1998).

Referensces

Chomsky, N. 1993. A Minimalist Program for Linguistic Theory. *The View from Building 20: Essays in Linguistics in Honor of Sylvain Bromberger*, eds. K. Hale and S. J. Keyser, 1-52. Cambridge: MIT Press.

Hayashishita, J.-R. 1997. On the Scope Ambiguity in the Scrambling Construction in Japanese. Manuscript, University of Southern California.

Hayashishita, J.-R. 2004. Syntactic Scope and Non-Syntactic Scope. Doctoral Dissertation, University of Southern California.

Hoji, H. 1985. Logical Form Constraints and Configurational Structures in Japanese. Doctoral Dissertation, University of Washington.

Hoji, H. 2003. Falsifiability and Repeatability in Generative Grammar: a Case Study of Anaphora and Scope Dependency in Japanese. *Lingua* 113 (4-6):377-446.

Hoji, H. and A. Ueyama. 1998. Resumption in Japanese. Manuscript, University of Southern California.

Hoji, H. and A. Ueyama. 2003. Resumption in Japanese: A Preliminary Study. Handout at WECOL 2003, held at University of Arizona, September 26-28, 2003. http://www.gges.org/work/hoji/WECOL-handout-3.pdf

Huang, C.-T. J. 1982. Logical Relations in Chinese and the Theory of Grammar. Doctoral Dissertation, MIT.

Lasnik, H. and M. Saito 1991. On the Subject of Infinitives. *Papers from the 27th Regional Meeting of the Chicago Linguistics Society*, 324-343.

Kataoka, K. 2004. Nihongo Hiteibun-no Koozoo: Kakimaze-bun to Hiteekoo-hyoogen (Syntactic structure of Japanese negative sentences: scrambling construction and negation-sensitive elements). Doctoral dissertation. Kyushu University, Fukuoka, Japan. (A slightly revised version will be published from Kurosio Publishing, Tokyo.)

Kataoka, K. 2006a. 'Neg-sensitive' elements, Neg-c-command and Scrambling in Japanese. *Japanese/Korean Linguistics 14*.

Kataoka, K. 2006b. Neg-Scope and Resumption: Their Implications for the Analyses of Scrambling. *Theoretical and Empirical Studies of Reference and Anaphora --- Toward the Establishment of Generative Grammar as an Empirical Science.* Granted by Grant-in-Aid for Scientific Research (B), Japan Society for the Promotion of Science. Grant No. 15320052

Klima, E. S. 1964. Negation in English. *The Structure of Language*, eds. J. Fodor and J. Katz, 246-32. N.Jersey: Prentice-Hall.

Kuno, S. 1980. The Scope of the Question and Negation in Some Verb-final Languages. *CLS* 16:155-169.

May, R. 1977. The Grammar of Quantification. Doctoral Dissertation, MIT.

May, R. 1985. *Logical Form: Its Structure and Derivation.* Cambridge: MIT Press.

Miyagawa, S. 2001. The EPP, Scrambling, and *wh*-in-situ. *Ken Hale: A Life in Language,* ed. M. Kenstowicz, 293-338. MIT Press.

Pollock, J.-Y. 1989. Verb Movement, Universal Grammar, and the Structure of IP. *Linguistic Inquiry* 20 (3):365-424

Reinhart. T. 1983. *Anaphora and Semantic Interpretation.* Chicago: The University of Chicago Press.

Ross, J. R. 1967. Constraints on Variables in Syntax. Doctoral Dissertation, MIT.

Saito, M. 1992. Long Distance Scrambling in Japanese. *Journal of East Asian Linguistics* 1:69-118.

Saito, M. 2003. A Derivational Approach to the Interpretation of Scrambling Chains. *Lingua* 113 (4-6):481-518.

Sells, P. 1984. Syntax and Semantics of Resumptive Pronouns. Doctoral Dissertation, University of Massachusetts, Amherst.

Ueyama, A. 1998. Two Types of Dependency. Doctoral Dissertation, University of Southern California. Distributed by GSIL Publications, USC, Los Angeles.

Yoshimura, N. 1992. Scrambling and Anaphora in Japanese. Doctoral dissertation, University of Southern California.

Non-veridical Uses of Japanese Expressions of Temporal Precedence

STEFAN KAUFMANN AND YUKINORI TAKUBO
Northwestern University, Kyoto University

1. Introduction[1]

The English temporal sentential connective *'before'* has two Japanese near-equivalents, *'mae'* and *'-nai uti'*. All three of these constructions have *non-veridical* readings (see below). However, they differ subtly in the implicatures associated with those readings. In this paper we discuss these difference in detail and sketch a formal analysis.

2. Some English Facts

2.1. Non-veridicality of *'Before'*-clauses

Both *before* and *after* combine with a clausal complement to form a modifier of the matrix clause. We refer to the embedded complement (the bracketed parts in (1)) as the *temporal clause*.

(1) a. *A* [before *B*]   [before *B*,] *A*
     b. *B* [after *A*]   [after *A*,] *B*

---

[1] We thank the conference organizers and members of the audience. This work was supported in part by the Japan Society for the Promotion of Science (JSPS, "The Logic of Everyday Inference and Its Linguistic Forms: With Special Reference to Quantificational Expressions, Conditionals, and Modal Expressions").

The role of the connectives is to locate the time of the eventuality denoted by the matrix clause relative to that of the temporal clause. There is a well-known asymmetry between 'before' and 'after' regarding the semantic status of the temporal clause: It is entailed by 'after'-sentences, but not by 'before'-sentences, as illustrated in (2a,b) (Anscombe 1964, Beaver and Condoravdi 2003, Heinämäki 1972, Heinämäki 1974, Ogihara 1995, Valencia et al. 1992).

(2)   a. I left the party before I got sick. $\not\Rightarrow$ I got sick.

      b. I got sick after I left the party. $\Rightarrow$ I left the party.

Consequently, 'B after A' entails 'A before B', but not vice versa:

(3)   a. I left the party before I got sick. $\not\Rightarrow$ I got sick after I left.

      b. I got sick after I left the party. $\Rightarrow$ I left before I got sick.

Thus English 'before'-sentences can be used in contexts in which the temporal clause is not known to be true, or even known to be false.

2.2.   Flavors of Non-veridicality

Non-veridicality in sentences of the form 'A before B' comes in two flavors: On the *non-committal* reading, the truth of B is not established. On the stronger *counterfactual* reading, the falsehood of B is established. Which reading arises in a particular case depends on contextual factors (i.e., what is known or presupposed) as well as the semantic relationship between A and B (e.g., the sentence must be counterfactual if A and B cannot both be true). Thus (4a) is most likely either veridical or counterfactual, since the speaker can be assumed to know whether he got sick. The third-person temporal clause in (4b), on the other hand, allows for a non-commital reading.

(4)   a. I left the party before I got sick.   *[verdical or counterfactual]*

      b. I left the party before Sue got sick.   *[may be non-committal]*

In contrast, (5) has a counterfactual reading for semantic reasons, regardless of contextual factors, since the matrix clause and the temporal clause cannot both be true (in the intended temporal relation).

(5)   Mozart died before he finished the Requiem.   *[counterfactual]*

In this paper we are mainly concerned with the counterfatual reading and the implicatures associated with it.

2.3. Likelihood Implicature

'*A before B*' may be true while *B* is false, but neither the truth of *A* nor the falsehood of *B* are sufficient for the truth of '*A before B*', even when *A* and *B* stand in the right temporal relation. In (6) (adapted from Beaver and Condoravdi 2003, henceforth B&C), the falsehood of the temporal clause is given, yet the sentence does not follow.

(6) [David never won a gold metal, but he once at lots of ketchup.]
     ↛ David ate lots of ketchup before he made a clean sweep of all the gold medals in the Sydney Olympics.

Similarly, (7) is not necessarily true, even though its matrix clause is.

(7) Squares had four sides long before David made a clean sweep of all the gold medals in the Sydney Olympics.

Thus counterfactual '*A before B*' does imply something about *B*, though not that *B* is true. Rather, the implicature is *modal*. Some differences aside, B&C, Heinämäki (1972), Ogihara (1995) and others all spell it out as the condition that *B* was *likely* at or just before the time of *A*. However, this characterization runs into problems in cases in which *A* itself is highly likely and implies the falsehood of *B*. An example is (8):

(8) [As he always does / as people around here always do,]
     Bill returned his books before they were overdue.

Here the given context implies that *B* was highly *unlikely* at the relevant time, yet the '*before*'-sentence is felicitous.

This problem is avoided by stating the implicature as a *conditional*, making the likelihood of *B* contingent upon the falsehood of *A*. There are two candidate forms for such an implicature: the past (predictive) indicative, and the present counterfactual. Based on (8), both seem viable: (9a) *was* true at the relevant past time and (9b) *is* true now.

(9) a. If Bill does not return his books, they will be overdue.

     b. If Bill had not returned his books, they would have been overdue.

Similarly, both conditionals corresponding to (5) are true at the respective times. In the next section, we take a closer look at the relationship between '*before*'-clauses and conditionals.

2.4. '*Before*'-sentences and Conditionals

The label "counterfactual" for the use of '*A before B*' presently under discussion suggests a close affinity between '*before*' and the counterfactual. However, the two are not equivalent: '*Before*'-sentences generally imply the corresponding counterfactuals, but not *vice versa* (the symbol '⤳' reads "implicates"):

(10) a. *'A before B'* ⤳ *'If had been ¬A, would have been B'*

  b. *'If had been ¬A, would have been B'* ⥇ *'A before B'*

The following scenario is a case in point.

(11) The speaker is on the bus from Kyoto to Tokyo. She gets off at Nagoya; the bus travels on. The next day the speaker hears that the bus had an accident and everyone on board was injured or killed.

  a. If I hadn't gotten off the bus, I would have been injured.

  [true now]

  b. If I don't get off the bus, I will get injured. *[was false then]*

  c. #I got off the bus before I got injured.

(11a) is true and felicitous in the given context, even though the accident was highly unlikely at the time of the antecedent. On the other hand, the unlikelihood of the accident means that (11b) was false. In cases which exhibit this mismatch between the present counterfactual and the past indicative, the corresponding *'before'*-clause patterns with the past indicative, not the present counterfactual.[2] Thus we conclude that *'A before B'* implicates that at (or just before) the time of *A*, the indicative conditional *'If A is false, B will be true'* is/was true.

3. Some Japanese Facts

3.1. Non-veridicality and Likelihood Implicature

The two Japanese formal nouns (*keisiki meisi*) *'mae'* and *'uti'* (with a negated complement clause) both correspond to English *'before'*:

(12) a. *B* mae ni *A*   *[lit. 'before B, A']*
      B before LOC

  b. *B* nai uti ni *A*   *[lit. 'while still not-B, A']*
      B NEG within LOC

'Mae' takes non-stative clauses as its complement. Its temporal meaning corresponds to English *'before'*. *'Uti'* combines with stative, progressive and negated clauses, generally meaning *'while still'*. Both require Nonpast tense in the complement clause. The locative postposition *'ni'* can be dropped in colloquial speech.

---

[2] Although it is sometimes assumed that present counterfactuals are equivalent to the corresponding past indicatives, this is not always the case (see Kaufmann 2005a and references therein).

Both of (12a,b) are like English *'before'*-sentences in having veridical and non-veridical uses, as well as non-commital and counterfactual uses in the non-veridical case. However, they differ in the implicatures of the counterfactual reading. Consider again the scenario in (11). The veridical use is illustrated in (13) (recall that the accident occurred):

(13) [Boku-wa] ziko-ga   {okoru mae-ni   / okora-nai
     I-TOP   accident-SUBJ   occur before-LOC   occur-NEG
     uti-ni   } basu-o   orita
     within-LOC   bus-ACC exit-PAST
     I got off the bus before there was an accident.

The non-veridical use in this example must be counterfactual. By assumption, the accident is not foreseeable at the time the speaker leaves the bus. This does not affect (14a), but it makes (14b) infelicitous:

(14)   a.   Kega suru mae-ni   basu-o   orita
          get injured before-LOC bus-ACC exit-PAST

      b.   #Kega si-nai   uti-ni   basu-o   orita
          get injured-NEG within-LOC bus-ACC exit-PAST

In this, (14a) patterns with the counterfactuals (11a) and (15):

(15)   Basu-o   ori-tei-nakat-tara   kega si-tei-ta   *[true now]*
     bus-ACC get off-PRF-NEG-COND get injured-PRF-PAST
     If I hadn't gotten off the bus, I would have been injured.

In contrast, (14b), like (11c) above, patterns with the past indicative conditionals (11b) and (16):

(16)   Basu-o   ori-nakat-tara   kega suru   *[was false then]*
     bus-ACC get off-NEG-COND get injured
     If I don't get off the bus, I will get injured.

In sum, *'B mae ni A'* implies the counterfactual, whereas *'B-nai uti ni A'* implies the past indicative.

More observations have been reported in the literature which we cannot address here for lack of space (see Kuno 1973, McGloin 1989, Ogihara 1995, and Terakura 1985 for more details). We mention only one additional fact which bears on the analysis.

3.2. Past and Future

We concluded from (14a) that *'B mae ni A'* does not implicate the (past) indicative. Things are different with future reference, however. Both forms in (17), like their English gloss, implicate the (present) indicative:

(17) Bakkin-wo {torareru   mae-ni   / torarenai uti-ni   }
      fine-ACC   take-PASS before-LOC   take-NEG within-LOC
      kuruma-wo ugokasoo
      car-ACC   let's move-CAUS
      Let's move the car before we are fined.
      ⤳ If we don't move the car, we will be fined.   [now]

With past reference, the difference becomes apparent again. (18) is
felicitous even if the car was parked in a spot that had never been visited
by the parking enforcer, and only after moving it did the speaker learn
that other cars parked next to it were ticketed. (18) does implicate the
counterfactual, however, as expected.

(18) Bakkin-wo torareru   mae-ni   kuruma-wo ugokasita
      fine-ACC   take-PASS before-LOC car-ACC   move-PAST
      We moved the the car before we were fined.
      ⤳̸ If we don't move the car, we will be fined.   [then]
      ⤳ If we hadn't moved the car, we would have been fined. [now]

For 'nai uti' in (19), unlike 'mae', the indicative implicature does carry
over to the past.[3]

(19) Bakkin-wo torarenai uti-ni   kuruma-wo ugokasita
      fine-ACC   take-NEG within-LOC car-ACC   move-PAST
      We moved the car before we were fined.
      ⤳ If we don't move the car, we will be fined.   [then]

Under our account, the presence of the indicative implicature with futurate 'mae' in (17) is not due to 'mae' per se. Rather, it arises for
pragmatic reasons, having to do with the inability to "look ahead" in
history, as opposed to the benefit of "hindsight" with regard to the past.

4. Analysis

4.1. Temporality

Due to space constraints, we ignore for the most part the role of aspectual classes, tenses, and the details of the semantic composition. The
main ingredients of the formal framework are from B&C, Condoravdi
(2002), Condoravdi (In press), and Kaufmann (2005b). We will write
'α' and 'β' for the *sentence radicals* obtained by stripping the atomic
sentences *A* and *B* of their tenses.

---

[3] Incidentally, the counterfactual is *not* implied by (19): The sentence is still felicitous if the speaker has since learned that he was wrong and the car would not have
been fined even if it had been left in place.

Let T be a set of atomic temporal instants, ordered by an "earlier then"-relation $<$ that is transitive, asymmetric and linear.[4] The denotation $[\![\alpha]\!]$ of sentence radical α is a function which, given a subset of T, returns "true" if α is true at some member of that set, and "false" otherwise. Tenses denote intervals $x \subseteq T$, determined relative to speech time S: the set of times preceding S for the Past, and its complement for the Nonpast. A simple tensed sentence is evaluated by applying the denotation of its radical to the tense interval x. Thus for instance, '$PAST(\alpha)$' is true iff α is true at some time preceding speech time.

Other elements besides tense, such as context, temporal frame adverbials and temporal clauses, impose further restrictions on the subset of T of which the radical is predicated. 'B mae' and 'B-nai uti' denote subsets $y \subseteq T$; their contribution as modifiers of the matrix clause consists in intersecting the interval x provided by tense with y, thus strengthening the resulting existential statement about α.

Regarding the denotation of 'B-mae', we adopt the definition B&C give for English 'before B'. There, the tense of B is inherited from A, and 'before B' is the set y of times preceding the *earliest* time in $[\![\beta]\!]$.[5] The assumption that B lacks its own tense is sensible for English in view of the obligatory Sequence of Tense in 'before'-clauses. For Japanese, in contrast, recall that B has obligatory Nonpast tense, and assume for simplicity that this Nonpast is semantically vacuous. Thus we are dealing with an expression 'B mae ni α', where B is the (vacuously) tensed temporal clause and α is the untensed matrix clause; the tense of the matrix clause makes an obvious further contribution, which we ignore here. Then the analogous truth conditions to those of B&C are as follows:

(20) 'B mae ni α' is true at time t if and only if there is some $t' \in [\![\alpha]\!]$ which precedes the earliest $t'' \in [\![\beta]\!]$.

B&C's definition of "earliest" ensures that (20) entails that B is true at *some* time. The combination with tense then adds the condition that t' must stand in the appropriate relation to t.

'B-nai uti' is slightly more complex, but semantically transparent. 'B-nai' is the negation of B, true of a set of times just in case it does

---

[4] Transitive: for all $t,t',t'' \in T$, if $t < t'$ and $t' < t''$, then $t < t''$. Asymmetric: for all $t,t' \in T$, if $t < t'$ then not $t' < t$. Linear: For all $t,t' \in T$, either $t < t'$ or $t' < t$ or $t = t'$. Transitivity and asymmetry jointly imply irreflixivity: For all $t \in T$, not $t < t$.

[5] B&C stipulate that all English sentence radicals denote sets of times which have an earliest time. They also rightfully point out that the definition must be refined for the case that B is an accomplishment: There, 'before B' may be the set of times preceding the earliest *culmination time* in $[\![B]\!]$.

not contain any instances of $[\![\beta]\!]$.[6] 'Uti' maps such intervals to themselves and adds the presupposition that they are right-bounded.[7] The resulting meaning is literally 'when still'; the combination with 'B-nai' yields 'when B is/was still false', equivalent to 'when B is/was not yet true'. Thus as far as its temporal meaning is concerned, 'B-nai uti ni α' is equivalent to 'B-mae ni α' in (20).

This subsection offered only rough outline of the temporal treatment. Further facts, such as restrictions on aspectual classes, cannot be accounted for without further complexity. We leave these elaborations for the full version of the paper and move on to the modal dimension.

4.2. Modality

Basics. As used above, the set T traces the history of one world (the actual one). The likelihood of a sentence is independent of its truth value at the actual world. We extend the above linearly ordered model of time to a *possible-worlds* model of *branching time* (see Kaufmann 2005b and references therein). Given a set W of possible worlds, each corresponds to an alternative history traced by T. A world-time pair or *index* $i = \langle w, t \rangle$ is a "snapshot" of world w at time t. Sentence radicals denote sets of indices. The truth of a simple tensed sentence is fully determined by the world of evaluation, but the interpretation of 'before'-sentences makes reference to alternative worlds if the temporal clause is not instantiated at the world of evaluation.

Branching time. The passage of time involves the elimination of possibilities. At each $\langle w, t \rangle$, the past up to t is fixed, but there are multiple possible continuations. Furthermore, for subsequent times t', fewer continuations are possible at $\langle w, t' \rangle$ than at $\langle w, t \rangle$. Intuitively, uncertainty about the future at $\langle w, t \rangle$ is partly resolved at $\langle w, t' \rangle$ by the events that came to pass during the time that elapsed between t and t'.

Modal bases. In Kratzer's (1981) terms, the set of alternatives at $\langle w, t \rangle$ is a *modal base (MB)*. Formally, an *MB* is a function from indices $\langle w, t \rangle$ to sets of co-temporal indices $\langle w', t \rangle$.[8] This set may comprise *historical* or *epistemic* alternatives, corresponding to objective or subjective uncertainty, hence to different readings of the modal implicature. We write 'MB_i^{+p}' (where p is a sentence) for that subset of MB_i at which p is true.

---

[6] In fact, B in B-nai uti is untensed; the Nonpast is expressed on the negative suffix 'nai'. We continue to write 'B-nai' for simplicity and uniformity.

[7] It is fairly common to attribute such a presupposition of a "phase transition" to temporal particles (Condoravdi In press, Löbner 1989, and others).

[8] Kratzer's definition of *MB* as well as *OS* (below) is more elaborate than this. Our simplification is purely for the sake of brevity.

Ordering sources. The *MB* determines which continuations of history are *possible*. To encode what is *likely*, we adopt from Kratzer (1981) the notion of an *ordering source* (*OS*). Formally, an *OS* is a function from indices $\langle w,t \rangle$ to *pre-orders* $\preceq_{\langle w,t \rangle}$ on the set of co-temporal indices $\langle w',t \rangle$.[9] For our purposes, we use two ordering sources: *Relative likelihood* is a "stereotypical" *OS*, one which ranks worlds by the degree to which they conform to the "normal" course of events: '$j \preceq_i j'$' means that j is more normal, or less far-fetched, than j'. *Overall similarity* is given by a "totally realistic" *OS*, one which ranks worlds by their similarity to the world coordinate of j.[10] Whereas likelihood is a time-dependent notion, overall similarity is assumed to be constant throughout a world's history.

Human necessity. Relative to a modal base *MB* and an ordering source *OS*, we say that a sentence *A* is a *human necessity* at i if and only if it is true at the most likely continuations under $\preceq_i$.[11]

4.3. Truth and Implicature

Using the notions just introduced, we account for non-veridicality and the implicature separately. First, definition (20) is modified to allow for non-veridical uses.

(21) '*B mae ni* α' is true at $i = \langle w,t \rangle$ with respect to modal base *MB* if and only if there is some t' such that $\langle w,t' \rangle \in [\![\alpha]\!]$ and t' precedes the earliest time t'' such that for some $\langle w',t \rangle$ in MB_i, $\langle w',t'' \rangle \in [\![\beta]\!]$.

The only substantive change from (20) is the existential quantification over alternative worlds in evaluating β. Clearly (21) is weaker than (20): The sentence entails that β is/was *possible* at the relevant time, not that it is true—nor, for that matter, that it is/was likely. The meaning of '*B-nai uti ni* α' is similar to (21).

The likelihood implicature is added separately as the condition that β (or, in the case of '*-nai uti*', the end of not-β) be a "human necessity" relative to $MB^{+\neg\alpha}_{\langle w,t' \rangle}$—in other words, that the conditional '*If* ¬α, *will* β' is true at t'. This is in line with the widely shared assumption

---

[9] A pre-order is transitive and reflexive (see Fn. 4 above).

[10] The notion of overall similarity is familiar from the literature on conditionals (Lewis 1973, Stalnaker 1968), but not very well defined. See (Kaufmann 2004, Kaufmann 2005a) for an analysis in terms of causal independence.

[11] This is a simplified statement. In general, there may not be a set of most likely continuations. For the general case it should be: "...if and only if for all $j \in MB$, there is a $j' \in MB$ such that $j' \preceq_i j$ and for all $j'' \in MB$ such that $j'' \preceq_i j'$, *A* is true at j''." The term "human necessity" is due to Kratzer (1981).

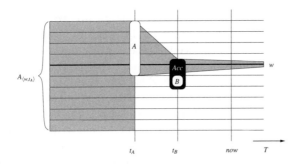

Figure 1.
(The grey area shows the alternatives of *w* at each time.)

that conditionals are interpreted in terms of modal operators, with '*if*'-clauses imposing restrictions on the modal base.

The difference between '*mae*' and '*-nai uti*' formally comes down to the choice of the ordering source with respect to which the implicature is calculated: In the case of '*mae*', it is totally realistic, thus the implicature is true iff *B* is true at the *most similar* α-worlds. In the case of '*-nai uti*', it is stereotypical, true iff *B* is true at the *most normal* α-worlds (from the perspective of *t'*).

Returning now to the "bus" scenario (11), recall the judgments about English (11c) and Japanese (14a,b), repeated here:

(11c) #I got off the bus before I got injured.

(14) a. Kega suru mae-ni   basu-o   orita
          get injured before-LOC bus-ACC exit-PAST

      b. #Kega si-nai   uti-ni   basu-o   orita
          get injured-NEG within-LOC bus-ACC exit-PAST

Figure 1 is an informal depiction of the scenario. Times flows from left to right; alternative worlds run parallel to the world *w* of evaluation. The grey area covers, for any index ⟨*w,t*⟩, the set of alternatives open at that time. The time *t'* at which the speaker got off the bus is labeled '*t_A*'. The accident ('*Acc*') is unlikely at *t_A*, but occurs at *t_B* in *w*. The closest non-*A* worlds to *w* (i.e., worlds at which the speaker did not get off the bus) are ones in which the accident happened, and in the closest ones among those, the speaker was injured ('*B*').

Now the implicature of (14a) is *true* because the most *similar* non-*A* worlds to *w* are ones at which the accident occurs. In contrast, the implicature of (14b) is *false* because the most *likely* non-*A* worlds from the perspective of *t_A* are ones in which the accident does not occur.

Notice that both sentences are semantically *true*; the infelicity of (14b) is explained by the falsehood of the implicature. This is a subtle but non-trivial difference between our account and that of B&C. Here, the truth value of the sentence and that of the implicature are determined by different sets of worlds (the whole modal base *vs.* the most likely/similar worlds); the sentence is true but its implicature is false. In contrast, B&C calculate both with respect to the subset of "reasonably probable" worlds in the modal base, attributing the infelicity of (11c) to semantic undefinedness, due to the fact that the temporal clause is not true in any of those "reasonably likely" alternatives. The ramifications of this difference remain to be explored.

5. Conclusions

Non-veridical expressions of temporal precedence constitute an intriguing set of data at the interface of modality and temporality. We have shown that in Japanese a distinction is lexicalized that has no analog in English, and we have demonstrated the utility of standard formal tools in the analysis of the observations. In future work, we plan to complete the picture by drawing into consideration other temporal connectives, such as Japanese 'toki', 'aida' and 'mama', as well as English 'while' and 'as long as', and others.

References

Anscombe, E. 1964. Before and After. *The Philosophical Review* 73:3–24.

Beaver, D. and C. Condoravdi. 2003. A Uniform Analysis of *Before* and *After*. *Proceedings of SALT XIII*:37–54.

Condoravdi, C. 2002. Temporal Interpretation of Modals: Modals for the Present and for the Past. *The Construction of Meaning*, eds. D. I. Beaver, L. Casillas, B. Clark, and S. Kaufmann, 59–88. Stanford, CA: CSLI Publications.

Condoravdi, C. In press. Punctual *Until* as a Scalar NPI. *The Nature of the Word*, eds. S. Inkelas, S. and K. Hanson. Cambridge, MA: MIT Press.

Heinämäki, O. 1972. Before. *Papers from the Eighth Regional Meeting, Chicago Linguistic Society*, eds. P. M. Peranteau, J. N. Levi, and G. C. Phares, 139–151. Chicago, IL: The Chicago Linguistic Society.

Heinämäki, O. 1974. *Semantics of English Temporal Connectives*. Doctoral Dissertation, University of Texas at Austin.

Kaufmann, S. 2004. Conditioning Against the Grain: Abduction and Indicative Conditionals. *Journal of Philosophical Logic* 33(6):583–606.

Kaufmann, S. 2005a. Conditional Predictions: A Probabilistic Account. *Linguistics and Philosophy* 28(2):181–231.

Kaufmann, S. 2005b. Conditional Truth and Future Reference. *Journal of Semantics* 22:231–280.

Kratzer, A. 1981. The Notional Category of Modality. *Words, Worlds, and Contexts*, eds. J. Eikmeyer and H. Riesner, 38–74. Berlin: Walter de Gruyter.

Kuno, S. 1973. *The Structure of Japanese*. Cambridge, MA: MIT Press.

Lewis, D. 1973. *Counterfactuals*. Cambridge, MA: Harvard University Press.

Löbner, S. 1989. German *Schon–Erst–Noch*: An Integrated Analysis. *Linguistics and Philosophy*, 12:167–212.

McGloin, N. H. 1989. *A Students' Guide to Japanese Grammar*. Tokyo: Taishuukan.

Ogihara, T. 1995. Non-factual *Before* and Adverbs of Quantification. *Proceedings of SALT V*:273–291.

Stalnaker, R. 1968. A Theory of Conditionals. *Studies in Logical Theory, American Philosophical Quarterly, Monograph: 2*:98–112. Oxford: Blackwell.

Terakura. 1985. English *Before*-clauses and Japanese Temporal Clauses. *Journal of Asian Culture* 9:199–215.

Valencia, V. S., T. von der Wouden, and F. Zwarts. 1992. Polarity and the Flow of Time. *Language and Cognition*, volume 3, eds. A. de Boer, J. de Jong, and R. Landeweerd, 209–218. Groningen: Uitgeverij Passage.

What Exactly Intervenes What?

AE-RYUNG KIM
Kyungnam University

1. Introduction

It has been observed that wh-phrases in-situ are subject to a linear constraint that a wh-phrase in-situ cannot be preceded by a scope-bearing element. Beck and Kim (1997) and Tanaka (1997) suggest an analysis based on data from Korean and Japanese, respectively.

(1) a. *$Amuto$ mues-ul   sa-ci   an   ha-ss-ni?   (Korean)
       Anybody   what-acc   buy-ci   neg   do-past-Q
       'What didn't anybody buy?'
   b. Mues-ul$_i$ $amuto$ t$_i$ sa-ci   an   ha-ss-ni?
       what-acc$_i$ anybody   t$_i$ buy-ci   neg   do-past-Q

(2) a. *$Taro$-$sika$ nani-o   yoma-nai-no?   (Japanese)
       T-only   what-acc   read-neg-Q
       'What did only Taro read?'
   b. Nani-o $Taro$-$sika$ t yoma-nai-no?
       what-acc   T-only   t read-neg-Q

The two sets of examples in (1) and (2) contain a wh-phrase and an NPI, a typical example of scope-bearing elements. A wh-question is unacceptable when the wh-phrase follows an NPI as in (1a) and (2a). The questions are saved if the wh-phrase scrambles as in (1b) and (2b).

The linear constraint is explained in two different approaches. One approach attributes the constraint to the existence of an intervener between Spec CP and a wh-phrase in-situ. I will call this approach "intervener approach" in this paper. Under this approach the constraint is commonly called the intervention effect. The other approach explains the constraint in terms of linear crossing of two movements. This approach will be called "LCC approach", naming after Linear Crossing Constraint suggested by Tanaka (1997). In this paper I will point out that the intervener approach treats the intervention effect in terms of interpretation and I will claim that it is on the right track, showing an empirical problem with LCC approach.

2. Two Approaches to the Intervention Effect

2.1. Intervener Approach

Following Beck (1996), Beck and Kim (1997) adopt LF movement for wh-phrases in-situ for interpretation. Based on the contrast between overt and covert wh-movements from German data as in (3), they claim that LF movement is blocked by an intervening negation.

(3) a. Wen$_i$ glaubt   niemand, daβ Karl gesehn   hat t$_i$?
       Whom believes nobody   that Karl seen   has
       'Who does nobody believe that Karl saw?'
    b. *Was glaubt   niemand, wen$_i$ Karl gesehn hat t$_i$?
        What believes nobody   whom Karl seen has?
       'Who does nobody believe that Karl saw?
    c. Was   glaubt   Luise, wen$_i$ Karl gesehn hat t$_i$?
       What believes Luise whom Karl seen   has
       'Who does Luise believe that Karl saw?

A wh-phrase wen moves across a negative quantifier niemand overtly in (3a), and the sentence is grammatical. In (3b) wen moves overtly to its clause and it is assumed to move to matrix clause at LF to take matrix scope. This covert movement crosses over niemand. A negation quantifier niemand is responsible for the ungrammaticality of (3b), which is confirmed by the sentence (3c), where niemand is replaced with Luise and the sentence is grammatical.

Beck and Kim (1997) claim that a negative quantifier forms a barrier, Negation Induced Barrier (henceforth NIB) and an LF (wh-)trace and its binder should not be intervened by an NIB at LF. They attribute the intervention effect to the NIB. The NIB blocks an appropriate binding between a wh-quantifier and its variable, trace. According to their analysis the sentences (1a) and (1b) would be structured as in (4a) and (4b) at LF, respectively.

(4) a. *$[_{CP}$ what$_i$[Q] [$_{NIB}$ anybody t$_i$ buy-neg]]   LF

b. $[_{CP}$ what$_i$[Q][t$_i$ [$_{NIB}$ anybody t$_i$ buy-neg]]   LF

In (4a) a wh-phrase and its trace is intervened by an NIB, while in (4b) they are not.

Pesetsky (2000) also explains the intervention effect in terms of intervener. He observes the intervention effect in English from data involving the violation of Superiority Condition.

(5) a. Which person bought which book?
    b. Which book did which person buy?

The sentence (5b) violates Superiority Condition, which requires to attract the closest wh-phrase in multiple wh-questions. When a sentence contains D-linked wh-phrases, the condition can be violated. Pesetsky (2000), however, claims that both sentences observe the Superiority Condition. He claims that what moves first is *which person* in both sentences. What is different is that a phrasal movement takes place first in (5a) but in (5b) a wh-feature movement takes place first and it is followed by the phrasal movement of *which book*. There are one overt movement involved in (5a) but in (5b) one overt movement and one feature movement.

Based on the example (6) and (7) below, crediting them to E. Kiss, Pesetsky (2000) points out that multiple wh-questions violating "apparent Superiority Condition" are subject to the intervention effect.[1]

(6) a. Which person __ did not read which book?
    b. Which person __ didn't read which book?

(7) a. Which book did which person not read __?
    b. *Which book didn't which person read __?

Multipel wh-questions are ambiguously interpreted between pair-list reading and single-pair reading but pair-list reading is stronger than single-pair reading. Let us concentrate our concern on only the pair-list reading in this discussion. The sentences in (6), which observe the Superiority Condition, have pair-list reading regardless of contraction of negation with the auxil-

---

[1] Sentences like (5b) and (7a)) are considered to be instances of violating the Superiority Condition in general. However, under Pesetsky's (2000) analysis they do not. For this reason he calls such examples cases of 'apparent Superiority Condition'.

iary. The position of negation makes difference, when there is violation of the apparent Superiority Condition as in (7). If negation moves to I tagging along with the auxiliary as in (7b), the sentence cannot be interpreted as pair-list reading.

According to Pesetsky (2000), (7a) and (7b) look different at LF as shown in (8a) and (8b), respectively.

(8) a. [$_{CP}$ Which book$_j$ F$_i$-C [$_C$ did] [$_{IP}$ F$_i$-**which person** buy not t$_j$]]

b. *[$_{CP}$ Which book$_j$ F$_i$-C [$_C$ did-not] [$_{IP}$ F$_i$-**which person** buy t$_j$]]

At the structures in (8), wh-feature of *which person* is placed at Spec CP marked 'F-C' and the wh-phrase stays in-situ. The difference between (8a) and (8b) is that the feature at Spec CP and the wh-phrase in-situ are intervened by negation in (8b). Pesetsky (2000) regards the lost of pair-list reading in (8) as manifestation of the intervention effect. He treats the feature at Spec CP as a quantifier and the wh-phrase in-situ as its restriction. He suggests a characterization of the intervention effect as in (9).

(9) A semantic restriction on a quantifier (including *wh*) may not be separated from that quantifier by a scope-bearing element.

Pesetsky (2000) consider a scope-bearing element as an intervener to the proper interpretation of wh-phrases in-situ at LF.

2.2. LCC Approach

Tanaka (1997) and Tanaka (2003) treat the linear constraint as being derived from an illegitimate arrangement of movement lines. He follows Watanabe (1992) in assuming invisible movements at overt syntax. A sentence like (10) involves two invisible movements.

(10) a. *Taro-sika* nani-o yoma-nai-no?   (Japanese)
         T-only   what-acc read-neg-Q
         'What did only Taro read?'
      b. Nani-o   *Taro-sika* t yoma-nai-no?
         what-acc T-only   t read-neg-Q

Tanaka (1997) posits that the operator of *nani* moves rightward to Spec CP and the negative operator of *Taro-sika* also undergoes rightward movement to Spec NegP at overt syntax. Their movements are represented as in (11a) and (11b).

(11) a.*[Taro-sika-t₁] [what-acc-t₂] buy-neg-Op₁-past-Q-Op₂

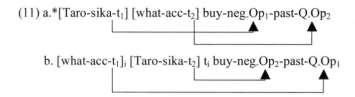

   b. [what-acc-t₁]ᵢ [Taro-sika-t₂] tᵢ buy-neg-Op₂-past-Q-Op₁

Tanaka (1997) suggests a constraint named Linear Crossing Constraint (henceforth LCC) to rule out (11a) as in (12).

(12) Linear Crossing Constraint

Suppose that Op_i precedes Op_{i+1} and that t_i, the trace of Op_i, precedes t_{i+1}, the trace of Op_{i+1}, then t_{i+1} cannot precede Op_i at S-structure.

To put LCC simply, it bans two A'-dependency lines from crossing at S-structure as in (11a). Tanaka (2003) points out that LCC could apply at LF if scrambling is not undone, which accords with Chomsky's (2000) elimination of LF component. LCC approach to the intervention effect is structure-based. It defines how the paths of the two movements should be arranged. According to LCC approach, the intervention effect results from an illegitimate arrangement of movement lines.

3. Insensitive to Intervention Effect

I have introduced two different approaches to the intervention effect: one regards an NPI preceding a wh-phrase in-situ as interfering the association of the wh-phrase and its quantifier at C; the other attributes the intervention effect to linear crossing of wh-movement and NPI movement. In this section I will introduce a new set of NPIs, which do not cause the intervention effect even though they precede a wh-phrase.

(13) a. Mary-ka UNICEF-e kibukum-ul *hanpunto* nae-ci an ha-ss-ta.
     M-nom UNICEF-to donation-acc a-red-cent make neg do-past-dec
     'Mary didn't donate a red cent to UNICEF.'
   b. *Mary-ka UNICEF-e kibukum-ul *hanpunto* nae-ss-ta.
     M-nom UNICEF-to donation-acc a-red-cent make-past-dec

(14) a. Mary-ka *hanpalcakto* wumciki-ci an ha-ss-ta.
     M-nom one-step move neg do-pass-dec
     'Mary didn't budge an inch.'
   b. *Mary-ka *hanpalcakto* wumciki-ss-ta.
     M-nom one-step move-pass-dec

The expressions *hanpunto* and *hanpalcakto* need to co-occur with negation as we can see from the ungrammaticality of (13b) and (14b). The expression

hanpunto and *hanpalcakto* could be understood similar with English NPIs 'a red cent' and '(budge) an inch', respectively.
These NPIs do not seem to produce the intervention effect.

(15) a. Nuku-ka UNICEF-e kibukum-ul *hanpunto* nae-ci an ha-ss-ni?
who-nom UNICEF-to donation-acc a-red-cent make neg do-past-Q
'Who didn't donate a red cent to UNICEF?'
b. [kibukum-ul *hanpunto*]$_i$ nuku-ka UNICEF-e t$_i$ nae-ci an ha-ss-ni?
donation-acc a-red-cent who-nom UNICEF-to make neg do-past-Q
c. *Hanpunto*$_i$ nuku-ka UNICEF-e kibukum-ul t$_i$ nae-ci an ha-ss-ni?
A-red-cent who-nom UNICEF-to donation-acc t make neg do-past-Q

(16) a. Nuku-ka *hanpalcakto* wumciki-ci an ha-ss-ni?
who-nom one-step move neg do-pass-Q
b. *Hanpakcakto*$_i$ nuku-ka t$_i$ wumciki-ci an ha-ss-ta.
one-step who-nom t move neg do-pass-dec

Although the NPIs scramble before a wh-phrase as in (15c) and (16b), they are grammatical. These expressions are NPIs in that they need to be licensed by negation, but they are insensitive to the intervention effect. For the sake of convenience I will call them 'insensitive NPIs' (NPIs insensitive to the intervention effect).

According to Tanaka's (1997) and (2003) analysis, the operator of an NPI should move to Spec NegP presumably for the feature-checking purpose. Since insensitive NPIs need to be licensed by negation we have to assume that their operators move to Spec NegP. Their precedence to a wh-phrase should cause linear crossing of two movements as shown in (17), producing the intervention effect.

(17) [NPI-t]$_i$ who-t [$_{VP}$ ... t$_i$ ...] Neg-$_{Op}$ Q-$_{Op}$

According to LCC approach, the intervention effect should apply to all the cases where an NPI precedes a wh-phrase because all the NPIs need to be licensed by negation. LCC approach cannot explain why insensitive NPIs do not cause the intervention effect.

4. Properties of Insensitive NPIs

4.1. Negative Intensifier

Now we need to examine why the NPIs introduced in section 3 do not produce the intervention effect. Let's find out their properties different from other NPIs. The NPIs *hanpunto* and *hanpalcakto* do not seem to function as substantives. They look like rather a quantifier of an NP. They can be omitted without changing the content of the proposition.

(18) a. Mary-ka UNICEF-e kibukum-ul *hanpunto* nae-ci an ha-ss-ta.
    M-nom UNICEF-to donation-acc a-red-cent make neg do-past-dec
    'Mary didn't donate a red cent to UNICEF.'
  b. Mary-ka UNICEF-e kibukum-ul nae-ci an ha-ss-ta.
    M-nom UNICEF-to donation-acc make neg do-past-dec
    'Mary didn't donate to UNICEF.'

(19) a. Mary-ka *hanpalcakto* wumciki-ci an ha-ss-ta.
    M-nom one-step   move   neg do-pass-dec
    'Mary didn't budge an inch.'
  b. Mary-ka wumciki-ci an ha-ss-ta.
    M-nom move   neg do-pass-dec
    'Mary didn't move.'

The NPIs in the sentences (18a) and (19a) are omitted in the sentences (18b) and (19b). Although two sentences of each pair are different in expressing the degree of negation, their truth conditions are same.

This property distinguishes them from other NPIs like NP-*pakkey* 'only'. It can also function as a quantifier of an NP as we can see in (20a). Its omission, however, changes the content of the proposition as in (20b).

(20) a. Mary-ka computer-lul *hantae-pakkey* sa-ci an ha-ss-ta.
    M-nom computer-acc one-unit-only   buy neg do-past-dec
    'Mary bought only one computer.'
   b. Mary-ka computer-lul sa-ci an ha-ss-ta.
    M-nom computer-acc buy neg do-past-dec
    'Mary didn't buy a computer.'

A sentence with an NP-*pakkey* must have negation but it expresses a positive proposition. In the sentence (20a) the NP-*pakkey* looks like a floated quantifier of the object and the sentence is positive. The quantifier can be omitted as in (20b), but the omission turns the sentence into a negative proposition.[2]

---

[2] An NPI *hanpunto* can also be used alone without accompanying its head. We may assume that its head is omitted. It may be possible because the semantic content of its head should be monetary and hence it is easily predictable. Even in this case *hanpunto* can precede a wh-phrase without causing the intervention effect.
(i) a. Mary-ka UNICEF-e hanpunto nae-ci an ha-ss-ta.
     'Mary didn't donate a red cent to UNICEF.'
   b. Hanpunto$_i$ Mary-ka UNICEF-e t nae-ci an ha-ss-ta.
     'Mary didn't buy anything.'

Unlike NP-*pakkey*, *hanpunto* and *hanpalcakto* is omissible without causing change in the content of the proposition. It means that they do not make contribution to the truth condition. Instead their function in a sentence is to intensify a negated part

4.2. Scope-Insensitive

When there are two scope-bearing elements, most of them interact with the other as in (21).

(21) a. Mary-to computer-man sa-ss-ta.   also > only
  'Mary also bought only computer.'
  b. Computer-man Mary-to sa-ss-ta.   only >also
  'Computer is the only item which Mary also bought.'

When *Mary-also* c-commands *computer*-only, the former takes the wide scope. The reversed order produces the reversed scope relation. C-command relation at S-structure determines the scope interpretation.
  NPIs also show the similar scope interaction.

(22) a. Mary-man *amuketto* sa-ci an ha-ss-ta.   only > not ∃
  'Mary was the only person who didn't buy anything.'
  b. *Amuketto* Mary-man sa-ci an ha-ss-ta.   not ∃ > only
  'There was not an item which only Mary bought.'

When an NPI *amuketto* comes after *Mary-only*, 'only' takes the wide scope as in (22a). When *amuketto* come before *Mary-only*, it takes the wide scope as in (22b).
  The insensitive NPIs, however, do not show such a scope interaction with another scope-bearing element.

(23) a. Mary-man UNICEF-e kibukum-ul *hanpunto*   nae-ci an ha-ss-ta.
  M-only UNICEF-to donation-acc a-red-cent   make neg do-past-dec
  'Only Mary didn't donate a red cent to UNICEF.'   only > not ∃
  b. *Hanpunto* Mary-man UNICEF-e kibukum-ul nae-ci an ha-ss-ta.
  'Only Mary didn't donate a red cent to UNICEF.'   only > not ∃

(24) a. Mary-to *hanpalcakto* wumciki-ci an ha-ss-ta.
  'Mary also didn't move a step.'   also > not∃
  b. Hanpalcakto Mary-to wumciki-ci an ha-ss-ta.
  'Mary also didn't move a step.'   also > not ∃

We can see from (23) and (24) that *hanpunto* and *hanpalcakto* are not influenced by structural relation with *Mary-also*. They are within the scope of *Mary-also* regardless of their c-command relation with *Mary also*. It seems that their scope is fixed within VP at least in the two cases (23) and (24).

We have seen that the NPIs *hanpunto* and *hanpalcakto* do not interact with another scope-bearing element. They are scope-insensitive. Since they are scope-insensitive they do not interact with the scope of wh-phrases. When a wh-phrase is preceded by an NPI whose scope is irrelevant to the interpretation of the wh-phrase, its interpretation is not blocked by the NPI, showing no intervention effect. We may conjecture that scope-insensitivity is responsible for the insensitivity to the intervention effect. It is inferred that scope interpretation is involved in producing the intervention effect. It means that the intervention effect is concerned about interpretation.

We can find a supporting argument in Hooeksema (2000). He points out that predicative NPIs like *my cup of tea* as in (25) fall within the scope of negation regardless of their position.

(25) a. It is not *my cup of tea*.

b. *My cup of tea*, it's not.

The scope of an NPI *my cup of tea* is fixed whether it is c-commanded by negation or it is topicalized, violating c-command constraint on English NPIs. It is implied from Hoeksma (2000) that a scope-insensitive NPI is relatively free in the structure.

Another supporting argument is found in the discussion of the intervention effect in English multiple wh-questions in Pesetsky (2000). He notices an exception to the intervention effect. Let's examine the contrast shown in (26a) and (26b).

(26) a. $^{??}$Which boy did only Mary introduce which girl to __?

b. Sue asked which boy only Mary introduced which girl to __.

The sentence (26a) fails to yield a pair-list reading, showing the intervention effect. In (26a) and (26b) the closer wh-phrase to C stays in-situ, violating Superiority Condition. According to Pesetsky (2000), however, the closer wh-phrase *which girl* undergoes feature movement first, and then the phrasal movement of *which boy* takes place. At LF the wh-feature at Spec CP and its restriction *which girl* are separated by a scope-bearing element *only Mary*. The same clause is embedded in (26b). Again this clause is supposed to be subject to the intervention effect. This sentence is, however, acceptable. If we put focus stress on *only Mary* it takes matrix scope. When (26b) receives the interpretation with *only Mary* receiving matrix scope, it could have pair-list reading, which means that the intervention effect disappears. We can see from (b) that a wh-phrase in-situ is not blocked for its interpretation by a scope-bearing element whose scope is outside of the scope of the wh-phrase. It indicates that the intervention effect is caused by the interference of an NPI whose scope is relevant to the interpretation of the wh-phrase.

5. Summary

I have dealt with a linear constraint shown in (27b), where a wh-phrase following an NPI is unacceptable. This paper names the constraint the intervention effect, following the most of the literature dealing with the phenomenon.

(27) a. Nuku-ka *amuketdo* sa-ci   an ha-ss-ni?
       Who-nom anything buy-ci neg do-past-Q
       'Who didn't buy anything?'
    b. *Amuketdo* nuku-ka sa-ci   an   ha-ss-ni?
       Anything who-nom buy-ci neg do-past-Q

In this paper I've introduced examples in which an NPI precedes a wh-phrase but which do not manifest the intervention effect, exemplified in (15c) repeated in (28).

(28) *Hanpunto$_i$* nuku-ka UNICEF-e kibukum-ul t$_i$ nae-ci an ha-ss-ni?
     A-red-cent who-nom UNICEF-to donation-acc make   neg do-past-Q
     'Who didn't donate a red cent to UNICEF?'

The example contradicts LCC approach, in which all NPIs preceding a wh-phrase produces the intervention effect because of the movement of NPIs to Spec NegP.

The NPIs insensitive to the intervention effect do not seem to make substantive contribution to the content of the proposition, judging from the fact that they are omissible without changing the truth condition of the proposition. These NPIs are not interactive with other scope-bearing elements including wh-phrases. The data with insensitive NPIs support intervener approach suggested by Beck and Kim (1997) and Pesetsky (2000). The data, however, ask the intervener approach to elaborate on the qualification of the intervener. Intervener approach regards all quantifiers or scope-bearing elements as an intervener to the interpretation of wh-operator at Spec CP and wh-phrase in-situ. As we saw, however, the intervener should be reduced to scope-interactive scope-bearing elements.

References

Beck, S. 1996. Quantified Structures as Barriers for LF Movement. *Natural Language Semantics* 4:1-56.

Beck, S. and S. Kim. 1997. On wh- and Operator Scope. *Korean. Journal of East Asian Linguistics* 6:339-384.

Chung, D. and H. Park. 1997. NPIs Outside of Negation Scope. *Japanese/Koorean Linguistics* 6:415-435.

Hagstrom, P. 1999. Decomposing Questions. Doctoral dissertation, MIT.

Hoeksema, J. 2000. Negative Polarity Items: Triggering, Scope, and C-Command. *Syntactic and Semantic Perspectives*, eds. L. Horn and Y. Kato, 114-146. Oxford, New York: Oxford University Press.

Kim, A. 2002. Two Positions of Korean Negation. *Japanese/Korean Linguistics* 10:587-600.

Kim, A. 2005. Compatibility between Korean NPIs and Licensers. *The Journal of Modern British and American Language and Literature* 35.2:209-227.

Linebarger, M. C. 1985. Negative Polarity and Grammatical Representation. *Linguistics and Philosophy* 10:325-387.

Pesetsky, D .2000. *Phrasal Movement and Its Kin*. Cambridge, MA: The MIT Press.

Saito, M. 1992. Long Distance Scrambling in Japanese. *Journal of East Asian Linguistics* 1:68-118.

Sells, P. 2001. Negative Polarity Licensing and Interpretation. *Harvard Studies in Korean Linguistics* 9:3-22.

Sohn, K. 1994. NPI as Focus Barriers: LCC or RM? *Proceedings of the Western Conference on Linguistics* 7:251-265.

Tanaka, H. 1997. Invisible Movement in *SIKA-NAI* and the Linear Crossing Constraint. *Journal of East Asian Linguistics* 6:143-188.

Tanaka, H. 2003. Remarks on Beck's Effects: Linearity in syntax. *Linguistic Inquiry* 34:314-323.

Yoon, H. 1994. Negation and NPI. *Explorations in Generative Grammar*, ed. Y-S. Kim, et al., 700-719. Seoul: Hankuk Publishing.

A Contrastive Study of Resultative Constructions in Korean and Japanese: From the Perspective of Historical and Cognitive Linguistics

YONG-TAEK KIM
University of Oregon

1. Introduction[1]

In this paper, I will argue that the distributional differences between Korean *-key* and Japanese *-ku/-ni* resultative constructions can be explained by suggesting that the *-key* resultative construction is an extension from the *-key* causative construction. This conclusion challenges previous works (Uehara et al. 2001, Washio 1997a, 1999).

My argument will take the following form. In section 2, I will show the definition of the resultative construction and its semantic feature. In section 3, I will posit research questions by pointing out the problems of previous studies. Section 4 will show distributional differences between *-key* and Japanese *-ku/-ni* constructions in general, and propose an alternating analysis for the distributional differences between *-key* and *-ku/-ni*[2] resultative constructions by suggesting that the resultative *-key* construction extended from the causative *-key* construction. Section 5 will support the analysis by

---

[1] I am deeply grateful to Professors Eric Pederson and Noriko Fujii for their valuable comments. Special thanks go to Professor Yoshihisa Nakamura for sending his papers. However, I remain responsible for any errors.

[2] The *-ku/-ni* distinction depends on the resultative phrase they are attached to; *-ku* with adjective and *-ni* with nominal adjective.

showing the relation between causative and resultative constructions from the perspective of historical and cognitive linguistics.

2. Resultative Constructions

The resultative construction (hereafter RC) shows a wide range of syntactic and semantic variation. In this paper I will focus on mono-clausal RCs which show overt morphosyntactic realization. These integrate a causing event and a resulting state:

(1) a. John pounded the metal flat.
    b. NP$_1$ V NP$_2$ AP
    c. = [John pounded the metal]$_{Event}$ CAUSE [The metal became flat]$_{State}$

It is well documented that prototypical resultative sentences are telic: they describe events with a definite endpoint (Rappaport Hovav and Levin 2001; Tenny 1994, among others). This is shown by the standard test in (2).

(2) a. John pounded the metal **for an hour/*in an hour.**   [atelic]
    b. John pounded the metal flat *for an hour/**in an hour.** [telic]

The RC in (2b) motivates the profile shift from action-profiling atelic event in (2a) to result-profiling telic event in (2b).[3]

3. Resultative Constructions in Korean and Japanese

RCs in Korean and Japanese have been analyzed mostly in comparison to those in English (Kim 1999, Kim and Maling 1998, etc. for the former, and Kageyama 1996, Washio 1997b, etc. for the latter). Several contrastive studies between -*key* and -*ku/-ni* RCs have been attempted (Uehara et al. 2001, Washio 1997a, 1999). However, it would seem that they have left much work undone.

RCs can be represented by so-called adverbializers -*key* in Korean and -*ku/-ni* in Japanese. Their syntactic structure is shown in (3a) and (3b) respectively. The English resultative sentence (1) is usually translated into Korean and Japanese as in (4K) and (4J) respectively in the literature.

(3) a. NP$_1$ NP$_2$ AP-**key** V
    b. NP$_1$ NP$_2$ AP-**ku/ni** V

(4) K.[4] (?)John-i   chelphan-ul   napcakha-**key**   twutulkyessta
    J.   ?John-ga   teppan-o   petyanko-**ni**   tataita
         John-NOM   metal-ACC   flat   pounded

---

[3] Langacker (1987) defines 'profile' as a substructure within the base that is designated and achieves a special degree of prominence while 'base' as the cognitive structure against which the designatum of a semantic structure is profiled. The concepts of circle and arc illustrate base and profile respectively.
[4] Each K and J in examples indicates Korean and Japanese.

'John pounded the metal flat.'

According to Washio (1997b), nine of 100 native Japanese speakers accepted (4K) (9%), forty-nine of them judged it unacceptable (49%), forty-two of them said it is quite marginal, though perhaps not completely unacceptable (42%). On the other hand, I asked twenty native Korean speakers to judge (4K). Fourteen of them accepted it (70%), and six of them said it is marginal (30%). No one said it is unacceptable.

Two questions arise: i) why are the translated examples (4K) and (4J) less acceptable than (1), and ii) why is (4K) more acceptable than (4J). Lexical semantic approaches (Kageyama 1996, Nitta 2002, to mention a few) argue that a resulting phrase can be used only with change-of-state verbs, and the main verb *tataku* 'pound' in (4J) is not a change-of-state verb since it is possible to say that pounding event does not affect the metal as shown in (5J). Therefore, (4J) is less acceptable than (1).

(5) K. John-i   chelphan-ul   twutulkyess-una napcakhay-ci-ci
     John-NOM metal-ACC pounded-but   flat-PAS-NMZL
     anh-ass-ta
     NEG-PST-DCL

    J. John-ga   teppan-o   tataita-ga   petyanko-ni **nar-ana-katta**
     John-NOM metal-ACC pounded-but flat   become-NEG-PST
     'John pounded the metal, but it didn't become flat at all.'

This approach can be supported by a following example as in (6):

(6) a. John-ga   teppan-o   petyanko-ni **naru-made**   tataita
     John-NOM metal-ACC flat   become-until pounded
     'John pounded the metal until it became flat.'

    b. John-ga   teppan-o   petyanko-ni tataki-**[nobasi]**-ta
     John-NOM metal-ACC flat   pound-spread-PST
     'John pounded the metal flat.'

When either a change-of-state verb *naru* 'become' as in (6a) or a result-denoting verb, such as *nobasu*, which forms a verb compound, as in (6b) is added to (4J), it becomes more acceptable.

This type of approach may be able to explain Japanese data. However, it cannot explain the typological differences of the RCs in (1) and (4) in which all verbs are non-change-of-state verbs as in (5).

First, I'll present a short answer to the first question, which is not the main concern of this paper. I suggest that the less acceptability of (4) is related with frequency: bi-clausal resultative constructions with conjunctives, such as -*tolok* and -*made* 'until' as in (7K) and (7J) or -*se* and -*te* 'cause-effect' as in (8K) and (8J) are more commonly used than mono-clausal resultative constructions with -*key* and -*ku/-ni* as in (4).

(7) K. John-i   [chelphan-inapcakhay-**ci-tolok**]   twutulkyessta
John-NOM   metal-NOM flat-become-until   pounded
J. John-ga   [teppan-ga   petyanko-ni **naru-made**]   tataita
John-NOM metal-NOM   flat   become-until pounded
'John pounded the metal so that it became flat.'

(8) K. John-i   chelphan-ul twutulkye-**se** napcakha-key   hayssta
J. John-ga   teppan-o   tatai-**te**   petyanko-ni   sita
John-NOM   metal-ACC   pounded   flat   did
'John pounded the metal so that it became flat.'

Korean and Japanese are known to exhibit remarkable structural commonalities in morphosyntax. Washio (1997a) argues that RCs in the two languages are allowed when the resulting phrase is not completely independent of the meaning of the verb as in (9) and (10):

(9) K. *kutul-un   kwutwu-patak-ul yalp-**key** tallyessta
they-TOP   shoe-sole-ACC   thin   ran
'They ran the soles of their shoes thin.'   (Washio 1997a: 245)
J. *karera-wa   kutu-no   soko-o   boroboro-**ni** hasit-ta
they-TOP   shoe-GEN   sole-ACC   threadbare   ran
'They ran the soles of their shoes threadbare.' (Washio 1997b: 20)

(10) K. John-un   pyek-ul   ppalkah-**key** chilhayssta
J. John-wa   kabe-o   aka-**ku**   nutta
John-TOP   wall-ACC   red   painted
'John painted the wall red.'

Then, why is *twutulkita* with RCs in Korean as in (4K) more acceptable than *tataku* with RC in Japanese as in (4J), although both of them are non-change-of-state verbs? Let's work on this question, the main focus of this paper, in detail in section 4 and 5.

4. The Distributional Differences between Korean -*key* and Japanese –*ku*/-*ni* Constructions

To have a better understanding of the distributional differences between Korean -*key* and Japanese -*ku*/-*ni* RCs, let's look at another example.

(11) K. John-un   [tali-ka   aphu-**key**]   talli-ess-ta
J. *John-wa   [asi-ga   ita-**ku**]   hasit-ta
John-TOP leg-NOM   painful   ran
'John ran [to the extent that/until] his leg became sore.'

Apart from whether (11K) is a RC or not, it is interesting that when the -*key* and -*ku*/-*ni* clause is embedded, the former does not need a change-of-state verb, whereas the latter without a change-of-state verb is unacceptable (Uehara et al. 2001). As we discussed in (6), the Japanese -*ku*/-*ni* construction becomes acceptable when change-of-state verb *naru* 'become' with conjunctive particle *hodo* 'degree' or *made* 'until' is added as shown in (12):

(12) John-wa   [asi-ga   ita-**ku   naru-hodo/made**]   hasit-ta
     John-TOP   leg-NOM   painful   become-degree/until   ran
     'John ran [to the extent that/until] his leg became sore.'

Previous studies (Uehara et al. 2001, Washio 1997a, 1998, 1999) assume that morpheme *-key* has some conjunctive-like property to link the embedded clause to the matrix clause unlike *-ku/-ni* morphemes without clear evidence. This lexical semantic approach cannot uncover cognitive and typological implications that the causative construction and the RC are closely related (Givon 1997:61, Goldberg 1995:81, to mention a few).

To put the conclusion first, I propose that the prototypical meaning of *-key* construction[5] [NP₁ NP₂ A/V-key V] is the causative construction, and the resultative *-key* construction is one of its extensions. Since the resultative *-key* construction inherits causal relations from the causative *-key* construction, it can express causal relations without a change-of-state verb. On the other hand, the prototypical function of *-ku/-ni* construction [NP₁ NP₂ A-ku/NA-ni V] is as an adverbial construction expressing manner or degree of verbal action. The prototypical causative construction is formed not by the *-ku/-ni* construction but by the morphological suffix *-(s)ase*. Therefore, *-ku/-ni* RCs need a change-of-state verb to show a causal relation. This can be supported by historical and cognitive linguistics.

5. The Relation between the Causative Construction and the Resultative Construction in terms of Historical and Cognitive Linguistics

The relation between the causative and the resultative construction will be discussed in terms of historical linguistics by working on the diachronic changes of the causative constructions in Korean in 5.1. It will also be discussed in terms of cognitive linguistics, particularly event profiling in 5.2.

5.1 Historical Linguistic Evidence: Diachronic Changes of {-i}[6] and {-key} in Korean

According to Choi (2000), Jeong (1998), Kim (1989), Kim (1996). and Park (1989), adverbializer {-i} used to be the most productive lexical and clausal

---

[5] Construction Grammar defines constructions to be any stored (typically highly frequent) pairings of form and function; according to this definition, words and morphemes are technically constructions as well (Goldberg and Jackendoff 2004:2).
[6] There is another adverbializer {-o/-u}. The allomorphs of {-i} are -i, -hi, -li, -ki; those of {-o/-u} are -o/-u, -ho/-(c)hu, -ko/-ku.

manner adverbializer as in (13) and (14) respectively until the late 16th C.[7]

(13) kh-**i** uysimhA-myen kh-**i** arom-i isi-li-ni
 great-AD doubt-if great-AD leraning-NOM exist-will-since
 'since you will learn a lot if you dobut a lot.'
 (*Mongsanhwasangpebeyaklok*, late 15th C, recited from Kim 1989:
 113; translation is mine)

(14) nwunsmu-lAl [syuken-ey kAtAk-**i**] hullinola
 tear-ACC   towel-LOC soggy drop
 '(I am) dropping tears to the extent that towel becomes soggy.'
 (*Tusienhay* 1481, recited from Jeong 1998: 742; translation is mine)

However, adverbial suffix *-key* started to be used with *hata* 'do' during the late 14th C and early 15th C, and has replaced the adverbializer *-i* since 16th C, as shown in (15), which is a modern translation of (13):

(15)*kh-i/khu-**key** uysimha-myen*khi/khu-**key** alm-i iss-uli-ni
 great-AD doubt-if great-AD learning-NOM exist-will-since
 'Since you will learn a lot if you doubt a lot,'

The adverbializer *-i* also used to express both direct and indirect causative construction as in (16a) and (17a) respectively until late 16th C. However, periphrastic causative *-key hata* 'do' started to be used during the late 14th C and early 15th C, and brought about much reduction of morphological causative constructions. Since late 16th C, it has become the most productive causative construction (Choi 2000, Kim 1996). The morphological causative constructions in (16a) and (17a) have been replaced by the periphrastic causative *-key hata* as in (16b) and (17b), each of which is their modern translations. The meaning of *sal-i-ta* has been reduced to direct causation alone as in (18) in modern Korean.

(16) a. palAl-ay pAy ep-kenul nyeth-**o**-si-ko   sto
  sea-LOC ship not.exist-since shallow-CAU-HON-and then
  kiph-**i**-si-ni
  deep-CAU-HON-since
  'Since there is no ship, (Heaven) made the sea shallow and then deep.'
       [*Yongpiechenka* 1445, translation is mine]
 b. pata-ey pay eps-ese yath-**key-ha**-si-ko   tto
  sea-LOC ship not.exist-cause shallow-CAU-do-HON-and then
  kiph-**key-ha**-si-ni
  deep-CAU-do-HON-since

(17) a. cyung sal-**i**-si-ko
  monk live-CAU-HON-and
  '(King) let a monk make a living (e.g. by giving some land)'

---

[7] 'A' in (20) and (21) indicates a vowel, which has disappeared in modern Korean.

[*Welinsekpo* 1459, recited from Choi (2000:311); translation is mine]
b. cung   sal-**key-ha**-si-ko
   monk live-CAU-do-HON-and

(18)   cung   sall-**i**-si-ko
        monk live-CAU-HON-and
        '(A doctor) brought a monk to life,'   [Modern Korean]

The diachronic changes of {-i} and {-key} is summarized in Table 1 (adapted from Kim 1996).[8]

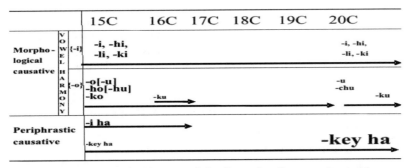

		15C	16C	17C	18C	19C	20C
Morpho- **logical** **causative**	V O W E L	{-i}	-i, -hi, -li, -ki				-i, -hi, -li, -ki
	H A R M O N Y	{-o}	-o[-u] -ho[-hu] -ko	-ku		-u -chu	-ku
Periphrastic **causative**			-i ha				
			-key ha				**-key ha**

Table 1. The Diachronic Changes of the Causative Construction in Korean

It seems that the resultative construction [NP$_1$ NP$_2$ A-key V] could be formed in modern Korean as the *-key* construction has become the most productive causative construction. This can be supported by the fact that bi-clausal constructions expressing resultativity have been the most proto-typical resultative construction, which I exemplified in (7) and (8), and the *-key* RC is still less acceptable than those constructions.

On the other hand, Japanese forms its causative construction not by *-ku/-ni* but by the morphological causative suffix *-(s)ase*, which has been in use since Late Old Japanese[9] (Narrog 2004), the most productive causative morpheme in modern Japanese, as in (19):

(19) K. John-i   Mary-lul   hakkyo-ey   ka-**key**   **hay**-ss-ta
         John-NOM   Mary-ACC school-to   go-CAU   do-PST-DCL

      J. John-ga   Mary-o   gakkoo-ni   ik-**ase**-ta
         John-NOM   Mary-ACC school-to   go-CAU-PST
         'John caused Mary to go to school.'

I have suggested that resultative *-key* construction is an extension from

---

[8] The font size of morphemes indicates their productivity.
[9] Late Old Japanese: 9th-11th C

the causative *-key* construction by showing historical changes of the *-key* construction. On the other hand, the prototypical function of *-ku/-ni* construction [NP$_1$ NP$_2$ A-ku/AN-ni V] is as an adverbial construction expressing manner or degree of verbal action. The prototypical causative construction is formed not by the *-ku/-ni* construction but by the morphological suffix *-(sa)se*.

5.2 Event Profiling: ACTION-profiling vs. RESULT-profiling Constructions

Kim (2006) proposes that biactant constructions (i.e. a verb of action involving two participants X and Y, each of which represents an agent and a patient prototypically) fall somewhere along a continuum of ACTION-versus-RESULT profiling of event structure. At one pole of the continuum one finds ACTION-profiling constructions such as those containing surface-contact-verbs (e.g. *touch*). At the other pole RESULT-profiling constructions such as those containing change-of-state verbs (e.g. *break*).

In terms of semantic properties, the action (i.e. X's control) is profiled rather than the result (i.e. Y's affectedness) in ACTION-profiling constructions since the result is not specified as shown in (20).

(20) *I touched the window, so it broke/but it did not break.

On the other hand, it is the Y's affectedness rather than the X's control that is profiled in RESULT-profiling constructions since types of action are not specified:

(21) I broke the window by hitting/throwing a stone, etc.

The semantics of ACTION-profiling and RESULT-profiling constructions are reflected in syntactic properties. First, passives of the ACTION-profiling constructions cannot express state as in (22), whereas those of RESULT-profiling constructions can as in (23).

(22) ??He did not want to buy the door because it was touched.

(23) He did not want to buy the door because it was broken.

Another syntactic property of biactant constructions is that ACTION-profiling constructions are more likely to occur with continuative aspect, while RESULT-profiling constructions are less likely to occur with it as in (24) and (25) respectively.

(24) I was touching the window.

(25) *I was chipping the china cup. [non-repetitive]

The continuum of biactant constructions can be summarized as in Figure 1.

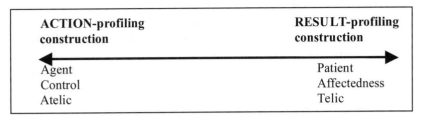

Figure 1. The Continuum of Biactant Constructions

5.2.1 The Causative and Resultative Construction: ACTION-profiling vs. RESULT-profiling Construction

The causative construction profiles causer's action, whereas the RC profiles resulting state of a patient in that the former does not necessarily entail the result as in (26a), whereas the latter entails it as in (26b):

(26) a. Mary-ka   John-i   chelphan-ul   napcakha-key twutulki-**key**
        Mary-NOM John-NOM metal-ACC   flat   pound-CAU
        hayss-una   napcakhay-ci-ci   anh-ass-ta
        did-but   flat-PAS-NMLZ   NEG-PST-DCL
        'Mary caused John to pound the metal flat, but it did not become flat.'

    b. *John-i   chelphan-ul napcakha-**key** twutulkyess-una
        John-NOM metal-ACC flat   pounded-but
        napcakhay-ci-ci   anh-ass-ta
        flat-PAS-NMLZ   NEG-PST-DCL
        '*John pounded the metal flat, but it did not become flat.'

The causative construction can occur with continuative aspect as in (27a), whereas the RC becomes less acceptable with it as in (27b).

(27) a. Mary-ka   John-i   chelphan-ul napcakha-key twutulki-**key**
        Mary-NOM John-NOM metal-ACC flat   pound-CAU
        ha-koiss-ta
        do-CONT-DCL
        'Mary kept causing John to pound the metal flat.'

    b. ?John-i   chelphan-ul napcakha-**key** twutulki-**koiss**-ta
        John-NOM metal-ACC flat   pound-CONT-DCL
        '*John kept pounding the metal flat.' [non-repetitive]

With these semantic and syntactic properties, it seems that the causative construction is ACTION-profiling construction, whereas the RC is RE-SULT-profiling construction.

5.2.2 The Continuum of -key Constructions: From Purposive to Degree to Causative to Resultative

In modern Korean, the -key construction has multifunctionality, expressing purpose, degree, causation, result, etc. The following is a good example to show its continuum along the purposive, degree, causative, and resultative constructions in that (28) can be paraphrased as (29).

(28) John-un   sinpal-i   talh-key   ttwiessta
      John-TOP   shoes-NOM   threadbare   ran

(29) a. John-un   sinpal-i   talh-key **ha-lyeko**   ttwiessta [**purposive**]
         John-TOP   shoes-NOM threadbare do-purpose   ran
         'John ran in order for his shoes to become threadbare.'
      b. John-un   sinpal-i   talh-**cengtolo**   ttwiessta [**degree**]
         John-TOP   shoes-NOM   threadbare-degree   ran
         'John ran **very hard** to the extent that the shoes become threadbare.'
      c. John-un ttwie-se sinpal-ul   talh-key   **mantulessta**[**causative**]
         John-TOP ran-cause shoes-ACC threadbare   made
         'John ran, and it made his shoes threadbare.'
      d. John-un   sinpal-i   talh-aci-**tolok**   ttwiessta [**resultative**]
         John-TOP   shoes-NOM   threadbare-PAS-until ran
         'John ran until his shoes became threadbare.'

The prototypical meaning of (28) is (29b). The phrase *sinpal-i talh-key* is a kind of idiom like *paykkop-i ppaci-key* (navel-NOM come.out-key), *pal-patak-ey ttam-na-key* (sole-LOC sweat-come.out-key), all of which mean 'very hard', modifying a verbal action. Therefore, (29b) is profiling AC-TION rather than RESULT. (28) can be interpreted as (29a) in a situation where John wants to make his shoes threadbare to ask his mother to buy new shoes. It is John's intention rather than ACTION or RESULT that is profiled. Therefore, I put it leftmost in Figure 2 below. In (29c), the speaker wants to express what made John's shoes threadbare, although it is a mar-ginal interpretation. It is causation that is profiled. The interpretation of (28) as (29d) is possible in a situation where the speaker wants to express John's threadbare shoes rather than his running. It is the result, or John's thread-bare shoes that are profiled. I put the causative construction between the constructions expressing degree and resultative since unlike the -key con-struction meaning degree, it still implies a resulting state, although it does not necessarily entail it. This shows that one and the same event can have different representations depending on a speaker's profiling of an event, or a speaker's construal. This can be summarized as in Figure 2:

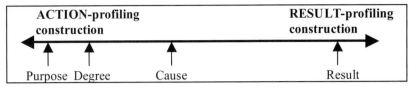

Figure 2. The Continuum of *-key* Constructions

In this section, I have shown the close relationship between the causative construction and the RC by working on the diachronic changes. This is supported by a cognitive analysis of biactant constructions as a continuum of ACTION-versus-RESULT profiling of event structure.

6. Conclusion

I have argued that the distributional differences between Korean *-key* and Japanese *-ku/-ni* resultative constructions arise because the former is the extension from the causative *-key* construction, whereas the latter does not express causative.

The distinction between Korean and Japanese RCs furthers our understanding of subtle differences in the expressions of resultativity in Korean and Japanese. It may have further implications for the relationship between causative and resultative constructions across other languages as well.

Abbreviations:
ACC: Accusative, AD: Adverbializer, AP: Adjective Phrase, C: Century, CAU: Causative, CONT: Continuative, DCL: Declarative, GEN: Genitive, HON: Honorific, INST: Instrument, LOC: Locative, NA: Nominal Adjective, NEG: Negative, NMLZ: Nominalizer, NOM: Nominative, NP: Noun Phrase, PAS: Passive, PP: Prepositional Phrase, PST: Past, TOP: Topic, V: Verb.

References

Choi, D. 2000. Kwuke Satong Kwumun uy Thongsicek Pyenhwa (Historical Development of Korean Causative Constructions). *Eoneohag* 27:303-27.

Givon, T. 1997. *Grammatical Relations: A Functionalist Perspective.* Amsterdam and Philadelphia: John Benjamins.

Goldberg, A. 1995. *Constructions: A Construction Grammar Approach to Argument Structure.* Chicago: University of Chicago Press.

Goldberg, A. and R. Jackendoff. 2004. The English Resultative as a Family of Construcitons. *Language* 80:532-68.

Jeong, J. 1998. Kolyesitay uy -i Pusa wa Pusahyeng (-i as Adverbializer and Derivational Adverbial Suffix in the Corea Dynasty). *Kwuke Ehwi uy Kipan Kwa Yeksa*, ed. J. Shim, 737-84. Seoul: Taehaksa.

Kageyama, T. 1996. *Dooshiimiron* (Theory of Verb Meaning). Tokyo: Kuroshio.

Kim, H. 1996. *Kwuke Phasayng Tongsa uy Thongsicek Yenkwu* (A Diachronic Study on the Derived Causative Verbs in Korean). Doctoral Dissertation, Kon-Kuk University.

Kim, J. 1999. Constraints on the Formation of Korean and English Resultative Constructions. *NELS* 29:137-51.

Kim, J. 1989. Pusahyeng Cepsa '-i' wa '-key' uy Thongsicek Kyochey (Historical Changes of Adverbial Affixes '-i' and '-key'). *Kwukekyoyukyenkwu* 21:113-149. Kyungpook National University.

Kim, S. and J. Maling. 1998. Resultatives: English vs. Korean. *Japanese/Korean Linguistics* 7, eds. N. Akatsuka, et al., 363-79. Stanford: CSLI Publications.

Kim, Y. (in preparation). The Interface between Cognitive Grammar and Construction Grammar: On the Conative Construction. Manuscript, University of Oregon, College of Arts and Sciences.

Langacker, R. W. 1987. *Foundations of Cognitive Grammar Vol.I: Theoretical Prerequisites*. Stanford: Stanford University Press.

Narrog, H. 2004. From Transitive to Causative in Japanese: Morphologization through Exaptation. *Diachoronica* 21(2):351-92.

Nakamura, Y. 2001. Nijuu-mokutekigo Kobun no Ninchi-kozo: Kobunnai Nettowaku to Kobunkan Nettowaku no Syorei. (Cognitive Structure of the Double Object Construction: A Case Study of Intraconstructional Network and Interconstructional Network). *Studies in Cognitive Linguistics* No.1:59-110.

Nitta, Y, 2002. *Fukushiteki Hyogen no Syosoo* (Various Aspects of Adverbs). Tokyo: Kuroshio.

Park, S. 1989. *Kwuke Pusahwaso {-i} wa {-key} ey Tayhan Sacek Yenkwu* (A Historical Study on the Adverb Formative {-i} and {-key}: With Focus on Function and Distribution). Master's Thesis, Seoul National University.

Rappaport, H. and B. Levin 2001. An Event Structure Account of English Resultatives. *Language* 77:766-97.

Tenny, C. 1994. *Aspectual Roles and the Syntax-Semantics Interface*. Dordrecht: Kluwer.

Uehara, S., Q. Li, and K. Thepkanjana. 2001. A Contrastive Study of Resultative Constructions in Japanese, Korean and Mandarin Chinese: A Cognitive Approach. *Proceedings of the 1st Seoul InternationalConference on Discourse and Cognitive Linguistics*:292-304.

Washio, R. 1997a. Kyelkwa phyohyen uy yuhyeng (A Typology of Resultative Expressions). *Language Research* 33:435-62. Seoul National University.

Washio, R. 1997b. Resultatives, Compositionality and Language Variation. *Journal of East Asian Linguistics* 6:1-49.

Washio, R. 1999. Some Comparative Notes on Resultatives. *Linguistics: In Search of the Human Mind*, eds. M. Muraki and E. Iwamoto, 647-707. Tokyo: Kaitakusha.

Syntactic Change from Connective to Focus Particles in Japanese

TOMOHIDE KINUHATA
Kyoto University

1. Introduction[1]

A great deal of work in the history of Japanese centers on change of meaning. Works within the theory called 'grammaticalization' are to be considered as a part of the study of semantic change as well, lending themselves to concepts such as 'concrete meaning' and 'abstract meaning.' Syntactic change , on the other hand, has been paid little attention even from a descriptive perspective, let alone from a theoretical point of view. The goal of this paper is to present a syntactic path from connective to focus particles and situate this change in a general picture with respect to the emergence of *kakari-musubi*, which, I believe, constitutes the fundamental study to construct a theory of the change of syntax.

In section 2, we have a brief look at previous studies on the grammatical items which we will refer to in the following sections. After proposing a syntactic path from connective to focus particles in section 3, we see the

[1] I am indebted to Satoshi Kinsui whose lectures at Osaka University inspired in me the conception of the present work. I would also like to thank Tadashi Eguchi, Hajime Hoji, Yoshitaka Kozuka, Eric McCready, Yukinori Takubo and Daiki Tanaka among many others including the audience of J/K 15, who have helped me understand the relevant issues.

historical data in terms of this path in section 4. Section 5 is devoted to analyzing the motivations for the change and its relation to the emergence of *kakari-musubi* construction.

2. Previous Studies and Problems

The fact that the historical studies in Japanese are mainly concerned with the meaning change is true of the words such as *naritomo* and *demo*, which we discuss in this paper. Konoshima (1966) refers to the historical change of *demo*, stating that '*Demo*... had changed into 'exemplification' from 'concessive' in its usage' (p. 351, translation my own). Yake (1997), claiming that *naritomo* had undergone the same type of change as *demo*, said 'we found examples of *demo* which, having lost its original fuction to constitute the conditional phrase, merely convey the meaning 'exemplification'(p. 37, translation my own).

I argue in this paper, admitting that their meanings have evolved into 'exemplification', that their change doesn't occur for a particular meaning, and a syntactic analysis gives a unified account for the phenomena at issue and explains the motivation for their semantic change as well.

3. Concept of the Syntactic Change

The syntactic change which I propose is the following process from Phase 1 through Phase 2 to Phase 3.

(1)   Phase 1   Phase 2   Phase 3

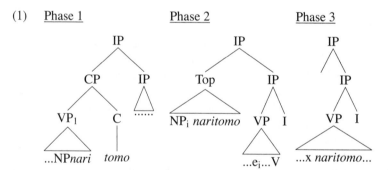

In Phase 1, *nari* is the head of the VP and *tomo* a subordinator. *Nari* and *tomo*, in phase 2, merge into one word which is base-generated in the higher position as 'Top'[2] , and the NP in the topic position, if it is an argument, has a relation to the empty category (zero pronoun) co-indexed with it in VP. In Phase 3, *naritomo* is inserted and attached to one of the elements under the VP (I assume here the 'attachment' analysis proposed by Kuroda 1979).

---

[2] I use the term 'Topic' as referring to an NP which occupies (and is assumed to be base-generated in) sentence-initial positions and (thus) can not focus the verb of the main clause.

Given the above assumptions, we can expect the following phenomena of the three stages in the historical materials of Japanese. *Tomo* takes a predicate nominal in Phase 1 and the subordinate clause has only concessive or conditional relation to the main clause. In Phase 2, *Naritomo* takes an NP which can be an argument or an adjunct of the main clause. *Naritomo* with the property of Phase 3 can focus the verb or the VP besides the NPs in the main clause. Let me turn to the empirical research based on this expectation in the next section.

4. Data

4.1. *Naritomo*

We see in the following that the three stages considered in section 3 show a close correspondence to what actually happened in the history of Japanese.[3]

The statistics related to the examples of *naritomo* I found are given in Table 1.[4]

	VP(S)	NOM	ACC	Oth	Adj	VP(M)	Total
Genji	18	1	0	2	0	0	21
Amakusa	2	3	5	3	5	0	18
Toraakira	9	5	39	18	23	10	104

Table 1. Distribution of *naritomo*[5]

The fact that most examples are distributed under VP(S) in *Genji Monogatari* can be accounted for, if we assume the structure of this period as in Phase 1. Some of these examples are illustrated below.[6]

---

[3] See 'Texts' for the chronology of materials in the tables.

[4] I won't touch upon the floating-quantifier-like construction such as '*oni futari naritomo turete* (bring two demons) (*Toraakira* Seirai)' in the following discussion. '*Oni* (demon)' is a host NP and '*futari* (two) *naritomo*' functions like a floating quantifier. I found 1 example of this type in *Amakusaban Heike* and 18 examples in *Toraakirabon Kyōgenshū*.

[5] Let me note the abbreviations used for tables. VP(S) in the upper line means that the NPs before *naritomo* function as predicate nominals of the subordinate clause. NOM, ACC, Oth and Adj refer to the NPs with *naritomo* which are interpretable as Nominative cases, Accusative cases, other cases or adjuncts of the main clauses respectively. 'Other cases' here includes examples which can be understood with case particles such as *ni*, *he*, *kara* or *nite* supplied. Examples are classified under VP(M) when they focus the verb or the VP of the main clause.

[6] I will use the following abbriviations for glosses. ACC(Accusative case), CAU(Causative), CLA(Classifier), CONC(Concessive marker), COND(Conditional marker), DAT(Dative case), DIR(Directive case), EMPH(Emphatic particle), FIN(Sentence final particle), GEN(Genitive marker), HON(Honorific expression), IMP(Imperative), LOC(Locative case), NEG(Negative), NOM(Nominative case), POL(Polite expression), Q(Question), TOP(Topic marker), VOL(Volition).

(2) a. kutiwoshiki shina <u>nari-tomo</u> ... kokoro mo tomari-namu-kashi
     humble   class   heart   also stay-Guess-FIN
     'Even if she were in the humble class, I would be attracted to her.'
                                                      (*Genji* Yadorigi)
   b. tatofi   makotoni fito   <u>nari-tomo</u> kitune kodama
      even if really   human   fox   ghost
      yaunomono-no   ajamukite torimotekitaru-nikoso-faber-ame
      something-NOM deceive   bring-Copula-POL-Guess
      'Even if it really were a human being, I think it was deceived and
      brought here by something like a fox or a ghost.' (*Genji* Tenarafi)
   c. ito   kataki   koto <u>nari-tomo</u>, waga if-amu   koto fa
      much difficult thing   my   say-Guess thing TOP
      tabakari-temu-ya
      accommodate-Guess-Q
      'Even if it's very difficult, will you accommodate my request?'
                                                      (*Genji* Ukifune)

Kutiwosikisina in (2a) can not be construed as an argument of the main clause.
Because the main clause 'I would be attracted to her' has no argument position for 'humble class', and thus it can only be a concessive clause. In (2b),
the object of *torimotekitaru* (bring) is the object they are looking at; a princess
called *Ukifune*. The speaker is wondering whether the property of *Ukifune* is
human or not. Incapable of denoting this object, *fito* before *naritomo* must be
a predicate of the subordinate clause.

Although we have examples interpreted as an argument of the main clause
in *Genji Monogatari*, they are few in the number and not incompatible with
the status of the predicate of the protasis as well. (3) are all the instances I
classified as arguments.

(3) a. imijiki mononofu adagataki   <u>nari-tomo</u>, ... utiwemare-nubeki
        extreme warrior   hostile enemy   smile-Guess
        shama-no   shi-tamafere-ba
        figure-NOM do-HON-COND
        'Because he has a figure toward which even the warriors or hostile
        enemies should smile.'   (*Genji* kiritubo)
   b. imijiki miti <u>nari-tomo</u>, omomuki-gataku oboje-tamafu
      extreme road   proceed-difficult think-HON
      'It would be difficult to renounce the world however precious it is,
      Genji thinks.'   (*Genji* Momidinoga)
   c. shebaki kakine-no   uti   <u>nari-tomo</u>, ... faru-no   fana-no
      small   hedge-GEN inside   spring-GEN flower-GEN
      ki-wo   mo uwewatasi
      tree-ACC also plant

'I would like to plant the trees which flourish in spring even though my garden is not so big.'　　　　　　　　　　　(*Genji* Usugumo)

Contrary to the situation in *Genji Monogatari*, the examples in *Amakusaban Heike* ranges evenly from VP(S) to Adj. I gave an example of subject in (4a), object in (4b), indirect object in (4c) and adjunct in (4d) with their counterparts in earlier versions of *Heike Monogatari*.[7]

(4)　a.　sanbiacu-nin-no　　　　　mono-no vchi　tare　　nari tomo
　　　　three hundred-CLA-GEN one-GEN inside someone

　　　　core-uo　sucoxi qiq-eba
　　　　this-ACC a little hear-COND
　　　　'If someone in that three hundred people hears this a little, '
　　　　　　　　　　　　　　　　　　　　　　(*Amakusa* 1-1)

　　b.　ima ychido　　　facanai fude-no　　ato-uo　　naritomo
　　　　one more again short　pencil-GEN trace-ACC

　　　　tatematçutte von votozzure-uo qi-cǒ
　　　　send　　　　news-ACC　　hear-VOL
　　　　'I want to send a short letter and hear the news about him.'
　　　　　　　　　　　　　　　　　　　　　　(*Amakusa* 1-8)
　　　　ima ichido fakanaki fude no ato wo mo tatematuri　　(*Kakuiti* 2)

　　c.　moxi izzucu-no　　　　　vra-ni　　naritomo cocoroyasǔ
　　　　if　somewhere-GEN　shore-LOC　　　relievedly

　　　　vochitçuita-naraba,
　　　　get setteled-COND
　　　　'If I get settled at some shore relievedly,'　　Amakusa 3-7
　　　　mosi idukuno ura ni mo kokoro yasuku otitukitaramu tokifa
　　　　　　　　　　　　　　　　　　　　　　(*Hyakunizikku* 7)

　　d.　nanitoyǒni naritomo vocoye-uo　sotto　　　idasa-xerare-i
　　　　somehow　　　　voice-ACC naturally let out-HON-IMP
　　　　'Please let out a cry in some casual way or other.'　(*Amakusa* 1-3)
　　　　ikasamanimo okoje no idubeu saurau　　　　　(*Kakuiti* 2)

Let me remark the fact that case-marker-attached NPs are used with *naritomo* as in (4b) and (4c). This evidently indicates that *naritomo* does not constitute the VP of the subordinate clause but the argument of the main clause. At the same time, in *Kakuitibon Heike Monogatari*, one of the earlier versions of *Amakusaban Heike*, we have no such example, which implies that these examples began to be used around the 14th or 15th century.

　I tentatively assume here that the NPs in (4) occupy the 'topic' position, because there is no instance focusing the verb of the main clause. But this

---

[7] See Kiyose (1982) on the relationship between *Amakusaban Heike Monogatari* and its earlier versions.

assumption raises the question of how case markers in (4b) and (4c) are licenced. I will return to this point in the next section.

So far, we have seen that *Amakusaban Heike Monogatari* has a larger variety of examples than *Genji Monogatari* does, except for the one focusing the verb such as (5). This is the difference between *Amakusaban Heike* and *Toraakirabon Kyōgenshū*.

(5) a. nikusa   mo nikushi, nabutte   naritomo yar-au
       hatefulness also hateful make fun of   *do-VOL*
       'I hate him very much and so I'll make fun of him.'
                                             (*Toraakira* Kuramamairi)
     b. yai koi,   mizu narito[8] nom-ashe-taraba   torikajesh-e
       hey come on water   *drink-CAU-COND get back-IMP*
       'Hey come on, if you let him drink water or did something, get it back.'   (*Toraakira* Imamairi)
     c. kotoba naritomo kawashe-ba   onaji koto-ja   fodoni
       word   *exchange-COND same thing-Copula since*
       fanaite nagusam-au
       talk   comfort-VOL
       'Since exchanging words is enough for us to feel comfort, let's talk and give comfort to each other.'   (*Toraakira* Finosake)

Naritomo in (5a) is attached to the verb '*naburu* (make fun of)', and a light verb '*yarou*' is inserted. Although *naritomo* in (5b) and (5c) are attached to NPs, these foci should be considered not as the NPs but as the VPs, given appropriate interpretations from the context. *Naritomo* in (5b) focuses the event '*mizu wo nomasu* (let him drink water)', as one of the actions to entertain a newcomer. '*Kotoba wo kawasu* (exchange words)' in (5c) is contrasted with other events such as '*kawo wo awasu* (look at each other)'.

From the observations so far, it follows that *naritomo* had changed from Phase 1 through Phase 2 to Phase 3.[9]

---

[8] *Narito* is a variation of *naritomo* found in Pre-modern Japanese.

[9] One might argue that the differences in distribution of examples between the texts in Table 1 are due to the amount of examples each text possesses; *Toraakirabon Kyōgenshū* has five times more instances of *naritomo* than *Genji Monogatari* or *Amakusaban Heike*, and thus has examples focusing the verb of the main clause. This argumentation might be applied only to the difference between *Toraakirabon Kyōgenshū* and *Amakusaban Heike*. Since *Genji Monogatari* is as long as *Toraakirabon Kyōgenshū*, the limited examples of the former should be attributed to the characteristics of *naritomo* in this text. However *Amakusaban Heike Monogatari* is shorter than them and we have to extend the research further. I have collected 47 examples from *Mōgyūshō* and *Chūkajabokushishō*, which were trascribed in the early 16th century. Different though their style of writing may be, I found a similar distribution with *Amakusaban Heike Monogatari*, except one example '*ta naritomo tukurite, tomo kaumo suru yauni seyo*. (Making a field, you should manage to live.) (*Mōgyūshō*, 4),' which seems to focus VP. Although we have to do more wide-ranging

4.2. Demo

Demo appears to follow a similar pattern to *naritomo*. It is, however, difficult to detect its change from Phase 1 to Phase 2 because we find few instances of it before the 17th century. Here we see the change from Phase 2 to Phase 3. The distribution of the examples is given in Table 2.

	VP(S)	NOM	ACC	Oth	Adj	VP(M)	Total
Toraakira	5	3	1	1	2	0	12
Chikamatsu	9	2	5	7	8	5	36

Table 2. Distribution of *demo*

Toraakirabon Kyōgenshū reflects the language in which *demo* was being under Phase 2. It had come to be used as a Focus marker in *Chikamatsu Jōruri*. The examples of 'Topic' are given in (6) and those of Focus in (7).

(6) a. soregashigami <u>demo</u> sheu yau mo nai
      I   *do* *way also NEG*
      'Even I cannot find the way to do.'   (*Toraakira* Fonekawa)
  b. yubi <u>demo</u> irowasu-mai-zo
      finger   *touch-NEG/VOL-FIN*
      'I won't make him even touch your finger.'   (*Toraakira* Fanago)

(7) a. kuzetsu <u>demo</u> shiyatta ka... kishoku <u>demo</u> warui ka
      quarrel   *do*   *Q*   *feeling*   *bad*   *Q*
      'Did you quarrel with him ... or does he feel bad?'
                           (Chikamatsu, Tanbayosaku)
  b. konata-no tsureai-ni   mo kotoba koso   kawas-azu
      you-GEN husband-DAT also word   *EMPH exchange-NEG*
      tomo   chiyotto kawo <u>demo</u> mi-tai
      CONC a little   *face*   *see-Wish*
      'Even if I cannot talk with your husband, I want to take a brief look
      at his face.'   (Chikamatsu, Meidonofikyaku)

In (7a), '*kuzetsu wo shita*' is contrasted with '*kisyoku ga warui*' as a reason for the absence of the hearer's boyfriend. '*Kawo wo miru*' is contrasted with '*kotoba wo kawasu*' in (7b).

4.3. Nara(ba)

Contrary to the change of *demo*, we can only see the change from Phase 1 to Phase 2 in *nara(ba)* as illustrated in Table 3.

research, I conclude here that the usage of *naritomo* focusing the verb was not common before the late 16th century.

	VP(S)	NOM	ACC	Oth	Adj	VP(M)	Total
Genji	54	2	2	0	0	0	58
Toraakira	72	12	4	2	5	0	95
Chikamatsu	18	2	3	0	2	0	25
Sharebon	38	7	3	6	6	0	60

Table 3. Distribution of *nara(ba)*

Most examples come under the category VP(S) in *Genji Monogatari*. Some of the examples are as in (8)

(8)   a.   waga yado-no   fana   shi   nabeteno iro   <u>nara-ba</u> nanikafa
        my   house-GEN flower EMPH normal   beauty   why
        sharani   kimi-wo   mat-amashi
        especially you-ACC wait-Guess
        'If the flower of my house weren't so beautiful, would I invite you
        especially?'   (*Genji* Fananoen)
   b.   ware, onna   <u>nara-ba,</u>   kanarazu mutubiyori-namashi
        I   woman   surely   get married-VOL
        'If I were a woman, I would surely get married to him.'
                                        (*Genji* Wakana)
   c.   mameyakanaru mikokoro <u>nara-ba</u> konofodo-wo   oboshishizumete
        honest   heart   this time-ACC hold back
        'If you are honest, I want you to hold back your emotion this time.'
                                    Genji Takekawa

Although the dominant use as predicate nominals remains the same, instances of NOM, ACC, Other and Adj increase little by little through the Premodern period. In addition, we have examples with case-marker-attached NPs used with *nara(ba)* in *Sharebon* as in (9).

(9)   a.   haimyo   de   <u>nara</u> ... Kinaga no kimi no yaitoya nado
        pen name LOC   *and the like*
        ha   yoku tohutta mono-jiya
        TOP well famous one-Copula
        "Kinaga no kimi-no yaitoya' is well known as a pen name.'
                                       Hokukwatūjō)
   b.   yausu   de <u>nara</u>, manzara fukai tokoro-e   mo
        appearance by   at all   deep   part-DIR also
        hamari-masu-mai
        fall into-POL-NEG
        'According to appearances, he won't go into the serious situation .'

(Hokukwatūjō)

However we don't have any examples of *nara* focusing the verb not only in the materials in Table 3, but also in the result gained from 'Google Search'. This is reinforced by the intuition that the examples below are deviant.

(10) a. Tarō ha   gohan-o   tabe (ha/ [??]nara) shi-ta.
          TOP dinner-ACC eat   *do-Past*
          'Taro ate dinner.'
      b. Yamada ha   Tanaka-o   naguri (ha/ [??]nara) shi-ta   ga   koroshi
          TOP   -ACC hit   *do-Past CONC kill*
          (ha/ [??]nara) shi-nakat-ta
                do-NEG-Past
          'Yamada hit Tanaka but did not kill him.'

5. Motivations and Related Phenomena

5.1. Motivations for Change

The motivations of these syntactic changes should be considered in two separate parts; the motivation for Phase 1 to Phase 2 and that for Phase 2 to Phase 3.

The former change contains the process where *nari* and *tomo* merge into one word and the nominal preceding the copula is interpreted as an argument (or an adjunct) of the main clause. We may wonder what could be the rationale behind the reintepretation from the predicate to the argument. I think that an answer may be found in the characteristics that Japanese has. Japanese has zero pronouns and is a verb final language. Kuroda (1999) and Kinsui (to appear) discuss the relationship between these characteristics and the reinterpretations of independent sentences as arguments of the main clause. Though there are still things that have to be explained, I confine myself here to pointing out the relevance with these studies.

As a result of the structural change, *naritomo* is not independent from the main clause in Phase 3. I think that the motivation behind this is that Japanese is a free word order language. Once the NP is interpreted as an argument of the verb, it is also probable to interpret it not as base-generated in the sentence-initial position as in (11a) but as preposed to that position by scrambling as in (11b). ('t_i' in (11b) represents a trace of movement)

(11) a. [NP$_i$ *naritomo* [$_{VP}$ ...e$_i$... V]
      b. [... [NP *naritomo*$_i$ [$_{VP}$ ...t$_i$...V]]

If the 'NP *naritomo*' is interpreted in the trace position in (11b), it is not unreasonable to assume that *naritomo* is inserted under the VP from the sentence-final position by the 'attachment transformation,' which enables *naritomo* to focus the verb of the main clause.

This 'scrambling' analysis leads us to the question whether the case-marker-attached NPs used with *naritomo* are base-generated in the sentence-initial position as proposed in 4.1, because it is usual to assume the case marker to be licenced under VP.[10] If this is the case, it seems reasonable to consider the relevant examples in *Amakusaban Heike* as taking a step forward into Phase 3.

One final remark. What triggers the semantic change from 'concessive' to 'exemplification'? This meaning transition had taken place in the process from Phase 2 to Phase 3. Since the 'concessive' meaning can only be expressed by a relation between two independent phrases, the structure of Phase 3, which doesn't have independent phrases especially if *naritomo* focuses the verb, forces *naritomo* to evolve its meaning into some other one. Consequently it happened to be 'exemplification'.

5.2. Emergence of *Kakari-musubi*

It is acknowledged that Classical Japanese has a syntactic pattern called *kakari-musubi* where the scope of a constituent marked with a *kakari* particle (e.g. *so, namu, ya, ka* or *koso*) is demarcated by a paticular predicate form (*musubi*, Rentai or Izen form).[11] I give a typical example of this construction in (12) in which a *kakari* particle is attached to the NP.

(12)   atamitaru tora ka foyuru
       hostile   tiger   bark
       'Does a tiger bark furiously?'   (*Man-yō-shū* 199)

Three sources are hypothesized about the origin of *kakari-musubi* ; namely 'annotative constructions' (Nomura 1995, 2002), 'insertion' (Sakakura 1993) and 'inversion' (Ōno 1993). Nomura (1995, 2002), discussing the disadvantages of the other two hypotheses, argues that the *kakari-musubi*, especially that with *ka* and *so*, traces its origin to the annotative clause such as (13).

(13)   umashakewo Miwa-no   fafuri-ga   ifafu sugi   te   fure
       -GEN priest-NOM bless Japanese cedar hand touch
       -shi tumi ka kimi-ni   afi-gataki
       -Past crime   you-DAT see-difficult
       'I cannot see you these days. I wonder if the reason is that I touched the Japanese cedar which a priest of Miwa shrine blesses.'
                                                            (*Man-yō-shū* 712)

---

[10] See Hoji (1985: chapter 3) among others.
[11] See Whitman (1997) among others for the structure of this construction.

In our framework, the process is considered as follows; [12] the annotative construction which constitutes a CP corresponds to Phase 1 and, through Phase 2 where the NP preceding *ka* can be interpreted as an argument of the main clause as in (12), *ka* can be attached to any element under the VP in Phase 3, including the verb of the main clause as in the examples below.

(14) yasumishishi wago ofokimi-no   ofomifune mati-<u>ka</u>-kofu-ramu
       my Emperor-GEN ship   wait- -long-Guess
       Shiganokarashaki
       'I'm wondering if Shiganokarashaki is waiting and longing for the
       ship of our emperor.'   (*Man-yō-shū* 152)

Since this change is assumed to occur in Pre-Old Japanese, our study gave empirical grounds that this process actually took place and reveals that it is not an impracticable idea, through the history of *naritomo, demo* and *nara(ba)*.

6. Concluding Remarks

In this paper I have proposed a syntactic path from connective to focus particles and argued that this change doesn't occur for a particular meaning, making reference to the emergence of *kakari-musubi*. More scrutiny should be given to the relevant changes and we have to clarify the resemblances and the differences between them, in order to build a theory for syntactic change.

Texts

Hoteiban Man-yō-shū Honmonhen (Hanawashobō, 8th C.), *Genji Monogatari* (Nihon Koten Bungaku Zenshū, Shōgakukan, 11th C.), *Heike Monogatari* (*Kakuitibon*) (Shin Nihon Koten Bungaku Zenshū, Shōgakukan, 13th C.), *Hyakunizikkubon Heike Monogatari*   Shidōbunko Kotensōkan 2, 13th C. , *Amakusaban Heike Monogatari Taishōhonmon oyobi Sōsakuin* (Meijishoin, 16th C.), *Ōkura Toraakirabon Kyōgenshū no Kenkyū* (Hyōgensha, 17th C.), *Sonezakishinzhū meidonohikyaku hoka gohen* (Iwanami Bunko, Chikamatsu Monzaemon, 18th C.), *Sharebon Taisei* (Chūōkoron, 18-19th C., Selecting 23 texts of Kyoto and Osaka dialect)

References

Hoji, H. 1985. Logical Form Constraints and Configurational Structures in Japanese. Doctoral dissertation, University of Washington.

Kinsui, S. to appear. The Interaction between Argument and Non-argument in the Historical Change of Japanese Syntax. *The History and Structure*

---

[12] The process in which a copula and C merge into one word is not involved in this change. This is because *kakari* particles can take NPs from the beginning.

of Japanese, eds. B. Frellesvig, M. Shibatani and J. C. Smith. Tokyo: Kuroshio Publisher.

Kiyose R. 1982. *Amakusaban Heike Monogatari no Kisoteki Kenkyū (Basic Study on Amakusaban Heike Monogatari)*. Hiroshima: Keisuisha.

Konoshima, M. 1966. *Kokugojoshi no Kenkyū: Joshishi no Sobyō (Studies on Japanese Particles: A Sketch of the History of Particles)*. Tokyo: Ōfūsha.

Kuroda, S.-Y. 1979. *Generative Grammatical Studies in the Japanese Language*. New York & London: Garland Publishing Inc.

Kuroda, S.-Y. 1999. Shubu Naizai Kankeisetsu (Head-internal Relative Clauses). *Kotoba no Kaku to Shūen: Nihongo to Eigo no Aida*, eds. S.-Y. Kuroda and M. Nakamura, 27-103. Tokyo: Kuroshio Publisher.

Nomura, T. 1995. *Ka* niyoru Kakari-musubi Shiron (A Tentative Assumption on *Kakari-musubi* with *Ka*). *Kokugo Kokubun* 64-9:1-27. Kyoto University Kokubungakukenkyūshitsu.

Nomura, T. 2002. Rentaikei niyoru Kakari-musubi no Tenkai (Development of *Kakari-musubi* with *Rentaikei*. *Nihongogaku to Nihongokyōiku, Shiriizu Gengokagaku 5*, ed. H Ueda, 11-37. Tokyo: University of Tokyo Press.

Ōno, S. 1993. *Kakari-musubi no Kenkyū (Studies on Kakari-musubi)*. Tokyo: Iwanami Publisher.

Sakakura, A. 1993. *Nihongo Hyōgen no Nagare (The Stream of Japanese Expressions)*. Tokyo: Iwanami Publisher.

Whitman, J. 1997. Kakarimusubi from a Comparative Perspective. *Japanese Korean Linguistics* 6, eds. J. Haig and H. Sohn, 161-178. Stanford: CSLI.

Yake, T. 1997. Kateijōkenkumatsukeishiki Shutsuji no Joshi ni Tsuite: *Demo*, *Naritomo* no Imikinōhenka (On Particles which Stem from Suffixes of Conditional Phrases; Change of Semantic Function with *Demo* and *Naritomo*). *Gobun Kenkyū* 84:28-38. Kyūshū University Kokugokokubungakkai.

Until in English and Japanese

KIYOMI KUSUMOTO
Hirosaki Gakuin University

1. Introduction[1]

A well-known puzzle about English *until* is the following: *until* modifies homogeneous predicates such as states and activities, but not achievements and accomplishments.

(1) a. He was sick until 2003.
   b. He slept until noon.
   c. * He arrived until noon.
   d. * He built a house until 2003.

The fact in (1) clearly shows that there is some restriction on the types of predicates that *until*-phrases can modify. Such a restriction seems to disappear in sentences with negation.

---

[1] For comments and discussion, I would like to thank Ikumi Imani, Makoto Kanazawa, Mayumi Masuko, and especially Chris Tancredi. This research is supported by the Grant-in-Aid for Young Scientists from the Japanese Ministry of Education, Culture, Sports, Science and Technology, to which I am grateful.

(2) a. He wasn't sick until 2003.
    b. He didn't sleep until noon.
    c. He didn't arrive until noon.
    d. He didn't eat a sandwich until noon.

How can we account for this contrast? Two types of answers have been given in the literature. Mittwoch (1977) argues that the contrast is reduced to scope interaction between *until*-phrases and negation. *Until* selects homogeneous predicates. This restriction results in the contrast in (1). Such a contrast disappears since negation makes everything homogeneous. Karttunen (1974), on the other hand, argues that there are two *until*s in English. One selects homogenous predicates, and the other selects punctual predicates and is a negative polarity item.

Both analyses seem to work cross-linguistically since Japanese *made* 'until' shows a similar distribution. In affirmative sentences, *made*-phrases are compatible with homogeneous predicates but result in ungrammaticality when modifying achievements and accomplishments.

(3) a. kare-wa ni-sen-san-nen-made byoki-dat-ta.
        he-top   2003-year-until   sick-COP-past
        'He was sick until 2003'

    b. kare-wa zyunizi-made nemut-ta.
        he-top   12-o'clock-until sleep-past
        'He slept until noon'

    c. * kare-wa zyunizi-made ki-ta.
        he-top   12-o'clock-until come-past
        'He came until noon'

    d. * kare-wa ni-sen-san-nen-made zibun-no ie-o   tate-ta.
        he-top   2003-year-until   self-gen house-acc build-past
        'He built his house until 2003'

All types of predicates are compatible with *made*-phrases under negation.

(4) a. kare-wa ni-sen-san-nen-made byoki-de-nakat-ta.
        he-top   2003-year-until   sick-cop-neg-past
        'He was not sick until 2003'

    b. kare-wa zyunizi-made nemura-nakat-ta.
        he-top   12-o'clock-until sleep-neg-past
        'He didn't sleep until noon'

    c. kare-wa zyunizi-made ko-nakat-ta.
        he-top   12-o'clock-until come-neg-past
        'He didn't come until noon'

d. kare-wa ni-sen-san-nen-made zibun-no ie-o   tate-nakat-ta.
    he-top 2003-year-until   self-gen house-acc build-neg-past
    'He didn't build his house until 2003'

In this paper, we will see that English *until* and Japanese *made* differ in crucial respects despite these apparent similarities. We will show that the differences revealed help us to choose the proper semantics of *until* (and *made*) among previous representative analyses. In doing so, we will provide a compositional semantic analysis of these lexical items.

2. A Difference between English and Japanese: Actualization Implications

One characteristic feature of *not...until* is that it invites a strong implication that the relevant event actually takes place at (or a little later than) the time denoted by the complement of *until*-phrases. For instance, the speaker of (5a) commits him/herself to not only the truth of (5b) but also that of (5c).

(5) a.   He did not arrive until noon.
     b.   He did not arrive before noon.
     c.   He arrived at (or a little later than) noon.

We call implications such as the one in (5c) *actualization implications* of (5a). One might claim that a similar implication holds for *until* in affirmative sentences. For instance, (6b) may be inferred from (6a).

(6) a.   He slept until noon.
     b.   He woke up at (or a little after) noon.

Both inferences seem reasonable. As noted in the literature (Declerck 1995, Karttunen 1974), however, they differ in that the implication in the former case is not cancelable, whereas the implication in the latter case is. Thus, denying the implication creates inconsistency in (7a), whereas the continuation in (7b) is fine.

(7) a. # He didn't arrive until noon yesterday. In fact, he didn't arrive at all.
     b.   He slept until noon. In fact, he slept all day that day.

Karttunen (1974) claims that the following contrast also shows the same point.

(8) a. # She didn't get married until she died.
     b.   She remained a spinster until she died.

The example (8a) invites an inference that she got married at the time of her death, and hence conflicts with our world knowledge. No such anomaly occurs in (8b).

There has been much debate as to whether such actualization implications are conversational implicatures, presuppositions, or entailments. The fact that these implications are not cancelable suggests that they are not mere conversational implicatures.[2]

To see whether they are presuppositions or entailments, consider the following sentence where the *not ...until* construction is embedded under a modal operator.

(9) It is possible that he didn't arrive until noon.

Modal operators are presupposition holes in the sense that a presupposition of the embedded sentence survives as a presupposition of the entire sentence (see Karttunen 1973, Schwarz 2005). Thus, the sentence (10a) implies both (10b) and (10c).

(10) a. It is possible that he is here again.
  b. It is possible that he is here now.
  c. He was actually here some time before.

This is because the sentence *he is here again* presupposes that he was here some time before and asserts that he is here now.

If actualization implications are presuppositions, the sentence (9) is predicted to have the same implication as (5a). This prediction is not borne out. The sentence implies that it is possible that he arrived at noon, but fails to imply that he actually arrived at noon. The conclusion derived here is that

---

[2] de Swart (1996) argues that the implications can be cancelled or suspended, based on the following examples:

(i) a. She said that she wouldn't come until Friday. In the end, she didn't come at all.
  b. I won't leave until Friday, if at all.

She claims that (ia) is consistent and that (ib) does not imply that the speaker will leave on Friday.

Her examples, however, do not show the relevant point, because the *until*-phrases are further embedded under a propositional attitude expression or a consequent of a conditional sentence.

The following examples show that such environments are not suitable for testing cancellability of implications. (iia) is consistent and the speaker of (iib) does not commit herself to leaving on Friday.

(ii) a. She said that Hans is a German linguist. But in fact he is not a linguist.
  b. I will leave only on Friday, if I leave at all.

The following examples show, however, the speaker of the (a) sentences does commit him/herself to the truth of the (b) sentences.

(iii) a. Hans is a German linguist.
  b. Hans is a linguist.
(iv) a. I will leave only on Friday.
  b. I will leave on Friday.

actualization implications are part of the meaning of *until*, not presuppositions. Japanese *made*, on the other hand, does not have such strong implications. The first sentence in (11) alone invites an inference that he actually came at or a little later than three. But denying it does not result in a semantic anomaly.

(11) kare-wa sanzi-made   ko-nakat-ta.
    he-top   3-o'clock-until come-neg-past

kekkyoku sono-hi kare-wa ko-nakat-ta.
After-all that-day he-top come-neg-past
'He didn't come until three. In fact, he didn't come at all that day.'

Accordingly, no contrast is found between the following two examples.

(12) a. kanozyo-wa sin-u-made   kekkon-si-nakat-ta.
        she-top   die-pres-until marry-do-neg-past
        'She didn't get married until she died'

    b. kanozyo-wa sin-u-made   dokusin-dat-ta.
        she-top   die-pres-until spinster-cop-past
        'She was a spinster until she died'.

The above facts suggest that one *until* analysis is not tenable for English *until*, for it cannot account for the existence of actualization implication, which should be attributed to the truth conditional semantic content of *until*. This leaves us to posit two *until*s for English, as argued in Karttunen (1974). Japanese *made*, on the other hand, may be given a straightforward account under one *until* analysis. A similar conclusion has been reached in Giannakidou (2002), which examined the Greek counterparts of *until*.

In what follows, we will first give the semantics of the homogeneous *until* in English (*until$_H$*) and Japanese *made*. We will then give the semantics of the negative polarity *until* (*until$_{NPI}$*) in English. In the final section, we will examine the source of the homogeneity requirement.

3. The Semantics of *until$_H$/made*

The semantics of *until$_H$* and *made* we propose looks like this:

(13) $[[\text{until}_H/\text{made}]] = \lambda t \lambda P \lambda t' \exists t'' \exists t''' [t'' \subseteq t \ \&\ t''$ is the right boundary of t''' $\&\ t''' \subseteq t' \ \&\ P(t''') \ \&\ \forall t'''' [t'''' \subseteq t''' \rightarrow P(t'''')]]$

Until-phrases operate on VP denotations (properties of times) and return the same type. They introduce a time interval whose right boundary is determined by the interval introduced by their first argument and assert that the events denoted by the VP hold throughout that interval.

Let us now compute the meaning of sentences with *until/made*-phrases.

(14) a.   He slept until noon.

   b.   kare-wa zyuunizi-made nemut-ta.
        he-top 12-o'clock-until sleep-past
        'He slept until noon'

Below we provide the structure of the English sentence. The structure for Japanese differs from it only with respect to its linear order, and thus the semantic computation goes exactly like that of English.

(15)

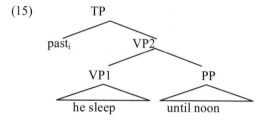

We assume that tenses represent temporal variables whose semantics is determined by variable assignment function, as in the following (see Partee 1973):

(16) $[[past_i]]^g = g(i)$

The rest of the computation goes as follows:

(17) a. $[[VP1]] = \lambda t[sleep(he)(t)]$

   b. $[[VP2]] = \lambda t \lambda P \lambda t' \exists t'' \exists t'''[t'' \subseteq t \ \& \ t''$ is the right boundary of t''' & $t''' \subseteq t' \ \& \ P(t'') \ \& \ \forall t''''[t'''' \subseteq t''' \rightarrow P(t'''')]] \ (\lambda t[sleep(he)(t)])$
        $= \lambda t' \exists t'' \exists t'''[t'' \subseteq noon \ \& \ t''$ is the right boundary of t''' & $t''' \subseteq t' \ \&$
        $sleep(he)(t'') \ \& \ \forall t''''[t'''' \subseteq t''' \rightarrow sleep(he)(t'''')]]$

   c. $[[TP]] = \exists t'' \exists t'''[t'' \subseteq noon \ \& \ t''$ is the right boundary of $t''' \ \& \ t''' \subseteq$
        $past_i \ \& \ sleep(he)(t'') \ \& \ \forall t''''[t'''' \subseteq t''' \rightarrow sleep(he)(t'''')]]$

The last line says that there was a time of his sleeping whose right boundary is sometime during a (contextually salient) noon and he slept throughout that time.

At first sight, the first existential quantifier introducing a time during the interval of the *until*-phrase is not necessary. In fact, a more simplified version has been proposed in the literature (e.g., Alexiadou et al. 2003).

(18) $[[until]] = \lambda t \lambda P \lambda t' \exists t''[t''$ is the right boundary of $t \ \& \ t'' \subseteq t' \ \& \ P(t'') \ \&$
   $\forall t''''[t'''' \subseteq t'' \rightarrow P(t'''')]]$

Consider the following example, however.

(19) kare-wa gogo-made   nemut-ta
     he-top afternoon-until sleep-past
     'He slept until in the afternoon'

Unlike *zyuunizi* 'noon', which is instantaneous, *gogo* 'afternoon' is an interval predicate. In order for the sentence (19a) to be true, until what time does he has to be asleep? It is certainly not the case that he has to be asleep all through the afternoon time. It is enough for him to sleep some time into the afternoon.

Let us turn to *made*-phrases in sentences with negation. Our proposal for Japanese is that there is only one *made* in Japanese. Thus the very same *made* is used in the following examples.

(20) a. kare-wa zyuunizi-made nemura-nakat-ta.
        he-top 12-o'clock-until sleep-neg-past
        'He didn't sleep until noon'

     b. kare-wa zyuunizi-made ko-nakat-ta.
        he-top 12-o'clock-until come-neg-past
        'He didn't come until noon'

Following Mittwoch (1977) among others, we assume that negation makes all types of predicates homogeneous. See also Sasahira (to appear) for recent arguments supporting negation as stativizer. Assuming structures like the following then, the homogeneity requirement of *made* is satisfied.

(21)

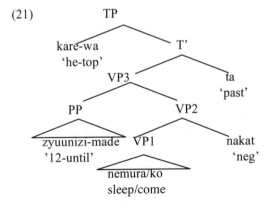

(22) a. $[[\text{VP3}]] = \lambda P \lambda t' \exists t'' \exists t''' [t'' \subseteq \text{noon \& } t'' \text{ is the right boundary of } t'''$
      $\& \ t''' \subseteq t' \ \& \ P(t'') \ \& \ \forall t''''[t'''' \subseteq t''' \rightarrow P(t'''')]](\lambda t[\neg \text{sleep(he)}(t)]$
      $= \lambda t' \exists t'' \exists t''' [t'' \subseteq \text{noon \& } t'' \text{ is the right boundary of } t''' \ \& \ t''' \subseteq t'$
      $\& \ \neg \text{sleep(he)}(t'') \ \& \ \forall t''''[t'''' \subseteq t''' \rightarrow \neg \text{sleep(he)}(t'''')]]$

    b. $[[\text{TP}]]^g = \exists t'' \exists t''' [t'' \subseteq \text{noon \& } t'' \text{ is the right boundary of } t''' \ \& \ t'''$
      $\subseteq \text{past}_i \ \& \ \neg \text{sleep(he)}(t'') \ \& \ \forall t''''[t'''' \subseteq t''' \rightarrow \neg \text{sleep(he)}(t'''')]]$

This yields the reading in which he was in a state of not sleep-ing/coming until noon.

Mittwoch's scope analysis predicts the other scope relation, namely the one in which negation takes scope over *made*-phrases.

(23)

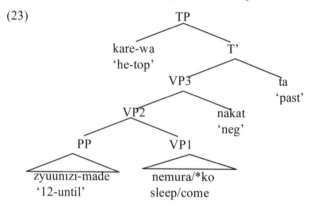

Since *made* requires homogeneity, this structure is available only for stative and activity predicates. The reading it yields is simply a negation of its affirmative counterpart. It is brought up by the following continuation.

(24) kare-wa zyuunizi-made nemura-nakat-ta. sore-yori hayaku oki-ta
he-top 12-o'clock-until sleep-neg-past that-than early wake-up-past
'He didn't sleep until noon. He woke up earlier than that.'

4. The Semantics of *until*_{NPI}

In this section, we propose the semantics of the negative polarity *until* in English. We have seen that sentences with *until* under negation such as (25a) means something like (25b).

(25) a. He didn't arrive until noon.
    b. He arrived at noon and he didn't arrive before noon.

In order to derive actualization implications from negative sentences, *until*_{NPI} itself has to have a negative meaning.

(26) $[[\text{until}_{\text{NPI}}]] = \lambda t \lambda P \lambda t' \exists t'' \exists t''' [\neg P(t'') \ \& t'' \subseteq t \ \& \ t'' \subseteq t' \ \& P(t''') \& \ t''' < t]$

The structure and the truth conditions of (25a) look like the following:

(27)

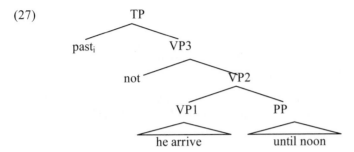

(28) $[[TP]] = \exists t''[\text{arrive(he)}(t'') \,\&\, t'' \subseteq \text{noon} \,\&\, t'' \subseteq \text{past}_i \,\&\, \neg\exists t'''[\text{arrive(he)}(t''') \,\&\, t''' < \text{noon}]$

The semantics correctly predicts the actualization implications.

5. The Homogeneity Requirement of *made*

The homogeneity requirement is often attributed to the lexical property of *until* in the literature. Our semantics of *until/made* proposed in the previous section also contains this requirement as its property.

(29) $[[\text{until/made}]] = \lambda t \lambda P \lambda t' \exists t'' \exists t'''[t'' \subseteq t \,\&\, t''$ is the right boundary of t'' $\&\, t'' \subseteq t' \,\&\, P(t''') \,\&\, \forall t''''[t'''' \subseteq t''' \rightarrow P(t'''')]$

There are reasons to doubt it, however, at least for Japanese *made*. Japanese has another lexical item *made-ni* 'by', which seems morphologically related to *made*. The distribution of *made-ni* differs from that of *made*, however. *Made-ni* is compatible with eventive predicates.[3]

(30) a. kare-wa zyuunizi-made-ni nemut-ta.
    he-top   12-o'clock-until-at sleep-past
    'He slept by noon'

---

[3] *Made-ni* is incompatible with adjectives but is compatible with verbal statives.

(i) * kare-wa ni-sen-san-nen-made-ni byoki-dat-ta.
    he-top 2003-year-until-at sick-cop-past
    'He was sick by 2003'

(ii) kare-wa san-zi-made-ni heya-ni i-ta.
    he-top 3-o'clock-until-at room-in be-past
    'He was in the room by three'

It has been argued that there are differences between adjectival states and verbal statives (see Rothstein 1999, Sasahira to appear). The semantics of *made-ni* may be sensitive to such differences.

b. kare-wa zyuunizi-made-ni   tui-ta.
   he-top   12-O'CLOCK-until-at arrive-past
   'He arrived by noon'

c. kare-wa ni-sen-san-nen-made-ni   ie-o tate-ta.
   he-top   2003-year-until-at house-acc build-past
   'He built a house by 2003'

This alone shows that *made-ni*, unlike *made*, does not have the homogeneity requirement. Also compare (30a) with (3b), repeated here.

(3) b. kare-wa zyuunizi-made nemut-ta.
       he-top 12-o'clock-until sleep-past
       'He slept until noon'

In order for (3b) to be true, his sleeping time has to last up to noon. On the other hand, (30a) simply asserts the existence of his sleeping time before noon. Therefore, the semantics of *made-ni* should be something like this:

(31) $[[made-ni]] = \lambda t \lambda P \lambda t' \exists t'' \exists t''' \exists t'''' [t'' \subseteq t$ & t'' is the right boundary of t''' & $t''' \subseteq t'$ & $t'''' \subseteq t''$ & $P(t'''')]$

If the meaning of *made-ni* is derived compositionally from that of *made* and *ni*, then the meaning of *made* should not have the homogeneity requirement built into it. We propose that the homogeneity requirement of *made* comes from the covert adverb of quantification 'always' which shows up in the absence of overt adverbs whose semantics is given below (cf. Rathert 2003):

(32) $[[always]] = \lambda q \lambda P \lambda t [q(P)(t)$ & $\forall t'[t' \subseteq t \rightarrow P(t')]]$

The structure for *kinoo made* 'until yesterday' looks like the following:

(33)

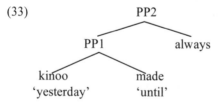

The computation goes as follows and we get the same meaning for *made*-phrases as the one we proposed in section 3.

(34) a. $[[PP1]] = \lambda P \lambda t' \exists t'' \exists t''' [t'' \subseteq$ yesterday & t'' is the right boundary of t''' & $t''' \subseteq t'$ & $P(t''')$)

   b. $[[PP2]] = \lambda P \lambda t' \exists t'' \exists t''' [t'' \subseteq$ yesterday & t'' is the right boundary of t''' & $t''' \subseteq t'$ & $P(t''')$ & $\forall t''''[t'''' \subseteq t''' \rightarrow P(t'''')]]$

There is no direct evidence to show that the homogeneity requirement of English *until$_H$* is also derived in this way. The closest English counterpart of *made-ni* is *by* and it does not seem to be morphologically related to *until*. As noted in Giannakidou (2002, 2003), a bigger picture emerges when we consider more cross-linguistic data. Languages such as Greek use one lexical item for homogeneous *until* and *by*, and employ another lexical item for negative polarity *until*. Examining differences and similarities among such languages is crucial to better understandings of the phenomenon.

References

Alexiadou, A., M. Rathert, and A. von Stechow. 2003. Introduction: The Modules of Perfect Constructions. *Perfect Explorations* vii-xxxvii. Berlin: Mouton de Gruyter.

Declerck, R. 1995. The Problem of *Not...Until*. *Linguistics* 33:51-98.

Giannakidou, A. 2002. UNTIL, Aspect, and Negation: A Novel Argument for Two *Untils*. *Semantics and Linguistic Theory* 12:84-103.

Giannakidou, A. 2003. A Puzzle about UNTIL and the Present Perfect. *Perfect Explorations,* eds. A. Alexiadou, M. Rathert, and A. von Stechow, 101-132. Berlin: Mouton de Gruyter.

Karttunen L. 1973. Presuppositions of Compound Sentences. *Linguistic Inquiry* 4:169-194.

Karttunen, L. 1974. Until. *Chicago Linguistic Society* 10:284-297.

Mittwoch, A. 1977. Negative Sentences with *Until*. *Chicago Linguistic Society* 13:410-417.

Partee B. 1973. Some Structural Analogies between Tenses and Pronouns. *Journal of Philosophy* 70:601-609.

Rathert, M. 2003. Universal-Existential Puzzles. *Perfect Explorations,* eds. A. Alexiadou, M. Rathert, and A. von Stechow, 363-380. Berlin: Mouton de Gruyter.

Rothstein, S. 1999. Fine-Grained Structure in the Eventuality Domain: the Semantics of Predicative Adjective Phrases and *Be*. *Natural Language Semantics* 7:347-420.

Sasahira Y. To appear. Negation as a Stativizer: Evidence from Japanese. *North East Linguistic Society* 36.

Schwarz, B. 2005. Scalar Additive Particles in Negative Contexts. *Natural Language Semantics* 13:125-168.

de Swart, H. 1996. Meaning and Use of *Not...Until*. *Journal of Semantics* 13:221-263.

Sekkaku

ERIC MCCREADY

Aoyama Gakuin University

1. Introduction[1]

This paper considers the semantics and pragmatics of the Japanese sentential adverbial *sekkaku*. The following example gives a feeling for what the adverbial means.

(1) sekkaku   gohan-o tukutta noni   tabete-kurenakatta
     SEKKAKU food-Acc made   CONC eat-recieved-not
     'Even though I made food, (he/they) didn't eat any.'

Based on examples like this one, native speakers often express the intuition that *sekkaku* means something like 'even though'. But, as it turns out, this is not correct: although the subordinate clause in (1) does mean something like this, it is because of the concessive subordinator *noni*, not the adverbial itself.

This paper will express a different thesis about the meaning of *sekkaku*. According to the analysis proposed here, *sekkaku*'s meaning

[1] I would like to thank Nicholas Asher, Makiko Irie, Tomohide Kinuhata, Yukinori Takubo and Satoshi Tomioka for helpful comments, as well as the audience at J/K 15. This research was partially supported by Japan Society for the Promotion of Science Grant #P05014.

has three distinct elements. First, *sekkaku* indicates, for the proposition ϕ in its scope, that the speaker takes ϕ to be positive. Second, if ϕ describes an agentive eventuality e, e is intentional. And, finally, it expresses that ϕ should ordinarily result in some other event ψ, which is also a positive one. The first part of the paper motivates these claims and provides a formalization. The second part of the paper considers the adverbial's distribution. *Sekkaku* is very restricted as to the kind of propositions it can apply to. In particular, it cannot modify conditionals, modalized sentences, negated sentences, objects of attitudes (in general), or futurates. An interesting connection can be made here to the adverbial *yoku(mo)*, as discussed by McCready (2004); this will be clarified later in the paper.

There is a complication that will make its presence known immediately. *Sekkaku* cannot modify matrix clauses, but only subordinate or relative clauses.

(2) * sekkaku   gohan-o   tukutta/tukurimasita
     SEKKAKU food-ACC made/made-HON
     'I made food ... '

It can be difficult to tell the meaning of *sekkaku* proper from the meaning of the element that heads the subordinate clause it appears in (in the present paper I will only consider subordinate clauses, though in principle I do not see why the analysis shouldn't extend to relative clauses as well). In terms of distribution, the need to place *sekkaku* in an embedded position can complicate the example construction, in that sometimes it can be difficult to embed certain elements regardless of the presence of *sekkaku* (for instance, some modals, cf. McCready and Asher 2006). The last part of the paper briefly addresses the reason for *sekkaku*'s need to appear 'low'.

Finally, a caveat before getting into the meat of the paper. *Sekkaku* in fact has three (possibly) distinct uses: as a propositional modifier, as in (3a), as a nominal modifier (3b), and as what appears to be a pure nominal (3c). This paper will concentrate on the propositional modifier use, ignoring the others. I believe that the use in (3c) is best understood as an instance of the propositional modifier use in which *sekkaku* modifies an ellipsed or null sentential complement which is recovered from context, an analysis also proposed by Watanabe (2001).

(3) a. Propositional modifier:
sekkaku   tukutta noni   tabenai no?
SEKKAKU made   CONC eat-not Q
'Even though I made this on purpose for you, expending a
lot of effort, you aren't going to eat it?'

   b. Nominal modifier:
sekkaku-no   umai sake
SEKKAKU-GEN tasty alcohol
'fortunately present liquour'

   c. Nominal:
sekkaku   dakara tabeyoo   yo
SEKKAKU so   eat-HORT YO
'We have it so let's eat it.' (very rough translation)

2. Meaning of *Sekkaku*

I construct a lexical meaning for *sekkaku* step by step, by considering successively more complex data. Watanabe (2001) independently
came to roughly similar conclusions (as pointed out to me by Yukinori
Takubo, p.c.), though his work is descriptive in nature. I will point out
places at which our analyses diverge when they arise.

The first thing to note is that *sekkaku* explicitly requires that the
proposition in its scope be something the speaker thinks is positive.
This can be shown by the contrast between (4), which expresses something good and is felicitous, and (5), which doesn't, and is not.

(4) sekkaku   gohan tukutta noni   (tabe-nai no?)
SEKKAKU food   made   CONC (eat-not Q)
'Even though I went to the trouble of making this food, which
was a good thing (aren't you going to eat it?)'

(5) ? sekkaku   asi-o   otta   kara   yasum-e yo
SEKKAKU leg-ACC broke because rest-IMP YO
'Since you went to the trouble of/were lucky enough to break your
leg, have a rest.'

We can formalize this straightforwardly using the predicate **good**
McCready (2005). **good**(p) is true just in case the speaker takes p to
be positive. Contextual information also plays a role in determining
whether something is or is not good; as a result, (5) will be understood
as negative in general. See McCready (2005) for discussion.

- $[\![sekkaku]\!]= \lambda p.[p \wedge \mathbf{good}(p)]$

Another persistent intuition about *sekkaku* often expressed by naive speakers is that whatever it modifies took place on purpose, i.e. intentionally. Adding this is simple. The new part of the following lexical entry states that the agent of the event described by p acted intentionally when doing that event.

- $[\![sekkaku]\!]= \lambda p.[Desc(p, e) \wedge \exists x[Agent(x, e) \wedge Intend(x, realize(e))] \wedge p \wedge \mathbf{good}(p)]$

But this is in fact too strong. *Sekkaku* can apply to sentences that lack agents altogether, as in the following example.

(6) sekkaku   kuri-ga   otiteiru   kara   hiro'oo
     SEKKAKU chestnuts-NOM fallen.down because pick.up-HORT
     yo
     YO
     'Since fortunately some chestnuts have fallen down here let's pick them up.'

Therefore we need to weaken our addition to the definition. However, if the eventuality denoted by a given sentence *does* have an agent, the sense of intentionality is always present.

The solution is straightforward. We will use a conditional statement that is a variant of the presupposition above.

- $[\![sekkaku]\!]= \lambda p.[p \wedge \mathbf{good}(p) \wedge \forall e \forall x[Desc(p, e) \wedge Agent(x, e) \rightarrow Intend(x, realize(e))]]$

Now the lexical entry states that, if there is an agent, she intended to realize e. This is as desired, for if there is no agent, as in (6), nothing is expressed about intentions. I should note that e here is not meant to be restricted to 'events': rather it should be understood as generic 'eventualities' of all sorts. The reason is that *sekkaku* can be used with stative sentences.[2]

---

[2] As noted by Watanabe (2001), however, *sekkaku* is not so good as a modifier of adjectives in the general case: people don't say things like *sekkaku aoi kara* 'SEKKAKU it's blue, so ...". I will not attempt to derive this restriction here, especially as I think that the situation is not quite this clear-cut. It seems that contextual factors can come into play to save sentences like this one in some circumstances.

(7) sekkaku   osake   katte-aru   kara nom-oo   yo
     SEKKAKU alcohol buy-RESULT so   drink-HORT YO
     'We're lucky enough to have some alcohol, so let's drink!'

The (semi-)final piece of the *sekkaku* meaning is its modal flavor. When *sekkaku* applies to a proposition ϕ, it does not only state something about ϕ. It is also associated with something that should (have) result(ed) from ϕ: eating food (given that it was made), collecting chestnuts (given that they have fallen), etc. Sometimes what exactly it is that should have resulted can be related to the content of the root clause, but sometimes not. We see this in the following examples. Here there is clearly no standardized relationship between making dinner and a fire starting, or between making dinner and not having dinner eaten. Rather, we get something like a denial of expectation between the subordinate clause and the main clause.

(8) a. sekkaku   gohan tukutteita noni   kazi-ni   nattesimatta
         SEKKAKU food   was.making CONC fire-DAT became
         'A fire started right when I was working on dinner.'

     b. sekkaku   gohan tukut-temo   tabete-kure-nakat-ta
         SEKKAKU food   make-CONC eat-receive-not-PST
         'Even though I went to the trouble of making food, she didn't eat any.'

How then is the identity of 'what should have happened' set? It seems to come from world knowledge. My guess is that the identity of q is in general drawn from scripts or world knowledge about typical sequences of actions; discussion of how world knowledge should be formalized, however, goes beyond the scope of this paper. Note though that on this (seemingly natural) analysis *sekkaku* includes a pragmatic element; this is unsurprising in view of other aspects of Japanese grammar (e.g. comparatives: Beck *et al.* 2004).

How should the modal flavor of *sekkaku* be characterized? There are a number of options. The one I will pursue here is simply to use a normality conditional $>$: given φ (the argument of *sekkaku*), then normally ψ. See e.g. Asher and Morreau (1991) or Halpern (2003) for more on such conditionals. Halpern in particular provides a version of normality conditionals that's relativized to agents, which is what we want here; this is the background logic I will assume (though I will not make it explicit here). '$\phi > \psi$' should thus be read 'if ϕ, then normally

ψ, according to the speaker'. In addition, *sekkaku* states that ψ is good. Adding the corresponding clause yields the new lexical entry below.

- $[\![sekkaku]\!]= \lambda p.[p \wedge \mathbf{good}(p) \wedge \forall e \forall x [Desc(p, e) \wedge Agent(x, e) \rightarrow Intend(x, realize(e))] \wedge \exists q[[p > q] \wedge \mathbf{good}(q)]]$

This looks quite good and accounts for speaker intuitions about the adverbial meaning. However, there is a complication stemming from the behavior of *sekkaku* under denial. Consider the following mini-dialogue.

(9) A. sekkaku   keeki-o   tukutta noni   ...
         SEKKAKU cake-ACC made   CONC
         'Even though I made a cake special ... '

     B. tigau daro?!
         wrong MOD
         'Yeah right!'

By his utterance, B might mean two things. He might mean 'it's not the case that the cake was made on purpose'; he might also mean 'No cake was made.' However, he certainly doesn't mean: 'Making the cake was not a good thing', or 'There is nothing that should result from making a cake.' Both of these latter meanings are possible in principle, according to our semantics (and on the assumption that denying one conjunct is sufficient to deny an entire sentence, which seems reasonable). Now it makes sense that we can't deny **good**ness: this is the judgement of the speaker, and as such she has privileged access to it (Mitchell 1986). The analysis gets this right. But the fact that the conditional ($^{\vee}p \rightarrow should(q)$) cannot be denied suggests that it is not part of the *asserted* content at all, but rather is presupposed. Implementing this proposal leaves us with the following representation, which gets the meaning of *sekkaku* right, but not the distribution, which I turn to in the next section.

- $[\![sekkaku]\!]= \lambda p\{\exists q[[p > q] \wedge \mathbf{good}(q)]\}.[p \wedge \mathbf{good}(p) \wedge \forall e \forall x [Desc(p, e) \wedge Agent(x, e) \rightarrow Intend(x, realize(e))]]$

3. Distribution of *Sekkaku*
This section will show that the distribution of *sekkaku* is extremely restricted, as already mentioned. Specifically, we will see that *sekkaku*

cannot modify conditional antecedents or consequents (though this latter fact follows directly from the inability of *sekkaku* to appear in root clauses), modal sentences, complements of attitude verbs (in general), negated sentences (in general), or non-past sentences interpreted as futurate. This paradigm is strikingly similar to facts reported by McCready (2004, 2005) for the adverbial *yoku(mo)* (also Japanese). I will point out some differences as we come to them. The end of the section will propose a generalization covering the facts and a presuppositional treatment. Let us now go through the restrictions one by one. Note that the environments in question are always embedded, for the obvious reason.

Sekkaku cannot appear in modalized sentence, whether they describe future (10a) or past (10b) possibilities. This indicates that the restriction is not temporal in nature. Neither the *sekkaku*($\Diamond\varphi$) scoping, on which *sekkaku* modifies the modal proposition, nor the $\Diamond(sekkaku(\varphi))$ scoping, on which it's stated that it's possible that *sekkaku*(φ), is available in these sentences. The situation here is identical to that of *yoku(mo)*.

(10) * asita   moti-o   sekkaku   tukuru kamosirenai kara
      tomorrow rice.cake-Acc SEKKAKU make   might   because
      kite   yo
      come.IMP YO
      'Tomorrow I might go to the trouble of making a ricecake, so come over.'

Sekkaku cannot appear in the antecedent or consequent of conditionals, and also may not apply to the entire conditional proposition. I do not show the consequent case: as it follows directly from the fact that *sekkaku* cannot appear in root clauses, it seems that the infelicity of *sekkaku* in this context has a different cause from the other two possibilities.

(11) a.   * [omae-ga   sekkaku   keeki-o   tukut-tara]   motiron
             you-NOM SEKKAKU cake-ACC make-COND of.course
           taberu yo
           eat   YO
           'If you go to the trouble of making a cake, of course I'll eat it.'

b. * taberu no   dat-tara   [sekkaku   gohan-o   tukuru]
    eat   NOMIN Cop-COND SEKKAKU food-ACC make
    'If you'll eat it, I'll go to the trouble of making some food.'

Interestingly, however, conditional antecedents all become felicitous when the sentence-final element *no da* is inserted in the conditional antecedent. This does not save *yoku-mo* conditionals, though.[3] The reason for this difference between the adverbials is not clear to me at present.

(12) [omae-ga sekkaku   keeki-o   tukutta n   dat-tara]
     you-NOM SEKKAKU cake-ACC made   NO Cop-COND
     motiron taberu yo
     of.course eat   YO
     'If you've gone to the trouble of making a cake, of course I'll eat it.'

(13) * [omae-ga yokumo   keeki-o   tukutta n   dat-tara]
       you-NOM YOKUMO cake-ACC made   NO Cop-COND
     motiron taberu yo
     of.course eat   YO
     'If you've had the unbelievable gall to make a cake, of course I'll eat it.'

Sekkaku cannot be used with futurates either. This makes some sense given what we've seen so far: *sekkaku* has been shown to be infelicitous with propositions that describe events that haven't actually taken place. This suggests that *sekkaku* (and also *yokumo*) is incompatible with indeterminacy, or *non-actuality*. Futurate sentences certainly fit this description, as they describe eventualities that haven't happened yet, by definition.

(14) * asita   moti-o   sekkaku   tukuru kara
       tomorrow rice.cake-ACC SEKKAKU make   because
     kite   yo
     come.IMP YO
     'Tomorrow I will go to the trouble of making a ricecake so come over.'

---

[3] The *yokumo* example given here is perhaps a bit pragmatically weird as well, but the situation carries over to *yokumo* more generally, as shown by McCready (2005).

Interestingly, however, it is possible to modify futurate sentences with *yokumo* and *sekkaku* if they are understood as referring to past decisions about future actions. For instance, I could use the subordinate clause (14a) (without *sekkaku*, and minus the concessive *noni*) to describe my decision yesterday to make *mochi* tomorrow. On such an interpretation sentences like these appear to be fine.

Using *sekkaku* in negated sentences is not so good either, in general.

(15) ? sekkaku   kurabu-ni ik-ana-katta   noni
       SEKKAKU club-DAT go-NEG-PST CONC
       ne-rare-na-katta
       sleep-POSS-NEG-PST
       'Even though I went to the trouble of not going to the club, I couldn't sleep.'

It's possible to interpret sentences like this one as a negative description of a positive event, however (cf. Miller 2003). Thus the subordinate clause in (15), for instance, might be understood as meaning 'Even though I deliberately skipped the club and went to bed early instead ...' rather than simply 'Even though I didn't go to the club ...' On this latter interpretation, *sekkaku* is fine, as is *yokumo*. The reason should be clear: on the 'negative description' reading, we are no longer talking about a non-actual/indeterminate event, but about something that actually happened (although we use a somewhat roundabout way of doing so). Thus the actuality requirement of the adverbials is satisfied.

As with *yoku(mo)*, *sekkaku* is not too good in true attitudes such as *believe*.[4] Again, the reason simply seems to lie in the nonactuality of complements of verbs like these. Note that a shift to verbs like *siru* 'know' does not improve matters, even though such verbs entail (or, according to some, presuppose) the truth of their complements: the reason may be that this entailment is the product of additional logical work (e.g. in modal accessibility relations) and, perhaps, doesn't hold directly enough for the actuality requirement to be satisfied.

(16) * biiru-o   sekkaku   kau to   sinzita
       beer-ACC SEKKAKU buy COMP believed
       'I believed you would purposely and fortunately buy beer.'

---

[4] It is fine in quotative sentences, however, as is *yokumo*. See McCready (2005) for details.

How should these facts be analyzed? The answer is straightforward, given the work of McCready (2004, 2005), who analyzed *yoku-mo* as presupposing that the proposition it applies to describes an *actual* eventuality: one that happened at a past time in the actual world. I will take precisely the same route here, adding this presupposition to the other elements of *sekkaku*'s meaning previously discussed.

- Final semantics for *sekkaku*:

  $[\![sekkaku]\!] = \lambda p.\{\exists q[[p > q] \wedge \mathbf{good}(q)] \wedge \exists e[\tau(e) = t \wedge t \leq n]$
  $\wedge\ Desc(e, p)\}[p \wedge \mathbf{good}(p) \wedge \forall e \forall x[Desc(p, e) \wedge Agent(x, e) \rightarrow$
  $Intend(x, realize(e))]]$

This lexical entry accounts for both the distribution and meaning of *sekkaku* in a way that is formally adequate (although I haven't given a formal semantics here for the normality conditional). It should be noted, though, that since I have adopted the same analysis I previously used for *yokumo*, the analysis here does not derive the subtle differences shown to hold in the distribution of *yokumo* and *sekkaku*. I hope that the analysis given here will prove flexible enough to do so, when these differences are better understood.

One interesting thing to speculate on is whether this difference might relate to the preference of *sekkaku* for appearing in subordinate clauses. It also seems that a connection can be made with other, similar, adverbials that have meanings concerning what one might term 'speaker affectedness' or speaker attitudes, which, in Japanese, often seem to come bundled with expectational meanings (statements about the expectedness or unexpectedness of a proposition). Further research is needed to clarify the connection between these two types of meaning, and to determine exactly what the differences are between elements of this kind.

4. Discussion

In this paper I have given a semantics for *sekkaku* that accounts for the sorts of proposition it can modify, as well as for its basic meaning. One element of its distribution remains mysterious, however. Why is *sekkaku* unable to modify root clauses? I do not at present have a definitive answer to this question. In this final section, however, I would like to explore some possibilities.

A first guess is that, since *sekkaku* needs a proposition describing an actual eventuality to apply to, it requires the material in its scope to be presupposed. Perhaps all the subordinate clauses it is good with presuppose their content. Matrix clauses would be out because they can simply be false, while (presupposing) subordinate clauses cannot. If this is right, we would have a straightforward explanation that follows from other facts about the adverbial.

Unfortunately, this simple explanation can't be right, for a number of reasons. First note that -*temo* clauses, which *sekkaku* commonly appears in (Koyano 1997), do not presuppose their content. Rather, they are more like concessive conditionals.

(17) Taro-ga   ki-temo   ore-wa   ika-nai   yo
     Taro-NOM come-CONC me-TOP go-NEG YO
     'Even if Taro comes, I still won't, man.'

And further, *sekkaku* can appear in relative clauses (as noted earlier), which clearly are not presupposed.

A presupposition-based explanation therefore does not go through. It seems reasonable to conclude that there must be something that matrix clauses lack—or have—that *sekkaku* requires—or is not compatible with. This could be something syntactic, semantic, or pragmatic in nature. A first possibility that springs to mind is an assertion operator of the sort discussed by Krifka (1992), who takes it to be correlated with existential closure on eventualities. Main clauses could well be associated with an assertion operator which subordinate clauses lack (in that it is present in the main clause, and so automatically takes scope over the subordinate content). Perhaps *sekkaku* requires a CP to intervene between it and this operator. This would account for why *sekkaku* can appear in relative clauses, which also have an intervening CP. However, it is not clear to me why *sekkaku* would be incompatible with an assertion operator, especially since this incompatibility could not be semantic in that the assertion operator would have to scope over *sekkaku* as well.

Another possibility comes from the fact that *sekkaku* includes a proposition q in its semantics (in the clause $p > q$). Maybe the matrix clause content is needed in inferring the content of q. Watanabe (2001) takes such a line, as far as I can tell; this is reasonable for him in that, on his analysis, q is associated directly with the content of the main clause, which means that without a main clause, we don't know what q should be. But I have shown above that the relationship between q and the main clause content is not as direct as this analysis would have it;

on my account, q follows from p and world knowledge or scripts. The main clause, for me, would be needed to provide information about the actual outcome of p; but, on the analysis as stated, it's not clear why this should be necessary. In any case, either of the possible analyses suggested here require additional evidence, which I don't at present have. I leave this issue for future research.

References

Asher, N. and M. Morreau. 1991. Commonsense Entailment: A Modal Theory of Nonmonotonic Reasoning. *Proceedings of the Twelfth International Joint Conference on Artificial Intelligence*, eds. J. Mylopoulos and R. Reiter, 387-392. Los Altos, CA: Morgan Kaufman.

Beck, S., T. Oda, and K. Sugisaki. 2004. Parametric Variation in the Semantics of Comparison: Japanese vs. English. *Journal of East Asian Linguistics* 13:289-344.

Halpern, J. Y. 2003. *Reasoning about Uncertainty*. Cambridge, MA: The MIT Press.

Koyano, T. 1997. Fukusi 'sekkaku' no yoohoo [Uses of the adverbial 'sekkaku']. *Nihongo, Nihonbunkakenkyuu [Studies in Japanese Language and Culture]*, Volume 7 of *Osaka Gaikokugodaigaku Nihongo Kooza [Osaka Foreign Language University Japanese Lectures]*. Osaka Foreign Language University.

Krifka, M. 1992. Thematic Relations as Links Between Nominal Reference and Event Domains. *Lexical Matters*, eds. I. Sag and A. Szabolcsi, 29-53. Stanford, CA: CSLI Publications.

McCready, E. 2004. Two Japanese Adverbials and Expressive Content. *Proceedings of Semantics and Linguistic Theory 14*, ed. R. Young, 163-178. Ithaca, NY: CLC Publications.

McCready, E. 2005. *The Dynamics of Particles*. Doctoral dissertation, University of Texas at Austin.

McCready, E. and N. Asher. 2006. Modal Subordination in Japanese. *Penn Working Papers in Linguistics 12.1*, eds. A. Eilam, T. Sheffler, and J. Tauberer, 237-249. Philadelphia, PA: PWPL.

Miller, P. To appear. Negative Complements in Direct Perception Reports. *Proceedings of Chicago Linguistics Society 39*.

Mitchell, J. 1986. *The Formal Semantics of Point of View*. Doctoral dissertation, University of Massachusetts at Amherst.

Watanabe, M. 2001. *Sasuga! Nihongo*. Tokyo: Chikuma Shinsho.

Verbs of the 'Put-On' Class and Their Peculiarity in Korean

MINJEONG SON
CASTL/University of Tromsø

1. Introduction[1]

Verbs of putting x on *one's body* are expressed in Korean by different lexical items depending on which body part is involved, as listed in (1).[2]

(1) a. ip-   'put x (e.g., clothes) on one's body'
     b. sin-   'put x (e.g., shoes) on one's feet'
     c. an-   'put x in one's arms'
     d. ep-   'put x on one's back'
     e. mwul-   'take x in one's mouth'
     f. ssu-   'put x (e.g., a hat, glasses) on one's head/face'

The verbs illustrated above are singled out as a separate verb class, i.e., verbs of the 'put-on' class (Son, To appear (a)), since their verbal behavior

---

[1] I would like to thank the organizers of the 15th Japanese/Korean Linguistics Conference in Wisconsin where this paper was presented and the audience of the conference for their comments and questions. I have also greatly benefited from the insightful comments, suggestions, and discussions with Satoshi Tomioka and Benjamin Bruening on this topic. All the shortcomings are my own.
[2] The list here is meant to be illustrative, not exhaustive.

is different from normal transitives in a number of constructions such as morphological causatives, morphological passives and the *-ko iss-* construction.[3]

The purpose of this paper is twofold: First, I provide explanations for the peculiar verbal behavior of verbs of the 'put-on' class. I shall argue that the peculiarity of these verbs, when occurring in the aforementioned constructions, is attributed to their syntactic and semantic properties that differ from normal transitive verbs. Secondly, I provide empirical support for a theory of syntactic decomposition of predicates by demonstrating that the peculiar verbal behavior of verbs of the 'put-on' class can only be explained by decomposing verbs into smaller syntactic pieces.

Section 2 illustrates how verbs of the 'put-on' class behave differently from normal transitives when they appear in morphological causatives, morphological passives, and an aspectual construction expressed by *-ko iss-*. In Section 3, I present the syntactic and semantic structure of verbs of the 'put-on' class, which postulates a locative-argument-introducing v_{APPL}. Section 4 demonstrates that the proposed syntactic and semantic structure of verbs of the 'put-on' class provides straightforward explanations for their peculiar argument structure patterns in the constructions mentioned above.

2. Peculiar Verbal Behavior of Verbs of the 'Put-On' Class

Let us first consider how verbs of the 'put-on' class are distinguished from normal transitive verbs (e.g., 'read') in terms of their argument structure realizations. One such difference is found in the argument structure of morphological causatives. When regular transitives are causativized, the causee, the agent of a non-causative counterpart, is realized as an agent, as in (2).[4]

(2) a. Ai-ka   chayk-ul   ilk-ess-ta.
     Child-NOM   book-ACC   read-PST-DC
     'The child read the book.'

    b. Inho-ka   ai-eykey   chayk-ul   ilk- *hi*-ess-ta.
     Inho-NOM   child-DAT   book-ACC   read-CAUSE-PST-DC
     'Inho made the child read the book.'

In (2b), the causee 'the child' is interpreted as an agent of reading a book, and the subject 'Mary' is interpreted as a causer that brings about the event

---

[3] Transitive verbs in comparison with verbs of the 'put-on' class are meant to be typical accomplishment verbs such as 'read' and 'destroy'.

[4] The causative suffix in Korean is realized in various forms, such as *-i, -hi, -li, -ki, -(i)wu, -kwu,* and *-chwu*. I will regard *-i* as the underlying form for these allomorphs.

— *the child read the book*. Thus, when a normal transitive sentence is causativized, thematic roles of the base sentence are retained in a causativized sentence. When verbs of the 'put-on' class are causativized, however, the causee, the agent of a non-causative counterpart, is realized as a location, rather than an agent. Consider (3), for example.[5]

(3) a. Inho-ka   wuntonghwa-lul   sin-ess-ta.
       Inho-NOM   sneakers-ACC   put.on.one's feet-PST-DC
       'Inho put the sneakers on (his feet).'

   b. Emma-ka   Inho-eykey   wuntonghwa-lul   sin-***ki***-ess-ta.
      Mother-NOM   Inho- DAT   sneakers-ACC   put.on-CAUSE-PST-DC
      'Mother put the sneakers on Inho's feet.'
      *'Mother made Inho put the sneakers on (his feet).'

As seen in (3b), the agent of (3a), *Inho*, is no longer interpreted as an agent when the sentence is causativized. Rather, it is understood to be a location where the sneakers end up at the end of the event.

Further differences between verbs of the 'put-on' class and normal transitive verbs are found in morphological HI passives and the *-ko iss-* construction. When these two constructions are associated with verbs of the 'put-on' class, derived predicates bear atypical argument structures.

Let us first consider morphological passives in which passive verbs associated with verbs of the 'put-on' class involve an argument structure that differs from normal transitives. In proto-typical passive constructions, thematic roles of the arguments are invariant regardless of whether the event involving them is expressed in the active or in the passive, as in (4).[6]

(4) a. Kwunin-tul-i   nalkun   cip-ul   hel-ess-ta.
       Soldier-PL-NOM   old   house-ACC   demolish-PST-DC
       'The soldiers demolished the old house.'

   b. Nalkun cip-i   kwunin-tul-eykey   hel-***li***-ess-ta.
      Old   house-NOM   soldier-PL-DAT   demolish-PASS-PST-DC
      'The old house was demolished by the soldiers.'

The sentences in (4) illustrate a regular active-passive alternation; when the verb *hel-* 'demolish' is suffixed with *-hi*, the theme of the active sentence is made a subject by passivization, and the agent is expressed in an optional

---

[5] Due to the different semantics of the causee in (2) and (3), a number of researchers (e.g., Kim 1998) divide morphological causatives into two types. See Son (To appear (b)) for further details.

[6] The passive suffix in Korean is realized in four different forms,-*i, -hi, -li,* and *-ki.* I consider *-hi* as the underlying form of these allomorphs, distinguished from the causative morpheme *-i.*

'by' phrase (-*eykey*-marked in Korean). The thematic roles of the arguments in (4) thus are invariant regardless of the different syntactic position of the arguments and different verbal morphology. However, when a member of the 'put-on' verbs are combined with the passive morpheme, the passive verb bear an argument structure that differs from normal transitives; the agent and the theme of the corresponding active sentence are realized in the passive as a location and an agent respectively. Consider (5), for example.

(5) a. Inho-ka   kikkei   ai-lul   ep-ess-ta.
       Inho-NOM   willingly   child-ACC   put.on.one's back-PST-DC
       'Inho willingly put the child on his back.'

    b. Ai-ka   kikkei   Inho-eykey   ep-*hi*-ess-ta.
       Child-NOM   willingly   Inho-DAT   put.on-PASS-PST-DC
       'The child willingly *got on* Inho's back.'
       *'The child was willingly put on Inho's back by Inho.'

As seen above, the agent of the active sentence in (5a), *Inho*, is no longer interpreted as an agent in (5b). Rather, it is understood to be a location where the subject 'the child' is situated at the end of the event. Furthermore, despite the passive morphology on the verb, the surface subject in (5b) is interpreted as a volitional agent, rather than a theme, given that the agent-oriented adverb 'willingly is associated with the surface subject.[7]

Another type of construction in which verbs of the 'put-on' class are found to be distinguished from normal transitives is the aspectual construction expressed by -*ko iss*-. The auxiliary verb -*ko iss*- is a combination of a non-finite connective morpheme -*ko* and the aspectual auxiliary verb *iss*- 'be'. The auxiliary verb -*ko iss*- can attach to various verbal roots. When it combines with an accomplishment verb, as in (6), it is prototypically used as a periphrastic aspectual marker which expresses a continuing process.

(6) Inho-ka   chayk-ul   ilk-*ko*   *iss*-ta.
    Inho-NOM   book-ACC   read-KO   be-DC
    'Inho is reading a book.'

Therefore, -*ko iss*- has generally been treated as a progressive marker, comparable to *be -ing* in English. However, when -*ko iss*- combines with verbs of the 'put-on' class, it can also express a continuation of a result state, un-

---

[7] On the basis of the semantic difference between (5a) and (5b), it has often been argued (e.g., Park 2001) that the combination of the verb and -*hi* in (5b) is formed in the lexicon, and that the surface subject is base-generated as an external argument, a unergative (lexical) approach. See Son (To appear (a)) for arguments against the lexical approach to HI-Passives.

like the English *be -ing*. Example (7), for instance, is ambiguous between a progressive and a result-state interpretation.

(7) Inho-ka   wundonghwa-ul sin-ko   iss-ta.
     Inho-NOM   sneaker-ACC   put.on-KO be-DC
    a. 'Inho is putting the sneakers on.'   (Progressive)
    b. 'Inho is wearing the sneakers.'   (Result-State)

As in (7a), when *-ko iss-* is used as a progressive marker, the sentence is interpreted as an on-going *process* which involves a dynamic and durative action of the agent. In contrast, when *-ko iss-* is used as an aspectual marker denoting a result state, as in (7b), the event denoted by the verb, 'putting on the sneakers', is completed at a prior time, and the result state of 'wearing them' holds at the utterance time.

We have seen thus far that verbs of the 'put-on' class in Korean show argument structure patterns that differ from normal transitive verbs in morphological causatives, morphological passives and the *-ko iss-* construction. The question that immediately arises then is what makes the verbs of the 'put-on' class differ from normal transitive verbs in their argument structure realizations. I argue that the distinction between verbs of the 'put-on' class and normal transitives in their verbal behavior is due to differences in their underlying syntactic and semantic structures.

3. The Syntax and Semantics of Verbs of the 'Put-On' Class

The analysis propounded in this paper adopts the framework of Distributed Morphology (Halle and Marantz 1994), according to which syntactic categories are purely abstract, having no phonological content. Only after syntax are phonological expressions, called Vocabulary Items, inserted in a process called Spell-Out, i.e., Late Insertion. I also assume, following Marantz (1997), that words to be category-less concepts, i.e., roots ($\sqrt{}$) (to adopt the terminology of Pesetsky 1995). They gain their categorical status by being associated with a functional head that determines their word category. For example, a verb is a root whose nearest c-commanding head is *v*. Another crucial assumption made in this paper is that there exist variants of *v* that determine eventiveness and argument structure of a sentence. These variants include v_{CAUSE}, v_{DO}, v_{INCHO} and v_{BE}, which roughly reflect semantic primitives that are drawn from a conceptual inventory provided by UG (cf. Harley and Noyer 2000).[8]

On the basis of the assumptions outlined above and a theory of syntactic decomposition of predicates (e.g., Hale and Keyser 1993), I analyze verbs of the 'put-on' class to be syntactic constructs, rather than syntactic

---

[8] See Son (2006) for detailed discussion of the variants of *v* and their semantic contribution.

atoms. The verb *sin-* 'put x on one's feet', for example, is not treated as a syntactic atom that enters into the syntax as a whole. Rather, it can be decomposed into smaller syntactic parts (or morphemes), namely a verb root, $\sqrt{sin}$, and an abstract verbal head, v_{APPL} that introduces a locative argument. The root projection ($\sqrt{P}$) denotes a core meaning component of the verb (e.g., *putting a shirt*), while $v_{APPL}P$ expresses where the theme is located at the end of the event. I further argue that verbs of the 'put-on' class do not require an external-argument-introducing verbal head, similar to the syntactic configuration of unaccusative verbs. Normal transitives, however, require an external-argument-introducing v, i.e., v_{DO}, which requires the DP in its specifier to be interpreted as an agent. Example (8) gives an illustration of the syntactic and semantic structure of each verb type.[9]

(8) a. Representation of Verbs of the 'Put-On' Class

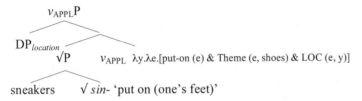

b. Representation of Normal (accomplishment) Transitives

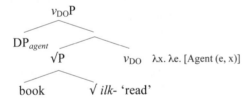

As seen in (8), verbs of the 'put-on' class and normal transitives have different syntactic configurations. Normal transitives are constructed by merging $\sqrt{P}$ with v_{DO}, the semantics of which is equivalent to Kratzer's (Kratzer 1996) Voice, as illustrated in (8b). On the other hand, verbs of the 'put-on' class are constructed by merging $\sqrt{P}$ with v_{APPL}, rather than v_{DO}, as in (8a). v_{APPL} denotes a relation between an individual and the event denoted by $\sqrt{P}$. The argument introduced by v_{APPL} is a positional endpoint of the theme, i.e., a location.[10]

---

[9] I assume that the entire verbal phrase is further embedded under a tense projection with the possibility of intervening aspectual/mood functional projections.
[10] The postulation of v_{APPL} in (8a) is motivated by the intrinsic meaning of the verbs of the 'put-on' class. See Son (2006) for further explanations.

It is important to note that verbs of the 'put-on' class in Korean are ambiguous between two meanings, an eventive meaning (e.g., (3a)), and a stative meaning, in which the subject is non-agentive. Consider (9), for example.

(9) Inho-ka   wuntonghwa-lul   sin-ess-ta.
    Inho-NOM   sneakers-ACC   put.on.one's feet-PST-DC
    a. 'Inho put the sneakers on (his feet).'
    b. 'Inho wore the sneakers (or Inho had the sneakers on his feet).'

Example (9) can describe either a dynamic event, in which *Inho* put on the sneakers, or a simple state, in which *Inho* had the sneakers on (his feet). With the eventive meaning, the subject *Inho* is interpreted as an agent and a location where the sneakers end up at the end of the action. With the stative meaning, the subject loses agentivity and is interpreted only as a location. The sentences in (10) with adverbial modification show further evidence that example (9) has two possible interpretations.

(10) a. Inho-ka   ku   wundonghwa-lul halwucongil sin-ess-ta.
        Inho-NOM   the   sneakers-ACC   all day   put.on-PST-DC
        'Inho wore the sneakers all day.'
        *'Inho put on the sneakers all day.'

    b. Inho-ka   ku   wundonghwa-lul himtulkey   sin-ess-ta.
       Inho-NOM   the   sneakers-ACC   with difficulty put.on-PST-DC
       'Inho put on the sneakers in a difficult manner.'
       *'Inho wore the sneakers in a difficult manner.'

I posit two different syntactic structures for the ambiguity shown in (9). I argue that the structure given in (8a) gives rise to the stative reading in (9b). This explains the non-agentive property of the subject in (9b), the structure of which is given in (11).

(11) Representation of (9b): Stative Meaning

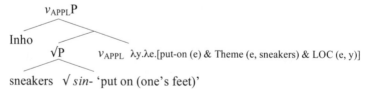

As seen in (11), the subject is base-generated as a location introduced by v_{APPL} and moves to the subject position, e.g., [Spec, TP], to satisfy the EPP feature of T. The structure in (11) then accounts for the non-agentive property of the subject when the verb has a stative interpretation (i.e., 'wear').

In order to produce the eventive meaning in (9a), in which the subject bears two thematic roles, agent and location, I argue that $v_{APPL}P$ merges with v_{RFL}, which, like other eventive verbal heads, introduces an agent argument and denotes an agentive event. What is unique about v_{RFL}, however is that its semantics specifies that the agent is identified with a location. In a technical semantic term, v_{RFL} in its semantics selects an open predicate with an unsaturated individual argument and states that the agent introduced by v_{RFL} is identified with this argument. This is formally represented in (12).

(12) v_{RFL} (with verbs of the 'put-on' class)
 $\lambda P_{<e,<s,t>>} \lambda x. \lambda e.$ ∃e' [P (e' ,x) & Agent (e,x) & CAUSE (e, e')]

v_{RFL} requires a predicate of type $<e <s,t>>$ as its argument and returns a predicate of the same type (i.e., $<e<s,t>>$). Due to its semantic specification, upon merging with $v_{APPL}P$ in (8a), v_{RFL} enforces a syntactic detransitivization of the $v_{APPL}P$, as shown in (13).

(13) Representation of sin- 'put on one's feet': Eventive Meaning

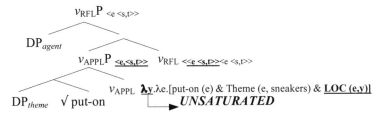

As seen in (13), no syntactic argument is projected in the specifier position of v_{APPL}. Were it to be projected, this would result in a type mismatch between v_{RFL} and $v_{APPL}P$; if the locative argument is saturated within the domain of $v_{APPL}P$, the $v_{APPL}P$ ends up with type $<s,t>$, a function from an event to a truth value. However, v_{RFL} requires an argument of type $<e<s,t>>$. A fully specified syntactic and semantic representation of the eventive sin- 'put on one's feet' in (9a) is given in (14).

(14) Representation of (9a): Eventive Meaning

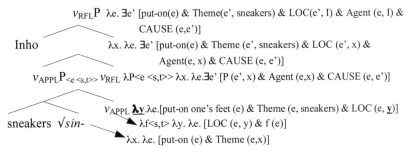

Since no DP is projected by v_{APPL}, the locative argument in the semantics of v_{APPL} remains unsaturated when we get to the interpretation of v_{APPL}P. By combining v_{APPL}P with v_{RFL}, the unsaturated argument, the location, is identified with the agent selected by v_{RFL}. These two semantic arguments then are saturated by the DP projected by v_{RFL}, *Inho*, and we arrive at the intended reading that *Inho* is both the agent and the location of the event.

In the following section, I shall show that the syntactic and semantic structure proposed for verbs of the 'put-on' class provide straightforward explanations for their argument structure patterns in morphological causatives and the *-ko iss-* construction in comparison to those of normal transitive verbs.[11]

4. Morphological Causatives and The *-ko iss-* Construction

On the basis of the syntactic structures posited for verbs of the 'put-on' class and normal transitives in (8), the different semantics of the causee in morphological causatives (e.g., (2) and (3)) can be accounted for straightforwardly. I assume that morphological causatives are produced by merging v_{CAUSE} with the underlying structure of base predicates, namely v_{APPL}P and v_{DO}P, as illustrated below.

(15) a. Verbs of 'put-on' (e.g., 3b) b. Normal Transitives (e.g., 2b)

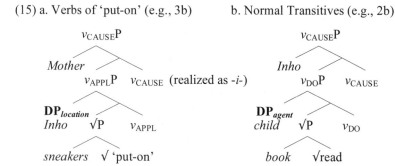

As shown in (15b), v_{CAUSE} in causatives with normal transitive bases takes an agentive-event-denoting v_{DO}P as its complement. This explains why the causee receives the agent thematic role; since the agent is explicitly expressed in the underlying structure of the base predicate, the external argument introduced by v_{CAUSE} cannot receive an agent interpretation but is interpreted as a causer. As illustrated in (15a), v_{CAUSE} in causatives with verbs of the 'put-on' class takes v_{APPL}P as its complement. This explains the thematic role of the causee as a location, rather than an agent. The semantics of

---

[11] Due to space limitations, I omit the discussion of morphological passives in this paper. Readers of interest in this matter are referred to Son (To appear (a)).

the causee as a location when verbs of the 'put-on' class are causativized thus is explained by the underlying syntactic configuration of these verbs that differs from normal transitives.

The analysis of the interpretative difference of *-ko iss-* advanced here relies on differences in the semantic and syntactic structure of a base verb with which the aspectual marker combines; whether or not verbs create ambiguity of *-ko iss-* hinges upon the possibility of a base verb having an ambiguity (i.e., different syntactic structures). We have seen earlier that verbs of the 'put-on' class are ambiguous between a stative and an eventive meaning, and that there exist two different syntactic structures available for these verbs. Normal transitive verbs, in contrast, are not ambiguous and thus have a single syntactic structure. Once the semantic-syntactic structures of 'put-on' verbs and transitive verbs discussed above are adopted, explanations for the ambiguity and non-ambiguity of *-ko iss-* follow straightforwardly.

Ambiguity of *-ko iss-* between a progressive and a result state is to be accounted for in terms of a functional head, realized as *-ko*, attaching to different syntactic structures that already exist for a base verb; the ambiguity of *-ko iss-* is attributed to two different structures available for verbs of the 'put-on' class, as shown in (16). I assume that *-ko* and *iss-* each projects its own functional phrases. Let us call *-ko* some type of Functional Phrase. I assume that the projection headed by the aspectual auxiliary verb *iss-* 'be' is an Aspectual Phrase (AspP).[12]

(16) Ambiguity of *-ko iss-* with Verbs of the 'Put-On' Class

a. *-ko iss-* (Progressive: 7a)   b. *-ko iss-* (Result State: 7b)

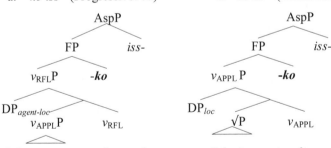

Inho is putting on the sneakers.   Inho is wearing the sneakers.

As seen in (16), the ambiguity of *-ko iss-* builds straightforwardly on the structural difference between a stative and an eventive interpretation of verbs of the 'put-on' class (e.g., (11) and (13)). I assume that *-ko* is seman-

---

[12] The analysis of the ambiguity of *-ko iss-* presented here is slightly modified from Son (To appear (c)).

tically vacuous and has only a syntactic function that picks out an eventuality-denoting constituent. The aspectual auxiliary *iss-* denotes a continuance of an eventuality picked out by *-ko*. Therefore, although the progressive and the result-state interpretations denoted by *-ko iss-* may be thought to be very distinct, they in fact have something in common; their commonality lies in the fact that they both focus on a durative situation, whether dynamic or static, that persists/holds at reference time. I argue that the result-state interpretation of *-ko iss-* (e.g., 7b) is a result of merging *-ko* with v_{APPL}P that denotes a state, rather than an (agentive) event. The *-ko iss-* construction represented in (16b) expresses a continuation of an eventuality denoted by the constituent picked out by *-ko*; the *state* of Inho wearing the sneakers continues at the reference time. The structure given in (16b) then accounts for the non-agentive property of the subject when *-ko iss-* is associated with a (result)-state. As seen in (16a), when *-ko iss-* merges with v_{RFL}P that contains an external argument, the sentence denotes a continuance of a dynamic event, rather than a (result) state; the *event* of Inho putting on the sneakers continues at the time of the utterance, which yields a progressive meaning. The presence of v_{RFL} in the structure then explains the agentive nature of the subject associated with the progressive interpretation.

With respect to normal transitives, there exists only one syntactic structure, unlike verbs of the 'put-on' class. Thus, *-ko* can only merge with the existing structure. This explains the non-ambiguity of the aspectual marker when normal transitive verbs are involved, as shown in (17).

(17) Normal Transitives: No Ambiguity, Only Progressive Meaning

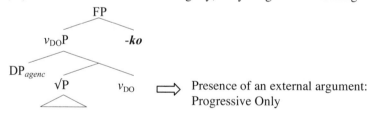

⟹ Presence of an external argument:
Progressive Only

5. Conclusion

This paper has shown that verbs of putting something on one's body part in Korean are singled out as a separate verb class due to their distinct verbal behavior in a number of constructions. I argued that the peculiar verbal behavior of these verbs is attributed to their syntactic and semantic properties that differ from normal transitive verbs; by adopting a theory of syntactic decomposition of predicates, I argued that verbs of the 'put-on' class are constructed by merging roots with v_{APPL} that introduces a locative argument, while normal (accomplishment) transitives are constructed by merging roots with an agent-argument-introducing v, i.e., v_{DO}. I further showed that verbs of the 'put-on' class are ambiguous between 'wear' and 'put-on' and posited two different syntactic structures for each verbal meaning. The current analysis of the verbs of the 'put-on' class has been shown to provide straightforward explanations for the argument structure patterns of morphological causatives and the ambiguity of -ko iss-, the phenomena of which have been considered to be independent from each other in the previous literature.

References

Hale, K. and Keyser, J.1993. On Argument Structure and the Lexical Expression of Syntactic Relations. *The View from Building 20: A Festschrift for Sylvain Bromberger,* eds. K. Hale and J. Keyster, 53-108. Cambridge: MIT Press.

Halle, M. and A. Marantz. 1994. Distributed Morphology. *The View from Building 20,* eds. K. Hale and J. Keyser. Cambridge: MIT Press.

Harley, H. and R. Noyer. 2000. Formal vs. Encyclopedic Properties of Vocabulary: Evidence from Nominalizations. *The Lexicon-Encyclopedia Interface,* ed. B. Peeters, 349-374. Amsterdam: Elsevier.

Kim, A. R. 1998. VP Complement of HI-Causative. *Japanese/Korean Linguistics 8,* ed. D. Silva, 445-458. Stanford: CSLI.

Kratzer, A. 1996. Severing the External Argument from its Verb. *Phrase Structure and lexicon,* eds. J. Rooryck and L. Zaring, 109-137. Dordrecht: Kluwer.

Marantz, A. 1997. No Escape from Syntax: Don't Try Morphological Analysis in the Privacy of Your Own Lexicon. *Proceedings of the 21st Penn Linguistics Colloquium.* University of Pennsylvania, Philadelphia, PA.

Park, S.D. 2001. Passive Constructions in Korean. *Harvard Studies in Korean Linguistics* IX:640-649

Pesetsky, D. 1995. *Zero Syntax.* Cambridge: MIT Press.

Son, M.J. 2004. The Syntax and Semantics of the Aspectual Marker -ko iss- in Korean. *Proceedings of the West Coast Conference on Formal Linguistics* 23, eds. V. Chand, A. Kelleher, A. Rodriguez and B. Schmeiser, 745-758. Somerville, MA: Cascadilla Press.

Son, M.J. 2006a. Causation and Syntactic Decomposition of Predicates. Doctoral Dissertation, University of Delaware.

Son, M.J. 2006b. Atypical Argument Structure of HI Passive in Korean. *Penn Working Papers* 12.1., eds. A. Eilam, T. Scheffler and J. Tauberer, 335-348.

Son, M.J. To appear. A Unified Syntactic Account of Morphological Causatives in Korean. *Proceedings of the 13th Japanese/Korean Linguistics.* Stanford: CSLI

Two Types of Modal Auxiliaries in Japanese: Two Directionalities in Inference

YUKINORI TAKUBO

Kyoto University

1. Introduction[1]

Modal auxiliaries in Japanese that express propositional modality have traditionally been classified into two subclasses: epistemic modals that include *daroo* (would), *hazuda* (should), *nitigainai* (must), *kamosirenai* (possible) henceforth the *daroo*-class modals, and evidential modals that include *yooda* (it appears), *rasii* (it seems), and possibly, *sooda1* (I hear) and *sooda2* (looks like), henceforth the *yooda*-class.[2] The distinction is based on the existence of overt evidence on which to base the inference for *yooda*-

---

[1] We thank Shigeru Sakahara, Hiroshi Mito, Tomohide Kinuhata and Matt Berends for pointing out various problems in the paper and improving the styles. This work is supported in part by JSPS Research Grant, Basic Research (B) No. 16320053 and Basic Research (A) No. 15202009.

[2] We use the term 'modal auxiliary' following the traditions of Japanese linguistics, although Japanese modals do not exhibit properties separating them from other predicates. We will also use 'modal predicates' or simply 'modals'.

class, as opposed to its absence for *daroo*-class (Miyake 1995, Morimoto 1994, Oshika 1995, Takubo 2001, Teramura 1984).

In this paper, we will first introduce some new facts concerning the distributional differences between the two sub-classes and propose structural differences that account for their distribution. We will then argue that the distinction among these two types of modals is related to the directionality of inference, which we express as a generalized form of modus ponens (i.e. inference of the pattern, $P{\rightarrow}Q$, $P \models Q$)), and its inverse. We will relate the differences in the direction of inference to the nature of the complement that they take and what the entire sentence, with the modal as head, denotes.

2. The Two Classes of Modals

2.1. Scopal Properties

The two subclasses differ in their scopal properties. *Daroo*-class modals must not include the conditional premise in their scope. In (1), only the consequent may be asserted.[3]

(1) Kootei buai-ga   sagar-eba, keiki-ga   yokunaru.
     Official-discount-NOM fall-if,   economy-NOM become-good
     Daroo
     would.
     'If the official discount rate goes down, the economy would improve.'

Yooda-class modals must include the premise in their scope, and thus can only serve as an assertion of a general conditional statement rather than a conditional inference (see (2)).

(2) Kootei buai-ga   sagar-eba, keiki-ga   yokunaru
     Official-discount-NOM fall-if,   economy-NOM become-good
     yooda.
     {appear. seem}

     'It appears (to be the case) that if the official discount rate goes down,

---

[3] *Daroo* has a non-epistemic usage, which allows a wh-word or a focused constituent in the premise, as in (i).

  (i) A: Kono natu **nani-o** ur-eba ii *daroo*.
     this summer-ACC sell-if good would
     'What do you think we should sell this summer.'
    B: **Eakon-o**   ur-eba ii *daroo*.
     air-conditioner-ACC sell good would
     'I think we should sell air conditioners.'

This usage is not possible with the other modals in the *daroo*-class. The conditional ending -*nara*, which never permits focus in the premise, can be used in stead of -*reba* ending to limit *daroo* to its epistemic usage. *Nara* conditionals cannot be used with *yooda*-class, as expected. See Takubo (2006) and references therein for further discussion.

the economy will improve (accordingly).'

That the two subclasses differ in their scope properties is further supported by the following facts. With *daroo*-class auxiliaries, the antecedent and the consequent in the conditional statement (1) can each be expressed by different speakers as in (3).

(3) A: Kootei buai-ga   sagatta-yo.
     Official-discount-NOM   fell- SFP
     'The official discount rate has been lowered.'

     B: Zya, keiki-ga   yokunaru   *daroo*.
        then economy-NOM   become-good would
        'Then, the economy would improve.'

Thus with *daroo*-class modals, the premise need not be included in the assertion of the sentence. With *yooda*-class, the assertion involves the conditional relation between the antecedent and the consequent, i.e., the conditionals involved denote a generic statement. So the consequent cannot be uttered independently of the antecedent. If they are separately asserted as in (4), the result is unacceptable.

(4) A: Kootei buai-ga   sagatta-yo.
     Official-discount-NOM   fell- SFP
     'The official discount rate has been cut down.'

     B: ??Zya, keiki-ga   yokunaru   *yooda*.
        then economy-NOM   become-good   appear
        'Lit. Then, the economy appears to improve.'

The distributional facts observed above can be accounted for if we assume that with *daroo*-class modals, the conditional premise is outside the scope of the modal and that with *yooda*-class, they are within its scope. Thus the structure of sentence (1) will be like (5) and that of (2) like (6), respectively.

(5) [Kootei buai-ga sagar-eba [[keiki-ga yokunaru] *daroo*]].
     'If the official discount rate goes down, the economy would improve.'

(6) [[Kootei buai-ga sagar-eba, keiki-ga   yoku naru] *yooda*].
     'It appears (to be the case) that if the official discount rate goes down, the economy will improve (accordingly).'

2.2. Inferential Properties

In this subsection, we show that the scopal differences between the two subclasses can be characterized in terms of the nature of inference involved.

The inference involved in the *daroo*-class is deductive, i.e., sentences headed by *daroo*-class modals are interpreted as the conclusion of the modus ponens deduced by the speaker. In the case of example (1), the major premise is the knowledge on the part of the speaker of the relation between interest rates and economy.

(7) Major premise: If the official discount rate is lowered, economy improves.
Minor premise: Official discount rate has been cut down.

Conclusion: Economy improves.

Daroo-class modals are attached to the conclusion inferred, given the major premise and the minor premise. The major premise is some general knowledge presupposed in the discourse and the minor premise can be given anew by the conversational partner. Given the nature of deductive inference, the major and minor premise are presupposed, and constitute old information, while the conclusion is asserted and constitutes new information. In terms of the informational structure, the conditional sentences with *daroo*-class auxiliaries can be represented as follows.

(8) [Kootei buai-ga sagar-eba, [[keiki-ga yokunaru] *daroo*]].

Old	New

'If the official discount rate has been cut down, the economy would improve.'

The informational structure we posit for *daroo*-class modals follows from our assumption that the conclusion is added anew to the knowledge base of the speaker by deductive inference.

The scopal properties proposed for *daroo*-class modals can be supported by facts concerning the expression *imagoro*. *Imagoro* denotes a counterpart of the utterance time on some time scale, as in *asita no imagoro,* (tomorrow at about this time). It can be used in referring to the utterance time itself when it identifies the time of an event displaced from the deictic location as in (9).

(9) John-wa   *imagoro* Seoul-ni   tuiteiru   *daroo.*
     John-TOP   about now Seoul-LOC   has-arrived would
     'John would have arrived in Seoul about this time.'

John's arrival in Seoul is the conclusion of the speaker based on some knowledge, e.g. his itinerary. The inference involved can also be expressed as a generalized form of modus ponens. An itinerary can be expressed as a function $f(t)=e$, i.e., a function from a set of time points to a set of events. Thus given the knowledge of an itinerary and a time point t_i, one can infer e_j at t_i. Here the time point is given but the event is conjectured. Modals in Japanese can associate a focus with a constituent in its scope, i.e., the constituents in its c-command domain.

The focused constituent receives a phonological salience and starts a phonological phrase. In (9), the expression for e may receive phonological salience. There must be an intonational break between *imagoro* and *Seoul-ni* in (9) and *imagoro* never receives phonological salience. The salience rather falls instead either on *Seoul-ni* or *tuiteiru*, suggesting that *imagoro* is not in the scope of *daroo*. The phonological phrasing may be represented as in (10), with the syntactic structure as in (11).

(10) {John-wa}   {imagoro} {Seoul-ni tuiteiru *daroo*}.

(11) [John-wa   [imagoro [[Seoul-ni tuiteiru] *daroo*]]].

In contrast, the inference involved in the *yooda*-class is abductive and identifies x, given y, namely f^1, which is the inverse function of f. Since x may not be uniquely determined given y, the inference only provides a most plausible candidate for explaining y in the context of utterance and is defeasible. Look at the situation in (12).

(12) Situation: Taroo looks at the newly published alumni newsletter and finds that one of his classmates has changed her surname.

    a. Kanozyo-wa   kekkon-sita   *yooda*.
         she-TOP   married   appear
        'It appears that she has got married.'

    b. #Kanozyo-wa   kekkon-sita   *daroo*.
         she-TOP   married   would
        'She would have gotten married.'

The knowledge used in the inference is the general practice in Japan about women changing names after marriage. The inference obviously is not modus ponens, because one cannot deduce from the knowledge that a woman has changed her name, that she has gotten married. In fact, *daroo* or *kamosirenai* cannot be used here, as shown by the inappropriateness of (12b). The inference involved is abduction, i.e., the inverse of deduction; which identifies a possible minor premise, given major premise and the consequent, involving the identification of a most probable candidate for causing the situation in question based on some general knowledge.

That *yooda*-class modals involve abductive inference can be further illustrated by the use of *imagoro*. With *yooda*-class modals, *imagoro* must be focused, with obligatory phonological emphasis on it as in (13).

(13) John-wa   ***IMAGORO*** Seoul-ni   tuita {*yooda/rasii*}.
     John-TOP   about now   Seoul-LOC   arrived {appear/seem}

The intonational pattern shows that *IMAGORO Seoul-ni tuita yooda* forms one phonological phrase, with the peak on *IMAGORO*, and gradually falling toward the end of the sentence including the modal, suggesting that *IMAGORO* is within the scope of *yooda* and receives focus. The phonological facts can be described if *yooda*-class modals utilize the inverse function, making it necessary to place focus on time. *Imagoro* used in *daroo*-class modals involves identification of an event e_j, given some general knowledge $f(t)=e$, and time t_i. We propose that with *yooda*-class modals, the inverse function $f^{-1}(e)=t$ is involved, which gives time given f and e. The new information, therefore, is the time point; with an event and the general knowledge being presupposed, giving an informational structure similar to pseudo-cleft, i.e. 'the time that John arrived in Seoul is this time (and not the time expected).' The informational structure and the intonational pattern can be accounted for if we assume the structure (14), with IMAGORO within the scope of *yooda*-class modals, which can be mapped to the phonological phrasing represented in (15).

(14) [John-wa [[*IMAGORO* Seoul-ni tuita] {*rasii/yooda*}]]

(15) {John-wa} { *IMAGORO* Seoul-ni tuita rasii/yooda}

The scope facts about conditionals can be accounted for in the same way. The whole conditional 'if p then q' must be in the scope of *yooda*-class modal as in (16).

(16) [[if p then q] {*rasii/yooda*}].

Unlike *imagoro*, which requires obligatory focus, the focus can be placed on any constituent within the scope. Given the abductive nature of *yooda*, 'if p then q' can be interpreted as providing an explanation for observed facts, say p & q. 'If p, then q-*yooda*' can then be understood as providing a major premise, or some general knowledge which serves to account for observed facts, the minor premise and the conclusion. Thus, (16) may be taken to express inductive inference.

2.3. Abduction in *Daroo*-class: *No* as a Scope Expansion Marker

In the preceding subsection, we have seen that *daroo*-class modals and *yooda*-class modals differ in the direction of inference involved, deduction in the former and abduction and induction in the latter. There is, however, a set of facts that seem to run counter to the generalization we have just made. If *daroo* is changed to *no-daroo*, abductive interpretation becomes possible as in (17).

(17) a. Kanozyo-wa kekkon-sita *no-daroo.*
          she-TOP   married   **no**-daroo (would)
          'It would be case that she has gotten married.'

b. Kanozyo-wa kekkon-sita (no) *nitigainai.*
she-TOP   married   **(no)**-must
'She must have gotten married.'

c. Kanozyo-wa kekkon-sita *no-da.*
she-TOP   married   **no**-copula
'It would be case that she has gotten married.'

Conditionals can also be in the scope of these modals, suggesting that they allow induction interpretation.

(18) [[Kootei buai-ga sagar-eba, keiki-ga   yokunaru] *no daroo*].
'It must be the case that if the official discount rate goes down, the economy will improve (accordingly).'

Morphologically, *no-daroo* can be considered to be the combination of *no*, a complementizer, and *daroo*. *No* places the preceding sentence in the scope of modals, thereby serving as a scope expansion marker. *Nitigainai* is more or less in free variation with *no nitigainai*, so it can be treated in the same way as *no-daroo* with regard to its scope properties. *Kamosirenai* generally must be preceded by *no* to allow scope expansion. We will call those *daroo*-class modals that allow abductive interpretation *daroo*-class b and those that do not, *daroo*-class a, for ease of reference.

One may conclude from these observations that the differences between the two classes of propositional modals lie in their scopal properties: *yooda*-class modals are wider than *daroo*-class modals, while the scope of the latter can be expanded by *no*. One may further like to reduce the difference in the directionality in inference to the scopal properties, by saying that narrow scope modals induce deduction and wide scope modals induce abduction or induction.

In the next section, we will show that the differences in the two types of modals cannot be reduced to their scope properties and that the *daroo*-class b has properties distinct from *yooda*-class. We will also show that the two classes differ in their reference to the knowledge base and the type of conclusion to be reached.

3. The Nature of Abductive Inference in *Yooda*-class Modals

The nature of minor premise is different in *yooda*-class and *daroo*-class b. For *daroo*-class b, as in *daroo*-class a, the speaker need not know the information expressed in the minor premise beforehand and it can be provided by the conversation partner. The speaker, therefore, may not be committed to the truth of the premise. *Zya* is a discourse connective used to indicate that the conclusion is based upon the premise that the conversational partner has just provided, indicating that the information was unknown to the speaker prior to the discourse session.

(19) A: Keiki-ga   yokunatta-yo.
economy-NOM   became-good -SFP
'The economy has been improving.'

B: *Zya*, kooteibuai-ga   sagatta
then official-discount-NOM fell
{*nodaroo, nitigainai/??daroo,kamosirenai*}
{it is that, it would be that, must/ would, could }.
'Then, the official discount rate must have been cut down.'

(20)   **Major premise** (general knowledge) :
If the official discount rate goes down, economy improves.
Minor premise: provided by the hearer
Economy improves

Conclusion by abduction:
Official discount rate has been cut down.

In contrast, *yooda*-class modals cannot be used with a sentence beginning with *zya*, indicating that the minor premise may not be provided by the conversational partner.[4]

(21) A: keiki-ga   yokunatta-yo.
economy-NOM   become-good -SFP
'The economy has been improving.'

B: *Zya*, kooteibuai-ga   sagatta {*??yooda, ??rasii*}.
Official-discount-NOM fell   {appear, seem}
'?Then, the official discount rate seems to have been cut down.'

Both the minor premise and the conclusion of the abductive inference must be provided by one speaker for *yooda*-class modals to be used.

(22) B: Kooteibuai-ga   sagatta {*yooda, rasii*}.
Official-discount-NOM fell   {appear, seem}
'The official discount rate seems have been cut down.'

A: Doosite.
why
'What is your ground for saying that?'

B: Keiki-ga   yokunatta.
economy-NOM   become-good
'The economy has been improving.'

In (22), B's utterance 'Kootei buai-ga sagatta {*yooda, rasii*}' is the conclu-

---

[4] The major premise cannot be provided by the conversational participant as a form of induction, either.

sion abductively drawn from the observation 'keiki-ga yokunatta.' The premise from which the conclusion is drawn must be B's own observation and cannot be provided by the conversational partner.

In the next section, we will show how the constraints on inference in the two types of modals can be expressed.

4. Evidential Nature of *Yooda*-class and Epistemic Nature of *Daroo*-class Modals

In this section we will show that all the characteristics of *yooda*-class modals can be derived if we assume that sentences with *yooda*-class modals, i.e., p-*yooda*, p-*rasii*, and possibly p-*sooda1* and p-*sooda2*, describe the current situations which are perceptible situation, i.e. that part of the speaker's reality in which the speaker knows the truth of all the propositions.[5]

We say that a proposition is 'settled' when its truth has already been objectively determined by the actual situation at hand (although the speaker may not know it).[6] When the speaker knows a proposition by past experience or deictically by perception, we say that s/he 'd-knows' it, and the proposition d-known to the speaker will be called a 'd-proposition'. D-propositions are all settled. We argue that unlike *daroo*-class modals, *yooda*-class modals express d-propositions and are not really modals that involve quantification over possible worlds, and that the inferential force comes from somewhere else.[7]

4.1. Evidential Nature of Y*ooda*-class Modals

We propose that A to be the definitive characteristics of *yooda*-class modals. In what follows we use YOODA as a cover term for '*yooda*-class modals'.

A. The proposition expressed by 'p-*YOODA*' must be a d-proposition.

Saito (2006) proposes that the following constraints hold between the complement of *yooda* and *rasii* and the whole sentences including the modals.[8]

---

[5] Miyake (1995) claims that *yooda*-class modals, within which he includes *yooda, rasii, mitaida, sooda*, and *toyuu*, express what he calls 'zissyooteki handan (empirical judgment),' that is, judgment based upon what the speaker experienced, and tries to relate the directionalities inference in evidential modals in Japanese to the type of judgment involved. Oshika (1995) makes similar observations.

[6] Cf. Kaufmann (2005) for more formal and precise definition of this notion.

[7] *Daroo*-class can co-occur with adverbs of quantification such as tabun (probably), kitto (certainly) , *osoraku* (perhaps), cannot modify *yooda*-class modals. If sentences with *yooda*-class modals are d-propositions, it is natural that they cannot be modified by these adverbs, just as proper names cannot be quantified.

[8] Takubo (2006) suggests that Saito's constraints can naturally follow by positing the lexical properties as follows:

p-*yooda*: look as if p   p→look as if p

B: Lexical constraints on *yooda* and *rasii* :

$p \rightarrow p\text{-}yooda$: {w: p=1 in w} ⊂ {w: p-*yooda*'=1 in w}

$p\text{-}rasii \rightarrow p$: {w: p-*rasii*'=1 in w} ⊂ {w: p=1 in w}

We will show that A and B will account for the evidential nature of *yooda*-class modals and why they invariably induce abductive (or inductive) reasoning.

From the lexical characterizations for *yooda* and *rasii* in B and the assumption A, the following corollaries can be derived.

C1: Hikyoo (simile) use is possible only for *yooda* and not for *rasii*.
Hikyoo usage of *yooda* is to be found in cases where p is false and p-*yooda* is true, i.e. where the speaker D-knows both ¬p and p-*yooda* as in (23).

(23) kono heya-wa   marude   taihuu-ga   kita   *yooda*.
     this room-TOP   as-if   typhoon-NOM   came   appear
     'This room look as if a typhoon had come.'

With *yooda*, this value assignment is possible because [p→p *yooda*] can be true even if p is false. *Rasii* cannot have this use because p cannot be false without making [p-*rasii*→p] false.

C2: P in p-*yooda* and p-*rasii* must be settled.
For p-*yooda* it is obvious that p must be settled. Given that p is the sufficient condition for p-*yooda*, if p-*yooda* is a d-proposition, and is thus settled, then p must be settled because{w: p=1 in w} ⊂ {w: *p-yooda*=1 in w}. For *p-rasii*, since {w: p-*rasii* =1 in w} ⊂ {w: *p* =1 in w}, just from the inclusion relation alone we cannot say that p is settled. However, since the speaker asserts p-*rasii* to be true when s/he says it, s/he is committed to the truth of the p-*rasii*. Then the cases where the premise p-*rasii* is false are excluded from consideration. Since p is the necessary condition for p-*rasii* to hold, in all the possible worlds where p-*rasii* is true, p must also be true. P, therefore, must be settled, when p-*rasii* is a d-proposition. The difference between *yooda* and *rasii* is that with *yooda*, the consequent of a conditional p-*yooda* is asserted, whereas with *rasii*, the premise p-*rasii* is asserted.

C3: P in p-*yooda* and p-*rasii*, cannot be a d-proposition.
In the case of p-*yooda*, by Gricean maxim of quantity, it is more informative to say *p* if the speaker knows p as his/her own knowledge prior to the utterance.[9] The speaker, therefore, cannot assert p-*yooda* if s/he knows p,

---

     p-*rasii*: typical sub-cases of p   typical sub-cases of p→p
[9] See Saito (2006) for details.

without violating the maxim of quantity.[10] In the case of *p-rasii*, it is redundant to say *p-rasii* when the speaker d-knows p. Since [*p-rasii*→p] is always true if p is true, asserting *p-rasii* fails to contribute new information.[11] Therefore, the complement of *yooda* and *rasii* cannot be a d-proposition.

From C1,C2,C3, it follows that for non-simile use of *p-yooda*, and *p-rasii*, propositions expressed by p must be settled but not known to the speaker, and those expressed by *p-yooda* and *p-rasii* must be known to the speaker either by past experience or deictically by perception, prior to the utterance. If the speaker does not know whether p is true or not, s/he can abductively infer p, given knowledge *p →p-yooda or p-rasii→p* and the minor premise given by *p-yooda*, which is a d-proposition. Inference, therefore, must always go from knowledge based upon what is already known to what is settled but not known, the reverse of the causation chain.[12]

Yooda-class modals relate the perceptible part of the current situation expressed by the predicate p-*YOODA*, and the situation outside it expressed by p, its complement. The inferential force comes from the lexical properties of each lexical item and where information expressed in the complement is located.[13]

4.2. Epistemic Nature of *Daroo*-class Modals

Daroo-class modals are always attached to the conclusion of the inference, which can either be deductive, abductive, or inductive, depending on the scope of the modals. The lexical characterization of *daroo*-class modals dictates that its complement must not be known to the speaker prior to the utterance and thus, is added anew to the knowledge base by inference. Premises can either be known to the speaker or can be new additions provided by the conversational partners. *Daroo*-class modals are not evidentials in the narrow sense, because they are not a description of the current state of affairs, but are epistemic in that they lexically code inference based on some knowledge base.

---

[10] When the speaker knows that saying p violate the territoriality of the hearer and thus has to behave as if s/he does not know the truth of p, it becomes possible to use p-*yooda* in place of p to respect the territoriality of the hearer (cf. Kamio 1990). Our characterization of *yooda* accounts for the fact that among the *yooda*-class modals, only *yooda* (or *mitaida*, the synonym of *yooda* in colloquial speech), can be used for this usage.

[11] *Rasii* can be used as a suffix taking a nominal to express prototypes, e.g. 'otoko-rasii(manly)', 'Tanaka-rasii (typical of Tanaka)' In the nominal taking cases of *rasii*, however, C3 does not hold. 'otoko-rasii otoko (manly man) is perfect, due to the difference in syntactic position.

[12] See Aksu and Slobin (1986) for relevant discussion.

[13] *Sooda* 1 (hearsay) does not involve inference because of its lexical properties. *Sooda* 2 (looks like) allows its complement not to be a settled proposition, allowing deductive inference. Both P-*sooda* 1, p-*sooda* 2, however, must be a d-proposition.

5. Summary

In this paper, we have shown the following:

1. The complement of *daroo*-class modals must not be a d-proposition.
2. *P-YOODA* must be a d-proposition.
3. The inferential force of *YOODA* can be operative only if the complement p is settled but is not a d-proposition.
4. The inferential force of *YOODA* when operative cannot be deductive because of 3.
5. The epistemic nature of *daroo*-class modals comes from 1 and evidential nature of *yooda*-class comes from 2-4.

References

Aksu, A. and D. I. Slobin. 1986. Development and Use of Evidentails in Turkish. *Evidentiality: The Linguistic Coding of Epistemology* (Vol.XX in the Series Advances in Discourse Processes), eds. W. Chafe and J. Nichols, 159-167. Norwood, NJ: Ablex.

Kamio, A. 1990. *Zyoohoo no Nawabari Riron* (The Theory of Territory of Information). Tokyo: Taisyuukan.

Kaufmann, S. 2005. Conditional Predictions: A Probabilistic Account. *Linguistics and Philosophy* 1:45-77.

Miyake, T. 1995. Suiryoo ni tuite (On Conjuecture). *Kokugogaku*, No. 183:1-11.

Morimoto, J. 1994. *Hanasite no Shyukan-o Arawasu Hukusi-ni tuite* (On Adverbs Expressing Speaker's Subjectivity). Tokyo: Kurosio Publishers.

Oshika T 1995. 'Hontaihaaku' *Rasii* no Setu (Theory of *Rasii* as 'Capturing Main Body'). *Miyazi Hirosi & Miyazi Atuko Sensei Koki Kinen Ronsyuu* (Festschirft for Professors Miyazi Hirosi & Miyazi Atuko's 70th birthday), eds., Oshika, T. et al., 527-548. Tokyo: Meizi Syoin.

Palmer, F. R. 2001. *Mood and Modality, Second edition.* Cambridge: Cambridge University Press.

Saito, M. 2006. Sizengengo no Syooko Suiryoo Hyoogen to Tisikikanri (Information Management and Evidentials). Doctoral Dissertation, Kyushu University.

Takubo, Y. 2001. Gendai Nihongo-ni okeru Nisyu no Mo-daru Zyodoosirui-ni tuite (Two Modal Auxiliaries in Modern Japanese). *Festschrift for Professor Umeda's 70th Anniversary,* eds. Nam & Punghyen et al., 1003-1025. Seoul: Thayhaksa.

Takubo, Y. 2006. Nihongo Zyookenbun to Modaritii (Japanese Conditionals and Modality). Doctoral Dissertation, Kyoto University.

Teramura, H. 1984. *Nihongo-no Sintakusu-to Imi 2* (Syntax and Semantics of Japanese Vol. 2). Tokyo: Kurosio Publishers.

Index

Japanese and Korean Linguistics

For a cumulative table of contents of the entire series, please visit

http://cslipublications.stanford.edu/ja-ko-contents/jako-collective-toc.html

where articles are grouped by the following subject categories:

Phonetics and Phonology
Syntax and Morphology
Semantics
Pragmatics, Discourse and Conversation
Psycholinguistics and Cognition
L1 and L2 Acquisition
Historical Linguistics, Language Change and Grammaticalization
Sociolinguistics and Language Use

For more information on other volumes in this series, please visit

http://cslipublications.stanford.edu/site/JAKO.html